How to
Complete
and Survive
a Doctoral Dissertation

How to Complete and *Survive* a Doctoral Dissertation

by DAVID STERNBERG

ST. MARTIN'S PRESS · *New York*

For information, write: St. Martin's Press,
175 Fifth Avenue, New York, N.Y. 10010
Manufactured in the United States of America

Library of Congress Catalogue Number: 80-28938
ISBN: 0-312-39605-8
ISBN: 0-312-39606-6 (pbk.)

DESIGN BY DENNIS J. GRASTORF

10 9 8 7 6 5 4

This book is for the tens of thousands of courageous ABDs confronting the great task in the years to come. ·

Table of Contents

A Finnish proverb goes, strong *sisu* (guts) will help get a person even through a gray rock. Now I chant "Sis-u, sis-u," inside my head as I lug myself up those weary hills toward the end of a long run.

RICHARD ROGIN, in *The Runner Magazine*

CHAPTER 1

The Loneliness of the Long-Distance Writer

THE DISSERTATION DOCTORATE: A LONG-STANDING AND POORLY UNDERSTOOD PROBLEM.

The status of ABD (All But the Dissertation) is the critical one in American graduate education. Since the 1960s its poignancy, sometimes permanency, has been growing. We all seem to know someone—a friend, relative, spouse, colleague—who is either filled with apprehension confronting the task fresh after completed course work or bogged down for years in stop-again, start-again efforts to finish.

Although dissertation woes are generally familiar in the context of the private lives of obscure graduate students, they have been know to obstruct revolutions and revolutionaries! Rosa Luxemburg's long-term lover and fellow political activist, Leo Jogiches, couldn't finish his dissertation, the cause of much wrangling between the two: "When she moved to Berlin, Leo stayed behind in Zurich, working at an interminable doctoral thesis which he never completed. Years went by . . . before she could persuade him to leave Switzerland and join her." [1]

No such prolonged crisis confronts the doctoral candidate in hard/life sciences or "professional degree" programs, where a full dissertation (see below for a delineation of the elements defining a full dissertation) is not required. It is in the social sciences, education, humanities and letters disciplines that people have their lives disrupted and even sometimes permanently scarred by a dissertation-writing experience.

1

American society is not aware, excepting personal acquaintance of particular ABDs, of the almost larger-than-life trials, fortitude, despair, courage and even heroics experienced in writing a doctoral dissertation. One never sees a TV program or movie, for example, about a handicapped, disadvantaged, full-time-employed, or alcoholic-addicted person who, against all odds, completes a dissertation in political science or educational psychology. Skating championships, law and medical degrees, attainment of political office, yes; doctoral dissertations, no. Nor is there any modern fiction about people writing dissertations, depicting them as central heroic or tragic characters caught up in a great struggle, or any "how-to-do-it" books.[2] Again, books abound about fiction writers as heroes, about studies of fiction "writers at work" and about how to write poetry, short stories and novels, even, recently, general nonfiction.[3]

The first, and only, nonfiction book about dissertation writing I was able to find was John Almack's *Research and Thesis Writing: A Textbook on Principles and Techniques of Thesis Construction for the Use of Graduate Students in Universities and Colleges,* published half a century ago! [4] This book is not without merit on the "mechanical" side of thesis construction, but, reflecting its times, it says absolutely nothing about the structural/bureaucratic and emotional dimensions ringing dissertation writing. It seems long overdue for a book on writing a dissertation in tune with its time, when such a project has to be understood to be as much of an emotional and human relations enterprise as an exercise in library research, hypothetheses construction, and gathering and analysis of data. Although not slighting the "mechanical" aspects of the dissertation, the greater weight of the present volume is toward sociological and personal issues that the dissertation writer must confront and master.

The frequency of the ABD status has become so large that it has been legitimated in its own right: Professional journals, like the *Employment Bulletin* of the American Sociological Association, frequently contain openings for an "instructor or assistant professor to teach introductory and family courses: ABD," or, "will consider M.A.; prefer ABD." A recent perusal of the Sunday *New York Times Careers in Education* section indicated the ABD status as an acceptable credential for teaching positions in history, psychology, human relations, bilingual-teacher education and English-language studies.

Implicit in these offerings is the understanding that one will soon get his doctorate or not be retained beyond a limited number of reappointment years in the teaching position, but understood as well is the hard fact that many will never complete the dissertation.* A social science trade joke, recognizing the limited mileage of the ABD, goes, "An ABD and fifty cents will get you a cup of coffee."

In the last years of the 1970s colloquia/workshops on "How to Write a Doctoral Dissertation" were held at major metropolitan New York graduate centers, including New York University and City University of New York (CUNY). All sessions played to standing-room-only crowds of graduate students. In March of 1980 Kingsborough Community College of CUNY advertised in *The New York Times* for a major doctoral-candidate workshop dealing with problems like writers' blocks, oral examinations, statistical analysis and publishing professional articles. In May 1980 the following advertisement appeared in *The New York Times:* "Doctoral Candidates. Can't get that dissertation off the ground? Enroll in intensive workshop, June 5-7 . . . Leave workshop with a detailed draft of your proposal. Limited to 7." This last workshop appears much closer to a business venture than the other more academic, nonprofit, sponsored ones. Profit-oriented dissertation "counseling," probably involving no small measure of actual thesis *writing,* appears to be growing in response to the desperation of many ABDs.

Most social science and some humanities doctoral programs themselves schedule (often require) anticipatory socialization for students near the end of their course work in the form of routine thesis prospectus or dissertation seminars, but veterans of these efforts are nearly unanimous in evaluating them as very little help for the great task. (Read on for reasons why in-department forums are ineffective.)

This book is intentionally entitled: "How to Complete *and Survive* a Doctoral Dissertation." Two potential emotional/career nightmares

---

* Throughout this volume the male pronoun and possessive pronoun—"he" and "his"—are used generically to refer to both male and female dissertation candidates. Since, as we shall soon see, nearly half the candidates are women, the writer wishes to disavow any sexist intention in using male nomenclature. Constantly substituting "he/she," or "one" or "the candidate" is awkward and tedious. Using "they" is just plain grammatically wrong, which wouldn't do in a "how-to" book concerned with writing. So I am more or less stuck with "he" and "his," and hope all men and women reading the book construe them as intending to embrace both human genders equally.

face the ABD: *Not* to finish is practically to guarantee a years-long, if not lifelong, mood of a flawed or somehow incompleted life, where the ABD is constantly explaining/rationalizing to others (e.g., university employers, colleagues, friends, spouses, lovers, family) and to himself just why he didn't finish. The emotional energy expended in often decades-long apologizing and soul-searching is incalculably debilitating and humiliating.

On the other hand, I have often heard ABDs remark (indeed, sometimes said it myself), "If only I could finish my thesis, my troubles would be over." Although such a statement has some validity, *finishing* often scars the successful laureate as well: All along the dissertation course, from initial topic selection and proposal to defense, are strewn potential dangers to self-preservation (dignity), *inter alia,* a sadistic (or lecherous) professor on one's committee; "selling your soul" to a committee which won't pass your thesis unless you excise what you consider to be its (and thus your) guts or add what you judge to be anathema; situations where the fieldwork data contradicts one's hypotheses and causes one to feel (wrongly, as the book will show) that the alternatives are either giving up the project or "fudging" the data; lying to or manipulating (thus depersonalizing) your sample in order to get data deemed "absolutely essential" for the thesis.

A last-stage emotional correlate of finishing is often postpartum dissertation depression, where the writer is so emotionally exhausted, that years of unproductive drifting can follow. One function of this book is to anticipate the surfacing of many of these emotionally crippling conditions and train the candidate in self-compassion and self-healing along the dissertation course.

Statistics of the Problem.

When I researched this book I discovered something akin to a "cover-up" regarding information about doctoral candidates in dissertation-required programs. Not only are there no national statistics on ABDs; there are no national statistics on how many students are enrolled in doctoral programs separate from master's degree enrollments. At the local level of particular universities, graduate registrars were either vague and defensive about hard statistics on this group or, even when eager to help, hard put to give satisfactory answers since

4

their coding categories did not include attention to this specific status. My review of much statistical data on universities (an enormous body of facts and figures on nearly every conceivable aspect of university programs, faculty and student characteristics), together with my interviews with registrars and educators, convince me that the dissertation doctorate is certainly the least understood institution in American higher education. (Some tentative answers to why this should be so come later in the chapter.) The statistical picture of the ABD problem in the United States that follows, then, was necessarily constructed by me through indirect measures, formula suggestions from prominent registrars, educators, statisticians at the National Center for Education and educated guesses from my own experience as a sociologist and dissertation adviser.

What we are trying to ascertain here is an estimate of the number of people currently in the same boat in the early 1980s. Table I gives the national statistics for graduate students, full and part-time, enrolled beyond the first year of graduate school in the twelve fields of study requiring a dissertation for the doctorate, as of 1976 (the last year for which figures were available when this book was written). Although a small portion of this population are master's candidates, the great majority are doctoral:

Table 1.1: Enrollments in Dissertation-Required Doctoral Programs, 1976

Field of Study	Beyond First Year Full-time Enrollment	Beyond First Year Part-time Enrollment Divided by Three
1. Area Studies	1,206	250
2. Communications	1,262	555
3. Education	29,942	26,936
4. Foreign Languages	4,015	907
5. Home Economics	1,108	520
6. Letters	10,524	3,280
7. Library Sciences	1,400	744
8. Psychology	10,789	2,336
9. Public Affairs and Services	10,057	2,419
10. Social Sciences	18,115	4,697

5

Field of Study	Beyond First Year Full-time Enrollment	Beyond First Year Part-time Enrollment Divided by Three
11. Theology	5,510	1,259
12. Interdisciplinary Studies	2,942	1,492
Subtotal	96,870	45,395

Total: 142,265 full-time *or* full-time-equivalent doctoral students in dissertation-required fields

Source: *Digest of Education Statistics,* National Center for Education Statistics, HEW, 1979, p. 95

Note that the part-time total was divided by *three* to get a full-time equivalent of that portion of the doctoral population which roughly controls for students who pursue doctoral courses well beyond the conventional two full-time years that most catalogs and authorities indicate as normative.[5] The total of 142,265 must be corrected additionally for growth in graduate student populations since 1976 (dissertation-required doctoral enrollments *are* growing, although not at a striking rate, despite general decline in college enrollments). A "medium growth" projection would be 1.5 percent per year.[6] To come up to 1981, then, the total would be 152,935 doctoral students.

The reader will have noted a large variance in enrollments by field. Education doctorate enrollments (about 60,000) account for nearly three times the next largest category, social sciences (23,000), followed by psychology, letters, and public affairs and services (each with about 13,000). The smallest fields are area studies, communications, home economics and library science, each with 2,000 or fewer candidates.

Do doctoral program enrollments differ substantially by sex? Despite considerable rhetoric from feminist quarters, the data do not support a general claim that women are discriminated against in current dissertation-required doctoral *enrollments*. Data is not available for assessing their proportionate representation as ABDs. We do know, however, that they still represent a minority of doctorates received: In 1973, 30 percent of doctorates granted in sociology went to women; in 1978, 37 percent.[7] Table 1.2 gives the percentage distribution of men and women enrolled in the twelve fields:

6

Table 1.2: Enrollments in Dissertation-Required Doctoral Programs by Sex, 1976

Field of Study	Male %	Female %
1. Area Studies	55	45
2. Communications	58	42
3. Education	42	58
4. Foreign Languages	39	61
5. Home Economics	15	85
6. Letters	51	49
7. Library Sciences	25	75
8. Psychology	55	45
9. Public Affairs and Services	54	46
10. Social Sciences	68	32
11. Theology	83	17
12. Interdisciplinary Studies	54	46

Source: *Digest of Education Statistics,* National Center for Education Statistics, HEW, 1979, p. 95

A totaling of male and female *full and part-time* students in 1976 comes to 116,806 men and 116,251 women, virtually a 50–50 split between the sexes. Of the twelve areas, only two were significantly male-dominated (defined as showing a skewed distribution of at least 60–40)—theology and social science—and three significantly female-dominated—foreign languages, home economics and library science. Increasing pressures from affirmative-action groups make it likely that the 1980s will see even further reductions in the enrollment inequalities by sex that do exist, as well as moves toward near-parity in degrees conferred.[8] In any event, the drastic biases against women candidates in "professional studies," such as medicine and law, have no real analogue in the dissertation-required fields. This may well be because sexism is always most evident in those institutional and educational sectors where the most money and power are implicated, and, by and large, regardless of the relatively high prestige attached to winning, say, an humanities or social science doctorate, these twelve fields rank relatively low on both financial and power scales. In my judgment, sexism practiced by faculty members against her ranks relatively low on the list of hurdles facing the female dissertation writer. Certainly, she may have to combat debilitating sexist attitudes on the part of an unsympathetic or often outright hostile husband who wants dinner on the table at six, no matter what the dissertation time schedule demands. But such problems can be dealt with in a way that historic institutionalized resistance to female membership in fields like medicine cannot. The major hurdles to completing and surviving a dissertation, discussed at great length in this volume, are not sex-linked.

Approximating the number of ABDs within the larger doctoral population is even chancier than estimating the number of doctoral students. I divided the population by *three,* reasoning that this would give the number of candidates who had most likely finished all (two full years) of their course work, and were either squarely up against the dissertation, or soon to be so after their last qualifying written and/or oral preliminary (to the thesis) examinations. This calculation yielded a figure of 50,978 ABDs. This is a very considerable figure in its own right, but an even more important point to stress is its perennial nature: Each academic year throughout the 1980s more than 50,000 *new* ABDs will be generated by the American graduate school system. We will have over half a million ABDs during the decade.

In this sense the ABD is in a very large boat with lots of company. It is one of the key paradoxes of the ABD that it is a "lonely crowd" status. Statistically large in numbers as ABDs may be, the context and contours of graduate education institutions, and perhaps the very structure of the dissertation doctorate itself (see discussion below), make almost all successful doctorates products of an individual, and usually lonely, agency.

If 51,000 ABDs per year is a reasonably close estimate, what is the completion, or success, figure? Again, as of this writing no research, certainly on a national scale, has ever been conducted. Certain individual departments in particular disciplines may have carried through studies of their own shops, but that information is available on a "need-to-know" basis only. The best, although far from entirely satisfactory, model one can use is an "in-out" scheme. Simply put, one asks how many finished-product doctorates come out as compared to

ABDs going in. Let's look first at the number of doctorates awarded yearly in the twelve areas:

Table 1.3: Doctorates Awarded in Dissertation-Required Doctoral Programs, 1976–1977

Field of Study	Number of Doctorates Awarded
1. Area Studies	153
2. Communications	171
3. Education	7,955
4. Foreign Languages	752
5. Home Economics	160
6. Letters	2,199
7. Library Sciences	61
8. Psychology	2,761
9. Public Affairs and Services	335
10. Social Sciences	3,784
11. Theology	1,125
12. Interdisciplinary Studies	304
Total	19,760

Source: *Digest of Education Statistics,* National Center for Education Statistics, HEW, 1979, pp. 112–116

Perusal of all the (albeit admittedly incomplete) available statistics leads to the conclusion that no matter how one cuts the pie, each year in the 1980s will see upward of 50,000 ABDs go in and about 20,000 earned doctorates come out of the graduate education machine. Obviously, one cannot simply compare brand-new ABDs of a given year with awarded doctorates for the *same* year to get a success figure, since normally it takes one to two years to write the dissertation. But, for example, we generated about 47,400 new ABDs in 1976; 19,760 doctorates were awarded the next year. Assuming the 1976 ABDs had now worked on their dissertations for at least a year, their finishing rate was about 42 percent. Obviously, there is some statistical distortion here, since all the 1977 awards were not conferred upon 1976 starters; some could have begun five years earlier. So one cannot talk

9

about cut-and-dried success and failure rates, given the often idio-syncratic time phasing of particular dissertation writers in particular fields and the far from satisfactory statistics. Still, a "catch-up" process that significantly alters the numbers does not appear to be operating; for every one hundred ABDs that go in, only forty-some doctorates come out, year after year.

The "in-out" figures vary drastically from field to field. Here are the percentages of finishers (based on 1976–1977 data) for the twelve fields:

Table 1.4: Ratio of Awarded Doctorates to Entering ABDs

Field of Study	Awarded Doctorates (in %) Entering ABDs
1. Area Studies	32
2. Communications	28
3. Education	42
4. Foreign Languages	46
5. Home Economics	29
6. Letters	48
7. Library Sciences	9
8. Psychology	63
9. Public Affairs and Services	8
10. Social Sciences	50
11. Theology	50
12. Interdisciplinary Studies	21

Source: *Digest of Education Statistics,* National Center for Education Statistics, HEW, 1979, p. 95; pp. 112–116

To get some understanding of what is behind the enormous fluctua-tions among finishers in different fields would require a book in its own right. Among the larger enrolled fields, psychology has the best track record, and public affairs and services egregiously the worst. Even operating with a relaxed and optimistic model of "catch-up," it seems likely that, at best, no more than about half of 1980s American ABDs will be getting their degrees.

It is my sense that university chairpersons, deans and even highest officials intuit these substantial nonfinishing rates (unparalleled in other kinds of graduate, undergraduate, indeed any type of American educational program) but do not undertake or commission a "body count" for fear that public access to such data would (1) reduce enrollments in graduate programs; (2) lead to student demands for far-reaching changes in graduate program guidelines and requirements; (3) threaten lucrative "maintaining matriculation" fees now paid by many ABDs for periods sometimes up to a decade; (4) entail faculty and administrative shakeups and housecleanings.

Even keeping in mind the caveat of not translating the in-out figures into success-failure rates per se, the probabilities of not converting the ABD into a Ph.D. in the candidate's foreseeably near future are alarmingly high. Certainly, if you are a five-year-old ABD pounding the pavement at your regional or national convention and avoiding old classmates with the embarrassment that "everybody finished but me" (one of a list of counterproductive dissertation myths discussed in this book), you are flailing yourself with a statistical unreality.

FOR WHOM IS THIS BOOK?

This volume is intended primarily for doctoral candidates in fields of study—ordinarily one of the twelve discussed above—where a dissertation is required. By a full dissertation is meant a thesis which requires (1) exhaustive library review/survey of related literature; (2) construction of a researchable problem, and related hypotheses, which makes some original contribution to the field; (3) experimental work and/or fieldwork with subjects and/or groups; (4) an elaborate methodology for analyzing the data collected; (5) a lengthy, literary write-up, analysis and discussion of the results of such experimental work or fieldwork; (6) a formal, oral defense of the dissertation before a committee. Non- or quasidissertation doctorates are those which require from none to some, but less than all of the above elements of a full dissertation.

Nondissertation fields include those such as medicine, dentistry and engineering. Law doctorates (the J.D.) often require a major senior paper for graduation, but this paper is not comparable in terms of the six elements to the scope and arduousness of a dissertation. Hard and

11

life science doctorates require a "dissertation," but the form and strict faculty supervision (see below) of these projects are not like a full dissertation. With disciplines such as letters, history, languages and philosophy we have a midground, where elements three and four are usually not salient, but the other requirements are in full force. Full dissertations must be written by candidates in the social sciences (here including psychology as a social science), public administration and in the majority of education doctorates.[9]

This book, then, will be relevant and useful for all kinds of doctoral candidates, except those in the so-called "professional" and hard/life science areas.[10] It will be instructive even for *them* in correcting any smugness or patronizing attitudes that many hold about the inability of so many dissertation candidates to finish. The book should also be helpful to those who have to "live with" a dissertation writer through his trials in understanding some of the enormities of the project and the accompanying strains to which a candidate is exposed.

Although a candidate writing a thesis in, say, French or comparative literature will not have to complete an "experiment," issues addressed in this volume—such as deciding to write a dissertation, building a dissertation file, how to get out of a dissertation depression and how to deal with one's proposal/dissertation committee—are as pressing for him as for a student writing a sociology, psychology or public administration thesis.

As already noted, there are over 150,000 full-time or full-time-equivalent students in relevant dissertation-required doctoral programs in any given year. In the broadest sense, the book speaks to all of these people. For purposes of answering just what a specific student might look for in the volume, we might break this population down into four groups: (1) students in their first or second year of course work who are still deciding about whether to write the dissertation, or, having already decided that fundamental question, are looking for a viable topic, or want some sense of what is in store for them; (2) students still doing course and/or qualifying examinations who have already concurrently started a dissertation; [11] (3) the 50,000-plus new ABDs generated each year by the American university system, faced with the immediate task of climbing the Matterhorn looming above them; (4) the "veteran" ABDs, still in a holding pattern of "maintaining matriculation," often five or more years after completion of their other requirements. No one knows the size of this last group; indeed, when I interviewd graduate registrars, the cover-up element seemed most prominent, perhaps, in the long-term ABD area.

THE DISSERTATION WRITER ADRIFT.

In the introduction to their generally valuable *Guide to American Graduate Schools*, Livesey and Doughty, both graduate registrars at one time or another at a major university, state that the dissertation is the most rewarding phase of a doctoral program. This is a most astonishing statement. I have never encountered a dissertation writer, most certainly while writing his thesis, who would acquiesce in such a judgment. When I ask my students or clients to word-associate to their dissertations, some combination of the following responses is typical: fear, agony, torture, guilt, no end in sight, indefinitely postponed gratification, "ruining my life, "I'm drowning in it," anxiety, boredom, hate, despair, depression, humiliation, powerlessness. Should the reader object that I may see a "deviant" part of the candidate spectrum, I would answer that discussions with successful colleagues in various fields over more than ten years have yielded the same kind of negative emotional response when recalling the days of our dissertations.

The truth of the matter is that, although the American educational system is characterized at almost all levels by "support systems"—remedial programs, tutors, counselors, pass/fail options—for students unparalleled in the world, virtually the entire support structure vanishes for doctoral candidates undertaking a dissertation in education, social science, humanities or letters. Abrupt withdrawal of the support system leads to the candidate's feeling some or most of the unhappy emotions listed above.

Interestingly, the support system continues intact for "hard" science and "professional" candidates. In physics or zoology, for example, Ph.D. candidates are assigned by their graduate mentors/advisers to pursue some relatively narrow and well-defined experiment for their dissertation project; in law or medicine, a senior-year long paper or comparable project may be required, but its proportionate weight in obtaining the doctorate is tiny compared to a dissertation in political science or educational sociology. Hard science and professional-degree candidates know that if they attend two to four years of classes

13

along with their mates and carry out the last-year project, closely supervised by their advising professor, they will—excepting contingencies like banana-peel slippage—almost always receive their doctorates. As we have already demonstrated, and as the ABD knows all too well, no such certainty is available to doctoral candidates in fields with which this book is concerned.

The degree of uncertainty and magnitude of eventual nonfinishers in "soft" science doctorates is astounding and puzzling, not only because of the contrast with "hard" science and professional doctorate prognoses, but because of the length and arduousness of predissertation course and examination work that dissertation-degree candidates must log. Certainly, a sociology or history candidate has put in as much, if not considerably more, work (often including acquisition of an M.A. en route) by the time he reaches the ABD status as the law student at the end of three years of law courses, but the law student is by then a Juris Doctor and the ABD has yet to *begin* the major project required for his doctorate! [12]

Professional students might counter with the fact that they must additionally pass state licensing boards, but, again, the reality is that the vast majority of medical and law college graduates pass the boards/bars, even though some of them must try a number of times. There is no analogue to this "second (or even third and fourth) chance" in dissertation doctorate "licensing." It is a rare event—of dissertation lore—for a candidate to be (fully) failed on his dissertation and then go out and try another one, partly because doctoral committees/programs do not generally allow it, but, more importantly, because the dissertation course is so long and debilitating that a second effort is almost unthinkable to the candidate.

People do not understand how matters stand for the dissertation candidate: his family has trouble grasping the magnitude of the task; friends may be sympathetic, but in a general way which gets to none of the nuances of the loneliness and uncertainty involved. Most often, relatives and friends cannot understand why your high school and college classmates got their law, medical, engineering or dentistry degrees right on schedule, and you seem to be floundering and having so much *angst*. Holders of professional and hard-science doctorates are generally patronizing toward the struggling ABD: the doctors and lawyers see it in terms of somebody snared by impractical or unprag-

14

matic projects; the scientists see the delays as inevitable results of fooling around with "fuzzy," "soft-headed" and nonrigorous ideas and methods. All too often, the candidate himself internalizes some of this derogation and impatience toward his own project.

From all the evidence I have been able to gather, ABDs seem to have been caught unawares by the problematic nature of finishing their degrees. That is, the typical ABD entered graduate school three to four years previously with high hopes and the feeling that the main victory had already been won: getting over the GREs and acceptance into a program. Up to this point, his situation is very similar to someone accepted by a law or medical school. Next follows involvement with course work and preparation for predissertation comprehensives. The concern is with doing well in both phases so that he will be allowed to write the dissertation, not that the dissertation will perhaps turn out to be near-impossible to write. Very often, even graduate students at the top of their classes and feeling confident and quite highly motivated right through completion of course work (even though interest seems generally to decline in graduate programs after the first year, including some professional programs) [13] describe their realization that the dissertation does not necessarily follow smoothly as "a hell of a shock," or "the sky falling in," or "a whole new ball game." The following section examines some of the most prominent features of the dissertation writer's adriftness and essays some account both of its timing in the doctoral course and its causes.

Specific Features of the ABD Problem.
Dissertation anomie. Only the statistically rare (e.g., a favored graduate or teaching assistant, often bitterly resented by the rest of the students because of his connections) among ABDs, or those approaching that status, doesn't get the message that nobody down at the department is seriously concerned with helping him work through a multiyear project on a continuous, serious basis. Dissertation anomie is the occupational disease of the ABD. Structurally, it is a dislocation between stated official goals of a doctoral program, on the one hand, and the unavailability of means—particularly faculty personnel, tutelage and support—for the candidate's successful pursuit of his goals. Psychologically, the dislocation is experienced by individual candidates in feelings of drifting, powerlessness and despair. Dissertation

15

anomie as internalized by ABDs cannot fairly be described as "pathological," "neurotic" or "deviant." It is the cluster of predictable feelings, given the structural dislocations in the programs.

Each kind of anomie has a "chronic" and "acute" phase. Departments appear to go through cycles of anomie: some years, under some chairpersons, the policing of and standards for writing dissertations might be tightened up, after a preceding period of slackness; when this occurs, a candidate writing during that latter administration will probably have a somewhat less anomic experience. But one can never count on continuities within the administration, either at the field of study/departmental level or the cross-discipline dean's level; both are subject to change of personnel and policy at any time. The only reliable constant is the possession of a set of dissertation-writing savvys, skills and attitudes which this book tries to teach.

Faculty unreliability. Why should the faculty and administration be dilatory or delinquent in helping future junior colleagues get over the last great hurdle to full membership in a discipline? One might understand the indifference of people (including relatives and friends) in terms of lack of interest in long-term intellectual projects that have less than dramatic practical "payoff," but this cannot account for faculty (near) indifference and reluctance to help.[14] Or can it? Wilensky demonstrated that American university professors were nearly as unread and "practical" oriented as nonacademics.[15] But giving faculty some benefit of the doubt, regardless of their general attitude toward matters of the mind, surely they must be interested at least in work in their *own* disciplines. Although this is usually more or less true (not without exceptions that every doctoral candidate can identify within his own department), it is not the same as saying that graduate professors are interested in students' doctoral dissertations.[16]

One can scale faculty from one to ten on dissertation interest and helpfulness. Excepting infrequent "round-robin" systems (as rare as round-robin chairmanships), where each graduate faculty member is assigned an equal number of dissertation candidates, a very large majority of faculty members constitutionally empowered by the university to be dissertation advisers, readers or committee members will score three or below on the scale. In every department there are one or two nines or tens, known to all candidates by the student grapevine, besieged by numbers they cannot adequately handle. Such men and women have a way of moving on, either through exhaustion, lack of recognition for their efforts by administrations or bitterness with colleagues who won't help with the load; so that even they cannot really be relied upon to see one through a lengthy endeavor, no matter how close one feels to them. The message bears repeating and will be driven home throughout the book: When it comes to doing a dissertation, the buck stops with the candidate and the resources he can bring to the project. Outside help will be appreciated and utilized when available, but the bottom line must be, "I am going to do this thing myself," so that if—usually when—allies withdraw their divisions, the dissertation front doesn't collapse.

Why isn't the faculty (consistently) helpful? From a sociological perspective, dissertation advising rates low as a career-promoting activity. People are promoted, given tenure, receive more attractive offers from other universities, principally in terms of what they *publish themselves*, certainly not for editing and advising the writings and publications of graduate students. Graduate professors will often baldly tell one as much.

Sometimes they offer a somewhat less self-interested and not totally specious reason for reluctance to get heavily involved with dissertation candidates. Advising a doctoral dissertation is a most time-consuming affair. Most of the ABDs who come to graduate professors about dissertations have only the fuzziest notions of what they would like to pursue as topics. Very often, after "fooling around" with half a dozen "pipedreams," the student vanishes, either quite literally into the limbo of "maintaining matriculation" from where many never return, or goes on to the next "sympathetic" professor, where the process starts all over again. Very quickly, say the professors, one gets cynical, or at least very cautious about commitment to an ABD.

For many professors, the ABD is viewed like the bookmen and women who come by their offices with regularity: one gives them a few quick minutes of partial attention and then gets rid of them, either by making a promise to "consider" a new book for course adoption or sending them down the hall to an unsuspecting colleague who is "really the person you should be talking to about this."

This faculty definition of the ABD as Fuller Brush salesman, interloper and time waster, combined with techniques for brushing him off, exacerbates dissertation anomie and often sets tragedies in motion. ABDs are run around from professor to professor in a downward spiral of powerlessness, increasing discouragement and embarrassment. ABDs who felt fairly comfortable with faculty during course work begin to feel like strangers in their own departments, cooling their heels in waiting rooms and becoming increasingly apologetic for taking up (more of) a professor's time.

Not infrequently, a professor will sign his approval to a dissertation proposal or prospectus (which he may or may not have read with care) of a persistent student to get him off his back, when the prospectus is not viable as a dissertation; somewhere along the way—usually longer than shorter given faculty's relaxed attitudes toward dissertation beginnings—a dissertation committee is going to veto the whole project, after the candidate has invested considerable work and hope. Most of the time, that candidate will walk away from the doctorate and become another forgotten casualty of American graduate education.

Lack of graduate student community. Four principal factors determine how much or how little student community, solidarity and support a given doctoral program will exhibit:

1. whether the program is located in a rural or urban university setting.
2. the size of the enrollment.
3. the percentage of doctoral candidates enrolled full- versus part-time.
4. the percentage of candidates with full-time or substantial part-time employment outside the program/university.

A megapolis-based, subway campus program with hundreds of matriculated students, many of whom are matriculated part-time and hold full-time jobs, will be the atomized/alienated/anonymous pole along a continuum of graduate student community/lack of community. A small (under fifty) rural program where the students all are sequestered in the same university town, enrolled full-time and usually working part-time in some capacity connected with the university, very often the program itself, will approach the *gemeinschaft* pole, where students will band together to study for courses, research projects and qualifying exams.

Fewer and fewer programs contain any longer all four of the opti-

18

mal elements for graduate student community; e.g., the *size* of rural-based enrollments is exceeding the limits necessary for most of the students to get to know each other well. Many programs in many disciplines, including the largest ones, contain all four of the negatively synergistic elements. The Midwest seems to be the major region of the nation where schools containing some measure of most of the optimal conditions can still be found, although there are many exceptions to this rule in the giant state universities.

Even with the presence of optimal conditions for graduate student community, surprisingly little seems to materialize. For reasons more closely scrutinized in Chapter Four, doctoral candidates have been reluctant to band together either during course or (especially) the later dissertation-writing stage. Attempts to organize graduate students to take a stand againt specific faculty or university policies have met with conspicuously less success than with undergraduate students. There is an abiding fear of graduate program faculty and a cultural norm of "doing your own time"; joining together can be labeled as "trouble-making," thus jeopardizing one's doctorate.

Added to fear of faculty retaliation has been an abiding sense of *competition* among doctoral candidates who have read into low finishing rates a kind of quota system which pits them against their fellow students. I argue in this book that no such quota system exists, and that others writing dissertations should be sought out to form support groups (see Chapter Seven). There indeed seems to be such a slowly developing trend in many universities and disciplines, both large and small, urban and rural. But for every presently developing enclave of doctoral student solidarity, there still exist countless undifferentiated masses of enrolled graduate students and ABDs who are going it almost completely alone. There is certainly a lonely, solitary component to writing a doctoral dissertation, but the size of this element may have been exaggerated by the dissertation subculture. In some instances, this loner view of the thesis has led to study groups, formed for various predissertation purposes, being terminated when ABD status has been reached—a most serious error.

Candidates' unpreparedness.[17] Faculty constantly complain that even graduate students at the ABD level are "unprepared" to write a dissertation. This statement is puzzling since it appears to discount the worth of the numerous theoretical, substantive and methodological courses that the student has negotiated in, say, sixty credits of his field of study. But I do not believe they mean unprepared in the narrower sense of having no grasp of the literature in the discipline, or unequipped to carry through statistical analyses of data, or unable to write with minimum clarity (although any or all of these failings may, in fact, characterize a minority of ABDs). Unprepared here means more in the way of *unsocialized* to the scope and meaning of a doctoral dissertation.

The idea and institution of a doctoral dissertation which foreran the current American model developed in Western Europe, principally in Germany and France (Johns Hopkins was its transplanter from the Old to the New university world). The European doctorate was an enormous project, often the capstone of a career, generally achieved later in life than in the American case, demanding a thesis of originality, great length (and thus years to write) and very often controversy. Doctoral dissertation defenses were, like hangings, public affairs (this public quality continues to a limited extent, even today), where any interested person could attend and even pose contentious questions from the audience to the candidate. It was not unknown for these defenses to break up in melées.

Nothing in the contemporary American student's prior twenty-year educational experience could possibly "prepare" him for a dissertation akin to the traditional model. Indeed, very few of the current supervising professors were any more prepared when they wrote *their* dissertations (never mind their bemoaning of decline of standards since their day). Credentialed faculty look back upon the dissertation like veteran marines see boot-camp days at Paris Island: a hell-and-brimstone initiation into the corps. And since the veterans went through hell (and it made better men of them), why shouldn't today's ABDs have to take it? Indeed, such attitudes about the initiation-like quality and function of the dissertation, usually unstated, may play a major role in faculty indifference to the ABD's plight. For all we know, distinguished docents like Weber in Germany, Freud in Austria and Durkheim in France may have held the same notions about their students struggling with their dissertations.

Transcending the revenge or "get-even" function that the thesis may—or may have—played for present and past faculty, there exists a widespread faculty conviction that the dissertation is the instrument that forges a full-fledged colleague out of a graduate student, in that it forces him to combine the disparate skills and ideas he has picked up in graduate courses into a coherent piece of professional work. The correlative attitude here is that one really has to go this route alone, forge the product oneself. This is the position that, with certain qualifications, I myself hold. In any event, the basic point to be underscored is that even those professors who have a positive and sympathetic attitude toward ABDs cannot be relied upon to work closely with the candidate, since they are apt to feel, partly through their own dissertation experience and partly because of professional convictions, that the dissertation is necessarily a lonely affair of the mind and heart. It may even be that, operating under this paradigm of the dissertation, they are not alarmed at the high "dropout" rate among ABDs, seeing in that process a kind of doctoral Darwinian natural selection and survival of the fittest.

Again, simply consider the American graduate student's reaction when facing such a "switch" in expectations right at the end of his academic career. From grade school through high school through college and graduate school (course work), students are officially and/or informally encouraged to pursue learning styles and goals almost diametrically opposed to those required for a dissertation (certainly in the European understanding of the doctorate, but even within the later American tradition, I believe). The American educational system encourages working together with peers.[18] Student peer groups devalue serious and sustained intellectual pursuit in favor of social and athletic skills. American teachers positively sanction memorization and rote learning of conventional wisdom, discourage or even punish creative and nonmidstream thought. Even colleges and universities have always weighted their curricula in favor of "practical" matters, with "free-floating" intellectual courses and enterprises much more often eulogized than practiced or funded.[19]

Nor is it generally true that the term papers of college or even graduate school prepare the student to some extent for the dissertation. Remembering the six elements of the dissertation (above), one need only reflect on numerous term papers (if indeed one can even recall them) distinctly lacking in these features. Graduate students themselves consistently report that their term papers are synthetic reports, where one takes an idea from X, a quote from Y, a prayer from Z. Rarely are the papers *analytical* or *critical* in a sense approaching the demands of a dissertation. The professors are, of course, implicated in this corruption; still hoping for the occasional well-researched and finely honed analytic performance, they have come to settle for some reasonable regurgitation of their lectures or assigned texts whose prose transcends word-salad. To insist on first-rate, carefully prepared papers would be (1) to fail many more people than the administration would allow; (2) to bring a double or treble load of end-of-term (just when one wants to start vacation) work upon the professor's shoulders in the form of rereadings of revised papers; and (3) to insure widespread unpopularity among even graduate students who simply are not "prepared" for such stringent demands and see them as "unreasonable," "sadistic" or as some kind of specific "personal" animosity toward particular students.

Then, too, term papers so often seem to be done in a rush, on the fly, started as the term is ending, competing with the demands of two or three other papers. Students sometimes appear to spend more time considering the color of the cover page or the style of plastic folder in which to encase the paper than in the contents itself. Such fast-food writing habits and schedules, so endemic to and reflective of our contemporary life-style in general, practically guarantee failure to write an acceptable dissertation, unless a candidate is prepared to make changes along the lines indicated in this book.

It is probably true that the *master's thesis* used to serve as a kind of anticipatory socialization halfway house between term papers of one kind or another and the dissertation.[20] However, in an attempt to streamline graduate programs and cut down on required years of matriculation (studies at the turn of the 1970s indicated that the average successful candidate in most disciplines was taking from seven–nine years after completion of his undergraduate degree to finish) in a time of tight money, inflation and aversion to "idleness" and "time wasting," the master's degree, and related thesis, is becoming extinct, at least as part of doctoral programs.[21] Although nowhere near as demanding as the dissertation, the master's thesis did require some attention to many, if not most, of the six elements of the full dissertation.

Most ironically, it is now being used primarily as a "terminal" degree to "cool out" students not considered by departments as "Ph.D. material." With an M.A. in hand one could—very often can, even today—get a research and even long-term (albeit usually not tenurable) teaching post. Today's "elite" ABD often doesn't have a master's degree to fall back upon should he fail or seriously delay in negotiating the dissertation. This all-or-nothing condition (where on paper and in employment reality all he has is his bachelor's degree) further increases the anxieties of the ABD status.

THE SCHEME OF THE BOOK.

This first chapter's intention is to give the ABD candidate, or any other person considering writing a dissertation, a general picture of the situation he faces along statistical, emotional, general interpersonal and faculty-relations dimensions. One theme that emerges very clearly is the statistical "togetherness" but personal "aloneness" of the dissertation-writing status. Another is the less than heartening rate of finishing the degree. A third is the generally lukewarm, at best, cooperation of the faculty in this large endeavor. The last is the "unpreparedness" of the typical candidate to mount the dissertation without some turnabout in his accustomed manner of approaching intellectual problems, studying, researching and writing. The remainder of the book is designed to help the candidate understand, face up to and surmount the hurdles that have been outlined.

The chapters constitute a dual-track, psychological-emotional *and* practical "guidebook," with the writer traveling shoulder-to-shoulder with the candidate along all the sequential stations of the dissertation course. Issues discussed at length include:

1. Deciding whether you really want to write the dissertation, involved herein a "cost accounting" of the career and emotional credits and debits.
2. Picking a dissertation topic that will "go."
3. Making the dissertation the top priority in your life: building a dissertation-writing frame of mind and place.
4. Building a dissertation file: the philosophy and construction code.
5. Writing a successful dissertation proposal, or prospectus, including picking a committee you can work with.
6. The dissertation itself: researching it, writing it and presenting it to the faculty.
7. Down in the dissertation dumps: how to get out.
8. The dissertation defense: how to pass it.
9. Beyond the dissertation: getting professional mileage out of it.

10. Beyond the dissertation: surviving it.
11. Myths versus realities about the dissertation: dangerous traps, bugaboos and myths about the thesis which have ensnared, weakened and defeated candidates.

The contents of this guidebook stem directly from the personal successful theses (four of them) experiences of the author, acquaintance with numerous dissertations of his colleagues in various fields, his extensive supervision of dissertations and M.A. theses over a period of twelve years, five years of a dissertation-therapy practice during which the writer has helped (but never *written:* the main input must always come from the candidate) a significant number of clients complete, or make significant progress on, dissertations in which they were previously bogged down for years.* Along the way, at relevant points and junctures, anecdotes and parts of "case studies" will be related (including the author's own dissertation), with which many a reader will surely identify, or at least empathize.

HOW TO USE THIS BOOK.

I assume that a person who has reached, or is nearing, ABD status is minimally literate, conversant with the basic theories and methodologies of his field, thoroughly experienced in library research, knows an *op. cit.* from an *ibid.* If one needs serious remedial work in any of these areas, one is ready for neither the dissertation nor this volume. So the book is in no way a "style manual" or "writer's tool" in the sense of a work like Crosby and Estey's *College Writing.*[22] *How to Complete and Survive a Doctoral Dissertation* does contain "nuts and bolts" on organizing a dissertation file, writing a proposal and the dissertation itself, but they are of a very different order from style, grammatical or citation guidelines. In this book usually even "mechanical" problems (e.g., constructing a file) are infused with equally important emotional themes (e.g., getting into an attitudinal frame of mind to keep your file humming along).

---

* In the following chapters I make liberal use of my own doctoral dissertation whenever I feel it is highly relevant to illustrating an important point. I also want the reader to bear in mind constantly that I have personally experienced most of the dissertation's travails.

How to use the book will depend, of course, at what station on the dissertation path the reader finds himself. Ideally, it should be read prior to, or just at the time of, reaching ABD status, so that all the chapters will be relevant to the candidate's unfolding experience. As the project moves along, specific sections, corresponding to the candidate's stage of development, should be consulted again. The book is designed to be a constant companion to the writer from start to finish, and beyond.

The book is equally relevant for long-term ABDs, since most of the time they are going to have to turn around their attitudes, working/writing habits and sometimes even a "no-go" topic, if they seriously hope to finish and survive.

It must be remembered from the start that the writer is, perforce, discussing the basic issues of a general dissertation's life history in American graduate schools; there are, of course, hundreds of particular programs which are bound to vary in detail and even sometimes in basic requirements. Still, I believe that the basic "variance" has been covered; naturally, a particular candidate in a particular program will have to make adjustments in the book's guidelines to tailor it to his department, its peculiar faculty composition, his particular dissertation and his own personality. Nonetheless, it is clear to me how similar "under the skin" are most programs' demands about dissertations. Certainly, the requirements of qualities and habits the *writer* must possess or cultivate to complete the dissertation are virtually identical throughout the nation.

So, I would have the reader turn to the book for information, strategies and reshaping of attitudes toward the great project. More generally, and perhaps most importantly, the book is intended to convey support and hope, without being Pollyanna-like; all too often, I have found, the doctoral dissertation candidate is his own worst enemy (as if he needed any more!), torpedoing himself with doomsday myths about the dissertation. Hopefully, this book will demythologize and remove some of the terror from the thesis experience. At the same time, it intends to train the candidate in anticipation and self-compassion, so that dissertation crises along the way don't take him unawares, throw him completely off, stall his progress or ruin the next five or ten years of his life.

Now, let's get on the dissertation course.

SUMMARY.

1. ABDs (All But the Dissertation) have become a substantial "minority group" in American society but have achieved very little public understanding, sympathy or support. Currently, each year some 51,000 new ABDs are produced, facing the task of carrying through a huge project for which they have been ill prepared, either in college or graduate school itself. The 1980s will see more than half a million ABDs generated, a substantial percentage of whom will never finish the thesis. If one adds to the new ABDs the large, if precisely undetermined, number of "veteran" ABDs who hang on year after year without progress, we see a large "social problem," perhaps even a crisis, in the midst of American graduate education.

2. The writer had to construct his own statistical picture of and projections for ABDs when he discovered that no national data on that specific status existed. Such a situation seems to be the combined result of "cover-up" and indifference factors. The author's statistical workup shows that more than half of all ABDs writing full-fledged dissertations never finish, although the percentages vary considerably from discipline to discipline. Such a high failure rate is startling in contrast with ABDs' prior successful completion of two to four arduous years of all other degree requirements, and with the infinitely lower failure rates for "professional," non-dissertation-required doctorates, such as law, medicine and dentistry. It is difficult to see how any other factor but the differential thesis requirement can account for the very different success rates. Men and women are about equally represented in the ABD population, although men are over-represented in doctorates conferred. But projections from 1970s data indicate that women will make substantial strides toward parity with men by 1990.

3. After completion of predissertation requirements, the candidate finds himself adrift, with accustomed educational support systems withdrawn to a degree unprecedented in American education at any level. Particular conditions implicated in this situation are dissertation anomie, faculty "unreliability," lack of a graduate student community and candidates' "unpreparedness" for the great task.

4. The book is addressed to (a) graduate students still doing course work, who want anticipatory socialization to the demands of the upcoming dissertation course; (b) the 51,000 new ABDs squarely up

against the thesis task; (c) the undetermined but large number of "veteran" ABDs; (d) families, spouses, lovers and friends of ABDs, to aid them in living with their candidate through this difficult time in his life by providing some in-depth background on the project with which he is wrestling; (e) graduate educators, administrators and faculty, in the hope that this exposition will prompt structural reforms of the callousness and even disrespect with which programs currently treat ABDs.

5. The volume is designed to be a constant companion or "guidebook" for the writer along all the major stations of the dissertation course: the initial deliberate decision to write the thesis; proposal; data collection; data analysis; actual writing of chapters; thesis defense; postdegree aftermath. Throughout, four essential dimensions of the project are consistenly treated and interwoven: "nuts-and-bolts" issues; emotional difficulties of the candidate caused by the thesis experience; possible changes and disruptions in interpersonal relations; strategies and tactics for dealing with dissertation-supervising faculty.

NOTES

1. Neal Ascherson's review of E. Ettinger's ed., *Comrade and Lover: Rosa Luxemburg's Letters to Leo Jogiches*, in *New York Review of Books*, March 6, 1980, p. 4.
2. In the early 1930s, George Stewart, an English professor at Berkeley, wrote a novel called *Doctor's Oral*, describing the disruptions in intimate relations, and anxieties generated by writing a dissertation. I am indebted to my former professor, Robert Bierstedt, for calling this book to my attention.
3. W. Zinsser, *On Writing Well: An Informal Guide to Writing Nonfiction*, 2nd ed. (New York: Harper and Row, 1980).
4. John Almack, *Research and Thesis Writing: A Textbook in Principles and Techniques of Thesis Construction for the Use of Graduate Students in Universities and Colleges* (Boston: Houghton-Mifflin, 1930).
5. H. Livesey and H. Doughty, *Guide to American Graduate Schools*, 3rd ed. (New York: Viking, Compass Books, 1975), page xx.
6. *Projections of Education Statistics* to 1986–87 (Washington, D.C.: National Center for Education Statistics, HEW, 1978), Table 9, pp. 28–29.
7. Wilkinson, "A Profile: Minorities in Sociology and Other Behavioral Sciences," American Sociological Association *Footnotes*, November

1978, pp. 6–8; "Women in the Profession: Data Sources for the Eighties, Sociologists for Women Society, SWS *Newsletter,* January 1980.

8. If the Wilkinson statistical trend continues in social science, 1990 should see equal numbers of candidates and conferred degrees for both sexes. For a more doubtful view of rapidly approaching parity, especially in doctoral *degrees,* see Dearman and Plisko, *The Condition of Education* (Washington, D.C.: National Center for Education Statistics, HEW, 1979), p. 231, and their "Projections of Degrees, by Level and Sex to 1987–1988," forthcoming management bulletin.

9. Usually, education doctoral dissertations have to do with some basic institutional element, such as faculty or student personnel, administration of some level of education system, instructing a particular type of student and the like. The substantive and methodological perspectives are ordinarily psychology, sociology, political science or public administration. See *Digest of Education Statistics,* Table 108 (on degrees conferred by field and subfield of study, 1976–1977), (Washington, D.C.: National Center for Education Statistics, HEW, 1979), pp. 113–114.

10. Even in the more rigorous sciences, a concern with writing lucid English for popular and lay audiences, as well as for colleagues, is growing, although it probably has not yet substantially affected dissertation style. See R. Barass, *Scientists Must Write: A Guide to Better Writing for Scientists, Engineers and Students* (New York: Wiley, 1978).

11. Although precise numbers are not known, pre-ABD dissertation starts are apparently not infrequent. See Livesey and Doughty, op. cit., pp. xxii–xxiii.

12. In the 1970s, in a little-known debate and decision, the Board of Higher Education of the City University of New York (CUNY) ruled that a J.D. qualified as a "doctor's degree" required to hold a tenured professorial line. I have always disagreed with this decision, since the J.D., in my judgment and experience, amounts to little more than an M.A., especially since no dissertation is required. The decision was made on lobbying and "political" grounds, rather than on academic ones.

13. Derek C. Bok, "A Challenge to Legal Education" *Harvard Law School Bulletin,* Fall 1979, pp. 12–15.

14. Cf., R. Hofstadter, ed., *Anti-Intellectualism in American Life* (New York: Knopf, 1963).

15. H. Wilensky, "Mass Society and Mass Culture," *American Sociological Review,* April 1964; see also Anderson and Murray, eds., *The Professors: Work and Life Styles Among Academicians* (Cambridge, Mass.: Schenkman, 1971).

16. When the term "graduate faculty" is used, a distinction has to be made

between the minority situation, usually in elite schools, where graduate professors teach and work only in the graduate program; and the much more usual case, where professors have assignments in both undergraduate and graduate, say, education or sociology programs. In the former cases, of course, faculty are much more apt to be forthcoming with supervision and guidance of theses.

17. Those candidates in the minority elite programs may be *partially* exempted from some of the remarks in this section on unpreparedness; but even there I would contend that the issues of the dissertation task are never squarely met in course work, term papers or class projects.

18. Educators never seem to discuss the inconsistencies between emphasis on peer group learning and phobias against "cheating." Particularly with young students, when "moral judgment" is not fully developed, a distinction between cooperation and cheating must be very difficult to see. Many students, I believe, carry a genuine lack of distinction right through college.

19. With the near-depression economics of the late 1970s and early 1980s, even the most traditionally liberal arts-oriented of universities, notably Harvard, have retrenched to a more "practical" focus on the Three Rs, giving way to the demands of many (corporate) employers (often endowers) and even many students that marketable skills be emphasized.

20. I wrote a 191-page master's thesis in sociology and found it helpful, up to a point, for doing my dissertation three years later.

21. The late 1970s saw a burgeoning of "uncolleges," where one spent all his time in the shop learning a skilled trade (machine, computer programming, TV or air-conditioning repairs) and was promised by television commercials there would be no "hassles" with useless drivel like foreign languages, history or sociology. The growth of "uncolleges" is certain for the 1980s as well. One wonders how their advertisements might strike, or tempt, a floundering ABD.

22. H. Crosby and G. Estey, *College Writing,* 2nd ed. (New York: Harper and Row, 1975).

CHAPTER 2

The Great Decision: Reordering Priorities and Choosing a (Viable) Topic

THE DISSERTATION: STARTING ALL OVER AGAIN

In medical or law school, the decision to *enter* these graduate programs is the last great decision, since faithful course attendance and examination passing virtually ensure acquisition of an M.D. or J.D. in four or three years' time. It is the crux of the ABD problem that dissertation-required doctorates demand an extra great decision—to write or not to write—and that the average candidate is unaware, until far down the program's line, of its importance and necessity. It is the failure to confront this decision peculiar to dissertation doctorates that accounts for more nonfinishes or long delays than any other single factor.

It is probably not exaggerating matters very much to assert that course work and even preliminary examinations, on the one hand, and writing the dissertation, on the other, have no relationship. Certainly, as we have seen, successful (even outstanding) performance up to the dissertation is no guarantee of completion of the degree. What the catalogs, deans and faculty don't tell the candidate is that graduate school success really involves the negotiation of *two* separate programs, one ending with passing course work and preliminaries (and sometimes obtaining a master's degree as well), and the other beginning with "applying" for admission to write a dissertation through submission of an acceptable proposal. In a very real sense, disserta-

30

tion writers are starting over again, and very little in their past two or three years of performance counts for much. That matters shouldn't stand this way (and many program spokespersons will indignantly howl that what I am claiming is false or exaggerated), that there should be continuity between the two parts of a doctorate, that it is unfair, even a disgrace and should be rectified forthwith—with all this the writer concurs. But the "two-program" model is here to stay for the foreseeable future, certainly going to span the reader's dissertation-writing experience. If the candidate wants to work to alter this system, fine. But do it after you finish your doctorate.

It is just this failure to understand that the dissertation and the preceding parts of the program are independent that makes questions such as "Do you really want to write your dissertation?" or "Have you thought through some changes in your life you are going to have to make while doing the project?" sound puzzling or even silly. "Of course I want to do my dissertation; I'm in graduate school, aren't I? I'm here to get my doctorate," the candidate will answer. But he or she has usually "bought" the "professional school" model of the doctorate, the one minus the zinger: the dissertation. Omission of the dissertation as its "own ball game" makes these questions and answers unreflexive to each other.

Cost Accounting the Dissertation.

The dissertation is definitely not for everybody, not even for all ABDs, particularly since most have failed to consider the independent demands and related skills and attitudes of that project. All ABDs, or near-ABDs, should undertake a serious "cost analysis" prior to undertaking the dissertation.[1] Involved in the equation are considerations such as one's goals/priorities in life, a sober appreciation of the specific demands of writing a dissertation, an honest inventory of one's *intellectual/literary strengths and weaknesses* vis-à-vis these demands, an inventory of one's *emotional strengths and weaknesses* vis-à-vis the dissertation demands, a projection of the "rewards" and "punishments" awaiting one along the dissertation way, and beyond. As the candidate reads through this book, he will get a fuller understanding of just what changes in life-style the dissertation is going to demand and be able to make a more reliable and convincing decision as to whether he possesses what Tom Wolfe has called, in another context, the "right stuff" for the task.[2]

Some Wrong Reasons for Writing the Dissertation.

I am terming those reasons which generally won't sustain a candidate through the project as "wrong." If you are contemplating a dissertation chiefly for one or more reasons akin to the following (selected) types, you are, my "actuarial" experience dictates, in for a great deal of trouble:

1. "I've got an exciting topic." More specific discussion about choosing a dissertation subject will ensue later in the chapter, but here let me state that, although an "exciting" topic (sometimes connected with a "chance-in-a-lifetime" research access) can serve as a first-stage motivator, all dissertation topics become predictably frayed, frustrating, often boring, infuriating for the writer at points down the course. When students tell me that their problem is that they picked the "wrong"—say, sociology—topic, I relate to them the agonies and ennui that fellow candidates who chose "in" topics on sex roles or more bizarre types of deviant behavior are experiencing. One picks a dissertation topic—a relatively secondary concern—after serious commitment to the primary goal of writing a doctoral dissertation; to reverse the sequence of these two decisions is to misunderstand the nature of the dissertation and invite nonfinishing.

2. "If I don't write the dissertation, I'll have wasted years of study and money." It is true in large part that you will have wasted both. I am not going to patronize you with talk about how learning is valuable in its own right, regardless of material reward (even though that is undoubtedly universally true up to a point), living as we are in the financially tight 1980s. But the dissertation is not like a business venture, or even like a professional school (business school included) where just "hanging in there" or "toughing it out" more often than not will pay off or bring you even. If an ABD's cost accounting yields debits in lack of skills and/or motivations for the long-distance dissertation, he should quit, or at the very least take some time off, do something else for a while, to rethink priorities and willingness to work on deficiencies. Better to waste two or three years than five or six.

3. "Everybody's expecting me to write it and get my doctorate." The problem here is that "everybody," including the candidate, until very

32

recently was operating on the doctorate *qua* law, medicine or dentistry model. These good folks, including one's nearest and dearest, don't understand about the extra requirement (any more than you really did). In any situation where one allows others in possession of less crucial intelligence than oneself to dictate a decision, a self-destructive delegation and abdication of agency and authority is being committed. In my experience, one can still—after very serious and thorough conclusions about the costs of a dissertation being too high, or one's "set" toward the task just not being up to it—walk away from two or three years of course work, certainly hurt for a while, but survive quite whole. Such is not the case after putting in an additional year or two on a dissertation with no end in sight. Those years are more than waste: each succeeding one bores into one's strength, making it harder and harder to walk away whole and get on to another task or profession where the prognosis is better and interest higher.

4. "I'm not quitting this one too." Oftentimes, candidates in dissertation-requiring programs have a biography of leaving other disciplines or careers. Such earlier abdications, changes of mind, reversals of field may weigh heavily on the state of mind of a candidate who is contemplating not pursuing the dissertation: "Here I go again. Another time of not seeing it through." I believe American society puts entirely too much pressure on its young adult persons to "find themselves," usually equating that discovery with hitting upon a lifetime job or career. The equation is quite false: many people who successfully pursue one line of employment never really "find themselves" in the sense of internally experienced feelings of gratification; on the other hand, many occupational "drifters" move from field to field, feel reasonably good about themselves and experience shame (not internal guilt) only when denigrated by others for their spotty employment records.

In any event, the dissertation doctorate is the worst place for a career-uncertain person to make his last stand, if that mood is his chief one for continuing in a program, since the dissertation prerequires the very kind of commitment which is most problematic in the case of this type of candidate.

The Right Reason for Undertaking the Dissertation.

Although one can catalog a list of wrong (insufficiently motivating) reasons for undertaking the dissertation, only one general "right" rea-

33

son exists: The candidate is deeply interested in his specific discipline and has every intention of pursuing a career within the field immediately upon (or at least soon after) completion of the thesis. This reason must not be confused with that of finding a "sexy" or "in" dissertation topic, which is a fleeting and often effervescent motivator.

One of the most troublesome aspects of the dissertation is the relative absence of short-term, even middle-term rewards. Dissertation writers constantly complain about not being able to see the end of the road as the months and seasons of proposals, research, analysis and writing go on. (There are certain ways, which the book will discuss, in which along-the-way rewards can be built in by the writer, but they only partially break up the built-in burden and dreariness of the thesis course.) The dissertation-writing situation parallels long-distance running in this respect. How do runners keep going, mile upon mile, in, say, a twenty-six-mile marathon? Experienced harriers, such as James Fixx, note that when their feet and souls begin to drag along the way, they constantly remind themselves that there were well-thought-out reasons for wanting to finish the race before they began; some even repeat these reasons to themselves right through the entire course of the run.[3]

It is my conviction that only the candidate's firm intention to become a full (the doctorate bestowing full membership) professional in his dissertation field, combined with his constant self-reminders of that intention and eventual gratification through the ups and downs of the long dissertation "run," is an adequate long-range reward for the task confronting him. Since the time I was in college, there was talk, and lore, about the so-called "gentleman scholar" (who in undergraduate school received the "gentleman's C" grades), who pursued graduate school and even the dissertation at his leisure, with no serious thought about finishing in a relatively limited time, or especial concern with taking up a career in the field. I have come to doubt that (a) such people exist, or (b) if they do, that they ever finish their theses. Even in the serious academic and research employment recessions of the 1970s and 1980s, almost all the earnest and committed dissertation writers I have known believed they would obtain (although very often not without a good deal of initial perseverance and disappointment at the start of employment search) a full-time "line" position.

34

This is to say that people who are in the dissertation game on "spec" are most often not going to make it. Those who believe they are going to "pick up" a dissertation doctorate and then "see what happens" are a particularly high-casualty group. I am not asserting that one cannot successfully negotiate a dissertation while working another job (including running a household with children)—there may sometimes even be advantages to such a dissertation-writing situation. But if one's *attitude* is leisurely and uncommitted to a definite switch in full-time employment to the doctorate field, the "moonlight" candidate has small hope of completing.

Let me point up again the distinction between interest in one's field and in one's dissertation subject. In the past few years I have had a number of clients in psychology Ph.D. programs who were interning as clinical psychologists/psychotherapists. Invariably, their dissertation topics and methodologies—whether they were matriculated in clinical psychology, educational psychology, counseling psychology or another specialty—were *experimental* projects. It is one of the dislocations of graduate psychology programs—parallel ones can no doubt be found in many of the disciplines with which we are concerned—that no matter what eventual subfield of psychology a Ph.D. pursues (a National Science Foundation report indicated that three-fourths of psychologists pursue "service" careers working with patients or clients, and only one-fourth "research" ones), he is almost always required to write an experimental-model dissertation.

My psychology dissertation clients always disliked, sometimes even hated, their dissertations because there was so little relationship (or the relationship was a *negative* one, as they saw it; the "objective" methods of the dissertation research and experiment were opposed to the "intuitive" approach in therapy) to their present and future work in psychotherapy. Thus, on top of the usual aversion to necessarily making the dissertation the center of one's life was the additional complication that the content, methodology and *ideology* of the topic conflicted with the substance, approach and ideology of their clinical work, even though the dissertation and their jobs were both in the general field of psychology. Yet, most of these persons finished their theses (most even came to "like" their dissertations, or at least feel terribly proud and gratified that they were able to complete them), because the doctorate was absolutely essential for them to become licensed as clinical psychologists. Each of these candidates possessed a very strong *general commitment* to psychology and was able, with struggle, to transfer that drive to a topic to which he or she was certainly less than committed. My input consisted in large part in getting these candidates to remind themselves constantly that the lifelong gratification of being "Dr. Jones," practicing their professions in a fully credentialed and societally prestigious manner, was worth an all-out eighteen-to-twenty-four-month effort now.[4]

Getting into the Driver's Seat of Your Dissertation.

As we have taken pains to note, American graduate schools, let alone lower-level systems of education, do not enculturate their students for the task of the dissertation. Accordingly, ABDs come to the dissertation assuming—to the problematic extent they think much about it at all—that their lives are going to proceed pretty much along SOP lines during their project. The dissertation is hazily adumbrated as not much more than a long term paper. Many candidates never get past this erroneous picture of the thesis, never get a handle on its true scope, never finish. The dissertation experience, until they give up, is one long puzzle for them: "Every time I go down to the department they find something else wrong, or something else for me to add. I can't understand it." Or: "I go to one professor, and she tells me I better take her course in theory construction before I continue my proposal; I go to another, and he tells me I need work in statistics. What's going on here? I feel like I'm getting the runaround."

What's going on is that the candidate is continuing to play the *reactive role* in which he has been so heavily trained by our school system, rather than taking the *active role* the dissertation demands. To do a dissertation one has to see the big picture: if you fail to have the grand design blocked out, then you are constantly at the compartmentalizing mercies of faculty and various advice givers, since they can capriciously change the shakily charted direction of your thought and inquiries. The candidate has to get into the driver's seat of his dissertation, and this means jettisoning long-seated, dysfunctional intellectual—and even life—styles. A main goal of this book is to plot out, in the following chapters, specific strategies and tactics for converting the typically shaky ABD from a reactive, passive, childlike taker of advice and instructions to an adult, autonomous forger of his own dissertation. Without such a "conversion," the thesis will rarely be completed,

36

or, even if completed, fail to bestow its chief potential benefit—aside from the doctorate—infusing the rest of one's life with a sense of achievement in completing an enormous project which so few men and women are able to negotiate.

Making the Dissertation a Top Priority in Your Life.

It is only when the dissertation is first or second on the ABD's priority list that he is able to devote to it the time, attention and motivation to grasp its big picture, or grand design. Only with the thesis constantly on one's mind can one "call the shots." Think of the candidate as a stagehand straining to push the "set" of his dissertation to the middle of his life stage. But a theater grip has to move props and set pieces around. Everything can't be center-stage; some must be moved upstage, downstage or even offstage for the duration of important scenes.

The successful candidate is going to have to rearrange his social and psychological priorities—and even relationships—during the dissertation course if he is to get on top of the thesis and drive it home to completion. Many, if not most, ABDs offer fierce resistance to setting a new scene onstage. And yet, nearly all the successful writers I have known had to make the dissertation close to an obsession (magnificent or otherwise). This is almost indescribably difficult to convey, especially to American students, who find the concept so alien. The idea of lovers, spouses, children, social life in general being relegated to a back burner, virtually put "on hold" for much of the dissertation course, is horrifying, often incomprehensible to people. Yet the rigors of the research and writing are such that a candidate has no strength, stomach or time for extensive quarrels, grand passions, backbiting. The "shutting down," or at least severe "cutback," of extradissertation concerns for the year or two of writing is poignantly if humorously underscored by a "personal" ad in the *New York Review of Books* (November 22, 1979): "33-YEAR-OLD ATTRACTIVE WOMAN, having just finished her doctorate, is ready to enjoy life again and would like to meet an adventurous man."

Friends and Lovers During the Dissertation:
Differential Association.

But, you may protest indignantly, do I seriously expect you to give up your husband, your lover, your family, your job? Believe me, none of these would be bad ideas, at least in certain cases. But I am not suggesting across-the-board cutting off of one's intimate and employment connections, even if this were possible. Rather, I am suggesting the need to create a "space" for oneself of relative tranquillity and freedom to think about and work on the dissertation. Management of one's particular extradissertation relationships has to be dictated by answering the question: "Is the content or tone of this relationship helpful, detrimental or neutral in getting my dissertation finished?" Depending on your biographical answers to these questions, you are going to have to nurture, withdraw from or accept various associations. Dissertation writing demands a kind of "differential association" with people determined by how they affect the progress of your thesis.[5]

Obviously, some detrimental dissertation associations can't be completely cut off: Your husband may be intractable about not supporting your need for dissertation space, but a good provider, father and lover. You'll need him, and want him, at a later date, after the doctorate is conferred. What you must do in the meantime is try to negotiate with *him* to give you some time off and with *yourself* to point mentally and emotionally in the dissertation direction without a new debilitating *guilt* burden of neglecting the family. Such alterations in associations or emotional investments in associations are possible only if you have genuinely put finishing the thesis virtually at the top of your list.

Dissertation time is no time for emotional crises in one's personal life; the crises of the dissertation are quite enough to bear and surmount. Candidates "swept away" by a new grand passion can get shipwrecked on the dissertation rocks. Actually, if one is totally committed to a dissertation, getting swept away is unlikely, but the early stages of writing (e.g., the proposal) are dangerous times; many candidates, frightened by the extent of the commitment, are seeking a way out.

Figure 2.1 delineates the salient status positions and corresponding role relationships a "typical" ABD is likely to possess and have to deal with. (Obviously, some candidates will not be incumbents of all of these statuses, although most will occupy some version of all or nearly all of them.) The doctoral candidate status is much further refined and analyzed in terms of specific role partners in Chapter Six, on presenting the unfolding dissertation to faculty (see Figures 6.1 and 6.2, below).

Plotting Your Differential Dissertation Associations.

Figure 2.1: An ABD's Status-and-Role Sets

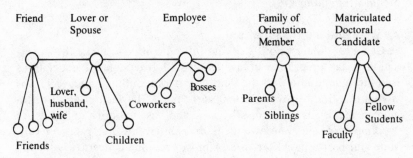

At the point of seriously undertaking the project, the candidate is urged to diagram his own differential association map/model, taking Figure 2.1 as a point of departure:

1. List your key statuses, and with whom you deal within them on a regular basis.
2. Evaluate each personal, family, student and work association (a) in terms of whether it helps, hurts or is neutral to dissertation progress, and (b) *in what specific ways.*
3. For each association map out a strategy for maximizing or minimizing your contacts (not merely on a numerical dimension, but in terms of emotional investment) during the dissertation writing.
4. Make the exercise an ongoing one; every couple of months re-evaluate both the nature of the associations and how well you have managed to deal with them in the interests of moving ahead with your dissertation.

Some of these alterations in your association model, first construed by the candidate as temporary, may turn out to be permanent. Sometimes the dissertation experience, by changing a person, permanently alters certain personal/social as well as occupational relationships. This is almost inevitable in a project demanding reaching way down inside oneself for resources perhaps never before realized. A dissertation has a way of making a *mensch* of a man or woman no longer satisfied with all of the old arrangements and associations in life.

There is, then, risk, but also promise in doing the dissertation. Any way one cuts it, the doctoral dissertation is not for the fainthearted (see Chapter Nine, "Beyond the Dissertation: Surviving It and Professionally Exploiting It").

Of Work and the Dissertation.

Can a candidate who is working full-time hope to make the dissertation a near top priority in his life, possibly rearrange his associations and life-style in line with the kind of program outlined above? This is a vital question for over 160,000 part-time ABDs facing the dissertation in the 1980s (part-time because the vast majority of them are working). No one *knows* what the differential finishing rates for full-time and part-time writers are. Almost everyone concerned with the issue *guesses* that full-timers have higher success rates, or, at the least, faster finishing rates. The reliability and validity of these hunches, observations and guesses are complicated by many "mixed" cases; an ABD may stop work, say, for a year to work on his thesis, then returns not having finished, or someone may continue to work and complete his dissertation.

I am cautious about overall negative correlations between working and effectively writing and finishing the dissertation. Some of that caution comes from my own dissertation experience: During at least half of my dissertation course (eighteen months from its start to finish), I held a part-time teaching job, which did not, upon reflection, impede my progress (although at the time I cursed it roundly and often for believing it to be doing so). Beyond my dissertation, I know that the most sustained, long-distance writing I did in the 1970s was during academic terms when I was teaching a four-course load.

Much depends upon the *nature* of one's employment. Going back to the differential dissertation association model, work can be classified as contributive, dysfunctional or neutral in reference to dissertation progress. Teaching or research jobs in the same or related field to one's thesis most often have a synergistic, positive effect on dissertation development. In my case, I used the classroom to get feedback from my students on problems I was having with my fieldwork. Having to delineate these issues in lecture form forced me to rethink and clarify them for myself. Then, too, sharing my work with my students was most stimulating and motivationally very crucial; students were awaiting the next episode in my dissertation research. The lectures I gave during my fieldwork were some of the most exciting, existential and "authentic" of my career. Students sense when you are talking about something you are actually carrying through, as opposed to giving a "secondary source" lecture.

One kind of dysfunctional job so physically and emotionally exhausts a candidate that the last thing on his mind is two hours of dissertation work after dinner. This kind of job creates the "weekend warrior" type of work style, where the candidate tries to give his project a few hours on the weekend (said hours being resented by the ABD himself who wants Saturday and Sunday to rest and recharge for Monday; his spouse and children, who want these hours shared with them). A *sine qua non* of progress is a regular, scheduled taking up of the dissertation cudgels. Weekend dissertation writing coupled with a physically demanding full-time job rarely yields a finished thesis.

Another kind of dissertation-disservice job involves soakage in forty hours of a chiefly antiintellectual or "practical" ambience. I would say that the majority of business and sales jobs fall into this category. The danger with such work locales is that they tend to instill in the candidate a cynicism, impatience and even deprecation toward the worth of his dissertation. Such debilitation is often as hindering to writing a dissertation as a physically demanding job. Although there is talk (there are even books) about the "academic marketplace," and although certain elements of dissertation negotiation (e.g., the proposal) have a definite contract element, the dissertation is not "doing business," in the sense of commercial affairs. The hustle, high-pressure sales techniques and ideology that "everybody and everything has its price" are most dysfunctional activity styles and attitudes for winning dissertation approval from a laid-back faculty accustomed to moving at a much more leisurely pace.[6]

There *is* one instance when a candidate can turn an aggressive business context to his advantage: when that site and its personnel are the subjects of his dissertation (see below in this chapter for choosing a dissertation topic). When this is the case, the "double agent" quality of the job can convert it into an exciting affair: one isn't really there as an employee, although that is one's "cover," but as a sociologist, political scientist, psychologist, recording the data for one's own purposes and project.

Sometimes a job has already conferred a relatively high status on the incumbent, to the extent that he may seriously resist the role reversal and role abnegation built into the status of ABD in his dealings with supervising graduate faculty. High-placed business executives, ranking police officers, supervisors of public agencies and lawyers—to name a few groups—have all had authority conflicts and stresses when concomitantly pursuing a doctorate. Although a teaching position is usually a dissertation-promoting employment (see above), in the case of a long-term ABD who has taught for many years, holds tenure and perhaps a high rank (cases of tenured professors without a Ph.D. were more common ten or twenty years ago, but can still be found), it is not conducive to rematriculating and/or completing the dissertation. A fifty-year-old professor, mistakenly addressed by students, staff and faculty as Dr. Jones for fifteen years, comfortable with his teaching situation, has very little to gain (and perhaps a good deal to forfeit: his position might be jeopardized if the question of his incomplete credentials was raised anew) by reseeking the doctorate.

There is, of course, the other side to the picture where a "halo effect" mechanism transfers the ABD's "outside" prestige over to the graduate program setting and creates deferential or collegial treatment from faculty. A few years ago, for example, an MD entered the doctoral program in sociology at an Ivy League university. Within a year, a number of the faculty were asking him for prescriptions. Without necessarily postulating a causal relationship, it is instructive to note that he negotiated the doctoral/dissertation course with unusual smoothness. In my own case, I would hazard that my possession of a law degree when I entered the New York University sociology graduate program gave me some "points"; I recall being asked for, and giving, occasional legal advice to professors during my course years. But any leverage I might have gained during predissertation years vanished for a number of reasons, perhaps most saliently the fact that *I* vanished for a year or two upon completion of my course work and preliminary orals, and returned to confront new faculty whom I had never counseled and who were unfamiliar with my extrasociology credentials.

Neutral jobs are those which neither promote nor hinder progress on the dissertation. Although I couldn't possibly catalog them all, by a process of exclusion they would include work which didn't leave one bone-weary and jobs where at least some "life of the mind" element existed. Many nonprofit organization and/or public service jobs would qualify here; in the private sector, publishing and advertising probably won't hurt you, although they may not help. A number of my master's and doctoral advisees over the years have used "neutral" work sites, especially public service agencies (e.g., drug control divisions, court staffs, social welfare departments) as successful theoretical focuses and data bases.

An employed reader/candidate is going to have to construct his own personalized calculus in evaluating his job as functional, dysfunctional or neutral for getting his dissertation done. Certainly, my classification and assignment of particular jobs to one category or another does not presume to be "airtight." Some teaching jobs are permeated with cynicism and antiintellectualism; some business positions are rich in analytic thinking and long-range planning (both necessary features in a dissertation). But, if only to use my observations as a point of departure, the fully employed candidate has to evaluate his job with a view toward maximizing its dissertation-promoting aspects and containing or defusing its dissertation-discouraging elements. If such a calculus "prints out" as highly negative, the candidate is either going to have to change his job or face inevitable discouragement and delay in the progress of his thesis. It is at such a decision junction that being in touch with the reasons for writing one's dissertation becomes imperative.

Setting Up a Dissertation Office.

The need to rearrange social and psychological life priorities during the dissertation course is facilitated and reinforced by (indeed, requires) creating an objective base, or "office," designed exclusively for this project. Developmental psychologists have demonstrated that children with their own rooms perform better in school than matched children without one. The quality of the room's furnishings, luxurious or rather sparse, seems unimportant in affecting learning; the privacy is paramount. There is every reason to believe that such differentials stretch into adult performance of intellectual tasks.[7]

The office should (1) be in a separate room, or at least place, and (2) devoted as completely as possible, during the life of the dissertation, to thesis matters. Both of these requirements may present problems of execution in a particular candidate's case. One's home or apartment may simply not have an extra room to convert into a dissertation office. A number of my clients lived with spouses in one-bedroom apartments. In each of these instances, they "carved out" a part of either the bedroom or living room, using some kind of room divider, such as bookcases or screens to isolate the office. Another ABD created an office under the loft bed she constructed in the bedroom. Particularly in the case of the bedroom office, it was agreed upon (eventually, but not without resistance) that the ABD's spouse would stay out of the bedroom during dissertation working hours. Until that ground rule was implemented, the office was so permeable and subject to interruption (from spouse) and even disruption (from children) that little sustained progress could be made.

It is also almost essential that the office not be the base for multiple enterprises, from paying bills, to letter writing, to collection and storage of mail, memorabilia and years of graduate school clutter in the form of notes, books and term papers. A desk and bookcase(s) in the "common area" of the home should do for these diverse activities and papers. The idea is to underscore both the "starting anew" and single-mindedness of the dissertation project. The clean desk signifies the clean slate of one's beginning. Every item that subsequently enters your office should be there only because of its necessity for and contribution to the dissertation. If this sounds like a rather "Spartan" organization plan, it is intended to; soon enough the office will begin to fill up.

So, the *privacy* of your office signifies to both you and those you live with the respect and importance you accord to your independent project. (It is most often the independent quality and implications of the dissertation course which cause a spouse or lover to resist the office rearrangement, not the specious reason that it is "inconvenient" or "unfair.") It also helps you get into the driver's seat of your dissertation by providing you with a dissertation space that is always waiting for you when you have scheduled time for work, or whenever you feel like (and you will) "just being" with your dissertation. Making the office *exclusive to the thesis* also underscores its uniqueness and importance, and gets one right down to a dissertation-writing frame of mind. No diversions await one in the office; one sits down and is squarely up against the task.

44

What should the office contain? You need a decent-size desk, one or more bookcases, writing materials and/or a typewriter, a filing cabinet (the building of a file is so crucial to mounting a dissertation that the next chapter is devoted to it), probably (à la Woody Allen in *Manhattan*) a tape recorder (the uses of which are discussed in Chapter Three) and perhaps a blackboard (particularly if you are a teacher and feel comfortable and familiar with getting down ideas in that fashion). Although, everything else being equal, the office should be as pleasant as possible, little time should be spent on interior decorating after the essential equipment has been set up. Establish privacy and exclusivity; further elaborations are usually "dissertation stall."

Dissertation Office Hours.

It is essential to set up a rather rigid schedule of hours to work each day (week) on the dissertation. You've set up an office; now you have to "punch in," with the important difference that *you* are the boss and have to police yourself in punctuality and attendance. The editors of the *Paris Review* have interviewed, since 1953, over fifty successful full-time novelists, essayists, poets and playwrights living in many countries to get a picture of how they worked at their craft.[8] Perhaps the most important common thread among such a diverse group of writers was that they maintained a virtually invariable daily writing time, five to seven days a week, for from two to four hours, and at the same time of the day (most often, mornings).[9] Another theme that emerged was how *systematic* and *businesslike* about their writing these people are (were), even in the case of those stereotyped as "unpredictable," "flamboyant," "wild" or "irresponsible" (e.g., William Faulkner, Ernest Hemingway, Henry Miller, Norman Mailer).

I have discovered that *some time each day* (or at least five days a week: even the most zealous candidate/writer has to reward himself with an occasional day of rest) at the office is the key effective variable. Optimally, the period should be a minimum of two hours, but this cannot always be arranged, particularly for full-time employed candidates. The point is that, say, ten hours a week spent in the dissertation office in two sittings (often at weekends) does not have the same punch as five two-hour sessions. What one needs on this job is to establish and maintain an ongoing rhythm and flow. Progress on the dissertation comes with day-to-day involvement: if you give it only two "shots" a week, half of your allocated time session is apt to be spent just "catching up" or reminding yourself of where you left off the previous week. So, in terms of progress, a two-session ten-hour input is going to yield closer to five hours, because of deductions for "maintenance." Thus, it is probably more effective to spend only one hour each day in the office (five hours a week) than a whole afternoon on both weekend days.

The writer will discover that he will often want to exceed his daily minimum time, particularly when things are humming. Whenever feasible, one should try to leave an hour's breathing space after the scheduled time limit to allow one to continue when the blood is up. On the other hand, the writer should never "leave the office early" on a day when the project isn't speeding along. Very often, I know from my own experience, a person can sit stalled at his typewriter or daydreaming for an hour and a half; suddenly a breakthrough can happen, and the next half hour is rapid, productive work. But you have to give yourself time, tough out some of the (seeming) doldrums if you are to be there to exploit the opportunity. Mark Twain once said, "The harder I work, the better my luck gets."

I rarely have a day anymore when nothing, or very little at all, comes out of two or three hours at my machine. But certainly, there are sessions when I am a good deal less than satisfied with what I have written. I make it a rule never to indulge in a past novice habit of angrily ripping up pages which I don't like and throwing them in the wastebasket. I find that the next day in the office I can almost always extract something from those imperfect pages which will, in fact, fit into my ongoing manuscript. Short of this, that output at least gives me a lead-in for the next day's hopefully more on-target production.

The discussion about time spent in the dissertation office has to be qualified with respect to library research and fieldwork that particular dissertations require. At certain stages of the dissertation, your work will undeniably require your being "out of the office" and "in the field" for days, or even weeks, at a stretch. Still, one always has to come back to the office to put together library and field research. During the fieldwork stage of my dissertation (lasting about nine months), I almost always spent an additional two or three hours (at the end of the day) in my office, reviewing my field notes, reminding myself what had to be followed up the next day, writing down impressions and hunches (see next chapter on "Building a Dissertation File" for a tabulation of these kinds of office activities). Despite the time demands of library attendance and fieldwork or conducting experiments, one must not relinquish a daily period at the dissertation office (although it may be necessary for limited periods to reduce the blocks of time); one must mind the store.

These guidelines about time apply to the employed ABD as well as the candidate who doesn't have to work during his dissertation course. The employed ABD is going to have to find ways to get in a daily hour or two at his office, even if this means confrontations with family and friends, and sacrifice of leisure, usually evening, hours for TV. If time is not found and a schedule not implemented, neither the working nor the nonemployed ABD is going to finish the dissertation. Additionally, there are going to be times with dissertations (particularly in social science and education fields) where the working candidate will have to take a few days off from employment, usually to gather data from subjects or groups who aren't available after 5 P.M. Again, during the writing of the dissertation, after all the data and statistical analyses are in, an employed ABD may want/need to take off some days or weeks to write "full-time" in the office. These contingencies must be anticipated and taken into account in evaluating the functional or dysfunctional effects of one's job on completing the dissertation.

Choosing a Dissertation Topic.

Contrary to a good deal of faculty and student mythology, the dissertation topic *per se* is at best a secondary factor both in determining whether a candidate finishes and the troubles he experiences at different stages of research and writing. Recall my argument about the topic as *dependent* variable, commitment to becoming a full-fledged member of the profession as the *independent, prior* one in the sequence of dissertation decisions. No matter how "exotic" the topic, e.g., "Swedish Prostitutes and Their Black American Pimps in Stockholm"; how "current" or "relevant," e.g., "Mary McCarthy and Susan Sontag: Contrasting Visions in Feminist Literature"; how obscure or arcane, e.g., "Effects of White Noise Occlusion of Voice Feedback on Superego Functioning"; all dissertations run into a predictable, common set of both "internal" problems, from hypothesis construction to sample issues, methodological difficulties, analytic contradictions and "external" difficulties connected with getting several faculty members

47

to agree upon not only the topic itself, but from what perspective and in what degree of emphasis and detail it should be pursued.

None of this is to say that one should not give careful consideration to the thesis topic. *Careful consideration* should be underscored here, because when a fresh ABD or near-ABD is buzzing with dozens of tentative topics, such consideration is going to render most of these inspirations unfeasible. One has to put four essential questions to every prospective topic:

Is it researchable? For a comparative-literature candidate, the issue might be whether relevant texts from other eras, countries or languages were available/accessible. For the psychology or sociology candidate, the key question is whether one has access to, or can gain admission to, topic-loaded samples or groups. For example, an undoubtedly worthwhile and "relevant" dissertation topic in social psychology would be "The National Security Council As a Small Group: A Test of Bales's Interaction Process Matrix." Bales and his associates, watching, recording and videotaping Harvard undergraduates for decades through one-way mirrors, have constructed a set of "laws" about how members will behave which they assert are generalizable to all small "task-oriented" groups. However, it is most unlikely that an ABD will get a chance to set up shop in a room adjacent to the NSC conference room, so that such a topic is going to have to be scratched and something a bit more pedestrian and a lot more accessible substituted, like *Tally's Corner: A Study of Negro Streetcorner Men.*[10] One must be virtually certain that the data for the dissertation will be available and accessible *when* the candidate comes around to the collection phase of his project. The timing of the operation is every bit as crucial as the topic per se in the calculation of its researchability. If the chances are higher than the .05 level that your target group or sample will disappear or disband six months or a year down the pike, or that its personnel will change, presenting you with members who may not "honor" their predecessors' generous offer of your entry (and such reversals transpire very often), then you must immediately drop that topic, no matter how attractive, and move on to the consideration of others.

Does it make a contribution to the field? Nearly all program catalogs makes some reference to the dissertation as required to "make a substantial contribution to the field (or to the literature)." Sometimes the qualifier "original" is added to the litany of the requirement. Although no one quite knows what these phrases mean—or, more accurately put, various faculty will differ as to their construction—they are not merely lip-service embroiderings. The *size* of the contribution bothers many dissertation donors: One of my clients, describing her education doctorate in nursing, told me, "I'm going to contribute my little mite here, and then somebody else her little mite there, and so on." This is what I would term "the dissertation-as-too-little" syndrome, where the ABD, steeped in the background of term papers and short-term projects, construes the dissertation as a kind of "quickie" to be knocked off in a few months. Other candidates initially (if they persevere in this attitude, they are in great trouble) see their dissertation as *the* contribution to the field. Here we have what I call the "dissertation-as-too-much," or "dissertation-as-*magnum opus*," syndrome. Although a dissertation must be a good deal more than a "mite" to be approved, it is, after all, in almost all cases the *first* large work in a candidate's career. The *tour de force* and the *magnum opus* come twenty or thirty years later. Although there can be no exact rules about how to find a middle ground between these two misconceived polar views of a dissertation, the ABD must reality-test this dimension of his dissertation. Generally, a resolution of this issue comes with day-to-day consideration of the issue in your "office," careful perusal of related literature, feedback from faculty and students.

Is it original? "Originality" gives many an ABD trouble as well, which is understandable, given the nonoriginal orientation of one's preceding educational exposure and experience. The problem is that rarely, if ever, has the student been asked to produce a sustained, serious input of his own. What the ABD has to be looking for in choosing an "original" thesis topic is "*daylight*," i.e., "after perusal and study of related literature, and appraisal of the scope and ambition of other recent theses in the field, do I find a hole, a gap, a missing link that my topic can contribute to plugging, bridging or forging?" For example, prior to my dissertation, there was a recent growing literature in socialization processes of health professionals; medical, dental, osteopathic and nursing students had been studied. In my Fuller brushman travels through the department, the chairman (interested in the sociology of occupations) mentioned that chiropractors' (a large group of some 23,000) education had never been studied. I did a calculus of researchability, contribution and originality and during the next twenty months researched and wrote my dissertation.[11]

The candidate must guard against panicking that the "originality" of his thesis has been extinguished or "scooped" by another ABD or professional sometime during the period of his research and writing. Suppose you are writing a dissertation on the sociology of the single life-style in Manhattan. One day you hear that another sociology student up at Columbia is doing his on "just the same thing," as your "commiserating" informer breathlessly puts it. Despair! Anguish! Everything lost! Nonsense, although many candidates go through a trauma like this, or are walking (and writing) around with a fear that the "bad news" is coming tomorrow. The truth, of course, is that *fifty* ABDs could write sociology dissertations on the enormous general topic of single or sex roles, or drugs, or homosexuality (and *have*), without the "daylight" or originality of any of them being trampled or usually even touched upon by the others. If you have chosen your "daylight" carefully, there is no chance that it will be occluded by another writer: to dwell on that kind of fear is "dissertation paranoia."

Will it blow up in your face? Will it come back to haunt you? A topic can qualify as researchable, contributory, and sufficiently original and still be rejected, or at least carefully reweighed, as potentially dangerous to your career, even, on occasion, to your personal safety. Dissertations which deal with unpopular ideologies or stigmatized or illegal groups are most apt to backfire in ways which are often unpredictable at the time of dissertation embarcation. I had little inkling of the threats from chiropractors about publishing my findings which were awaiting me at the end of the dissertation trail (see Chapter Nine for details). I was not to know that chiropractors would object, to the point of threatening me, to my publishing as a book my dissertation about chiropractic student culture. Journalist Anthony Thomas probably didn't expect the magnitude of attack from the Saudis and the NATO countries following the screening of his "dissertation" on contemporary sex roles in Saudi Arabia ("Death of A Princess," 1980); one of my sociology colleagues, worried himself half to death over supervising faculty's moralistic and sexist disapproval of his mid-1960s "insider" study of a militant homosexual organization.

Although I was not able to heed my own advice, I would counsel (perhaps precisely because of my own woes in this area) against doing a doctoral dissertation with even a slight smell of its topic putting off one's thesis committee or threatening one's career or safety. The dissertation, and doctorate it confers, is simply too pivotal and difficult a career step to make it any more problematic by introducing gratuitous elements of risk and anxiety. If one is thick-skinned, it is fine to pursue controversial research *after* obtaining at least some corona of protection and status which the doctorate confers.

Of Fate and the Dissertation Topic: José Moreno and the Dominican Revolution. Although superficially it appears that people hit upon an eventually viable dissertation topic through many routes—from "chance," to "out-of-the-blue," to methodical planning—ultimate topics almost always come out of extensive soaking in the literature and prior research of one's field, and are traceable consequences of that immersion. It may be arguable whether the final choice is determined by "fate" or "being in the right place at the right time," but prior to that right moment or right idea come months, even years, of selective reading and thinking about dozens of related issues.

An exception, which ultimately proves the rule about topics resulting from a long deliberative planning and screening process, was José Moreno's dissertation-turned-book, *Barrios in Arms: Revolution in Santo Domingo.*[12] In October of 1964 Moreno arrived in Santo Domingo with the intention of writing his dissertation for Cornell University's sociology department on structural anomie in formal Dominican organizations, such as labor, agricultural and "social welfare" groups. In the spring of 1965, when the revolution broke out, all the organizations he planned to study in his proposal were in disorder—so he studied, perforce, the revolution instead! Thus, once in a while your topic can be decided by a massive social upheaval, rather than a thesis committee or extensive library investigation.

But even though all his original proposal planning went down the drain, Moreno was able to use his general sociological skills to write an incisive and competent treatise on the role of various small (interest) groups in shaping the contours and coalitions of the rebellion. This highly unlikely turn of dissertation events only serves to underscore the point that particular topics are much less crucial to the thesis decision and writing process than a general competence grounded in the theory and methods of one's discipline.

Other avenues to picking a topic. Most often, a prospective candidate who is excessively worried about his specific dissertation topic, who feels bewildered about the vast array of choices confronting and confusing him, hasn't yet paid his dues in terms of soaking in the field.

If you feel that you have done this groundwork but are still shaky about nitty-gritty procedures for selecting a topic, let me finally suggest a few paths that have worked for some people:

1. Although, as noted in Chapter One, master's theses are being phased out of doctoral programs, you might just have had to write one (as I did). I have known of fine Ph.D. dissertations that have been "spun off" from master's thesis material. Not all M.A. theses have this potential for expansion and have to be scrutinized in terms of the substantial contribution and originality criteria. If there has been a few years' interval between the master's thesis and the dissertation, there may also have been a significant switch in faculty. Such a turnover might provide another kind of "daylight" for the M.A.-turned-doctorate, in providing it with new readers who would be less apt to see it as just a "rehash" of the master's. In any case, you should never consider the expansion as "an easier dissertation" because it won't turn out that way: the additional theoretical and methodological problems that you will have to confront and resolve in expansion will be very similar to those of a brand-new dissertation topic.

2. A candidate in search of a topic can read other recent successful proposals and dissertations in his department to determine acceptable standards of contribution, originality, competence and literary worth. Reading other proposals is often heartening, especially when a candidate is living with "the dissertation-as-too-much" myth. It is also advisable to correlate proposals whose topic and style seem related to what one might personally undertake with the particular faculty member(s) they were written for, in an attempt to find professors whose views and standards you can work comfortably with on a dissertation committee. Whether such faculty are still in your program (or whether they will continue to be in it two years hence when you are finishing up) or will be able to take you on are, of course, questions that have to be investigated. My own position is that although one may pick a thesis topic with a particular professor's counsel, encouragement and approval (indeed, such approval is often required), one should *never* pick it because that faculty member is going to see one through the two-odd years of the project. The topic must be

above "politics and personalities," stand alone on its own and the candidate's merits of researchablity, contribution and originality. Too many circumstances can intervene (and repeatedly have) in your relationship with a faculty member, from a falling-out you may have with him, to his losing or changing his position in the program or the department, to his leaving (for good, or taking a sabbatical) "just when you needed him most."

Although it is advisable to choose *tenured* full or associate professors as chief advisers, on grounds of more authority and less chance of departure, they certainly won't turn down a better job offer to stick around supervising your dissertation. Even in today's depressed academic market, there is still considerable lateral movement near the top.

Whenever possible, discuss program dissertations that appeal to you with their authors. This may often be difficult because such persons may have left for parts unknown, or you may feel reluctant to call them since you didn't really know them, or because you really *did* know them and are embarrassed because they've finished and you haven't. My clients have experienced very good luck in contacting earlier finishers in their programs. Almost invariably, such successful candidates have been very willing to share their time and dissertation experience with another candidate. Writing the thesis is such an enormous undertaking and triumph that it is apt to be on the finisher's mind for years hence. Convince him that you are seriously involved in the same great task, and he will most often embrace you. This eagerness to help is interestingly contrasted with the reluctance to help on the part of the faculty, primarily, I believe, because of the status differentials involved in the latter case, whereas the new Ph.D. can still recall in an instant his until-recent ABD status.

What you will get from the successful recent candidate in your program is an insider's story of everything from the mechanics of the thesis, to the operation of the stages of the dissertation course, to (depending on your relationship with the new finisher) personality profiles on various committee members. You will see quite quickly that the final "neat" version of his proposal, data gathering and analysis were, in fact, preceded by months of the "messy" issues with which this book is concerned. My position is that the candidate should write his dissertation with the bottom-line assumption that *nobody* is going to help him. Within that general guideline, recent successful candidates are better sources for advice and counsel than the graduate faculty, as outrageous as that assertion may appear to the uninitiated or naive.

3. A minority of candidates have previously worked with a particular professor, either as teaching or research assistants, the latter "RAs" sometimes connected with a grant won by the faculty member. Sometimes students take or are offered "spinoffs" from the mainline grant data pool to "work up" as their own dissertations. There is nothing inherently wrong with this approach to topic selection, although professors do have a way of leaving a program and taking their grants with them. I have personally seen too many cases of grant-spinoff nonfinishing to be overenthusiastic about such a selection process. Besides the "principal investigator's" outright departure, grants can and do get canceled, "fellows" upon whom the RAs are bestowed can fall out of favor with the investigator and not be reappointed. Again, the same basic rule is appropriate: If you are working on a grant and you are given a section of the data for your thesis, ask yourself, "Where would I and my thesis stand if the grant and its administrator were to disappear tomorrow?" If your answer in terms of research-ability, contribution and originality is, "My thesis stands just fine, and independent," go right ahead. Otherwise, if you are still at the initial topic-deciding stage, find a topic that can stand on its own feet.

SUMMARY.

1. Failure to examine thoroughly the reasons for which one wants to write the dissertation, and the changes its execution will force in life-style, is a major cause of nonfinishing. Starting candidates are usually unaware that writing the thesis is like beginning a new program—starting all over again—which has little connection with the "old" one of courses and preliminary examinations, and whose success or failure hardly correlates with performance in the predissertation program.

2. The dissertation is definitely not for all ABDs, and a particular person contemplating the project must candidly "cost account" his intellectual and emotional strengths and weaknesses in the face of what the dissertation will demand.

3. There is a range of "wrong" reasons for mounting a dissertation, all of which share the common flaw that they are not sufficiently motivating over the long run of the dissertation course. The only "right" reason for pursuing the dissertation is the candidate's deep interest

and commitment to his field, combined with his intention to pursue a full-time career in the discipline upon completion of the degree.

4. Getting into the driver's seat of one's dissertation involves making the thesis a top priority in life and correspondingly reducing for the length of the project, the scope of other spheres of relationships, such as intense love affairs or various emotional crises. The reader is presented with a model of differential dissertation association for maximizing or limiting those relationships with people which promote or reduce allocation of the dissertation to high priority.

5. Can one complete a dissertation while employed full-time? The answer depends on the kind of job which is held, since "work" is not of one piece. Various work conditions, sites, ideologies and ambiences which contribute to, work against or are neutral to dissertation progress are discussed.

6. It is essential for the ABD to set up a dissertation "office," devoted exclusively to the thesis and off limits to family and friends during working hours. Symbolically, the office testifies to and reinforces the candidate's single-minded, serious and ongoing commitment to his dissertation. Regular "office hours" and probably new writing habits, treated in the text, have to be instituted.

7. One's dissertation topic usually comes out of intimate familiarity with a discipline over a good deal of time, rather than from a "brainstorm." A well-trained candidate should be able to write a dissertation on any of a range of topics in his field, directing onto them his general theoretical grasp and methodological skills. A final topic is ordinarily culled from a list of potential ones according to how well it meets the standards of: 1. researchability; 2. contribution to the field; 3. originality; 4. stability (with no potential to blow up in one's face). For those having inordinate difficulties in selecting a topic, the chapter suggests a number of approaches.

NOTES

1. The long-term ABD must also, alas, undertake such an accounting. Although the writer is the last to advocate "quitting," there are most definitely a minority of cases where cutting one's losses is the only alternative to destroying one's life.

2. The "right stuff" was the combination of skills and emotional attitudes that determined, so the candidates believed, which test pilots would be chosen as the first astronauts. See Tom Wolfe, *The Right Stuff* (New York: Farrar, Straus and Giroux, 1979).

3. James Fixx, *The Complete Book of Running* (New York: Random House, 1977), p. 92.
4. It is undeniably one of the thrilling moments in life to receive one's doctorate. Although it is fashionable to play down the title and its use, almost all the Ph.Ds I know use their title with (deserved) pride. As a motivator and anticipatory socializer, I often address my graduate students and clients as "Doctor" and try to get them to see themselves with that status in the not-too-distant future.
5. In criminology, "differential association" is a model for predicting criminal behavior by frequency, priority, intensity and duration of contacts with other people disposed or opposed to law-breaking behavior. See Sutherland and Cressey, *Criminology* (New York: Lippincott, 1978).
6. This nonhurried pace, incidentally, seems to characterize the publishing world as well and exasperates many writers. But it has to be lived with.
7. Cf., Virginia Woolf, *A Room of One's Own* (New York: Harcourt, Brace and World, 1929). Although the volume is concerned with feminist independence, having a room/space of one's own is equally applicable and vital to dissertation independence and autonomy.
8. George Plimpton, ed., *Writers at Work, The Paris Interviews, Four Series* (New York: Penguin Books, 1977). The description of writing as "work" is most apt in the present dissertation-writing context.
9. A variation on the time standard is a fixed minimum word or page output per day, the writer generally stopping when, but not before, that quota is met. Hemingway, for example, kept a large chart of his daily word output, averaging around 500—"so as not to kid myself." When he missed a day to go fishing, he doubled up the next.
10. Elliot Liebow, *Tally's Corner* (Boston: Little, Brown, 1967). Anthropological and sociological literature is rich in "participant observation" studies of various groups. Oftentimes, such groups really don't want to be scrutinized, and researchers have to use great ingenuity to get access/ entry. But difficulties have to be contrasted with near-impossibilities: the majority of studied groups are powerless people. For reasons that have to do with the political structure of modern societies, no systematic observational studies of high-level decision-making groups have been conducted.
11. David Sternberg, "Boys in Plight: A Case Study of Chiropractic Students Confronting a Medically Oriented Society," unpublished doctoral dissertation, New York University, 1969.
12. José Moreno, *Barrios in Arms: Revolution in Santo Domingo* (Pittsburgh: University of Pittsburgh Press, 1970).

CHAPTER 3

Building a Dissertation File: Philosophy and Construction Code

The key to completing a dissertation is not brilliance or even inspiration, but organization. Indeed, many a long-term ABD is overloaded with brilliant insights which keep him darting in various noncumulative directions; the definitive quality of brilliance is a short, blinding illumination that quickly burns out. This is precisely *not* what the ABD writer needs. What he does need is a master *plan* in the form of some kind of filing system which keeps him on the right track(s), helps him evaluate his progress on various dissertation fronts, keeps him on keel, "flash-freezes" occasional "brilliant" insights so that they can be reconsidered within the framework of the total plan.

I suspect all serious researchers and writers (at least nonfiction ones, and probably many novelists, as well) keep files at the nerve and communications centers of their "offices." [1] Yet, the concept is foreign or vague to most beginning ABDs, who continue to surprise me with blank responses to my questions about how they are coming along with their files. A dissertation candidate must have a file, and it has to be seriously constructed at the time a topic is decided upon, *prior* to undertaking both the proposal/prospectus and the dissertation itself. Because the file is so vital to success with the dissertation—and because its rationale and format are so poorly grasped by most beginning writers—it requires its own chapter.

Various metaphors can be used to describe the function of the file in negotiating a dissertation project. One can see it as the "scaffold" which supports the writer and his dissertation during the erection of the thesis. I like to conceive of it as a "vehicle" which the candidate builds and then "rides along" to the end of the dissertation. In my own theses and book-writing experiences, I have discovered that the vehicle metaphor is much more than that; as my file grows, it eventually *becomes* the particular project.

There is no doubt that one way in which we humans are moved and motivated is by seeing *tangible growth* as a consequence of our efforts. For the gardener, growth is measured by increase in flower size; for the weight lifter, inches on the triceps; for the dissertation writer, thickness of one's file. If the reader sets up his file properly from the start, he will discover many times down the dissertation course the "lift" pulling out his filing drawers can give him.

HOW TO BUILD A DISSERTATION FILE: HEADINGS, PROCEDURES, DISCUSSION.

What follows is a kind of "starter set" of essential file headings upon which any given candidate can build, elaborate, revise to suit the needs of his own particular discipline, program, topic, thesis style, relations with faculty and students, and personality. Note immediately that the file is much more than a straightforward nuts-and-bolts blueprint or recording system (although it is, of course, both of these, as well): it is a "life history" of the dissertation, taking into full account the human and emotional sides of the project. Note, too, that some of the file headings will have (or already have had) their own chapters—or at least chapter sections—in the book, e.g., choosing a topic, severe problems during the dissertation course, strained relationships with proposal and/or thesis committee. I certainly do not claim that my particular system is the only way to set up a file, only that it has worked for many candidates (including myself). I do believe that wherever one begins, he or she is going to end up with a file and headings quite akin to those outlined here, since ultimately it is the common nature of the dissertation demands that tell.

Dissertation Log.

A running time sheet of hours spent in the office, library and field should be assiduously kept. Such a log is important in its own right as a motivator and will play a part when the candidate periodically reviews his progress (or lack of it), or has to rebudget his time in light of job demands or new phases of his dissertation (e.g., spending more time in the field than in the office, or *vice versa).*

Choosing a Dissertation Topic.

Ordinarily, this won't be a very thick file, since the candidate will have settled on a topic at about the time the filing system is set up. But there should be an account of how—through a sifting process and calculus of researchability, contribution and originality—you finally decided to go with your topic. This will be important in the days of "dissertation doubt" you will confront from time to time over the next year and a half: "Why did I have to pick this damn topic?" or, "If only I'd chosen a topic like X did." If you have the record available, you can go back and read and review exactly *why* you carefully and patiently selected "Sartre's Contribution to Existentialism" (which is currently torturing you), instead of "Camus' Views on Nihilism" (which is currently attracting you).

Timetable for Proposal, Experiment, Fieldwork, Statistical Workup of Data, Write-up, Defense.

Although one rarely meets the originally blocked-out deadlines in an exact fashion and must revise them in the face of unforeseen circumstances and delays, a master time plan—and a quite delimited one, at that—is essential to avoid the no-end-in-sight syndrome so common to the dissertation course.

Relations with Proposal-and-Dissertation Committee Members.

Although "personalities" are not as important as the candidate's own steady and thorough input into his dissertation (and also because specific members often change through the dissertation course), one must certainly deal with them on a more or less regular basis throughout the phases of doing a dissertation. Even though less than sanguine relationships with faculty can rarely defeat a highly competent thesis, strained situations with one or more members can definitely delay completion and make the project period very unpleasant, just as good relationships with advisers and members can expedite and lessen the emotional burden of writing (at the very least, not *add* to it). Accordingly, a *dissertation differential association calculus* should be worked out (and constantly *updated)* with each relevant faculty member evaluated in terms of whether he is promoting, obstructing or neutral to the dissertation's progress. Then strategies should be worked out to maximize or minimize contacts with faculty according to how they were scored.

Comparative Proposals and Dissertations from Other Successful (Recent) Candidates in the Program.

The guideline uses to which these sources can be put for constructing one's own proposal and thesis were discussed in Chapter Two. Prior successes should be scrutinized with the aim of answering questions such as, What content and ordering of sections does the department approve and prefer? How thorough a review of the literature is required? What kinds of methodological designs and variables, what kinds of statistics keep coming up? How long is the average proposal or dissertation? How extensive, and at what level of literary quality, are the "critical" reviews of the literature, analysis and discussion sections?

The Dissertation Proposal.

Herein, a heading for each important, discrete section of the proposal. Chapter Four is devoted to the various dimensions of constructing a viable proposal.

Contacts and Arrangements for Subjects and/or Groups in Your Experiment or Fieldwork.

ABDs are generally not prepared for the unreliability of data-source contacts. A vague promise from a colleague, for example, to give you half an hour of his introductory psychology class to administer your instrument "anytime you want" often never comes through, or the half hour isn't half enough, or you need to go back for a second session (which he can't give you), or the cross section of the sample is not representative. People have to be very seriously pinned down; commitments (sometimes on a *quid pro quo* basis) have to be obtained from colleagues, fellow researchers, friends, contacts in school systems, for the provision of a specific number of subjects on specific dates for specific/sufficient amount of (often classroom) time. When-

60

ever possible, "backup" data sources should be arranged, so that fall-throughs don't catch the researcher in an "all-or-nothing" trap which may seriously delay the dissertation.

Troubleshooter File.

At what junctures in the project do intellectual problems or contradictions keep recurring? For example, no matter how often she reworked the proposal, one of my clients couldn't convincingly relate her two latter hypotheses to the first two. Another dissertation writer continued to have trouble in constructing a valid measure for "will to live" in connection with her dissertation on "Locus of Control Among the Terminally Ill." How can such difficulties be resolved? By altering the hypotheses, changing the methodology? Perhaps they cannot be solved, but at least "lived with"? Candidates should beware of the myth of the "perfect dissertation" (discussed later in this volume).

Serendipity/Inspiration File.

As work moves ahead, unexpected and/or contradictory ideas and data are going to arise. The experienced (read successful) researcher uses even contradictory and superficial-appearing "doomsday" data to advantage—rather than despairing (which is what the inexperienced ABD has a pronounced tendency to do)—banking it for an "alternative" explanation of results. Most "finished" behavioral science work is, contrary to methodology textbook righteousness, revisionist. (See Chapter Five for elaboration of serendipity in thesis writing.)

Devil's Advocate File.

Here one raises himself the hardest, most unjust, off-the-wall questions which proposal and defense committee members are likely to raise, and prepares answers. Since the candidate generally comes to know more about his particular topic than anyone else on earth before he is through (often a dubious distinction among one's friends: I found, for example, during my dissertation that people at parties had a way of excusing themselves when I turned to an in-depth discussion of the world of chiropractors), eventual faculty questions can be fielded if the devil's advocate brief has been kept up and current, with both questions and answers.

"Ventilation" File.

Regularly, the candidate should get down (and to some extent *out* of his system) the *passions* of the dissertation, be they love, hate, boredom, frustration, anxiety, fear. Anthropologists and sociologists have long encouraged and practiced such ventilation about different phases of research, from relations with one's sample, to one's colleagues, to one's own writing.[2] During my research with chiropractic students, I kept a "journal" where I recorded prominent and recurrent *feelings* that kept surfacing; about once a month I summed these up in a memorandum for my ventilation file. During much of my fieldwork, I was in real danger of being expelled from the chiropractic college due to—what I termed in the dissertation—"chiropractic paranoia." This created enormous anxiety and occupied much of my journal. Then, too, in my role of "house sociologist" and general confidant to both students and faculty, I became "wise" to several cases of miscarriage of justice (in terms of grades, allotted transfer credits, suspensions from school) that reflected specific faculty-student animosities or vendettas. To retain my credibility as an objective observer and keeper of confidences, there was nothing I could do about these ethically troubling situations without jeopardizing further access to my sample, and thus completion of my dissertation. During some of these episodes, the ethical/human side of me was at war with the careerist side: the battle was fought in the journal. Researchers are constantly running into these kinds of ethical/emotional dilemmas.[3] Of course, a particular candidate's ventilative issues will be determined by the nature of his project and what steps are required, but even if fieldwork or an experiment isn't involved, plenty of emotional issues will surface. Whatever the structural demands of a given dissertation, the personality of a particular writer is the key intervening variable: another researcher in my place at the chiropractic college might not have been bothered by what I perceived as major conscience questions and have focused on different emotional qualms, e.g., personality conflicts with certain abrasive faculty or students.

"How'm I Doing?" [4]

About once a month an evaluative memorandum should be written by the researcher to himself, taking stock of the general progress of the various thrusts of the project. This memorandum should be written "cold," *before* work on the master review/progress file (see below), for a sense of how much the candidate is carrying in his head about his dissertation. Acquisition of a "gestalt" view of one's thesis is a major step toward completion, since henceforth whatever data one confronts in the office, library or field can be efficiently discarded or incorporated in line with whether they fit the big picture. Carrying the dissertation in one's head is also vital for the dissertation defense (see Chapter Eight, below).

Dissertation Group File.

The issues of formation, format, maintenance and uses of a dissertation support group are discussed in depth in Chapter Seven. If a candidate joins such a group, he must keep two subfiles on it. One must be a record (preferably taped) of the group's comments during sessions specifically devoted to his thesis. The other should be summaries, supplied by other members in the form of abstracts, outlines, statements of particular problems, of fellow group members' projects.

Successive Drafts of Dissertation Chapters.

In almost all cases, the candidate is going to have to write at least two versions of each dissertation chapter. All drafts, earlier and later, should be kept together for comparative purposes. At the point when a chapter has been more or less finalized, a copy should be made and placed for safekeeping in some location other than one's office. Dissertation horror lore abounds with stories about the careless or unfortunate ABD who loses the only copy of his completed dissertation to a fire, theft, flood, the destructive rage of a vengeful spouse, drunken movers, eviction.[5] In an actual case with which I am acquainted, a psychology candidate lost his only copy in a robbery of his briefcase. Totally shattered, he retired to a Mediterranean island for the better part of two years, returned to New York City, wrote a new thesis (undoubtedly making multiple copies this time of developing chapters) and is now a successful psychoanalyst (perhaps specializing in disaster victims). Where the second copy is placed is determined by the candidate's worst fear: a friend of mine, terrified of fire, kept a copy of his dissertation manuscript in the refrigerator, wrapped in plastic; another acquaintance, apprehensive of burglary, kept a copy in a heavy safe. Excepting some unusually developed paranoia like the above cases, the best place to keep a legible copy is in a bank safety-deposit box.

Master Review/Progress File

1. Title a separate blank page for each of the salient headings in your file.
2. Provide a date slot for each page.
3. Xerox twelve–fifteen copies of each page.
4. Every month, without fail, the writer should date one set of the headings, and type or write in work progress and problems—carried out, confronted, resolved, unresolved—during that month for each file heading.

This is a most effective technique for overviewing which parts of the dissertation are forging ahead, standing still or lagging behind (more of this in Chapter Five on researching and writing the dissertation). These reviews lead to intensified or reduced efforts in one heading area or another in the forthcoming month. The writer must always precede a given monthly master review write-up with a review of at least the *prior* month's progress file. The key to cumulative progress is the sense of continuity that such a developmental comparison allows.

The master review/progress file is one where no time skimping should be tolerated. Of course, in a given month, one will normally have much more to say under some headings than others (sometimes because some files are right "on time," sometimes because no progress has been made). It is not at all inordinate that two or three entire office sessions should be spent on your review. Sometimes the exercise will flow beautifully; other months it will be a halting and painful business. Whatever the tone of a particular month's review writing, it must be pushed through.

Recently I attended a trial lawyers' review workshop in New York. The keynote speaker, a distinguished trial attorney, devoted his entire presentation to the development of an unexpected assertion that the bedrock of successful trial lawyering was *list keeping*! He detailed his own list-keeping styles, subjects and procedures, complete with an account of his continual checking and cross-listing. At first the relatively young audience of attorneys seemed skeptical about or bored by his insistence upon the centrality of a listing or filing scheme to presenting a winning case—anticipating probably that he would talk of the brilliant cross-examination, surprise witness or dramatic summing up. As the talk wore on they became, I believe, convinced, if not fascinated, that routine, day-to-day organization and collation of material was fundamental to a sound trial case. I, of course, could not help but be struck by the similarity between starting lawyers and beginning ABDs, the latter being as initially skeptical and unimpressed by repeated stress on a matter as routine or banal as the dissertation file, when the greener fields of boundless theories and inexhaustible inspirations lay before them.

Index File.

You must have an index file of your substantive files. Number the file folder as soon as you begin a new entry, and transcribe its number and title onto your master index sheets. A master index is indispensable when the files proliferate, and you want to find something quickly, or cross-file, in your cabinets. Always keep your files in *seriatim* order.

I can hear an early-stage dissertation writer saying, "All of this seems a pretty elaborate filing system for the three pages of a mini-proposal that I have at the moment!" But you will be astonished at how quickly your materials will grow as you work in earnest on your dissertation. The filing system reverses the ordinary dictum of "form follows function" with a sequence of "function follows form," based on my repeated observations that setting up an adequate and comprehensive operations base—or file—motivates, even forces, the ABD to go out into the world and gather the materials of his dissertation.

On cross-filing. As your files develop, it will strike you that some subjects, under whatever heading they started off, are equally weighted on, or appropriate under, two or more headings. Cross-filing may then be indicated. Now, one has to proceed with caution in cross-filing: in the largest sense, all sections of one's thesis are interrelated (or they better be), all cross-filable. Taken to an extreme, one could drown in an orgy and compulsion of filing, producing a brilliant ingrown file, but no dissertation. Never cross-file (i.e., place a duplicate copy of key ongoing materials under two or more headings), unless you feel a recurrent "tugging" with more or less equal force from two different headings. Cross-filing decisions are best made after the master/review progress file has been completed for a given month.

To give the reader some taste of a possible cross-file (obviously, the particular combinations for peculiar disciplines, topics and writers are vast) that cuts across many fields of study, consider a situation that might (often does) arise within the context and interfaces of file headings entitled "Relations with proposal and dissertation committee members" and "Ventilation." Dilatory ABDs often wake up to the fact that they have neglected their "fence mending" down at the department, that they are out of touch with faculty members with whom they worked and studied during predissertation days and perhaps do not even know faculty currently in charge of the doctoral program. It is most difficult for the candidate to reestablish connections with a department which he may not have visited for a year or two; every day he further delays, the resistance and embarrassment are enhanced. Here is an ideal problem for cross-filing and cross-solving. Use "Relations with committee members" to plot out strategies for effecting a rapprochement; use "ventilation" for getting out the humiliation and rage you may feel in taking up the Fuller Brush Man role. A strategy that has often proved effective in both reintroducing and reinstating oneself with the faculty and allaying some of one's most troubling "reentry" emotions is what I term "dissertation confession." Suppose you are a two-year-old ABD and have done very little toward a dissertation proposal, have not visited your department for about a year and the chairperson has changed. The very best approach is to schedule an appointment with the chairperson and "lay it on the line" with him. You acknowledge that you have delayed, give some reasons for such delay, recount for him the pain you have been undergoing in not making progress, reaffirm your intense commitment to finishing and promise to submit a proposal within some reasonable time limit.

The face-saving aspect of this approach is that it is truthful. Stopping short of begging for mercy, one asks for compassion. Most chairpersons see themselves as "shepherds" of their faculty and graduate student flocks. They like to play the "father/mother confessor" role. More often than not, they have heard such "confessions" or "repentances" frequently in the past; very likely, they personally experienced delays and doubts about their own dissertations. So, in this problem context, one can usually expect a sympathetic response—rather than indifferent or hostile—from faculty. You may well be off the hook, provided that you do, in fact, demonstrate some tangible written proof of progress before your memory begins to fade once again from the chairperson's mind.

The File and a Tape Recorder.[6]

A tape recorder is very valuable for certain aspects of the file and actual writing of the dissertation: In getting down an idea that can occur at any time of the day, office hours or not, but which you do not have time to develop at the moment. Sometimes such flashes relate directly to the file or chapter you are presently working on (say, a spied contradiction in your analysis or a required addendum); nearly as often they refer to work you "completed" weeks ago, or work coming up in the weeks ahead. In any event, try never to switch file horses in midstream: keep to the flow of your present work, and deal with the "intruder" later; it's there waiting on the cassette for subsequent calm and unobtrusive consideration.

Certain specific file headings lend themselves to the oral dimension, most particularly:

"How'm I doing?" Some candidates prefer to talk out, rather than write down, their monthly off-the-top-of-the-head summing up of their dissertation. Upon playback, they are able to ascertain how their presentation will sound to others, such as a thesis committee or dissertation adviser, and which parts of the thesis are still thin or less than convincing.

Devil's Advocate File. Every month after the dissertation is well underway, prepare a list of "The Ten Bitchiest Questions," read each onto the tape and proceed to answer them. Upon feedback, ask for each whether your response would satisfy a faculty interrogator. Did you sound confident? Shaky? Irritated? Proposal and dissertation defenses (about which more will be written in later chapters) are staged affairs, presentations of self with the aim of being accepted, "getting over." In the specific area of answering cantankerous, malicious or even stupid faculty questions, the candidate's best strategy is to take on all such comers as if they were serious and reasonable queries, worthy of in-depth and good-natured answers. The candidate should strive with his answers to create an atmosphere of collegial community with his examiners—all of you interestedly promoting the advancement of the discipline, at the moment through the vehicle of a dissertation. If your side of the presentation is convincing, it will be very hard for faculty not to "play along," to treat you as anybody less than a soon-to-be full colleague. Judge your audio performance in accord with such collegial-sounding criteria.

Ventilation. Most people find it more natural and satisfying to talk or laugh or cry or scream about their feelings than to write about them. Ventilation sessions cannot be scheduled like other file tapings; emotions don't know timetables. Whenever a strong dissertation emotion comes upon you—be it impatience with an adviser who is holding you up by reading your chapters at a maddeningly slow pace, anger with your husband who isn't keeping up his commitment to take over the children and household chores to give you your full time in your office, outrage over how one of your fieldwork sample was treated by a superordinate that day, frustration with inability to find a satisfactory analytic statistic for a key section of your data—get it down on tape.

Dissertation group discussions. Tape the sessions devoted to your thesis, since such a record is much more comprehensive than note taking. It will also allow you to gauge the effectiveness of your oral presentation in a context not too different from faculty appointments, hearings and defense regarding your dissertation.

Which tapes to save. My own habit is to label and save all cassettes I make in the office on a particular large project. Certainly, the candidate must keep, at the very least, taped material on the specific file headings discussed above. The exclusive goals of all the files and all the tapes are finishing and surviving the dissertation. Repeated reviews of all previous "How'm I doing?" devil's advocate and dissertation-group tapes give you a sense of developmental progress on your journey toward its end, and hone your speaking and debate skills for coping with defense hearings. Review of the ventilation tapes helps you to anticipate and better cope with dissertation traumas further down the line. ("Hey, I talked about that two months ago; let me go back and see how I felt about and dealt with it then.")

What to Tape and What to Write Out.

The tape recorder, as valuable as it is for the purposes noted above, has its limits as a dissertation tool. After all, the medium of the thesis is the written word, and even though there are crucial oral episodes, like discussions with dissertation committee members and the formal defense, the talk about the thesis is based on what the candidate has put down on paper in the form of working "position papers" on key issues of theory and methodology, and successive drafts of thesis chapters.

Written documents allow for scrutiny and overview nearly impossible with tapes. Inconsistencies and *non sequiturs* abound in even the best lectures. When the candidate sits down to write (about) his dissertation, he is clearly up against it, cannot "wing it" or "bullshit" his way through a talk-show version of his project. This *confrontational* quality of writing—where the words stare back at you, often with reproach on first draft—is part and parcel of the dissertation enterprise. It taps directly into the loneliness corona surrounding dissertation writing: only the candidate sitting in his office hour after hour, reviewing and redrafting what he has put to paper, can eventually get it right.

Your file becomes your severest critic and your greatest ally. Its contents force you to revise—and revise again—your written versions; its contents insist that matters are not as simple as you have presently put them, that certain areas need embellishment or refinement. On the other hand, the work and investment that have gone into your file over the months will yield the capability to get the writing "right" that the file-qua-critic is demanding.

SUMMARY.

1. Organization, rather than brilliance or intuition, is the most necessary dissertation-writing attribute. An extensive file is the bedrock of a successful dissertation project. The file is the objectification of organization. During its construction, the candidate practices and further develops the required organizational skills.

69

2. The file can be seen as a "vehicle" which one constructs and then "rides along" to the dissertation's end. To be fully effective, it must be set up at the time a thesis topic is finalized, and prior to writing the proposal and dissertation proper.

3. The chapter provides the candidate with a "starter set" of essential dissertation file headings, including assembly instructions, upon which he can elaborate according to his own peculiar project needs. The headings embrace nuts-and-bolts topics, emotional problems of the dissertation, interpersonal issues and diplomatic relations with advising and supervising faculty—all of which are expanded upon in subsequent chapters of the volume. Selected headings discussed include: a dissertation log; a timetable for various phases of the thesis; relations with proposal and dissertation committee members; contacts and arrangements for subjects and/or groups in one's experiment or fieldwork; a troubleshooter file; a serendipity/inspiration file; a devil's advocate file; a "ventilation" file; a "How'm I doing?" file; a dissertation-support-group file; a master review/progress file.

4. The uses and art of cross-filing in promoting the dissertation are considered, along with illustrative examples.

5. Tape recording is indicated as a valuable adjunct method in the building of certain files, especially "How'm I doing?"; the "devil's advocate file; "ventilation"; and dissertation-group discussions.

NOTES

1. For interesting, even exciting, accounts of how two social scientists set up files for their projects, see C. Wright Mills, *The Sociological Imagination* (New York: Oxford University Press, 1959), Appendix; and "Profile" on Robert K. Merton, *The New Yorker,* January 1961.

2. Cf., Napoleon Chagnon, "Yanamamö Social Organization and Warfare," in Fried *et al.,* eds., *War: The Anthropology of Armed Conflict and Aggression* (New York: Doubleday, 1967); Hammond, ed. *Sociologists at Work: Essays on the Craft of Social Research* (New York: Basic Books, 1964); and A. Shostak, ed., *Our Sociological Eye: Personal Essays in Society and Culture* (Port Washington: Alfred, 1977).

3. Cf., L. Humphreys, *Tearoom Trade: Impersonal Sex in Public Places* (Chicago: Aldine, 1970); and Wolf and Jorgensen, "Anthropology on the Warpath in Thailand," *New York Review of Books,* November 19, 1970.

4. "How'm I doing?" is apparently New York Mayor Edward I. Koch's daily query to constituents and city officials. "Profiles (Mayor Edward I. Koch—Part I)," Ken Auletta, *The New Yorker,* September 10, 1979.

5. The nineteenth-century explorer, anthropologist and poet, Sir Richard Burton, had a large part of his manuscripts destroyed (burned) by a wife enraged with their "immoral" contents and Burton's behavior. See Alan Moorehead, *The White Nile* (New York: Dell, 1966).
6. For a provocative argument for restoring certain presently lost dimensions of meaning to literature by reinstituting reading aloud as a regular exercise in university criticism courses, see R. Shattuck, "How to Rescue Literature," *The New York Review of Books,* April 17, 1980.

CHAPTER 4

The Dissertation Proposal

GETTING INTO THE PROPOSAL WITHOUT DELAY.

Timing of the proposal and dissertation effort bears stressing right at the start of the chapters devoted specifically to proposal and dissertation. One should strike while the iron is hot, that is to say, almost immediately after the final preliminary orals are negotiated.[1] "Taking a deserved rest" at this point has condemned many candidates of my acquaintance to additional years of dissertation labor, which might have been avoided if they had pushed directly on when the blood was up and the faculty familiar with and favorable toward their recent progress. I know in my own biography that an R & R year abroad after my orals, when I was completely out of touch with my department faculty, was a major contributor to delaying my thesis completion for nearly two years. In academia, leaving your university situs with matters up in the air—be it an incompleted dissertation, undecided tenure, an uncertain promotion—practically insures that the departer, upon return, will find himself a victim of the adage about what can go wrong, will go wrong.

WHY IS THE PROPOSAL SO IMPORTANT?

The dissertation proposal, known in some programs and departments as the dissertation prospectus, is crucial to, and linked with, the total dissertation-writing process in five ways: (1) Its construction is the process by which one decides definitely on the viability of a topic;

(2) It establishes a "contract" with the faculty that applies/extends to the dissertation itself; (3) It is a "trial run" for the dissertation, a "minidissertation"; (4) Its successful negotiation puts most ABDs "over the top" of the dissertation course; (5) It establishes the tone and pattern of relationships with dissertation-supervising faculty.

THE PROPOSAL AS TOPIC-DECISION PROCESS.

Contrary to dissertation mythology, the choice of topic is not an inspirational point in time, but a rather extended process, with two major phases.[2] In the first phase, one culls from various sources a list of possibles. Such a culling, remember, already assumes a basic grounding in the discipline, obtained from several years' soaking in the field. In the second phase, the ABD has to test his most compelling first choice against the criteria of researchability, contribution, originality, and potential explosiveness. The proposal is a systematic, extended exploration of one's topic, from statement of the problem all the way through anticipated analytic procedures (discussed below in the chapter). Quite literally, the candidate is saying to himself (or better be!), "I propose [intend] to spend the next eighteen months of my life buried in this topic. Here you [the "you" refers first to the candidate himself, then to his adviser and hearing committee] have x number of pages justifying such a large expenditure of time and energy. Is my proposal convincing?"

THE PROPOSAL AS CONTRACT.

Dissertation proposals, like matrimonial ones, are accepted or rejected. To further the parallel, both are sometimes initially turned down, but second or third overtures (often with revised terms) are accepted. In marriage law, it used to be that an acceptance of a proposal was itself a contract, and either party's failure to comply was actionable by the person still willing to carry through. Domestic proposals contracts have dwindled from law and usage just when dissertation proposal contracts have emerged. The core of the dissertation proposal contract says—although not in just these words and much more explicitly in some programs than others—"We [faculty] accept your proposal to carry out a specified project, known as a doctoral dissertation. If and when said project is completed within the guidelines of your proposal, we promise to approve your dissertation."

Before I consider the most important implications/issues of the proposal as a contract, how widespread, the reader wants to know, is the contract quality of dissertation proposals within American doctoral programs? As one might expect from the discussion in Chapter One, there has been no professional research of this question about the dissertation, anymore than of half a dozen other key issues or phases. Then, too, the contract element, if studied, would emerge in numerous shadings and emphases from university to university; like our local police departments, each university, public or private, is more or less sovereign unto itself (even within the *same* state or city university system, various campus graduate schools within the same discipline will have different rules and requirements for course work, qualifying examinations and dissertations), especially in this kind of internal or domestic matter. Thus, after reviewing the following general discussion of the contract considerations in the proposal, an ABD must try to ascertain where his own college and/or program stands on the issue.

Certainly, the general idea of the dissertation as contract between candidate and graduate faculty is established. In the late 1960s, Washington University (St. Louis) sued (unsuccessfully) to take back a social science doctorate on the grounds that the writer had used unethical research methods, thus violating a vital element of the contract between him and the graduate faculty and therefore vitiating the contract; in the 1970s, Columbia University sued (successfully) for the return of a Ph.D. granted to a candidate who had plagiarized his history dissertation, again on the grounds that such a violation rendered the university's commitment to go through with the contract null and void. It should be said that dissertation contract *court law* is very sparse—probably no more than half a dozen cases on one issue or another of the thesis—but its rare formal invocation does not negate its existence or authority within the university framework; occasions when candidates have threatened to take legal action against a department (or specific members of a department) for unwarrantedly denying or delaying their doctorates are far more numerous, but almost always they are "settled out of court." I trust it is understood that I am not promoting litigation as a main-line method of getting one's dissertation approved. The occasional court's notice of dissertation disputes is presented in order to drive home the usually implicit contractual elements of a dissertation/doctorate undertaking. In all contracts, the state is a "silent partner," whose say is invoked only when remedies between the explicit contractors have failed.

An impressionistic survey of dissertation doctorate programs in reference to the contractual element in the narrower, more specific area of the proposal itself leads to the tentative conclusion that most programs recognize a contract, but to varying degrees of explicitness. In some departments, for example, the catalog, special doctoral candidacy rules and thesis committee regulations state very clearly that acceptance of a dissertation proposal (in a formal hearing) is both preliminary to and mandatory for a candidate, and binding upon the department. In many—perhaps still most—programs, the contract element of the proposal (including by just which administrative process it will be accepted or rejected) is less explicit. In less explicit departments, however, discussion with graduate faculty will usually uncover a willingness to act upon such assumptions, even though these academics are loath to construe them in "vulgar" or "mechanistic" business-type frameworks.

Certainly, then, there is enough contract background to dissertation proposals and dissertations themselves—some of it implicit instead of explicit, most of it university-based rather than court-based in terms of promulgation, interpretation or enforcement, should a dispute arise between the contracting parties—that a contemporary candidate is warranted in proceeding *as if* a dissertation proposal contract is in force once his committee approves his proposal. In the generally zero-sum model of power and authority in which he finds himself in relation to dissertation-supervising professors, the contract element is perhaps the only "guarantee" of some substance upon which he can rely.

Putting the dissertation proposal and the dissertation within the broad context of American contract law—even with the qualifications and modifications dictated by the unusual university setting and status of the particular contracting parties—gives the ABD some clout against two nightmarish eventualities that he encounters often in his dreams, and sometimes in reality:

1. As I have already pointed out, the ABD has absolutely no assurance that the men and women evaluating his original proposal and/or sitting on the dissertation committee will *continue* to serve during the several years of his project. (In some departments member-

75

ship is the same for both committees, in others partly the same, and in still a third category of program, completely different. Then, too, regulations are modified by personnel developments; a political science graduate department may stipulate that both committees be populated by the same faculty, but resignations may make this impossible.) What would (and does) happen if, say, the two sympathetic members of your three-person proposal committee resign from your anthropology department at Indiana University to become codirectors of the Maori Research Institute in Christ Church, New Zealand, replaced by two urban anthropologists who are, at best, uninterested in, at worst, hostile to, your dissertation critiquing the HRAF (Human Relations Area Files)?

Under contract law, parties succeeding, inheriting or buying contracts from earlier or original contractors are bound by those contracts' obligations. Major exceptions to such a rule are so-called "personal service" contracts; e.g., an opera singer sells her contract to sing in *Carmen* to someone who cannot carry a tune; the Met is not bound to let the latter ruin its winter season. Nor would Indiana's anthropology department be obligated to honor your selling your rights and obligations embodied in a dissertation proposal to a bona fide nonmatriculated purchaser. But a new Met manager, administration or even ownership would have to honor the prior management's contract with an opera singer, and the anthropology department at Indiana must honor its dissertation contract with you, regardless of changes in its personnel and their specialties.

In the instant case, the departure of the two faculty best acquainted with your topic is going to make the dissertation even lonelier than it always is, anyway, but this is a far cry from a situation where the department could renege on its commitment, citing a lack of qualified faculty to continue supervision. Most of the time when a candidate is put in left-in-the-lurch circumstances approximating this example, departments allow—sometimes even encourage and support—his acquiring an outside adviser (who may even become a dissertation committee member pro tem). Without necessarily heating up the issue by specifically citing protection in contract law, the candidate should be aware of his rights (almost always departments stress *your* duties and requirements *you* have to meet; almost never, like landlords, do they emphasize or acknowledge *their* obligations toward doctoral candidates), and be prepared, if necessary, to make demands on his department to live up to its side of the dissertation proposal agreement.

2. The ABD has no assurance that the hypotheses of the proposal are going to "pan out" in the predicted direction. There is much dissertation lore surrounding this issue: what one does if the data go astray; how a thesis committee will rule; what kind of cyanide pill works fastest. Although I want to save for Chapter Five, the bulk of discussion about how to handle "negative" or "contrary" findings with a more constructive, sanguine, less Hamlet-like response than suicide, let me note here that the contract assumptions of the dissertation proposal surround one's undertaking to *test* propositions and hypotheses which have been reached through logical, orderly and deductive canons of thought legitimated in one field or another. Neither the contract nor any (social) scientific model demands that the *results* of such testing be in a particular direction. Indeed, the very core of the intellectual and scientific enterprise is that the data be allowed to fall, and stand, as they may. There is much talk about how dissertation committees don't like—may even reject—theses in which one's own hypotheses are disconfirmed (even in the face of statements made all the time in texts and classes demonstrating that a refutation of theories represents a contribution in its own right). I know of no case in which a dissertation was turned down primarily for disconfirmation of hypotheses, excepting instances where the hypotheses were "straw men."

Toward a Contract Model of the Dissertation Proposal.

American faculty in arts and sciences are far more used to the intrusion of legal review and process into their "ivy towers" than an outside observer—and many inside students—suppose. A year does not pass in a university when several faculty do not bring grievance procedures (mediated and pursued by their teaching unions) and/or lawsuits (pursued after union remedies have stalled or failed) to compel reversals on negative reappointment, tenure or promotion decisions.

Indeed, some of the candidate's own dissertation supervisors may have been at one time or another party to one of these grievances/suits. Although faculty lose these appeals more often than not, a substantial minority win. University administrations make every effort to keep the news of such victories from the general college community;

77

most undergraduate students, and even many graduate/doctoral ones appear unaware of internecine struggles (excepting cause célèbre cases) among and between faculty and administration going on just below the surface of college life. A lesson for the ABD, if he doesn't know it already, is that his graduate faculty is rifted by many professional and personal antagonisms, most of them stemming from tenure and promotion battles that have been fought out over the years preceding his entrance upon the departmental scene.[3] If the candidate fortuitously picks two implacable faculty enemies to sit on his committee, his dissertation will be delayed in the cross fire of hostile career memories.

Curiously, the contractual/grievance model employed by faculty has not been formally or substantially extended to ABD-supervising-faculty relations and disagreements. The explanation for the near total absence of grievance procedures and a systematic view of the proposal and dissertation as a contractual relationship has to do with the anachronistic state of student-faculty relationships in dissertation doctorate programs, compared with such status relationships in other schools and colleges within the contemporary American university. The 1960s and 1970s witnessed enormous upheavals in traditional status relationships between students, faculty and administration, particularly at the undergraduate level, although graduate students, too (even some professional school students—law, medical, but rarely engineering students) fought alongside their undergraduate brothers and sisters.

When the dust settled in the 1970s, undergraduate students had made substantial advances toward "parity" with faculty and administration, manifested in many forms—from establishment of "advocacy" departments of counseling, to severe reins on professors' traditional near-totalitarian control over how much or little students might participate in classes, to no-fail and pass/fail grading systems, to requirements for full-scale, quasijudicial hearings before students could be suspended, to student participation in appointment and policy decisions, including matters of curriculum and hiring of faculty, deans and presidents.

The dust clearing in graduate dissertation programs did not give the same picture. Graduate departments are still almost medieval in terms of faculty-student relationships, especially when compared to undergraduate shops. Graduate students have more to lose than under-graduate chains; they can—and sometimes do—lose their *doctorates*. The greater stake that doctoral students have in their studies, including the dissertation, combined with the awful uncertainties about negotiating the thesis, cause these students to be meeker, more bewildered, less directed toward banding together to meet faculty in a united front. The faculty, in its turn, exploits the underdog position of the graduate students in order to maintain a status quo of nearly zero-sum authority arrangements.

The 1980s will see some movement toward emancipation of the doctoral candidate. Dissertation programs cannot singlehandedly turn back the forces of educational history. The 1980s ABD can count on more support for his accepted proposal as contractual, or quasicon-tractual, in nature. In practical terms, this means that faculty will be less arbitrary and more cautious about taking unfavorable action on a dissertation completed in line with the approved proposal, conscious of possible, even probable, in-university or general legal challenge lurking in the background. More court cases will surface; a few departments may institutionalize grievance procedures. The beginnings of "dissertation" law may emerge, following on the heels of em-bryonic "dissertation therapy" of the 1970s (see Chapter Seven for elaboration). But the 1980s are probably too soon for full implementation of a contract model for the dissertation; there still exists a very strong graduate faculty lobby for the view of the ABD as a lone figure, almost an explorer, who has to come up with a unique and mighty product—one which cannot and should not be judged or confined within narrow legalistic parameters of a contract model.

THE PROPOSAL AS "MINI-DISSERTATION."

As the candidate works on his proposal, questions about how full or complete it must or should be will keep coming up. Three criteria must be met: 1. Does it fulfill the committee's minimum demands for approval? 2. Is the writer realistically able to convert the stages of the approved proposal into the real thing? 3. Does the proposal "cover all the bases," at least in rudimentary form, of the dissertation, regardless of faculty's acceptance of it and the adequacy of its several parts? It is the latter two standards which candidates so often neglect, much to their dissertation distress down the course.

79

An old con maxim goes, "Don't do the crime, if you can't do the time." Don't write a Madison Avenue proposal that sounds and looks good, laced with all the current sociologese or psychologese that isn't tooled for gearing into the dissertation.[4] Even if the committee should pass such a proposal, the candidate will find himself up against a blank wall when he tries to "deliver" on a "contract" he signed without possession of an adequate "plant" or resources for production. I have seen a number of cases of candidates locked into, trapped by, an approved proposal which they never "really meant"; none of them finished his dissertation.

A thorough proposal is very nearly a mini-dissertation. Most of the time a candidate will want to write a longer version than his committee wants, or even likes. If the department is doctrinaire about maximum pages, the ABD should nonetheless "let it all hang out" in his first drafts and edit down for committee consumption, saving the longer drafts for incorporation into the body of the full dissertation. "Letting it all hang out" means exploring as fully as one can, at this time, the issues of the thesis (the parts a proposal should contain are treated later in the chapter). Although some of the issues will change—or your answers/resolutions will change—down the path of the dissertation, initial in-depth explorations in the proposal will usually stand the test of time: very rarely will one be confronted by a whole new world of objections or hurdles.

Of course, some sections can be outlined only in general form, e.g., statistical procedures; others must await the collection and analysis of the data, e.g., discussion of results. My personal counsel—and custom—is to explore even these sections in a proposal (these parts are for my eyes only). That is, I assume certain data will pan out as predicted by my hypotheses; then I run them through my statistical tools (making very sure I understand both the mechanics and assumptions of these statistics); next, I write an analysis and discussion section in line with one direction of statistical outcome. Sometimes I follow up with a devil's advocate trial run, where I assume that the data pans out in an unpredicted direction. The idea, of course, is to *anticipate* as many issues as possible, so that one isn't thrown into a panic at a later stage.

Other sections of the proposal—e.g., review of the literature, rationale for the study—can be slotted, virtually intact, into the dissertation itself. This assumes, of course, a very thorough, "mini-dissertation" job on the proposal. You will even find that one of your "alternative versions" of an anticipatively written analysis/discussion section will generally fit the dissertation as well (although more cutting and editing may obviously be necessary).

I like to see fifty or more pages to a proposal. It is all right, too, if it is wordy, loquacious, even gushy; such excesses can always be edited. One has to have a large corpus, sufficient material *to be able to cut.* An excess of pages is a minor problem, compared to too few. Terse and "economic" proposals, on the other hand, make me suspicious of a candidate's failure to sink into his subject, to look deeply into the topic's waters. I sense a continuation of the term-paper mentality being carried inappropriately into the realm of the great project.

Many faculty advisers, I know, tend to preach a limited, brief, introductory-phase view of the proposal. A tactful student can officially take this short-sighted advice but should pursue the proposal as if it were, in fact, the dissertation. If necessary, two "sets of books," or files, one for presentation to the proposal committee and another for personal, more extensive use and consumption, can be kept. "Collapsing" the proposal and dissertation will protect a candidate against promises he cannot keep and cut the completion time of the dissertation by as much as half.

There is a final way in which the proposal may function as a "trial run" for the full dissertation: although there is much variation in format, formality, rigor and composition of committee from field to field and within departments of a given discipline, today most ABDs have to defend their proposals at some kind of official hearing. Some of these hearings are very similar in style, substance of interrogation and faculty membership to the trial the candidate will face in his final dissertation defense. Oftentimes, one can get "early warning" at the proposal hearing about which faculty are going to be difficult in passing chapters of the thesis and at the final defense, and prepare accordingly. (See below, "The Dissertation Defense," Chapter Eight, for detailed discussion of strategies and preparation for the final defense, and, by implication, the proposal hearing.)

AN ACCEPTED PROPOSAL AS OVER THE TOP.

In my experience, the dissertation proposal is most often a greater hurdle in the dissertation venture than the dissertation itself. Although neither I, nor anyone else, have hard statistics on this point, I would hazard that the failure rates for proposal and dissertation are vastly different: the great bulk of nonfinishing ABDs are candidates who never negotiate an approved proposal; most completers of an accepted proposal, on the other hand, finish their dissertations in (relatively) short order.

In an endeavor where the rewards and gratification along the way are minimal, achievement of an approved proposal has to rank as the first prominent reinforcement. Candidates invariably experience a tremendous second wind upon completing the proposal. "All the months I was struggling with the proposal, I felt like I had nothing," as one of my clients put it. "Then they [the committee] approved it, and the sky opened up, and my feelings went from nothing to everything. For the first time, I felt I had something to work with. I began to believe I was going to finish the damn thing." The accepted proposal is a vote of confidence in your project by the men and women who are authorized to grant your doctorate. The candidate's internalization of this confidence generally allows him to do the dissertation research and writing in a less anxious, self-doubting mood than during the proposal, particularly if the proposal has been written in the mini-dissertation form outlined above.

Prior to the late 1960s, it was unusual to hear of committee decisions on proposals and dissertations that weren't black or white; candidates passed or failed.[5] Failure was less "final" at the proposal stage, of course—usually, one could go out and do another proposal—but *conditional passes,* although not unknown, were not frequent. By the 1970s, such conditional passes, "subject to [major or minor] revisions," had become facts of life and SOP at many major universities.[6] There is every indication that conditional passes will be common in dissertation decisions throughout the 1980s.

A proposal accepted, subject to revisions and changes required by faculty, should be construed by the candidate as a victory and as affirmative action. Even an acceptance subject to *major* changes is still basically an acceptance. There is absolutely no reason for despair when conditions are imposed, even though I have seen candidates go into damaging downspins after such faculty actions. Prescribed thesis-promoting activity at this juncture is to carry out forthwith those amendments, additions, deletions, elaborations on which thesis committee members *seriously* insist.

It is an art in itself to discern just which faculty objections and suggestions have to be incorporated in a second draft. If the candidate

82

is given a memorandum by his adviser and/or the proposal committee, summing up the hearing and enumerating demanded changes, less leeway is afforded (often a blessing, rather than a burden). But if, as is most often the case, the proposer is supposed to rely on notes from or memory of the hearing regarding points made by several members, then negotiation and diplomacy become very crucial in reworking a proposal.

In both proposal and dissertation defenses, faculty input is motivated by a number of distinct reasons. Certainly, not all suggestions made to the candidate are serious demands for amendment. Often, a committee member's critical comments are really directed toward other colleagues on the committee with whom he is conducting a long-term polemic which preceded you by years; or he is demonstrating to his colleagues (sometimes "superiors" who will make a decision on his tenure or promotion) in this semipublic forum that he is current with the field. Or he is making *pro forma* points, because that is what committee members are expected to do in this role.

Since a substantial, albeit unascertained, number of suggestions were never intended by the critics themselves to be followed through by candidates—indeed, thesis members *forget* the majority of off-the-top-of-their-heads points within hours or days of the hearing—the candidate has to separate the wheat from the chaff to avoid wasting debilitating weeks, even months, on revisions that the demanding member has long forgotten. After waiting a few weeks, the candidate has to put on his Fuller Brush Man hat at this juncture (although his heel cooling will be shorter now, since he has gained an enormous increment in status through finishing the proposal) and meet with each of the committee members individually. During these interviews, some modified version of the old army maxim about "never volunteering" should be pursued: don't "volunteer" criticisms about your proposal; don't remind a professor of his contributions to your prospective work load. If he really believes that certain changes are necessary, he will bring them up again himself. Otherwise, they can normally be quietly dropped, or at worst given very light "pen service" in your amended version.

In these one-on-one encounters, it is often possible for the candidate to challenge a professor's demands successfully, particularly if, during the interval between hearing and interview, the candidate has rehearsed a persuasive argument. A more vexing issue is that of two

83

professors demanding contradictory incorporations in the proposal: X wants you to stress Hegel's view of history; Y insists upon Marx's. There is no easy way to solve or reconcile these demands; patient negotiation is necessary, with the candidate feeling his way as best he can between the members. One point is clear, however: one should make every effort to resolve all such major inconsistent demands at the *proposal stage*. But the peculiarly flexible nature of the proposal dissertation "contract" makes complete resolution at the earlier stage doubtful. Thus, Chapter Six deals in depth with reconciliation issues still surviving or newly emerging at the later dissertation phase.

Summing up, conditional pass of a proposal is a triumph and turning point in getting the dissertation done. Most often, the "conditions" for complete approval are not well defined or set by the initial hearing and are open to a great deal of paring down, negotiating and defusing through the candidate's initiative in individual talks with committee members and/or his adviser. It is essential for him to get a consensus among faculty about the main directions—substantive and methodological—of his dissertation, if he is not to be stalled time and again during its writing. Thus, even if a proposal were unconditionally accepted from the first hearing, it is imperative for the candidate to make the rounds of the committee members to head off irreconcilable expectations in fulfilling his dissertation "contract." Finally, even though nobody really *likes* criticism of his work, and even though the first reaction of most of us to it is annoyance, the candidate will come to value some faculty objections as contributing to a better dissertation. So to at least some extent, the proposal examination is genuinely an intellectual, dissertation-promoting stage, although that aspect usually gets lost during the anxiety-laden hour or two of the hearing itself.

WHAT TO DO ABOUT AN INVIABLE OR FAILED PROPOSAL?

A dissertation can be aborted at the proposal stage through self- or faculty determination. After putting in considerable work, the ABD may himself determine that too many unforeseen theoretical, methodological or faculty-relations obstacles stand in the way of completion.[7] Or the thesis committee may unconditionally reject the proposal—a not uncommon or especially surprising occurrence, given the tentative precontract negotiations at this point between candidate and faculty.

In the majority of terminations at the proposal stage, excepting extraordinary conditions—such as an ABD's already having devoted more than a year to the proposal, or implacable faculty hostility to a particular candidate which would be transferred to any number of further attempts—another attempt is indicated. The same advice cannot be given for someone who has been unconditionally failed on a completed dissertation (see Chapter Eight, "The Dissertation Defense," for discussion of a rejected thesis, and the distinction between a failed defense and a failed dissertation).

THE PROPOSAL AS ESTABLISHER OF "DIPLOMATIC RELATIONS" WITH THESIS-SUPERVISING FACULTY.

The writer has taken pains to warn the candidate that he cannot unqualifiedly count on faculty to be consistently interested or present during the unfolding stages of the dissertation. Perhaps some hyperbole was involved, if just to stress that even with a "helpful" or "supportive" faculty the ABD is going to find the burden of all major decisions and initiations on his own shoulders.

There *is* some measure of faculty continuity in most individual dissertation course histories: more often than not, your initial thesis adviser "lasts" through your proposal, research and writing, and defense; more often than not, at least the majority of your original proposal committee remain on the faculty and are there for your defense. Of course, their continued *presence and formal connection* with your project differ sharply from the *content* of those relationships in terms of promoting, obstructing or not affecting, one way or the other, the progress of your thesis.

The establishment and maintenance of "diplomatic relations" with relevant dissertation-supervising faculty entail an ongoing "differential dissertation association" calculus (see Chapters Two and Three for a general outline of that accounting system for interpersonal relations) which spans the four major moments of the dissertation: proposal; research; writing; and defense.[8] Accordingly, the book's discussion of the candidate's relationships with faculty must extend through a number of chapters (particularly Four through Eight), where different problematics of relationships are apt to be correlated with earlier or later moments (e.g., the farther along one moves on the dissertation course, the more likely that "maintenance" issues replace norm-establishment ones as most prominent). In this chapter, I want to alert the candidate to faculty-relationships questions that must be faced in the initial moment of the dissertation proposal.

CHOOSING A DISSERTATION ADVISER: MINIMUM QUALIFICATIONS.[9]

Most of us would have little trouble conjuring up a "dream adviser," just like we can produce on cue a pretty detailed fantasy picture of the "Mr. or Ms. Right" we seek in our personal lives. The ideal adviser would be (like the ideal scout and/or scoutmaster) loyal, true, brave, courteous, kind, helpful. But the candidate is not going to find his "dream adviser," any more than his real lovers are going closely to approximate "Ms. Right." So what should one be realistically seeking in a proposal/dissertation adviser?

The bottom-line requirement of the adviser is that he *be there* for the length of one's project. In my judgment, all other attributes are secondary (albeit sometimes very important) to this consideration. The same adviser (even a diffident one; the instance of an actively *hostile* one is another story), the same "warm body," is a crucial consistency/continuity-impelling vector through the moments of a dissertation. In numerous ways, it stamps the project as "serious" and to be "reckoned with" in the eyes of other faculty. The candidate, of course, can never be sure that his selection will remain in the program for the course of his project. But at the minimum, he should ask key probability questions (sometimes discreetly addressed to third parties, not the adviser), such as, does he have tenure? If he doesn't, is he up for it? And if so, does it appear likely he will receive it? Is he planning a sabbatical? An unpaid leave of absence? Is his health good? Is he near retirement?

The Dissertation Incest Taboo.

All other considerations are secondary, with the exception of a faculty member who is either clearly hostile to you (wishes you ill) or wants to establish a "personal" sexual relationship with you. It is most inadvisable for a candidate to go to bed with his or her adviser, or even to allow that possibility to hang temptingly in the air. The reasons for such avoidance are instrumental; they have little to do with the conventional arguments about "exploitation" of students (usually female, but by no means always; there are many cases of female faculty having relationships with male advisees) by faculty. Graduate students are, after all, consenting adults, many of them in their thirties, or even older. There is little reason to doubt that *both* faculty member and student are "getting something" from the relationship. If the student could be reasonably sure that such an intimate relationship would promote her/his dissertation, fine. And by this I don't mean that one's adviser-lover would bend dissertation requirements or write the dissertation for the candidate. Such "Blue Angel" conceptions of faculty-graduate student affairs are most naive; they happen that way in movies, not in the graduate anthropology department. By "promotion" of one's dissertation, I mean motivating a faculty member to read one's proposal and dissertation chapters with critical care, to make sound suggestions, to provide advice with key methodological and analytic questions that emerge. Unfortunately, love and passion don't generally yield such critical increments. Totally contrary to the stereotype, an adviser who loves you may do more damage to your dissertation than an indifferent one: he or she will be pushing just those kinds of romantically disorganized and nonroutine concerns that you have determined (through your careful decision to write a dissertation and construction of a file; see Chapters Two and Three) to postpone and avoid. These are the dissertation-obstruction problems of the "happy stage" of a love affair with your adviser. If—usually when—you or the adviser become disenchanted, ensuing rages, jealousies, avoidances practically insure that your dissertation will be doomed (if the adviser is, as very often happens, the "only person" qualified to supervise your particular topic) or very seriously delayed (pending your finding a new adviser). The world is more full of potential lovers than of dissertation advisers. Intersample contamination is strongly counterindicated.

The Size of the Adviser Pool.

Looking for a dissertation adviser with traits beyond the minimally required ones of continued presence and friendly detachment is affected by the *size of an available pool* of faculty. The pool of potential advisers is determined in a given department by (1) size of the faculty; (2) percentage of faculty assigned to or interested in supervision of dissertations; (3) the number of serious dissertation-writing candidates; (4) the nature of one's topic. These conditions were discussed in Chapters One and Two. In some programs a candidate will have a reasonably large (maybe three or four) potential group to pick from;

in others he may have only one, or, indeed, be put on a "waiting list." Of the four conditions, an ABD has control only over the fourth; don't relinquish that control by picking an arcane topic "in search of an unfindable adviser." Graduate faculty are less interested in what your topic is than in how you treat it from the special angle of political science, history or sociology. The dissertation is seen as training to be a general "journeyman" or "utility man" member of a given field. A sociology ABD, for example, should be able to write a thesis on homosexuality, or suicide, or homicide, or "born-agains," or Wall Street law firms with equal facility, using the conceptual and methodological tools of the sociological trade.[10] An ABD must always determine whether his proposed topic fits squarely within the category of mainline concerns of his discipline, thus guarding against extra difficulties in getting an adviser (the usual ones being quite enough) in his program.

Choosing an Adviser: Additional Desirable Qualities.

Assuming one has some leeway to "shop around" for an adviser, one can look for certain dissertation-promoting attributes, although it is certain no adviser will possess all of them. There is the added difficulty of not being well-enough acquainted with a prospective adviser to get any accurate picture of his advising potential; even if you knew him as an instructor and liked his lectures, his adviser role may be very different from his teacher function. It is advisable, then, to pursue multiple meetings with a prospective adviser in an attempt to fill in some of the blanks. Sometimes student peers can provide very useful information on advisers' styles. If you do know other ABDs who are currently under tutelage, or recent "post-docs" who did their theses under someone you are considering, by all means contact them (per the discussion in Chapter Two).

Dissertation-promoting qualities to be sought after in an adviser include:

1. At least moderately interested in your subject. Ideally, he might be someone whose own work is in the same or related area. Occasionally, a faculty member is phobic about a certain specialty or methodology in his field—an English professor detests Faulkner, a psychology teacher believes the TAT is witchcraft. One would have to be mad or masochistic to seek out the former with a proposal for "In

Praise of *As I Lay Dying*," the latter with a dissertation on "Toward Increased Validity of Projective Tests: the Case of the TAT." If on the other hand, a particular faculty member is known to specialize in one's contemplated topic, it is most diplomatic to seek him out as an adviser, if just to give him "right of first refusal." He may, in fact, not want to supervise your dissertation, may plead a work overload, but to go over his head or bypass him on his specialty is inviting trouble; he may show up at your defense with less than benign interest in your passing.

2. Reads papers and chapters within a reasonable time after submission.

3. Reads materials with a critical eye, offering ample comments and suggestions.

4. Accessibility. One wants an adviser whom one is not terrified to call for a chat from time to time, and someone who will give you an appointment to discuss key matters (like the latest submitted chapter) before the onset of another Ice Age.

5. Someone who knows his own mind, makes a decision and sticks with it. A wishy-washy adviser who continues to change his mind about key directions or thrusts in one's dissertation is a most dissertation-discouraging individual. Often, the wishy-washy adviser is very "friendly" and "personable," a "real nice guy," and students gravitate, understandably, to him, to their eventual regret.

6. Someone who "means business," who sees the proposal and dissertation—either explicitly or implicitly—as the performance of a "contract," outlined above in the chapter. It is far better to have a "grump" or even a surly person as adviser, who means business and possesses an integrity around that understanding, than a nondirective "Rogerian," an amiable person with no clear view of the "business" nature of the dissertation.

7. Someone who is respected by other faculty, preferably both professionally and personally, but at least professionally. An adviser can greatly facilitate the action taking on one's dissertation by other committee members if he has some clout in the department. Likewise, the adviser, as one's dissertation "rabbi," can protect and steer the candidate in the dangerous waters of the proposal hearing and dissertation defense, if he is forceful and has the esteem of his colleagues.

8. Someone who is respected as a "tough" methodologist. In many

departments, research specialists—often statistics and computer people—possess inordinate status and power because of the ideological aspirations of social science fields to be "just like" the hard sciences. Although it is by no means resolved that, say, anthropology's, psychology's or sociology's most appropriate or fruitful future direction is toward further quantification and empiricism, there is undeniably a current bias in that direction. Accordingly, the "research man" or "stat woman" often has the final say (the analogy—probably misconceived at bottom—is to the architects of a bridge or dam checking with civil engineers to see if the design will "go") on a given proposal.

Often these "scientific" types are not especially pleasant to deal with. They have an inclination to rewire one's thesis in a manner that takes the "soul" or "guts" out of it. On the other hand, they can be very useful in helping one write up a virtually "unbreakable" proposal contract, precisely because of their perhaps compulsive rigor. Whether one laments or praises their current entrenchment, they must be dealt with by proposal time. If such a person is not one's thesis adviser (chairperson of one's committee), every effort should be made to incorporate him as a second or third member; otherwise, the specter of his sitting on the final defense and torpedoing the dissertation (because of exaggerated deference afforded to him by less quantitative-oriented faculty members) hangs over your dissertation-writing days.

CHOOSING THE REST OF THE PROPOSAL/DISSERTATION COMMITTEE.

Selecting the other members of a thesis committee is subject, of course, to the same personnel limitations of a given department. Just how the candidate should obtain the other members varies from program to program: in some, the adviser sounds out prospective faculty; in others, the chairperson assigns faculty; in still others—probably the majority—the candidate has to go round to their doors.[11] Other members should possess the same qualities sought in the principal adviser, although because of the secondary role that second and third readers usually play, such attributes are less crucial. Perhaps most ABDs' engagement of remaining thesis committee members is a hasty affair, often arranged by telephone or letter. I have had clients who have *never met* one or another of their committee well into writing their proposals. At best, one gets two people who are "lukewarm" about his project, not expecting to do an awful lot of work with it down the stretch. However, the strategies which this volume counsels make the rest of the committee more important than often considered. Central to the "contract" is getting chapter-by-chapter approval by all committee members (see Chapters Five and Six). Thus, no matter whether these faculty are assigned or selected by the candidate himself, the ABD must establish a working relationship with them early on in the thesis course. Although secondary members may not be as apt as one's main adviser to make far-reaching demands for changes (not that it doesn't happen sometimes), their traditionally passive role can create major problems by their dilatoriness about reading and/or approving one's chapters. The chances of such delays are much reduced by getting to know the other members and convincing them that you "mean business." Established interpersonal relationships also aid the candidate in preparing the defense for his proposal hearing, over which these very faculty are going to preside.

WHAT SHOULD A DISSERTATION PROPOSAL LOOK LIKE?

In keeping with the preeminent emphasis of this book, much has been said in the chapter about the human relations and emotional dimensions/significances of the proposal, those aspects of the project which are undeniably so important and, equally undeniably, never systematically examined. In any event, the bottom line is what is set down on paper. What should the proposal contain? What sections should it have? What are advisers and faculty looking for? What *don't* they want to see? What sort of writing style is required?

In addressing these questions, I have drawn on sources with which I am intimately familiar, mostly (but not exclusively) from social science, and even more particularly from my own proposal and dissertation. Aware that the volume purports to cover to some degree the entire discipline spectrum of full-dissertation doctorates, I have tried to make the illustrations generalizable to other fields. Nuts-and-bolts discussion ensues where necessary, mostly in sections about statement of the problem, and hypotheses, and in methodological and statistical design, but not, I trust, to excessive/particularistic detail. Indeed, too much "cookbook" material would be patronizing; the ABD is no fool, unprepared as he may specifically be to write a proposal and dissertation. Then, too, each project always exhibits an idiosyncratic and personalized component, demanding individual creativity in design and implementation that can never be more than partly indicated or captured by formulae. What follows is a "factoring out" of key features and sections that characterize successful/approved proposals. I also flag along the way recurrent unacceptable tacks, approaches, "wrong trees" up which ABDs often bark. Remember that my working list of proposal sections could not possibly match the diversity of formal specifications contained in particular programs. Nevertheless, I have tried to touch all the main bases of a proposal regardless of what "aliases" they may be traveling under in given university and department bulletins.

Writing Style.

In sociology, the satirical term "sociologese" has been coined by pundits to describe an unnecessary elaboration of "insider" vocabulary and style that is often unintelligible to the uninitiated. Similar ritualistic vocabularies exist in most fields, from psychology to economics to literary criticism. Although a minimum frequency of "passwords" may be *de rigueur* (consult other prior proposals in your department on this issue), a good guideline in writing both proposal and thesis is to employ a style that is accessible to the "educated layman," as well as to the graduate committee, who tend to be irritated or turned off (or themselves don't understand) by too much "insider" terminology. Certainly, if you have any hopes to convert your dissertation into a *book,* avoidance of discipline linguistic codes is imperative. (See Chapter Nine on "Beyond the Dissertation: Surviving It and Professionally Exploiting It.")

Appearance of the proposal should reflect and support its literary quality. Chapter Eight stresses the absolute necessity of a professionally packaged and typed dissertation for a successful defense, but the student is advised to establish an earlier image of seriousness and commitment with a professionally typed proposal available for faculty during its hearing.

Review of the Literature.

In my view, the review of the literature is perhaps the single most important section of a dissertation proposal, even though many ABDs see it as something you "tack on" when the real work is finished. In truth, a properly executed critical review of the literature lays the foundations from which the rationale for the study, statement of the problem and hypotheses, and design of the research emerge.

Specifically, the review should accomplish four tasks: (a) establish a picture in the eyes of faculty readers of the candidate in full grasp of his subject; (b) connect the specifics of the dissertation topic with larger themes, "the big picture," in the discipline; (c) provide all-important "daylight" for the ABD's topic as an original contribution; (d) generate the end-of-proposal or dissertation bibliography.

(a) There is nothing better than a long, complete, thoughtful review of the literature in conveying to faculty the image (and reality) of a candidate who means business, in the driver's seat of his dissertation. Conversely, a skimpy review of the literature confirms preconceived faculty suspicions that ABDs are unprepared for and/or not seriously committed to the dissertation. Of course, mere length, without relevance, can bury a proposal itself; proposers will sometimes go on for pages with citations that recite the litanies of a field but are unrelated to the specific topic in hand.

(b) The candidate might see himself as film director: as his proposal film opens, the "big picture" is laid out; as the footage unfolds, the camera "pans in" on more specific locations, actors, themes, targets that will carry the picture, tell the story. The proposal writer is aiming toward a "zeroing in" on his topic, but he cannot *start* there—although many students make the mistake of beginning with very specific materials that should have been preceded by pages of introduction and gradual panning in.

Years ago, a sociology ABD decided to do his dissertation on homosexual behavior in men's rooms, so-called "tearooms." [12] The reason why he picked that exact topic (perhaps because he had access to the sample) is not crucial here; what is crucial is his "big picture" justification for this research subject.

He proposed to document numerous acts of fellatio that rest-room gays committed on each other. But the dissertation was in sociology, not pornography; how to make the transition, forge links to sociology? His review of the literature could not start with, say, observations of homosexuals in gay bars, excerpts from Gerald Walker's novel, *Cruising,* or Master and Johnson's *Sexual Inadequacy,* taking this last-mentioned team to task, perhaps for methodological shortcomings or ideological blind spots, even though there might be occasion for all these citations at the pan-in stage of discussion. All this type of literature—no matter how richly descriptive, clinically useful, "fascinating,"—is too close to sex for sex's sake, rather than sociology's, to constitute an acceptable theoretical starting point.

A classic and recurring sociological theme, starting with E. Durkheim's research in *Suicide* at the turn of the century, is that much apparently internally motivated behavior, like homicide and suicide, is at least partially determined by external social causes, structures and contexts. A newer, but certainly related, theme is that many social statuses which sociologists have usually assumed to be "fixed"—like sex and race—are, in fact, dependent upon social context: when context changes, statuses are mutable.

The tearoom researcher had to start off his review of the literature with an account of the introduction of these major themes into sociology, as well as their later stages of elaboration, including key researches in one tradition or the other. Slowly, he narrows his focus from work on "deviance" and "ascribed" (unchangeable) statuses in general down to "sexual deviance," and most specifically to homosexuality. Only with a more or less "unbreakable chain of evidence" can he present a convincing case for his sociology proposal.

Thus, this dissertation proposed to examine one kind of homosexual activity in light of two "red thread" themes in sociological theory and research. Of course, to test these particular propositions, the ABD had to observe his sample in at least one more context. Thus, the review of the literature develops, dictates, leads to an *appropriate methodology*. At a later date (having ascertained their addresses by noting their automobile license numbers in the rest-room parking lots), our ABD visited their homes in the role of census taker. He documented that the great majority of them were "happily married," "family men," lending additional empirical support to sociology's assertions that both "deviant" behavior and some "ascribed" statuses are situation-specific.

A proposal sequence has been described in which the ABD worked "backwards" (in his mental processes, not in how he put it down on paper), a person with a situation or sample in search of a "big picture." In my experience, some of this working-backwards process is inevitable; nor is there anything "unscientific" about it. I never knew a case where one generated a dissertation topic by starting with per-mutating and combining basic postulates of a field. Through some biographical blend of elements outlined in Chapter Two, ABDs find themselves with a list of topics and samples that may be viable. A major part of determining whether they will, in fact, "go" is checking them out in a review of the literature for their solid connections/linkages with enduring large themes and research in one's field.

(c) Not only must the ABD demonstrate continuity between his project and important work that has gone before, but some input of originality as well. With this task the proposer might see himself as a running back looking for a hole in the defense, or "daylight" through which to break with his contribution.[13] The "line" here consists of the standing studies related to the candidate's proposed research. Al-though I have already indicated (Chapter Two) that there is nothing inherently doomed about a replication of another project (such re-peats are squarely within the canons of both science and social sci-ence), faculty tend to resist the idea, unless one intends to challenge an important study whose conclusions have come to be accepted as gospel.

Imagine for a moment that historian A. J. P. Taylor had written *The Origins of the Second World War* as his dissertation. His proposal committee might have been concerned with his merely going over old ground in turning over once more the "familiar," well-documented, diplomatic, political and military events in Germany, England, France, Poland, and Czechoslovakia during the 1930s. But Taylor provided "daylight" for his dissertation with the (then) startling and controversial thesis that, contrary to nearly unanimous conventional historical wisdom, Adolph Hitler was not the prime mover of events, that his role had been largely reactive, not active. Taylor proposed to go over once more (replicate) all the key prewar historical documents and sources, but with an eye to drawing utterly different conclusions.

Ordinarily, however, "dissertation daylight" is found by going through a hole in the line, rather than knocking over a defender who is standing his ground. At the time I was selecting a dissertation topic, research in medical sociology was booming. My review of the litera-ture indicated that the training/socialization experiences of many health professionals had been recently studied. Sociologists had done field research of medical, dental, osteopathic and nursing students. But a big hole was gaping for chiropractic students. The studies of the other health groups had documented the very-to-relatively-high prestige of these professions, already communicated to these students during training days. I took the facts that (1) no recent work had been done on a large group of health practitioners; (2) chiropractors were making concerted efforts to professionalize; (3) they were held in relatively low occupational esteem (even stigmatized) by the American public and even personally possessed discouraged occupational images; and I combined them into a "daylight" package which proposed to investigate an occupational group with the rather rare dual loading on professionalization *and* stigma. In my dissertation I was able genuinely to compare and contrast the experiences of my chiropractic students with other groups of in-training health students by bouncing my findings off previous research case studies, as well as by conducting some original research with medical and dental students.

(d) Nothing is more dramatically and forcefully effective in summing up and reminding faculty readers, as they draw to the conclusion of your proposal or dissertation, of the enormous amount of research and thinking invested as page after page of a tightly typed bibliography. Not only should the bibliography be as massive as it is legitimate, but it should be technically impeccable in the mechanics of citation style—buttressing the picture of the candidate as totally professional and workmanlike.

Rationale for, Significance, and Implications of the Study.

Persuasive justification for one's subject should flow right out of a critical review of the literature, done along the lines indicated above. Usually, the significances of the study are multiple—some primary, others supplemental. "Contributions to knowledge" in the field (as the catalogs sometimes put it) have to be made in the areas of theory, empirical findings and methodology, although the first two are generally more primary and necessary than the third. In both "tearoom" and chiropractic student studies, participant observation was an important research tool. Both writers, in very different ways, found it necessary to amend and innovate traditional procedures in line with fieldwork conditions if the groups being observed were not to balk and act out of character because of perceived intrusions by the sociologists.[14] These methodological strategies and refinements made a contribution to the long and still developing tradition of participant observation in anthropology, sociology, criminology and psychology. They could not have stood alone as rationalizations, however: Humphreys primarily had to make a case for "tearoom trade" as further validation for the sociological perspective on deviance; Sternberg had to bring together what were formerly considered rather unrelated fields of sociological inquiry—professionalization and stigma— in the unique case of chiropractic education.

"Implications of the study" have to do with how the findings of one's dissertation might be used practically. In political science, public administration and education lingo, they often go under the name of "public policy." In many dissertations, implications have to await the outcome of data analysis to be set down fully; it will be more strategic to some theses than others to outline them at the earlier proposal stage. Many disciplines have had an uneasy time with "pure" and "applied" aspects of their fields. There was a time when anthropology eschewed "value judgments" and suggestions in ethnographies; sociology firmly distinguished between its "value-free" research findings and uses of its findings by social workers; academic psychology was doctrinaire about the intrusion of practical or "clinical" aspects into pure psychological research. But the last decades have seen increasing fusion of theory and practice, and although pockets of conservative resistance still exist, today it is appropriate, even advisable, to incorporate convincing implications of one's research into a proposal and/or dissertation.[15]

- If your social psychology experiment indicates that people are much less apt to act on their prejudices (here in terms of refusing hotel rooms to Chinese-American couples) when having to deal with minority group members face-to-face—as opposed to letter or telephone—then interpersonal confrontation tactics emerge as more effective than once-removed communications media for successfully implementing civil rights and affirmative-action programs.[16]
- If your history dissertation persuades that Hitler did not start the second world war, a policy implication for diplomacy is that the current rage for "psychohistory"—seeing nations in terms of Mao's China or Sadat's Egypt—may be misleading and should be balanced with greater attention to nations' superpersonal political, economic and military structures and ideologies.

- If your sociology dissertation demonstrates that the same men are straight in some groups and gay in others, then the strong potential of group therapies as change agents for sexual identities is suggested.

Statement of the Problem and Hypotheses.

What one comes to here is a formulation of the key problematic or issues which continued examination of the topic, in light of related literature and research, repeatedly yields as compelling questions. Related to this "statement of the problem" are procedures necessary to test out the truth probability of competing "answers" to the problem. Such procedures are known as hypotheses and are stated in the form of provable or disprovable assertions. To move from the abstract to the concrete plane here, let me return to my dissertation.

After a relatively short—albeit intense—time with my sample of chiropractic students, I was able to document a model of the chiropractic student under bombardment from "negative messages" about his occupational choice everywhere he turned in his life: he had heard down at the school that chiropractors were "starving"; girl friends and their parents were unhappy with his selection ("It's enough he's not Jewish, but to be a chiropractor, too!"); he was sometimes accosted at parties; the AMA continued to attack chiropractic; New York State (in 1968) continued to refuse it licensure; even classmates and faculty were "down" on the occupation. In short, the whole "rosy future" outlook documented by sociological observers of another group of health students—medical students—was replaced for my sample with a doomsday outlook.[17] Review of my field notes from the earliest weeks already shows me preoccupied with the problem, "Why do they stay on?" or, "How do they fend off the bad news?"

Although other issues were to emerge as well, the questions of why and how these chiropractic students pursued their studies in light of the multidimensional social opposition, even stigma, confronting them remained the central problematic of the dissertation. The thesis came to revolve around processes of identity management and stigma denial, themes with which some contemporary sociologists (like E. Goffman) and social psychologists (like L. Festinger) are deeply concerned.

Next, I had to propose a reasonable and testable answer to my stated central problem. Through my participant observation of the sample, I became convinced that chiropractic students (and graduate chiropractors as well) adopted a "self-over-other" defense mechanism, which allowed them to see themselves as successful "solo practitioners," "individual entrepreneurs," "heroic loners," whose especial talents and resolution would make them successes, even if the profession as a whole was "going to hell in a basket" (as one student put it to me). Later on in the thesis I was to use this "self-over-other" cultural theme of chiropractic to account at least partially for the relative lack of formal organization among chiropractors, as opposed to both MDs and dentists.

But how to "prove" the prevalence of such a defense mechanism operating to ward off intimations of an unhappy career? Hunches from "talk" I had heard in my fieldwork were not in themselves going to persuade my thesis committee. So I constructed a set of hypotheses: "The set of hypotheses which follow are essentially a series of probability statements, based on a sociological model of how respondents should score their personal chances versus their peers' chances in several crucial areas for chiropractors if the underlying theory in the research is to be confirmed. Each hypothesis is tested by a corresponding *pair* of situational questions concerning one sector (e.g., relations with family, medical doctors, success on licensing examinations) or another. One question in the pair asks the student to evaluate the chances for the typical chiropractor or student; the other question asks him to evaluate his own prospects." I then went on to list fourteen hypotheses, along with citations to the full text of the corresponding questions contained in one of the questionnaires I gave to my respondents. Here were some of them:

1. Respondents will predict higher incomes after ten–fifteen years for themselves than for the average chiropractor.
2. Respondents will predict greater success for themselves on chiropractic sections of state licensing examinations than for fellow candidates.
3. Respondents will predict that negative newspaper publicity about chiropractors in general would have more harmful effect on their fellow chiropractors' practices than on their own.
4. Respondents will indicate that their own families and friends have more fully accepted their decision to become chiropractors than have the families and friends of other classmates.

5. Respondents will indicate that they have been less subject to unpleasant social confrontations because of their status as chiropractic students than their fellow students

6. Respondents will predict friendlier relations with MDs for themselves than for other chiropractors.

7. Respondents will predict a better chance for themselves becoming members of nonchiropractic hospital staffs than for other chiropractors.

Can statement of the problem and related hypotheses really be so fully elaborated at the proposal stage of the dissertation? Certainly, the discussion of hypotheses construction and testing must be continued into the next chapter (on the dissertation per se) and spans both proposal and thesis writing itself. How refined the theory and hypotheses must or can be at proposal time is a function of (a) a particular program's demands; (b) the nature of one's topic and methodological design; (c) the researcher's relationship to his sample or subjects. At proposal time, my statement of the problem and several—but not all—of the hypotheses were already in existence, although not in finished form. Some of the hypotheses came only after months more of day-to-day contact with my sample, as I got to know all the ins and outs of their subculture.

With a "tighter" or more "rigorous" psychology dissertation experiment, for example, where the ABD conducts his fieldwork on a "one-shot" basis with university student samples, it is often possible, even required by the thesis committee, to have finalized hypotheses in position at proposal time. Already settled statistical procedures to test the hypotheses are also much more likely to be present in the experimental dissertation proposal. For most of us in other fields, both hypotheses and statistics will tend to be more open-ended, and dicier. In keeping with this book's contract view of the proposal and dissertation, however, it is certainly advisable to nail down by finished proposal time as much of the theoretical/hypothetical/statistical structure as is realistic under the conditions of a particular dissertation.

Methodological and Statistical Design.

In this final major section, the candidate must spell out the operational procedures with which he proposes to test his hypotheses. In my chiropractic student study, for example, I had to indicate the size and characteristics of my sample, dealing along the way with the question

100

of "representativeness." My methodolological design paralleled the theoretical model I had delineated and specified in the preceding sections on Statement of the Problem, Definition of Terms and Hypotheses:[18]

Figure 4.1: Hypothesized Self-Over-Other Model of Chiropractic Adaptation

Independent Variables	*Intervening Variable*	*Dependent Variable*
Negative and Stigmatic Messages About Chiropractic From Various Societal Sectors	Adaptive Defense Mechanism	Self-Over-Other Attitude Set re Personal Future As a Chiropractor

Negative and Stigmatic Messages About Chiropractic ———→ Defense ————————→ Set re Personal

---

I had to indicate the ways in which I was going to "operationalize" both the independent and dependent variables; the intervening variable was not measurable, but inferred (per the logic of social science) from the demonstrated relationship between the independent and dependent ones.[19] Both independent and dependent variable measures were "complex" ones, composed of more than one indicant. Negative messages were documented by newspaper and medical articles critical of chiropractic to which students were exposed; many references to such messages which I either overheard among student and faculty talk or which were reported directly to me (I designed a system to quantify these oral references to stigma); and in questionnaire items given to the entire sample, asking them to report the frequency of exposure to unhappy news about their profession in various social contexts outside the school. The dependent variable, self-over-other-attitude set, was measured and documented by responses to a series of paired questions, introduced above, in a second questionnaire to the students.

To take one hypothesis—respondents will predict higher incomes

101

after ten–fifteen years for themselves than for the average chiropractor—the second questionnaire presented the sample with two items:

---

1. How much would you say the *average chiropractor* starting out today can expect to be earning per year 10–15 years from now?

(check one)

a.____under $10,000
b.____$10,000 up to $20,000
c.____$20,000 up to $30,000
d.____$30,000 up to $40,000
e.____$40,000 up to $60,000
f. ____$60,000 up to $100,000

2. How much do *you estimate* that *you yourself* will be earning per year as a chiropractor when you've been out in practice 10–15 years?

(check one)

a.____under $10,000
b.____$10,000 up to $20,000
c.____$20,000 up to $30,000
d.____$30,000 up to $40,000
e.____$40,000 up to $60,000
f. ____$60,000 up to $100,000

Discussion of analysis of the data from these questions will be left to the next chapter on the dissertation itself, as will more detailed treatment of the trials and tribulations of questionnaire and experiment design. Let us say here only that it still remained for me to ascertain whether the distribution of data was in the expected direction at a statistically significant level, giving support to empirical existence of the Figure 4.1 model.

Even though *implementation* of the statistical design has to await the postproposal stage of collection of data, and even though the original statistical design may have to be modified along with subsequent in-the-field-dictated alterations in original hypotheses (see

Chapter Five for more on this), at least its bare bones have to be laid out in the proposal. Further, it behooves the candidate to understand the logic and mechanics of his statistical tools at the time he presents his proposal for approval. If you are going to use a Q-Sort, a semantic differential, an F Scale, a Pearsonian r, an analysis of variance, a sign test (the one I used in analysis of my fourteen hypotheses) in your experiment, be prepared to justify and explicate it in depth when the second reader on your committee begins to probe you about possible objections to its use in your research case.

Pilot studies or procedures become an issue for some dissertations, particularly those in psychology (and psychology-oriented education theses), where one has to pretest or create an instrument which will measure an independent or dependent variable. If subjects are going to be asked to play a game or do a task, it is always necessary to carry out dry runs to get the procedures straight, find out how much time is needed, anticipate "confounding errors" that subjects are likely to commit.

If you want to administer a "will to live" attitude scale to terminally ill patients for your nursing dissertation, you won't find it in the literature. You will have to construct it yourself. In that process you will have to utilize qualified judges to sort out the good indicators from the "duds" in the original larger pool of possible questions you thought up to tap the variable of will to live. Those pilot studies that yield the instruments which test your hypotheses must be conducted by the time of your proposal defense. There are sundry other kinds of preliminary testings, on the other hand, which will be carried out during the time of dissertation research. Prior to administering two finalized questionnaires to my sample, for example, I "tried out" earlier versions of certain sections of both on selected students, recent graduates and faculty, and modified the substance and/or style of many of them in accordance with the feedback I had received.

SUMMARY.

The dissertation proposal is crucial to and connected with the total dissertation-writing course in five ways:
1. In constructing it, one definitely seals his dissertation topic.
2. The proposal establishes at least a quasi or "equity" contract with

faculty that extends to the dissertation itself. Although the contract law of dissertations is in flux, varies in acceptance or adoption from one university to another, will probably never develop as tightly or explicitly in the university setting as contracts in business—because of unique, open-ended, creative, elements inherent in dissertation research and writing, and not native to the commercial world—it nonetheless has precedent and linkages in related university contexts (e.g., grievance hearings re tenure and promotion), is gaining in recognition and offers some assurance to an ABD that if he produces a dissertation substantially consistent with the terms of an accepted proposal, faculty will approve it.

3. A long, thorough, well-documented and detailed prospectus, exceeding the minimum requirements of a particular program, is recommended; such a proposal will serve, in fact, as a "mini-dissertation," much of which can be incorporated in the subsequent formal dissertation with only minimal changes: chapters or sections on review of the literature, theory, hypotheses construction, rationale for the study, and even methodology.

4. Of the ABDs who do not finish, the majority seem never to have gotten as far as having a proposal approved. It would appear, then, that getting a proposal accepted has a motivating and successful prognostic value disproportionate to its length (in terms of both pages and time) in the dissertation course.

5. Although continuity is not total, generally, one's original thesis adadviser and (usually) two other committee members who pass on the proposal stay on as the dissertation's judges. Such formal continuity says nothing about the quality of supervision, which can vary from excellent, through mediocre, to poor, with the modal experience in the mediocre/indifferent category. Guidelines for picking suitable, helpful advisers and committee members are outlined, along with a list of optimal supervision qualities to be sought after, even though the latter traits are often less than abundant in the available adviser pool of a given department.

What should a dissertation proposal look like? What elements should it contain? What are faculty looking for? The author offers a "composite" picture of a proposal, drawing on various sources (including his own dissertation), predominantly in the social sciences, to illustrate successful versions of key sections or components in a thesis prospectus. Recurrent unacceptable tacks and wrong trees up which ABDs often bark are also flagged.

NOTES

1. Some candidates may have already sketched out a proposal during the last year of course work. The same rule, in any event, applies to them: move ahead after orals on that foundation with all deliberate speed.
2. Refer to Chapter Two for an extended discussion of picking a viable topic.
3. For a harrowing account of the struggles ripping one graduate department apart (this one the sociology department at the University of New Mexico) by its then-chairmen, see R. Tomasson, "Hell in a Small Place: Extreme Conflict in One Sociology Department," in A. Shostak, ed., *Our Sociological Eye: Personal Essays on Society and Culture* (Port Washington: Alfred, 1977), pp. 266–281.
4. For a parallel overemphasis on campaigning and deemphasis on carrying out the job once elected, see Joe McGinniss' account of Richard Nixon's first successful presidential campaign, *The Selling of the President* (New York: Pocket Books, 1968).
5. Actually, pre-1970's approval procedures for *proposals* were very haphazard, rarely contained overt or even implied contract elements. In many programs, a formal proposal was not even required. A state of chaos existed, probably producing even higher nonfinishing rates for the dissertation.
6. Interestingly, in architecture there has been a decades-long tradition of candidates failing their first attempt at licensing examinations, to the extent that it is almost expected. Since most candidates pass on the next try, one suspects some element of "initiation rites" in the testing.
7. My original dissertation proposal on cultural perceptions of crime in Sweden was aborted when it fell into the hands of a methodologist who insisted on converting it from a theoretical study into a content analysis of Swedish newspapers! At that point, I had no stomach left for continuing with it. It still lies to this very day in a filing cabinet back drawer, one of the sadder uncompleted projects of my career. All academics, scholars and writers accumulate a number of similar stillborn efforts during their careers.
8. The term "moment" is used here with the connotations of both history and physics: a major period or force within a larger totality.
9. In some programs, the term "sponsor" is used instead of adviser.
10. Being a "generalist," in addition to a specialist in a few fields, is, in fact, expected of full-fledged professors. There have been many occasions, for

example, when I have been asked to "fill in" for colleagues in a sociology of the family, religion, methodology or statistics course, although none of these are my "specialties," because of the prevailing assumption that one can bring his general grasp of the field to bear on subfields.

11. In many crowded, understaffed departments, there is a "waiting list" for other committee members as well as advisers. Quite often, a candidate won't have a complete group until his proposal is finished.

12. In this composite proposal example, I draw on the research of L. Humphreys' *Tearoom Trade* (Chicago: Aldine Press, 1970), and more generally on a field known in sociologese as "ethnomethodology," which seeks to discover the taken-for-granted (unrecognized) norms by which people conduct their everyday lives. I never saw Humphreys' proposal and am "reconstructing" what it might have looked like in certain sections to meet the demands of a doctoral thesis committee. Likewise, I am making "educated guesses" about his thought processes in building a proposal.

13. Cf., basketball great "Doctor" Julius Erving's remark, "You play to daylight; sometimes it's there, and you take it." CBS, May 1980.

14. Humphreys had to assume the role of voyeur—"watchqueen"—to maintain access to his sample; Sternberg had to agree to let fledgling chiropractic students "adjust" him, as an act of faith and trust. In most participant observation studies, the researcher has to make creative, often uncomfortable, occasionally downright dangerous adaptations. Such adaptations account for the color and richness of many of these studies, but also for their frequently precarious quality.

15. Cf., Clyde Kluckhohn, *Mirror for Man: A Study of Human Behavior and Social Attitudes* (New York: Premier Books, 1961).

16. R. LaPiere, "Attitudes Versus Action," *Social Forces,* 1934. A common-sense way of putting LaPiere's basic finding, which has been corroborated in many social contexts over the years, is that folks have a much harder time turning you down when you are eyeballing them. An important implication for *dissertation-promotion policy* is that faculty are less likely to reject a candidate's proposal and/or thesis chapters if he has the courage continually to discuss the project with them in their offices, rather than by phone or memoranda. Again, I stress the importance, this time substantiated by a tradition of findings in social psychology, of regularly keeping your oar in down at the department, no matter how unpalatable the prospect.

17. In his volume, *Boys in White,* Becker had demonstrated the cheery and confident tone of University of Chicago medical students researched by him and his colleagues. (Chicago: University of Chicago Press, 1961.)

Employing a sociological pun, I entitled my dissertation, "Boys in Plight."

18. Some programs, notably psychology ones, require a formal section putting forth definitions of terms used in the hypotheses. As far as I am able to determine, most other fields have no formal rule about such a section per se, but it is, of course, vital for the proposal's and dissertation's lucidity that key hypotheses and methodological/statistical terms and concepts be predefined before being introduced in their respective sections of discussion.

19. This volume assumes a certain minimal research competence on the ABD's part. A reader who is fuzzy on the relationship between independent, intervening and dependent variables needs remedial reading in one or more good social science methods textbooks.

CHAPTER 5

The Unfolding Dissertation: Researching and Writing It

Chapter Four flows into Chapter Five, just as writing the proposal and the dissertation should be conceived of as two parts of a larger procedural unit. Although in the present chapter the emphasis is on the latter moment, the reader will see that much of the discussion of Chapter Four is, *mutatis mutandi,* relevant here as well.

Although an approved proposal is certainly an occasion for champagne, the importance of pushing on almost immediately—without resting upon one's laurels—with the research and writing of the dissertation cannot be overemphasized. By approved proposal time, the ABD who has implemented the work habits and attitudes detailed in earlier chapters of this book will have found the pace and momentum to carry him the rest of the way, provided he doesn't slacken.

There are four main components in executing the dissertation: (1) collection of data; (2) analysis and interpretation of one's findings; (3) writing the dissertation chapters; (4) presenting the unfolding dissertation to supervising faculty. Each of these involves many subissues, of which the most important, recurrent and vexing will be examined in this and the following chapter.

COLLECTION OF DATA.

How simple such a short phrase makes it all sound! So unlike the complexity, messiness and often tediousness of the real task. The methodologies of dissertation data collection can be broken down into three major categories. Non-social science dissertations, e.g., humanities and letters, generally pursue the first style of methodology, whereas social science theses range across all three approaches.

1. Research which involves on the writer's part no original collection of data directly from samples of people "out there." In one way or another, the data sources have been compiled or produced by somebody else. In humanities, letters, philosophy and history dissertations, first-order research involves perusal of primary sources like documents, original manuscripts and letters; and secondary sources such as texts, histories, monographs. In behavioral sciences, political science, public administration and education dissertations using a theoretical/methodological perspective of one or more of these disciplines, primary sources for data collection are survey, public opinion and census materials; and public documents such as legislative and administrative reports and judicial cases. The dissertation writer recollects, researches the spectrum of related data sources to pull out those ideas and facts which tend to substantiate his statement of the problem and hypotheses.

It is an interesting and much-debated (although unresolved) question as to whether such research can be called *empirical,* regardless of how thorough and exhaustive its execution, or whether that usually hallowed but occasionally scorned term is reserved for original collection on the part of a researcher. Sometimes the issue becomes not just interesting but crucial, e.g., when a department requires that a dissertation be "empirical," or involve "original research." Is, for example, an anthropology dissertation, "Contrasting Premarital Sexual Foreplay Among Three MicroAsian Folk Societies," based on computer data from the HRAF (Human Relations Area Files) "empirical"? Or can a sociology dissertation, "Differential Social Mobility Aspirations of Middle-Class and Working-Class Black Women," based on survey data from the NORC (National Opinion Research Center), be styled "original research"? There is no blanket answer to these questions. Generally, departments and programs which have gone "big" on computer methodologies and a "scientific" image would endorse such methods as empirical. Indeed, many social science departments nowadays either insist on or prefer the utilization of survey and/or census source data to the exclusion or radical deemphasis of other "contaminated" person-based sources of data collection.

2. Research which involves limited and highly structured—nonethe-

less essential—collection of data directly from living, breathing subjects or samples. This approach is characterized by a one- or two-shot, in-and-out-again gathering of data. In psychology dissertations, it is seen in experiments where student subjects are given a defined time to carry out some task, often under two or more experimental conditions. In sociology theses, it is most often found in the administering of questionnaires to groups of respondents (often classes of students). A dissertation on social mobility attitudes among black women might gather its data directly in this manner as opposed to using NORC sources (although, generally, the thesis would partake of both sources for comparative and complementary purposes).

Common to all limited fieldwork approaches are a lack of rapport with subjects and a very low risk factor in terms of permanent damage to one's methodology design. In the typical case, the candidate "borrows" a colleague's or fellow student/teacher's introductory class in psychology or sociology for half an hour to conduct an experiment or hand out a questionnaire. One doesn't know the respondents and, more likely than not—with the limited exception of returning to administer a second phase the following week—will never encounter them again. This is not to argue that the candidate must not exercise due preparation and care in designing his experiment or questionnaire (including pretesting) and obtaining his respondents—certainly, he must—but the chances of his being expelled from his fieldwork site before he collects the necessary data are very small (as contrasted with continuous collection of data from real people over a period of time: see below). If a class should unaccountably take umbrage with one's questionnaire and balk at filling it out, the researcher need only "clean up his act" to avoid a repeated reversal and take his questions to a new group. If the sample turns out to be too small or unrepresentative again, one moves on to another college class with a larger number of anonymous faces. In none of these instances of limited original empirical work is any individual setback with particular subjects fatal—inconvenient, time-wasting, infuriating, yes, but fatal, no. Its low-risk factor, combined with its genuine kernel of "real-life" research, are undoubtedly major factors in commending it to many behavioral-science candidates as an acceptable compromise between a person-disassociated dissertation based exclusively on already-gathered survey material and a person-permeated dissertation based largely on information gathered through continuous intimate interaction with one's sample, entailing recurrent hazards to completion of one's methodology and, ergo, one's dissertation.

3. Research which involves long-term, continuous contact with subject groups from whom data is being collected. This fieldwork approach is most typical in anthropology but is also found with some frequency in sociology, social psychology and certain education dissertations (those employing "participant observation" methodologies derived from social science).

There is an enormous literature on the pros and cons of such field studies, involving issues about whether they are truly "scientific," whether they are ethical (particularly if the researcher has not identified himself as such) and whether they are viable in light of high-risk factors of expulsion from the group before the data is collected. An ABD contemplating a field study dissertation should heed the following warnings:

a. Don't study a group which is illegal or stigmatized. In either case, the chances of (and anxieties about) expulsion are far too great.

b. Don't study a group whose center of (symbolic) existence involves activities and attitudes which outrage you. Your staying time in that kind of site can be counted in a week or two.

c. Don't study a group where you have to conceal your true role and researcher identity. This avoidance is especially important if the group is engaged in illegal activities but holds even for groups pursuing lawful ones. If, for example, the research site for your study on "Bet with Your Head, Not Over It: A Study of Gambling Activities of OTB Employees" is your *own* OTB office where you are employed as a clerk, you had best be prepared to change jobs—or at least branches—when the study comes to light and your cover is blown. Nobody likes a spy—even apart from what he or she writes—and hostile or cold shoulder reaction is the norm in these cases.

d. Don't study a group whose existence, membership, leadership are all in doubt in terms of stability and continuity. Many juvenile gangs, for example, of a type which Yablonsky has termed a "near-group" because of fast-shifting and fast-breaking changes in personnel, are poor candidates due to their here-today-gone-tomorrow composition.

e. Don't write your dissertation about a group for which no substitutes can be made, should you be expelled. If a certain type of group is the sole representative of its kind, say, the Women's Medical College of Pennsylvania (now called Medical College of Pennsylvania) in Philadelphia, dissertation time is not the right time to field-research it. Without knowing any specific details about the college, I would guess that officials might be very sensitive indeed about letting a male observer wander about at will, fearing negative sexist publicity from his study. Even if they granted entry in the most cordial manner, they might well have second and third thoughts (as did the chiropractic college I studied) six months down the road with the ABD past the point of no return and no alternative women's medical college to turn to for study if expulsion should occur. A very resourceful, uphill dissertation *might* be salvaged along the lines of "Closing Ranks: A Case Study of Feminist Associational Reaction to Perceived External Threat," but I, for one, wouldn't want to try to write that one.

Adherence to these avoidance policies still leaves room for many field studies, although the pool is definitely narrowed. Becker did a field study of medical students, Smigel of Wall Street law firms, Montagna of prestigious accountant firms in New York City.[1] All faced certain entry and maintenance (continuing access) problems, but the groups were all both legal and very sure of themselves; furthermore, they were all replaceable: Montagna could have gone to other accounting firms; Becker to another medical college.

The reader may object that my caveats exclude many important and socially valuable topics of study. True. If you have spunk and a flair for excitement and the eye of the storm, all the more research power to you. But save your illuminating undercover participant observation of a professional auto theft ring for your first book *after* you have obtained your doctorate in criminal justice, on a more mundane topic with a safer methodology. With this sequence of projects, you'll possess sufficient salary and prestige as an assistant professor of criminology to extricate yourself from a possible charge of accessory to grand theft, stemming from your research role in a criminal enterprise!

On balance, the ABD is not advised to pursue a thesis whose primary research design calls for extended participant observation of a group upon whose continued goodwill he is dependent for collection of indispensable dissertation data (an exception has to be made in the case of cultural anthropology, where ethnographic field studies are required by some programs). *Adjunct* fieldwork, which complements the validity of primary-methods data gathered through survey and/or questionnaire materials, is desirable, when available, for adding another dimension to one's study. But hypotheses testing should not, in my judgment, depend, on a first-line basis, on the successful sustained execution of fieldwork.

Researching a dissertation within the boundaries of the first two methodological approaches outlined—using data not collected by the candidate, or employing strictly limited originally collected data—leaves plenty of room for variations by individual styles and ingenuity: e.g., it is an art all in itself to design a tight, probing, valid and reliable questionnaire or experiment. Then, too, many public policy and social science issues are best (sometimes exclusively) testable by survey and questionnaire methods, e.g., political opinion, voting preferences, demographic trends, social-class structure, the effectiveness of school systems and programs in delivering services to students.

How Much Data to Collect?

It is very important to remind oneself continually to what purposes data are being collected, regardless of method. The most relevant guideline here is whether they bear on confirmation, rejection of, qualification of proposed hypotheses. Other relevant data would be "background" materials on, for example, social characteristics (age, sex, ethnicity, social class) of respondents, or administrative rules and regulations of an organization which yielded a picture of its social structure. It is generally better to collect too much rather than too little, within the tolerance limits of one's sample—and oneself—particularly with one- or two-shot questionnaires or experiments, where the respondents will not be available to retest if holes or unexplored issues surface two months later in the analysis stage of the dissertation.

In stressing abundance of data, "fishing expeditions" are not recommended. After all, one has a set of hypotheses and procedures to draw on in pinpointing data targets. Nevertheless, hypotheses have a way of becoming altered with progress of the dissertation (see fuller discussion below in hypotheses-testing section); key questions are posed in somewhat different ways; incoming data and theoretical models work back upon each other. The ratio of eventually used (in the final version of the dissertation) to originally collected data is most often not impressively high, although there is a good deal of variation among different researchers within and across disciplines.

In my study, I presented the chiropractic students with two questionnaires containing 177 items, many of them scales and multiple section questions. I was able to get nearly all of them to fill out these vast instruments because of my established, long-term relationship with them (one desirable consequence of certain field studies). I had upwards of 400 pieces of comparative data for each respondent. Certainly, I did not use anywhere near all of it in my analysis and write-up. But when the questions were originally drawn, each was included because I felt it was relevant to getting a finely detailed picture of my respondents' backgrounds and their world of the chiropractic college in a systematic and empirical way, confirming many of my impressionistic and *ad hoc* field observations. I then drew on this large pool of material to block out my thesis with a good deal of confidence that I knew what I was writing about. Many of the questions whose data did not appear in later versions of the dissertation were not "wasted" or "superfluous," since they were either stepping-stones along the way of analysis or aided in closing off theoretical deadends or analytic blind alleys.[2]

ANALYSIS AND INTERPRETATION OF FINDINGS FROM THE DATA.

The reader will remember from Chapter Four that I had presented my sample with various self-other questions designed to tap a self-over-other adaptation to the anticipated career tribulations of practicing chiropractic. Two items (see page 102 of Chapter Four) asked the students to predict their own and the average chiropractor's income after ten to fifteen years in practice. Let me continue with that example, as well as bring in others, to introduce four key issues of analysis and interpretation: determining statistical significance; handling troublesome, inconsistent or contradictory data impacting on the thesis from without (e.g., other books, studies); dealing with negative (to hypotheses confirmation) results generated from one's own data collected for the dissertation; whether, when and how to use computers in processing and analyzing data.

Statistical significance.

The self-over-other tendency was startling with the income items: the students predicted a median income of $52,500 for themselves and $28,400 for the average chiropractor. Looked at another way, fifty-two of the seventy-five in the sample predicted self-income at least one category higher, often two or even three. There were twenty-one ties and two cases where the individual predicted a higher income for the average chiropractor than himself.

Still, the final step in scientific testing of the hypothesis—that the "respondents will predict higher incomes after ten to fifteen years for themselves than for the average chiropractor"—was to determine whether the distribution of 52–21–2 was statistically significant in the expected direction. The *null* hypothesis (the nullifying or devil's advocate hypothesis, it might be instructively conceived as here) for each of my fourteen hypotheses was that chiropractic students predict their own career success to be no greater than the typical chiropractor or chiropractic student.

In specific statistical terms, the null hypothesis states that for any pair of self-other questions, students will choose the same amount of success for themselves and others, i.e., tied scores on any pair of questions, except for some error which is assumed to be random. Random error here means that students would be as likely to pick other over self, as self over other. For Hypothesis One, and the other thirteen, I employed a nonparametric statistic, the *sign test,* to ascertain whether the standing null hypothesis should be rejected in favor of my own hypotheses. In this manner, twelve of my fourteen hypotheses were confirmed, ten of them at the .001 level of statistical significance, one at the .01 level and one at .02, giving strong support to the empirical existence of the Figure 4.1 model in Chapter Four. Let me remind the reader that a .001 significance level finding means that the data distribution on a given item could have come about by chance less than one time out of 1,000, and that, ordinarily in social science, researchers accept a .05 or .01 level of significance as strict enough.

Descriptive Versus Analytic (Power) Statistics.

Whatever your hypotheses and field, you are generally going to come down to the question of using a statistic for determining significance. This is not a statistics text and does not purport to discuss the various power tools appropriate to different orders of data, and experimental and questionnaire designs. But the candidate should be cautioned against confounding in his research the related but distinct elements of magnitude, direction and significance. Suppose your dissertation in social psychology theorizes that authoritarian group therapy is singularly effective in rehabilitating drug offenders.[3] Further suppose your collected data look like this:

Table 5.1: Group Therapies and Recidivism

	Non-Recidivists	Recidivists	Totals
Authoritarian Group Therapy	60	40	100
Laissez-faire Group Therapy	50	50	100
Control Group (no therapy)	40	60	100

The magnitudes of the cell figures tilt in favor of confirming your hypotheses, although they are certainly not overwhelmingly persuasive of the efficacy of authoritarian as opposed to less directive group therapy. The direction of the data (authoritarian-receiving sample tending toward predicted non-recidivist pole) is also anti- null hypothesis. But however you operationalized the independent variables of the two kinds of therapy and measurement of recidivism, the resulting statistics in the table are all in the realm of *descriptive* statistics. An *analytic* statistic, or power statistic, as it is sometimes termed—in this particular case chi-squared—is necessary to determine whether the patterning of magnitudes and directions among and between the various cells is statistically significant. For example, it might turn out that the difference between success rates of the authoritarian and laissez-faire groups is not statistically significant, but that differences between either of these therapy-exposed groups and the control group are significant. Such results would have to lead to a rejection or modification of your hypothesis, with the "serendipitous (see below for more elaboration of serendipity) suggestion that an atmosphere of concern and support which made the addicts feel special seemed more important and efficacious than any particular therapy approach per se.

Sometimes the question of "near significant" or "approaching significance" findings comes up. One meets such phrases and discussion not only in dissertations but in journal articles and papers. Suppose an intracell chi-squared analysis of the data in Table 5.1 yields a .08 level

116

of "significance" for the distribution of cases between authoritarian and laissez-faire results. If the writer is "pushing" the efficacy of the authority therapy thesis, there is going to be pressure for him to use the "near-significant" argument in his discussion. Social-scientifically, it is unjustifiable, since statistical significance is by predefinition a zero-sum game, just as you don't *nearly* have an orgasm or make a putt. On the other hand, certain social science departments and their research bureaus are known to take and permit certain liberties in so-called "trend" interpretations. If the candidate comes up against "near significance" with his findings, he might consult the prevailing standards of other current dissertations and methodologists in his program in making a decision about pursuing the discussion. A way around near significance is sometimes to "collapse" the data categories into fewer ones, viz., if a three-by-two cell distribution (above) yields near-significant results, collapsing it into a two-by-two one often results in significance.

The Bogy of Disconfirming Evidence

ruining one's dissertation parallels the fear of somebody else coming along and "scooping" the candidate. But there is more reality to the surfacing of negative, challenging, unexpected results during continuing review of the literature and data analysis than there is to the virtually impossible chance of a candidate really being scooped on his thesis (see discussion in Chapter Two, on this point). As a matter of fact, I never knew a dissertation, including my own, where everything turned out just as expected along the lines of the proposal. Challenges to one's theoretical model and hypotheses can come from "without" and "within," from library sources one continues to pursue even during analysis and write-up, or from the data itself. Very often the "negative data" results from pursuit of both external and internal materials. But I have never come across a case where "negative results" ensued in rejection of a candidate's dissertation, even though ABDs continue to believe that such circumstances are fatal and not infrequent. I confronted such a challenge during my own dissertation research.

In my case, the field site data were coming in nicely, i.e., analysis of self-other items were yielding strikingly confirmative results of a self-over-other tendency prediction for rosy futures as chiropractors. I was feeling quite pleased and confident. At the same time, I continued to—

what law students and lawyers would call—"Shepardize" my case: canvass all studies, literature (lawyers preparing a brief check the latest appellate decisions bearing on their case through Shepard's recording system) related to my topic. Although I had done a good deal of groundwork for my proposal in areas like professionalization, adult socialization, stigma, I was bound initially to neglect others, whose importance would emerge only as my fieldwork, data collection and analysis proceeded. The candidate must disabuse himself of the narrow notion that data for one's study is confined to the originally collected materials yielded by his methods design; *all library literature* bearing on the problem is also data. Of course, "all the data is never in," and at a certain point one has to stop reading and collecting and write a final draft; but input should be sought after right up to the point of setting down a final version.

One afternoon toward the end (at least at the time I believed it was the end) of my data analysis, I had left my dissertation office for a Shepardizing/browsing session in the Columbia University social science library. I was attempting to find a better, more social-scientific-sounding label for the self-over-other tendency in my data. I had jotted down a list of cue words to check against the literature; e.g., egoistic, autistic, self-evaluation. Somewhere between autistic and self-evaluation, I ran across a string of psychology articles reporting that, in general, American subjects tend to elevate/score themselves over others in testing situations. Suddenly in the Columbia library I went cold. What had begun as a search for a felicitous term or phrase had turned into a thesis crisis.

Wasn't it entirely possible (even probable) that the consistent elevation of self over other in various questionnaire problematic contexts of an upcoming chiropractic career stemmed not from my hypothesized "solo" adaptation to and distancing from the negatively perceived chiropractor herd, but from the pedestrian tendency of people to rate themselves better than their peers on anything from reading ability, to friendliness, to attractiveness?

I relate this episode because sooner or later the current dissertation writer is going to experience a similar cold sweat of jeopardy to his whole project. Reflecting back on those events, I see that my crisis was unnecessarily extended and intensified because (a) I had, in understandable ABD eagerness for certainty, come to a psychological "closure" in the thrust of my thesis, putting all my eggs and energies

118

in the basket of the self-over-other mechanism, not playing enough with alternative frameworks or keeping open to challenging objections; (b) I immediately assumed that my thesis committee knew everything there was to know about the ins and outs of psychological literature on self and other scoring evaluations and would, as one person, peremptorily raise this fatal objection to my thesis. As it turned out, the committee hadn't the foggiest notion that such an "autistic factor" existed in testing. It was *I* who informed them about it. Fortunately, after I calmed down and thought matters through, I was able to use the factor in a "serendipitous" manner to reinforce and nail down my dissertation.[4]

By stating that I self-exacerbated the crisis, I don't mean to say that one didn't exist. I had stumbled on a serious objection to my whole model, no doubt about it, and I had to find a way out. Whether or not my adviser and other supervising faculty knew about this literature was not ultimately a first-order issue. But on a very practical level, I couldn't go into a thesis defense with my rear so egregiously unprotected; even a slim chance of one of the five being acquainted with the autistic test-taking tendency and making the damaging connection, vetoing my thesis in which I had single-heartedly and -mindedly invested almost two years of my life, was an infinitely greater chance than I was willing to take. Besides, and more important, I still believed that my thesis about a peculiar self-over-other tendency operating among chiropractors was accurate. True, I had perhaps become doctrinaire about the mechanism, as heavily involved dissertation candidates and researchers in general are apt to get about their projects; on the other hand, I had given the matter intensive and long-term investigation and reflection. Confronting this issue, then, became more than covering my rear or getting my thesis "through"; its resolution meant intellectually vindicating and defending a project into which I had poured my best.

What saved me at the time, however, was not Librium or psychotherapy, or even a triggering of the autistic tendency! What saved me was my file. As distressed and depressed as I was, I sensed that somewhere in that vast pool of intelligence I had collected lay a resolution. So each day I forced myself to spend my usual time in the office, reading over my notes, memoranda on theory and methodology of the dissertation. To this day I don't know how it came to me; I simply know that the right dissertation synapses eventually got wired because

I kept at the file, activating connection after connection. It came to me that the only way to "factor out" the "autistic constant" in test taking was to compare my chiropractic students with other health students. If I could show that, say, medical and dental students demonstrated a significantly smaller tendency toward self-over-other evaluation on career context questions, my thesis that a peculiar self-other defense mechanism was an intervening variable in the chiropractic student case would still be viable.

It took me such a long time to come around to this "inspiration" because only weeks before I had considered the dissertation nearly done, all the data in, the analysis finished. At one level or another, I was ferociously resisting opening up questions, most certainly gathering new data with new samples. However, once I came to the realization that some comparative research was the only way out—that there *was* a way out—I gathered myself for a last research effort. After weeks of new entry and access problems, I managed to get permission to administer a short questionnaire to a few classes at my university's medical and dental colleges. I presented these health students with self-other, paired, income-prediction questions identical to those asked the chiropractic student sample. Both the dental and medical students, particularly the latter, demonstrated a startling and statistically significant reduction of the self-over-other income prediction which had been so rampant and near-universal with my chiropractic group.

Completion of my thesis was delayed some three months. But the comparative research generated two final chapters of the dissertation, including a final "implications" one, where I speculated whether chiropractic's continued "solo practice" ethic (which I had amply documented) would allow it to survive in an age where other major health professions were all moving toward bureaucratic, group-practice organization and ideology. Neither of these last chapters, of course, had been contemplated by my proposal. Yet my committee made no objection to these additions, indeed, praised them as innovative adaptations and elaborations of the proposal's theoretical and research models. This is by way of saying that modifications in methodology and adjustment, and even revision, of hypotheses during the dissertation research and analysis are probably more the rule than the exception. No matter how well one pre- or pilot researches his topic for the proposal, later intensified exposure, as well as continued reexamination of the issues, is going to force changes in one's model.

"My Own Data's Coming Out Wrong."

My challenge came from *external* data. As we saw, I ultimately stood ground with the validity of my original thesis and findings about students' individualistic defense mechanisms, although I had to elaborate and extend my methodology in its defense. I would have faced a different hurdle if my original sample of chiropractic students had not exhibited a significant self-over-other elevation in line with my hypotheses. Let us turn to *internal* challenges to the dissertation, which are perhaps more frequent than the external type of my case. What do you do when the majority of your hypotheses are either not being significantly confirmed by your own collected data, or, worse, are indeed being disconfirmed?[5]

One alternative is to play it straight: report the disconfirming results, and rely on the scientific ethos and the contract model of the dissertation and proposal, i.e., you carried through assiduously the methodology of a design the proposal committee approved. That the hypotheses were rejected makes its contribution to the field in closing off an ultimately dead-end research direction.

My sense is that such an approach washes better in a hard science experiment/dissertation—where the rigor of an ineluctable scientific logic and procedure is more seriously followed—than in social science and education dissertations, although a particular, say, psychology ABD's department may be an exception to this rule of thumb and accept as sufficient negative results produced through "honest" procedures.

The largest obstacle to getting such negative results accepted, no matter what the discipline, is the suspicion cast upon one's *hypotheses*—either that they were badly developed in relation to your specific topic and/or in connection with earlier work in the field, or, more frequently, that they were straw men. If one is disposed to defend against these objections, stand by the authenticity and logic of the original model even in the face of incoming negative results, then it doesn't do to close the dissertation on a downbeat. The writer must essay one or more explanations for the inconsistency between his pre-

121

dictions and the empirical results (I believe that even in the hard sciences *some* reconciliation is expected).

One reconciliatory tack to take is methodological: the measuring design and instruments used were not sufficiently discriminatory or biased the results of the data (e.g., non-mutually exclusive items on a questionnaire, scales or tests of low reliability or validity, nonrepresentative samples of respondents). The difficulty here, of course, is that you yourself designed—or at least chose among the various established measures—the research instruments for your project. Criticism of your own measures has a hollow or masturbatory ring to it; criticism of someone else's venerated measure (viz., the Likert Scale in social psychology, the Guttman Scale in sociology, the Thematic Apperception Test in psychology) as the culprit is likely to be better received but probably won't be sufficient in itself to pull you out of the negative data hole. Your committee's response may well be, "Now that you have recognized the insufficiencies of your methodology, go back and do the research (experiment) with an appropriate, valid and reliable instrument."

A strategy more promising than mere reporting of chips-fall-where-they-may disconfirming results is a "full-scale inquiry" into the causes—theoretical and methodological—for such an outcome. (How full and to what scale depends on how many of the hypotheses have been defeated: generally, if the majority of one's hypotheses are sustained by the data, "limited" explanations for the failure of certain others to pan out can be legitimately designed.) It is perfectly legitimate in both science and social science to learn by experience; tirades, especially by social scientists, against so-called *"post factum"* construction and modification of theory, measuring instruments and data analysis ignore the centrality of such reciprocal activities in scientific work.[6] Methodology textbooks, particularly introductory or "low-level" ones, often push a rigid, self-righteous and prissy research checklist model, where you (a) state your hypotheses; (b) operationalize instruments to measure the variables; (c) carry out the data collection along the prescribed operational lines; (d) analyze the results; (e) write up your findings. Nothing is wrong with this research model as an "ideal type." As a matter of fact, it is a mandatory starting point for a dissertation proposal, and, generally for research projects, pursued throughout one's career. But to insist on these steps as being the whole story—that they must be unidirectional, followed in this exact sequence, that hypotheses or methodology can never be varied once set in motion along the original lines—is mechanical, and childish. Worse, it doesn't approximate the majority of actually conducted worthwhile research where people find that they have to make changes in both their assumptions and research procedures as they come to know their subject more intimately.[7]

The ABD *should* follow the ideal-type model of sequential research steps his first time through. Initial data results will determine how he is to proceed from that point. If all or most of one's hypotheses are beautifully confirmed at this stage, congratulations, Doctor. For most of us, matters will not run quite so smoothly, and some adjustments will have to be made, including modifying hypotheses, analyzing the data in novel ways, even administering new instruments.

- Recall in the chiropractic student case that, even though the data came out "right," the writer had to add an entirely new research direction to his study, never contemplated in the original proposal, in order to defend his central hypothesis from straw man charges.
- Recall in the drug group-therapy research that the candidate had to revamp his models for both the treatment and etiology of drug addiction when it transpired that "Rogerian" group treatment was as effective as the originally favored authoritarian treatment. In this case, elaboration of the original model could be made, using the initial data pool from the three condition groups. Although the laissez-faire treatment groups were originally seen merely as a second-condition control, the finding that Rogerian groups were almost as effective in treating drug addiction as highly directive ones necessitated the researcher's examining the control data to factor out its commonalities with the favored variable (e.g., both made the addict feel special, attended to).

It is most important to drive home the point that every candidate is going to face his own peculiar crisis with his data, and that he is going to have to call upon his own ingenuity and resourcefulness to get through it. It is a dysfunctional dissertation myth to believe that "nobody else is going through this hell"—since almost every candidate is experiencing his idiosyncratic version of the crisis. It is another debilitating myth to believe, "The data's come out wrong. I'm through." The preceding crisis examples were offered as antidotes to this second kind of despair, not so much for nuts-and-bolts guidelines but as an affirmation that a candidate steeped in and committed to his project will find a way, and that such a path will fall within current, more flexible paradigms for legitimate research procedures.

Nonetheless, a thorny faculty-relations issue is involved in "revisionist" dissertation research. If the proposal is construed by one's program as a contract, might not radical departures from its theoretical, methodological and analytic stipulations be interpreted by supervising faculty as fundamental enough violation to render the dissertation contract "null and void"? One must consider, first, how closely one's particular department adheres to the contract model. In any event, the charge of "radical departure" can be avoided if one initially executes the steps of the proposal as originally contracted. Having shown "good faith," one can then go on to demonstrate that realistic adaptations were necessary in light of developing conditions to carry out the *spirit* as well as the *letter* of the contract. In the dissertation case, the spirit of the contract implies that the candidate will produce a work which fully explores his topic. Such exploration often involves innovation and originality which cannot be foreseen at the time of proposal contract. There exists, as a matter of fact, support in equity contract law for subsequent modifications in performance, especially in cases of creative and artistic services. All but the least imaginative of dissertations would appear to fall within this category.

The Computer: To Use or Not to Use?

The issue whether to use computer technology in the data-processing and/or analysis stage of a dissertation is usually a serious one only in social science dissertations. Even in these areas, there are sharp differences of opinion and preference on the part of supervising faculty (and particular candidates) as to whether the computer should be a main-line or first-order methodological tool.

Certain computer services of the 1980s are undeniably potentially valuable to many fields of dissertation candidates at the *proposal stage:* increasingly, university libraries are subscribing to bibliography data banks, so that a candidate working up a comparative literature proposal for "The Concept of Time As Relative: Continuities Between the Work of James Joyce and Mario Vargas Llosa" will be able (soon, if not yet: some fields, e.g., psychology and anthropology, currently have more fully developed data banks than others) to cue a computer with key words and phrases, such as "non-linear time in literature," "early twentieth-century Irish literature," "late twentieth-century Peruvian literature," "commentaries on Joyce," "commentaries on Llosa," and within a few days and for a few dollars obtain an overview printout of the available antecedent materials bearing on one's topic. Obviously, many of the printout items will turn out, upon examination, to be irrelevant or only secondarily relevant, but almost always one finds the wheat with the chaff, especially if the cue phrases have been designed with the help of a librarian trained in this type of data-recovery procedure. Such an approach to review of the literature is immensely quicker and more efficient than traditional methods of consulting individual reference books, guides, indexes to the periodical literature of one's field. Of course, ultimately, there is no substitute for sitting down and reading the germane sources; no computer can do that for you (nor is recourse to computer summaries of materials sufficient). But the computer can zero in on key sources quite rapidly.

At later stages of the dissertation, one can use the scanning function of the computer as a "Shepardizer" to keep up with the concurrent developments in the area of one's topic right up to the time of dissertation defense. Sometimes periodic scanning will add valuable citations, even analytic suggestions.

So the use of the computer for preliminary and sustained scanning of the literature relevant to a topic, in whatever field where such a service is already available, is certainly not an issue. Controversies and anxieties arise when the computer is considered for the *main role* in a study as assembler and/or analyzer of the data. Generally, only social science-model dissertations, with elements of experiment, controls, table-partialling, correlation and the like, are amenable to computer approaches. Even within social science dissertations, the appropriateness or necessity for computer analysis will vary according to the nature of research materials (see beginning of chapter): survey data, demographic data, large-scale, large-sample questionnaire data are all good candidates for computer processing. The larger that observational data, collected firsthand, looms, the less the importance or even legitimacy of the computer; computer processing of Goffman's subtle observational studies of mental patients in *Asylums* or Nance's observations of the *Gentle Tasaday* of the Philippines strike all but a few among us as absurd.[8]

The issue of computer research in dissertation data has to be set in the ideological context of social science graduate departments. There is a "computer culture" in the air and corridors of many programs that surfaced in the mid-1960s and continues with added vigor into the 1980s. The denizens of such cultures, mostly graduate students and some faculty, appear to spend a rather large part of their days hanging around the computer room, awaiting the latest "run" on their data. An untutored listener hears much esoteric shoptalk, or "computerese." Sometimes one feels he has mistakenly wandered into a *dental* clinic, what with all the orthodontics and periodontics-sounding terminology of "bytes," "bits" and "chips." Graduate faculty differ in their stance toward the computer culture. Generally, although there are many exceptions in both directions, older faculty tend to be far less enthusiastic than younger professors. Such indifference, hostility or suspicion stems from one of two sources: fear, because the older people simply were never trained in computer programming or analysis, don't care to start now and are defensive about their ignorance in this "growth" area; a sense that the prominence of computer *methods* has led to the prominence of computer, technician-like *minds,* less sensitive to the humanistic considerations which have to feed the social sciences if they are going to research social matters with any depth beyond quantitative accuracy.

A particular candidate is going to have to check out the salience of the computer culture in his program when deciding just what to write and whom to approach as a possible adviser. There are departments where one almost has to do a dissertation with the computer as a large if not exclusive research tool. If the department is computer-obsessed, probably the issue along that dimension of picking an adviser is moot. In many other programs, one finds a large computer force, with a substantial enclave of dissenters. If one is disinclined to use the computer approach for one reason or another, sufficient faculty validation can usually be found in such "mixed" departments. I would venture that few if any major social science graduate programs today are "anticomputer" in emphasis. Although I personally view this as a lamentable, in some ways pseudo-scientific, development of the past two decades, dissertation facts must be faced. The fascination and adulation that Americans in general have with gadgetry, "hardware," science, science fiction is shared, quite expectedly, by American "social scientists."

The reader will have divined that my own feelings about computers in social science and humanities research are mixed. Most certainly, it is advisable, even mandatory, for literature scanning. When I wrote my doctoral dissertation (1968) computers were still "optional," even in analyzing questionnaire data. Years before, I had taken a mini-course in very rudimentary computer procedures (e.g., counting-sorting), but little had stayed with me, nor with, I believe, my fellow students. Looking back, I see now that computers would have sped up considerably my hand cross-tabulations and hand correlation calculations for my sample. I do not believe that five computers using five "languages" would have furthered my theoretical formulations at all. My bias is still for doing sociological matters with my own hands and touch. Transfer of too many functions to the computer room sanitizes and depersonalizes social reality for me. I don't even regret doing all the tabulations and correlations myself; I liked—and continue to like—the direct contact with my subjects, even if it took more time to work through the data that way. Of course, to a substantial degree we are talking about life-style preferences and values here: I would rather drive a shift car and continue to use a mechanical typewriter because I like the feel and contact involved, the sense that I still have an important direct and physical part to play in making the machine work. Alienation is perceiving the machine as separate, independent, alien to one. I believe that computers often alienate, sometimes even subordinate, their regular users. Computer-caused "dissertation alienation" (see Chapter One for other types of dissertation alienation) is a possible, although not inevitable, outcome of the ascendancy of the computer culture in social science departments.

Like it or not, many readers of this volume are going to have to incorporate some computer methodology into their dissertation research and methodology. The two major caveats should be: 1. Don't get "swept away," and 2. Don't get terrified.

1. During the dissertation course, a particular kind of student can get "led astray" by the "fascinating" world of computer hardware, its whirring discs, its printout chatter. There is a whole science-fiction, "Space Odyssey" corona to the computer to which many contemporary American students are susceptible. The danger for the ABD is that he can get so caught up in the *means* of the computer culture that he forgets about its *ends* in relation to the dissertation, pursuing a kind of *Endless Summer* quest for the "perfect run." Such seemingly endless tinkering, which can keep an ABD submerged and entangled in

miles of printouts for years, is actually abetted by certain "empiricist" departments (sometimes styled "social science bureaus") where the researcher, not having developed a prior theory, is encouraged to try run after run until he "comes up with something." If the researcher, on the other hand, had a well-thought-out theoretical model to start, descent to the computer room and its rituals can lead to an orgy of running all variables against each other, in which excess the clean lines of one's original hypotheses-testing design are obliterated.

The guideline that emerges from a discussion of such hazards is: Never go to the computer with an open agenda. Use the computer for performance of specific tasks related to the completion of one part or another of your dissertation. It is equally dysfunctional to the dissertation to become a first-rate programmer for its own sake, as it is to become a grand and glorious filer as an end in itself.

2. Many students, and faculty, are terrified of the computer. Indeed, computer folks are able to get a leg up on the rest of us by exploiting that fear; they possess some powerful, specialized, "scientific" skills to which we don't have a clue. It is undoubtedly true that for most of us the uneasiness revolves around our relative unfamiliarity with higher mathematics at which we weren't much good but considered (especially during high school and early college) awesome and the summit of intelligent endeavor. The irony is that in the status order of mathematical fields, computer and statistical math rank very low! There are also very serious questions about the validity or (limited) applicability of mathematical procedures in research about people, but most of us can only intuit objections to mathematical models of social behavior, since we don't have the math that the specialists keep urging upon us.

This is not the place for an essay demystifying the computer and/or mathematics subcultures in social science, although some have been written.[9] It is clear, however, that knowledge about how the computer works greatly mitigates anxieties about it. So the doctoral candidate is encouraged to take at least one basic course in various kinds of computers and their languages. Understanding that a binary computer, for example, is, when you come down to it, only a "yes man" or a "no man," possessing a most limited and rigid "authoritarian personality," (any given computer statement is a zero-sum alternative), no matter what kind of program function it is performing, counteracts reifying or apotheosizing tendencies among the uninitiated.

But ultimately, it is really not very important for dissertation candidates using the computer to understand how the computer works; it seems unlikely a defense committee would question you on COBOL, or ASSEMBLER languages. Even if someone demanded a detailed explication of FORTRAN in relation to your computer runs on analysis of variance, the others on the defense would probably button him up. What you must understand are *the theory and mechanics of the statistic you are having the computer process,* not the theory and mechanics of the computer itself. In all but the most computer-fanatic programs, it is perfectly acceptable to take one's data to a computer consultant, specialist or technician, and ask him to run a program for, say, multiple regression analysis of your data. You don't have to have the foggiest notion of how he wrote up the program so that the IBM could understand it. Remember, the machine is just doing infinitely more quickly what we used to do by sitting down at a desk for a couple of weeks with reams of graph paper, rulers, pencils and maybe bifocals. What you must understand are the assumptions, mechanics and pitfalls of the Pearsonian r in general, and specifically in reference to *your* data. Then you must understand the meaning of all the printout categories, columns, rows, subtotals, totals from the computer. This is not the same as understanding how the computer *works*; it is knowing where to look in the computer's presentation (printout) for the results of tasks the programmer has directed it to perform. The computer will tell you what the coefficients of correlation are and which are significant. It is a wholly *noncomputer* task and responsibility, however, to evaluate the meaning of the results within the framework of your sample's size and characteristics in relation to the theory and limitations of your statistic. The thesis committee, then, may well ask hard questions about pre- and postcomputer stages of data processing, analysis and conclusions.

WRITING THE DISSERTATION CHAPTERS.

Actually writing the chapters themselves is the goal of all one's proposal construction, data collection and data interpretation. This volume does not pretend to coach dissertation candidates in literary competence per se, although some hopefully useful counsel on thesis-writing habits, attitudes and pace was offered in Chapter Two.[10] Rather, what I do here is anticipate briefly certain important questions/decisions/issues that the writer will face as he finally finds himself in the position to do the chapters: the number of chapters the dissertation should minimally include; the necessity of outlining chapters prior to writing them; readiness of a chapter or section to show to faculty; timing the writing of various chapters—which to write first; finding a typist who is not only technically competent but sufficiently adaptable to handle a long-term job which is far from ordinary or straightforward.

What Chapters Should the Dissertation Contain?

Generally the dissertation chapters should parallel the *proposal* sections, adding materials on then-anticipated, now-completed methodological implementation, data presentation, data interpretation and implications. In most instances, the critical review of the literature, statement of the problem, rationale for the study, hypotheses and methodology sections of the proposal (see Chapter Four) will be transferable (sometimes intact, more often amended, but still recognizable, due to postproposal-stage further reading, on-site-dictated modification of methodology, analysis-stage revision of hypotheses and related changes in statistical procedures). The function of a full, extensive proposal as the "grundrisse" (Marx's famous notebooks upon which *Das Kapital* was to be based) for the dissertation is once again underscored.

Outlining the Chapters.

The prolific mystery writer Donald Westlake, recently stated that he never outlines or plots his books, isn't sure where they are going.[11] Perhaps this omission explains their generally zany quality, and perhaps some fiction writers can successfully proceed without outlines (although *The Writers at Work* interviews—see Chapter Two—cast doubt even on successful fiction writing without outlining), but the ABD who doesn't outline his chapters confronts a jungle of serpentine false paths and starts which will exhaust him. The magnitude of the materials, especially of collected and analyzed data, is potentially overwhelming.

The outline for a given chapter should factor out of the myriad notes, memoranda, accumulated data, on a given part of the dissertation, the basic infrastructural posits upon which you build the chapter. These logically progressive and interrelated themes allow you to determine just which materials will now be selected out of the large total pool and used in pursuing and elaborating a major direction. Comparison of various chapter outlines allows one to determine whether the "plot" is flowing consistently, or possesses redundancies or contradictions.

I have never met a (fiction or nonfiction) writer who *likes* to outline; a little like Listerine, it is a procedure you hate to use, twice a week. Even today, I still catch myself trying to sneak out of outlining an article or chapter. The tendency is still there—especially when I am excited or eager to jump right in—to "let it all hang out" or "play it by ear," relying on existential flow to make things right. Invariably, I find I must go back, write an outline and redo the entire draft.

When to Show Chapters to Faculty?

Correctional authorities have long debated the optimal sentence time for an offender—that elusive temporal point which is long enough to do the most rehabilitative good and, at the same time, the least recidivist harm. No one knows just where that happy line falls for prisoners; nor do we know within reasonable limits of confidence how long a doctoral candidate should hold off on submitting his chapters in order to effect the most gain from the delay and the least detriment to progress and approval.

At every stage in the thesis course, this book has counseled against waiting too long, since experience has shown that substantial delays or postponements at any juncture (from serious work on the proposal soon after completion of all other course work through all subsequent stages) result in a multiplied delay in finishing the dissertation as a whole.

Still, one must show some restraint when it comes to chapter submissions to the thesis committee. It has been my experience as a dissertation adviser and editor/consultant for several publishers that the reader's attitudes and appraisal of a manuscript are disproportionately shaped by the first draft which comes to his attention. If the first impression is unfavorable, successive drafts—even substantially revised ones—never quite erase the memory or smell of the first stinker. A rule of thumb would be only to submit chapters after a second draft, or when one can state he has given it his "best shot." If one belongs to a dissertation group (see Chapter Seven), the candidate should incorporate major useful criticisms before taking a draft down to the department.

Should you submit chapters one at a time or in blocks of two or three? I argue in the next chapter that, when possible, each chapter should be approved by a majority of the thesis committee before proceeding to the next (along the lines and logic of the contract model). However, there are programs whose policies won't allow such maximum candidate-protective procedure; the ABD will be asked to hand in a couple of chapters together, or even occasionally a "solid draft" of the whole dissertation. If your department asks for all of it—or even half of it—at one time, you still have to exercise the same care for best-shot quality, must not rush through it once over lightly, in the mistaken belief that it's just a first shot: Heed the warning above about first impressions. The "whole thing" departmental preference is most disadvantageous to the candidate, spiraling his worry that he may be writing chapter after chapter of an ultimately unacceptable version of a dissertation. Short of its being firm, unbending program policy, one should make every attempt to renegotiate submission procedures with his adviser along the lines of one or two at a time.

In What Order Should the Chapters Be Written?

Many writers actually write the last chapters of a book first; this may be particularly true of mystery writers. Many *readers*—myself included—read the last sections of a book first thing off the bat: to see if the outcome and conclusions reached by the author are interesting, startling or valuable enough to warrant following through 200 pages of development. With dissertations, one almost has to write first (at least one draft of) the chapters dealing with data collection and interpretation (see detailed discussion above), not just because these are the "meat" of the thesis, but because execution of these dissertation components will restructure the content and format of other chapters and sections—e.g., critical review of the literature, statement of the problem, hypotheses, rationale for the study, even though these latter topics officially precede methodology, data-processing, analysis and interpretation, and "discussion" in chapter order. My preference, dictated by the "hydraulics" of the parts of the dissertation system, is to rework chapters on the bibliography and theory—after all, the proposal, if done properly, was a first draft of these chapters—after doing a first draft of the "meat" chapters.

Writing Versus Submission Order.

The questions of writing order and submission order are distinct. If one is lucky enough to have an enlightened and reality-oriented dissertation committee, it is advantageous to submit the methodology and hypotheses-testing chapters first; if the faculty approves these infrastructure chapters, there is no way, short of an intervening decline into senility, that they are going to fail you on superstructural chapters, such as critical review of the literature. The reverse is not unfailingly true; many a negotiator of preliminary chapters, including the one on theoretical models, has been brought up short by faculty rejection of the central procedures and analysis chapters. Enlightened committees being rare birds, the candidate is most likely going to have to submit the chapters in standard *seriatim* order. Notwithstanding, substantial drafts of the central chapters should precede redrafting of the other chapters, if the latter are to make consistent sense in the final draft of the entire dissertation.

Finding and Keeping a Suitable Typist.

Even the most proficient of amateur typist dissertation writers will want to have those versions of chapters shown to faculty professionally typed. Additionally, candidates who write in longhand may want intermediate versions typed up to get a better sense of how they flow. Thesis typing demands special technical and emotional skills. Manuscripts, especially social science ones, are apt to be filled with tables, charts, figures, diagrams, graphs that require enormous care in getting rows and columns of figures in the right places. The nature of dissertation research and writing practically guarantees that the candidate will have to make *changes* in materials already submitted to and typed up by one's typist. The ABD should make it quite explicit to his prospective typist that sudden alterations, sometimes eleventh-hour ones, can be expected. Although one's typist is not on twenty-four-hour duty, there is an on-call requirement to dissertation typing (e.g., your committee is scheduled to read your data-analysis chapter tomorrow, and you've discovered two sections which simply must be changed and retyped today) not involved with most manuscripts. If the typist is not willing to live with this changing—and often overtime and irregular-hour—situation when you spell it out, you must look elsewhere.

The other consideration with a dissertation typist is, parallel to the bottom-line requirement for one's adviser, that he/she is staying put in your location for the working period of the thesis—anywhere up to two years. It is most unsettling and delaying to project completion to change typists in mid-dissertation, since the initial typist will have learned your whole style of abbreviations, editorial markings, grammatical and spelling quirks, which the second typist will now have to learn anew.

I recommend "shopping around" for a dissertation typist, not in the sense of getting the best price, but finding a sanguine combination of technical, attitudinal and stable-residence qualities. Money should be very little object here, since the project is so vital to the rest of one's working life.[12] Actually, a good dissertation typist can sometimes transcend his/her official role and function as a help agent and friend in times of dissertation distress or frenzy (see Chapter Seven). Unless you are absolutely strapped for money, I advise *paying* someone to do the job, rather than having it typed as a "favor" by a friend, lover, secretary or spouse. These various unwary acquaintances and intimates are not going to put up with the peculiar demands dissertation typing will make on them, so your thesis may be delayed, and/or your friendship jeopardized.

Often, the best way to get the proper typist is by referral from a friend or colleague who has done his dissertation or a similar long manuscript. I contacted my dissertation typist in that fashion. For the following six or eight months I lugged myself and chapters up five floors to his Greenwich Village apartment. But his competence, availability and even input into the manuscript (questioning here, editing there) were worth the foot-pounds and dollars expended. Sometimes the working relationship forged in the fire of dissertation writing develops into an extended one, where the typist/colleague handles subsequent books (this was not the case with me and my typist, since he went on to become a child psychoanalyst!), dispensing with the hassles of writer and typist having to get to know each other with every major new project.

SUMMARY.

There are four major components in executing the dissertation: (1) collection of data; (2) analysis and interpretation of one's findings; (3) writing the dissertation chapters; (4) presenting the unfolding dissertation to supervising faculty. This chapter deals with the first three components, and their most important subissues.

(1) The candidate has a choice between three general data collection approaches:

a. procedures which involve no collection of original data on the ABD's part, e.g., using library sources or survey data;
b. research which involves limited and highly structured data collection from subjects or groups, e.g., administration of questionnaires to classes or experiments to college student subjects;
c. long-term continuous collection of data from groups, e.g., participant observation.

The advantages and disadvantages of each approach are considered. The hazards of using participant observation as one's primary dissertation data collection method are detailed; the candidate is advised to opt for some combination of a. and b. approaches.

Some standards for determining just how much data to collect are offered, with an argument for gathering too much material rather than too little, since a filtering and sifting process inevitably occurs from the time of initial collection to eventual selection of those data for inclusion in the later dissertation drafts.

(2) The author considers with the reader how to handle four problematic issues/situations, most of which he will confront in his analysis and interpretation of the data:

a. determining whether one's hypotheses are confirmed by the evidence at statistically significant levels; herein of the difference between descriptive and analytic (power) statistics; and the concept of "near-significance";
b. handling troublesome, inconsistent or contradictory data impacting on one's dissertation from "external" data sources; herein of the uses of "serendipity" to extricate oneself;
c. dealing with hypotheses-disconfirming results from "internal" data, i.e., one's own originally collected data; herein of controversial postproposal, during-research hypotheses revisions, and additional data collection not indicated or foreseen at proposal time;
d. whether, when and how to use computers in processing and analyzing dissertation data; the author offers a demystification of computers and an analysis of computer subculture norms and ideology to calm the typically frightened, uninitiated ABD as he approaches the machine room.

135

(3) Important questions and strategies involved in actually writing the dissertation chapters are considered:

    a. just what chapters should/must the dissertation minimally include;

    b. the necessity of outlining chapters prior to drafting them is underscored;

    c. how to determine when a chapter is "ready" to show to faculty;

    d. scheduling the writing of various chapters—which to write first and which subsequently; herein of the difference between order of writing and presenting to faculty;

    e. the importance of patiently contracting with a typist who is reliable, emotionally adaptable and flexible enough for solid performance on the long-term and often odd-working-hours dissertation.

NOTES

1. Howard Becker et al., *Boys in White: Student Culture in Medical School* (Chicago: University of Chicago Press, 1961); E. Smigel, *The Wall Street Lawyer: Professional Organization Man?* (Glencoe: The Free Press, 1964); Paul Montagna, "Bureaucracy and Change in Large Professional Organizations; A Functional Analysis of Large Public Accounting Firms," unpublished doctoral dissertation, New York University, 1967.

2. Collected data not incorporated in the dissertation can sometimes find a place in articles or books subsequently spun off. See Chapter Nine.

3. For the past two decades, one influential school, Synanon House, has insisted that narcotic addicts are best cured by exposure to a firm, patriarchal, family-type therapeutic community. Cf., L. Yablonsky, *Synanon: The Tunnel Back* (Baltimore: Penguin Books, 1967).

4. I understand serendipitous data to refer to unexpected findings in research. Often, they initially appear contrary or inexplicable in relation to one's paradigm. But often, too, they can be turned to one's advantage.

5. Note the stress on *majority*; in my study, twelve of fourteen hypotheses were confirmed, two rejected in favor of the null hypothesis.

6. Cf., "Isaac Newton and the Fudge Factor," *Science,* February 1973; Robert Merton's discussions of the interplay between theory building and research data, as well as his praise for serendipitous analysis (both of which themes contradict, in my view, his attack upon and rejection of

what he terms *post factum* theory building). *Social Theory and Social Structure* (New York: Free Press, 2nd ed., 1968).

7. Hammond, ed., *Sociologists at Work: Essays on the Craft of Social Research* (New York: Basic Books, 1974).

8. E. Goffman, *Asylums: Essays on the Social Situation of Mental Patients and Other Inmates* (Chicago: Aldine, 1961); J. Nance, *The Gentle Tasaday* (New York: Harcourt Brace Jovanovich, 1975).

9. See, for example, R. Bierstedt's vintage demystifying critique of S. Dodd's mathematical models of society, in "Real and Nominal Definitions in Sociological Theory," In L. Gross, ed., *Symposium in Sociological Theory* (Evanston, Illinois: Row, Peterson, 1959).

10. Somehow or other, the candidate must bring to the dissertation project a minimum level of writing ability. Absent this, the case is futile. Most ABDs clear this hurdle. It *may* be possible to improve beyond bare competence by consulting books such as Zinsser, *On Writing Well: An Informal Guide to Writing Nonfiction*, 2nd ed. (New York: Harper and Row, 1980).

11. *New York Times Book Review* section, April 13, 1980.

12. By this point, the candidate has so much time and money invested in the dissertation project that hesitating or obsessing over an indispensable expenditure of, say, $500 is myopic. Besides, the IRS may allow typing and xeroxing costs as a deduction for job training (check the current regulations).

CHAPTER 6

The Unfolding Dissertation: Diplomatic Relations with Your Committee

Relations with faculty, as one's dissertation unfolds, can be the most anxiety-creating component of the process because the candidate has the least control over this element. Earlier chapters have had much to say about the generally unsatisfactory and often haphazard departmental conditions under which one selects, or is assigned, a proposal/dissertation committee. Naturally, the problems emergent from such selection circumstances at the proposal stage tend to continue into the dissertation stage, although now, necessarily increased contact with second and third committee members may actualize or exacerbate difficulties and conflicts which were latent at proposal time. The candidate faces two basic sets of dissertation negotiation issues: 1. those with the committee/department as a whole; 2. those with individual members of his committee. The first set involves structural conditions and strategies that almost all candidates will face—normal, inevitable bases everyone has to touch, inevitable hurdles one has to jump. The second set often gets us into the psychological context of the "abnormal": here, contract negotiation and general human relations skills which stand the candidate in good stead for the first set of issues are of limited use; most often, the candidate has drawn a particular kind of "problem professor" through chance, and dealing with him/her effectively may require psychotherapeutic skills which most ABDs don't possess. Because these second-set problems are so idiosyncratic and tinged with psychopathology, they are much less amenable to general suggestion or solution.

ISSUES WITH THE COMMITTEE AS A WHOLE.
Keeping in Touch Down at the Department.

I have noted a tendency on the part of dissertation writers to cut down—or off—their communications with their committee and department. Immersion in the thesis necessarily creates a sense of going it alone, a reluctance to show it or share it with anybody before it is done. Such commendable unswerving attention to the materials of the dissertation per se has, however, to be tempered with action along the contract and diplomatic fronts of the dissertation course.

It is absolutely essential that the candidate present his unfolding dissertation, preferably *chapter by chapter,* for approval to as many committee members as possible (again, preferably to all of them, but always to the adviser and second most interested faculty member). Remember that the collected and analyzed data are most probably going to dictate important changes from the original proposal's theory and methodology. Assuming the contract model is explicitly—or, more often, implicitly—in effect in one's program, the "other party" must be consulted when the candidate is introducing alterations in his performance. The ABD has to go into the defense with all chapters having been "initialed" by his committee.

What the candidate wants, then, is a reasonably prompt and careful reading of his chapters. Under the best of conditions, faculty's response to these needs is problematic, but nothing is better calculated to ensure compliance with neither of them than a low to nonexistent profile down at the department. I realize that many ABDs are most reluctant to "make the rounds" of their committee for reasons outlined in earlier chapters. There is no getting around the need for a certain minimum of face-to-face meetings with the adviser and committee members. On the other hand, some of one's lines of communication can be sustained/supplemented by progress letters, notes or phone calls.

The particular importance of the departmental secretary as a conduit for getting through to the chairperson and other faculty is rarely recognized. Like court clerks and bailiffs in the judicial system, he/she is often the real manager of everyday program business. I have known departmental secretaries to make or break an ABD's thesis by reliably and sympathetically conveying messages from him to the "boss," or "forgetting" about them. Departmental secretaries are also important—even determinant—in scheduling times for defenses and even arranging which faculty (sympathetic or hostile) end up hearing one's dissertation. Without being unctuous (but not embarrassed either; it's part of "taking care of business" and protecting oneself) about it, the candidate should make a reasonable effort to get on friendly terms with the departmental secretaries and administrative assistants. ·

Being Pulled in Different Directions.

It is not uncommon for different members of one's committee to prefer or even demand that the dissertation stress different areas or, worse, treat the data from irreconcilable perspectives adhered to by one or another professor. Elaborating other areas is not so devastating a demand to comply with as writing a thesis from contradictory angles.

You might ask whether the dissertation proposal wasn't designed to head off just these kinds of dilemmas. Proposal approvals often *do* avoid the worst of them. On the other hand, second and third members tend to read and even hear the proposal (at the hearing) with less than the keenest attention and interest (recall the manner in which they are recruited).

Postproposal appointments with individual members may be helpful in bringing out contradictory demands of faculty which were incompletely voiced at the hearing. Even so, it is in the nature of faculty attitudes toward dissertation supervision that the first time other-than-adviser members of a committee really take the work in progress seriously, read it with care, generate objections to it may be when the candidate starts bringing full chapters around. Perhaps only then do many faculty believe the *candidate* is serious about it. In any event, such "delayed reaction" on the part of the other members is all the more reason for making sure each chapter is presented in turn to all members before drafting the next one. It is usually pointless to argue that postproposal faculty objections violate their end of the contract, because of the peculiarly "flexible" nature of this type of contract. Only in the (very rare) case where a committee member completely reversed his endorsement and rejected the proposal—rather than demanded changes—would recourse to legalistic interpretation of the proposal be called for, and probably decided in the candidate's favor.

Before dealing with "irreconcilable demands" about how he should write his thesis, a candidate must ascertain whether the demands are truly mutually exclusive and, even if they are, whether both faculty members "mean business" with their required lines of thesis inquiry. For example, in sociology almost all substantive fields in which a dissertation might be written can be approached from the "functionalist" or "conflict" perspective, institutional interpretations which have been conventionally construed as contradictory in their assumptions. Since most graduate faculty subscribe to one version or another of these two positions, it is not uncommon for an ABD to feel torn in two directions by committee members of opposite functional/conflict persuasions. However, recent sociology has witnessed the emergence of a "hybrid" model which posits institutional structure and process as determined by both cooperative and conflictive moments.[1] This accommodative paradigm has extricated many a recent political science or sociology ABD from a theretofore genuine thesis dilemma.

If the demands of two thesis supervisors are truly irreconcilable, then one has to look to how committed the faculty members are in sticking to or enforcing the implementation of their positions in one's dissertation. Mention has already been made of offhand, casual critiques and suggestions—most of which are quickly forgotten—"thrown out" at the proposal drafting and hearing stages. Getting to the bottom line of committee members' requirements for a dissertation involves the aforementioned round of postproposal appointments, where a candidate has to probe subtly, prod gently, particular faculty's recall of points raised earlier, objections, suggestions for inclusions. I say subtly because dissertation annals are filled with stories about candidates' "volunteering" for months of extra research and writing. If, after this round of reinquiry, one of the members backs off from his position, or neglects to mention his earlier insistence on, say, a functionalist approach, while the other faculty member continues to be outspoken in requiring a conflict perspective of theory and methodology, this particular problem *may* be laid to rest. It is always possible, on the other hand, for the functionalist advocate to raise again his objections at a later point in the dissertation, for example, after he sees the first chapter. If the dilemma reappears, one has to pursue a strategy of *role-partner confrontation*.

Resolution Through Role-Set Analysis.

Chapter Two contained an extensive discussion of the ABD's critical social relations, summarized by Figure 2.1. Let us recall and further elaborate here the *student* status of that configuration:

Figure 6.1: The Role Set of the ABD's Student Status

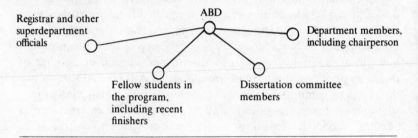

Figure 6.2 presents an enlargement and differentiation of an ABD-thesis committee segment of the role cluster where role conflict and strain are present:

Figure 6.2: The ABD and His Thesis Committee

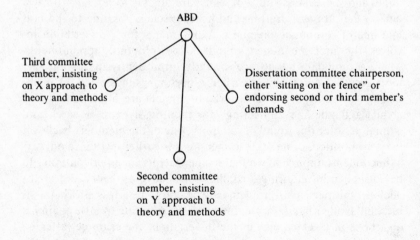

Robert Merton had devised strategies for minimizing or defusing contradictory demands made on a status incumbent by his role partners.[2] When possible, compartmentalization of interactions with various partners is useful: e.g., a young woman dates various men on different evenings; presidential candidate Lincoln talks abolition to Pennsylvania voters, and protection of slavery to the Georgia electorate. Another strategy, possible in some contexts, is to heed some role partners and relatively ignore others: faculty tend to invest more time and interest in publishing and research roles, for example, than in dissertation supervision, after a calculation that the latter activity counts for little in career mobility.

But neither compartmentalizing or avoidance of some role partners' demands are going to work for an ABD if he has already gone "one-on-one" with his several committee members and determined that two or more are adamant about his pursuing contradictory approaches in his dissertation. Given this type of situation, Merton suggests the approach of throwing the *incumbent's problem into the role partners'* laps. Indicated strategy is the ABD's presenting the dilemma before the entire committee. The argument runs that it is unconscionable for a committee to place a good-faith candidate in an impossible middle, not of his own doing, especially after his proposal has been passed. By laying the entire issue out on the table in the presence of all the role partners, it is hoped that the depth and pain of the dilemma will be seen by everybody. There may well be a fight among the committee, but resolution, at least for the candidate, of the issue should result. Such resolution may entail the resignation from the committee of the member whose position lost, but, given his continuing hostility, his departure is desirable.

The ease with which committee-member role conflicts can be resolved depends on the stance of the adviser. If he takes Y's or X's side, just from the social-psychological principle of "two-against-one," capitulation by the odd-person-out might be predicted, particularly since colleagues are generally (but not always) deferential to the position of the primary dissertation adviser. If one's adviser is diffident or undecided (either generally or on the specific controversy), matters get stickier. In such a case, the candidate must persuade him that he is more comfortable in writing the dissertation from one angle rather than the other and calmly suggest that it is, in fact, the adviser's duty in the role set to facilitate the dissertation by supporting the candi-

143

date's endeavor. How successful these final negotiations will be is too often dependent on the "personal relationships" between candidate and adviser to suit this writer, but with this particular thesis snag, matters sometimes boil down to such personality factors.

If all strategies, including confrontation of role partners, fail to resolve the issue, the only place left to go, it seems, is the department chairperson. Such recourse should be taken only after it is very clear that all other remedies have been exhausted. One danger is wounded *amour propre*: academia is unfortunately filled with prima donnas; "going over the head" of this type of supervising faculty member may result in his continual sniping at your dissertation effort in large and small ways for the next year. The other danger is closing ranks: the chairperson may be bureaucratically opposed to "departure from channels" and refuse to intervene. Nonetheless, for some small minority of ABDs, there will come a time when "going to see the man," with all its possible backfires, is the only path left.

Faculty Demands for Unanticipated Revisions.

Sometimes the problem is not inconsistent demands from faculty role partners, but one or more dissertation committee members insisting that the candidate revise his thesis, often in ways to which he is strongly opposed and/or which will require months more of research and writing time. It is in the nature of the flexible proposal/dissertation contract that one must be prepared for at least some modification requirements on the part of faculty; after all, I have tried to indicate that the candidate *himself* will probably see the logic and need for alterations as the research and analysis of his data proceeds. The difficulty becomes acute when the writer's changes are not coincident with those demanded by faculty.

The candidate is tightrope walking—at both the proposal and dissertation stage—between alienating his committee by entertaining no version of the dissertation but his own, and becoming servile (and hopelessly confused) by bending to every whim or suggested change in direction thrown out by one committee member or another. Although the following discussion urges capitulation if matters come to either that or indefinite suspension of concluding, an ABD should certainly stick to his guns until it becomes quite clear that the committee is not buying his arguments. In my experience, committees will often accede, even against their own views and objections, to the candidate's preferred treatment of basic issues, if they perceive him as on top of the material, and if he persists in a dignified and firm manner.

Although I won't repeat them here, one must follow indicated procedures (see preceding section) for establishing (a) just how new and/or conflictive faculty demands actually relate to the current version of the dissertation; sometimes they can be accommodated or incorporated without excessive difficulties; (b) just how serious and mandatory the committee's demands for change are.

After the candidate has completed the calculus of determining just what revisions simply "won't go away," they should be slotted into primary and secondary/tertiary categories of importance. The latter category, no matter how such changes irk one as silly, capricious or just plain wrong, should be completed forthwith. It is dissertation-destructive to take any kind of stand on matters that do not go to the heart or guts of the dissertation and/or require relatively little extra work. If you are planning to derive a book or a number of articles from your dissertation, you can note that these materials will be excised from the published versions.

Primary required revisions are of two types in terms of their emotional consequences: (a) "affectively-neutral" revisions and/or additions in methodology or theory. A faculty member may insist upon inclusion of another control group, or more elaborated discussion of an alternative theoretical model, or execution of additional statistical procedures in the analysis of the data. I have in mind here various operations which may require substantial library or field research—some of which the candidate may well believe are not necessary—but which are still generally "resonant" with the central themes of one's own draft. In my judgment—after one has made very sure that such changes are unconditionally expected—these types of primary revisions should be carried through without a whimper, sustained by the knowledge that one is generally "home free" on their completion.

(b) "affectively-laden" revisions and/or additions. One of my acquaintances wrote his sociology dissertation on bureaucracy under a leading "authority" at a major eastern university. His theoretical paradigm was a Marxist/conflict one; the adviser's was a hard-line anti-Marxist functionalist view of bureaucracy. It took three drafts and almost four years for my friend to finish. He knew all along that the adviser would veto the Marxist versions (the first draft was polar Marxist, the second one, "temperate" Marxist) but felt that to write the dissertation which the adviser would approve would be to cut the theoretical and ideological guts out of it, and to "sell his soul" through such a capitulation. I have no doubt that the approved third draft contained the adviser's rather than my friend's sociological voice on bureaucracies (although the distance between the two in this particular case was perhaps an extreme, atypical illustration of student-adviser "dissertation dissonance.") I would take issue, however, with the need for so much self-questioning and agony of four dissertation writing and revising years, and certainly with the *dissertation myth* that he had "sold his soul," a feeling which still continues to bother him years later.

Lying behind the dissertation myth of "selling out" is an exaggerated notion of the importance of one's dissertation. It is related to the myth of the dissertation as perfect, or as *magnum opus.* People's souls are simply not consigned to the devil, or even purgatory, for the "misdemeanor" sins committed against others, self or conscience in writing a doctoral dissertation. My friend had lost sight of the only reason for writing a dissertation: to get a doctorate. The dissertation became a "symbol" for him of progressive political identity, righteous opposition to the oppression of dissenting students by Establishment faculty and Lord knows what else. During the three years that he held out, he was consigned to insecure part-time teaching positions; wiser in my view to have given in, and then, with the credential problem behind, to write a streak of books pursuing the polemic. In fact, he is now writing such books, but three or four long years later than they might have been produced.

No more than the observer in the "tearoom" could my friend convincingly plead shock, surprise or indignation at the "goings on" of his adviser. Indeed, he had been the adviser's fair-haired boy through much of his earlier course work, and even qualifying examinations. While, as I have pointed out, faculty do have a way of cutting students loose as soon as they become ABDs (which *is* grounds for legitimate shock), they rarely change their theoretical and ideological stripes. Certainly, this particular ABD knew in depth the functionalist views of bureaucracy held by his adviser. Put in this context of preknowledge, the earlier drafts seem almost like kamikaze dissertation missions.

In my current view of "dissertation ethics," the inherently relatively minor social and human-relations consequences of doctoral research exercises, combined with the *self-chosen, insider, and achieved status of the ABD*, relegate "soul-searching" to the categories of dissertation diversion and dissertation self-sabotage.

ISSUES WITH INDIVIDUAL COMMITTEE MEMBERS.

With just a little bit of bad luck, the student is going to run into at least one of the "bad apples" depicted below, where faculty conflicts and differences about the dissertation can get "personal." However, one has to be very careful before reaching a judgment that the essence of a difficulty with a faculty member stems from specific "chemistry" between him and the candidate. The odds are against a personalistic interpretation in large-enrollment doctoral programs, since, as we have seen, faculty are skeptical or reluctant about getting involved in students' projects; they doubt serious student intentions, and proposal and dissertation supervising score few points for faculty careers. *Dissertation paranoia* consists largely of misinterpreting the general skepticism, cynicism, indifference or even outright hostility that graduate professors often develop toward ABDs as more specifically, even exclusively, focused on a particular candidate. Of course, it is not pleasant to be the target of even generalized negative and dysfunctional attitudes and actions, but if Professor X is a bastard to *all* his advisees, one deals with the problem in a different manner than if one is being singled out. For example, the possibility of a successful protest to the chairperson is greatly enhanced if five ABDs will attest to disturbed behavior or maltreatment on the part of the same faculty adviser (although when the chips are down, doctoral students rarely will take the chance of uniting in protest for fear of being ejected from a program where faculty have nearly all the power).

But whether your "bad apple" exhibits character aberrations in general or with you in particular, there is no easy management of the problem. The offending character trait should be considered in terms of the differential dissertation association calculus; if, for example, the thesis committee member is heavily into S and M in his leather-lined den at home but is able to tear himself away from such fantasies long enough to critique your analysis of variance helpfully down at his bare-walled office, go right on by his extra-dissertation deviance. Sometimes character aberrations of graduate professors can actually

147

be very *useful* to the ABD: I have found methodologists (as a group, certainly with exceptions) to be startlingly fussy, overcautious, compulsively self-doubting types. Psychoanalysts would call them "anal." On the other hand, if one can get past all that, these people are excellent for designing airtight, fail-safe experimental designs.

Unfortunately, there are other faculty members whose personality problems cannot be defused as irrelevant to the progress of a dissertation or used to promote its progress actively. Here I can only signal some of the most common types of "problem professors," whose socio- or psychopathologies can be most disruptive to a dissertation. The ABD should be on the lookout for such faculty and avoid them from the start if possible; otherwise, make every effort to replace them as thesis committee members if matters have gone too far. To attempt a list of specific tactics for avoidance or replacement would be doomed to banality, since the variations for particular interpersonal contexts and conflicts between problem professors and ABDs are so enormous. The ABD must weigh the variables of his own role relation with his unwelcome partner, set in the larger frame of departmental politics, in deciding how to solve this stubborn and unfair (unfair even within a general context of unfairness) obstacle to dissertation completion. Here is a "Least Wanted List" of dissertation problem professors:

The "Young Turk" Professor,

who has recently received his doctorate. Anxious to identify himself with his new faculty reference group and put distance between himself and the old student peers, this type of junior faculty member can break one's dissertation chops in a manner less frequently found among older, somewhat more compassionate faculty veterans. Socialization to the new collegial group may involve, in his marginal, immature view of matters, being "tough" with the graduate students from whose ranks he has recently departed. His career aspirations and hang-ups can easily translate themselves into your dissertation hang-ups and delays, produced by his hypercriticisms.[3]

The "Career ABD" Professor,

who himself took a decade to write a thesis—often because *his* angry adviser had preceded *him* with a ten-year-long effort—and at some level wants you to live through the same hell he (and his predecessors) did. Such a dissertation delayer may well not be in touch with these feelings and couch his thesis-advising neurosis in authentic-sounding rationalizations, such as "soak in it some more," or "these things can't be rushed," which are certainly sage enough counsel up to a point—which he always exceeds. There isn't much an ABD can do with this type of entrenched character disorder. If such a professor ends up as your adviser, you must make every effort to replace him.

The Sadistic Professor,

who uses his position of faculty power to ventilate upon an ABD personal and career rages in a manner that entails little risk of being censored or sanctioned. This is a most virulent type of problem professor who can conceal much of his pathology under catch phrases like "demand for rigor," "upholding of standards," and the like. With such a man or woman the candidate has to take action, either by joining with fellow students similarly tortured, or by denouncing him to other professors and/or the chairperson.

The Sexist Professor,

(man or woman) who converts the dissertation into a flirtation, emptying conferences of any value for furthering the thesis. Obviously, there are degrees of unacceptable and dysfunctional behavior in this area. Like American society in general, academic society is overwhelmingly sexist in climate. A female ABD is bound to be exposed to a certain amount of patronizing and manipulative behavior from male thesis committee members. Some women recently reported hostile and thesis-delaying behavior on the part of male *homosexual* graduate faculty. The cross-combinations of intergender sexism are rather numerous in late twentieth-century academia. But sexist banterings, pseudo-chivalry, "dirty jokes" and innuendos, as annoying and offensive as they undoubtedly are, are not in and of themselves threatening enough to the thesis to cause a search for new committee members. An ABD has to have a thicker skin than *this*, whether dealing with faculty, respondents or groups being researched. It is only when the sexual dimension (or tension) becomes the *core* of the role relationship between ABD and faculty member, occluding attention to the dissertation, that a change must be made.

Feminists may be unhappy with my position here, but this book is concerned almost exclusively with completing the thesis: deep-rooted sexism is still a fact of graduate university structure and hierarchy. Parts of it (like pseudo-chivalry) can actually be exploited by a woman. Time is probably on the side of feminism, but I believe the feminist ABD has to suspend her struggle for that ongoing cause during two years of the dissertation struggle since the latter will demand every bit of her energy, strength and interest. Writing her dissertation within a context of sexist faculty-student relations is not "selling her soul," contrary to some conventional rhetoric on this point. Two years later, she can return to the battlefield with the added ammunition of the doctorate in hand.

The "Hamlet-Complex" Professor,

who doubts every version of your thesis, often rejecting his own earlier endorsements of which research tacks to pursue. This type of faculty member can delay and frustrate a candidate to desperation with advisory approaches such as, "All the data is never in," or, "The question can be looked at from virtually an infinite number of angles," or, "On the one hand this, but on the other hand . . ." or (maddeningly), "Let's go back to square one, for argument's sake. Suppose you started with X model instead of Y. What kind of data would you collect then? [this after four months of data collection along lines of model Y] Have you given that alternative some thought?" Generally, such men and women are neurotic doubters in their own lives and projects.

It is true that doubt and skepticism (as texts on the logic of scientific inquiry constantly point out) are part and parcel of scientific advance, and neurotic doubting can hide behind these venerated scientific cautions, up to a point. But there comes a time when one has to take a chance (all science is ultimately based on probability; not certainty, but assumptions), go with one thought-through version of theory and related research, and rest one's case. Otherwise, dissertations would remain forever locked in your office desk with you as the only reader. Faced with a neurotic doubter on your committee, the best strategy is to use his doubts as long as they pose legitimate objections or critiques to your dissertation direction; but when the point of usefulness is passed, then one must take a firm stand against getting sucked into the professor's vortex of infinite uncertainty. Psychotherapists have found

150

that doubters (fundamentally persons with low ego-image) respect, even welcome, limits and lines drawn by others. The candidate has to say, "Enough is enough," politely, but with strength and conviction.

The "Passive-Aggressive" Professor,

who superficially presents himself as "friend" of the candidate but contradicts that goodwill by large and small acts of dissertation sabotage. Often he "promises you anything" but gives you nothing, or worse. Passive-aggressive professors don't like students and/or specific role obligations, such as dissertation supervising. On the other hand, they feel guilty about such role aversions. *Passive,* indirect aggression is the compromise between hostility and guilt. It surfaces in behavior such as unreasonable delays in reading one's unfolding chapters, or violation of a promise to support your dissertation's stance in negotiations with other committee members. In dealing with the delays and even perfidies of such professors, the candidate's best weapon is exploitation of the guilt component of this neurosis. When push comes to shove, the passive-aggressive's need for conveying a socially conformist, norm-abiding image will generally prevail over his indirect aggression (at least long enough for you to get him to read your materials).

The Jealous or Envious Professor,

who senses, sometimes accurately, that you are already, or potentially, cleverer in the field than he. Thus, you are perceived as a threat to him, and every possible action will be taken to head off your completion. As with several of the previously noted hard-core neurotic types, there isn't much constructive reasoning together to be achieved with a green-with-envy supervisor, and whenever possible one has to replace him, or at least relegate him to a back-burner committee status.

Problem Professors, Candidates' Problems and the Psychoanalytic Subculture.

In actual cases, advising professors often possess more than one dissertation-destructive trait. For example, continued dissatisfaction with successive drafts of your work may stem from a combination of a professor having spent ten years in the dissertation-writing salt mines himself, combined with a compulsive self-doubting neurosis; one could have a psychoanalytic field day speculating on the reciprocal causes and effects of neurotic doubting, perfectionism and a history of ten years down in the dissertation dumps. Whatever the problem, the ABD's major effort must be spent on eliminating or minimizing it. Elimination of such a problem professor is the preferable course; it dispenses with the need to practice "psychotherapy" where the need to practice dissertation writing is already quite demanding enough. If one has to "live with" a nonreplaceable problem professor, the candidate willy-nilly gets caught up in some "lay" psychoanalyzing and psychotherapeutic "cooling-out" techniques.

I have noticed that in some fields students *and* faculty actually seem to expect—even *like*—some of these interpersonal problem processes, particularly in psychology. Many of my psychology doctoral candidates (most often those in some version of a clinical program) appear to see their dissertation difficulties as rooted in the "father complex" or "passive-aggressive" neurosis of their advisers as in any matters to do with the substantive and methodological issues of their experiments. I suspect that the culture of clinical psychology is a kind of "intervening variable" in a few selected fields of dissertation course and negotiation, although ABDs may overemphasize it, to the neglect of the objective issues of their projects. Beyond psychology programs, it is my strong but undocumented impression that ABDs in *all* fields are overrepresented in the population of psychotherapy patients.[4] To what extent they are in therapy because of the dissertation problem is also very difficult to determine. It may also be that graduate *faculty* are overrepresented as an occupational group as patients. All this is by way of saying that a significant minority of ABDs and professors may well be wrapped up in the "cult of personality," whatever the field of dissertation, and that such involvements spill over to the student-adviser relationship, producing a measure of both the interpersonal difficulties I've outlined, as well as suggesting potential resolutions.

My own view is that such "hidden-agenda" extra-dissertation interpersonal processes, where both students and faculty see themselves "working through" emotional blocks, are dangerous to a candidate, since they tend to root success of the thesis in the shaky ground of personal friendships and "understandings" (which, as we have seen, are subject to radical reversal, change and even disappearance), rather than in compliance with the proposal and dissertation contract. The "psychoanalytic factor" is most salient in elitist programs, particularly in the northeast (most particularly in New York City, the seat of psychoanalytic sub-culture and practice). Looking to the rest of the nation, I believe ABDs are less likely to encounter it; even when present, its urgency or prominence for successful negotiation of the dissertation course will probably be comparatively small. Even in psychoanalytic culture departments, the ABD should make every effort—albeit avoiding pariah-like labels of "not being in touch with himself" or "hostile"—to put the dissertation project back on the clearer tracks of his proposal contract. That is, unless he too is caught up in notions of the dissertation as encounter group or therapy. If such is the case, my experience predicts an additional dimension of dissertation *tsures* diabolically conducive to ABD anomie.

THE "PANZER DIVISION" ANALOGY OF AN UNFOLDING DISSERTATION.

Let me conclude the two chapters on the struggle to write the dissertation in perhaps appropriate martial fashion. My advisees find the "dissertation army" analogy useful:

Figure 6.3: Assault on the Doctor's Degree, Earlier Campaign Phase

COMPLETED DISSERTATION

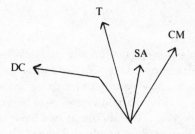

The dissertation army is composed of one's various major files. The goal of the struggle and campaign is to reach completion and defense. No matter how closely strategists study Clausewitz, some divisions always move ahead of or straggle behind others. For example, in the ABDs' battle for the dissertation (see Figure 6.3) his theoretical elaboration (T) and sustained contact with committee members (CM) may forge ahead of his statistical analysis (SA) of incoming data, and his data collection (DC) might not simply be behind battlefield schedule but actually deviate from the dissertation scheme. As "general" of all the "divisions' of the file, the candidate must keep deploying and repositioning divisions and maintaining supply lines (i.e., here input into various files), so as to end up with the following alignment of his dissertation army:

Figure 6.4: Assault on the Doctor's Degree, Later Campaign Stage, Nearing D Day

COMPLETED DISSERTATION

Without pursuing the metaphor excessively, ultimately the arrows/ thrusts (see Figure 6.4) represent chapters of the dissertation developed out of major files.

SUMMARY.

Presenting the dissertation to the faculty can involve two basic kinds of problems: 1. structural issues with the committee as a whole, that most candidates face, one way or another, as a matter of dissertation course; 2. difficulties with a particular professor that take one into the realm of psychology, and often abnormal psychology.

The first category of issues prominently includes:

    a. prompt presentation of unfolding chapters of the dissertation to faculty for prompt critique, suggestions, requests for revisions and approval;

    b. managing and reconciling conflicting thesis demands made by different committee members, as to which theoretical and/ or methodological directions to develop;

c. responding to requests for revisions, including how to determine which faculty demands, made by which faculty, are "negotiable" and which are "firm";

d. managing ethical or emotional qualms about having "capitulated" or "sold out" in making faculty-required revisions which go against the grain of one's political ideology, or against strongly held convictions about what the dissertation has genuinely demonstrated.

The second category of faculty-presentation problems concerns individual committee members who exhibit some kind of character disorder or neurosis which spills over to and contaminates the thesis advising, supervising, or judging relationship.

A list of "least-wanted" professors is presented, along with some brief analysis of probable etiologies of their disorders, and general advice for freeing oneself from their dissertation-detrimental clutches. On the least-wanted roll are: the "young Turk" professor; the "career ABD" professor; the sadistic professor; the sexist professor; the "Hamlet-complex" professor; the passive-aggressive professor; the jealous or envious professor.

The candidate is cautioned about the dissertation hazards of involving himself in a psychoanalytic subculture, present in some departments—particularly psychology ones—which make "virtues" out of some of the disorders displayed by faculty and convert substantive issues of the dissertation into elusive and mutable "personal" and "psychogenetic" ones.

In the last section of the chapter, a "Panzer division" metaphor of the dissertation's "assault" on the doctor's degree is represented by two final figures.

NOTES

1. Ralf Dahrendorf's "Toward a Theory of Social Conflict," *Journal of Conflict Resolution*, 11, 1958, was a seminal article in developing the hybrid model. Such a position was at first vigorously rejected by the powers-that-be of functionalism (e.g., R. Merton) but eventually accepted as mainstream. One is tempted to suggest that this hybrid model arose as much to resolve the conflicts of sociology ABDs caught between two supervisors on opposite sides of the functionalist-conflict paradigm as to resolve the contradictions in sociological theory per se!

2. Robert Merton, *Social Theory and Social Structure,* 2nd ed. (New York: Free Press, 1968).

155

3. Recall my earlier suggestion (Chapter Four) that recent graduates of one's doctoral program are a good source of support and information for the ABD. But the reference was not to such people who are superordinates in *your* doctoral program. As "young Turk" assistant professors across town, they may be devils; in the role of until recently "student peer" in your program, they may be helpful angels. The paradox exists only when one doesn't take into account the two different social status contexts that are operative.
4. See Chapter Seven for a discussion of whether psychotherapy is effective in helping dissertation depression.

CHAPTER 7

Down in the Dissertation Dumps: How to Get Out

THE DISSERTATION WAVE.

Figure 7.1 schematizes the dissertation course as a "wave," with the writer sometimes down in the dumps, or troughs, of one or more of the "three Ds"—dissertation depression, doubt or desperation—and sometimes riding the crests of relative elation or satisfaction with the project.

Figure 7.1: Troughs and Crests of the Dissertation Wave

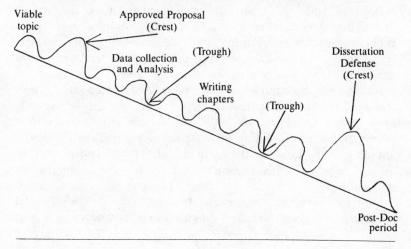

There are two vectors to the dissertation wave's course; one undulates, the other moves steadily downward. The most striking crests are achievement of an approved proposal and successful defense of the thesis, with selection of a viable topic, completion of major data collection and their corresponding analysis, and completion of various dissertation chapters other important high points. Troughs are the between times; when, for example, the data isn't panning out the way you hypothesized, you feel overwhelmed by what's left to be done, you're having trouble with your thesis committee. Note the *trough* trend—Post-Doc—at the end of the dissertation rainbow. Contrary to dissertation mythology, all problems are not vanquished by successful finishing. The book will have more to say about the dangers of post-dissertation depression and defeatism in Chapter Nine, which deals with surviving and professionally benefiting from a thesis.

The downward sweep of the wave figure is designed to convey an image of dissertation momentum building which generally makes successive stages easier; however, one has to stop way short of any assertion that matters are a "slide" from accepted proposal phase onward; there are too many instances of a candidate becoming trapped in a deep trough of fieldwork crisis, data analysis problems, a contrary chapter on discussion of the experiment, to talk about principles of increasing ease in the dissertation course. Trends, certainly; laws, no.

DISSERTATION DUMPS: NORMAL OR PATHOLOGICAL?

Before examining specific dissertation depressions, discouragements, desperations, doubts, let us consider for a moment their clinical connection. Not infrequently, dissertation writers exhibit symptomologies resembling or even duplicating clinical pictures of the neuroses—such as anxiety and hysteria—and even some of the psychoses—such as depression or paranoia. ABDs deep into a thesis will often report that they feel on the verge of a nervous breakdown, or that they are "going crazy." A reader unfamiliar with dissertation course and moods, including a pre- or new ABD, may protest that I am surely exaggerating matters with talk of neuroses and/or psychoses as dissertation-related or even caused. But those in the soup know differently.

Most candidates experience one or more very painful classical symptoms of various clinical syndromes. In my experience, however,

158

these psychopathological symptoms are paradoxically normal and predictable for the dissertation course. It may be true that a certain small percentage of ABDs are "round the bend" before they ever get their hands on a proposal and data analysis, and that such tasks exacerbate a preexisting emotional condition, but I believe that the vast majority of emotional disturbances exhibited during dissertation days date their origins within the thesis period and from the unusual stresses of the course. An analogous situation exists with prison homosexuality: most released prisoners return to preincarcerated heterosexual behavior upon release. One can talk about temporary or condition-based homosexuality. In the same way, one can discuss the "temporary insanity" of the ABD, with the assumption he will be his old nonsymptomatic self when the defense is done. On the other hand, we know that unusually traumatic and prolonged isolating social contexts (e.g., concentration camps, prisons, "reeducation"/brainwashing, solitary confinement) can permanently alter detainees' psyches, particularly if they are not deprogrammed upon release. There is the very real danger that some portion of the lonely, traumatized dissertation writer population may carry dissertation pathology beyond completion into their postdoctoral lives. Accordingly, this chapter identifies the most prominent dissertation emotional disturbances for the reader; offers some etiological light within the framework of the dissertation condition; considers a range of agents, strategies and therapies for heading them off at the start, coping with them once they beset a candidate, or making sure their presence doesn't continue beyond completion of the dissertation.

A CLASSIFICATION OF DISSERTATION ANXIETIES AND DEPRESSIONS.

Candidates' dissertation-caused or -activated anxieties and/or depressions manifest themselves in one or more of three spheres: negative and gloomy feelings about the dissertation itself, particularly about its doubtful outcome; a diminishment of self-esteem; a real or believed deterioration in relationships with significant others, for which the demands of the dissertation are blamed. Within each of these large areas we can list more specific problems. For each we can then further inquire as to whether they are primarily *dissertation myth-derived*: *candidate caused,* through deficiencies in work habits,

159

filing, or motivation; or almost *inevitable consequences* of the structures and processes of the dissertation course. Strategies for overcoming or containing them will vary according to etiological category.

Doubts About the Dissertation Itself.

- "I picked the wrong topic." As we have seen earlier, there is almost no such thing as the wrong topic, particularly at the Chapter-Four stage of the candidate's dissertation, when so much groundwork and prior committee approval and validation (e.g., accepted proposal and earlier chapters) have already been won. *The wrong topic myth* has to be clearly recognized as just that. Recognizing this, the candidate must make every effort to put this type of self-sabotaging anxiety out of his mind.

- "The data's come out wrong." Chapter Five took pains to point out that when one is talking dissertation and research data, "right" and "wrong" are not terms which accurately describe the realities of analytic procedure. Almost invariably, at least some of the data does not pan out according to initial hypotheses and model, and one must revise and often reenter the field with new measuring instruments. A candidate suffering from "wrong data" anxiety or depression has overbought the myth of the *a priori dissertation,* which introductory methodology texts and formal departmental guidelines most often push.[1] What is necessary here is a restructuring of attitudes toward acceptable/prevailing scientific procedure, with an emphasis on serendipity and the revisionist models outlined in Chapters Four and Five of this book.

- "Nothing comes; I can't write another word; the well's gone dry." Periods of blockage are inevitable in long-distance writing, but the intensity of depression and despair will be aggravated if the ABD suscribes to the *myth of the easy dissertation,* that others are gliding right through with no blockages. A negative self-fulfilling prophecy is often seen in blocked periods: the more one bemoans stoppage, the more pronounced it becomes. The only way out here—a procedure which requires much courage—is to put in the daily time at the office whether the juices are running or not. If you've laid the groundwork with your files, it's virtually impossible that your dissertation well of ideas is truly exhausted; immersion in the files will—a few days sooner or later—prime the pump once more. The absolutely *worst* possible path is to lay off the thesis, take some kind of R & R; upon return from a three-week break, in my experience, the trail will be colder than ever.

- "I can't see the end; I'm overwhelmed by what's still left to do; I'm never going to finish the damn thing." There is no gainsaying that the dissertation is a very long project with many hills to ascend. One might liken the experience to that of explorers who, expecting the source of the Nile over the next hill, reach its crest only to find another hill, and so on. But the analogy really doesn't hold, since the ABD has a "map" for his dissertation course in the form of proposal and file which expeditionary forces don't possess. The "map" allows him to look ahead and see the dissertation course as finite and finishable.

The *myth of the perfect dissertation* may be aggravating matters here. No dissertation, or, for that matter, no book, is ever "perfect," or absolutely finished. All successful doctoral candidates and book writers can think of ten important changes they would have liked to have made within days after a project's final defense or press date. But ten changes later, the dissatisfaction would be renewed. I often suspect that after, say, two drafts of a dissertation, further revisions don't make a thesis better, merely different. One is reminded of Camus' character in *The Plague,* who spends his life rewriting the first sentence of his novel—endless versions of horses trotting down the Champs Elysées. Candidates with relatively low ego-strength are peculiarly vulnerable to the "neurosis" of compulsive "dissertation revision," (beyond the bounds of necessary changes in hypotheses in line with emerging data), too eager to pursue self- or faculty-suggested "new angles" past the call of duty and dissertation. In some cases, such ABDs may have a low self-esteem problem, which denies their deserving the doctorate: compulsive revisions can ensure the validation of such unworthy ego-images.

- "I've left something out." The candidate is haunted by the fear that faculty is going to jump on just the one study, experiment, dissertation, monograph which challenges his thesis—and which he has accordingly either downplayed or omitted from his presentation—and is consequently going to reject his 335 pages *in toto.* The truth is closer to faculty rarely knowing the details of the specialized issues of a dissertation and the candidate being the world's expert in the area. Certainly, *something* is always going to be left out, but that a particular deletion will be pounced and

161

focused on by a wrathful faculty is a manifestation of dissertation paranoia.

- "I've been scooped." Belief that another ABD has beaten you to your "exclusive" is an erroneous transfer of either journalistic or hard science hazards to social science, arts and humanities fields. I have detailed at some length the virtual impossibility of another candidate's even coming near your model and methodology in the disciplines to which this volume is addressed, even in the improbable event of the titles of two dissertations being very similar: as we have seen, there is enormous room—indeed, need—for variety, multiplicity and even replication of studies within most topics. Lying behind "I've been scooped" anxiety is sometimes the *myth of the ultimate or definitive dissertation,* which says once and for all everything worthwhile and possible about a given area or topic.

Bewildered and Negative Feelings About Oneself.

- "What have I got myself into? I must have been crazy to take such a job on." It is common for candidates deep in a dissertation to suffer second thoughts about the soundness of their initial judgment in undertaking the thesis, especially when the current dissertation mood is "no end in sight." This uncertainty about the thesis decision is bad enough, but people show a marked tendency to generalize it to questioning their decision-making competence in other areas of their lives—areas in which, prior to the dissertation course, they may well have felt confident and secure.

Part of the process of restoring faith and credibility in one's judgment is to dispel the "no end in sight" mood by a return to proposal and file "maps" (see above). Consider as well how antithetical the decision to write the dissertation was to any kind of spur-of-the-moment, "inspirational," "off-the-wall," or "crazy" choice. Chapter Two depicts in detail the full range of extremely rational and deliberate *planning* that antedates the proposal and continues into later phases. When a candidate is in mid-dissertation doldrums, he has to "get back to basics," remind himself that a whole history of dissertation development—involving countless days of proposal writing, negotiations with faculty, questionnaire design, file building, field work, memorandum writing, chapter drafting—preceded today's urge to rip up Chapter Three because the last section just won't flow, and that he will survive and vanquish a day's or a week's frustrations and doubts. Getting back to basics also involves reviewing the *reasons* for which one undertook the dissertation. At the start, they were substantial and deliberate; then, too, the candidate (especially if he read this volume) went into the vast project with his eyes open. Unless one's life circumstances have changed substantially since the initial decision a year or eighteen months earlier, the validity of the reasons for pursuing the dissertation should be up-to-date, still in force, compelling.

- "Why do I continue to torture myself?" A candidate caught in the no-end-in-sight trap may shift his self-critique from his possessing poor judgment to his being *masochistic*. Candidates' friends and relatives, seeing him in long struggle, often offer this kind of pop psychology diagnosis; indeed, a candidate's analyst may come up with this type of interpretation! But diagnoses of the ABD-as-masochist, whether made by the candidate himself or others, are almost invariably wrong. Masochism is the intentional imposition of pain upon oneself. Psychoanalysts see it as self-punishment for a range of sins and guilts, more often imagined than real. Dissertation writing, on the other hand, is the intentional imposition of a large project upon oneself. Psychoanalysts and others would do well to see it accurately, as goal-directed self-growth, commitment to achievement. It is true that *pain* is common to both masochism and dissertation writing, but the contexts, uses and symbols of that pain are entirely different in the two situations. But it would appear that some psychoanalysts "buy" the ABD patient's fantasy version of the infinity of the dissertation; from that empirically erroneous perspective it is easy enough for a misdirected and misinformed therapist and his candidate patient to spin a clinical picture of the patient-as-masochist, torturing himself by continuing with work he will never complete.

It is crucial that a mid-dissertation-depressed ABD see his pain as functional, not masochistic, no matter what outside observers believe. Essential to the pain-as-functional perspective is rejection of the myth of the dissertation as endless. The masochistic trap, especially when pursued and elaborated with "professional help," inaccurately and diabolically converts a rational, noble, realistically obtainable and even heroic enterprise into a garden-variety neurosis or psychopathology. If an ABD catches himself in masochistic diagnosis, he must shake it off; if friends suggest it, he can laugh it off; if his analyst takes this tack, he must cut him loose. Pursuit of the *dissertation-as-masochism myth* in therapy is indeed masochism itself: blaming and criticizing oneself for untold work on a futile project (the entire analysis is masochistic because the assumption of futility of the project is dead wrong). In my judgment, an ABD who gets sucked into this direction of "therapy" is lost: every session in the dissertation office is subsequently seen as "throwing good money after bad."

It alarms me to speculate over the number of dissertations sabotaged by analysts pursuing the masochist interpretation. The danger is greatest when the therapist himself has not written a full dissertation (i.e., psychiatrists, MSWs, counselors with various non-doctorate credentials). Lack of familiarity with the unique world of the dissertation—including its immensely deliberate and planned nature, the multiplicity of tasks involved, the extensive filing system required, the thoroughness of the initial decision/commitment to write the dissertation, the predictable, chartable crests and troughs of the course—makes it very likely that an analyst will misinterpret "normal" dissertation responses in the context of "neurotic" or "disturbed"—here, specifically, "masochistic." His reference points are from a world where people's everyday activities simply do not include a project as rigorous, demanding, hazardous and solitary as a doctoral dissertation.

- "If I ever finish, I'll never write another thing in my life." One hears such threats often enough from ABDs. Should such pronouncements be taken seriously? I have seen enough cases of "burnt-out" candidates who never mount another serious piece of work in their field to dismiss such intentions merely as fleeting dissertation delirium. In certain dissertation disciplines—notably clinical psychology, where the candidate practices full-time psychotherapy upon receipt of his doctorate—additional long projects are not normally part of the career; the psychology ABD's last-ditch view of the dissertation may be motivated at the time by frustration or desperation, but it is also realistic and legitimated by career norms. For the rest of us, it is a very dangerous attitude, susceptible to self-fulfilling prophecy, since part and parcel of our English, political science, history or sociology trade is to continue writing articles, monographs, books.

It is paradoxical that an exercise presumably designed to launch a career can, not infrequently, stunt or destroy it.[2] Persons who get trapped in the burnt-out view of themselves are suffering from lack of dissertation perspective. They are usually victims of some admixture of the *dissertation-as-perfect, dissertation-as-magnum opus* and *dissertation as home-free myths.* An ABD already in the grips of cynicism must remind himself of the professional scheme of things: the dissertation is the *first* in a series of written projects he is going to have to (and, one hopes, want to) produce as professor of literature, anthropology or educational sociology. Although the most immediate, and often humiliating, supervisory strictures of adviser and thesis committee will be absent in later works, other enforcers of standards replace them, e.g., referees for journal articles; editors in publishing companies; senior faculty members, judges for fellowships, travel grants, research grants. Regard your dissertation as your debut, not your swan song. Regard many of the objections that supervising faculty raise as an introduction to the rules of your discipline's game, rules which you may as well get used to, since you will confront them time and again in the following thirty years.

- "Bob and Carol finished, and I'm the dummy who's left behind." ABDs often begin to question their abilities as well as their judgment during the dissertation, particularly when they begin to compete with program cohorts in terms of finishing dates. One has, first of all, to keep dissertation mortality rates in mind: if Bob and Carol finished, chances are high that Ted and Alice didn't. More important, dissertation writing is not really a "group sport," but much more like an individual one. As we have noted, programs do not set a quota system for how many degrees they will confer: if you show up a year after Bob and Carol with an acceptable dissertation, you won't be closed out. If the dissertation is any kind of competition at all, it is one with *yourself,* on the order of a marathon, where, with the exception of a few stars, the goal is simply to finish.[3] Behind the self-devaluation related to peer group comparison and competition may very well lie adherence to the *dissertation as home-free myth*: Bob and Carol have made it, can rest on their laurels, are above the struggle. The reality is, of course, quite to the contrary; the dissertation stage is the *least competitive* one in an academic career. Upon receipt of the doctorate, buyer's market competition is awaiting one in faculty appointments, promotion, tenure, publishing contracts and grants. In the sweep of a three- or four-decade career, the fact of some peers finishing the dissertation a year or two sooner or later

165

than others is not very significant, no matter how maddening it may seem at the time to the "left-behind" ABD. Again, putting the dissertation phase in the wider context of a long career, accompanied from start to finish by new projects, tests and challenges for *everybody* in the field, should help the candidate avoid the self-flagellation of dissertation envy over earlier finishers, in favor of renewed attention to the development, at one's own rhythm, of one's own thesis.

Negatively Affecting Relationships with Others.

- "I'm becoming an ass kisser." There is no gainsaying that the realities of faculty-candidate dissertation politics entail for almost all students a certain amount of kowtowing and self-effacement. Attention to the strategies for presentation of dissertation self—outlined in detail in Chapters Two, Four and Six—will protect against the worst of quasi-feudal graduate faculty liberties and/or abuses. The successful candidate has a fierce desire for completion, combined with a realistic intelligence about the social context of the dissertation. He should not allow the anticipated situation-specific need for subordinate role playing to be generalized into any revised and deprecatory evaluation of self as "ass-kisser." So long as his relationships with friends, family and fellow workers outside the dissertation zone are not altered toward the temporary accommodative pattern maintained with faculty, one's general integrity, in my view, remains intact.

    However, the candidate should not delude himself with the inaccurate consolation that upon finishing his doctorate, the days of ingratiation are necessarily over: hierarchical, bureaucratic academia is characterized by wheelings, dealings and power plays. Often, the comportment of an untenured assistant professor toward senior faculty is indistinguishable, in its tenor of subordination and humiliation, from that of an ABD toward his thesis committee. Ultimately, as Merton has suggested, occupational contexts and pressures can shape, or reshape, personality, and the temporary self-effacement of dissertation politics can become, over time, a permanent posture in dealing with both academic colleagues and with others outside the career zone. A certain undetermined number of professors do develop the accommodative seed of dissertation days into a way of life.

166

• "It's coming between me and Jack/Jill." Dissertation times are trying ones for family and love relationships. There seem to be two ways in which the dissertation can cause rifts between intimates. The ABD's devotion to the dissertation—his time spent in the office, at the library, in the field—drastically reduces the time spent theretofore with others. He becomes an absentee spouse, father, lover, locked in his office, or grudgingly spending Sunday afternoon in the park with the family, but preoccupied with how his computer runs are going to pan out on Monday. Secondly, during the course of the dissertation, the ABD changes certain of his fundamental values and perceives himself to have "outgrown" a spouse or lover. This type of dissertation disruption is discussed in Chapter Nine. Of course, in some instances, the two disruptive patterns interact and reinforce each other: an ABD who believes she is growing apart from the previously shared *Weltanschaung* of her husband buttresses this perception by spending radically less time with him, "away" on dissertation business.

I think that tensions around ABD role absenteeism are more common than serious estrangements from previous values, although the latter must not be minimized (often, value conflicts remain latent for a long period, are not so blatant as physical withdrawal of a person). There are no terribly good ways around the reality of dissertation withdrawal from loved ones. The book has stressed the necessity for a large block of time reserved for being alone with the great project. Family and lovers, not similarly engaged with their own task, are almost certain at times not to "understand," even when they generally profess support and concern for the ABD's success.

In certain serious respects, living with an ABD wrapped up in his thesis is like living with a handicapped or "problem" person (e.g., an alcoholic). Support and information groups have been formed by and for close relatives of many of these problem categories (e.g., spouses of alcoholics, disabled persons, released mental patients). These groups parallel those formed by the "problem" persons themselves. Later in this chapter I discuss possibilities and prospects for ABDs banding together in dissertation therapy/support groups. An important adjunct to that development (still embryonic) would be establishment of groups for ABDs' mates and lovers. That such plans sound farfetched or even facetious to some readers reflects, I believe, general ignorance in the United States about the plight of probably 100,000 ABDs each year, struggling to write a difficult and lonely dissertation with little or no support system provided by graduate education programs. In the absence of such group developments, ABDs must take other tacks to familiarize intimates with the contours of their projects, if dissertation-caused differences and rifts are to be prevented from escalating. Books already exist about *How to Live with an Alcoholic* and *How to Live with a Schizophrenic.* The present volume might profitably be given to dissertation spouses for information on "How to Live with an ABD."

● "The dissertation's breaking up that old gang of mine." In a less intense vein, dissertation disturbances of friendships parallel those for intimate relations. Through the process of differential dissertation association, the candidate will be spending less time with certain acquaintances, because of the across-the-board reduction of socializing during dissertation writing, combined with a discovery that some friends are nonsupportive, uninterested or even, in some cases, detrimental to the project. In a sense, people's attitude to your heavy involvement in the thesis, curtailing time spent with them, becomes an unintentional test of their true feelings for and understanding of you and your aspirations. At dissertation's end, some of the predissertation members of your friendship network may be absent.[4] On the other hand, *new* friendship bonds may be formed, particularly with other contemporary dissertation writers.

A subcategory of problem here might be the changing nature of the ABD's relationships with and feelings for his fellow employees. Involved again is the general issue of the candidate's simply taking some of his capital out of almost all his roles, from family to friends to work. Beyond that, however, depending, of course, on the nature of the job and its degree of intellectual isomorphism with the dissertation, a candidate may wake up in mid-dissertation to the fact that he doesn't have "that much in common" with his fellow employees.

Dissertation estrangement from some friends on or off the job, through current recognition of theretofore latent intellectual and philosophical differences, should not be the cause for self-blame or critique along the lines of a candidate feeling "traitorous" or that he has "taken on airs"; although it is not uncommon for people to whip themselves with these self-recriminations. Attenuation of friendships are always *triste,* and sadness is an appropriate response. But there is every reason to believe that one will meet new friends, probably find another kind of employment as well, more empathetic with the postdissertation self, values and interests.

Reification, Alienation and the Dissertation-As-Enemy.

Whether candidates are disturbed by problems with the dissertation itself, self-image or dissertation-precipitated changes of relationships with others, an underlying attitude seems to be that the dissertation has taken on a life of its own, beyond the control of its creator (à la Dr. Frankenstein's monster: I have, in fact, heard advisees exasperatedly use this specific literary image to describe their feelings about their theses. Indeed, with some changes in Mary Shelley's plot, we might recast MD Frankenstein as *ABD* Frankenstein doing a dissertation in biochemistry or physiology!). Whether the dissertation stubbornly won't come out right, overwhelms one with its demands, deflates one's self-image, diabolically fouls up relationships with lovers, families, friends or work, the sense of it "being out to get me" is there.

People have, apparently, a universal tendency toward reification—assigning too much power to abstractions—in most spheres of human activity, from economics to religion to family organization and, inferentially, to doctoral dissertations as well. Reification is characterized by amnesia about who created social products. Forgetting that we frail imperfect humans forged them in the first place leads to a sense of powerlessness, rage and a misconception that such products are timeless, immutable, and demanding in perfection beyond our abilities to comply. When a candidate reifies his doctoral dissertation, he is vulnerable to all these dysfunctional attitudes toward the thesis that accompany reification in any other area. The only way to get on top of a "runaway dissertation" is thoroughly to refresh one's memory about the personal origins of the proposal and Chapters One through Five. This is accomplished by once again immersing oneself in the dissertation file, to trace the project's genesis and development up to the present time in your own notes, memoranda, questionnaire construction, cross-filing.

WHOM CAN I TURN TO?

The remainder of this chapter is devoted to a consideration of various resource persons—counselors, self-help strategies and dissertation-writing peers—to whom a candidate might resort in times of the dissertation-directed, self-directed or other-directed emotional pains outlined above. In light of his own dissertation situation, a candidate will have to appraise which resource—or combination of resources—is likely to help him and be *available* to him.

Technicians: Methodologists, Statisticians, Computer Programmers.

Particularly in the social sciences, dissertation candidates have recurrent difficulty with the methodological, statistical and computer aspects of the project. In my view, the major cause of these problems is the quality and/or scope of graduate courses offered in nuts-and-bolts areas. All doctoral candidates are required to take four or five such courses, supposedly to prepare them for methodologically designing their theses. But the course sequences are more often than not uncoordinated with each other, or pay excessive attention to small, isolated, discrete techniques and studies in and for themselves, rather than pointing toward their utility or relevance in an upcoming thesis. There is, as best as I can make out, a near absence of anticipatory socialization for the methodology and statistics of the dissertation, and a graduate student can get an "A" in all of these courses and still face the dissertation as a methodological illiterate.

As noted earlier, consultants are usually available for a fee to provide the instruction that was owed a candidate in his course work: how to design a methodology and statistics tailored to his thesis. Although such "outside help" should be sought only as a "last resort," that stage comes rather quickly for most candidates, since other remedies—particularly program-affiliated methodologists—often prove unsatisfactory. That is, such methodologists are most reluctant to give time, attention and advice to the specific details of one's methods, statistics or computer runs. Remember, the formal assumption holds that the ABD learned all those nuts and bolts in the "stat-meth" courses; why should the experts be bothered to repeat such instruction? After one or two tries down at the department, the ABD gets embarrassed—by faculty's adherence to the counterfeit stand that such matters were already taught, and thus deficiencies are the candidate's fault and hence his responsibility for removing—and looks elsewhere for guidance. It is an open question whether faculty should be informed of resort to extradepartmental technicians. Certainly, they know that perhaps a majority of social science candidates use them, but straitlaced departments probably would prefer to let sleeping methodologists lie: the self-serving image of the ABD going out and designing his dissertation completely on his own, equipped with a full complement of appropriate skills taught him in his courses, is then preserved. Under some circumstances, I could even envision a scenario where a program or committee out to "get" a particular candidate might seize upon evidence of his use of various consultants (and it is entirely possible that an ABD might want two or three for various stages of the methodology) as evidence of "cheating" or not writing his own dissertation. In most instances, the resort to consultants is par for the course in social science work; faculty engage in it all the time, usually acknowledge such advice at the beginning of published research papers. But a kind of "double standard" exists for faculty and ABDs in this area. Just how stringent those standards are, and where lines are drawn for legitimate versus illegitimate dissertation aid and comfort are hard questions, but the ABD consulting outside technicians should keep possible disclosure difficulties in mind, and probably his mouth buttoned.

For whatever help you go to your technician, it is imperative to get him to explain the metatheory behind a method or statistical tool he employed, exactly what the statistical tests demonstrated in terms of your hypotheses, what the limitations of particular employed instruments are in relation to reliability and validity.[5] If you don't fully understand the first or second time around, keep at him. This is what you are paying him for out of your hard-earned coolie-wage adjunct professor salary. The last thing you need is a replay of the impatient methodology professor down at the department. Although the defense committee won't want an explication of FORTRAN or a mathematical proof for Chi-squared, they may well want to probe your grasp of the hazards of Chi-squared with small samples, or your handling of the reliability issue in your use of the Q-Sort or semantic differential scales.

Sympathetic Professors.

As I have indicated in earlier chapters, the sympathetic, interested professor—be he adviser, thesis committee member, departmental chairman or other faculty person—is an unreliable, rare, and generally highly problematic commodity in the dissertation-help stockpile. You might get delivery on one; then again you might not. If you do, he may run like a Packard but just as easily turn out to be a lemon, or get "recalled." By all means give this direction several tries—you probably would, in any event—but be cautious, just as "the other side" is careful and noncommittal. Even if you "connect" with a helpful faculty member, take his aid on a day-by-day basis, utilizing it for what it is contemporarily worth, but keeping in mind Chapter One's accounting of faculty unreliability, departures, absenteeism and even hostility when it comes to helping with dissertations. A calculus of dissertation politics also dictates that the candidate be careful if the sympathetic professor is not a member of his committee. For many hierarchy-obsessed faculty, extended consultations with such a professor might be considered as "going over my head," or "not going through proper channels," even though the indignant complainer hasn't lifted a finger to help, either substantively or emotionally, with the project. At all costs, avoid *addiction* to any faculty help, since your "supply" can be cut off at virtually any time through a multitude of circumstances over which you have no control.

Another danger here is that the sympathetic professor can stray into the murky waters of psychotherapy. A dissertation-depressed candidate may or may not benefit from therapy at this point (see section below), but it should *never* come from a faculty member in one's doctoral program. With the exception of some cases in clinical psychology programs, he is unqualified and might unwittingly exacerbate dissertation problems by introducing "red herring" suspicions about your emotional stability to thesis committee members. Faculty are all too ready to account for dissertation delay in terms of individual psychopathologies of candidates, since this approach allows them to ignore the roles of program structural deficiencies and absence of support systems in depressing, debilitating and delaying dissertations, conditions for which *they* are responsible.

Sympathetic and Supportive Students.

Dissertation dumps is a time when the candidate's self-esteem is low; often, he is being "dumped on" by his graduate professors. During 1968, when I was doing both the fieldwork and analysis of data for my dissertation, I was also teaching sociology part-time at Queens College. In that period I hit my deepest troughs with both a fieldwork crisis and then an analysis one, where the validity of my empirical findings came into question. On more than one evening I built my lectures in Introductory Sociology around my research traumas with my chiropractic student sample and site. In a very personal and immediate way I was able to show my students what "doing sociology" really meant, including the hazards, dilemmas, pains and triumphs along the way from fieldwork to analysis. In a certain real sense, one class in particular functioned like a kind of group adviser or sounding board for me, making suggestions how I might handle one or another type of obstacle. At a certain point in the course, this particular class began to anticipate eagerly my account of how matters had fared in a given week. I believe I managed to convey all of the traditional areas and issues of an introductory course in a very unusual, alive and engaging manner; those semesters, with my own research and career on the line, may well have been my finest teaching hours.

And *both* parties got something valuable: I gave my students a rather unique course, and they in turn led me toward solutions—sometimes, while lecturing, "daylight" would come to me—and a renewed sense of self-worth. When *I* doubted that I could finish the dissertation, or that the thesis was worth finishing in any event, *they* rushed in to affirm confidence in their professor and the importance of his project. Just when my graduate professors were taking me down a peg, about my dissertation in particular and, inferentially, about my sociological competence in general, my students gave me back my sense of being a good teacher and my conviction about the "rightness" and "deservability" of getting my doctorate to become a full-fledged professor. It was a most moving experience. I recommend sharing dissertation research with one's classes to any ABD who is teaching subjects that lend themselves to legitimate exploration through the vehicle of the dissertation. Sometimes a number of courses so lend themselves: I could certainly have centered sociology courses in methodology, medical sociology, social psychology and perhaps deviance around my research of semistigmatized chiropractic students confronting a medically oriented society.

Of course, one must take care not to give an excessively ego-oriented or maudlin presentation; it is important to give a full account of the theories and facts of the research problem, as well as the emotional aspects. But presentation of autobiographical materials as one important element alongside more objective features appears increasingly in social science research.[6] I have repeatedly contended in this volume that perhaps the sharpest pain of dissertation writing is its generally lonely and unshareable quality: friends, spouses, lovers, work colleagues, families, cocktail party guests, often even advisers and committee members, don't want to hear about the thesis. But in one's students, there exists a captive and potentially interested and caring audience with whom one can share one's "obsession."

Self-help Techniques.

Certain train-yourself activities can be very useful in inculcating the "pack animal" set of the dissertation routine. Nobody is going to finish a dissertation who doesn't have an attitude of getting back to it day after day, month after month, regardless of how well things flow or get bogged down in the office during a given period. In my experience, the endurance, tenacity and long-range rhythm developed from the pursuit of the long-distance category of sports such as running, swimming and skiing (cross-country) can often be transferred over to the motivational rhythm and long-range drive vital to sustaining dissertation performance. I realize that many ABDs cannot or will not entertain such self-help counsel because of already demanding work and family schedules, physical limitations (although age is certainly not necessarily one of them) or plain distaste for taking up sports which they feel are boring and/or tedious. Enough, however, would be interested and aided to justify a brief discussion.

I can relate my own writing projects, including my dissertation, to my regular pursuit of long-distance running over the past fifteen years.* In running, if you persevere, you get to a point—within limits—where you could run indefinitely: the finish of your daily—say, seven-mile—run isn't much on your mind in the fifth mile as any desperate sort of goal (maybe years ago when you started running it was), since you've long since developed the conviction that you'll be running distances like this three to five times a week for many years to come. You become comfortable within your run, the more you see it as just another segment of a lifelong activity. The reader, of course, knows me well enough by this chapter to recognize that far from advocating the dissertation as a lifelong activity, I believe it should be finished

---

* The reciprocities I have personally experienced between writing and running are no doubt among the reasons I entitled the first chapter of this volume "The Loneliness of the Long-Distance Writer."

174

from proposal to defense in a maximum of two years. But remember that the dissertation is only the first of many "runs" or projects for the typical ABD. To get into a long-distance frame of mind and perspective during dissertation time can create an invaluable career mood that equips one with a confident, receptive and engaged attitude toward new long works over the following thirty years.

But the existential mood developed in long-distance running can help not only with subsequent projects, but with the dissertation itself. The more I give myself up to my run, let myself merge into and participate with the paths of Central Park, the more effortlessly I flow and finish. Each time I begin to brood about *The Finish,* my pace is broken, the run becomes a burden. And so it seems to be with writing a dissertation: the more the candidate is immersed in his files, flowing with his fieldwork, humming along on his office typewriter, deep, deep in the very stuff of the dissertation and conversely, less preoccupied with the magical/mystical *Finish* date, the faster the thesis is going to move ahead to completion. Obviously, this running/writing illustration is not designed to devalue the booklong insistence on organization and planning as fundamental to dissertation success. The point to be made—which many dissertation finishers and professional writers would affirm—is that, perhaps paradoxically, when one has planned and outlined, and planned again, what has to follow is, as Philip Roth might put it, a "letting-go," a self-absorbed merging with one's dissertation materials.

Psychiatrists and Other Types of Psychotherapists.

Many dissertation writers are in one type of therapy or another, although it is impossible to know what percentage entered at the time of—and principally because of—dissertation depressions and anxieties.[7] The general question, in any event, is how effective is psychotherapy in getting a candidate back in motivated harness to finish the thesis. All I can do here is point up some issues which cut across the multitude of individual and group schools and approaches in which a candidate may be involved.

The greatest dissertation danger in psychotherapy is the tendency of analysts to relegate immediate dissertation griefs of the candidate to a secondary or symbolic dimension, insisting that sessions be spent on the "underlying," "psychogenetic," "developmental" processes, often dating back twenty or more years, which, they claim, account for the

ABD's present emotional discombobulation about Chapter Three of his thesis. I am not arguing for a total abandonment of psychogenetic character development interpretation, but for a redress of the balance between the role of biographical process *and* contemporary objective difficulties with the project. It may well be that you are resisting finishing the thesis because you don't want to face adult roles (prolonged self-infantilization), or because your father's perfectionist standards have penetrated and paralyzed your sense of self-esteem and worth ("I can't write anything good enough"), but, not withstanding the presence of such hang-ups, the data coming out contrary for five of your eight hypotheses is not to be casually dismissed as "secondary" or "transient" by an analyst who wants to "get down to the root of the problem."

When the data is coming out wrong, or one is in danger of being kicked out of one's field site, or the second reader is making the candidate's life hell with psychopathic or sadistic vacillation, that *is* the root of the problem, and any therapist who won't turn all his interest, concern and support to those matters on their own terms and in and for themselves is dissertation-destructive. Time enough when the immediate realistic dissertation crisis is past to get back to the extirpation of a twenty-five-year-old Electra complex. Recall my insistence in Chapter Two about the need for pushing the dissertation to the center of your life. Upon accomplishing this very difficult rearrangement of your life-style and priorities, the last thing you need is an analyst or fellow group therapy members misdirectedly trying to push it to the sidelines again by insisting you are acting "obsessively" or "compulsively."

Some years ago I wrote a series of articles on the radical criminal trials of the early 1970s.[8] One striking theme was how the radical defendants insisted that their lawyers be not only competent, but politically radical like them so that they would truly understand the nature of the struggle. It may well be that dissertation writers need analysts and/or fellow group therapy members who are "like them," having written or engaged in the process of writing a full dissertation.

A person looking for a "like me" therapist to work with during the dissertation course will not actively seek first time around an MD psychiatrist or MSW. The two largest categories of therapist remaining are Ph.D.s certified as clinical psychologists, and "Ed. Docs" who have received certification. At least these last groups have ordinarily written full theses. Even so, one has no guarantee that after fifteen years out in practice they are still "up" on the world of dissertation requirements and regulations. This selection *caveat* is by no means airtight. One can hit upon a psychiatrist who happens to be a researcher and writer as well, who will treat substantive dissertation difficulties at their face value; or one can have bad luck with a Ph.D. "Rolfer" who only dimly remembers his dissertation days and insists upon attacking misalignments of your cartilage and faciae instead of those of your data. Still, as a pretty good rule of thumb, therapists who themselves wrote dissertations are less apt to go off the deep end of misinterpreting the range of dissertation-based woes outlined above as psychopathological and psychogenetic-based disturbances, and more apt to deal with them forthrightly and intensively, as predictable byproducts of the unique dissertation-writing structural context and its unusual demands.

People in psychotherapy are notorious for forgetting that therapists are *their agents*. An ABD who *knows* that what's bothering him the most is his repeated inability to write an acceptable version of his proposal on "Economic Theory in the 'Young Marx' " cannot continue with an analyst who purports to "know better" than he about what his "real" problems are. Now, analysts can refuse to deal with substantive thesis difficulties for two different reasons. First, they can psychoanalyze, symbolize or deemphasize the dissertation, in the manner just depicted. Second, very commonly, they can claim lack of competence: "I've got a Ph.D. in psychology. I don't know the young Marx from the old one." I believe the ABD has to terminate with the first kind of reluctant analyst. Matters are more complicated with the second. Even though the therapist might not be able to help with the specific details of a field outside his own training, one can certainly capsulize for him the gist of the problems encountered, which he should be able to grasp and connect up with the general model of dissertation writing that he pursued in his own case. Some dissertation dumps have less to do with substantive issues of data and analysis, and more to do with feelings of reduced self-worth and deteriorating relations with others. If the latter woes are preoccupying a patient/ABD, a therapist must be willing to bring them to the center of the analytic hour, working on them in and for their own right.

But the world of the ABD is so unusual, the origins of dissertation pathologies so often misunderstood, that even the most sympathetic and eager-to-help therapist, not abreast of dissertation writing, may fail to provide satisfaction. This is another way of saying that conventional psychotherapy may not be effective in treating dissertation difficulties, may even be dysfunctional to progress. My own counsel to the ABD in—or seeking—conventional therapy is to practice once more the calculus of differential dissertation association and ask questions like, Did the analyst write a thesis himself? Is he current with dissertation-writing requirements? Does he have any other patients who are writing dissertations? Has he indicated a willingness to put my dissertation difficulties at the center of our work together? Will he read my dissertation materials, or at least some sections of them? Does the therapy group he wants me to join have any members who are also writing theses? Of course, the ABD is the final judge, but I would counsel that if he gets more than one "no" to the above questions, he should seek help elsewhere for emotional problems related to the dissertation. Because ABDs have been encountering too many "no's" to these kinds of questions from conventional therapies and therapists, some of them have turned for help to a new field, "dissertation therapy."

Dissertation Therapists.

I have no idea how many psychotherapists, psychoanalysts and counselors do dissertation therapy, either as a speciality within a larger general practice or exclusively. When I began this work in the late 1970s, I knew of no other persons in New York similarly engaged (although undoubtedly there must have been at least some others of whom I simply had not heard). More recently, one meets the odd psychologist with a dissertation patient or two, or reads an occasional counseling advertisement (e.g., in the *Village Voice* or *New York Review of Books*) for individual or group professional dissertation counseling/therapy.

No attempt will be made at this point to outline how dissertation therapists operate, first, because the "sample" of us is so small that I would, in any case, only be relating how *I* work; and secondly, because the entire *volume* is precisely a booklong description of what I do. Hopefully, if you read the book, you won't need a dissertation therapist! Indeed, accurate alternative titles for the book might be "The Portable Dissertation Adviser," or "The Portable Dissertation Therapist." I have tried to distill for the ABD the most useful disserta-

178

tion writing and surviving wisdom I have accumulated with advisees and clients over the past twelve years.[9]

Even though dissertation therapy might reasonably be thought of as a "growth industry," given the meager or unsatisfactory resource/support persons and systems presently available, there are several reasons why, in my judgment, only limited growth will take place:

1. The speciality demands of the practitioner a formidable combination of psychotherapeutic, generalist intellectual, methodological, editorial and human relations skills (of which the exercise of some contradict the exercise of others) which can be developed only over a long period of time.

2. Within the already limited pool of potential dissertation therapists, the rewards (monetary and otherwise) are probably perceived as too uncertain or not large enough, given the demands of such work, to lure many recruits.

3. The work is inordinately time-demanding. Unlike "straight" therapy, one must spend about two hours reading the client's materials for every hour of personal consultation.

4. Fees must, accordingly, be medium to high, putting the dissertation therapist beyond the budget of perhaps most ABDs.

5. Dissertation therapy is draining. Even if one is lucky enough to get interesting dissertations, serious, regular, critical attention to them cannot help but take energy and creativity away from one's own projects.[10] I have discovered that my maximum number of clients at any time is three; beyond that very small sample, I am drained, unable to give my best to additional ABDs, or to my own writing.

6. The dissertation therapist has no power. In a sense, the dissertation therapist is the adviser the ABD wishes he had down at his program, the adviser he can't get, except for the rarest of cases, for all the structural reasons outlined in this book. But the dissertation therapist has no connection with the committee and department (in fact, the client may be anxious that his consultations are confidential, unknown to anyone, most particularly his program). If dissertation therapist and client together work up a dissertation proposal which the therapist thinks is acceptable, how do matters stand if the official adviser and/or committee turn it down? Obviously, the therapist cannot intervene; he has no standing. The specter of such a rejection (which sometimes happens despite the best efforts of therapist and ABD) is always in the minds of seasoned thesis therapists and forces them to take

179

caution in accepting candidates whose projects or capacities they doubt. The tendency of the client to become very dependent and trusting toward the thesis therapist, combined with the brute fact that he has no control whatsoever over the decision-making processes of the candidates' thesis supervisors, puts the dissertation therapist in a perpetually vulnerable position.

7. The dissertation therapist as doppelgänger. There he sits in his Eames chair, in the shadows, unknown to the program committee, "control running" his ABDs. The "legality" of dissertation therapy is not entirely clear. How would the candidate's program construe his consultation with the shadow adviser? Would it be construed as cheating—the doppelgänger therapist as ghost writer? I suspect that certain departments would take dissertation therapy in stride, seeing it as a cross between an ABD consulting a technician and psychotherapist (which in a general way is not too far wrong), whereas others would see it not unlike the illegal term-paper-writing enterprises that have flourished on college campuses.

Clients are referred to me by psychologists, other clients, psychiatrists, but I have not had a referral, inquiry or objection from dissertation-supervising faculty or doctoral programs. Whether such silence implies ignorance that therapists like myself are working with some of their candidates, recognition and tacit approval, recognition and disapproval—tempered with guilt about faculty-created conditions causing the need for outside support services—I cannot say. But added to the feelings of powerlessness and uneasiness about the dissertation therapist role is an uncertainty about its "legitimate" status in the eyes of those supervising faculty who must ultimately decide the client's dissertation fate.

For one or more of the above reasons, then, one would not expect a growing pool of dissertation therapists to be available for ABDs in trouble in the 1980s; (and the ABDs visiting the extant ones will continue as a tiny percentage of the whole). *Leaderless peer group dissertation therapy,* however, to which we will now turn, seems to me a much more promising direction for helping large numbers of contemporary dissertation writers in distress.

Fellow Doctoral Students in the Same Boat.

The 1970s witnessed both a marked shift in traditional psychotherapies from individual to group forums and an unprecedented wide-scale use of group process in many kinds of consciousness-raising movements (e.g., women's, men's, gays' groups). Recently, there have been reports of the group context being used with dissertation writers: a faculty-directed group in a school psychology doctoral program in New York; a psychologist-directed private group for doctoral candidates in Manhattan; a leaderless group of dissertation writers in social psychology at Brandeis; a sociology group at New York University. I have indicated my skepticism about the efficacy and/or widespread availability of either conventional psychotherapists or dissertation therapists for helping with dissertation problems. With all the yet-to-be-solved obstacles in creating viable dissertation-help groups, certain of their subspecies emerge as potentially the most effective "external" support resource for the most number of ABDs. Although they began among psychology candidates, there is no reason to limit their development to that field, especially since the most effective support groups do not operate on a psychotherapy model.

Should a dissertation group be directed or leaderless? If directed, what kind of person should be the facilitator? If leaderless, of what should the membership and format consist? Since dissertation groups are in their infancy, answers to all these questions and the issues they entail are empirically "up for grabs." My own experience as a group leader or member (with prisoners, alcoholics, in general private practice, as member of a men's C-R group) is considerable, but I have never conducted dissertation groups *per se* (occasionally, a person in a general group has been an ABD); nor do I believe that many others in the early 1980s have had long-term, in-depth participation, either as leaders or members, with several dissertation groups. My observations and suggestions, below, about the formation and process of such groups involve "educated guesses" extrapolated from my familiarity with dissertation difficulties and professionally directed and self-help groups in general.

If the group is led, who should do the supervising? Much depends upon the *goals* of the group. In one New York school psychology doctoral group, candidates under the direction of faculty prepare specific dissertation sections to be presented at scheduled meetings of the group. All members are candidates in that particular program. This arrangement seems ideal for nuts-and-bolts aspects of the dissertation: since group leaders are also the duly authorized thesis supervisors, their acceptance of your production in the group is virtually identical with approving sections of your thesis. But program-mandated groups of this sort can probably be counted on two dissertation-

181

typing hands. Beyond their scarcity, they do not lend themselves to exploration and ventilation of the *emotional* dimensions of the dissertation course, their tone and direction being almost exclusively rational and "instrumental." Supervising faculty, after all, do not see their role here as therapists, nor the groups as therapeutic or consciousness-raising ones. Most certainly, they will not tolerate "personal" attacks on *them,* a venting of pent-up rages that every ABD worth his salt has accumulated.

Finding a suitable leader who is not a supervising faculty member, especially for dealing with emotional issues of the dissertation, involves the problems discussed in preceding sections. If the leader is a psychiatrist or clinical psychologist, he is apt to misinterpret dissertation-specific hang-ups within the inappropriate framework of conventional nosology. If the leader is a dissertation therapist, the same difficulties outlined in the preceding section about his position, potential and status in working with individual candidates stand for his working with dissertation groups.

As the situation now stands, and can reasonably be projected to continue for years to come, supervised dissertation groups, of either the substantive nuts-and-bolts type or emotional-support category, will not be available to the great majority of ABDs as a mainstream support resource. Depending upon the nature of the group, particularly the difference between instrumental/goal or affective/emotional priorities, the reasons for lack of access run the gamut from failure of most departments to offer work-in-progress groups as part of their doctoral programs, to unavailability of proper and competent leaders to run therapy-oriented dissertation groups, to graduate students' well-known limited cash flow.

Guidelines for Forming and Sustaining a Dissertation-Support Group.

In the face of these realities, *leaderless* peer dissertation groups appear to be the subspecies most likely to flourish and survive. What follows is a "program" to guide ABDs in setting up their own dissertation-support group. Remember that my guidelines are general and largely untested in this particular sphere. Particular groups will undoubtedly have to tailor their procedures and development along the lines of their own needs, memberships, emerging experiences. There is no absolute "right" or "wrong" manner in which to proceed. The bottom line is that members' dissertations should be pushed along to completion; the only reason for the group is dissertation progress. My program is offered, like my suggestions for setting up a dissertation file, as a "starter set" to get a group going. Feel free—in fact, expect—to alter, contradict, elaborate on it in ways which will enhance its dissertation-promoting function. Be forewarned that group construction is a difficult task which demands persistence and motivation. Special obstacles exist with a dissertation group, since all members are initially programmed to have little patience, interest in, or time for anybody else's dissertation problems. On the other hand, the special tenacity and motivation that ABDs possess (otherwise they wouldn't be ABDs pursuing such a momentous project) may serve them in good stead in making a self-help group work. If you are suffering with your dissertation and have exhausted other avenues of aid and comfort, certainly it is worth a try to reach out to your *compañeros* in the dissertation struggle. Although parts of the dissertation agony may indeed, as I have argued, be basically "unshareable," the size of that irreducible private portion is undetermined; it may be smaller than I, or you, think.

Specific Considerations.
   Members should be recruited among dissertation writers in the same general field, although not necessarily from the same program. Although all ABDs face some common problems in negotiating the dissertation, there are too many peculiar discipline-specific hurdles to expect anthropology, history and comparative-language ABDs to work together to mutual benefit in a dissertation group. If nothing else, lack of training in others' fields would be a great barrier to communication and aid. If members are all cadres from the same *department,* one has the double advantage of their sharing not only the discipline but the specific subculture of program requirements and faculty sociometrics in which they must negotiate their dissertations. But drawbacks to exclusive intradepartment membership might be: potential for excessive, dysfunctional rivalry among program "siblings"; reluctance to discuss faculty-specific gripes for fear of *soplones)* (squealers: see below for more on confidentiality agreements in dissertation groups); possible disapproval or suspicion of the group by conservative faculty, who might construe it as protest, or even cheating. Cross-departmental groups have the advantage of bringing to attention different angles and ways out of or around common discipline dissertation problems, to which a department-centric group

might be blind. Members might also feel less reluctant to speak out in cross-department groups.

Since both kinds of groups have certain credits and debits, group formers will have to weigh their relative merits in terms of the circumstances of their own programs. The recruitment process will vary from feeling out peer ABDs (who were perhaps study group members from pre-ABD stages of the program) to advertising in college and local newspapers.

An optimum maximum size should be four or five members, since particular people will not want to wait more than four weeks (even getting self-obsessed and possessed ABDs to wait that long will be a problem) for their night, and because members will not be able responsibly to keep up with issues and developments in more than three or four other theses. On the other hand, less than four is undesirable, since the number of potential relationships, or advice pathways, among members is drastically reduced. Table 7.1 gives the reader some guidelines for manageable lower and upper limits to dissertation group size. Keep in mind that if you want to end up with a permanent group of four or five reliable candidates, initially you have to contact seven or eight, since a couple will probably drop out after a few meetings.

Table 7.1: Increase in Potential Relationships with an Increase in Group Size

Size of Group	Number of Relationships
2	1
3	6
4	25
5	90
6	301
7	966

Source: W. Kephart, "A quantitative analysis of intra-group relationships," Hare (ed.) *Handbook of Small Group Research,* 2nd ed., New York: Free Press, 1976, p. 218

Meet weekly on a round-robin, home-and-home basis in each other's dissertation offices. When the group members come to your office, they will reinforce your sense of legitimacy and commitment to the often isolated and cut-off-from-others dissertation project. They may also give you valuable suggestions for streamlining your office or filing system. You will probably feel rather proud when the group comes to you and sees how you operate. That pride is a mighty dissertation motivater. On the other hand, visiting other members' offices is heartening as an antidote to dissertation isolation: "Hey, I'm not the only person in the world holed up in a home office with a big file, trying to write something nobody around me understands." What is created by these visits is a shared sense of professionalism and pride about dissertation writing which works against the low self-esteem that ABDs often develop. Meeting in each other's home offices also helps to dispel dissertation myths, sometimes suscribed to by families, spouses, lovers, that their ABD is some kind of a kook/loner, the only one in the world on this mad venture. Here they have before their eyes a *group* of persons all taking the dissertation business most seriously. Group visibility may take some of the "heat" off: hubby may not complain so much the next time you demur from a Friday night out on the grounds of dissertation business in the office.

All group members must be provided with detailed abstracts of everybody's dissertation in progress. And members must pay unswerving attention to studying them just prior to a particular member's "night up." If the group is delinquent in this vital "homework," the group is sure to break up, starting with the departure of the first person for whose presentation they have failed to prepare.

If a member intends to discuss specific substantive problems of his work that are not explicit in the abstract, he should provide members in advance with a description and summary of the gist of the problem.

Any particular week's meeting should be reserved for one, or at most two, candidates to present their work in progress and related difficulties. It is preferable that members of the group be at different stages— from proposal, to collection and analysis of data, to writing chapters, to preparation for defense—rather than, say, all beginning or just about completing. Those farther along can anticipatorily socialize those at an earlier stage. On the other hand, the relatively fresh and undiluted enthusiasm that beginners bring to the group can be helpful to tired or discouraged mid-dissertation members, who often have lost sight of how far they have come and are reminded now by seeing how far the beginners have to go.

185

On a given person's night, the problem may be focused primarily on substantive issues of the dissertation itself, a member's self-feelings or interpersonal difficulties related to dissertation life. The presenter will find that a surprising amount of advice and support will surface, angles on and solutions to the difficulty that the presenting member never considered. Although discussion will range near and far, two rules, sometimes difficult to interpret or enforce, must be held to: all discussion must be related to the task of completing members' doctoral dissertations; *the group must not do psychotherapy,* if for no reason other than the fact that the members are not trained therapists. Since emotional problems related to the dissertation will frequently occupy the group's attention, it is very easy to stray into psychoanalytic and psychotherapeutic waters. Most leaderless support groups formed around one problem or task—e.g., men's, women's, minorities', gays' consciousness-raising groups—quickly come to the psychotherapy crossroads. Those groups which take that path almost always deteriorate into internecine pop-psychiatric warfare and disband. A theme common to most of the C-R and many of the "deviant" (alcoholic, drug-addiction) support groups is that the psychogenetic misinterpretation of their problems and behaviorial patterns is foisted on them by other groups, obscuring the structural, sociological conditions they face, in whose context their speciously "sick" or "disturbed" behavior is actually rational and appropriate. This is the tack the dissertation group must take when it approaches a given member's "dissertation psychopathology." Instead of seeing a candidate's difficulties in personality and personalistic terms, the group must closely analyze the very real dissertation pressures under which a member is operating, as well as explode the dissertation myths under which he or others may be laboring in labeling him, say, "masochistic" or "obsessive." (Consider the ease with which an uninformed psychotherapist could misinterpret the absolutely essential need for an intricate and complicated filing system and religious time in the dissertation office as "obsessive-compulsive behavior.")

Members must make every effort to attend all meetings (like the dissertation itself, meetings that facilitate its progress must become a top life priority) and "put away" preoccupations with their own theses when other group members are "up." As I have already noted, the inner-directed set of the dissertation writer is going to make total focusing on the other person's project very tough, at least in the beginning. If, however, members are able to reach the "takeoff" plane, they will discover what all successful C-R, self-help and support groups find: "It's your night even when it's not your night." In a given session, nonpresenters who are involved and listening attentively will hear about *their own* dissertation problems being wrestled with by their peers. Indeed, the similarity of thesis difficulties, both in substantive and emotional keys, and in etiologies is precisely why support groups are able to work.

Presentation schedules will occasionally have to be altered to help a particular member who is facing a critical dissertation problem. Perhaps a member must meet with his thesis committee the following week for a hearing on his proposal, or the final defense has been pushed ahead two weeks, or her husband is threatening to leave her on grounds of adultery, citing the dissertation as corespondent.

Role playing is very useful in many dissertation crises contexts. If the group member doubts his oral performance capacity with faculty, the other members can take the roles of proposal hearing or final defense faculty and subject the candidate to a full-dress (and full-time: the group should devote the, say, two hours of the session to the member) rehearsal. Devil's advocate questions should abound; with this particular kind of "psychodrama," it is helpful if at least some of the others in the group are in the specific program with the protagonist, since they will have insider intelligence about the personalities, quirks, theoretical and methodological preferences, as well as interrogation styles of his committee members.

Jill's marital rift with Jack can also be handled with role-playing, where other members take the parts of her husband and children. I believe that both-sex groups work best, since many of the interpersonal dissertation problems center in one way or another around disrupted relationships with loved ones of the opposite sex, or with families. It is very important to have both men's and women's points of view about issues like role absenteeism or reduced sexual enthusiasm available when candidates confront a "home revolt" along these lines.

Upon unanimous agreement, the group may sometimes invite outsiders to attend. Guests would generally be of two types:

Intimates, usually spouses or lovers, of a member who is experiencing home difficulties because of disagreements over the obtrusive dissertation. Bringing in a spouse or close relative to get "both sides of the story" has numerous precedents in many self-help group therapy and marriage-counseling settings. Often, when the relative/outsider sees his beloved ABD defended and supported by three or four other men and women facing similar difficulties, there will develop a willingness to reach some accommodation or compromise during the dissertation course. Not that the fellow member will always come out smelling like a rose! A female group member may go along, at least part of the way, with an irate "abandoned" guest wife and insist that the dissertation-writing husband can make significant adjustments in his schedule to effect *rapprochement* without stalling the thesis' progress.

Guest speakers who have somthing special or unique to contribute. Such persons might be a member's acquaintance who is a specialist in the methodology and statistical analysis of the group's field, or a recent dissertation finisher, or a "sympathetic professor."

All dissertation "victories" and rites de passage—*be they acceptance of a proposal, completion of chapters, setting of a date for the final defense—should be formally acknowledged by the group.* All such milestones should bring a shared celebration, if only a toast with wine. Every within-course victory is an enormous motivater not just for the particular member achiever, but for all other persons in the group as well. Each success reinforces the conviction that the dissertation group is effective; which reinforces commitment to and involvement with the group; which leads to further victories—and so an upward spiral emerges, with all members being carried nearer to completion.

Since sensitive "personal" material is going to come up repeatedly, the issue of confidentiality should be discussed from the start and agreed upon. How far to go with confidentiality is a tricky matter. May one confide in lovers and spouses, for example? I have found that people invariably do, no matter what the strictures of their vows, so mum's the word, except for close family. There will undoubtedly be times when particular supervising faculty, perceived as the instant dissertation completion obstacle, either by the candidate himself or other members, will be commented on and analyzed in—putting it discreetly—less than sympathetic terms. The danger is that a group member will be reluctant and or afraid to speak out about a faculty member if he fears that such comments will get back to a particular professor or department, threatening his own or other group members' position in the program. There is no foolproof, airtight guarantee against information being leaked. One could like awake nights thinking up *unintentional* permutations of ways in which "slanderous" materials could get out. But beyond exercising reasonable care, such sleepless nights would be exercises in *dissertation paranoia*. Obviously, you don't spill your guts about problems with *anybody* in the group, be they problems with family, spouses, friends, dissertation professors, on the first few nights—or even during the first months—of meetings. Usually, over time—after it becomes clear which people have signed on for the long haul—groups develop a strong subculture of commitment and trust, especially when members see some progress toward goals. I think it is relatively rare and unlikely that "snitches" would remain long-term members of such groups. In any event, an informer would jeopardize his own program position as much as anyone else's in the group. Needless to say, any member found "telling tales" must be expelled from the group, and this should be understood from the first sessions.

Don't abandon the group without giving it your best shot. A group worth its salt always takes time to gel. Essential dissertation-completion attitudes are patience and endurance. Practice, indeed develop, those traits by sticking through the troughs of the group's development. The group instrument that will emerge will almost certainly cushion some of the blows of the dissertation course and speed up its finish.

Being Your Own Best Dissertation Friend.
Some of the resources delineated in this chapter for coping with dissertation disturbances will work better than others for particular people. My own belief is that leaderless dissertation support groups are likely to be the most effective of the change-agents involving help from other persons. But I have to reiterate my caution that the candidate cannot rely on the certainty of *any* of these outside agents coming through to save the day. Even with a good support group, one must never turn off, or even idle, his own dissertation motor; the group could have a major disagreement and disband tomorrow. So the chapter ends where the book began—with the insistence that some irreducible part of the dissertation is always going to be private and that one must be fully prepared to go it alone. The most reliable (because you have complete control over it) and probably most effective "therapy" in times of dissertation trouble and despair is staying with your file, spending prescribed time each day in your office, soaking in the project. Here we confront once more the existential loneliness of the long-

distance writer. If the candidate has the courage to live through it, the "insurmountable" problems will be solved and one day become dissertation lore to pass on to the next generation of candidates, including perhaps one's own ABD son or daughter.

SUMMARY.

1. The dissertation course is conceptualized in Figure 7.1 as an undulating wave with troughs of depression and doubt, and crests of enthusiasm at points of completing major phases, such as the proposal, especially difficult stretches of analysis or sticky chapters. The overall direction of the wave is downward, in that each successive stage from proposal completion onward is generally easier (although not without the possibility of at least temporary serious reversals further along) because of accumulated momentum, success and motivation.

2. An argument is advanced that most "disturbed" or "psychopathological" behavior exhibited by candidates during dissertation research and writing stems from "normal" response to excessive, "abnormal" dissertation pressures, rather than from deep-seated, prethesis personality problems. There is, however, a danger that dissertation-precipitated disturbances can persist beyond the end of the thesis if preventative measures, outlined in the present and in the final chapters, are not exercised.

3. Dissertation-caused anxieties and/or depressions are focused in three spheres: (a) negative feelings about the dissertation itself, particularly its doubtful outcome; (b) a diminishment of self-esteem; (c) a real or believed deterioration in significant other relationships, in which the demands of the dissertation are seen as the culprit. A listing of these disturbances is followed by an inquiry as to which are dissertation-myth derived; candidate-caused, through deficiencies in work habits or motivation; or predictable consequences of the structures and processes of the dissertation course.

4. The common and dysfunctional tendency of ABDs to reify their dissertations, converting them into objective enemies, is analyzed.

5. The second half of the chapter offers an extensive inventory and appraisal of various resource persons, facilitators, counselors, self-help strategies and dissertation-writing peers to whom or to which a candidate might turn in painful, emotional times described in the text. These include: technicians; sympathetic professors; one's own supportive students; self-help techniques, particularly long-distance

sports; psychiatrists and other psychotherapists; dissertation therapists; and support groups of fellow dissertation writers. A thorough evaluation of the effectiveness of psychotherapists and dissertation therapists is conducted, concluding that dissertation support groups are potentially more effective and certainly more available to large numbers of ABDs than either of the other two resources. Guidelines for forming and sustaining an effective dissertation support group are provided.

6. The chapter concludes with the author's assertion that, even though dissertation groups may prove particularly helpful, the candidate's best and most reliable resource in times of dissertation dumps is the accumulated wisdom and "capital" of his file. He is commended to immerse himself in it on a regular schedule, even when matters seem blackest or most circular; solutions will emerge. Once again, the inevitability of the ABD's having to go at least some of the painful distance alone comes to the fore.

NOTES

1. One wonders when *methodology textbooks* will give doctoral students a more accurate picture of the revisionist and reciprocal nature of theory and research as American high school *history books* have begun to explode sanitized, storybook versions of American history. See, Frances Fitzgerald, *America Revised; History Schoolbooks in the Twentieth Century* (Boston: Little, Brown, 1979).

2. See Chapter Nine for elaboration of strategies to prevent postdissertation self-destruction.

3. The only situation in which time becomes a factor is where an ABD delays so long, he plays out the total allowed (usually ten years) program matriculation time. Even then, extensions are usually granted.

4. In a classic study, Merton and Lazarsfeld demonstrated that friendships have a minimal chance of surviving the explicit recognition of deep differences on basic issues and values. "Friendship As Social Process: A Substantive and Methodological Analysis," in Berger et al., eds., *Freedom and Control in Modern Society* (New York: Van Nostrand, 1954), pp. 21–54.

5. For an elaboration of what the ABD has to learn from his consultant about the theory of statistics as opposed to the mathematics and machinations of particular statistics and computer programs, see Chapter Five.

6. See A. Shostak, ed., *Our Sociological Eye: Personal Essays in Society and Culture* (Port Washington: Alfred, 1977).

7. Let it be clear that I am focusing on explicitly recognized dissertation

doubts, difficulties, anxieties. If an ABD, God love him, is not particularly bothered by the dissertation, these sections on therapy and the dissertation are not for him; and primal scream, Rolfing, transactional analysis or Sullivanian approaches may be just right for whatever extra-dissertation ill ails him.

8. D. Sternberg, "The New Radical Criminal Trials," *Science and Society,* Fall 1972.

9. What I have attempted to do for dissertation writing in this volume, Martin Shepard tries to do for psychotherapy in his *The Do-It-Yourself Psychotherapy Book* (New York: Wyden: 1973).

10. The theses are often more interesting to the *therapist* than the writer, since the former approaches them afresh, unweighted down with the history of tediousness experienced by the candidate.

CHAPTER 8

The Dissertation Defense

THE DEFENSE: FORMALITY OR SERIOUS LAST STAGE?

In dissertation subculture, the defense is painted in two contradictory ways: 1. It is a "piece of cake," a mere formality, where the thesis committee more or less "rubber-stamps" a foregone acceptance of the dissertation. Under this view, the defense is rather congenial, almost festive, and the ABD, past the serious part of initiations, is heartily accepted into the fraternity of doctorate holders in his field. 2. The defense is a threatening, grueling two or more hours of adversary proceedings, where the (usually) five faculty members lean toward stopping the ABD from entrance into the fraternity unless he fights like an intellectual tiger.

It is difficult to know for certain which of these two contexts more closely approximates the mood and meaning of the "typical" defense of the 1980s. Much, as we have already seen in the book, depends on the specifics of particular programs and the individual relationships that an ABD has with faculty. When I defended my thesis in the late 1960s, the mood at New York University, at least in social sciences, was "piece of cake." And yet I was apprehensive about the defense: so much had not gone as expected at prior stages that I was not ready to believe in the "in-like-Flynn" model. Then, too, two additional, non-thesis committee members were assigned to my defense. One of these persons I wasn't acquainted with; the other had a reputation as being very difficult with candidates. It was also unsettling that so few candidates came up each year; surely, I thought, with only six or seven doctorates awarded (with over one hundred people at one or another stage of doctoral studies), the defense must be a formidable checkpoint. Years earlier, my preliminary comprehensive orals had been an ordeal, and it just did not seem logical that at this final point the relentless faculty would lie down and die.

It should be noted that my predefense intelligence was not very reliable, since so few got through that the pool of successful candidates to question was small, and at the time I was writing, all of my ABD peers were atomized and isolated from each other: we formed no dissertation consciousness-raising or support groups which might have collectively acquired a better picture of how serious or rigorous the defense was likely to be.

MY OWN DEFENSE ORDEAL.

It turned out that my defense was the very devil itself. Each man had his own copy of my 400-plus-page dissertation, although I had no idea how closely the two non-committee members had studied it. We sat around a long conference table, with me at the head (or *foot,* as I certainly experienced it more accurately an hour into the hearing). For a while things went well; I fielded questions about the sample, methodology and fieldwork quite handily. Then the "spoiler" turned his guns on me. He singled out one section of my hypotheses testing and began his own dissertation on how it was faulty, or wrongheaded, or didn't prove what it was supposed to prove. I do not remember just what the objection was, most certainly because of traumatic amnesia. I do recall trying desperately to understand his argument in order to make a coherent response, but failing. To this day I don't know if the other committee members understood either, or pretended to understand to save face or to avoid a picture to me of a faculty divided. I do know that this fellow began to turn the defense against me. I remember the frustration and despair that hit me, the sweat of fear that drenched my shirt: Here I have devoted my life for nearly two years to this dissertation, here I know more about chiropractic student culture than any man alive; and this son of a bitch, picking out three or four pages of my 422, is going to sink me! I remember also thinking about my wife's celebration party for me that night, to which she'd invited probably one hundred folks, and how mortifying it was going to be explaining what happened to me when

194

they arrived to congratulate me. It is not the profoundest piece of advice, I hope, that I offer the reader in this volume, but still a self-protecting one: Don't schedule a defense celebration party for the same night as the defense.

Again, I'll never quite know why the "spoiler" didn't succeed. Perhaps the others felt he was picking on me or were irritated that he took up so much time with points they didn't grasp. The three committee members knew how I had put my heart and energy into the project, knew I grasped the subject better than my interrogator, regardless of his superior debate style and my momentary intellectual paralysis. The close contact I had maintained with my committee, showing them chapters of the dissertation as I went along, probably saved the day. Somehow we got off the sticking point and moved rather desultorily through half an hour more of questioning.

Then, as the custom is in these matters, I was asked to step outside while they made their decision. The fifteen or so minutes I waited in a corridor or empty classroom seemed like hours. With every passing minute I was more certain they had rejected my thesis, or at least my *defense* of it (more below on this distinction). After an eternity, my adviser came out and said, "Congratulations, Doctor." By that point I was more flooded with relief than joy; I actually cried. Afterwards, the defense committee took me for the traditional success drink. The spoiler did not attend. Although nothing very substantive was mentioned, I knew it had been a near thing.

At least it had been a near thing in having my dissertation accepted unconditionally. I know now that the worst that could have happened would have been the committee's insisting I make certain changes to satisfy, in this case, the one unrelenting member. I understand now that ultimate full acceptance had never been in jeopardy—I had simply done too much competent sociological work for them to have turned it down—but my lack of information about other than zero-sum defense outcomes, combined, I believe, with the faculty's own informal *ad hoc* procedures about passing, failing or conditionally passing dissertations at that time, caused me much grief, most of it squeezed into the two-hour defense and subsequent fifteen minutes of waiting for the jury to come in.

Shortly after my defense, I began hearing about people who passed subject to "major" or "minor" revisions; I have since known of several cases where a candidate was failed outright and irreversibly (at various universities). It would require a study in its own right, and in any event there is no data available, to inquire as to whether dissertation defenses in general have moved closer to the adversary model over the past couple of decades. But my comments in this chapter about preparing intellectually and emotionally for the defense are in line with my booklong abiding point of view in dissertation matters: Assume that the defense committee is out to torpedo you, that you are going to have to go it alone on the defense with no allies on the committee. Preparing your defense in line with these assumptions, you will come to the hearing with your best possible case. If the defense turns out to be congenial and uneventful, what a pleasant surprise—but never count on it.

PREPARATION.

The old medical joke about the operation being a success but the patient dying has its dissertation analogue in the thesis being a success but the defense a disaster. At first look, it appears that the mere researching and writing of the dissertation is itself a most adequate preparation for a little two-hour defense (what are two hours, after all, compared with two intensive years?) with five people, none of whom know half of what the candidate does about his subject. And yet, paradoxically, it may be just that excessive expertise, relative to faculty, that can backfire (as in my case) with a professor who wants to make it clear who's boss.

A candidate must prepare for the defense in *three* areas: 1. total mastery of the substance of the dissertation; 2. "packaging" of the dissertation for the social ritual of the formal defense; 3. cultivation of a set of self-protective and realistic attitudes about the defense which will carry the ABD through both the predefense period and defense itself with relative equanimity. The operative word in preparation is *defense*—taken very seriously and literally—of both the dissertation and the sensibilities of its writer.

Readiness on Substantive Issues.

Regular attention to one's devil's advocate file (see Chapter Three) right up until the time of the defense is an optimal approach for keeping at one's fingertips the most difficult or probing questions examiners are likely to put. Devil's-advocate-file exercises should be supplemented with devil professor role playing in the candidate's dissertation group.

Packing the Dissertation for the Defense.

The defense candidate has to keep in mind that the faculty's approach to the dissertation is far different from his own. The ABD is obsessed with it; whereas total faculty man-hour attention to it probably hasn't amounted to one week's time in the candidate's office. All his wrestling with details of data-gathering, slightly variant statistical approaches, tedious assembly of bibliography and footnotes, proofreading couldn't interest them less. As outrageous as it seems, from the amount of blood, sweat and tears shed by the candidate, my sense is that the defense committee readers go right on by about 75 percent of the material.[1] What, then, do they tend to focus on? They look to the big picture, to a sense of what the dissertation is contributing to the field and to it's original elements (see discussion in Chapter Four). The candidate's packaging preparation should be in these areas.

An important and almost universally neglected aspect of packaging is the two- or three-page single-spaced *abstract* that University Microfilms requires at the beginning of all dissertations. Programs vary as to whether that abstract has to be included at the time of the defense, or whether one can write it up after a successful defense. My counsel is to make it the first item that hits the defense reader's eye: a terse yet complete overview of the dissertation, including the statement of the problem embedded in the key concerns of the discipline, a conveyance of its contribution and originality, the hypotheses developed from the problem, the methodologies employed in gathering and testing hypotheses-related data, the major findings, discussion of the results and implications of the study for the field. The abstract should lift the central themes from each chapter, condensing each into no more than a paragraph or two.

Dissertation defenses have a "shotgun marriage" aspect to them. They almost always seem to be set up a day before the spring term is over, with half the faculty packing their suitcases for the next day's summer trip to Formentera. It becomes a very real problem for the candidate to get the five required warm bodies together for the two hours. Usually, three of them have to be the thesis committee, with the other two from the department or a "sister" department (say, an anthropologist attending a sociology defense). More often than not, mere chance (along with a little help from the program's secretary) as to who happens to still be in town and available on June 31 at two in the afternoon—rather than any logical connection of a member's interests or specialities with the candidate's thesis—determines who sits in the fourth and fifth defense chairs. Certainly, one cannot gear any extensive preparation to these latecomers to the dissertation scene. It may well be that, given the structure of their general university obligations—in which serving as fifth reader of a dissertation can hardly place in the top rungs of priority—combined with the fact that they may not receive your 300-page, 30-table dissertation until a few days before the defense (there are true and not infrequent stories about defense members seeing the thesis for the first time when they sit down at the examining table), the abstract is the *only* part of the dissertation they read! Under these circumstances, the need for and utility of a clear and convincing abstract with some clout should be very apparent.

Aside from orienting, impressing and maybe pacifying eleventh-hour faculty arrivals at the dissertation, repeated revision of the abstract by the candidate throughout the dissertation course puts the 25 percent the defense hearing will concentrate on at the top of his inventory. To repeat my advice from Chapter Three, once a month throughout the dissertation course, starting with the proposal stage, the candidate should sit down with a tape recorder and recount, off the top of his dissertation head, the story of his thesis. Any given oral abstract should then be played back to test its credibility both to the candidate and the awaiting reference group, the defense committee. At a number of points, the entire series of monthly abstracts should be chronologically played back, so that the ABD gets a sense of the development and the stages of his project. After ten or twelve of these, telling one's dissertation story to the committee that final afternoon should be almost second nature. If one should happen to get rattled during the defense, long-term recital training should ensure carrying it off anyway.

Appearance of the dissertation is another aspect of packaging for faculty that is often neglected (although in a minority of cases it is *overdone*). Although an IBM Selectric-typed dissertation won't carry a word-salad dissertation, the average reader wouldn't throw it aside anywhere nearly as quickly as a less elegantly typed version. With borderline dissertations (which the author most definitely does not counsel settling for) a beautifully typed thesis might even win the day. In any event, the final draft of the dissertation which the committee uses should be professional typed (as should the final version of the proposal). The cost of three-to-five hundred dollars is a most justified and necessary expense. It makes absolutely no sense for a candidate to have given years of his life to a dissertation and then balk at spending a few hundred bucks to have it presented and packaged with style. As a matter of fact, one's dissertation *deserves* a first-class presentation. If you are reluctant to have it typed up properly, this should give you some signal that perhaps the thesis isn't yet up to par.

A first-rate abstract and professionally typed version of the dissertation have postdefense professional uses as well: universities sometimes ask professorial candidates to include an abstract and even, for people under serious consideration, a copy of the entire dissertation in their application papers; if you want to adapt your dissertation for publication as a book, you must have a professionally typed version to send around to interested publishers.

The point here is that all readers of the dissertation, from defense committee, to employers, agents, editors or publishers, get a sense of how the candidate *himself* views the quality of his project as reflected in its physical representation. Our trade, after all, is practised with and mediated by typewritten documents; there is no getting around this central fact of modern scholarship. When a candidate pays scant or sloppy attention to this norm, his faculty readers have a tendency, not without a certain justification in this context, to label or prejudge him, and *a fortiori*, his dissertation, as "unprofessional."

THE DEFENSE STATE OF MIND.

Until quite recently, patients signed their consent to operations without surgeons informing them of the procedures or risks of particular surgery. Patients awaited surgery in ignorant terror. After years of malpractice lawsuits by operees demanding, but not being awarded, damages for "complications" from operations, the courts evolved the tort doctrine of "informed consent," which holds that it is the doctor's duty to describe the operation. including what could go wrong, before the patient can give his permission. In most doctoral programs, it is the responsibility of the candidate to start the defense's wheels rolling; of course he needs the permission of at least his adviser, who presumably has made a judgment that the dissertation as it now stands is either acceptable or has gone about as far as it can go within its present framework of development (the distinction between the two will be discussed in a moment). In some ways, the typical ABD facing his defense is like the patient facing his operation, particularly under the old model of "uninformed consent," in that he has neither a clear picture of what will likely transpire nor of what could go wrong. In such a state of defense darkness, we have the breeding ground for predefense terror, during-defense paralysis and shock, and postdefense depression and outrage.

"Uninformed consent" is most likely to characterize those ABDs who have failed to gain approval of successive stages and chapters of the dissertation from crucial committee members, have failed to pursue the contract model of the dissertation (in many programs the during-dissertation supervision and validation guidelines are still so vague that a candidate can go ahead with the bulk of his thesis unscrutinized by faculty); have refrained from joining any kind of dissertation support group. Keeping in close touch down at the department and keeping in close contact with dissertation-writing peers is a synergistic process which anticipatorily socializes the ABD to his defense, reduces the "great blank" (A. Moorehead's term for uncharted Australia) of the final trial. But since many ABDs, either by personal decision or structural laxity of their program, continue to shy away from regular interaction with faculty during the dissertation course and/or refrain from joining with other students in the same boat, defense terror and shock are likely to continue. However, the following pages attempt to spell out the options open to the committee and some of the dynamics of the defense hearing, to alert and prepare the unwary ABD.

If a candidate has pursued the contract model to the full, he has relatively little to fear, since the three supervising faculty have accepted the thesis at least in its general thrust, and they constitute a majority of the defense committee. Any subtraction from three-person prior approval—say, one member sitting on the fence about the validity of your methodology—greatly increases the chances of defense obstacles. The opposite-polar case is going in without *anybody*'s approval. It sometimes happens that even when a candidate keeps in contact with his committee, these faculty will not make a commitment at a given point, want to "wait and see." Such reluctance may not be delinquent or dilatory on the part of supervising faculty; they may feel the product is a borderline "hard" case. In such an event, unwilling to take a firm stand, they may prefer to "throw it into the lap" of the final defense committee of five. This is a position of extreme jeopardy for an ABD, almost a Russian roulette model of the defense, where one has no allies and the moods or caprices of any of the five can push the group decision in one direction or the other. I believe that if an ABD follows the "game plan" outlined in this volume, his chances of finding himself on such an end-of-dissertation spot are, if not impossible, at least quite slim.

DEFENSE COMMITTEES' OPTIONS AND THE ALL-OR-NOTHING MYTH.

Head-in-the-sand ABDs approach the defense with the *all-or-nothing myth* (which may have some *reality* in their particular cases if they have assiduously avoided faculty approval of the basic outline of their thesis): "either they grant me my doctorate 'at five in the afternoon' or they flunk me." I have already noted that the trend in defenses is toward passing with revisions required. Different programs use various terminologies, but there are five categories of defense result: 1. Unconditional pass, with no revisions, except changes in typos, or semicolons and commas. I believe the frequency of this outcome to be on the wane. 2. Conditional pass, subject to minor revisions, larger than commas and spelling. A candidate might be asked to run another set of tests on his data, or elaborate on a critique of certain theories, or further develop implications for the study in the last chapter. I believe that this second category may today be the modal one. 3. Conditional pass, subject to major revisions, where whole chapters or sections of the dissertation have to be rewritten, reanalyzed or even re-researched. This third pass is not an insignificant number and is growing. 4. Occasionally a candidate, through nervousness or speaker's block, fails his *presentation*, even though the faculty *passes his dissertation*, with or without revisions. The author knows of several cases of just such a mishap. This type of failure was always cured, either by another defense or by some innovative faculty approach, viz., with a particularly formal-group-shy candidate, individual professors contrived to examine him about his dissertation over lunches and dinners. The departure (at Harvard) from the conventional examination was justified on the grounds of the dissertation itself being outstanding.

201

5. Complete failure of the thesis, where the committee judges that no amount of revision will cure defects in the thesis because its core is unsustainable. People who fall into this last category are truly dissertation tragedies and often never recover from the blow. The final section of the chapter addresses coping with this situation.

Candidates should make every effort to ascertain the range of options for their specific program, and further, if possible, what the "percentages" are in terms of where recent prior defenders were allocated, along the option spectrum. If one is not in constant touch with faculty and ABD groups, he may well have to go in to the program chairman and ask him outright. Obviously, inquiring about the empirical distribution among the formal categories is a much more delicate matter, perhaps better pursued among fellow students (although student grapevines, as opposed to dissertation support *groups,* can be notoriously or hysterically misleading on this score).

The point is to replace the terror of the all-or-nothing myth with a quite different pre-, during and post-defense attitude which accepts any outcome from numbers one through three as a victory. (Even the rare fourth outcome is usually only a temporary setback.) Certainly, one is trying for a number one, but the odds (and each department has to be checked individually to get accurate ones) are more in favor of a conditional pass, with most often minor—but not infrequently major—revisions. The outcome of the defense, then, parallels the outcome of the proposal hearing, where I argued (in Chapter Four) that approval subject to changes was still a major victory. I realize that a conditional defense pass is existentially more of a letdown, coming at the end when one smells victory, than a conditional proposal pass, so much earlier in the game. But, again, by this point the ABD has waited and worked so long that "running the few more miles" (see the analogy between dissertation writing and long-distance running developed in Chapter Seven) of the revisions should be taken in stride. The momentum to negotiate the revision "gun lap" will only be lost if the candidate goes in with all his eggs in the unconditional pass basket.

DEFENSE DYNAMICS AND ALIGNMENTS.

The favorite defense-lore story has to do with how, either unintentionally or by the candidate's design, two or more of the defense committee become involved in a lengthy debate with *each other* over some point generated by the dissertation and forget about questioning the student. At the end of two hours, he emerges as unconditionally passed without being especially examined. This is a kind of countervailing myth to the defense horror story of a candidate being mercilessly battered by a unified and relentless faculty five for a couple of hours. Although both versions are apocryphal, they both touch upon the theme of intracommittee relations and interaction during the defense. How should the candidate perceive the five persons facing him over the defense table in a manner calculated to expedite a successful defense? As a committee of the whole? As a tightly knit group with a common perspective? As a temporary aggregate of individuals with no shared view?

We have already seen that the administrative procedures for committee formation almost guarantee that the five will not be one group, in the sense of having shared an antecedent developmental history centered on concerns of the candidate's dissertation. For defense purposes it is best, and most accurate, to break down the five into one *group* composed of the three long-standing dissertation committee members (although not necessarily united in attitudes, interests or level of concern about a dissertation: the adviser might be highly involved, the other two thesis committee members only nominally engaged) and two last-minute visiting firemen *individuals*, with problematic connections both to one another and to the "Gang of Three." Dissecting the committee in this initial fashion does connect in some sense with the "divide and conquer" defense tale recounted above.

I believe that in almost all cases—unless one has special credible intelligence to the contrary—the candidate should "play" to the thesis committee group within the defense five. The ABD has had by this point an involved experience with the three, beginning with a hearing on his proposal (not unlike the dissertation defense, in many respects) and continuing through the research and writing of the dissertation, where all along, if he pursued the contract model of the thesis, he kept them current with unfolding developments. The last two members of the defense committee share none of this dissertation history: in a fundamental sense, the group alignment is the candidate plus his thesis committee, against the two *pro-tem* faculty judges, notwithstanding quite different official demarcations. The latter two may well not even have *read* substantial parts of the dissertation.

This structural realignment of groups within the dissertation defense doesn't yield inevitable or universal increments for all candidates. Specific circumstances of programs and peculiar relationships with one's committee have to be weighed. If the committee has been hostile for two years of supervision, the candidate's being part of the "in group" here will not protect him from their pursuing that animosity into a trying defense. If the committee has been indifferent to his project, "in-group" status will not provide much protection against overzealous attacks from the last two faculty, although the tendency of even disgruntled members of a group to unite against a "common enemy" sometimes accrues to a defense candidate. Thus, the author does not mean to counteradvise the original defense rule of thumb that the candidate should expect the hearing to be an adversary one. It is nonetheless true that in those cases where one has had a "good" regular relationship with his committee (probably a minority situation, and, in any event, open to the hazards of subjective misevaluation by the candidate), he can anticipate the majority of the final committee to be in his corner.

In my own case (see above), I went into my defense with my thesis committee on my side, although this unity developed only after prolonged negotiations, accommodations, stages and struggle over a year and a half of my dissertation course. The fourth member was a person known to be tough, and perhaps a "hatchet man," but I had never taken a course with him, so I had no specifics with which to work. I had never met or known anything about the fifth man. Even had I been inclined to do so, there was no time to "case" the final two, since there couldn't have been more than a two- or three-week interval between their appointment to the committee and D day. As matters transpired, Number Four tried, and almost succeeded, in torpedoing me. He was aided by his collegial reputation for being quite brilliant. What saved me was the dissertation-specific group realignments, where my thesis committee (but not with alacrity: they let me roast for an hour) eventually took my side, even against their esteemed colleague.

Although one's historical experience with his committee may allow him to rely on a generally sympathetic stance toward his dissertation, this does not imply an easy defense; one still must prepare thoroughly with devil's advocate training geared to anticipating the most difficult queries which the three are most likely to pose. For reasons outlined above, no preparatory time should—or usually can—be devoted to the final two faculty. It is always possible that the defense examiners will get off on a tangent and dispute/debate among themselves, leaving you without much more to do than look engaged or impressed, or that the member whom you dreaded most gets replaced because of illness with Ms. Milquetoast, or that because it's a beautiful summer day outside, the board okays you in an hour and a quarter to get to the beach. Still, anybody who comes in without preparing for and expecting very hard questions does so at his dissertation peril.

DURING THE DEFENSE: WHAT TO EXPECT AND HOW TO COPE.

The normal format has the candidate seated at one end or another of the table in some type of seminar room. I believe it is important to *rehearse* the scene when possible. Most often, you can learn from the departmental secretary a week or two in advance exactly *where* the defense will be held. I was able to do this. Go to the room during a vacant hour and sit down just where you'll probably be asked to sit during the actual defense (one way to insure this seating on D day is to get there earliest).[2] Then run through the story of your thesis, exactly as you've done with your tape recorder for the file (it might be a good idea to tape this version as well, for listening to prior to D day). It may even be possible to get your dissertation group to come down to the examination room and role-play the committee.

Although we don't have a situation where the candidate can really be in control, small doses of student direction can be carved out. For instance, it is important to be physically comfortable during the defense. You might very well want to ask faculty for permission to remove your coat if it makes you feel tight or restrained. Or you might want to provide yourself with a pitcher of water to guard against getting dry during the session. If you are comfortable using a blackboard in making points—either through employing it in lectures and/ or dissertation office work—try to get janitors to move one in for your defense. I have always found the latter group of grossly undervalued university workers to be very decent and accommodating in helping me with stage adjustments.

Usually, faculty will ask you questions on a round-the-table basis, with each member posing an uninterrupted series and segment of questions, and the adviser acting as moderator and "anchorman." It is putatively his job to make sure matters don't get out of hand by particular faculty interrupting each other's questioning time or taking over the meeting. Advisers/facilitators have varied success in this role; generally, the more involved your adviser is with you, the better he will do in this respect. The round-robin format tends to break down in most cases after the first hour or so, with a concomitant increase in cross-fire questions.

Remember that some inquisitors are more equal than others—normally the Big Three—and that it is correspondingly more crucial to give satisfactory responses to thesis committee members. (I maintain this, notwithstanding the—I believe—unusual turnabout of questioner importance in my own defense case.) Remember, too, that to pass you do not have to respond adequately to *every* question; I've never attended a dissertation where candidates didn't flunk at least a couple of questions (which is not surprising considering that *dozens* of questions are usually posed). You do have a very important and reliable ally sitting in the room, not in a chair but on the table: *the dissertation itself,* with all its completion, presence, facticity, embodiment of long-term thinking, research, analysis and conclusion. It is *prima facie* evidence and expert witness to your qualifications for the doctorate. If the going gets rough or the defense seems to be going against you, try to get the committee and your rattled self back to basics: open up your 300-page tome and remind them—if necessary by reading chapter and footnote—what the defense is at bottom all about: the written document of your researched dissertation. You may not speak so well, you suggest tactfully, because of the pressures of the defense situation, but let the faculty focus on the permanency of your research, rather than on the transiency of a nervous oral presentation.

What does a candidate do if he suddenly goes plain blank, most likely because he sees the tide going against him? I suggest excusing oneself from the defense for a few moments to visit the loo. Often, with some cold water in the face and five minutes' respite, you can come back and turn it around. But won't the committee think it strange? Maybe, maybe not. After all, students are constantly excusing themselves from classes to visit the bathroom; we professors often take a five-minute break during a lecture and leave the room; nominated Cabinet members excuse themselves during Congressional confirmation hearings; in your own defense, members of the committee may themselves drift in or out, or come in late, or leave early. Even if your committee should consider your departure a bit unusual, and even be onto why you took the break, so what—if the alternative is sitting there and suffering the sinking of your dissertation ship? Coaches have always known the effectiveness of a "time-out" for stopping the momentum of the other team. It is most possible that a defense time-out can break the faculty momentum against you; on your return a whole new area, with which you feel more confident to deal, might be broached. If during the last hour you acquit yourself with competence, nobody is going to weigh your mid-defense break seriously in voting whether to pass you (indeed, most will have forgotten it).

AFTERMATH.

If you are fortunate enough to win an unconditional pass, aftermath is no more than correcting some spellings and grammar (if that), and filing the appropriate number of finished xeroxed copies with your department and the registrar/recorder office. Passes subject to minor or major revisions entail further minor to major substantive dissertation work, and, in the case of passing subject to major changes, another decision about how and when to continue.

If you pass subject to minor revisions, get right on the case. No momentum should be lost here; usually, you can satisfy amendment requirements within a month or two. Precisely as with a proposal passed subject to revisions, make the rounds of the defense committee to "nail down" exactly what they really insist on being altered or elaborated. Remember from our discussion in Chapter Four that some of the suggestions and objections offered are soon forgotten by the questioners; the art of discovering how much they remember and how much they have forgotten is treated there.[3] Sometimes the adviser is delegated by the others to sum up required amendments and police their implementation. If this is program procedure, it is an easier route for the candidate, since the other four defense members will generally sign a final OK without perusal of the changes upon the assurance of the adviser that matters have been altered in accordance with their defense wishes. With the adviser supervising all revisions, the trick becomes to negotiate with *him*, in terms of what he recalls as the salient objections.

Whether he has to make the rounds of the entire defense committee or consult mainly with the adviser, the candidate is guaranteed a more sympathetic reception from faculty than at the much earlier stage of discussion of proposal revisions. Now he has gone through the fire of the defense and is nearly one of them. The candidate should keep in mind this definite and favorable change in his professors' perception of his status and prestige when he sits down at the revision bargaining table. I believe this attitude change applies—although perhaps with more reservation—even to the candidate passing with major revisions. It would be very difficult to draw precise and satisfactory lines between passes subject to minor versus major revisions. Certainly, there is some overlap in the middle, and some programs might go one way or another in a borderline case. Minor revisions generally go to secondary and tertiary matters of substance and methodology: one is asked to elaborate on a theory, thicken a bibliography, further refine the statistical workup and analysis of one section of data. But although changes are a good deal more than cleaning up some preposition-ending sentences or a sloppy abstract, the defense committee has accepted all the major components of the dissertation, and the candidate is "home free." Major revisions, on the other hand, speak to the committee's dissatisfaction with one or more primary components of the thesis: they may be dubious about the theoretical framework; or they may believe the testing of hypotheses was too thin; or that the analysis and discussion section was weak or unconvincing.

The diplomatic procedures for determining just what changes are "nonnegotiable" is the same with this conditional pass as with the pass subject to minor revisions, although in this case the candidate has more at stake since the level of demand is initially higher, whatever the ultimate conditions of the settlement. This means that a skillful candidate negotiator could conceivably knock months off revision work by obtaining a "strict interpretation" (narrow) of the defense committee's demands. It is indeed possible, because of the "give" in the postdefense picture of what happened, for a candidate, for all practical purposes, to turn a pass subject to major revisions into one subject to minor changes, regardless of official labels to the contrary.

If after revision negotiations on a pass with major changes, it becomes clear that, say, another eight months to a year of serious sustained work is still required, many ABDs will no doubt have to deliberate continuing immediately, even going on at all. My own counsel would be to push on through your discouragement as long as you have reasonably tight assurances from the committee that if you make specified revisions they will pass you once and for all. Although it is impossible at the present stage of American graduate education to rely fully on a contract theory of the dissertation in any strict legalistic sense, faculty will almost invariably honor a revision deal made with a candidate who has gone as far in the dissertation course as to have obtained a conditional pass in a full-scale defense.

Is there another formal oral defense after major revisions are made? I have no reliable data on this question, because there is no common policy discernible among the multitude of doctoral programs and committees. Some programs may require some kind of postrevision hearing, but whether it involves the formality of five examiners is doubtful. More common would be the candidate's being asked to meet informally with individual (or a couple of) members of the defense committee to have a "last round" on key revisions. From what I know of these postrevision "mini-defenses" (styled in some elite Ivy League programs as "chats"), I don't believe they are very formidable, or even really of a serious adversary nature at that late point.

A FAILED DISSERTATION.

What, finally, about the case we all dread but don't discuss very often—unconditional rejection of the thesis? It is true that one can pursue appeal and grievance procedures—sometimes full-scale lawsuits—to try to turn around the program's rejection of a thesis. But precedent and the assumption of competence and sound academic judgment on the part of graduate faculty is very much in the appellant's way. If your claim is one of personal discrimination (because of sex, race or serious personal animosity) against you, and thus against your thesis, by one or more thesis or defense committee members, and you can marshal *proof* of that discrimination (either through written documents or witnesses: and witnesses are very hard to come by, since professors, like MDs, will hardly ever testify against each other; and fellow graduate students withdraw at the last moment for fear that testimony will damage their own relations with faculty and jeopardize their dissertations), you have some moderate chance of winning a reversal or new hearing. If you seriously appeal a failed dissertation either on grounds of faculty's academic incompetence (you are arguing that at least five of the graduate faculty, after a judgment based on collective discussion, are wrong about your failure to perform the dissertation contract), or on grounds of personal discrimination, but without solid proof, you are guaranteeing yourself years more of hell, with little chance of ultimate vindication or victory—years which would much better be devoted to picking up the pieces and developing in a new direction.

That "direction"—except in the rarest of cases or circumstances—should *not* be another attempt at a doctoral dissertation, at all costs *never* in the same program, since the failed candidate and the faculty have definitely had it with each other. If another dissertation is mounted, it should come, in my judgment, only after much soul-searching reflection about the pain and life costs of a possible second rejection: years of one's career life have already been wasted, consolatory talk about "having learned something from the experience" being the thinnest and cruelest of sops. Intensive support psychotherapy seems to me much more unarguably indicated and valuable in helping one learn to live with a rejected thesis, than as help in writing one.

SUMMARY.

1. Dissertation subculture portrays the final defense in two contradictory fashions. One version sees it as a mere formality where the faculty judges "rubber-stamp" a foregone acceptance. The other views it as a serious, grueling, adversary procedure where the ABD must fight vigorously to pass a hostile committee. Most real defenses fall somewhere in the middle of these polar constructs, but the candidate is advised to prepare for the most difficult and unsympathetic reception, so that he can take in stride any defense climate which develops.

2. Preparation for the defense has to be conducted in three areas. First, the candidate must possess mastery of all substantive materials. Exercises with the devil's advocate file and "devil professor" role playing in one's dissertation group are useful in acquiring complete reign over materials.

Second, the dissertation must be strategically packaged for committee members. Important packaging elements include: a lucid and comprehensive abstract which appears at the front of the dissertation and, which may be the only part of the thesis read by latecomer defense committee faculty; professionally typed, impeccably edited and corrected copies of the thesis available to judges prior to the defense date.

For reasons which are not entirely clear, past candidates have made little concerted or systematic effort anticipatorily to obtain intelligence about what goes on in the defense, and so a folklore version, accented with fear, has been handed down from one ABD generation to the next. So, third, the ABD can reduce his trepidation about the defense by investigating its format, process and faculty decision options. Later sections of this chapter provide him with some of that information.

3. Defense committees have five decision options: a. to pass the dissertation unconditionally; b. to pass it requiring minor revisions; c. to pass it requiring major revisions; d. to pass the thesis but fail the candidate's unsatisfactory oral presentation and defense; e. to fail the thesis completely, with a judgment that no amount or direction of revisions will make it acceptable.

Passes subject to some kind of revisions are becoming modal. The candidate is urged to prepare himself mentally for construing even a pass requiring major revisions as basically an ultimate acceptance of his thesis. Failure in presentation of an otherwise acceptable thesis is almost always curable by a second formal or informal defense.

4. The conventional, official view of the student candidate set off against a united faculty defense group of five is challenged and replaced by a *realpolitik* model, where the defender is aligned with his long-term committee against—or at least in distinction to—the last eleventh-hour members of the oral defense. Such a realignment calls for an adjusted ABD defense plan, where the candidate plays basically to his thesis committee majority within the larger panel of judges.

5. A typical defense format, in terms of concrete elements such as seating arrangements, duration of the hearing, styles of faculty questioning (round-robin turn-taking versus cross-fire) is described. "Rehearsal" tactics, including visiting the examination room if possible, are indicated. The author anticipates common during-defense crises, such as "going blank," inability to answer particular questions, relentless attack by one judge who is turning the tide against the candidate, and offers some tactics for saving one's defense.

6. Procedures for converting passes with conditions to final passes are outlined. Strategies for negotiating or reducing demands for changes which faculty made during the defense—bargaining processes which are facilitated by the fact that a complete record or transcript of a dissertation "trial" is rarely kept—are discussed. Usually, another formal defense is not scheduled, but revisions are reviewed in informal

meetings with individual defense committee members, or with the adviser deputized to police changes.

7. The chances for overturning a truly failed thesis through appeals or grievance procedures are slim. A second dissertation effort is ordinarily counteradvised. At any cost, if undertaken, it should never be written for the same faculty and program as the first. The usefulness of support psychotherapy in the aftermath of dissertation failure seems less debatable than its effectiveness in helping a candidate successfully to finish.

NOTES

1. Even though the adviser and two other thesis committee members presumably read most of one's thesis, they probably retain, at best, 25 percent. But which quarter? Ah, that is the preparation question.
2. I *still* visit lecture rooms assigned for my courses some days prior to the first day of teaching to get a feel for size and ambience. I sometimes reshape my approach, depending on this reconnaissance.
3. Records of dissertation defenses are very hit or miss. I have never attended one that was taped, nor do we find dissertation stenographers transcribing the minutes. Individual faculty and the adviser/chair may take more or less systematic notes, but certainly talk of a full record is silly. This means that there is indeed room for negotiation about required changes, since a full, objective account of the whole proceedings is not available.

CHAPTER 9

Beyond the Dissertation: Surviving It and Professionally Exploiting It

DISSERTATION DAMAGE.

The ordeal of the dissertation course threatens postcompletion damage to the candidate in one or more of three different ways:

1. Loss of self-esteem, self-respect and self-confidence, the varied manifestations of which were discussed in detail in Chapter Seven, accompanied by counsel for avoiding or at least containing them.

2. Postdissertation paralysis, where the dissertation becomes the end of a career rather than the beginning. Here the candidate spends the next decade locked into a postmortem *angst und dram,* with no time, interest or energy to produce any new piece of work. The productive paralysis extends far beyond writing and researching: the burnt-out, lying-low professor's teaching is uninspired, his counseling of students unenthusiastic. If he becomes a graduate faculty member, he is likely to pass his indifference and negativism on to a new generation of ABDs, perpetuating the tradition of lack of support for dissertation writers.

Postdissertation atrophy is best countered in the manner of rehabilitation for all paralyses: exercise. The indicated exercise is pushing on with a new project after a very brief rest—long-term layoffs are counterindicated. Whether the new Ph.D. should strike off in a new direction or quite soon take up his dissertation for professional exploitation (discussed below) depends on how effectively the writer was able to employ the kinds of strategies for counteracting dissertation traumas, neuroses and disruptions outlined in this book.

213

3. Disrupted and sometimes irrevocably ruptured intimate relationships with spouses, lovers and close friends. Dissertation writing is, as Chapters Two and Seven spelled out, a "high-risk" occupation for divorces and breakups. The best way to avoid them is to attempt to bring your mate or lover into your project. There are styles for effecting this: informing him/her about it on a regular basis, including asking the partner to read and give feedback on sections and chapters as you write them; invitations to occasional meetings of your dissertation support group; having the partner actually work with you on some parts of the dissertation. My wife worked actively with me on a number of key areas of my research: she was responsible for my filing system being as thorough and effective as it was; she shared the enormous hand-tabulated correlation and table-partialing of the data; she provided invaluable angles of analysis when the data seemed to turn against me and my hypotheses. As it turned out, her involvement didn't save our marriage, but it did prevent its last two or three years from deteriorating into the kind of dissertation disaffection and role absenteeism detailed in Chapter Seven. Whatever the style of engaging the nonwriting partner, the idea is to limit as much as possible the other's feeling shut out from a large, unknown, even secret part of your life which is increasingly perceived as coming between you, or taking you away from him/her. How successful the ABD is in bringing the other into the dissertation enterprise depends on the idiosyncratic intellectual and emotional disposition of a particular partner.

In a certain number of cases, individuals will go their own ways after the dissertation. Others will stick with each other, hoping that time will bring matters back to the *ante status quo*. If the partner has continued to see the dissertation as alien and enemy, resisting attempts to bring him/her in, preferring a strategy of "just waiting until it's over" to cure estrangements the prognosis is poor for the two getting back together in the same old predissertation way. Postdissertation life is going to be a series of *new* extended career projects for the successful candidate (albeit probably not so tinged with desperation and anxiety as the dissertation) which the other may well experience as more of the same relationship diminishment.

An ABD who wishes to avoid the "I gave you the best years of my life" confrontation two years after the dissertation has to refrain from making promises he can't or won't want to keep. This entails disabusing one's partner of the idea that if he/she is just patient another year,

214

"it'll be all over," conveying instead that sustained work and a certain amount of role absenteeism will never be "over," from now on are an integral part of your intellectual, professional and emotional life. He/she may not accept this scenario for your future relationship and may decide to part company. The alternatives to honesty are subsequent years of squabbles, guilt-laying by one's partner which cripples every productive enterprise, mutually reinforced and spiraling resentment.

If a spouse or lover cannot accept your postdissertation pursuit of long-term serious writing and research—and this involvement is very important to you (which one would presume it to be for the great majority of persons who took on a task as demanding and unusual as the dissertation)—he or she may not be the "right" person for you in the years to come. The pain or resentment of living with a person who doesn't possess a kindred need to pursue intellectual projects, or at least respect and sympathy for such endeavors, must be experienced to be fully understood. At some point an individual, of course, has to make his own choice, weighing the pros and cons of continuing. It must be acknowledged that some persons of mighty intellect and drive toward publishing choose to stay with mates who are homebody types. Freud's wife kept, by all accounts, a comfortable bourgeois home but does not seem to have been a close intellectual confidante. Marx's wife appears to have offered more in the way of emotional than intellectual companionship. But both of these women were certainly sympathetic to their husbands' continuing projects, if not actively participant in them. A certain amount of complementariness between instrumental/intellectual and expressive/emotional roles in a marriage may be very functional, so long as both partners respect the other's values and worth.

SURVIVAL KIT: DISSERTATION MYTHS V. REALITIES.

Most severe ongoing and postdissertation disturbances develop because the ABD loses perspective about his problem/project and overreacts in desperation. Faulty perspective is often caused by the candidate believing in and living by dissertation myths reviewed in this volume. Postdissertation problems are the historical and biographical culmination of difficulties and distresses developed along the dissertation course; they do not spring from the brow of the defense committee's final inquisition. If such an accumulation, then, is to be prevented, or at least minimized, survival precautions have to be instituted from the start and practiced all along the journey of the thesis. One effective survival technique is neutralization of candidate- and dissertation-destructive myths. What follows is a brief restatement of the major recurring dissertation myths that the book has dissected, along with antidotal realities for neutralizing their detrimental effects on the student at the ABD and postdissertation stages:

1. *Myth:* "I've picked the wrong topic. It's not going to work."

Reality: If you've selected the topic with the care outlined in this volume, it is most unlikely that it will not prove viable. Almost all ABDs believe at one time another along the course that their particular topic was "wrong."

2. *Myth:* "I picked a dull topic."

Reality: Down the dissertation course, all theses go through stages of being perceived as dull or boring by their writers, no matter how exciting, "in" or relevant they appeared at proposal or research time. For their writers, regardless of evaluation by outsiders, all theses are equally dull and tedious in the framework of required research, statistical workup, analysis, writing, rewriting detail.

3. *Myth:* "X had an easier dissertation than mine."

Reality: There never was an easy dissertation. Although your problems and X's may vary both in substantive areas (he had a devil of a time with theory construction, you with statistics) and timing (twice he had to revise his proposal, you had to do two unanticipated pilots for your measuring instruments), the degree of difficulty roughly balances out in the end.

4. *Myth:* "Everybody's finished but me."

Reality: Half or more of the ABDs in your program who started the dissertation when you did haven't finished, either. Nor is there any "quota system," so that even if you do finish a year or two later than some of your cohorts, you'll receive your degree.

5. *Myth:* "Y over at Berkeley scooped me. There goes my thesis."

Reality: The journalistic analogy is invalid for doctoral dissertations. Ten people can, and would, write ten theoretically and methodologically independent dissertations on the same general topic in social sciences, education, humanities or literature.

6. *Myth:* "The faculty is out to get me."

Reality: If faculty have a dissertation supervision vice, it is almost always *indifference,* rather than persecution. It may be that in a given case one particular professor is hostile to a candidate, but to posit a conspiracy of several faculty plotting an ABD's downfall, given the low priority of dissertation supervision for faculty career mobility, is to suffer from dissertation delusions of grandeur.

7. *Myth:* "I'm ruined. The data aren't panning out."

Reality: Outside of "fairy tale" introductory methodology books, the data never pan out with no hitches on first testing of hypotheses with original instruments. In the real world of dissertation writing, everybody has to use a range of *postfactum* adjustments, which are the general norm in social, life and physical sciences.

8. *Myth:* "I'm all alone with an unshareable problem."

Reality: On a purely statistical level, you have the company of over 50,000 other men and women starting out each year to write a dissertation. Although there is undoubtedly an unshareable, lonely core to dissertation writing, its proportion and importance relative to the entire thesis apple can be reduced by reaching out to significant others, particularly a dissertation support group, and receptive spouses, lovers and close friends.

9. *Myth:* "I'm selling my soul to the committee."

Reality: Souls are lost and saved in matters much larger than dissertation negotiations. The faculty-demanded accommodations and revisions that one makes with so much pain (soul-searching) during dissertation days will appear trivial upon five-years-hence reflection (if, indeed, one remembers them at all), especially if one has transacted two or three subsequent major projects.

10. *Myth:* "It won't come in any good, anyway. Ph.D.s are driving taxis."

Reality: You *knew* jobs were tight when you began last year, committed to finishing. So chances are that the recent not-worth-the effort argument reflects a rationale for quitting a tough project, rather than a reevaluation of economic circumstances and possibilities.

11. *Myth:* "When it ends, my career troubles are over."

Reality: Your dissertation is the first in a series of similar long-term projects you will be pursuing throughout your career. Many of the difficulties or "troubles" you have experienced with the thesis are built into academic professions which reward people principally on the basis of their continued production of dissertation-type scholarship and research. Added to the basically noncompetitive conditions of dissertation writing will be the "trouble" of contesting with colleagues for a limited number of tenureships and more senior professorships. The dissertation should be seen as anticipatory socialization for the norms, demands and rewards of an academic career, rather than some kind of "one-shot" discontinuous effort by whose completion the new Ph.D. will have "arrived" once and for all.

It is also doubtful that troubles will be over with lovers and spouses on the issue of your continuing need for large swaths of time in your office for subsequent projects. In truth, you won't be able to "go home again," to the halcyon predissertation, preprofessional days of graduate student existence. And you won't *want* to. You may very well be able to work out a satisfactory new arrangement with family and loved ones, but time for yourself is going to have to be a nonnegotiable condition of the treaty.

12. *Myth:* "Once it's done, I'll never look at the damn thing again."

Reality: Although you may well lay off the dissertation for some undefined period immediately after completion, most candidates find themselves coming back to the thesis for a range of utilitarian purposes and emotional reflection. Dissertation exorcism or banishment attitudes reflect the dissertation-as-enemy theme, which makes it harder to finish; the enemy syndrome can also blind the finisher to his richest and most accessible source of professional capital angrily banished to the back of a filing cabinet.

GETTING PROFESSIONAL MILEAGE OUT OF YOUR DISSERTATION.

The most prominent national policy theme of late twentieth-century America is conservation and maximum exploitation of existing resources and capital. At an individual level, the largest resource or source of capital that the new Ph.D. is likely to possess is his recently completed dissertation.[1] The candidate has made an enormous investment in this project, a kind of "risk venture" that has now paid off. Although he cannot rest for a career on the laurels of this one success, it would be foolish not to exploit it for purposes and payoffs beyond receiving the doctorate. Even if you "hated" your dissertation and swear never to cast eyes upon it again, that mood will pass, and you will want to make use of your large resource in one or more of the following ways:

Publishing It As a Book,

not just in University Microfilms, Michigan. The potential for a dissertation being converted to a book varies enormously with field and subject. Although I played down the specific topic of a disserta-

218

tion as being of primary importance in the decision to write a thesis, a candidate looking way ahead, with serious ambitions and expectations to convert his dissertation into a book, must consider the market for his topic. Of course, even such farsightedness in no way guarantees—or even increases the chances—that a publisher will want to publish an "in" topic dissertation three or four years later; the topic may have "peaked" by then, or the manuscript may be judged of insufficient quality.

Even if a publisher is interested in a dissertation-as-book, editors will insist that it be changed in numerous ways, the most important involving a "translation" from dissertationese to readable English. Then, too, even important, well-researched dissertations display a choppy and sometimes contradictory content and style which reflect the candidate's efforts to meet the demands of various thesis committee members.

People who are "sure" that somebody is going to contract for their dissertations sometimes keep double books—write one version of the thesis for the committee and their degree and another for Random House. My own sense is that this procedure, in the context of the already numerous demands of the dissertation, is too taxing for most ABDs and may well delay the dissertation itself by dividing one's energies. My inclination would be to set up a "conversion" file, where one would annotate areas that would require deletion, elaboration, change in style to qualify for a book; however, such a file should not become a major project in itself during the dissertation course.

It can happen that you *won't want* to publish your dissertation as a book, at least not for a good while, even if offers are made. Your materials may be perceived as damaging, offensive or occasionally even libelous to the group you researched, regardless of how scientifically ethical or objective you considered your procedures and conclusions. When the subjects of your history, political science or sociology dissertation don't come out smelling like roses, it might even be *dangerous* to publish as a book, as opposed to burying your findings in the University Microfilm archives. Contrary to conventional wisdom, one can publish *and* perish!

In my own case, several high-placed chiropractors got wind that my dissertation was critical of their professional organization (it *never* evaluated the therapeutic efficacy of chiropractic itself). On a number of occasions, it was indirectly communicated to me that my own health (chiropractic and otherwise) would be best guaranteed by letting the dissertation lie unpublished. At one point, representatives of one of the chiropractic associations offered to buy my manuscript "for publication." I knew, of course, that what they really wanted was the legal copyright to the materials, so they could prevent it from being published. I refused their offer. Within six months after my dissertation defense, I received serious interest about the thesis from a New England university press but did not pursue this tentative offer, primarily out of fear of unpleasant consequences, including physical retaliation, from the chiropractic profession. Although I used the dissertation in many of the ways discussed below, I never converted it to a book.* As time went by and I became engaged in other areas of sociology, my enthusiasm for such a conversion waned. In my judgment, if one is going to turn dissertation into full-scale book, the iron should be struck while relatively hot, within, say, a year of completion. Otherwise, one is going to encounter large mental obstacles to gearing up and reinvolving on such a complete and detailed scale.

Writing Articles or Book Chapters from the Dissertation.

Although getting a book out of your dissertation is the exception, reworking two or three chapters into journal articles or chapters for edited volumes is common enough to be the rule. The two advantages of this use of the dissertation are: you don't have to reinvolve yourself with the enormous job of reworking the style, organization and substance of the entire thesis; and, for better or for worse, journalese and dissertationese in a given discipline are more or less cognate, eliminating the need for much translation.

The Dissertation As an Important Credential for Teaching or Research Appointments.

It is quite common for employers to ask new Ph.D.s to include their doctoral dissertations (initially the too-often neglected abstract will be required; if the candidate gets to the final rounds of decision, he may be asked to send along the full thesis) in application materials. On more than one occasion I have seen a candidate land an assistant professorship primarily on the grounds of the hiring committee's being impressed with a fine dissertation from a "good" program. Al-

---

*It is ironic that its only major appearance in print comes in this present book on dissertation writing over a decade later.

though the dissertation is frequently crucial in obtaining one's *first* full-time "line, tenure-track" position, it can sometimes be influential as well in later career decisions, such as tenure, promotion or offers from other universities. Almost like the mystique surrounding the Phi Beta Kappa key, there is a kind of continuing corona around the first-rate dissertation which can open many academic and foundation doors for its author.

As an Entrée into the Speciality Area of the Thesis.

The ABD takes a very deep dive indeed into one or more subfields of his discipline. Not only does he become one of the nation's foremost specialists in his selected area during the dissertation course, but he often has occasion to correspond with or meet personally the established leading lights of the speciality to get advice or references concerning fine theoretical and/or methodological problems he has encountered. In my own case, I became a close colleague with a number of prominent medical sociologists, one or two of whom offered to take me on their grants as a "post-doc." Several of my clients have pursued, at my suggestion, correspondence with recognized researchers in their dissertation areas. I have no doubt this will multiply research or teaching opportunities for them. Specialities within disciplines are subcultures within subcultures. If you hook into one of their networks by virtue of your dissertation, the grapevine will spread it about, and you will be sought after. It should be stressed that most often the new Ph.D. has to take the initial step, creating advertisements for himself by contacting the currently recognized authorities in the field.

The Dissertation/Doctorate As Essential for Eligibility for Tenure-Track Professorships.

Until even the early 1970s it was possible to land a tenured university teaching job without the doctorate. Higher education lore is rich in tales and humor about how this was achieved (for even then, the formal rules of most departments required the doctorate for appointment to the rank of assistant professor or above, and for tenure): fifty-year-old men vowing to their university presidents that they would reregister in Ph.D. programs tomorrow; cleverly concocted cases for professors possessing the "equivalent" of an earned doctorate through work and/or experience in the field; sworn affidavits about the ABD

221

defending his dissertation the week after tenure is conferred (a defense which never materializes); even downright lying about possessing a doctorate, when the candidate dropped out of graduate school at a pre-ABD stage. Although it still happens that somebody occasionally squeezes through, enforcement of and adherence to the doctorate-required rule has tightened up to the point of near-universal application. This may be the university-sphere manifestation of post-Watergate aboveboard administrative policies. Even if one managed to be the exception here, his tenure would be limited to the specific university where he squeezed by, in effect sentencing him to career "life" in a particular department.

As a Model for Further Large Scholarly Projects in One's Career.

In the first chapter of this volume I argued that the majority of ABDs are at a loss to research and write the dissertation, because nothing in their theretofore graduate or undergraduate education has prepared them for such a vast and original enterprise. Willy-nilly, the dissertation serves as the great apprenticeship in a given field of intellectual craftsmanship. But the apprenticeship is not the classic one of serving under a master tradesman or senior guild member, since, as we have seen, the graduate faculty is generally unevenly or nondirectively related to one's project. The apprenticeship is a *self*-apprenticeship, where, cut off from pre-ABD graduate faculty support and guidance systems, the candidate has to use his ingenuity and improvisation to solve his dissertation problems.[2] In ways I cannot even count my dissertation has served as a model for me in writing a number of books and long articles. My contemporary style of organization of sections, presentation of materials forcefully to support arguments, analysis of data, construction of tables, figures, diagrams and much much more, all are rooted—not without modification over the years, of course—in that trial of fire and two years' time. I believe most Ph.D.s would similarly link their later work to foundations in their dissertations.[3] The groundwork function of the dissertation for a productive career in one's discipline cannot be overstated.

As a Source for Lectures for Years to Come.

In Chapter Seven I recounted how I used my dissertation as a main subject and departure point for several courses I was teaching during that time. Those lectures had a special vitality because I was living them as I taught them. But the lecture uses of one's dissertation out-live the existentialism of its writing days. A good dissertation is at root not about the culture of law students, or the validity of the Rorschach Test versus the TAT, or a reexamination of party alignments under the Weimar Republic; one starts, of course, with a specific topic, but during the course of the next two years one has to confront all the "big" problems of sociology, psychology, political science or history, with which the field has been engaged, most often for generations. So whatever the specific putative topic, in writing a dissertation one really writes, simultaneously learns, *por la libre,* his own version of the field. In a very real way your dissertation is your own interpretation, reading of, "textbook" on your discipline.

Because of the ABD intensity of your involvement and research, as well as the lonely and self-reliant conditions you must write it under, it may very well turn out to be the deepest and most comprehensive examination of all moments of the field you will ever conduct. Thus, there is a wealth of objectified knowledge capital contained in the dissertation about the ongoing—often "timeless"—core problems and issues of a discipline. Since it is probably your best, certainly your broadest, shot, there is every reason to use and reuse it for lecture materials far beyond the formal parameters of its subject. I have come to believe that the rap against professors constantly harking back to their twenty-year-old notes is often unwarranted. If the basis of those notes is their dissertations, supplemented by more recent literature touching on the same fundamental issues, students are probably get-ting a valid version of a particular course, buttressed by historical connections and continuities, and drawn from the stage in the teacher's career where he most thoroughly investigated matters.

The Dissertation As Support and Validation of Self.

The preceding seven uses of the dissertation dealt with quite spe-cific career objectives. Now we come to three final functions of the dissertation, this and the next one which go to the emotional plane, and number ten which relates to the sociocultural one.

When I first drafted a list of dissertation myths and realities, I in-cluded the "myth," "You'll want to be proud of your dissertation when you look back at it over the years." But although this cannot be a major reason for writing it (indeed, I would contend that overatten-tion to this aim during the research and writing period could lead to

223

delay in pursuit of the *magnum opus* or perfect dissertation—which led me initially to classify it as one of the myths), it is nonetheless very true that long-term pride in the dissertation has important functions.

All of us, no matter what our prior accomplishments, positions or titles, suffer periods of self-doubt about our capacities and strengths. In such times, the dissertation is there as a permanent proof and reminder that one carried through to completion a very large, brave and demanding intellectual and emotional task. I vividly recall crises of self-doubt about my ability or fortitude to produce further major efforts in sociology or fiction, where I turned to the sheer and imposing largeness of my dissertation proper and its files for self-confirmation and validation: "My Lord, look what a work you produced!" Soon thereafter, I would open a new file and start banging away with a new ribbon and a new long-distance project.

The Dissertation As Changing One's Life.

I also believe there is much truth in the maxim that "finishing the dissertation will change your life." This is not to be confused with the aforementioned *myth,* "When it ends, my career troubles are over," but getting the degree does give one a new, prouder, self-esteeming image. It is of course true, as one of my colleagues put it, that if you check yourself in the mirror on the day following your defense you won't see a new person. There are related humorous (humorous at one level, sad at a deeper one) stories about persons who have undergone cosmetic surgery and then been disillusioned and disappointed that their social lives were not drastically ameliorated. But the analogy between getting one's dissertation and getting a "face lift" does not hold in terms of expectable consequences, precisely because the former was achieved and the latter passively received. Obtaining one's degree grants a passport to new circles of friends and colleagues, fundamentally changing the future direction of one's crucial life experiences.

Carrying On the Intellectual Tradition.

In most fields, one has to write the dissertation to be a full-fledged professor. Acquisition of the doctorate, then, allows a person to pursue full-time the life of the mind and train others in such an endeavor. In modern society, with increasingly antiintellectual values being exhibited by our young people, some of us have to "mind the cultural store," serve as role models for the intellectual craftsmanship, discipline and dialectic embodied in dissertations, if a tradition of thinking and scholarship is going to survive. It is in contributing to this vital survival task that dissertation writing and subsequent professing in the university is still a noble undertaking both for self and society, ultimately worth the hassle, pain and loneliness the ABD has to live through to get there.

SUMMARY.

1. The ordeal of the dissertation course threatens postcompletion damage to the candidate in one or more of three different ways: 1. continued loss of self-esteem and confidence; 2. postdissertation paralysis or atrophy, with the doctorate holder unable to produce subsequent work; 3. disrupted or irrevocably ruptured intimate relationships with spouses, lovers or close friends. These last disruptions are analyzed in a framework oriented to the Ph.D.'s future and calculated to reduce the guilt about changed feelings which are so often self- or other-imposed.

2. Postdissertation damage is the historical culmination of difficulties and distresses developed along the dissertation course. If such an accumulation is to be minimized, survival precautions must be instituted early on and practiced all along the journey of the thesis. One effective technique is neutralization of those candidate- and dissertation-destructive myths exposed throughout this book. Here twelve of the major myths are recapsulized, accompanied by their antidotal dissertation realities.

3. Consistent with our national 1980s resource conservation and exploitation emphasis, the completed dissertation is evaluated as the new full-fledged professional's greatest single resource or "capital investment" for his unfolding career. From that perspective, the chapter offers a list of major uses to which the dissertation can and will be put: 1. publishing it as a book; 2. writing articles or book chapters derived from it, if conversion to an entire published volume proves, as it most often will, unfeasible; 3. as an important credential for teaching or research appointments, at both the first and later stages of one's career; 4. as an entrée into the speciality area of the thesis; 5. as essential for tenure-track professorships; 6. as a model for one's subsequent scholarly projects; 7. as a long-term source for lectures.

The preceding uses of the dissertation were specifically related to career opportunities, objectives and problematics. Two more serve emotional functions, and a last relates to socio-cultural contribution. These are: 8. the dissertation as support and validation of self in subsequent years; 9. the dissertation as changing one's life, in the sense of conferring a travel visa into new collegial and friendship networks and circles; 10. licensing one to carry on the intellectual tradition. At a time in our society where intellectual values and pursuits are increasingly under the gun, some men and women have to "mind the cultural store," serve as role models for the intellectual craftsmanship and diligence embodied in dissertations, if a coherent tradition of thinking is to be perpetuated.

Notes

1. Conversely, an alarming amount of lost capital and wasted energy, both for our graduate educational system and the particular casualties affected, is represented in the high rates of nonfinishing for the dissertation doctorate. Although beyond the aims of this volume, plans for restructuring doctoral programs greatly to increase completion percentages are a pressing educational need.
2. In contemporary Cuba, a term one hears frequently is *por la libre,* which refers to myriad ingenious and imaginative ways which the Cubans devised to replace worn-out parts for industry, agricultural machinery, homes and autos denied to them during embargos. The ABD, exposed to a kind of faculty "embargo," often operates perforce *por la libre.*
3. Compare Darwin's assertion that the five years he spent as a young man on the *Beagle,* cruising the South American coastline were far and away the most important formative years in his life, determining all that was to come later in his theoretical modeling and research styles. Nora Barlow, ed., *The Autobiography of Charles Darwin* (New York: Harcourt, Brace, 1959), p. 76.

Index

227

229

Outlining the chapters of the dissertation, 130–31

Pain-as-functional perspective, 163–64
Paralysis, postdissertation, 213
Paris Review, 45
Perfect dissertation, myth of the, 161
Personal relationships, 37–39
  negative effects of dissertation on, 166–69
"Passive-aggressive" professors, 151
Pilot studies or procedures, 103
Postdissertation problems, 213–18
Pride in the dissertation, 223–24
Privacy of dissertation office, 43–45
Professional-degree candidates, 13–14
Professional mileage from dissertation, 218–25
Professors, *see* Faculty
Professorships, tenure-track, 221–22
Progress file/master review, 64–65
Proposal, 72–105
  accepted, 81–84
  appearance of, 92
  chapters of the dissertation and, 130
  conditionally passed, 82–84
  as contract, 73–79
  "contributions to the field" section of, 96–97
  "diplomatic relations" with supervising faculty established by, 85–86
  file on, 60
  "implications of the study" section of, 97–98
  importance of, 72–73
  length of, 81
  "methodological and statistical design" section of, 100–3
  as mini-dissertation, 79–81
  rationale for the study in, 96
  rejection of, 84–85
  "review of the literature" section of, 92–96
  second draft of, 82–84
  statement of the problem and hypotheses in, 98–100
  style of, 92
  timing of, 72
  as topic-decision process, 73
Psychology
  experimental-model dissertations in, 35–36

interpersonal problem processes with faculty in, 152–53
Psychoses, 158–59
  See also Emotional problems
Psychotherapy
  support groups and, 186
  See also Therapy
Publication of the dissertation as a book, 199, 218–20

Reification, 169
Relationships, *see* Personal relationships
Research appointments, dissertation as a credential for, 220–21
Research assistants, 54
Review, master/progress file, 64–65
Review of the literature, computers and, 125
"Review of the literature" section of the proposal, 92–96
Revisions
  affectively-laden, 145–46
  affectively-neutral, 145
  compulsive, 161
  faculty demands for unanticipated, 144–47
Role absenteeism, 167
Role-partner confrontation, 141–44
Role playing in support groups, 187
Role-set analysis, 142
Running, long-distance, 174–75

Sadistic professors, 149
Self-doubt, 162–66
Self-effacement, 166
Self-help techniques, 174–75
Self-validation and confirmation, dissertation as source of, 223–24
"Selling out," dissertation myth of, 146, 217
Sexism, enrollment inequalities and, 7–8
Sexist professors, 149–50
Sociology, functionist and conflict perspectives in, 141
Spouses (or lovers)
  negative effects of dissertation on, 167–68
  postdissertation problems with, 214–15
  at support group meetings, 187–88
  See also Intimate relationships
"Statement of the problem" section in proposal, 98–100

Praise for *Eleanor Roosevelt, Fighter for Justice*

★ "An eye-opening journey through Eleanor Roosevelt's life, career, and social justice work . . . An engaging biography that will greatly enhance middle school collections."
— *School Library Journal*, starred review

★ "Engaging and thought provoking."
— *School Library Connection*, starred review

"An indisputably timely book."
— *Publishers Weekly*

"This biography of Eleanor Roosevelt portrays her as a tireless champion of the underdog and a high-profile advocate for civil and human rights . . . A muscular and admiring profile in moral courage."
— *Kirkus Reviews*

"A worthwhile introduction to one of America's most prominent social activists."
— *The Horn Book*

"An inspiring account of Eleanor Roosevelt's untiring involvement with the major issues of her time."
— *Shelf Awareness*

"Cooper claims her own authorial turf by focusing on Eleanor Roosevelt's championing of civil rights."
— *The Bulletin of the Center for Children's Books*

ILENE COOPER

ELEANOR ROOSEVELT

FIGHTER FOR JUSTICE

HER IMPACT ON THE CIVIL RIGHTS MOVEMENT, THE WHITE HOUSE, AND THE WORLD

ABRAMS BOOKS FOR YOUNG READERS ★ NEW YORK

For Isabel Baker, Laura Bernstein,
Jerry Eichengreen, Beth Elkayam,
Susie Greenwald, and Phyllis Victorson,
dear friends and strong women, each of whom
works hard to make the world a better place

All photographs are courtesy of the Franklin D. Roosevelt Library and Museum, Hyde Park, New York, with the following exceptions: pages 21, 91, 120, courtesy of the Library of Congress; page 112, courtesy of the National Archives.

Excerpts from "Address by Mrs. Franklin D. Roosevelt–the Chicago Civil Liberties Committee," page 158, courtesy of the Estate of Eleanor Roosevelt.

The Library of Congress has cataloged the hardcover edition as follows:

Names: Cooper, Ilene, author. Title: Eleanor Roosevelt : her impact on the civil rights movement, the White House, and the world / by Ilene Cooper.

Description: New York : Abrams Books for Young Readers, 2018. | Includes bibliographical references and index.

Identifiers: LCCN 2017058795 | ISBN 9781419722950 (hardcover with jacket)

Subjects: LCSH: Roosevelt, Eleanor, 1884-1962--Juvenile literature. | Presidents' spouses--United States--Biography--Juvenile literature. | Civil rights movements--United States--History--20th century--Juvenile literature. | Civil rights workers--United States--Biography--Juvenile literature. | Women civil rights workers--United States--Biography--Juvenile literature. Classification: LCC E807.1.R48 C68 2018 | DDC 973.917092 [B] --dc23

Paperback ISBN 978-1-4197-3683-4

Originally published in hardcover by Abrams Books for Young Readers in 2018

Text copyright © 2018 Ilene Cooper

Book design by Sara Corbett

Printed and bound in U.S.A.

10 9 8 7 6 5 4 3 2 1

Abrams Books for Young Readers are available at special discounts when purchased in quantity for premiums and promotions as well as fundraising or educational use. Special editions can also be created to specification. For details, contact specialsales@abramsbooks.com or the address below.

Abrams® is a registered trademark of Harry N. Abrams, Inc.

ABRAMS The Art of Books
195 Broadway, New York, NY 10007
abramsbooks.com

CONTENTS

PROLOGUE

In June 1958, seventy-three-year-old Eleanor Roosevelt, a former First Lady of the United States, was driving through the hills of Tennessee. She was on her way to speak at the Highlander Folk School, an acquaintance at her side, a pistol near her hand. The gun was for protection. The Ku Klux Klan, one of the most dangerous hate groups in the United States, had placed a bounty on her head: $25,000 to kill Eleanor Roosevelt.

Eleanor, the widow of President Franklin Delano Roosevelt, was one of the most admired women in the world. She had earned that popularity by championing the causes of those who needed help getting the rights they deserved: the poor, women, immigrants, refugees. Eleanor's background was one of wealth and entitlement, yet emotionally, she knew what it was like to struggle. Her own insecurities translated into a desire to help others, but to turn her good intentions into action, she had to dig deep inside herself.

Perhaps her most controversial stand was her strong support of African Americans and their fight for civil rights. Many people in the United States turned their heads from the injustices—and the dangers—black people faced. Once she committed herself to the cause, Eleanor Roosevelt did not turn away. Turning away was not her style.

But as much as Eleanor was admired in some quarters, in others she was despised. From 1933 to 1945, when President Roosevelt died in office, Eleanor was a First Lady like no other. She didn't like staying at the White House presiding over luncheons and teas—although she did plenty of that, too—she had things to see, do, and fix. Those who disliked the president and his programs were also appalled that Eleanor had a life of her own—and one that involved being an outspoken advocate for the underdog at a time when prejudices were everywhere. After President Roosevelt died, during an unprecedented fourth term of the presidency, Mrs. Roosevelt kept on fighting injustice.

The Highlander Folk School in Monteagle, Tennessee, where Mrs. Roosevelt was headed that June day, had a decades-long history of working for social change in the country. During the 1950s, activists like Rosa Parks and Martin Luther King Jr. attended sessions on nonviolent protest there. The school had invited Mrs. Roosevelt to speak as part of a civil rights program about ways to protest unfair and immoral social conditions. She probably thought her visit to the Highlander School would just be another of the dozens of speaking engagements she made every year. But then the FBI advised her that a secret informant had told the agency that the Klan intended to stop the speech "even if they had to blow the place up."

The longtime head of the Federal Bureau of Investigation, J. Edgar Hoover, was no friend of Mrs. Roosevelt. He thought she was a dangerous liberal, and he ordered the FBI to follow her activities, bug her phone conversations, and keep a file on what she said and what was written about her. This dossier was begun in 1940, and by the time of her death in 1962, it was more than three thousand pages long!

When the FBI gave Mrs. Roosevelt the news of the threat against her life, they also informed her that if she decided to speak at the Highlander Folk School they could not protect her. Whether they couldn't—or wouldn't—Eleanor Roosevelt understood that if she made the trip to rural Tennessee, she would be on her own. The situation was dangerous, but she believed in the Highlander Folk School's mission and the cause of the civil rights movement.

So to Tennessee she went, determined as usual, but this time with a gun at her side.

ANNA HALL WAS THE BELLE OF HER DEBUTANTE SEASON.

1

GRANNY

Poor little rich girl. If ever a child fit that description, it was young Eleanor Roosevelt.

She was born on October 11, 1884 into a very privileged world. Her mother, Anna Hall, and her father, Elliott Roosevelt, came from wealthy families that were pillars of New York society. Eleanor's early years were lived in city town houses with fashionable addresses and country homes on expansive grounds. She was surrounded by servants and wore dresses made of velvet and lace. There were sea voyages, pony cart rides, plenty of dolls and toys. But one thing Eleanor didn't have: her mother's affection.

"My mother was one of the most beautiful women I have

ever seen," wrote Eleanor as the opening sentence of her auto-biography. This was not just the opinion of an impressionable little girl. Anna Hall Roosevelt, graceful and with striking patrician features, was considered to be one of the great beauties of her day.

Anna's family was among the early arrivals in the country that would eventually become the United States of America. One relative helped draft the Declaration of Independence. Another, in 1787, signed the United States Constitution.

The family of Elliott Roosevelt also had roots in America that were deep and wealthy. Elliott was handsome and personable, and as a boy, it seemed as if he would go far. His older brother, Theodore, was a sickly child who suffered with asthma, so it was Elliott who came first in sports and games.

But then something changed. Theodore decided to exercise and strengthen his body. As he grew stronger, Elliott seemed to become weaker, and he began suffering from all sorts of nervous ailments. By the time they were young men, Theodore took his place as the leader of his family—and eventually of the country. Theodore Roosevelt went on to become the twenty-sixth president of the United States. Elliott devoted his life to good times, travel, dances, and drinking. Lots of drinking.

Still, when Anna Hall and Elliott Roosevelt decided to marry—Anna, only nineteen, Elliott, twenty-three—it seemed like an excellent match: shimmering stars from the same cloistered social circle, a joining of two distinguished families, both partners with enough resources to have a life of style and ease.

Ten months after their 1883 wedding, Eleanor was born. For Elliott, she was "a miracle from heaven." Perhaps Anna had thought that at first, but by the time Eleanor was two, she had given her little daughter a less-than-flattering nickname: Granny. It was a name, Eleanor would say, that made her want to "sink through the floor in shame."

Eleanor describes herself in her autobiography as a shy, solemn child who rarely smiled. This was not the sort of behavior that would have endeared her to Anna, who preferred charm and gaiety. She didn't understand her dour little daughter, and she was disappointed that Eleanor hadn't inherited her good looks. As an adult, Eleanor said that she knew she was "ugly," though photographs show a pleasant-looking, if plain, child. Nevertheless, her sense that her mother disapproved of her was a burden she carried throughout her life.

FIVE-YEAR-OLD ELEANOR AND
HER ADORING FATHER, ELLIOTT

Elliott, though, remained enchanted with his little daughter. Even after the birth of his sons, Elliott Jr. in 1889 and Hall in 1891, his daughter, whom he nicknamed Little Nell, remained his favorite. He loved spending time with her, and when he was away, he wrote her long letters about all the wonderful things they would do when they were together. It comforted and delighted her to receive notes from Elliott in which he remembered the trips they had already taken and offered promises of more: "through the Grand snow clad forests over the white hills, under the blue skies, as blue as those in Italy."

Her father became the center of Eleanor's world. "With my father," she remembered years later, "I was perfectly happy."

Anna, however, was not happy. The fairy-tale version of married life that had been predicted for her and Elliott turned out to be an illusion. It was not long into the marriage that Anna began to suspect that Elliott's drinking was a bigger problem than she could handle. His behavior was erratic, and his trips away, sometimes for pleasure, sometimes to attempt to break his addiction, bore holes into their family.

ELEANOR HAD A LIFELONG LOVE OF HORSES. HERE SHE'S AT GRANDMOTHER HALL'S SUMMER HOME IN TIVOLI, NEW YORK, IN 1894.

Eleanor didn't understand why her father was gone so often, but cherished the time they had together, much of it centered on their mutual love of horses and dogs. But on at least one occasion, Elliott took the opportunity to show Eleanor a very different side of life. Members of the upper classes were expected to be charitable to those less fortunate than themselves, and the Roosevelt family took their responsibility seriously. Both Elliott and his father, Theodore Sr., were supporters of a charity called the Children's Aid Society. One of the society's projects was providing places where the many young boys hawking newspapers on the streets of New York could sleep or get a hot meal for a small fee.

On Thanksgiving and Christmas, the boys enjoyed a free holiday dinner—turkey, ham, potatoes, and pie, the kind of food they rarely saw. One year, when Eleanor was about six, her father brought her to help serve a Thanksgiving dinner to scruffy boys with nicknames like Crutcher and Jake the Oyster at the Newsboys' Lodge. This was an eye-opening event for a little girl who lived in luxury.

Eleanor was also struck by her father's personal generosity. One night he left their house wearing his finest coat. He returned, shivering, his coat gone. Eleanor asked what had happened to it, and he told her he had given it to a "a small and ragged urchin" who needed the coat more than he did.

Through these experiences, and after attending other charitable functions with her family, Eleanor became aware that while her life was blessed with plenty, there were plenty of others who lived in poverty. These lessons, and the importance Elliott put on helping those less fortunate, were planted early and deep.

Wealth was not very helpful to Elliott Roosevelt, however. Each year his drinking became worse and his actions more outrageous. Anna tried to hold her household together while struggling with her own health issues. Then in 1892, while Elliott was away, she came down with a case of diphtheria, an infection that begins with a sore throat and headache. In Anna's case, it ended with death. She was twenty-nine years old.

AFTER ANNA'S DEATH IN 1892, THE CHILDREN'S ONLY PARENT WAS THE TROUBLED ELLIOTT.

It is telling that on hearing the news of her mother's death, Eleanor's first thought was that now her father would be coming home. And though he did return for the funeral, it had already been decided that his children would be best off living with Anna's mother, Eleanor's grandmother, Mary Hall. Eleanor later realized what a defeat this must have been for her father to be separated from her and the boys, to be seen as unable to care for his own children. But at the time, his eight-year-old daughter listened closely as he told her that some-day she would make a home for him and they would travel the world together—"somehow it was always he and I."

This vision of life with her father (she wasn't quite sure where her brothers fit into the picture) helped sustain her when she moved into Grandmother Hall's large New York City brownstone home (in the summer, the family spent time at the Halls' country home in upstate New York, Tivoli). The household was dominated by Eleanor's young aunts and uncles, a rowdy crew in their late teens and twenties who always had drama happening in their lives. Grandmother Hall dealt with the chaos by going inside her bedroom and firmly closing the door.

Eleanor's brothers, five and seven years younger than she, didn't provide much company, and though her aunts and uncles were kind, they were focused on themselves. Elea-nor spent a good deal of her free time living inside her head, spinning daydreams in which she was the heroine and her father was the hero.

In May of 1893, only six months after her mother died, there was another loss. Her brothers both came down with scarlet fever. She was sent to Tivoli so she wouldn't catch the illness, too. There, Eleanor received a telegram from her father telling her that though Hall was getting better, Elliott Jr. was gravely ill and would likely be joining Anna in heaven. The four-year-old died a few hours later.

A little more than a year later, the news was even worse. Nine-year-old Eleanor received the shocking announcement from her aunts that her father was dead. They did not tell her that he had died from complications after attempting suicide.

Eleanor remembered later that she wept and wept, but the following morning she returned to her dreamworld, where her father still lived. She was content to spend much of her time there. "I knew in my mind that my father was dead, and yet I lived with him more closely, probably than I had when he was alive."

The next five years were a difficult and lonely time for Eleanor. Already shy, now she became fearful—of the dark, of displeasing people, of failure. Her life revolved around school and the occasional outing. She also liked to read, and as she grew older, she was left alone to choose what she wanted from the extensive Hall library. That is, until her grandmother started asking questions about books she thought might be unsuitable for a girl of Eleanor's age—then they would disappear. That's what happened to Charles Dickens's *Bleak House*. Eleanor tried to find the novel for days.

A huge disappointment for Eleanor was her grandmother's decision to allow only occasional visits with her father's family, the Roosevelts. Being with her exuberant Uncle Teddy and his family was exhilarating and very outdoorsy—far different from what she was used to at her grandmother's house. But Grandmother Hall, having lost control of her own children, decided to be a stern disciplinarian with Eleanor and Hall. Eleanor described her grandmother's child-rearing theory this way: "We were brought up on the principle it was easier to say no than yes."

So it came as a surprise to Eleanor when she was fifteen that Grandmother Hall told her, "Your mother wanted you to go to boarding school in Europe, and I have decided to send you." It is more likely that Grandmother Hall felt that her children, often wild in their ways, could become a bad influence on Eleanor now that she was a teenager, and so she wanted Eleanor out of the house. "Suddenly life was going to change for me," Eleanor remembered.

She was to attend a school outside London, England, called Allenswood Academy. To leave behind the pain and sorrow of her early life was liberating for Eleanor, but she was also leaving every person and place she had ever known. She would be alone in a school across an ocean, and making new friends was something she did neither easily nor well. It must have taken every bit of strength she had to muster the courage to go. But by now Eleanor knew one thing about herself: "Anything I had accomplished had to be done across a barrier of fear."

2

FINDING HERSELF

After a long ocean voyage, "lost and lonely" fifteen-year-old Eleanor was dropped off at Allenswood Academy by an aunt. In her suitcase was a packet of her father's letters tied with ribbon. But Eleanor didn't have much time to feel sorry for herself. She had entered a dizzying new environment, and she quickly realized she needed to step up.

The headmistress at the girls' school was handsome, silver-haired Mademoiselle Marie Souvestre. She was the kind of woman whose "eyes looked through you," Eleanor later reflected, "and she always knew more than she was told." An avant-garde educator who taught her lessons with intensity

A FIFTEEN-YEAR-OLD ELEANOR AT THE TIME SHE WAS SENT TO ALLENSWOOD

and enthusiasm and prized curiosity in her students, she was also a feminist who wanted her students to know that they could have happy, fulfilling lives, with or without marriage.

The women's movement—the push for women to have equal rights to men, including the right to vote—had been around for more than fifty years by the time Eleanor arrived at Allenswood in 1899. Most people in Eleanor's world were more comfortable with the status quo. Women, at least upper-class women, were raised to be helpmates to their husbands and mothers to their children. Even among the well-educated, few had careers.

Mlle. Souvestre had a different idea. She thought women and girls should be able to think for themselves, find ways to make a difference in the world, and she wanted to instill in them "courageous judgment, and . . . a deep sense of public duty." It was from Mlle. Souvestre, Eleanor later noted, that she learned one of her life's guiding principles: that the "underdog should always be championed."

Almost immediately upon her arrival at Allenswood, Eleanor became Mlle. Souvestre's favorite. One of the rules of the school was that French was the primary language to be spoken.

Eleanor's first nanny had been French, and so as a toddler she'd learned the language before learning English. This fluency gained Eleanor a coveted spot at Mlle. Souvestre's dinner table, where she spoke with her teacher in the woman's native tongue. She was also invited to her teacher's study with other select students to discuss—also in French—literature and poetry.

Teacher and student, over the next three years, became exceptionally close. They traveled across Europe together, and Mlle. Souvestre,

MADEMOISELLE MARIE SOUVESTRE WAS ONE OF THE GREATEST INFLUENCES ON THE LIFE OF ELEANOR.

who was in her early seventies, left it to Eleanor to handle all the arrangements. Those responsibilities gave her a new sense of confidence. Eleanor was also thrilled by her teacher's spontaneity; Mlle. Souvestre readily threw away plans if something more interesting presented itself. After years of doing what she was told, the idea that decisions could be made according to what one found appealing was wonderfully liberating. "Never again," she later wrote, "would I be the rigid little person I had been theretofore."

There was one more thing that Eleanor learned from Mlle. Souvestre. It might seem minor, but it went a long way to boost the girl's confidence: She taught Eleanor how to dress fashionably. For years Eleanor had been embarrassed about her clothes. She had grown very tall very early, yet her grandmother insisted that her skirts remain short, like a child's, although the dresses of other girls swept the floor. When she was finally allowed to dress more age appropriately, her clothes were usually made over from her aunts' hand-me-downs.

Mlle. Souvestere frankly told Eleanor she didn't think much of her clothes. While they were in Paris, she insisted that her student have a dress made just for her. At first, Eleanor was doubtful. She had been taught to be frugal, but Mlle. Souvestre wanted her to have a dress she'd be proud to wear. A flattering, dark-red evening gown was made. Decades later, Eleanor still remembered the joy she felt wearing that dress, and thought fondly of it as the article of clothing that had given her "more satisfaction than . . . any dress I have ever had since."

ALLENSWOOD ACADEMY WAS A SCHOOL WITH THIRTY-FIVE STUDENTS, GIRLS BETWEEN THE AGES OF THIRTEEN AND NINETEEN. THE SCHOOL WAS LOCATED NEAR WIMBLEDON COMMON, OUTSIDE OF LONDON. ELEANOR CAN BE SEEN IN THE BACK ROW, FIFTH FROM THE LEFT.

Often a teacher's pet is not popular with other students. Happily, this wasn't the case for Eleanor. Her fellow students admired her and valued her friendship. Having friends who enjoyed her company and looked up to her was something new for Eleanor, and she relished it. During her three years at Allenswood, Eleanor forged a new, more confident version of herself. Gone were the nervous headaches that had plagued her in New York. She no longer bit her fingernails to the quick. She would have loved nothing more than to stay at school for another year. Nevertheless, in 1902, Eleanor had to return home for a reason that she was dreading. It was time for the eighteen-year-old to make her debut in New York society.

The social season started in November, and young women

in the best families were expected to "come out" into society at fancy balls and exclusive dinners and luncheons. Eleanor's mother, Anna, had been the belle of her social season, and Eleanor was sure her debut would be unfavorably compared with her mother's success, which it was. It was also upsetting to know that the whole point of the season was to focus young women on finding suitable husbands.

Eleanor understood what Mlle. Souvestre meant when she had written to her student upon her return, "Protect yourself, my dear child . . . from . . . society's demands. There are more quiet and enviable joys than to be among the most sought-after women at a ball." Eleanor knew, however, she didn't have any choice in the matter.

The first dress ball she attended was "utter agony." But as the party-filled weeks went on, Eleanor began to feel more comfortable. Her sympathetic manner and intelligent conversation gave her some popularity, even if it was generally with the older crowd rather than her contemporaries. And although she still considered herself homely, she had a willowy figure and luminous blue eyes in her favor.

Eleanor had a lifelong frenemy (though no one knew that word then) in her cousin Alice, the eldest daughter of Theodore

Roosevelt, who was then president of the United States. As a
child, Eleanor had been in awe
of her confident cousin. Alice,
pretty, brash, and outspoken,
considered Eleanor a bit of a
bore—but also a rival for her
father's affections. Theodore
Roosevelt cared deeply for his
niece.

Alice also thought Elea-
nor's descriptions of herself
were made to gain sympathy.
"She was always making her-

ELEANOR AND HER COUSIN ALICE,
THE DAUGHTER OF PRESIDENT THEODORE
ROOSEVELT, WERE TOTAL OPPOSITES:
ELEANOR, RESPONSIBLE, SERIOUS,
AND SHY; ALICE, BRAZEN AND CHATTY.

self out to be an ugly duckling," Alice later observed about
Eleanor during her cousin's debut year, "but she was really
rather attractive." She added, "It's true that her chin went in a
bit, which wouldn't have been so noticeable if only her hateful
grandmother had fixed her [protruding] teeth."

It wasn't all parties and teas for Eleanor after her return
to New York. She took on the responsibility of overseeing
the boarding-school education of her bright eleven-year-old

brother, Hall, whom she had showered with letters while she was abroad, and she took charge of the family's New York City town house, where she lived while her aunts and uncles flitted in and out.

Then Grandmother Hall decided the town house was too expensive to maintain, so she closed it up and moved to Tivoli. Elliott Roosevelt had run through most of his money before he died, so Eleanor only had a small inheritance to live on. Once more, she was at the mercy of relatives to take her in. Now it was her cousin and godmother, Mrs. Susie Parish, who gave her a place to live. The feeling that she never had a home of her own was something Eleanor struggled with well into adulthood.

Anxious to find a way to make her life more meaningful, Eleanor joined the Junior League. This was a newly formed organization of young socialites, like herself, who wanted to work on the many problems that faced the millions of immigrants who were flooding New York City. Jewish, Irish, Italian, they came to the United States fleeing danger and poverty or in search of a better life. They did find opportunity and freedom, but there was also uncertainty; crowded, unsanitary living conditions; and for those who found work—and that included children—endless hours of toil for low wages.

Eleanor wanted very much to help. But unlike many of the Junior League members who were content to hold fund-raising events, Eleanor was determined to be personally involved. She had never forgotten how, as a child, she had gone with an uncle to bring Christmas presents to children living in the worst part of the city, Hell's Kitchen. She had tagged along with her young aunts when they volunteered at a mission in another poor part of town, the Bowery. The Thanksgiving visit to the Newsboys' Lodge remained an outstanding memory of her father and a reminder that he often told her to grow up to be a woman he could be proud of. During the winter of 1903, Eleanor began volunteering at the settlement house on Rivington Street in New York's Lower East Side.

Settlement houses were like community centers where neigh-borhood residents

THE RIVINGTON STREET SETTLEMENT HOUSE WAS LOCATED ON NEW YORK CITY'S LOWER EAST SIDE, A PART OF TOWN OVERFLOWING WITH IMMIGRANTS WHO NEEDED HELP ADJUSTING TO THEIR NEW LIVES.

could go to takes classes to learn English and get help in practical pursuits like finding jobs and honing household skills. Young children were offered day care, and teaching little ones was where Eleanor found her niche, conducting classes in exercise and dance. Eleanor admitted that at first she didn't know what she was doing, but that didn't stop her from trying.

She also got to see firsthand, as one of her biographers put it, "misery and exploitation on a scale she had not dreamed possible." The people who came to the settlement house lived crammed together in tiny, dingy apartments called tenements. The bathroom facilities for these tenement dwellers were outdoors and shared by all the residents.

Sometimes Eleanor was frightened to be out on the dirty, dark streets of the Lower East Side, but she got great joy from the children she taught. When a father of one of her students gave Eleanor a small present because the child enjoyed her classes so much, Eleanor felt a "glow of pride."

But teaching wasn't the only way that Eleanor was involved with the immigrant community. While she was working at the Rivington Street Settlement House, a study was made of the working conditions of poor immigrant women and girls who earned money sewing garments in factories. The shocking report showed that working fourteen hours a day, six days a week for a wage of six dollars was not uncommon. Eleanor joined the National Consumers League, a group that wanted to change things, including by putting limits on child labor and pushing enforcement of the law allowing only a sixty-hour workweek.

Eleanor took on the job of inspecting these unsafe factories, called sweatshops, where women and girls labored over their sewing machines. "I was appalled . . ." she wrote in her autobiography. "I saw little children of four or five sitting at tables until they dropped with fatigue."

Something was stirring in Eleanor Roosevelt. The ideals of Mlle. Souvestre and Elliott's hopes for her were becoming realized in her work with the women and children of the immigrant community. Being useful, she found, was immensely satisfying.

But other feelings were stirring as well. Perhaps to her surprise, she had caught the fancy of a handsome young man, a distant cousin, and he wanted to marry her. She was only nineteen and he just a few years older, but that didn't matter, nor did the objections of his mother.

Eleanor was in love, and she could think of nothing more wonderful than becoming Mrs. Franklin Delano Roosevelt.

THE ENGAGED ELEANOR
AND FRANKLIN IN 1906

LOSING HERSELF

"Oh! Darling, I miss you so . . .
So very happy in your love dearest, that
all the world has changed for me . . ."

YOUR DEVOTED LITTLE NELL

Eleanor's signature in this 1904 letter to Franklin said as much as the loving words. Her father had called her Little Nell. Now she was sharing the cherished nickname with someone else who said he loved her.

How did Eleanor and Franklin get together? In some ways, they'd known each other practically all their lives. The large Roosevelt family tree had many branches. The couple were not only fifth cousins, but Eleanor's father, Elliott, was also Franklin's godfather—though he must have rarely seen him, since he didn't spend much time with his own children. Family lore recounted how Eleanor and Franklin had met on a visit when she was just two—the little boy gave her a piggyback ride. Over the years, they saw each other occasionally at family functions. Once, when she was fourteen and he sixteen, he asked the shy wallflower to dance at a party, a gesture that earned her gratitude.

Their relationship had its more serious beginning when they met by chance on a train in 1902, the summer before her debut into society. Franklin would start his junior year at Harvard in the fall. At Franklin's invitation, Eleanor rather nervously joined him and his formidable mother, Sara. Afterward, the young couple struck up a correspondence and then found reasons to be together—a lunch here, a dance there—though rarely unchaperoned. Well-brought-up young women were not supposed to be alone in the company of single men.

Soon the couple's feelings for each other began to grow. Being in the same social circles, they could be together at parties and balls, and Eleanor was also invited to parties at Franklin's family's summer home on Campobello Island in New Brunswick, Canada. Still, they tried to keep their budding relationship under wraps. It was in 1903, during a football weekend at Harvard, that the couple snuck away long enough for Franklin to propose.

Thousands, maybe millions, of words have been written about the relationship of Eleanor and Franklin Roosevelt and how different they seemed, at least on the surface. Certainly their childhoods had been almost polar opposites: Eleanor, an orphan, at the mercy of relatives, and without a home to call her own. Franklin, the cherished child of two devoted parents who gave him almost anything he wanted and doted on his every accomplishment. His growing-up years were idyllic, spent in the family home, Springwood, in Hyde Park, New York, on the banks of the Hudson River. He went swimming and boating in the summer, ice-skating in the winter, and all through the year enjoyed discovering the lush natural world that was right outside his window.

In personality and appearance the young couple seemed to be opposites as well. Where Eleanor was plain, shy, serious, and burdened with responsibilities before she was even a teenager, Franklin was handsome, outgoing, eternally optimistic, and carefree. One story has it that when Franklin proposed to her, Eleanor wondered aloud what he saw in her.

What he saw, as he put it even before they were courting, was a young woman with "a very good mind." As Franklin came to know Eleanor better, he was impressed with her intuitive and sympathetic nature. Perhaps inspired by his cousin Theodore, Franklin had big plans for his future, and he wanted a wife who was not just a pretty decoration but someone in whom he could confide. In answer to her question, he told her he was sure he could become something "with your help."

Despite the couple's differences, they held important values in common, and these were a bond. Franklin felt, perhaps not as deeply as Eleanor, but felt nonetheless, the importance of doing good. He would, on occasion, accompany her home after her classes at the Rivington Street Settlement House—an endeavor he supported—and his conscience was stirred by what he saw. Once, he went with her to take an ill student home and was shocked to see firsthand what tenement life was like. "My God," he said, "I didn't know people lived like that."

At Harvard, Franklin had written a paper about his family and their long history in America and concluded that their success came, in part, because of their sense of civic responsibility: "Having been born in a good position, there was no excuse for them if they did not do their duty by their community." His father, James, whom he much admired and who had died when Franklin was eighteen, had also urged him to think about his responsibilities to other people.

His mother, Sara, however, wanted him to think mostly about his responsibility to her. Sara Delano was twenty-six when she married James, who was then twice her age. Nevertheless, they were a congenial couple, and when Franklin was born, Sara felt her world was complete. She not only adored her only child, she wanted to keep him close; so much so that while other boys of his social class entered boarding school at twelve, she kept him home for another two years. When he started at Harvard, she took an apartment in Boston to be near him.

Having been around Sara and hearing the family gossip, Eleanor probably knew how tightly his mother tied Franklin to her apron strings. If not, Alice, with her sharp tongue, might have told her. She described him derisively as a "good little mother's boy." Eleanor probably wasn't even terribly surprised that after Franklin confessed to his mother that he'd proposed, Sara insisted they postpone the announcement, during which time Sara would take Franklin on a cruise.

ELEANOR'S WEDDING PORTRAIT.
SHE AND FRANKLIN WERE
MARRIED ON MARCH 17, 1905.

Although she didn't quite come out and say it, the purpose of the trip was to make Franklin forget about Eleanor.

Despite all of Sara's machinations, in the end she couldn't stop the wedding, which was to take place on March 17, 1905. Theodore Roosevelt had promised to give his niece away at her wedding, but since he was president, the event was hard to fit into his busy schedule. The date was chosen because he was going to be in New York for the St. Patrick's Day parade. After he was done marching, he would escort Eleanor down the aisle.

The wedding took place in a relative's home, a lavish affair with two hundred guests and six bridesmaids, including Alice. No one had considered that with the parade route so close to the wedding, the guests would have trouble reaching the house. Eleanor remembered years later, "A few irate guests arrived after the ceremony was over!" Those in attendance saw a stately Eleanor, dressed in satin and lace, carrying a lily of the valley bouquet, escorted down the aisle by her uncle, the president. Waiting at the altar was her handsome groom.

When the ceremony was over, President Roosevelt congratulated Franklin for keeping the name in the family and made a beeline for the refreshments. To Sara's indignation, the guests followed the witty, outspoken president and left the bride and groom standing alone. Eleanor shrugged it off. "I do not remember being particularly surprised at this," she recalled later. She and Franklin followed the laughter into the next room.

★

After a three-month honeymoon in Europe, Eleanor came home pregnant, and the first of their children, Anna, was born in 1906. After that, the babies came in rapid succession: James (1907); Franklin, Jr. (1909), who died at eight months old; Elliott (1910); another Franklin (1914); and finally John (1916).

Eleanor was uncomfortable with motherhood, and it showed. She veered from being too strict with her children to trying avant-garde methods of child-rearing—like rigging up a wire contraption to hold Anna outside a window after she read that fresh air was good for babies!

Without a real childhood of her own to use as a blueprint, she didn't know how to play with her children or be light-hearted around them, though sometimes she tried. Franklin, by contrast, with his big, boisterous personality, delighted in rolling around with his chicks, as he called them. But whether

ELEANOR AND FRANKLIN ON THEIR HONEYMOON IN SANREMO, ITALY

he was home or, as was often the case, busy with work, Eleanor was left to be the disciplinarian.

As adults her children described their mother as distant, dutiful, but unable to enjoy them. Eleanor, looking back, said that regretfully she didn't know anything about being a mother.

Sara took full advantage of this weakness. In many ways, often quite brazenly, Sara undermined Eleanor's mothering. She hired the help, who were loyal to her, won the children over with gifts and trips, and convinced herself she was more important to the children than their mother. She once told her grandson John, "Your mother only bore you. I am more your mother than your mother is."

Though her appropriation of the young Roosevelts may have been Sara's most outrageous action, it was at the top of a very long list of slights, insults, and overbearing behavior. The year Eleanor and Franklin married, Sara gave the young couple a Christmas gift—a drawing of a New York City town house that she was building for them. Actually, there were to be two town houses, one for them and one for Sara. The houses were connected by sliding doors through adjacent walls on three different levels.

Eleanor, afraid of displeasing Sara, went along with the decision to live so close together, but the house would remain a sticking point between them. Sara never stopped coming through those connecting doors. Eleanor remembered bitterly, "You were never quite sure when she would appear, day or night."

THE DRAWING OF THE TOWN HOUSE THAT SARA WAS HAVING BUILT FOR ELEANOR AND FRANKLIN. IT'S SIGNED, "FROM MAMA."

And where was Franklin in all this? Pretending as if the acrimony wasn't happening. Eleanor came to realize that no matter how much she longed for her husband's support, he wasn't going to take sides. He disliked unpleasantness and assumed eventually the two women would work things out.

Eleanor's unhappiness went on for years. Her frustrations and anger boiled into what she would call her "Griselda moods," named after a put-upon wife in Chaucer's *The Canterbury Tales*. The harder she tried to be the dutiful wife,

ELEANOR'S DISSATISFACTION
WITH HER LIFE LEFT HER THIN AND
UNHAPPY. EVEN AFTER SHE GAINED
MORE CONTROL OVER HER LIFE,
BOUTS OF DEPRESSION WOULD
CONTINUE TO PLAGUE HER.

mother, and daughter-in-law, the more disagreeable—and depressed—Eleanor became.

Meanwhile, Franklin was forging ahead in his career. He had gone to Columbia Law School and supported his family while living in New York working at a law firm.

But being a lawyer didn't really suit the outgoing Franklin. He had higher ambitions, and the example of his cousin, President Theodore Roosevelt, showed him that politics might be a way to satisfy both his ego and his desire to be in public service.

In 1910, the Democratic Party asked him to run for the New York State Senate as a candidate from the Hyde Park area. Franklin was eager to take up the challenge, but the fact that he was a political novice showed. The first time Eleanor heard him make a speech, he spoke so slowly and his pauses were so long, "I worried for fear he'd never go on." Speaking style notwithstanding, he won, becoming the first Democrat to take the seat in thirty-two years. The town house was rented out and the family moved to Albany, the state capital. Eleanor hadn't been especially keen on Franklin getting into politics, but it did have one advantage: Sara didn't move with them. Nevertheless, she kept her presence felt with frequent visits.

Albany was a revelation for Eleanor. She thought politics

and government were going to be her husband's work. But as she soon learned, the politician's wife also had a role to play. Eleanor had to conquer her shyness and become Franklin's helpmate, hosting teas and luncheons and calling on the wives of allies and sometimes rivals. At first, for Eleanor this was just doing her wifely duty. As she put it, "Duty was perhaps the motivating force of my life . . . I looked at everything from the point of view of what I ought to do, rarely from the standpoint of what I wanted to do." But slowly, she became interested in what made government work and in the men—almost exclusively men—who pulled the political levers.

She looked for ways to be involved. She made social connections with government officials and their wives and figured out ways for Franklin to make political alliances, even with enemies. During Franklin's time in the state senate, Eleanor made it a practice to invite both sides of a political dispute to her home and make friends with everyone involved. "The first requisite of a politician's wife," she said, "is always to be able to manage anything." As one friend put it, "She was playing the political game far better than anyone else," but it was a game built on her real interest in people and her growing realization that the idea of championing the underdog was resurfacing as an important part of her life. As her success in political life grew, she began to build a strong base of political support for Franklin—and eventually for herself.

When it was time for Franklin to run for reelection, a man who would become an important influence on both Roosevelts stepped into their lives, Louis Howe. Howe saw a great future for Franklin Delano Roosevelt far beyond the New York State Senate. Howe became Franklin's closest adviser and helped him win his reelection race in 1912.

Initially, Eleanor, as she put it, "was not favorably impressed." A short, scrawny former newspaperman with a pockmarked face, a remnant of a serious childhood accident, Howe called himself one of the homeliest men in New York. And while

LOUIS HOWE, TRUSTED ADVISOR OF BOTH FRANKLIN AND ELEANOR, DRESSED CASUALLY AT HIS HOUSE ON HORSENECK BEACH IN MASSACHUSETTS

people did say he looked like a troll, it wasn't his looks that bothered Eleanor: It was his nonstop cigarette smoking that drove her crazy. He befouled the air and left ashes all over her house—and himself. It took a while for Eleanor to appreciate his political skill and personal devotion to the Roosevelts.

During the 1912 election, Franklin had campaigned hard not just for himself but for the Democratic candidate for president, Woodrow Wilson. Though loyally sticking with their party, this decision was awkward for Franklin and Eleanor because Theodore Roosevelt was running as a third-party candidate. Cousin Alice, though she remained friendly, especially with Franklin, never quite got over this betrayal.

Another family issue for Eleanor in 1912 was the marriage of her brother, Hall. Only twenty, he had been an excellent student at both his boarding school, Groton, and later at Harvard. Hall seemed to be making his way in the world, and his wife-to-be was a beauty. At the wedding, Eleanor said she "felt as if my own son and not my brother was being married." But despite his academic success, Eleanor was worried about her brother. It was clear that Hall was very much his father's son: He drank too much. She was right to be concerned. His drinking would get worse as the years went by.

It was only a few months after Franklin's reelection to the state senate that the new president, Wilson, rewarded his election loyalty by appointing him—at only thirty-one years old—assistant secretary of the navy. The job in the new administration was a huge step up from state politics, and, in fact, was the same job that had launched Theodore Roosevelt's political career culminating in the presidency. The secretary of the navy, Joseph Daniels, Franklin's boss, noted that fact in his diary with the hope, "May history repeat itself." Clearly some people were already seeing great things ahead for Franklin Delano Roosevelt.

While her husband got to work in March of 1913, Eleanor was left with the huge job of moving her family to Washington, D.C. Once again Eleanor was nervous about change, but building on the skills she'd learned in Albany, she learned her way around Washington and figured out how to navigate D.C. society's strict protocols. She also felt much more confident as a mother (and as in Albany, happy to be away from Sara's prying eyes). Franklin Jr. and John, who were born during this time in Washington, were raised by a much more relaxed mother.

Theodore Roosevelt, more forgiving than his daughter, was proud that Franklin held his old position in the navy. He recognized what others did—that Franklin, with his ability, wit, and charm, was a rising political star. In 1916, Woodrow

Wilson was reelected as World War I was raging in Europe. Wilson's position had been one of American neutrality, but when Germany sank American ships, the United States entered the war on April 6, 1917. Franklin's position at the navy now became even more important.

Once the United States was in the war, Eleanor noted, "the men in government worked from morning until late into the night. The women in Washington . . . began to organize . . . to meet the unusual demands of wartime." For Eleanor that meant volunteering at naval hospitals and at the Red Cross canteens, doing everything from making sandwiches (and once almost slicing off a finger while cutting bread) to supervising volunteers to washing floors. Getting out in the wider world— outside of politics—made her happy and broadened her perspective. "I became a more tolerant person, far less sure of my own beliefs . . . I knew more about the human heart."

Eleanor had her hands full juggling the responsibility of children, her volunteer work, and the role of political hostess. She had servants to help run the house, but in 1914, she hired pretty twenty-two-year-old Lucy Mercer as her social secretary. Lucy, from a good but poor family, needed the work and did her job efficiently and with good humor.

Eleanor became very fond of Lucy, and so, as it turns out, did Franklin. Eleanor was not always in D.C., especially during the brutal, humid summers. She would take the children to stay with Sara at Springwood, or all of them would travel to Campobello Island.

The attraction between Franklin and Lucy grew, and they began a romance that flourished during Eleanor's absences. Some in Washington guessed about

LUCY MERCER, CIRCA 1915

the affair; others knew—including Alice, who took a certain amount of glee in dropping veiled hints to Eleanor. When Franklin canceled a trip to see the family on Campobello Island during the summer of 1917, Eleanor became suspicious.

In September 1918, the bottom dropped out of thirty-four-year-old Eleanor's world. Franklin came home after a work-related trip to Europe feeling unwell. Eleanor unpacked his bags. Tucked away, she found a packet of letters tied with a piece of velvet ribbon. As she read them, she

43

realized they were love letters from Lucy. The letters were the confirmation she'd been dreading. Eleanor immediately marched into Franklin's sickroom, letters in hand, and told him she would give him a divorce. Divorce was frowned upon at that time, but an angry Eleanor was ready to take that step.

Franklin may have wanted to marry Lucy, but reality intruded in the forms of Sara Roosevelt and Louis Howe, who'd moved to Washington to work for Franklin. Sara was furious. She told her son if he did something as scandalous as abandoning his wife and children, she'd snap her purse shut: Franklin would not have access to her considerable wealth. Louis, who believed that someday Franklin would be president, told him divorce and remarriage would mean his political career was over.

Franklin decided to stay in his marriage, and Eleanor agreed—with the stipulation he would never see Lucy again. Though the couple was going to stay together, Eleanor, shattered by the deception, was determined their life together would now be on a new footing. She appreciated Franklin's skill as a politician; she felt he had an important role to play in government and in the country. He was the father of her children, and she understood that in some way, she was going to have to continue in the role of his wife. But Franklin was no longer her great love, or if he was, she could no longer admit it.

Things were going to be different. Eleanor knew she would now have to decide what *she* wanted to do with her life—and then figure out a way to do it.

WITH NO MOTHER OF HER OWN, ELEANOR TRIED HARD TO FORGE A RELATIONSHIP WITH SARA. ALTHOUGH THERE WERE HAPPY MOMENTS AND TIMES OF AGREEMENT, ELEANOR FELT LIKE SHE WAS IN A DECADES-LONG TUG-OF-WAR WITH HER MOTHER-IN-LAW.

4

A LIFE TO BE LIVED

nce they decided to stay together, Franklin and Eleanor tried to mend the cracks in their marriage. Yet the deceit ate away at Eleanor, literally—she developed a form of anorexia. She also lost a good deal of the hard-won confidence she had worked for over the years. Still, she was ready to turn around her life. One defining moment came when she attended the funeral of Grandmother Hall at Tivoli in 1919. During the service, Eleanor pondered her grandmother's unhappy, unfulfilled existence. After being widowed, Mary Hall had done little with her life but try—unsuccessfully—to cope with her children. What a waste. Eleanor came away with one conclusion:

"Life was meant to be lived." And lived to the fullest on one's own terms.

FRANKLIN, SARA, ELEANOR, AND THE FIVE ROOSEVELT CHILDREN IN 1920

Eleanor set about making changes. For her own interest, she took typing and business classes. And she began taking charge of her household, to Sara's annoyance. In 1919, Eleanor dismissed all the white servants Sara had hired over the years and replaced them with black staff. Years later she wrote that perhaps it was "the Southern blood of my ancestors [who had owned slaves], but ever since I had been in

Washington, I had enjoyed my contact with such colored people as came to work for me. I never regretted the change which I made when I completely staffed my house with colored servants." This statement showed a naïveté about race relations, generally and personally.

Despite her previous interest in the plights of immigrants, Eleanor paid virtually no attention to the difficulties of African Americans, who faced prejudice every day. It would be almost two decades before she came to this understanding, despite her awareness of the great turmoil in the black community.

In 1919, while Franklin was serving as assistant secretary of the navy, terrible race riots rocked Washington, D.C. African American soldiers who thought fighting in World War I would open job opportunities or somehow decrease prejudice came home to even more segregation. As one historian put it, "The benefits of the war to make the world safe for democracy was restricted to whites."

The Ku Klux Klan was active, and not just in the South. Racial tensions spiked. In most cases, whites attacked blacks, and blacks fought back in more than thirty cities across the country during that hot summer. Washington, D.C., was one of them. Eleanor, who was at Campobello with the children, was worried about Franklin's safety, as her letters show: "No words from you and I'm getting anxious because of the riots. Do be careful not to be hit by stray bullets." The next day she added, "Still no letter or telegram from you and I'm worried to death."

Eleanor's and Franklin's concern in their continuous correspondence was for his personal safety. They didn't mention the riots in Washington, D.C., that left fifteen people, both white and black, dead, and many, many more injured. Nor did they discuss why the riot in Washington, D.C., was only one of dozens of race altercations across the United States that year. These riots and the lack of protection from law enforcement galvanized the African American community, and a new civil rights movement was born, though Eleanor and Franklin seemed oblivious to it.

Through much of Eleanor Roosevelt's adulthood, a thread emerged. She began to care for repressed communities when she came to know their members as individuals. As a young woman, she had casually made anti-Semitic comments; prejudice against Jews was common in her social circle. Her feelings changed when she made close friends who were Jewish. In 1919, she didn't know any African Americans except as servants. She may have felt sympathy for those who had been killed or wounded, as a general matter, but she had little interest in the root causes of black anger.

If the plight of African Americans was not a concern to Eleanor, there was one cause that caught her full attention after World War I. Eleanor became involved in the push for women's voting rights.

The fight to get women the right to vote in the United States had been going on since the 1850s. Women's suffrage had never been of much interest to Eleanor. She had always assumed men were "superior creatures" and could handle the voting. It was actually Franklin who became a suffragist first, in 1912. He was a state senator when a bill allowing women to vote in New York was presented to the legislature, and he backed it. Franklin's stance woke Eleanor up. It soon became apparent to her that the progressive reforms she was interested in seeing come about—better working conditions, child welfare laws, improved housing—would have more of a chance of happening if women could vote.

In 1920, the Nineteenth Amendment to the U.S. Constitution was ratified, and women were granted the right to vote (although some states had granted this previously). In less than three months, women were allowed to vote in a national election for the first time. Eleanor enthusiastically voted, and she also decided to get more involved by joining the League of Women Voters. The league's purpose was to inform women about issues and encourage them to get involved in the political process. Eleanor's talent for leadership was quickly recognized, and she was soon appointed to the league's board.

There was another important element to the 1920 presidential election for the Roosevelt family. Franklin, who had left his navy job to return to politics, was chosen to run for vice president on the Democratic ticket with presidential nominee James Cox. Once again, Eleanor was again asked to play the role of political wife, now following Franklin on the campaign trail. The long train trips around the country bored her at first. One of her chief jobs was motioning to her husband when he talked too long. His oratory had vastly improved since his first speeches, but he never spoke for five minutes when he could stretch it to ten.

Louis Howe saw more important work for Eleanor, however. Over the years, he had remained indispensable to Franklin, and Eleanor had come to appreciate his skills and overlook the cigarette ashes. Louis, for his part, had always been impressed by Eleanor's brains and instincts. He sought her input during the 1920 campaign, giving her early looks at Franklin's speeches and encouraging her to voice her opinions. He made sure to introduce her to both the politicians and newspaper reporters they met as they crossed the country, and she made friends in both groups. And perhaps just as important, he taught her how to speak in public effectively.

BEFORE TELEVISION, AND LONG BEFORE SOCIAL MEDIA, CANDIDATES FOR NATIONAL OFFICE CONDUCTED CAMPAIGNS BY RIDING TRAINS ACROSS THE COUNTRY, STOPPING IN CITIES AND TOWNS TO TALK TO VOTERS.

All Eleanor's insecurities came back in front of an audience. Her hands shook, her high voice could become screechy. Sometimes she would giggle from sheer nervousness. Louis, experienced in the ways of campaigns, worked with Eleanor and gave her simple rules she could follow that both calmed her and made her a much better speaker. His advice was: "Have something you want to say, say it, and sit down."

Almost everyone knew that the Cox-Roosevelt ticket didn't have much chance of winning, and it did lose to the Republican, Warren G. Harding, who became the twenty-ninth president. But during that campaign, Louis and Eleanor forged an unbreakable bond. Here was someone, Eleanor felt, who understood her and knew how to channel her energies. Louis was insistent in his belief that Franklin would be president of the United States and told Eleanor when Franklin's term was finished, he would make *her* president!

After Franklin's vice presidential loss, the family returned to their town house in New York City, and he to careers in both law and business. He hadn't made much money during his years in government and was eager to support his family without help from Sara.

For Eleanor, her confidence restored, the time had come to truly take back her life. Along with the League of Women Voters, she joined other progressive women's organizations dedicated to social change. Through this network, she made friends who broadened her horizons about everything from poetry to politics. These "New Women," as they were nicknamed, reminded Eleanor of Mlle. Souvestre and her ideas and ideals. Often unmarried or living with other women in same-sex relationships, members of Eleanor's circle were passionate about social reform and were not afraid to organize for political power. Eleanor felt comfortable with these bright and dedicated friends. They exemplified her goal of living life on one's own terms, and she was inspired by them. They were responsible, as she put it, "for the intensive education of Eleanor Roosevelt."

Then, in the summer of 1921, something happened that turned Eleanor's life upside down and threatened to dash every one of Franklin's political dreams.

It was August, and the Roosevelt family was on Campobello Island. They had spent a busy day sailing, swimming, even helping put

FRANKLIN AND ELEANOR ON CAMPOBELLO ISLAND. FRANKLIN'S PARENTS HAD HAD A HOME THERE SINCE 1883, AND IT BECAME A SUMMER HOME FOR ELEANOR AND FRANKLIN'S FAMILY. HERE THE COUPLE ENJOY THE BEACH IN 1920, THE SUMMER BEFORE HE CONTRACTED POLIO.

out a small fire on one of the neighboring islands. Franklin came down with a chill, and then he began running a fever. He went to bed, but the next morning he noticed his legs weren't working properly. Horrified, he soon realized that he was paralyzed from the waist down.

The local doctors were not able to make a diagnosis as Franklin's high fever grew worse. Finally, a specialist was brought up from New York. He gave the family the devastating news. Franklin had infantile paralysis—polio. Though the disease mostly struck children, adults were certainly not immune. Today, vaccination has wiped out polio in the United States, but in the 1920s, there was no cure and almost no treatment. It was a disease that frightened everyone, and the Roosevelts were no exception.

Eleanor sprang into action. She became Franklin's devoted nurse, exhausting herself. A doctor told her, "You will surely break down if you too do not get immediate relief." Eleanor did get assistance from the ever-present Louis Howe. Together, they took care of Franklin—bathing and massaging him, even brushing his teeth—until they could move him back to New York. Franklin, an optimist by nature, assumed that eventually he would fully recover, and Eleanor became his cheerleader.

It slowly dawned on all the Roosevelts that this wasn't to be. Over time, Franklin taught himself to shuffle his heavily braced legs forward for short periods, as long as he was holding on to someone's arm or on crutches, and to stand if gripping a lectern while giving a speech. But despite the appearance of movement, he never really walked by himself again. Although the public rarely saw it, Franklin spent most of his waking hours in a wheelchair.

Sara had been in Europe during the first few weeks of Franklin's illness. Upon her return, and as his prognosis became less hopeful, she argued—strongly—there was only one thing to do. Franklin must return to the place he'd loved since boyhood, Springwood in Hyde Park, and live quietly. Eleanor and Louis Howe were violently opposed to this notion of what his life should be. Louis still saw a great political future for him, while Eleanor knew that being idle and solitary was against everything in Franklin's outgoing nature.

One of Franklin's doctors, George Draper, witnessed "the intense and devastating influence of these high-voltage personalities on one another." A polio specialist, he found himself in the middle as Sara argued that her son should be treated as an invalid. Eleanor angrily replied that "if he fights he may overcome his handicap."

This was one battle Eleanor won and Sara lost. Dr. Draper told Eleanor she was right and that Franklin should live as normal and vigorous a life as possible. Though he'd spend the next several years recuperating, Franklin kept his hand in politics, staying active in both local New York happenings and on the national scene. In 1924, his rousing speech at the Democratic National Convention nominating Alfred E. Smith for president marked his full-time return to the political stage.

Once the dust of the medical crisis began settling, Eleanor and Franklin continued trying to find a way to lead their lives, apart and together. Franklin, in an effort to find relief and new treatments for his legs, began spending time first in Florida, then in Warm Springs, Georgia, where he eventually set up a sanitarium to help himself and other polio sufferers.

Eleanor did not care for the South—she didn't like the heat, the bugs, and the more casual lifestyle. Now approaching middle age, she spent most of her time in New York. She began to untangle herself from Sara—she even blocked the connecting doors to the town houses!—and took more responsibility for her children.

One stark realization was that Franklin could not be the same kind of father he was before his illness, especially to the younger boys, Franklin Jr. and John, who were only seven and five years old when their father contracted polio. The older children, Anna, James, and Elliott, had witnessed their father's physical agony as he'd tried to rehabilitate himself. They had been shocked, and Anna had become furious with her mother when she gave Anna's town house room to Louis during the first weeks after the family returned to New York from Campobello. But the three eldest could cope. "It began to dawn on me if the two youngest boys were going to have a normal existence," Eleanor wrote later, "I was going to have to become a good deal more companionable . . ." That she did, spending more time with them, and even taking the boys camping.

Even with all that was going on her life, Eleanor didn't slow down when it came to the causes that were ever more important to her. Her deep interest in politics and reform movements led her to become an ardent member of the New York State Democratic Committee. She edited the *Women's Democratic News*, a political newsletter, and perhaps most controversial, became a member of the Women's Trade Union League in 1922. This group, which some considered aligned with radicals, wanted women to form unions so they could insist on better working conditions. Eleanor not only raised money for the group, she also hosted parties for working-class women who, she felt, could use some fun in their lives.

ELEANOR ON CAMPOBELLO ISLAND IN 1925 WITH HER FRIENDS MARION DICKERMAN AND NANCY COOK

During the 1920s, Eleanor Roosevelt became a working woman as well. Along with her friend Marion Dickerman she bought the Todhunter School for upper-class girls in New York City, where she began teaching history and literature. It was a wonderful experience for Eleanor, who was able to emulate her heroine, Mlle. Souvestre, and in response received the same affection and respect from her own students. Decades later, one of those students stated emphatically, "And I never forgot a damned thing she ever taught me!"

Building on what she'd learned at Allenswood, Eleanor considered her main job was to get her students to think for themselves. It wasn't enough for them to regurgitate the lessons she taught. She demanded to know what *they* thought. In her literature courses, she made sure her students read women authors, and her educational goal was to lead her students "into an enlivened understanding of every possible phase of the world where they were going."

Still, as in many of her stands, there was contradiction. Though she believed wholeheartedly in public education (and that teachers, mostly women, were not paid enough), Todhunter was an expensive private school, the sort of place her own children went to.

In 1928, Franklin—often called by his initials FDR in newspaper headlines, a nickname that stuck—ran for and won the governorship of New York State, and Eleanor had to give up some of her own political work to take on the role of the state's First Lady. She still continued to take the train from Albany, the state capital, to Manhattan once a week to stay for several days of teaching. "I like teaching better than anything else I do."

It was a great source of pleasure to Eleanor that during his term, she and Franklin developed a serious working partnership. Since his mobility was limited, he often sent her out into the state to learn about the workings of various agencies and programs. One of her first visits was to a state hospital. When she returned, Franklin began asking her questions. "'What was the food like?' I said, 'Oh, I looked at the menus and they seemed very adequate.' And he said, 'I didn't ask you about the menus. I asked you what the food was like. You should have looked in the pots on the stove.' After that I was much better as an inspector."

One more thing happened during those years that made Eleanor's life easier and happier. She had never really felt comfortable at the Hyde Park estate. Springwood was Sara's house. Franklin came up with the idea to build a stone cottage on a piece of his land for Eleanor, Marion Dickerman, and their friend Nancy Cook (who was also a financial partner in Todhunter). The house, named Val-Kill after a nearby stream, was a sanctuary for Eleanor and where she lived when she was at Hyde Park. It was, at last, a home that she could call her own.

But there was another house calling—the White House. Eleanor knew that running for the presidency had always been

Franklin's long-term plan. It was not hers. Eleanor was content with the life she had and did not look forward to living in the White House fishbowl, where her every move would be watched and commented on. Nevertheless, in 1929 a national event occurred that rocked the United States to its core: The stock market

ELEANOR'S COTTAGE AT VAL-KILL WAS HER SANCTUARY FOR DECADES.

crashed, and the Great Depression began. People lost their savings and their jobs, and they watched the economy collapse. For a while, it looked as if the country might collapse as well, and the Republican president, Herbert Hoover, seemed unable to do much about it.

In 1932, Franklin ran for the presidency on the platform of a New Deal for Americans. If he won, he would have no less a job than repairing and restoring a broken country. Whatever her personal feelings, Eleanor knew she had to support the man she felt could handle that enormous job. And that man just happened to be her husband.

5

REACHING

OUT

"The only thing we have to fear is fear itself!" This long-remembered line from Franklin Delano Roosevelt's inauguration speech in March of 1933 heartened the unemployed, impoverished, and worried citizens throughout the United States suffering through the third year of the Great Depression. But the new president knew that words would have to be followed by actions. After he took office, Franklin determinedly set out to get the country back on its feet.

The first one hundred days of Franklin's administration were a whirlwind of activity. They had to be, as the country was in crisis. A quarter of the workforce was out of work, more

FRANKLIN AND ELEANOR
RIDE TO HIS INAUGURATION
ON MARCH 4, 1933.

than a million people were homeless, banks were failing, and savings had disappeared. In those one hundred days, Franklin ignited his New Deal. He pushed fifteen major bills through Congress that attacked the Depression from all sides: banking, industrial changes, farm aid, employment, and social welfare. He spoke to the public in radio "fireside chats," and his calm and optimistic tone buoyed listeners across the country.

FRANKLIN DELIVERS HIS SIXTH FIRESIDE CHAT IN 1934.

Sometimes it seemed that the New Deal had formed an "alphabet soup" of agencies. There was the CCC, the Civilian Conservation Corps, providing jobs for young men in forestry and other conservation services; and the WPA,

THIS WELL WAS THE ONLY SOURCE OF WATER IN A TENNESSEE TOWN
UNTIL THE TENNESSEE VALLEY AUTHORITY HELPED MODERNIZE THE AREA.

the Works Progress Administration, employing millions to work on infrastructure projects like roads and bridges, while artists and writers and musicians carried out arts projects. The Tennessee Valley, a part of the country particularly hard-hit, was provided flood control and electricity by the TVA, the Tennessee Valley Authority.

The goal of these agencies and others was to provide direct relief to Americans. Some of the programs worked, others did not. A few, like one to regulate agricultural production, were ruled illegal by the courts. In 1935, Social Security was established, giving many older Americans a monthly stipend to help secure their futures. Though the Depression dragged on for years, finally ending with America's entry into World War II, the quick actions Franklin took did stabilize the country.

Eleanor, as always, did her duty. She had been correct about the fishbowl that was Washington, D.C. Everything she said, did, and even wore was scrutinized. Despite any personal discomfort, she soon realized that there was much she could do to help her country through this crisis, even though she had no formal title other than First Lady. But that was enough.

As he had done as governor of New York, Franklin used Eleanor as his eyes, ears, and legs. He started her traveling on a national scale, both to view actual conditions in the country and later to report on the progress his programs were making.

ELEANOR PUT HER STAMP ON THE ROLE OF FIRST LADY, TRAVELING THROUGHOUT THE COUNTRY—EVEN DOWN IN THE COAL MINES—AS AN ACTIVE PARTICIPANT OF HER HUSBAND'S ADMINISTRATION.

Sometimes she would go to the sites of federal relief projects unannounced, so she could see the real situations, not versions prettied up for the First Lady. It seemed Eleanor was everywhere: in rural areas, in crowded tenements, in national parks, in prisons, even down in a coal mine.

A problem arose when the head of the Secret Service discovered the independent First Lady was not going to allow an agent to accompany her on her travels. One day, he came to Louis and tossed a revolver on his desk and said, "Well, all right, if Mrs. Roosevelt is going to drive around the country alone, at least ask her to carry this in the car." In her autobiography, she reported, "I carried it religiously . . . I asked a friend, a man who had been one of Franklin's bodyguards in New York State, to give me some practice in target shooting so that if the need arose I would know how to use the gun." It took a good deal of practice, but Eleanor did become knowledgeable about handling guns.

ELEANOR LEARNS HOW TO SHOOT A GUN.

★

Republicans, who didn't like the Roosevelts and their activism, along with some members of the press, made fun of Eleanor and her travels. (A newspaper published a half-joking prayer, "Just for one day, God, please make her tired.") But most Americans admired her efforts. They began to feel she was a friend and started writing her letters. Before bed, after long days that might include a visit to a CCC camp or hosting a dinner for foreign dignitaries—or both!—she would try to answer her mail. "From March 1933 to the end of the year, I received three hundred one thousand pieces of mail . . . ," she reported. "The variety of the requests and apparent confidence that I would be able to make almost anything possible worried me."

Though she could not, of course, answer most personally, she did reply to a cross section, referred others to the proper government agencies, and sometimes offered advice or even money to those who sounded desperate.

She also continued a practice she had started during the 1920s, getting paid for writing books and newspaper columns and guesting on radio programs. A First Lady receiving wages was unheard of, and though Eleanor did receive criticism about this, especially from Republicans, her writing proved extremely popular—and profitable. The money allowed her to continue giving money to the charities of her choice.

Through her travels and writings, Eleanor was in touch with everyday people and seemed to have her finger on the pulse of the country. She continued to be particularly interested in women's issues, while a new focus was the youth of America. She was concerned that the United States was in danger of losing a whole generations of young Americans—"a stranded generation," she called them—disillusioned with an economic system that had let them down and left them with little hope for the future.

ELEANOR AT SHE-SHE-SHE CAMP FOR UNEMPLOYED WOMEN IN BEAR MOUNTAIN, NEW YORK. THE FIRST LADY WAS THE DRIVING FORCE BEHIND THE CAMPS. THE CIVILIAN CONSERVATION CORPS WAS DESIGNED FOR YOUNG MEN ONLY, WHOSE WORK INVOLVED FORESTRY AND UTILIZING THE COUNTRY'S NATURAL RESOURCES. ELEANOR MADE SURE THERE WERE PROGRAMS FOR JOBLESS WOMEN AS WELL.

It was Eleanor's determination and persistence in lobbying her husband, as well as others in the administration, that led to the formation of another successful entry in the alphabet soup of commissions: the NYA, the National Youth Administration, or as Franklin affectionately called it, "the missus organization." NYA programs gave grants to high school and college students to help them stay in school, and those who had dropped out could apply for job-training programs. Using a similar "family" metaphor, the head of the program in North Carolina echoed a sentiment heard around the country in a letter to Eleanor. "Out here we think of the NYA as your government child. Certainly no member of the alphabet family is more popular."

Despite her history as a politically astute reformer and champion of the underdog, there continued to be one group that didn't receive much of Eleanor's attention. She was in her forties and First Lady of the United States before she began to seriously look at the problem of racism in America and the injustices faced by its African American (then called Negro or colored) citizens. But once she did, she was determined to help.

Why was racism still such an issue almost seventy years after the end of the Civil War in 1865? The Thirteenth Amendment to the Constitution, ratified in December 1865, ended slavery. The Fourteenth Amendment, ratified in 1868, gave former slaves citizenship and all persons born in the United States equal protection under the law. The Fifteenth Amendment, ratified in 1870, said that race could not be used as a reason to deny the right to vote—for men only, of course; women wouldn't get the vote for another fifty years.

Northern troops occupied the South until 1877, a period called Reconstruction, and enforced these laws. One of the results was that African American men were elected to public office. Another result was the simmering anger of many white citizens who had lost not only the war, but their way of life. When the troops left the South, ways were found to disenfranchise black voters and return political and economic power to whites.

A system of strict segregation was set up in which blacks were kept separate socially from whites and in subservient positions. African Americans in the Southern states had to defer to white people, eat in their own establishments, go to their own schools, sit separately in public venues, use public bathrooms for blacks only, and even drink from their own water fountains.

Other parts of the United States had their own forms of segregation. Some were codified into law, for instance, the separation of blacks and whites in hotels and a prohibition on intermarriage; other restrictions were more a matter of custom than regulation. These laws varied in different Northern and Western states. In the South, they were more uniform and harsher, and the penalties for breaking them often more severe. These were called Jim Crow laws, named for a stage character insulting to blacks.

During the hard times of the Depression, there wasn't much for whites or blacks, but African Americans always got the shorter end of the stick. Nevertheless, there were groups fighting hard for change against sometimes dangerous, always overwhelming odds. The best known was the NAACP, the National Association for the Advancement of Colored People. Founded in 1909, its goals included political, educational, social, and economic equality under the law.

With her sensitivity to people, especially those whose lives were difficult through no fault of their own, it would seem Eleanor should have been an early supporter of African American rights and groups like the NAACP. So why wasn't she?

As with many people, her racism began in childhood. Eleanor's paternal grandmother, Martha Bulloch Roosevelt, was raised in the South before the Civil War, where she had lived on a plantation. Though Martha had died a few months after Eleanor's birth, the girl grew up hearing romanticized stories from her great-aunt Annie, Martha's sister, about the Bulloch girls' happy childhood in Georgia. As a part of plantation life, the sisters had young slaves, called shadows, who waited on the girls and slept at the foot of their beds. As a girl, Eleanor enjoyed the tales. She never thought about the stories from the enslaved children's points of view.

But even as an adult, she didn't consider African American sensitivities. One of her biographers has speculated that approaching middle age, the only blacks she knew were servants. Her road to racial sensitivity was not only slow but uneven. As late as 1936, even after her ideas about social justice had begun to broaden, she could be thoughtless. One example—she was still using the offensive term *darky*, and in her autobiography, no less.

Eleanor was put on the defensive by a young African American woman, a graduate of Tuskegee University, who saw the word *darky* while reading a magazine excerpt of Eleanor's autobiography. She wrote to the First Lady: "I couldn't believe my eyes" when I came across the "hated" and "humiliating" term. The writer continued that it was even more shocking having been written by a women she admired so much.

Eleanor responded, "*Darky* was used by my Georgia great aunt as a term of affection, and I have always considered it in that light. I am sorry if I hurt you." A chastised Eleanor asked, "What do you prefer?"

VISITING NEW DEAL PROGRAMS TO SEE HOW THEY WERE WORKING WAS AN IMPORTANT PART OF HOW ELEANOR SAW HER JOB AS FIRST LADY. HERE SHE IS VISITING A WPA AFRICAN AMERICAN NURSERY SCHOOL ON DES MOINES AVENUE IN IOWA IN 1936. MANY OF THE NEW DEAL PROGRAMS IN BOTH THE NORTH AND SOUTH WERE SEGREGATED.

The awakening of Eleanor's social consciousness had begun with her charity visits as a child and working at the Rivington Street Settlement House as a young adult. Later, issues like child labor and workers' rights captured her attention and energy. But for many years, she only saw herself doing good works from a position higher than those she was helping. She didn't consider them as equals.

It was over the course of her adulthood, especially after she became First Lady, as she traveled and talked, observed and learned, that Eleanor began seeing the common humanity she shared with people of all races. As one historian put it, "She was not afraid to allow herself to change and become a better, more accepting, more balanced and informed person."

This was perhaps most true when it came to her willingness to stand by the side of those fighting for their civil rights. Her personal friendships with individuals of color finally brought Eleanor to a greater understanding of what African Americans endured, and in many ways this shocked her. The White House was to become her new schoolhouse, the place where she would truly begin to learn what it meant to be black in America.

A NEW STANDARD FOR UNDERSTANDING

A very different Eleanor Roosevelt came to Washington, D.C., in 1933 than the one who had lived there when her husband was the assistant secretary of the navy during World War I, almost twenty years before. This Eleanor realistically understood her shortcomings, but she had also developed many strengths. Two of the most important were her ability to spot inequalities and a willingness to do something about them.

One of the first things she did after her husband's inauguration was to visit the slums of Washington, D.C. The crusade to dismantle the filthy alley slums of D.C., home to mostly African Americans, had been led by another First Lady, Ellen

Wilson, the first wife of President Woodrow Wilson. The housing, constructed in hidden alleys behind the stately homes and public buildings of Washington, had long been declared a health hazard because the horrendous conditions there bred disease.

Eleanor, during her first stay in Washington, knew of Mrs. Wilson's efforts but hadn't done much to support them. Now, the new First Lady learned that things had not changed since Mrs. Wilson died in 1914. (On her deathbed, Ellen Wilson was told a law had been passed that would clear the slums, but World War I intervened and nothing was done.)

On a blustery March day in 1933, Eleanor, in one of her first acts as First Lady, toured the alley slums. Accompanied by a longtime crusader for better housing, Charlotte Everett Hopkins, who had urged the visit, she was driven through a small crevice opening into a rotten world of crumbling wooden tenements, home to twelve thousand blacks and one thousand whites. There was no running water and only outdoor bathrooms. The rarely collected garbage was a magnet for well-fed rats that darted everywhere.

Eleanor didn't just look on this visit, she listened. The residents described the horrors of life in the dirty tenements,

the indignities, the disease, the desperation. These shocking sights and conversations convinced the First Lady to
take on the crusade of decent housing. She talked about it,
wrote about it, and a year later she spoke at the first National
Housing Conference, calling out slumlords as "thoughtless
people" who would force others to live in squalid conditions
"just to make a little more money." She took her post of hon-
orary chairman of the Washington Committee on Housing
seriously, helping to pass legislation that created the Alley
Dwelling Authority of 1934, which tore down and rebuilt or
renovated the inadequate housing.

Eleanor's concern with decent housing led to one of her
pet projects, a planned community in West Virginia called
Arthurdale. The Appalachia area was one of the poorest in a
country that was almost drowning in poverty. Lorena Hickok,
Eleanor's close friend and a newspaper reporter now working
for the Roosevelt administration, had been sent to inspect
conditions in various parts of the United States. The worst
she had seen was a coal mining area called Scott's Run in West
Virginia. The name "Run" came from the stinking waste that
trickled down the side of the hills. Hickok reported, "Along the
main street through the town, there was stagnant, filthy water,

which the inhabitants used for drinking, cooking, washing, and everything else imaginable."

A COAL MINING FAMILY IN WEST VIRGINIA

Eleanor came to see for herself. She met a community of starving people who talked to her about what it was like to live in abject poverty. Despite different settings, the problems of poor people in rural West Virginia and urban Washington, D.C., were very similar.

In one shack she saw a little boy who held a white rabbit close in his arms, obviously his pet. Eleanor recounted how his sister told her, "He thinks we are not going to eat his rabbit.

81

But we are." Hearing that, the boy fled down the hill, still clutching the rabbit to his chest.

Eleanor used this story to help raise money for the new community of Arthurdale. What began as an idea to move out-of-work coal miners to West Virginia farmland became a planned community, where the residents could farm as well as work in light industries. Franklin got behind the program, and Congress approved twenty-five million dollars for the project, with hopes it might possibly serve as a prototype for other such communities. Still, there were critics aplenty who disapproved of why and how so much money was being spent.

ELEANOR MEETS WITH THE RESIDENTS OF THE NEW ARTHURDALE COMMUNITY IN 1935.

The first prefabricated homes in Arthurdale were ready for occupancy in 1934. Thanks in part to Eleanor's fundraising efforts among her wealthy friends, Arthurdale became a true community, with a clinic and good schools. She used her connections to bring a furniture factory and a vacuum cleaner assembly plant to the area.

In the end individual families benefited from Arthurdale, but the area as a whole did not. Congress turned against the project, finding it too expensive to continue financing. By 1941, Eleanor herself conceded that money had been wasted, but, she thought, money had also been saved: "I have always felt that many human beings who might have cost us thousands of dollars in tuberculosis sanitariums, insane asylums, and jails were restored to usefulness and given confidence in themselves."

There was one aspect of the Arthurdale experience, however, that shocked her. Even though whites and blacks had been living together in poverty in the region for decades, white residents of Arthurdale refused to allow African Americans to join them in their new community. Six hundred families, including two hundred black families, originally applied for housing, but the first fifty families, chosen by a committee from the University of West Virginia, were all white.

These first families formed the Arthurdale Home-steaders Club, which was allowed to make its own rules for their community. The First Lady requested that the next group of residents be more diverse, but the Homesteaders Club refused, writing her that they were "thoroughly opposed to Negroes as residents, and we feel that we should not risk the loss of respect we have gained in the community by admitting Negroes." They also made the point that the community would need separate schools, since West Virginia law forbade integrated schools.

This was an eye-opening turn of events for Eleanor. She was now starting to understand just how corrosive the systematic segregation of African Americans was. Unlike many Americans, even liberals and progressives who preferred not to look at the problem, she saw racism for what it was: a disease to the body of the United States that needed to be examined and cured.

To that end, Eleanor began to surround herself with people who were already working on the cause of civil rights, though that name had yet to be commonly given to the movement. One of those people was a woman she had met in 1927, an African American educator named Mary Jane McLeod Bethune.

ELEANOR CAME TO REGARD MARY JANE MCLEOD BETHUNE AS ONE OF HER CLOSEST FRIENDS.

Mary was the fifteenth of seventeen children born to a pair of former slaves in South Carolina. The only child in her family to attend her local one-room schoolhouse, she'd come home, after walking five miles back and forth, to teach her family what she'd learned each day. Her teacher helped her get scholarships to continue her learning. As an adult, she dedicated herself to education and starting schools for blacks.

Now married to another educator, Mary first encountered Eleanor at a meeting of the National Council of Women in 1927. She was the last to arrive in a room filled with white women, and she wasn't sure where she should sit. Later she remembered how Sara Roosevelt got up from her seat, took her arm, and led her to a chair between her and Eleanor. "I can remember, too, how the faces of the Negro servants lit up with pride when they saw me seated at the center of that imposing gathering." Whatever Sara's other faults, she was not a racist, mostly because her father, an educator, taught tolerance rather than prejudice. This encounter over time led to a fast friendship between the Roosevelt women and Mary Jane McLeod Bethune.

Another person who came into the First Lady's orbit was Walter Francis White, the head of the the NAACP. Walter, of mixed European and African heritage, had blue eyes and light hair and could easily have passed for white. Instead, he spent his life fighting injustice against African Americans.

Walter was among a small group of notable black leaders and educators who were invited by Eleanor to a dinner meeting at the White House in January 1934. She wanted it known that the Roosevelt administration was interested in their concerns. For over four hours in a no-holds-barred conversation, the participants discussed and debated the problems facing their race. As one historian put it, "Never before had black leaders been invited to discuss unemployment, lynching, unequal expenditures to educate children, and the failure to provide housing, sanitation, and running water."

The group decided that as much as they would like to tackle the huge issue of segregation, there was a more immediate problem to focus on—making sure that blacks got their fair share of the New Deal programs, which at the moment was not happening.

Franklin was wheeled in after midnight to say hello to the group and offer his support. But in the coming years, it would be Eleanor, not Franklin, who kept the issue of civil rights front and center in the Roosevelt administration. As one participant in that unprecedented evening meeting put it, Eleanor "set before all of us a new standard for understanding and cooperation in the field of race."

There was one more person who came along a few years later and helped the First Lady open her eyes. She was one of Eleanor's many correspondents, a young African American woman named Pauli Murray.

Pauli first saw Eleanor in 1933, when the First Lady was visiting a camp for unemployed women in upstate New York. Shy and nervous about meeting the president's wife, she

A YOUNG PAULI MURRAY, WHO WOULD
BECOME A LIFELONG FRIEND

hid behind a book she was reading. After the visit, Pauli was called out by the camp's director for her disrespect. When she wrote to Eleanor in 1938, she used this incident to remind the First Lady that she was "the girl who did not stand up" at Camp Tera.

Her note to Eleanor was attached to a copy of a letter she'd sent to President Roosevelt about being denied admission to her state school, the University of North Carolina, because of her race. In it, she wrote with eloquence, passion, and sadness about what it felt like to be black in America. "Twelve millions of your citizens have to endure insults, injustice, and such degradation of spirit that you believe impossible as a human being . . . Can you, for one moment, put yourself in our place and imagine the feelings of resentment, the protest, the indignation, the outrage that would rise within you to realize that you, a human being, with the keen sensitivities of other human beings, were being set off in a corner, marked apart from your fellow human beings?"

Pauli, who had copied Eleanor because she thought there was better chance of the First Lady reading the letter than her husband, closed by noting that segregation "isn't my problem alone, it is the problem of my people, and in these trying days, it will not let me or any other thinking Negro rest."

This letter, the first in series of letters between the two women that would last until the end of Eleanor's life, was yet another thread in the tapestry of anger and despair that she now saw as the plight of African Americans. As the First Lady of the United States, she decided to use her position to work side by side with black leaders who were leading the charge for their equal rights.

Eleanor Roosevelt now firmly believed that by making the country a better place for its African American citizens, it would become a better place for all its citizens.

THE SPUR

Eleanor thought it was important to show African Americans they had a friend in the White House. Though the struggle was theirs, it was useful to have a backer who had the president's ear. She kept her eye on New Deal legislation to make sure laws were evenly applied to both blacks and whites. She also tried to use her influence to make sure African Americans were placed in significant positions in New Deal agencies. Neither of these issues was always met with success.

There was one civil rights fight, however, that had particular urgency. It pitted Eleanor against Franklin, beginning in his first term in office and continuing throughout his presidency. It concerned a despicable American tradition: lynching.

Lynching was the hanging (sometimes with burning, torture, and dismemberment) of usually minority men, women, and young people by mobs. Lynchings were all too familiar after the Civil War and through the years

CROWDS GATHER IN WACO, TEXAS, TO WATCH THE 1916 LYNCHING OF JESSE WASHINGTON.

leading into World War II. One of the most horrifying things about public lynchings was that they were often festive public spectacles, with both adults and children in the audience. One newspaper called them "carnivals of death." Sometimes postcards were sold as souvenirs of the events.

Although about 85 percent of victims during this time period were blacks and the lynchings happened mostly in Southern states, other minorities, such as Mexicans and Chinese Americans—as well as whites—were also targeted, and states including Minnesota, California, and New York were places where lynchings occurred.

The NAACP, among other organizations, was anxious to have a federal law passed against lynching, and two senators, Robert F. Wagner of New York and Edward P. Costigan of Colorado, proposed a bill to make lynching a federal crime. Eleanor was a staunch backer of the law, and tried to get Franklin to put his considerable presidential weight behind its passage. But this turned out to be impossible.

It wasn't that Franklin didn't believe in the merits of the bill. He did. He had spoken out about lynching in one of his radio fireside chats on December 6, 1933, saying, "We know that it is murder . . . We do not excuse those in high places or low who condone lynch law." But the Costigan-Wagner Bill posed a huge political problem for him. The Senate was controlled by Democratic senators from the South. If Franklin came out too strongly for the anti-lynching bill, he would anger those senators who felt the federal government had no right to interfere in what they considered issues of states' rights.

It's hard to understand how the murder of people in the most brutal way possible would be something that lawmakers could disagree about. But since the Civil War, the Southern states were hypersensitive to federal interference. It was also true that since Reconstruction, the Southern states were looking for ways to take away rights, including voting rights of African Americans. To that end, Southern state governments disenfranchised voters by charging poll taxes and administering literacy tests. When that didn't work, there was always intimidation.

African Americans who were lynched were often not accused of any real crimes but rather of behavior considered impudent or inappropriate by the social structure, for instance, a black male whistling at a white woman or a person of color not acting with enough deference to whites. Sometimes the charges were made up or used to take property from African Americans. Lynching frightened people and kept them in their place.

In 1933, there were twenty-eight lynchings; twenty-four of the victims were black. Walter White of the NAACP continuously discussed with the First Lady the progress of the Costigan-Wagner Bill and asked her to press the president for his support. She tried, but in May of 1934, she wrote White a letter saying, "The President talked to me rather at length today about the lynching bill. As I do not think you will either like or agree with everything that he thinks, I would like an opportunity of telling you about it . . ." She also offered to set up a meeting with the president.

Franklin was famous for using his charming personality and telling amusing anecdotes to defuse uncomfortable situations. That's what he tried to do when he joined Eleanor and his mother, Sara, during a meeting they had set up with Walter White on May 7, 1934. Franklin tried to explain why politics made it impossible to support the bill. Walter argued with him. The president became frustrated.

He turned to his wife. Had she coached Mr. White? Franklin asked. Eleanor mildly suggested they continue talking. Then the president turned to his mother, "Well, at least I know you'll be on my side." Sara "shook her head." No, she was on Walter's side.

Franklin threw up his hands. Finally, he firmly explained the political realities to Walter: "I did not choose the tools with which I must work. But I've got to get legislation passed by Congress to save America. . . . The Southerners, by reason of the seniority rule [in Congress], are chairmen or occupy strategic places on most of the Senate and House committees. If I come out for the anti-lynching bill now, they will block every bill I ask Congress to pass to keep America from collapsing. I just can't take the risk."

Walter White did get Franklin's assurance that if the

bill came to his desk he would sign it. But the bill was never passed.

In October of 1934, a black man, Claude Neal, accused of murdering a white woman, was taken from a jail in Alabama and moved back to Florida, where the crime had been committed. Neal's captors were so bold, the lynching was advertised in advance, so people could come out to watch. News of the lynching spread across the country through newspapers and radio. Soon the Florida governor was receiving telegrams telling him to stop this tragedy in the making, but he and other local authorities did nothing. The crowd that came to watch numbered perhaps in the thousands, and those holding Neal, fearful of a riot, decided to lynch him in private. But first they tortured him in horrible ways, including cutting off parts of his body.

After the deed was done, the waiting crowd demanded the body and inflicted more damage. The mob's anger spilled over, and people began burning whatever property they could find in the area that belonged to blacks. It took the arrival of the National Guard to quell the anger.

This horrifying event galvanized the black community and its supporters. In fact, this disgusting episode disturbed people all across the United States, and support for the anti-lynching bill grew.

A protest meeting at New York City's Carnegie Hall was planned, and Walter White wanted the First Lady to speak. She informed Franklin about the meeting and told him she was inclined to take part, but said she would do whatever he thought best. The president told her that to make that speech would be political "dynamite." Eleanor apologized to Walter and stayed away.

THE RELATIONSHIP BETWEEN ELEANOR AND FRANKLIN WAS A COMPLICATED ONE, BUT THEY ALWAYS RESPECTED EACH OTHER AND DID THEIR BEST TO SUPPORT ONE ANOTHER, SOMETIMES WITH VARYING DEGREES OF SUCCESS.

Franklin admired his wife and rarely told her not to do something. Eleanor had once asked Franklin if he minded her speaking out. "No, certainly not," he answered genially. "You can say anything you want. I can always say, 'Well, that's my wife, I can't do anything about her.'"

Yet he could also make it clear, as with the dynamite comment, when something was not in the best interest of him or his administration. One of Eleanor's roles, as she saw it, was to be her husband's conscience. She had a way of looking at him and saying, "Now, Franklin . . ." or leaving notes and articles for him. She expected him to learn about and hopefully act on the issues she brought to him. Yet she also understood—and often told those who wanted her support on a range of issues—that Franklin was the president, not she. He was the only one to make the ultimate decisions on matters of state.

During the early spring of 1935, the Costigan-Wagner Bill was brought to the Senate floor. The Southern senators prepared to filibuster the bill. That meant this bloc would hold the floor and make sure no other legislation could pass until the anti-lynching bill was killed. Franklin, who continued to need his New Deal legislation passed, would not say anything against the filibuster, which went on for several weeks before the sponsors of the bill agreed to withdraw it. Eleanor wrote to a disappointed Walter, "Of course, we will all go on fighting."

The anti-lynching bill was debated again in 1937; Republicans in Congress supported the bill, and the House passed it, moving it along to the Senate. Eleanor implored her husband to support the bill, but the president once again insisted he needed the Southern Democratic senators for help with his other legislation. There was another filibuster. This time, during the long days of talking, the First Lady watched from the Senate gallery "in silent rebuke of the shameful tactic." The bill died in the Senate later that fall. Other attempts were made to pass anti-lynching legislation during Franklin's terms in office, but all met the same fate.

There were efforts to pass an anti-lynching bill in succeeding years. All failed until 1946, after Franklin's terms had ended.

The failures of the anti-lynching bills were deeply disappointing, but Eleanor continued to push her husband for more support on the overall issue of civil rights. Louis Howe, her ally and supporter, had died in 1936, but she found several strong supporters in the administration, including Harold Ickes, the secretary of the interior, and presidential adviser Aubrey Williams, who called himself a Southern rebel because though he was from the South, he championed African Americans' rights. Many other members of the president's inner circle, however, disliked Eleanor's outspoken views on race relations and resented the way she tried to push her agenda with him.

Eleanor never in doubted that Franklin respected her views and appreciated her efforts. It was also clear her husband often found her to be relentless and even annoying at times when it came to her pursuit of causes she believed in. She once noted, perhaps sadly, "He might have been happier with a wife who was completely uncritical. . . . Nevertheless, I think I sometimes acted as a spur, even though the spurring was not always wanted or welcome. I was one of those who served his purposes."

IT NEVER HURTS TO BE KIND

President Roosevelt won reelection for a second term in 1936 in a landslide, losing only two states. One element in his sweeping win was the support of the African American community. Traditionally, African Americans had voted for the Republican Party, the party of Abraham Lincoln, who had freed the slaves. Herbert Hoover had received the majority of their votes in the 1932 election, but the New Deal legislation of the Roosevelt administration, as well as Eleanor's personal advocacy for African American concerns, was swinging their votes to the Democrats.

With four more years of a Roosevelt administration ahead of her, Eleanor was again ready to use her position as First

Lady to advance the cause of civil rights in ways large and small.

Moving a chair might not seem like a big deal, but it was in 1938, when Eleanor was attending the Southern Conference for Human Welfare in Birmingham, Alabama. On the first day of the large gathering, white and black attendees had mixed freely. When the police commissioner, Eugene "Bull" Connor—later to become infamous for his cruel treatment of civil rights protesters—got wind of this, he sent police to the auditorium the next day to make sure segregation laws were enforced.

The police arrived at municipal auditorium and told the participants they had to segregate themselves according to race. Eleanor, who had taken a seat next to her friend, Mary Jane McLeod Bethune, was informed personally that she needed to get up and move to the white section. The First Lady had her own solution to the problem. She picked up her chair and placed it in the center aisle, on neither the black nor the white side of the room. And there she sat for the rest of the program.

At Eleanor's suggestion, Mary had already been appointed to an important post in the Roosevelt administration. She was named director of Negro Affairs for the National Youth Administration, where she successfully oversaw programs that helped tens of thousands of young black people find jobs or be accepted in job training programs. The governmental appointment didn't stop Mary's other civil rights activities, and because she was friends with the First Lady, her concerns got a fair hearing at the White House.

There was, however, something about the relationship between the two women that bothered Eleanor. It was her habit to give her women friends a friendly peck on the cheek when she greeted them. Yet she didn't kiss Mary, and she knew it was because she didn't feel comfortable kissing a black person. One day, without thinking about it, she kissed her. Eleanor's daughter, Anna, reported years later that this kiss was a personal milestone for her mother.

Another prominent African American woman was affected by the actions of the First Lady. The opera singer Marian Anderson was known around the world for her magnificent contralto voice. She had already sung for a small group at the White House. But in 1939, Anderson's manager wanted to hold a concert in Washington, D.C. The only venue large enough to hold the anticipated crowd was Constitution

Hall, which was owned by the Daughters of the American Revolution (DAR), a group of white women descended from those who fought in the Revolutionary War or aided in gaining independence from Britain. The organization informed Anderson's manager that Constitution Hall was "not available to Negro artists."

Marian Anderson said she was "shocked beyond words to be barred from the capital of my own country after having appeared in almost every other capital of the world."

Eleanor was a member of the DAR, and she was disgusted when she learned that the group had refused to let a black artist, and a distinguished one at that, perform at Constitution Hall. She resigned from the organization, writing in her letter, "You had an opportunity to lead in an enlightened way, and it seems to me that your organization failed."

Both Eleanor and Franklin encouraged the secretary of the interior, Harold Ickes, to arrange for an outdoor concert for Anderson on the steps of the majestic Lincoln Memorial. Then, the First Lady used her contacts in radio to have the concert broadcast across the country. On April 13, 1939, Secretary Ickes introduced Marian Anderson with the words, "Genius knows no color line."

ELEANOR'S ROLE IN HAVING MARIAN ANDERSON SING AT THE LINCOLN MEMORIAL INCLUDED HER SUGGESTION THAT THE NAACP USE THE RADIO BROADCAST OF THE EVENT TO RAISE MONEY FOR THEIR ORGANIZATION. HERE SHE MEETS WITH THE SINGER IN JAPAN IN 1953.

With the statue of Abraham Lincoln behind her, the singer began her concert with "My Country, 'Tis of Thee" and ended it with the Negro spiritual, "Nobody Knows the Trouble I've Seen." Seventy-five thousand people, black and white, turned out that Easter Sunday to hear Marian Anderson sing.

Eleanor's outreach to African Americans did not go unnoticed, especially when they were invited guests to the White House, a place built with slave labor. Notable African Americans had visited the White House before. Abraham Lincoln had met with abolitionists Frederick Douglass and Sojourner Truth there during the Civil War. Educator and author Booker T.

Washington was the first African American to be invited for dinner then, by Theodore Roosevelt in 1901. But Eleanor made the White House even more inclusive. As early as 1934, she was making her social agenda clear by inviting both political friends like Mary McLeod Bethune and Walter White and everyday African Americans to the private quarters of the White House for meals and other social events.

This continued throughout the president's time in office. The "People's House," as the building has been nicknamed, became socially integrated. One of her guests was her correspondent and now a social activist and Howard University law student, Pauli Murray. The young woman and the First Lady often challenged each other's opinions. Though they agreed on big issues, there was a generational rift, with Eleanor sometimes urging moderation and caution on the impatient Pauli, whom the First Lady once dubbed "a firebrand."

The day Pauli was invited for the first time to the White House for tea in 1943 was full of mishaps. The aunt who was to accompany her had taken ill, so she invited a friend. The friend's husband showed up on an army leave unexpectedly, so Pauli made arrangements with the White House for him to attend. But then he decided his uniform was too wrinkled for such an important occasion, so teatime had to be pushed back once more. When the trio arrived at the White House, they realized they had forgotten their admission cards!

Pauli was exhausted and embarrassed by the time the First Lady greeted them and led her guests outside to a table on the South Portico. There, she later remembered, the comforting smell of magnolia trees and honeysuckle calmed her down. Eleanor's sensible ease made Pauli think she might appreciate the story of why they were so late. Sure enough, the First Lady, listening to Pauli rattle off the disasters, "burst into spontaneous laughter."

Pauli would go on to do important things as a lawyer, writer, activist, cofounder of the National Organization for Women, and the first African American Episcopal priest. Her friendship with Eleanor endured.

During the first eight years of her husband's administration, the First Lady spent many hours visiting black schools and churches and speaking at conventions of black organizations. Though she had support from the public in many quarters—for instance, 64 percent of those polled approved of her resignation from the DAR—a wide swath of people across the country vilified her, and in the nastiest of terms, because of her stand on civil rights. Eleanor's response was often to invoke the Golden Rule to try to make these critics understand that they should treat others, no matter their race, as they would like to be treated.

One of the events that caused a stir was a party she threw for black girls from a local reform school. When she had toured the school, she found the conditions there deplorable. She invited some of the girls to a lawn party at the White House, where cake and lemonade was served. Eleanor received much criticism over the invitation, but she mildly replied, "I feel if these girls are ever to be rehabilitated and, as far as possible, returned into community living prepared to meet the difficulties of life, they need much more than they are getting. Therefore, it seems to me as every young person enjoys an occasional good time, these youngsters should have an occasional good time."

In 1938, she received a letter from a woman who was upset after seeing a photograph of the First Lady serving food to a black child at a Hyde Park picnic. Eleanor wrote back in her commonsense way: "Surely you would not have refused to let her eat with the other [visitors] . . . I believe it never hurts to be kind."

Her involvement with the cause of African Americans'

civil rights did not mean she had forgotten about other people who needed her help. During Franklin's second term, the First Lady kept her eye on the plight of immigrants, issues affecting the poor, especially as they concerned the New Deal, affordable housing, and she did everything she could to fight the discouragement of the young. This kept her popularity high among the majority of the public.

The Depression continued throughout the 1930s. Sometimes the economy was better, then it would sputter again—1937 was a particularly bad year when unemployment rose sharply. Still, most people, thanks to the aid of the federal government and its New Deal programs, felt more optimistic.

That didn't mean African Americans were getting their fair share of New Deal programs and jobs; often they were not, despite Eleanor's efforts. Still, some white people across the country felt she was doing too much for African Americans.

The First Lady was particularly disliked in the South, where her liberal stands on race offended the very fabric of that society. Lies were spread about her—it was whispered she was starting "Eleanor Clubs" that encouraged black women to quit their jobs as maids—but her own actions were quite enough to raise ire. Sometimes, it was the mildest of events that made people mad. Even a photograph of Eleanor giving a little African American girl a flower from a bouquet the child had presented to the First Lady was used against her throughout the South. Ironically, the same picture was also distributed in the North in African American communities to show them her solidarity.

ELEANOR'S FRIENDS AND FOES AGREED ABOUT ONE THING: SHE WAS TIRELESS. SHE ALWAYS SEEMED TO HAVE TIME FOR ONE MORE APPEARANCE OR TO ANSWER ONE MORE LETTER. HER VISIT TO THE NATIONAL YOUTH ADMINISTRATION IN MAINE IN JULY 1941 SHOWED HER CONTINUED COMMITMENT TO NEW DEAL PROGRAMS.

No matter the criticism she received, the First Lady was determined to keep traveling throughout the country pushing back on the injustices she saw. "Eleanor Everywhere"—that was her nickname. Everywhere even included prison. In her autobiography, she told the story of the time she had to leave the White House for a Baltimore prison visit so early that she didn't have time to say good morning to her husband. Franklin asked her assistant where she was, and the woman replied, "Prison." The president smilingly shook his head. "I'm not surprised, but what for?"

There was an unfortunate personal aspect to the criticism Eleanor received. Often those who railed against her interests and goals, both press columnists and private citizens, also made fun of her looks, her voice, and her mannerisms. Newspaper cartoons emphasized her buck teeth and weak chin.

But Eleanor was smart enough not to show her detractors she cared. She would laugh off unflattering photos and paved the way for other women who wanted to be in the public eye by telling them not to take anything personally and to "develop skin as tough as a rhinoceros hide."

9

WAR CLOUDS

During President Roosevelt's second term, a huge dark cloud was looming on the horizon: war. Across the Pacific, Japan was arming itself and preparing to invade China. Across the Atlantic, Adolf Hitler and his Nazi Party had risen to power in Germany. The Nazis were terrorizing their country's Jewish population and casting covetous eyes on neighboring countries. Germany annexed the Rhineland in 1936 and then Austria in 1938. It took Czechoslovakia in 1939. When Germany invaded Poland in 1939, England and France, who had a mutual protection pact with Poland, declared war on Germany.

HITLER AND OFFICERS STAND IN FRONT OF THE EIFFEL TOWER
AFTER THE NAZIS STORMED INTO PARIS IN JUNE 1940.

President Roosevelt understood that he would have to prepare the United States for war, even though there was strong
sentiment against fighting a war in Europe. There had been
more than fifty thousand U.S. combat deaths in World War I
(and a total of more than ten million military deaths for all
countries), and the feeling in the United States was one of isolationism. Americans did not want to fight foreign wars.

Franklin had to be careful how he presented the issue

of foreign affairs to the public. It was like walking a political tightrope. He had to strengthen the country and ready it for war if war should come. But he was also considering something no other president had ever done—running for a third term in office. He had to convince the potential voters of the 1940 election that war was neither inevitable nor his first choice as a course of action.

As the world situation grew increasingly tense, the First Lady was also worried. She had seen firsthand the horrors caused by World War I. But she was also well aware of the tragedies that were unfolding in Europe and elsewhere. On a personal level, she was concerned because she had four sons who would be eligible for military service. Her children were all grown by now. Their childhoods, which they remembered as troubled, had not made them happy adults. All five experienced marriage, divorce, and remarriage. They sometimes felt torn between their parents, especially Anna, who was a confidant to both Eleanor and Franklin. The Roosevelts had five grandchildren by 1939, with more to come. Eleanor worked hard to be a more confident and compassionate grandmother than she had been a mother.

She decided the best thing she could do at this time was

to be more "everywhere" than ever, hitting the road on speaking tours where she discussed everything from foster care to New Deal progress to civil liberties. As with her former racial bigotry, it had not been unknown for Eleanor to display the strains of anti-Semitism she had grown up with and that were prevalent throughout the United States. Now, however, after all that she had seen and heard, her eyes were wide open to the horror of prejudice.

In a major speech delivered to the American Civil Liberties Union in March 1940, she said that religious and racial prejudice "are a great menace because we find that in countries where civil liberties have been lost, religious and race prejudice are rampant." Freedoms of speech, of religion, of the press, and the freedom to follow one's own conscience were precious and needed to be defended not just by the government, but by everyone. These truths, as she saw them, became Eleanor's moral pillars for the rest of her life.

With the turbulent world situation, Eleanor understood why the president had to focus his attention on foreign affairs. But she was also concerned that domestic problems like civil rights would fade into the background as events heated up in Europe and around the world.

She was right. World events did inevitably take center stage. But there were also many civil rights issues that affected the run up to World War II, and Eleanor was ready to offer her help as always. As one historian put it, "Eleanor refused to be insulated and shielded from a problem. The more perilous it was politically, the more twisted its roots in history, custom, and law, the more urgent [she thought] that it be ferreted out, confronted, and dealt with."

Racial injustice was one of those problems that not only affected people at home, but also elicited an uncomfortable and unwelcome response in the world. Adolf Hitler, for instance, pointed out that the United States had little standing to complain about Germany's treatment of Jews when it had such a sorry record on its black citizens. Eleanor sorrowfully noted his point: "It seems incredible when we are protesting the happenings in Germany to permit intolerance such as this in our own country."

Despite the prejudice African Americans faced in the United States, they answered the call to serve their country in times of war. African Americans had fought in all American wars. Through the Civil War, they fought in both all-black and integrated units. After the Civil War, segregation entered the armed services. Nevertheless, thousands of African Americans volunteered to fight during World War I. Few, however, saw combat because the army believed they were more suited to manual labor than fighting. After the war, interest in serving plummeted, and the number of African Americans in the armed services was dismal.

The situation in the navy was uniquely unfair. Young black men were in the service, but they were only allowed to be messmen. As messmen, all they were allowed to do was make beds, do laundry, and perform menial tasks for other sailors. In essence, they were servants—with no chance for advancement.

In September 1940, Congress passed the Selective Training and Service Act. It required men between the ages of twenty-one and thirty-five to register with their local draft boards. The armed services were also encouraging men to enlist. Nevertheless, not everyone was being encouraged.

Eleanor began to receive letters and hear about the indignities—and sometimes the dangers—that faced African American men who wanted the right to fight. A letter came from a doctor who was refused a commission because he was black. A high school teacher, in Charlotte, North Carolina, who had gone to a recruitment center to get information for his students, was beaten by whites. A dentist who came to enlist was informed, "Hell, if you said you were colored I would have saved you a trip . . . There are no colored dentists in the Dental Corps."

One group of enlisted men decided to make their dissatisfaction known. Fifteen navy messmen wrote an open letter to the *Pittsburgh Courier*, a black newspaper. "Our main reason for writing is to let all our colored mothers and fathers know how their sons are treated after taking an oath pledging allegiance and loyalty to their flag and country. . . ." The letter went on to describe what awaited African Americans in the navy and advised parents not to let their sons join. They ended by saying, "We take it upon ourselves to write this letter regardless of any action the Navy authorities may take."

The authorities were quick to take action. The men were jailed and then dishonorably discharged from the navy. That didn't stop messmen from other ships from writing their own letters in solidarity detailing their own similar experiences.

Congress did pass a law in 1940 that made it easier for African Americans to enlist in the armed services, but there were provisions in the law that also made it likely they could also be turned down. For instance, the law said men inducted into the army had to be deemed "acceptable," a nebulous term that could be used to turn black enlistees away. Civil rights leaders wanted to make sure there would be some teeth in this law.

Eleanor urged a White House meeting. Nothing happened. So in September of 1940, she wrote a pointed memo to her husband from the Greenwich Village apartment she kept in New York. She'd just finished speaking to a conference of African Americans. She'd begun her speech, "You know, better than any other people, that [American Democracy] is not perfect . . ." But she told the audience how hopeful she felt that Americans were moving along "the road to better understanding." Finally, she pledged her "faith and cooperation to make this a better country."

In writing to Franklin, she told him that public sentiment was growing among blacks and whites about the unfairness that was apparent in the armed services. Eleanor also noted, "This is going to be very bad politically, besides being intrinsically wrong."

The president listened. He called a meeting for September 27, 1940. Among the participants was A. Philip Randolph, "a commanding figure," who had organized the Brotherhood of Sleeping Car Porters (the first labor union led by African

Americans) in the face of great obstacles. Walter White was also there. Walter, interestingly, had been pushing a proposal to have a volunteer, integrated army, since there were many white men who said they *were* willing to serve alongside blacks. Also attending were the secretary of the navy, Frank Knox, and assistant secretary of war, Robert Patterson.

ELEANOR WITH A. PHILIP RANDOLPH (LEFT) AND NEW YORK MAYOR FIORELLO LA GUARDIA

Randolph told the assembled group that blacks felt they weren't wanted in the services. White "emphasized that . . . an army . . . fighting allegedly for democracy should be the last place to find undemocratic segregation."

Franklin tried to counter by saying the new law passed by Congress would give blacks more opportunities to serve, but Randolph pointed out the law's deficiencies. The president offered a few suggestions that seemed to indicate he was moving forward on the issue of integrating the services, and Randolph and White left with high hopes for progress. Nevertheless, the military men in attendance, and others who had gotten wind of the meeting, all gave a thumbs-down to the idea of integration.

One of the army's top generals, George Marshall, deplored the idea of "experiments which would have a highly destructive effect on morale." Secretary of the Navy Knox firmly told the president that his job was to prepare the navy for a war on two oceans. If he had to spend his time trying to integrate it as well, he would have to resign.

DESPITE THE CONTROVERSY OVER INTEGRATING THE ARMED SERVICES, AFRICAN AMERICANS WERE INSTRUMENTAL IN THE FIGHT TO WIN WORLD WAR II. HERE, MILES DAVIS KING, A CREWMAN ON THE *U.S.S. TULAGI* CARRIES A LOADED MAGAZINE FOR HIS GUN EN ROUTE TO SOUTHERN FRANCE IN 1944.

A week after the meeting was held, nobody was satis-fied. Randolph and White had heard nothing from the White House. Once again they asked the First Lady to intervene, which she did, but the statement the War Department finally issued merely said that Negro units would be formed in the major branches of the services and that there would eventu-ally be a flight training program for blacks.

And then this blow: "The policy of the War Department is not to intermingle colored and white enlisted personnel . . . This policy has been proved satisfactory over a long period of years . . . to make changes would produce situations destruc-tive to morale." Integration of the armed forces, the policy said, was not in the best interest of the country or of national defense.

This caused an uproar in the African American commu-nity. Adding insult to injury, one of the president's advisers made it seem as if the civil rights leaders at the meeting were in agreement with the War Department's statement—which they certainly were not!

Franklin had to issue a statement denying this was the case, but that was just a small bandage on a big problem. The NAACP encouraged its members to organize protests. The

1940 election was just around the corner, and the president again needed black votes. He quickly promoted one of the only blacks of high rank in the army, Colonel Benjamin Davis, to brigadier general and gave assurances that desegregation options were still being looked at.

These efforts calmed things somewhat in the African American community, but sentiment was also running high in other parts of the country that did not want integration. The president and First Lady once again received angry letters, some calling them horrible names. Nevertheless, Franklin Delano Roosevelt did win his third presidential term in 1940. The race against Republican Wendell Willkie, who was for integration of the armed services, was hotly contested, but Franklin won handily. Still, after the election, some of Eleanor's closest friends in the African American community remained angry about the president's hesitations on civil rights issues.

Pauli Murray wrote to the president and First Lady comparing Franklin, who used "vague and general language" about race, to Willkie, who clearly stated racial prejudice was like "imperialism."

Eleanor fought back. "I wonder if it ever occurred to you

that Mr. Willkie has no responsibility whatsoever? He can say whatever he likes and do whatever he likes, and nothing very serious will happen." Had he been elected president, she noted sharply, Willkie would have had to deal with the Southern bloc in Congress and angry segments of the public, just as Franklin did. She let her personal bitterness show when she added that for someone as well versed in the political system as Pauli, "your letter seems to me one of the most thoughtless I've ever read."

In her reply, Pauli admitted that, yes, her letter was rude and reckless. But it was written from a place of "desperation and disgust." She wrote a long letter, detailing her frustrations, and the First Lady's anger softened. She invited Pauli to New York to talk things over in person. A nervous Pauli was relieved when Eleanor greeted her at the door of her apartment with a hug. She had come to argue but left with her "militant armor replaced by unreserved affection." They agreed to continue their dialogue.

President Roosevelt spent a good deal of time during the first two years of his unprecedented third term trying to rally support for England, which was virtually alone in the fight after Belgium, Luxembourg, and the Netherlands were invaded by Germany in May of 1940. France was lost in June. Germany turned on its ally, the Soviet Union, invading in June of 1941. It seemed inevitable that the United States would soon be dragged into another world war.

Just as the armed services needed to be mobilized, the defense industries that would build the ships and planes, manufacture guns and ammunition, and provide numerous other necessities of war, had to be beefed up. This meant that for the first time since 1929, there would now be plenty of jobs, and African Americans expected they would benefit. Individual lives and whole communities would be vastly improved with more employment opportunities. Many African Americans had been trained in New Deal programs for more skilled jobs, and were now ready to take them.

But instead of opportunity, what they often received was more racism. One Kansas City steel company noted that they hadn't had a black employee in twenty-five years and didn't intend to start now. An aviation company stated that "Negroes will be considered only as janitors."

There were many ways of keeping people out of jobs. Black applicants would receive high scores on defense companies' entrance exams, but they still wouldn't be hired, or they'd be pushed aside by whites who had much lower scores or who had no training at all. This happened throughout the country.

The African American community decided to take things into their own hands. A. Philip Randolph went to several civil rights groups, including the NAACP and the Urban League, with an idea. They would organize a ten-thousand-man march on Washington, right down Pennsylvania Avenue between the White House and the Capitol building, to protest racial discrimination in war industries, as well as the larger issue of segregation.

There were doubters among some who Randolph approached. Could ten thousand people really be counted on? But in African American communities, the enthusiasm for the march grew. This was a chance for people who felt they were being ignored to make their voices heard. Randolph upped the number of how many would come to Washington, D.C., on July 1, 1941, to march. Now it would be one hundred thousand!

This caught the White House's attention. The last thing Franklin wanted was a massive march in a summer-hot city that could lead to violence. Eleanor, who had been speaking at African American colleges and other venues during the spring, apprised the president of what was happening in the black community. Eleanor told Franklin about how upset people were about the difficulties they had getting access to defense jobs, and he agreed that the walls put up against them weren't fair.

As July 1 grew closer, it became clear to those in the Roosevelt administration that the march was happening. The president had already taken the unheard-of step of making, as one historian put it, "the first official call for what later became known as affirmative action." He wrote his aides ordering them to take "Negroes up to a certain percentage in factory order work. Judge them on quality." The president didn't like the fact that "first-class Negroes are turned down for third-class white boys."

This request went out to companies, but Randolph and others knew the time for requests was over. Eleanor was not in favor of the march. She too worried that there would be violence on the streets of Washington. The First Lady made direct pleas, in meetings and in person, to call off the march. Randolph, while appreciating her position, declined. Finally Franklin agreed once again to schedule a meeting between Randolph, Walter White, and members of his administration.

It took place at the White House on June 18, a few weeks before the march. As usual, Franklin tried to charm and placate Randolph and White, but Randolph remained firm. When asked by the president what he wanted done, Randolph replied, "We want you to issue an executive order making it mandatory that Negros be permitted to work in these plants."

The president demurred. He couldn't do it. What if other groups asked for the same thing?

Well, one of his aides who was present wondered, so what if they did? Maybe it would be best to include *all* groups in the executive order.

The negotiating went back and forth over the next day. Eleanor became involved, too. She was up on remote Campobello Island, but she walked the half mile down to the telegraph office where there was a telephone to read the last draft to Randolph. Executive Order 8802 stated that both employers and labor unions were "to provide for the full and equitable participation of all workers in defense industries, without discrimination because of race, creed, color, or national origin." A Fair Employment Practice Committee would be set up to oversee the order.

The one-hundred-thousand-man march was called off.

FIGHTING AND DYING

A date which will live in infamy." That's how Franklin described December 7, 1941, the day Japan launched a devastating air attack on U.S. naval ships and military facilities at Pearl Harbor, Hawaii. He spoke these words the following day as he asked a joint session of Congress for a declaration of war. Within an hour of his speech, Congress issued that declaration. Four days later, Germany and Italy declared war on the United States.

For Americans, World War II had officially begun.

Isolationism was now forgotten, and men all over the country went to their local recruitment offices to enlist. In the first years of the war, black men—volunteers and those who were drafted—were usually assigned to service units that helped supply and maintain troops on the front lines. As the war dragged on, the government needed men, black and white, to take the place of fallen infantrymen, pilots, and officers. Still, throughout the war, the problem of segregation remained.

From the first moments of battle, servicemen of color distinguished themselves. The argument that black men in the navy were only capable of being messmen was turned on its head when one of the heroes of Pearl Harbor was a black sailor, Dorie Miller. Miller carried his captain through raging flames to safety, and then without weapons training, picked up a machine gun and began firing at Japanese planes. At first, the navy only wanted to give him a commendation for his actions, but on May 11, 1942, Franklin approved the Navy Cross for Miller, that service's third-highest award at the time.

World War II brought almost unbelievable stresses for Franklin and Eleanor. On a personal level, there was concern about their four sons serving in the armed forces. Elliott in the Army Air Corps, James in the Marine Corps, and Franklin Jr. and John in the navy. Eleanor said, "I imagine every mother felt as I did when I said goodbye to the children during the war. I had a feeling that I might be saying goodbye for the last time."

In the fall of 1941, Sara died at age eighty-seven. Franklin keenly felt the loss of the mother who adored him. Eleanor was sympathetic, but her feelings about Sara remained unresolved. "I kept being appalled at myself because I couldn't feel any real grief," Eleanor told her daughter, Anna, and that seemed "terrible" after their long relationship.

Just a few weeks later, Eleanor had the emotional task of sitting by the bedside of her dying brother, Hall, who had battled alcoholism for decades. "My idea of hell, if I believed in it, would be to . . . watch someone breathing hard, struggling for words . . . and thinking this was once the little boy I played with and scolded. He could have been so much and this is what he is . . . in spite of everything, I've loved Hall . . ."

Meanwhile, the fate of the world was on Franklin's shoulders. There was no guarantee that the United States and its allies, Great Britain and the Soviet Union, would win the war.

Instead of the war drawing the president and the First Lady closer together, it pulled them apart. Franklin was, naturally, consumed with war plans. Eleanor didn't know how to make herself useful in this new situation. Sometimes, she vehemently opposed his decisions.

In February 1942, Franklin signed an executive order that

effectively allowed the internment of Americans of Japanese descent. Even though they had done nothing wrong, because they looked the same as America's enemies, they were considered a danger. More than one hundred thousand Japanese Americans would eventually be moved from their homes, lose their property, and be relocated in camps.

JAPANESE AMERICANS WAITING TO BE TAKEN TO AN INTERNMENT CAMP IN SALINAS, CALIFORNIA

Eleanor disagreed with internment, wrote against it, and visited a Japanese camp to observe the conditions in 1943. She made a short speech there that noted while she could understand "the bitterness" of those who had lost loved ones to the

Japanese enemy, she felt that the issues of Japanese Americans must be looked at "objectively . . . for the honor of our country." For the First Lady, that meant emptying the camps as soon as possible. Though some camp residents began to leave at the end of that year, the camps were not fully closed until 1946.

There was also disagreement with the president on the subject of refugees. She had been interested since the late 1930s in helping Jewish refugees trying to escape Hitler's Germany find a home in the United States. But until the bombing of Pearl Harbor, public opinion remained isolationist and unwelcoming of refugees. The United States took in about one hundred thousand refugees from 1933 to 1940. This was a larger number than any other country, but only a small percentage of those trying to flee.

Eleanor focused her efforts on bringing Jewish children to the United States from Europe. Franklin didn't spend much time on the problem of European Jews specifically, maintaining the best way to save the Jews was to win the war. Nevertheless, by 1943 both Roosevelts knew what much of the public did not: The Jews were not just being taken to labor camps as Nazi propaganda claimed. They were being systematically murdered.

Eleanor was greatly disturbed by Franklin's tightening of

immigration laws, which his administration said reduced the chance of Nazi spies entering the country. Of course, it also reduced the number of frantic refugees. In 1941, Eleanor said to a friend, "One of the things that troubles me is that when people are in trouble, whether it's the dust bowl or the miners . . . the first people who come forward and try to help are the Jews. Now in these terrible days . . . why they don't they come [to help the Jewish people]?"

ELEANOR SAW FOR HERSELF THE DESTRUCTION THAT NAZI BOMBS HAD CAUSED LONDON WHEN SHE VISITED IN 1942.

Feeling her presence at home was not helpful to her husband, Eleanor spent time traveling during the war years. She made a three-week goodwill trip to England in 1942, winning friends among the British people.

DURING A TRIP TO ENGLAND IN 1942, ELEANOR MET WITH KING GEORGE VI AND QUEEN ELIZABETH.

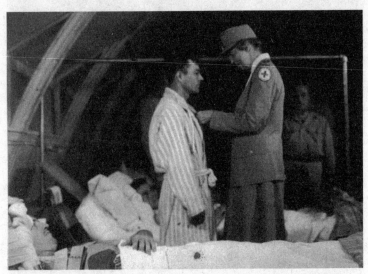

ELEANOR VISITED THE TROOPS—ESPECIALLY THOSE WHO WERE WOUNDED—BRINGING THEM COMFORT AND THE SINCERE THANKS OF THE PRESIDENT FOR THEIR SACRIFICES.

In 1943 she took a controversial trip to the Pacific theater of war, where the fighting was especially intense. The admirals and generals thought her trip would be a nuisance, but her visits with the service people in the field and those injured in hospitals brought comfort and a bit of home to them—and

ELEANOR FLEW MORE THAN 23,000 MILES IN THE ARMY TRANSPORT PLANE TO PLACES THROUGHOUT THE SOUTH PACIFIC, FROM NEW ZEALAND TO FIJI TO AUSTRALIA.

admiration for her. One soldier who heard her speak said, "We liked this speech . . . it was good to hear a kind lady saying nice things." Even Admiral William Halsey, one of her most vocal critics, later admitted, "She did more good than any other person or group of civilians, who passed through my area."

Yet even with her nonstop travels, the "Negro" question, as it was called then, was never long out of Eleanor's mind. In the United States, there was continued racial unrest during the war years. There were still lynchings, prejudice in hiring and employment, and segregation throughout American society. Eleanor continued to work alongside African American leaders in their fight for civil rights.

One issue that caught her attention occurred in Detroit, Michigan. The Sojourner Truth housing project was built for blacks working in defense industries, but white workers demanded the housing for themselves. At the request of civil rights leaders, Eleanor lobbied her husband, and eventually—after violent racial encounters—the project was given to its intended residents. Later in 1943, more racial rioting broke out in Detroit, and some put the blame directly on the First Lady, accusing her of trying too hard to mix the races and the "coddling of Negroes." Used to attacks, Eleanor replied, "I suppose when one is being forced to realize that an unwelcome change is coming, one must blame it on someone or something."

Letters continued to flood the White House accusing the First Lady of being a troublemaker who stirred the pot of racial division. Most of the criticism came from whites, but African Americans also didn't like the way she sometimes counseled restraint or patience. One historian later said she could, at times, "sound patronizing." The president, as usual, was content to let Eleanor take much of the heat on the issue of civil rights so he could continue running the war and the country.

One of the knottiest racial problems concerned the armed services in the South, where transportation and use of base facilities was a big issue for black military personnel. These service people now included African American women. In 1942, Congress approved the creation of the Women's Army Auxiliary Corps. These women served as stenographers, postal clerks, and truck drivers, as well as in other noncombat roles. African American women served in segregated units. Two of the training centers for the WAACs were in the South, one in Georgia, another in Louisiana.

Since buses and trains in the South were segregated, black service people were often at the back of the line when it came to getting tickets. If they didn't return to their bases on time, they were considered AWOL—away without official leave—and penalized.

In other cases, blacks were at stations where they couldn't buy food because there were no segregated facilities and they weren't allowed to eat with whites. In one instance, German prisoners of war were served in a station lunchroom because they were white, while black Americans had to eat in the kitchen! It's no wonder the soldiers asked themselves what kind of democracy they were fighting for. All this was particularly shocking for African Americans who had been raised in the North and hadn't had to live under stringent Jim Crow laws.

Eleanor fought hard to make sure the War Department looked at the busing situation. She noted, "These colored boys lie side by side in the hospitals . . . with the white boys and somehow it is hard for me to believe that they should not be treated on an equal basis."

At last, the War Department agreed with her. On July 8, 1944, they issued a directive stating all transportation owned and operated by the government would be available to all military personnel regardless of race and regardless of local customs. This did not cover private transportation companies, but it was a big first step.

In 1944, further progress was made in desegregating the navy. A new secretary of the navy, James Forrestal, had ambitious plans for integration. Although by now the navy had allowed blacks to serve as more than messmen, these new jobs did not, as a rule, place them on ships. Instead, black sailors were often placed at docks, moving equipment and loading ships.

A tragedy occurred in Port Chicago, California, in July of 1944, as six hundred men, mostly black, were loading ammunition and bombs onto ships. A giant explosion destroyed the pier and killed more than two hundred black sailors and injured hundreds more. This event spurred Secretary of the Navy Forrestal to move even more quickly on with his plans. His directive on "Negro Naval Personnel" stated that no inherent differences existed between blacks and whites and that each member of the navy would be trained according to his abilities and promoted on the basis of his performance.

Eleanor was pleased with the forward motion, but there was one branch of the service that had her personal attention: the first unit of black combat pilots, the Ninety-

Ninth Pursuit Squadron. Trained in Tuskegee, Alabama, near the Tuskegee Institute founded by Booker T. Washington, they were also known as the Tuskegee Airmen.

The program had been initiated in 1941 after a black pilot who had been denied a place in the Army Air Corps won a legal battle, and a combat-training program for blacks was court ordered. Though obligated to train black pilots, there was nothing that said the Army Air Corps had to use them. So by 1942, not one of the thousand pilots that had been trained had seen active service.

The First Lady was well aware of this situation—demoralizing to the men involved, and wasteful when it came to helping the war effort. She wrote several times to the secretary of war, but still the airmen sat idle. Eleanor wanted to show her concern personally and struck up correspondences with both faculty and random airmen. She was particularly taken with one of the young fliers, Cecil Peterson, and asked him to keep her informed about how things were going. They wrote back and forth for three years. Cecil told her, "Your letters and gifts are inspiring and have prompted me to be a better soldier." He also asked her to tell the president, "there's a private down here rooting for him."

As a more public display of support, Eleanor went flying with Charles A. Anderson, a Tuskegee Airman, in Alabama and insisted a photograph be taken. The news got national coverage, and the First Lady used the picture and reporting to convince the president to activate the Tuskegee Airmen's unit.

Finally, in 1943, the Tuskegee Airmen were sent overseas to fight in both North Africa and Europe. They performed brilliantly. In over fifteen hundred missions, they shot down more than two hundred enemy aircraft without losing any of their own planes to enemy fire. As a group, the Tuskegee Airmen won over one hundred Distinguished Flying Cross medals.

A turning point in World War II came on June 6, 1944. The Allied forces, one hundred fifty thousand strong, landed on the beaches of Normandy, France, and went on to liberate Europe.

If running for a third term was unprecedented, running for a fourth presidential term was almost unthinkable. Franklin, however, was determined to see the war to a successful conclusion as president. On November 7, with Harry S. Truman as his running mate, he won once more.

But Franklin was ailing. Polio—and its long-term effects on his body—was just one of his medical issues. He suffered

from high blood pressure, coronary heart disease, and conges-
tive heart failure, all exacerbated by his chain-smoking and
his stress. Just a few months after his inauguration, he died at
his retreat in Warm Springs, Georgia, on April 12, 1945. He did
not live to see the Allies' victory over Germany only a month
later in May 1945. In August, victory over Japan was achieved
after the dropping of atomic bombs on the Japanese cities of
Hiroshima and Nagasaki.

Though Franklin had been suffering with many ailments,
all of which contributed to his worsening health, he died from
a cerebral hemorrhage while having his portrait painted. Eleanor was at a speaking engagement when she was told to return
to the White House immediately. "I did not even ask why," she
later remembered. "In my heart I knew . . ." Anna and her husband, John Boettiger, along with presidential aide Steve Early
gave her the news. As for the four Roosevelt sons, they were all
on active duty in war zones. She cabled them with the news.
"He did his job to the end as he would want you to do. Bless
you all, and all our love."

Eleanor, along with Steve Early and the president's personal physician, flew to Warm Springs to escort the body home
by train. As Franklin's coffin left Warm Springs, the president's

friend Graham Jackson, an African American musician, took out his accordion and played the mournful spiritual "Goin' Home."

As the train rolled along the tracks back to Washington, Eleanor looked out the window and was gratified to see people, black and white, waving and holding signs of sympathy. The comfort of those signs was marred by the news offered by one gossipy Roosevelt cousin who had been present when the president died. Franklin had not been alone, she informed Eleanor. At his side was his old love, Lucy Mercer Rutherfurd.

This information blindsided Eleanor. Franklin's long-ago promise to her, that he would never again see Lucy, had been broken. Now she was learning this news at a moment of intense grief. She was further upset to find out her daughter, Anna, had facilitated a number of visits between him and Lucy at the White House over the years at her father's request.

Eleanor didn't have too much time to dwell on this betrayal, though she did confront Anna when she returned with the president's body to the White House. Her daughter tried to make her understand that she had been caught between two parents, but Anna worried her strong bond with Eleanor was now severely strained.

The next days were hectic. Eleanor had to plan the funeral and move out of the White House so the new president and his family could move in. When now-president Truman asked Eleanor if there was anything he could do for her, she replied, "Is there anything we can do for you? For you are the one in trouble now."

Franklin's funeral, with two hundred friends and relatives in attendance, took place in the East Room of the White House. His body, accompanied by Eleanor, was then taken by train to be buried in the garden of his beloved Hyde Park estate. Along the route, just as on the journey from Georgia to Washington, Americans of all colors, religions, and creeds stood alongside the tracks, crying and holding American flags. At his burial, Eleanor asked that the last words he had written in a speech that he never gave be included: "The only limit to our realization of tomorrow will be our doubts of today. Let us move forward with strong and active faith."

On April 20, 1945, Eleanor left the White House. Now a widow, no longer the First Lady, when she arrived at her apartment in New York City, she was startled to see a group of reporters at her door.

Eleanor shooed them away. "The story is over."

11

TURNING THE PAGE

But the story was not over. A sixty-year-old woman as engaged and vital as Eleanor Roosevelt was not going to stay at home with her beloved knitting. A new chapter of her life was just beginning.

In December of 1945, President Truman asked Eleanor to be one of the United States delegates to the newly formed United Nations, which was about to hold its first meeting in London. At first, Eleanor said no. Then, after prodding from the president, she said she would think about it. Finally, "with fear and trembling," she said yes. She realized that, as someone who hated war and loved peace and who felt strongly that the countries of the world should function as neighbors not adversaries, she had much to bring to the table.

Her male counterparts on the delegation—and they were all males—saw it differently. Some of them disagreed with her politically, and some of them didn't like her personally. Eleanor was fully aware that sexism was also part of the equation. She knew "that as the only woman, I had better be better than anybody else . . . I knew that if I in any way failed, that it would not just be my failure. It would be the failure of all women. . . ."

The hostility against Eleanor was evident from the first. The men on the committee made snide comments, and in meetings, they often ignored her opinion. But Eleanor wasn't one to be ignored. She continued to speak up and make her points.

As one of her UN assignments, she was the U.S. representative tasked with tackling the massive worldwide refugee problem. Close to a million people had been displaced during the war. The Soviet Union demanded that Soviet refugees and refugees from countries that were now in their sphere of influence, like Poland and Hungary, be returned to their home countries. But many of those refugees did not want to live under those repressive Soviet regimes. Others, who had

ELEANOR ADDRESSING THE GENERAL ASSEMBLY AT THE UNITED NATIONS IN JULY 1947

spoken against the Soviet Union or communism, feared they would be imprisoned or killed.

Eleanor's Soviet counterpart on the committee insisted these refugees be returned, but thanks to her ability to debate and persuade, the United Nations General Assembly voted to allow refugees to live where they preferred. This was a big victory for refugees' freedom of movement and for Eleanor herself. Her biggest critic in her delegation, U.S. senator Arthur Vandenberg, was finally persuaded as well. He now saw Eleanor's talent and value. "I want to take back everything I ever said about her," he declared, "and believe me it's been plenty!"

The UN delegation, on which she served for six years, wasn't Eleanor's only area of activity. As always, her concerns were wide and varied. She took great interest in the Jewish victims of the Holocaust and lobbied for the Jewish people to have their own state. Israel was recognized by the United States in 1948.

ALTHOUGH A SUPPORTER OF ISRAEL, ELEANOR ALSO SPOKE OF AND WROTE ABOUT HER CONCERNS FOR THE COUNTRY'S ARAB POPULATION. HERE SHE VISITS WITH A BEDOUIN BOY IN BEERSHEBA, ISRAEL, IN 1959.

She also traveled the world to see the living conditions of women and offer her support for women's rights. She visited with heads of states. At home she joined a board that oversaw Wiltwyck, a school for abused boys. After so many years in the public eye, she knew how to gather support for the causes she believed in, through her writings, her speeches, and media appearances.

ONE OF THE POSTS ELEANOR TOOK ON AFTER FRANKLIN'S DEATH WAS BOARD MEMBER OF THE WILTWYCK SCHOOL FOR BOYS. IN 1947, SHE BROUGHT A GROUP OF BOYS TO VAL-KILL FOR A PICNIC.

But despite her many concerns and interests, she never neglected the fight for civil rights. After their contributions to winning World War II, African Americans were unwilling to go backward. The issue heated up during the 1950s and '60s. African Americans were sick and tired of segregation. They wanted full voting rights, educational and employment equality, and the same access to public facilities that was available to whites. Black citizens were entitled to the Declaration of Independence's promise of "life, liberty, and the pursuit of happiness." It was time—past time.

Eleanor Roosevelt remained active in the cause she had taken up while she was First Lady. And with Franklin gone, she no longer had to worry about political concerns. She joined the boards of the NAACP and CORE (the Congress of Racial Equality) to help the progress of the civil rights movement. She used her influence with Harry Truman in 1948 to have him become the first president to speak at the NAACP convention. He made his speech, joined by Eleanor, on the steps of the Lincoln Memorial.

Eleanor continued her "My Day" newspaper column, which she had begun writing in 1935, along with a question-and-answer column in the *Ladies Home Journal* called "If You Ask Me." She used these columns, her other writings, and her speeches to discuss civil rights, trying to explain how discrimination, segregated schools, and efforts to repress the black vote through roadblocks like poll taxes were the opposite of what America should stand for.

During the Montgomery Bus Boycott, when the black citizens of Montgomery, Alabama, refused to ride public transit until it was integrated, she met with Rosa Parks. Parks had sparked the boycott in December 1955 by refusing to move to the back of the bus. Eleanor also worked with Dr. Martin Luther King Jr. to raise money for the boycott.

Dr. King was her first guest on her 1959 television show, *Prospects of Mankind*. And when he was arrested during a protest march and thrown into a Georgia jail in 1960, she defended him in her columns, noting this action would lose the United States respect in the eyes of the world.

IN 1958, ALONG WITH SINGER AND ACTIVIST HARRY BELAFONTE, ELEANOR LOOKS AT ONE OF FRANKLIN'S QUOTES MEMORIALIZED IN BRUSSELS, BELGIUM.

Dr. King admired Eleanor greatly, and she admired him. King's "insistence that there be no hatred in this struggle" was, in her view, "almost more than human beings can achieve." As for his part, he wrote to her in 1962, "Once again, for all you have done, and I'm sure will continue to do to help extend the fruits of Democracy ... please accept my deep and lasting gratitude."

As the fight for civil rights grew more intense during the early 1960s, Eleanor seesawed between feeling buoyed about the progress that had been made and distressed at the increasing violence against the protesters.

But her own struggle was almost over. In 1960, Eleanor was diagnosed with aplastic anemia, a blood disease. In 1962, she was given a course of steroid drugs that led to her heart failing. She died that year at her home in New York City on November 7, at the age of seventy-eight. The world mourned her death, and Dr. King eulogized her by saying, "The impact of her personality and its unwavering devotion to high principle and purpose cannot be contained in a single day or era."

Three months after her death, her last book, *Tomorrow Is Now*, was published. In it she made her final call to get involved in the civil rights movement: "Staying aloof is not a solution, but a cowardly evasion."

Eleanor Roosevelt was no coward. When the FBI informed her in 1958 that the Ku Klux Klan had placed that $25,000 bounty on her head, they told her it would be best if she canceled her appearance at the Highlander Folk School. She thanked them for the information and then made plans to go anyway.

ELEANOR CONDUCTS A CLASS AT THE HIGHLANDER FOLK SCHOOL
AND CHATS WITH THE ATTENDEES.

Eleanor flew to the Nashville airport where she was met by another older woman, and they drove to the Highlander Folk School in rural Tennessee, her pistol on the seat between them. As one historian put it, "And here they are. They are going to go through the Klan. They're going to stand down the Klan . . . they drive up at night through the mountains to this tiny labor school to conduct a workshop on how to break the law."

Fortunately, the Klan didn't confront them. Maybe they knew who they were dealing with.

Until her death, Eleanor Roosevelt probably did more than any other white person to change the course of race relations in the United States. In part, that was because she had access to presidents—not just Franklin, but also Harry Truman and later John F. Kennedy—who had the power to make things happen. But it was also because she was able to explain to everyday citizens, through her speeches, columns, books, radio and television appearances, and even personal letters, how corrosive segregation was, not just to African Americans, but to the country as a whole.

On a more personal note, her friend Pauli Murray said after Eleanor's death, "The great lesson Mrs. R. taught all of us by example was largesse, generosity—her heart seemed to me as big as all the world."

As a child, Eleanor lived in her own world of dreams and terrors. As an adult she fought for what she believed in, overcame her fears and prejudices, and helped others do the same. Perhaps she described her life best: "You gain strength, courage, and confidence by every experience in which you really stop to look fear in the face. You must do the thing which you think you cannot do."

Again and again, Eleanor Roosevelt did just that.

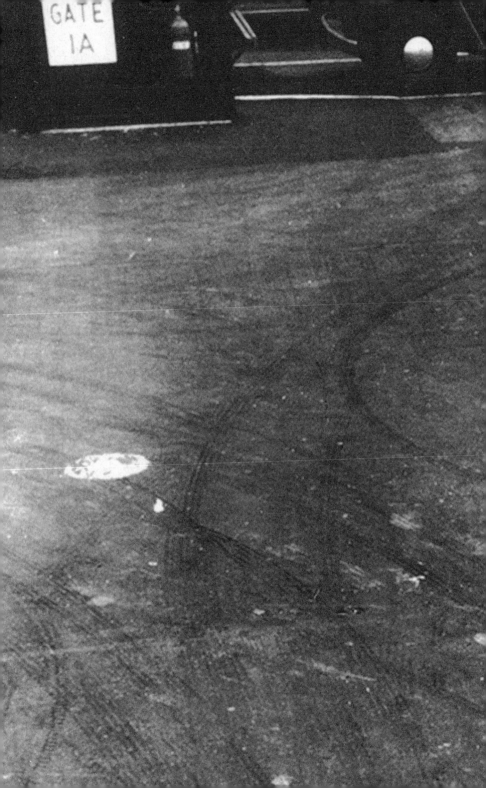

ELEANOR LEAVING LAGUARDIA
AIRPORT IN 1960, SUITCASE IN
HAND, STILL ON THE GO

ELEANOR IN HER OWN WORDS

EXCERPTS OF "ADDRESS BY MRS. FRANKLIN D. ROOSEVELT—
THE CHICAGO CIVIL LIBERTIES COMMITTEE,"
MARCH 14, 1940*

The numerals in brackets refer to the paragraph number of the speech.

[2] Now we have come here tonight because of civil liberties. I imagine a great many of you could give my talk far better than I because you have first-hand knowledge of the things you have had to do in Chicago, over the years, to preserve civil liberties. But I, perhaps, am more conscious of the importance of civil liberties in this particular moment of our history than anyone else, because, as I travel through the country and meet people and see the things that have happened to little people, I am more and more conscious of what it means to democracy to preserve our civil liberties. All through the years we have had to fight for civil liberty, and we know that there are times when the light grows rather dim. Every time that happens democracy is in danger. Now, largely because of the troubled state of the world as a whole, civil liberties have disappeared in many other countries. It is impossible, of course, to be at war and to maintain freedom of the press, freedom of speech, and freedom of assembly. They disappear automatically. And so, in some countries where ordinarily these rights were inviolate, today they have gone. And in some other countries, even before war came, not only had freedom of the press, freedom of assembly, and freedom of speech disappeared, but also freedom of religion. And so we know that here in this country we have a grave responsibility.

* THE COMPLETE SPEECH MAY BE FOUND AT VOICESOFDEMOCRACY.UMD.EDU/ELEANOR-ROOSEVELT-ADDRESS-BY-MRS-FRANKIN-D-ROOSEVELT-THE-CHICAGO-CIVIL-LIBERTIES-COMMITTEE-4-MARCH-1950.

[7] There are many times when, even though there is freedom of the press and freedom of speech, it is hard to get a hearing for certain noble causes. I often think that we, all of us, should think very much more carefully than we do about what we mean by freedom of speech, by freedom of the press, by freedom of assembly. I sometimes am much worried by the tendency that exists among certain groups in our country today to consider that these are rights are only for people who think as they do, that they are not rights for the people who disagree with them. I believe that you must apply to all groups the same rights, to all forms of thought, to all forms of expression, the same liberties. Otherwise, you practically deny the fact that you trust the people to choose for themselves, in a majority, what is wise and what is right. And when you do that, you deny the possibility of having a democracy. You have got to be willing to listen, to allow people to state any point of view they may have or to say anything they may believe, and then to trust that, when everyone has had his say, when there has been free discussion and really free, uninfluenced expression in the press, in the end the majority of the people will have the wisdom to decide what is right. We have got to have faith, even when the majority decides wrongly. We must still hold to the fundamental principles that we have laid down and wait for the day to come when the thing that we believe is right becomes the majority way of the people.

[11] I think we should begin much earlier to teach all the children of our nation what a wonderful heritage of freedom they have–of freedom from prejudice–because they live in a nation which is made up of a great variety of other nations. They have before them and around them every day the proof that people can understand each other and can live together amicably, and that races can live on an equal basis even though they may be very different in background, very different in culture. We have an opportunity to teach our children how much we have gained from the coming to this land of all kinds of races, of how much this has served in the

development of the land. Yet somehow I think we have failed in many ways to bring early enough to children how great is their obligation to the various strains that make up the people of the United States. Above all, there should never be race prejudice; there should never be a feeling that one strain is better than another. After all, we are all immigrants–all except Indians, who, we might say, are the only inhabitants of this country who have a real right to say that they own the country. I think that our being composed of so many foreign peoples is the very reason why we should preserve the basic principles of civil liberty. It should be easy for us to live up to our Constitution, but there are many groups among us who do not live up to what was written in that Constitution.

[12] I am very much interested to find that in our younger generation there is a greater consciousness of what civil liberty really means. I think that is one of the hopeful things in the world today: that youth is really taking a tremendous interest in the preservation of civil liberties. It is a very hard period in the world for youth because they are faced with new problems. We don't know the answers to many of the problems that face us today, and neither do the young people. But the problems are very much more important to the young because they must start living. We have had our lives. The young people want to begin, but they can't find a way to get started. Perhaps that has made them more conscious of civil liberties. Perhaps that is why when you get a group of them together, you find them fighting against the prejudices which have grown up in our country, against the prejudices which have made it hard for the minority groups in our country.

[13] The other night someone sent up a question to me: "What do you think should be done about the social standing of the Negro race in this country?" Well, now, of course I think that the social situation is one that has to be dealt with by individuals. The real question that we have to face in this country is: what are we doing about the rights of

a big minority group of citizens in our democracy? That, we all have to face. Any citizen of this country is entitled to equality before the law; to equality of education; to equality at earning a living, as far as his abilities make that possible; to equality of participation in government, so that he may register his opinion in just the way that any other citizen can do. Now, those are basic rights, belonging to every citizen in every minority group. We have got, I think, to stand up and be counted when it comes to the question of whether any minority group is not to have those rights, because the minute we deny any of our basic rights to any citizen, we are preparing the way for the denial of those rights to someone else. Who is going to say it is not right today to do this or that? Who is going to say it is not right tomorrow? And where does it stop? We have to make up our minds as to what we really believe. We have to decide whether we believe in the Bill of Rights, in the Constitution of the United States, or whether we are going to modify it because of the fears that we may have at the moment.

[15] I should like to remind you that behind all those who fight for the Constitution as it was written, for the rights of the weak and for the preservation of civil liberties, there was a long line of courageous people. And that is something to be proud of and something to hold on to. But its only value lies in the premise that we profit by it and con- tinue the tradition in the future; that we do not let those people back of us down; that we have courage; that we do not succumb to fears of any kind; that we live up to the things we believe in; that we see that justice is done to the people under the Constitution, whether they belong to minority groups or not; that we realize that this country is a united country, in which all people have the same rights as citizens; and that we are grateful for that; and finally, that we trust the youth of the nation to herald the real principles of democracy-in-action in this country and to make this even more truly a democratic nation.

TIME LINE

ELEANOR ROOSEVELT'S LIFE
AND MAJOR DOMESTIC AND FOREIGN EVENTS
DURING THAT TIME

1884 Eleanor is born on October 11 in New York City.

1892 Eleanor's mother, Anna, dies, leaving behind three young children.

1893 Eleanor's brother, Elliott Jr., dies.

1894 Eleanor's father, Elliott Sr., commits suicide.

1899 Eleanor embarks on her education at the Allenswood Academy in England.

1901 Vice President Theodore Roosevelt becomes president after President William McKinley is assassinated.

1902 Eleanor returns from Allenswood to make her debut in New York society.

1903 The Wright brothers make their first powered flight at Kitty Hawk, North Carolina.

1905 Eleanor and Franklin Roosevelt are married on March 17, with President Theodore Roosevelt officiating.

1906 Daughter, Anna, is born.

1907 Son James is born.

1908 Henry Ford introduces the Model T automobile.

1909 Son Franklin Jr. is born in March but dies in November.

1909 The National Association for the Advancement of Colored People, the NAACP, was founded by W. E. B. Du Bois.

1910 Son Elliott is born.

1910 The Roosevelt family moves to Albany, the capital of New York, after Franklin is elected to the state senate.

1912 Woodrow Wilson is elected president.

1913 The Roosevelt family moves to Washington, D.C., after Franklin is appointed assistant secretary of the navy by President Woodrow Wilson.

1914 Son, also named Franklin Jr., is born.

1916 Son John is born.

1916 Jeannette Rankin of Montana becomes the first woman elected to the United States Congress.

1917 On April 6, the United States declares war on Germany, beginning U.S. involvement in World War I.

1918 Eleanor begins work for the American Red Cross.

1918 Eleanor discovers Franklin's affair with Lucy Mercer.

1918 World War I ends on November 11.

1920 Franklin runs as vice president on the Democratic ticket. After he loses, he works as a lawyer in New York.

1920 Women are granted the right to vote upon ratification of the Nineteenth Amendment to the Constitution.

1920 Warren G. Harding is elected president.

1920 Commercial radio begins broadcasting in the United States.

1921 While vacationing at the family's summer home in Canada, Franklin is stricken with polio.

1922 For the next five years, Eleanor is an active participant in progressive organizations such as the Women's Trade Union League, the League of Women Voters, and Women's Division of the New York State Democratic Committee.

1923 Warren G. Harding dies of a heart attack, and Vice President Calvin Coolidge becomes president.

1924 J. Edgar Hoover is appointed to head the FBI.

1926 The radio network NBC begins, followed by CBS the next year.

1927 Eleanor, along with her friend Marion Dickerman, buys the Todhunter School in New York City and begins teaching there.

1927 Charles Lindbergh is the first person to fly nonstop across the Atlantic Ocean.

1927 The first "talking picture," *The Jazz Singer*, is released.

1928 Franklin is elected governor of New York. Eleanor moves to Albany and assists her husband.

1928 Herbert Hoover is elected president.

1929 The stock market crashes, plunging the country into the Great Depression.

1932 Amelia Earhart flies solo across the Atlantic Ocean.

1932 Franklin is elected president of the United States.

1933 Eleanor assumes the role of First Lady. She takes on a number of projects, including advocating for the Arthurdale community, traveling throughout the country to observe the effect and efficiency of New Deal programs, and writing a newspaper column and books.

1933 Adolf Hitler becomes chancellor of Germany.

1934 Eleanor begins advocating for the African American community.

1936 Franklin is elected to his second term as president.

1939 Germany's invasion of Poland starts World War II in Europe.

1939 At the New York World's Fair, Franklin speaks via an invention new to most people, television.

1940 The Germans march through Europe continues.

1940 Franklin wins an unprecedented third term as president.

1941 Japan bombs Pearl Harbor, triggering the U.S. entry into World War II, fighting against Japan, Germany, and Italy.

1941-1945 World War II rages with battles throughout the world, and the Holocaust, the systematic murder of Jews and others, moves into high gear.

1941-1945 Eleanor spends the war years visiting the troops and promoting the Tuskegee Airmen, an African American unit of the U.S. Army Air Corps.

1944 Franklin wins a fourth term as president.

1945 Franklin dies in Warm Springs, Georgia, on April 12.

1945 Germany surrenders on May 7, ending the war in Europe.

1945 The United States drops atomic bombs on the Japanese cities of Hiroshima and Nagasaki. Japan announces its surrender on August 15, 1945.

1945 President Harry S. Truman appoints Eleanor to the newly formed United Nations.

1947 Eleanor becomes chair of the Commission on Human Rights of the United Nations, which issues a Universal Declaration of Human Rights.

1952 Dwight D. Eisenhower is elected president of the United States.

1952-1957 Eleanor travels the world. Her visits include Israel, India, Thailand, and the U.S.S.R.

1960 John F. Kennedy is elected president.

1962 Eleanor dies of heart failure after contracting aplastic anemia and tuberculosis of the bone marrow.

NOTES

PROLOGUE

vi   "even if they had to blow the place up" www.pbs.org/wgbh /americanexperience/features/primary-resources/eleanor-fbi/2/.

vii   Information on the history of the Highlander Folk School can be found at www.tnhistoryforkids.org/history/in-search-of /in-search-of/highlander.2522958.

vii   Information on Eleanor's visit can be found at www.neh.gov /humanities/2000/januaryfebruary/feature/eleanor-roosevelt.

1
Granny

1–2   "My mother was one of the most beautiful . . ." Eleanor Roosevelt, *The Autobiography of Eleanor Roosevelt* (New York: Harper Perennial, reprint edition, 2014) 3.

3   "a miracle from heaven . . ." Joseph P. Lash, *Eleanor and Franklin: The Story of Their Relationship Based on Eleanor Roosevelt's Private Papers.* (New York: W. W. Norton, 1971) 21.

3   "sink through the floor . . ." Roosevelt, *Autobiography,* 9.

3   "ugly" Candace Fleming, *Our Eleanor: A Scrapbook Look at Eleanor Roosevelt's Remarkable Life* (New York: Antheneum Books for Young Readers/Anne Schwartz, 2005).

4   "through the Grand snow-clad forests . . ." Eric Burns, *Someone to Watch Over Me: A Portrait of Eleanor Roosevelt and the Tortured Father Who Shaped Her Life* (New York: W. W. Norton/Pegasus, 2017) 76 (galley).

4   "With my father . . ." Roosevelt, *Autobiography*, 5.

6   "a small and ragged urchin" Burns, *Someone*, 12.

8   "somehow it was always . . ." Roosevelt, *Autobiography*, 9.

9   "I knew in my mind . . ." Russell Freedman, *Eleanor Roosevelt: A Life of Discovery* (New York: Clarion Books, 1993) 15.

10   "We were brought up on the principle . . ." Roosevelt, *Autobiography*, 6.

10   "Your mother wanted . . ." Lash, *Eleanor and Franklin*, 73.

11   "Suddenly life . . ." Roosevelt, *Autobiography*, 20.

11   "Anything I had accomplished . . ." Lash, *Eleanor and Franklin*, 6.

2
Finding Herself

12   "lost and lonely" Roosevelt, *Autobiography*, 20.

12   "eyes looked through you . . . and she always knew . . ." Ibid., 22.

14   "courageous judgment . . ." Lash, *Eleanor and Franklin*, 80.

14   "underdog should . . ." Ibid., 80.

15–16   "Never again would I be . . ." Roosevelt, *Autobiography*, 31.

16   "more satisfaction . . ." Ibid., 29.

18   "Protect yourself . . ." Blanche Wiesen Cook, *Eleanor Roosevelt: Volume 1, The Early Years, 1884–1933* (New York: Penguin, 1992) 123.

18   "utter agony" Lash, *Eleanor and Franklin*, 93.

19   "She was always . . ." Cook, *Volume 1*, 128.

22   "misery and exploitation . . ." Lash, *Eleanor and Franklin*, 98.

22   "glow of pride" Freedman, *Eleanor Roosevelt*, 34.

23   "I was appalled . . . I saw little children . . ." Lash, *Eleanor and Franklin*, 100.

3
Losing Herself

25   "Oh! Darling, . . ." Cook, *Volume 1*, 139.

27   "A very good mind" Lash, *Eleanor and Franklin*, 101.

28   "with your help" Ibid., 98.

28   "My God . . ." Ibid., 135.

28–29   "Having been born . . ." Ibid.,119.

29   "good little mother's boy" Ibid., 103.

31   "A few irate guests . . ." Roosevelt, *Autobiography*, 50.

32   "I do not remember . . ." Ibid., 50.

34   "Your mother only bore you . . ." Fleming, *Our Eleanor*, 24.

35   "You were never quite sure . . ." Lash, *Eleanor and Franklin*, 162.

37   "I worried for fear . . ." Roosevelt, *Autobiography*, 63.

38   "Duty was perhaps the motivating force . . ." Ibid., 66.

38   "The first requisite . . ." Cook, *Volume 1*, 191.

38   "She was playing the political game . . ." Lash, *Eleanor and Franklin*, 192.

39   "was not favorably impressed" 67.

40   "felt as if my own son . . ." Cook, *Volume 1*, 197.

41   "May history repeat itself." Ibid., 200.

42   "the men in government . . ." Freedman, *Eleanor Roosevelt: A Life*, 58.

42   "I became a more tolerant person . . ." Roosevelt, *Autobiography*, 93.

4
A Life to Be Lived

48   "Life was meant to be lived" Roosevelt, *Autobiography*, 104.

48–49   "the Southern blood of my ancestors . . ." Cook, *Volume 1*, 251.

49   "The benefits of the war . . ." Ibid., 250.

50   "No words from you . . ." Cook, *Volume 1*, 252.

50   As a young woman . . . One discussion of Eleanor's feelings toward the Jews appears in this book review of *FDR and the Jews* by Richard Breitman and Allan J. Lichtman at jewishstandard.timesofisrael.com/eleanor-roosevelt-and-the -jews but is also mentioned in other sources. Her casual anti-Semitism was a hallmark of America's upper classes and what is remarkable is not her prejudice but her evolution. In *Eleanor Roosevelt: A Life of Discovery*, Russell Freedman comments that Eleanor knew virtually no blacks.

51   "superior creatures" Fleming, *Our Eleanor*, 43.

54   "Have something . . ." Roosevelt, *Autobiography*, 124.

55   "for the intensive education . . ." Roosevelt, *Autobiography*, 113.

56   "You will surely break down . . ." Cook, *Volume 1*, 309.

57   "the intense and devastating influence . . ." Hazel Rowley, *Franklin and Eleanor: An Extraordinary Marriage* (New York: Farrar, Straus and Giroux, 2010) 117.

58   "if he fights . . ." Fleming, *Our Eleanor*, 47.

59   "It began to dawn on me . . ."

61   "And I never forgot . . ." Cook, *Volume 1*, 399.

61   "into an enlivened understanding . . ." Ibid., 405.

61   "I like teaching better . . ." Ibid., 399.

62   "What was the food like . . ." Freedman, *Eleanor Roosevelt: A Life*, 87.

5
Reaching Out

64 "The only thing we have to fear . . ." www.pbs.org/wgbh /americanexperience/features/bonus-video/presidents-enemy-fdr.

69 "Well, all right . . ." Roosevelt, *Autobiography*, 176–177.

70 "Just for one day . . ." Fleming, *Our Eleanor*, 72.

70 "From March 1933 . . . the variety of requests . . ." Roosevelt, *Autobiography*, 171.

71 "a stranded generation" Blanche Wiesen Cook, *Eleanor Roosevelt: Volume 2, The Defining Years, 1933–1938* (New York: Penguin, 1992) 269.

72 "the missus organization" Fleming, *Our Eleanor*, 92.

72 "Out here . . ." Cook, *Volume 2*, 271.

75 "I couldn't believe my eyes . . ." Lash, *Eleanor and Franklin*, 522

76 "*Darky* was used. . ." Ibid., 522.

77 "She was not afraid . . ." jewishstandard.timesofisrael.com /eleanor-roosevelt-and-the-jews.

6
A New Standard for Understanding

80 "thoughtless people . . . just to make . . ." Cook, *Volume 2*, 156.

80–81 "Along the main street . . ." Cook, *Volume 2*, 130.

81–82 "He thinks . . ." Roosevelt, *Autobiography*, 178.

83 "I have always felt . . ." Cook, *Volume 2*, 151

84 "thoroughly opposed . . ." Cook, *Volume 2*, 139.

86 "I can remember . . ." Ibid., 159.

86–87 "Never before . . ." Ibid., 153.

87   "set before all of us . . ." Ibid., 153.

88   "the girl who did not stand up" Patricia Bell-Scott,
The Firebrand and the First Lady: Portrait of a Friendship
(New York: Knopf, 2016) 29.

88   "Twelve millions of your citizens . . ." Ibid., 27.

89   "isn't my problem alone . . ." Ibid., 27.

7
The Spur

91   "carnivals of death" The Editorial Board, "Lynching as Racial
Terrorism," *New York Times*, February 11, 2015, www.nytimes
.com/2015/02/11/opinion/lynching-as-racial-terrorism.html.

92   "We know that it is murder . . ." Blog of the Franklin D. Roosevelt
Presidential Library and Museum; "Eleanor Roosevelt's Battle
to End Lynching," blog entry by Paul M. Sparrow, Director,
February 12, 2016, fdr.blogs.archives.gov/2016/02/12/eleanor
-roosevelts-battle-to-end-lynching/.

93   "The President talked to me . . ." Lash, *Eleanor and Franklin*, 515.

94   Had she coached . . . "Well, at least I know . . ." The incident of the
Roosevelt-White meeting is reported in Cook, *Volume 2*, 181.

94   "I did not choose the tools . . ." Ibid., 516.

96   "dynamite" Ibid., 516.

97   "No, certainly not. . . . " Doris Kearns Goodwin, *No Ordinary
Time: Franklin and Eleanor Roosevelt—The Home Front in
World War II* (New York: Simon & Schuster, 1994) 164.

98   "Of course . . ." Cook, *Volume 2*, 246

98   "in silent rebuke . . ." Blog of the Franklin D. Roosevelt
Presidential Library and Museum; "Eleanor Roosevelt's Battle
to End Lynching," blog entry by Paul M. Sparrow, Director,

February 12, 2016, fdr.blogs.archives.gov/2016/02/12/eleanor
-roosevelts-battle-to-end-lynching/.

99 "He might have been happier.... Nevertheless..." Roosevelt,
Autobiography, 279.

8
It Never Hurts to Be Kind

101 Blog of Real-Time News from Birmingham; "The Week in
Birmingham History: Eleanor Roosevelt Faced Off Against Bull
Connor." Though reported in a number of books about Eleanor,
this article gives the fullest account: www.al.com/news
/birmingham/index.ssf/2014/11/the_week_in_birmingham
_history_23.html.

102 The insight about Eleanor kissing Mrs. Bethune appears in Lash,
Eleanor and Franklin, 523, and was reported in an interview he
conducted with Eleanor's daughter, Anna Roosevelt.

103 "not available to Negro artists." Blanche Wiesen Cook, *Eleanor
Roosevelt: Volume 3, The War Years and After, 1939–1962*
(New York: Viking, 2016) 34.

103 "shocked beyond words..." Ibid., 34.

103 "You had the opportunity to lead..." www.pbs.org/wgbh
/americanexperience/features/biography/eleanor-anderson.

103 "Genius knows no color line" www.youtube.com
/watch?v=mAONYTMf2pk This clip features highlights
of the Anderson concert.

105 "a firebrand" Bell-Scott, *The Firebrand*, xviii.

106 "burst into spontaneous laughter" Bell-Scott, *The Firebrand*, 114.

107 "I feel if these girls..." Lois Scharf, *Eleanor Roosevelt: First
Lady of American Liberalism* (Boston: C.K. Hall, 1987) 107.

107   "Surely you would not . . ." Lash, *Eleanor and Franklin*, 521.

109   "I'm not surprised . . ." Roosevelt, *Autobiography*, 193.

110   "develop skin as tough as a rhinoceros hide" Fleming, *Our Eleanor*, 104.

9
War Clouds

114   Religious and racial prejudice "are a great menace . . ." Cook, *Volume 3*, 248.

115   "Eleanor refused to be insulated . . ." Lash, *Volume 3, 521*.

115   "It seems incredible . . . Cook, *Volume 3*, 34.

117   "Hell, if you said you were colored . . ." Goodwin, *No Ordinary Time*, 166.

117   "Our main reason for writing . . ." Ibid., 167.

118   "You know, better than any other people . . . the road to better understanding . . . faith and cooperation . . ." Cook, *Volume 3*, 357.

118   "This is going to be very bad politically . . ." Lash, *Eleanor and Franklin*, 530.

118   "a commanding figure" Goodwin, *No Ordinary Time*, 161.

119   "emphasized that . . ." Cook, *Volume 3*, 362.

120   "experiments which would . . ." Goodwin, *No Ordinary Time*, 169.

121   "The policy of the War Department . . . This policy . . . to make changes . . ." Cook, *Volume 3*, 363.

122   "vague and general language" Bell-Scott, *The Firebrand*, 100.

122   "imperialism" Ibid., 100.

123-23   "I wonder if it ever occurred to you . . . your letter . . ." Ibid., 101.

123   "desperation and disgust." Ibid., 102.

123   "militant armor . . ." Ibid., 102.

124 "Negroes will be considered only . . ." Goodwin, *No Ordinary Time*, 246.

126 "the first official call . . ." Ibid., 249.

126 "Negroes up to a certain percentage . . ." Ibid., 249.

127 "We want you to issue an executive order . . ." Ibid., 249.

127 "to provide for the full and equitable participation . . ." Ibid., 252.

10
Fighting and Dying

128 "A date which will live in infamy" www.youtube.com /watch?v=W6ScDXwYjWA.

129 "I imagine every mother . . ." Fleming, *Our Eleanor*, 115.

130 "I kept being appalled . . ." Goodwin, *No Ordinary Time*, 274.

130 "My idea of hell . . ." Cook, *Volume 3*, 427.

131–32 "the bitterness . . . objectively . . . for the honor . . ." www.nps .gov/articles/erooseveltinternment.htm.

133 "One of the things . . ." jewishstandard.timesofisrael.com/eleanor -roosevelt-and-the-jews.

136 "We liked this speech . . ." Goodwin, *No Ordinary Time*, 463.

136 "She did more good . . ." Ibid., 465.

136–37 "coddling of Negroes . . . I suppose . . ." Ibid., 446.

137 "sound patronizing" Lash, *Eleanor and Franklin*, 676.

138 "These colored boys . . ." Goodwin, *No Ordinary Time*, 522.

140 "Your letters and gifts . . ." Fleming, *Our Eleanor*, 123.

140 "there's a private down here . . ." docs.fdrlibrary.marist.edu /images/p7742.jpg.

142 "In my heart . . ." Cook, *Volume 3*, 575.

142 "He did his job . . ." www.nytimes.com/learning/general /onthisday/big/0412.html?mcubz=0.

143   "Goin' Home" time.com/photography/life/.

144   "Is there anything . . ." Goodwin, *No Ordinary Time*, 605.

144   "The only limit . . ." Cook, *Volume 3*, 577.

144   "The story is over" Fleming, *Our Eleanor*, 131.

11
Turning the Page

145   "with fear and trembling" Eleanor Roosevelt, *On My Own: The Years Since the White House* (New York: Harper & Brothers, 1958) 299.

146   "that as the only woman . . ." Fleming, *Our Eleanor*, 135.

148   "I want to take back . . ." Joseph P. Lash, *Eleanor: The Years Alone* (New York: W. W. Norton, 1972) 47.

152   "insistence that there be no hatred in this struggle" kingencyclopedia.stanford.edu/encyclopedia/encyclopedia /enc_roosevelt_anna_eleanor_1884_1962.

152   "The impact of her personality . . ." Epitaph for Mrs. FDR. *New York Amsterdam News*, November 24, 1962.

153   "Staying aloof . . ." www.gwu.edu/-erpapers/teachinger/lesson -plans/notes-er-and-civil-rights.cfm.

154   "And here they are . . ." www. neh. gov/humanities/2000 /januaryfebruary/feature/ Eleanor Roosevelt.

155   "The great lesson . . ." Bell-Scott, *The Firebrand*, 352.

155   "You gain strength . . ." Eleanor Roosevelt, *You Learn by Living: Eleven Keys for a More Fulfilling Life* (New York: Harper Perennial, reprint edition, 2016).

BIBLIOGRAPHY

*Denotes books of interest for young people

BOOKS

Bell-Scott, Patricia. *The Firebrand and the First Lady: Portrait of a Friendship*. New York: Knopf, 2016.

Burns, Eric. *Someone to Watch Over Me: A Portrait of Eleanor Roosevelt and the Tortured Father Who Shaped her Life*. New York: W. W. Norton/Pegasus, 2017. (Galley)

Cook, Blanche Wiesen. *Eleanor Roosevelt: Volume 1, The Early Years, 1884–1933*. New York: Penguin, 1992.

———. *Eleanor Roosevelt: Volume 2, The Defining Years, 1933–1938*. New York: Penguin, 1999.

———. *Eleanor Roosevelt: Volume 3, The War Years and After, 1939–1962*. New York: Viking, 2016.

*Fleming, Candace. *Our Eleanor: A Scrapbook Look at Eleanor Roosevelt's Remarkable Life*. New York: Atheneum Books for Young Readers/Anne Schwartz, 2005.

*Freedman, Russell. *Eleanor Roosevelt: A Life of Discovery*. New York: Clarion Books, 1993.

Gerber, Robin. *Leadership the Eleanor Roosevelt Way: Timeless Strategies from the First Lady of Courage*. Portfolio, 2003.

Goodwin, Doris Kearns. *No Ordinary Time: Franklin and Eleanor*

Roosevelt—The Home Front in World War II. New York: Simon & Schuster, 1994.

Lash, Joseph P. *Eleanor: The Years Alone*. New York: W. W. Norton, 1972.

——. *Eleanor and Franklin: The Story of Their Relationship Based on Eleanor Roosevelt's Private Papers*. New York: W.W. Norton, 1971.

Roosevelt, Eleanor. *On My Own: The Years Since the White House*. New York: Harper & Brothers, 1958.

——. Chadakoff, Rochelle, ed. *Eleanor Roosevelt's My Day: Her Acclaimed Columns 1936–1945*. Seattle: Pharos Books, 1989.

——. *The Autobiography of Eleanor Roosevelt*. New York: Harper Perennial, reprint edition, 2014.

——. *You Learn by Living: Eleven Keys for a More Fulfilling Life*. New York: Harper Perennial, reprint edition, 2016.

Rowley, Hazel. *Franklin and Eleanor: An Extraordinary Marriage*. New York: Farrar, Straus and Giroux, 2010.

Scharf, Lois. *Eleanor Roosevelt: First Lady of American Liberalism*. Boston: C.K. Hall, 1987.

WEBSITES

Eleanor Roosevelt and the Jews: jewishstandard.timesofisrael.com /eleanor-roosevelt-and-the-jew

New Deal Network: newdeal.feri.org/index.htm

Week in Birmingham History: www.al.com/news/birmingham/index... /the_week_in_birmingham_history

National Archives Forward with Roosevelt—the blog of the Franklin Delano Roosevelt Presidential Library and Museum: fdr.blogs .archives.gov/2016/02/12/eleanor-roosevelts-battle-to-end-lynching

Marian Anderson sings at Lincoln Memorial: www.youtube.com
/watch?v=mAONYTMf2pk

The King Center/Eleanor Roosevelt: kingencyclopedia.stanford
.edu/encyclopedia/encyclopedia/enc_roosevelt_anna
_eleanor_1884_1962

Eleanor Roosevelt/Humanities: www.neh.gov/humanities/2000
/januaryfebruary/feature/eleanor-roosevelt

Tennessee History for Kids: www.tnhistoryforkids.org/places
/highlander

Speech to Congress, December 8, 1941: www.youtube.com
/watch?v=W6ScDXwYjWA

Eleanor Roosevelt: Undo the Mistake of Internment: www.nps.gov
/articles/erooseveltinternment.htm

New York Times: www.nytimes.com/learning/general/onthisday
/big/0412.html?mcubz=0

AUTHOR'S NOTE

When I began writing this book, I thought I knew a good deal about Eleanor Roosevelt. Certainly, I was aware of her unhappy childhood, the ways in which her husband's extramarital affair affected her personal relationships, and how her unrelenting work as First Lady had bought her both high praise and intense vilification. I also knew that one of her great interests was in the civil rights movement.

What I didn't know was how late Eleanor came to her involvement in this cause. It was not until 1933, as Franklin Roosevelt began his first term as president during the Depression, that she began to understand the corrosive effects of the United States' subjugation of its black citizens. Eleanor came to see how detrimental this bigotry was to both African Americans and the country as a whole. In the process, she became more aware of her own feelings and prejudices.

This is the story of Eleanor's evolution—how she used her megaphone and access to power to help those already on the front lines of social justice movements further their causes. At various points in her life, Eleanor Roosevelt was broken and had to remake herself. It was this growth that allowed her to evolve and to realize that she shared a common humanity with those determined to secure their inalienable rights. Fighting injustice became her life's work.

Note: I struggled with which names to use for the people in this book. It seemed almost too forward to call Eleanor Roosevelt by her first name, especially later in life. But Eleanor the girl—the one who was orphaned and often fearful but tried hard to do her best— remained an important part of the woman she became, so I primarily use Eleanor throughout. Consequently, for the most part, I also use first names for others.

ACKNOWLEDGMENTS

It is always a pleasure to work with Abrams Books for Young Readers because of the care and diligence the staff put into each book. I'm particularly grateful to my editor, the smart, savvy Howard Reeves, who keeps pushing in the best possible way; and to the awesome Emily Daluga, whose patience is endless and her ability to keep the train on the track is remarkable. Abrams is known for its beautiful book making and here the thanks go to associate art director Pamela Notarantonio and the book's designer Sara Corbett. I would also like to thank the staff at the Franklin D. Roosevelt Presidential and Museum in Hyde Park, New York, especially archivist Patrick Fahy, whose help with locating the book's many photographs was invaluable. A special appreciation to Lila Freeman and Vic Glazer who drove me to Hyde Park—in a blizzard!—and, as always, to my husband, Bill Ott, for his support and the endless cups of tea.

INDEX

Note: Page numbers in *italics* refer to illustrations.

CONSTITUTIONAL LAW

IN A NUTSHELL

Third Edition

By

JEROME A. BARRON

Lyle T. Alverson Professor of Law
National Law Center
The George Washington University

C. THOMAS DIENES

Patricia Roberts Harris Research Professor of Law
National Law Center
The George Washington University

ST. PAUL, MINN.
WEST PUBLISHING CO.
1995

Library of Congress Cataloging-in-Publication Data

Barron, Jerome A.
    Constitutional law in a nutshell / by Jerome A. Barron, C. Thomas Dienes. — 3rd ed.
        p.   cm. — (Nutshell series)
    Includes index.
    ISBN 0–314–06379–X
        1. United States—Constitutional law.   I. Dienes, C. Thomas.
II. Title.   III. Series.
KF4550.Z9B35   1995
342.73—dc20
[347.302]   95–4798
                                         CIP

ISBN 0–314–06379–X

TEXT IS PRINTED ON 10% POST CONSUMER RECYCLED PAPER

 PRINTED WITH SOY INK

For Kim
And
For Jonathan, David, and Jennifer

*

FOREWORD TO THE THIRD EDITION

In this third edition, we continue once again the task of providing a short summary of constitutional law. The task has become somewhat difficult. The instability of precedent—always a matter of controversy in constitutional law—is highlighted by some of the featured cases in this edition. In *Planned Parenthood of Southeastern Pennsylvania v. Casey*, the Court managed by a fragile margin to retain the battered shell of *Roe v. Wade*. We try to explain in some detail that the real significance of *Casey* is that it established a new and imprecise undue burden standard for evaluating the constitutional validity of abortion regulation. Undue burden may mean one thing for Justice O'Connor, another for Justice Stevens, and still another for Justice Scalia.

In *R.A.V. v. City of St. Paul*, Justice Scalia set the Court on a new course in First Amendment law. No category of speech, even categories hitherto thought unprotected such as "fighting words," was entirely "invisible" to the protection of the First Amendment.

A dramatic example of the way in which new directions in constitutional law have been forged since the second edition of this book in 1991 is the case of *United States v. Lopez* decided on April 26, 1995. In *Lopez*, the Supreme Court, per Justice Rehnquist, in a remarkably activist 5–4 decision seemed to return the Commerce Clause to its limited pre-1937 interpretation. In adopting this interpretation, the Court conceded that it dispensed with the certainty which had previously characterized Commerce Clause adjudication—legislation enacted under the Commerce Clause had been entitled to deference and, therefore, to validation. This apparently is no longer true.

We were fortunate in being able to include the *Lopez* case in this third edition since we were putting this book to bed just as it was announced. The cutoff date for this Nutshell was April 28, 1995.

Our discussion of the new cases shows that Justices O'Connor, Souter, Kennedy and Scalia are developing their own unique approaches to bitterly contested constitutional issues. For example, Justice Scalia's ideas on standing as reflected in his opinion for the Court in *Lujan v. Defenders of Wildlife*, are discussed in some depth. Analyzed in substantial detail is Justice O'Connor's opinion for the Court in *New York v. United States*, an opinion which manifests her continued allegiance to the importance of a doctrine of state sovereignty even in the context of the exercise of the federal commerce and spending powers.

As these justices refine their constitutional philosophies, they have been joined by colleagues newer to the Court. Justices Thomas, Ginsburg, and Breyer have replaced Justices Marshall, White and Blackmun. In some cases, the constitutional philosophies of these newcomers has become evident at least in certain areas of constitutional law.

Where a basis for defining their views exists, we try to indicate to the student the nature of that evidence and the significance it will have for the future course of constitutional law.

Basically we attempt in this edition—as we have in previous ones—to explain the new cases in terms of the changes that they make in existing constitutional law and of their likely scope and impact for the future. Where certainty exists, we have striven to point that out but where doubt or uncertainty are all one can say, we have felt obliged to point that out too.

Even at the risk of losing a leaner product, we have declined to discard the necessary discussion of the fundamental constitutional precedents of the past. We have scuttled discussion of some decisions which have not proved to have an enduring quality in order to make room for new decisions which appear to be of greater importance. Our goal as in the past has been brevity, simplicity, and candor.

Where a principle of constitutional law can be stated without equivocation, we have done so. Where ambiguity is present, we have felt that we owe the student a duty to acknowledge it. As always, as we move from one edition of this Nutshell to the next, we find that our most demanding critics and our most rigorous editors are our students.

JEROME A. BARRON
C. THOMAS DIENES

Washington, D.C.
April, 1995

*

OUTLINE

OUTLINE

*

TABLE OF CASES

References are to Pages

XVII

TABLE OF CASES

TABLE OF CASES

TABLE OF CASES

TABLE OF CASES

TABLE OF CASES

TABLE OF CASES

TABLE OF CASES

TABLE OF CASES

*

THE CONSTITUTION OF THE UNITED STATES

1787

Preamble

We the People of the United States, in Order to form a more perfect Union, establish Justice, insure domestic Tranquility, provide for the common defence, promote the general Welfare, and secure the Blessings of Liberty to ourselves and our Posterity, do ordain and establish this Constitution for the United States of America.

Article I

Section 1. All legislative Powers herein granted shall be vested in a Congress of the United States, which shall consist of a Senate and House of Representatives.

Section 2. [1] The House of Representatives shall be composed of Members chosen every second Year by the People of the several States, and the Electors in each State shall have the Qualifications requisite for Electors of the most numerous Branch of the State Legislature.

[2] No Person shall be a Representative who shall not have attained to the Age of twenty five Years,

and been seven Years a Citizen of the United States, and who shall not, when elected, be an Inhabitant of that State in which he shall be chosen.

[3] [Representatives and direct Taxes shall be apportioned among the several States which may be included within this Union, according to their respective Numbers, which shall be determined by adding to the whole Number of free Persons, including those bound to Service for a Term of Years, and excluding Indians not taxed, three fifths of all other Persons.] The actual Enumeration shall be made within three Years after the first Meeting of the Congress of the United States, and within every subsequent Term of ten Years, in such Manner as they shall by Law direct. The Number of Representatives shall not exceed one for every thirty Thousand, but each State shall have at Least one Representative; and until such enumeration shall be made, the State of New Hampshire shall be entitled to chuse three, Massachusetts eight, Rhode Island and Providence Plantations one, Connecticut five, New York six, New Jersey four, Pennsylvania eight, Delaware one, Maryland six, Virginia ten, North Carolina five, South Carolina five, and Georgia three.

[4] When vacancies happen in the Representation from any State, the Executive Authority thereof shall issue Writs of Election to fill such Vacancies.

[5] The House of Representatives shall chuse their Speaker and other Officers; and shall have the sole Power of Impeachment.

Section 3. [1] [The Senate of the United States shall be composed of two Senators from each State, chosen by the Legislature thereof, for six Years; and each Senator shall have one Vote.]

[2] Immediately after they shall be assembled in Consequence of the first Election, they shall be divided as equally as may be into three Classes. The Seats of the Senators of the first Class shall be vacated at the Expiration of the Second Year, of the second Class at the Expiration of the fourth Year, and of the third Class at the Expiration of the sixth Year, so that one third may be chosen every second Year; [and if Vacancies happen by Resignation, or otherwise, during the Recess of the Legislature of any State, the Executive thereof may make temporary Appointments until the next Meeting of the Legislature, which shall then fill such Vacancies.]

[3] No Person shall be a Senator who shall not have attained to the Age of thirty Years, and been nine Years a Citizen of the United States, and who shall not, when elected, be an Inhabitant of that State for which he shall be chosen.

[4] The Vice President of the United States shall be President of the Senate, but shall have no Vote, unless they be equally divided.

[5] The Senate shall chuse their other Officers, and also a President pro tempore, in the Absence of the Vice President, or when he shall exercise the Office of President of the United States.

[6] The Senate shall have the sole Power to try all Impeachments. When sitting for that Purpose, they shall be on Oath or Affirmation. When the President of the United States is tried, the Chief Justice shall preside: And no Person shall be convicted without the Concurrence of two thirds of the Members present.

[7] Judgment in Cases of Impeachment shall not extend further than to removal from Office, and disqualification to hold and enjoy any Office of honor, Trust, or Profit under the United States: but the Party convicted shall nevertheless be liable and subject to Indictment, Trial, Judgment, and Punishment, according to Law.

Section 4. [1] The Times, Places and Manner of holding Elections for Senators and Representatives, shall be prescribed in each State by the Legislature thereof; but the Congress may at any time by Law make or alter such Regulations, except as to the Places of chusing Senators.

[2] The Congress shall assemble at least once in every Year, and such Meeting shall be on the first Monday in December, unless they shall by Law appoint a different Day.

Section 5. [1] Each House shall be the Judge of the Elections, Returns, and Qualifications of its own Members, and a Majority of each shall constitute a Quorum to do Business; but a smaller Number may adjourn from day to day, and may be authorized to compel the Attendance of absent Members, in such

Manner, and under such Penalties as each House may provide.

[2] Each House may determine the Rules of its Proceedings, punish its Members for disorderly Behavior, and, with the Concurrence of two thirds, expel a Member.

[3] Each House shall keep a Journal of its Proceedings, and from time to time publish the same, excepting such Parts as may in their Judgment require Secrecy; and the Yeas and Nays of the Members of either House on any question shall, at the Desire of one fifth of those Present, be entered on the Journal.

[4] Neither House, during the Session of Congress, shall, without the Consent of the other, adjourn for more than three days, nor to any other Place than that in which the two Houses shall be sitting.

Section 6. [1] The Senators and Representatives shall receive a Compensation for their Services, to be ascertained by Law, and paid out of the Treasury of the United States. They shall in all Cases, except Treason, Felony and Breach of the Peace, be privileged from Arrest during their Attendance at the Session of their respective Houses, and in going to and returning from the same; and for any Speech or Debate in either House, they shall not be questioned in any other Place.

[2] No Senator or Representative shall, during the Time for which he was elected, be appointed to any civil Office under the Authority of the United States, which shall have been created, or the Emoluments whereof shall have been increased during such time; and no Person holding any Office under the United States, shall be a member of either House during his Continuance in Office.

Section 7. [1] All Bills for raising Revenue shall originate in the House of Representatives; but the Senate may propose or concur with Amendments as on other Bills.

[2] Every Bill which shall have passed the House of Representatives and the Senate, shall, before it become a Law, be presented to the President of the United States; If he approve he shall sign it, but if not he shall return it, with his Objections to the House in which it shall have originated, who shall enter the Objections at large on their Journal, and proceed to reconsider it. If after such Reconsideration two thirds of that House shall agree to pass the Bill, it shall be sent together with the Objections, to the other House, by which it shall likewise be reconsidered, and if approved by two thirds of that House, it shall become a Law. But in all such Cases the Votes of both Houses shall be determined by Yeas and Nays, and the Names of the Persons voting for and against the Bill shall be entered on the Journal of each House respectively. If any Bill shall not be returned by the President within ten Days (Sundays

excepted) after it shall have been presented to him, the Same shall be a Law, in like Manner as if he had signed it, unless the Congress by their Adjournment prevent its Return in which Case it shall not be a Law.

[3] Every Order, Resolution, or Vote, to Which the Concurrence of the Senate and House of Representatives may be necessary (except on a question of Adjournment) shall be presented to the President of the United States; and before the Same shall take Effect, shall be approved by him, or being disapproved by him, shall be repassed by two thirds of the Senate and House of Representatives, according to the Rules and Limitations prescribed in the Case of a Bill.

Section 8. [1] The Congress shall have Power to lay and collect Taxes, Duties, Imposts and Excises, to pay the Debts and provide for the common Defence and general Welfare of the United States; but all Duties, Imposts and Excises shall be uniform throughout the United States;

[2] To borrow money on the credit of the United States;

[3] To regulate Commerce with foreign Nations, and among the several States, and with the Indian Tribes;

[4] To establish an uniform Rule of Naturalization, and uniform Laws on the subject of Bankruptcies throughout the United States;

[5] To coin Money, regulate the Value thereof, and of foreign Coin, and fix the Standard of Weights and Measures;

[6] To provide for the Punishment of counterfeiting the Securities and current Coin of the United States;

[7] To Establish Post Offices and Post Roads;

[8] To promote the Progress of Science and useful Arts, by securing for limited Times to Authors and Inventors the exclusive Right to their respective Writings and Discoveries;

[9] To constitute Tribunals inferior to the supreme Court;

[10] To define and punish Piracies and Felonies committed on the high Seas, and Offenses against the Law of Nations;

[11] To declare War, grant Letters of Marque and Reprisal, and make Rules concerning Captures on Land and Water;

[12] To raise and support Armies, but no Appropriation of Money to that Use shall be for a longer Term than two Years;

[13] To provide and maintain a Navy;

[14] To make Rules for the Government and Regulation of the land and naval Forces;

[15] To provide for calling forth the Militia to execute the Laws of the Union, suppress Insurrections and repel Invasions;

[16] To provide for organizing, arming, and disciplining, the Militia, and for governing such Part of them as may be employed in the Service of the United States, reserving to the States respectively, the Appointment of the Officers, and the Authority of training the Militia according to the discipline prescribed by Congress;

[17] To exercise exclusive Legislation in all Cases whatsoever, over such District (not exceeding ten Miles square) as may, by Cession of particular States and the Acceptance of Congress, become the Seat of the Government of the United States, and to exercise like Authority over all Places purchased by the Consent of the Legislature of the State in which the Same shall be, for the Erection of Forts, Magazines, Arsenals, dock-Yards, and other needful Buildings;—And

[18] To make all Laws which shall be necessary and proper for carrying into Execution the foregoing Powers, and all other Powers vested by this Constitution in the Government of the United States, or in any Department or Officer thereof.

Section 9. [1] The Migration or Importation of Such Persons as any of the States now existing shall think proper to admit, shall not be prohibited by the Congress prior to the Year one thousand eight hundred and eight, but a Tax or duty may be imposed on such Importation, not exceeding ten dollars for each Person.

[2] The privilege of the Writ of Habeas Corpus shall not be suspended, unless when in Cases of Rebellion or Invasion the public Safety may require it.

[3] No Bill of Attainder or ex post facto Law shall be passed.

[4] No Capitation, or other direct, Tax shall be laid, unless in Proportion to the census or Enumeration herein before directed to be taken.

[5] No Tax or Duty shall be laid on Articles exported from any State.

[6] No Preference shall be given by any Regulation of Commerce or Revenue to the Ports of one State over those of another: nor shall Vessels bound to, or from, one State be obliged to enter, clear, or pay Duties in another.

[7] No money shall be drawn from the Treasury, but in Consequence of Appropriations made by Law; and a regular Statement and Account of the Receipts and Expenditures of all public Money shall be published from time to time.

[8] No Title of Nobility shall be granted by the United States: And no Person holding any Office of Profit or Trust under them, shall, without the Consent of the Congress, accept of any present, Emolument, Office, or Title, of any kind whatever, from any King, Prince, or foreign State.

Section 10. [1] No State shall enter into any Treaty, Alliance, or Confederation; grant Letters of

Marque and Reprisal; coin Money; emit Bills of Credit; make any Thing but gold and silver Coin a Tender in Payment of Debts; pass any Bill of Attainder, ex post facto Law, or Law impairing the Obligation of Contracts, or grant any Title of Nobility.

[2] No State shall, without the Consent of the Congress, lay any Imposts or Duties on Imports or Exports, except what may be absolutely necessary for executing its inspection Laws: and the net Produce of all Duties and Imposts, laid by any State on Imports or Exports, shall be for the Use of the Treasury of the United States; and all such Laws shall be subject to the Revision and Controul of the Congress.

[3] No State shall, without the Consent of Congress, lay any Duty of Tonnage, keep Troops, or Ships of War in time of Peace, enter into any Agreement or Compact with another State, or with a foreign Power or engage in War, unless actually invaded, or in such imminent Danger as will not admit of delay.

Article II

Section 1. [1] The executive Power shall be vested in a President of the United States of America. He shall hold his Office during the Term of four Years, and, together with the Vice President, chosen for the same Term, be elected, as follows:

[2] Each State shall appoint, in such Manner as the Legislature thereof may direct, a Number of

Electors, equal to the whole Number of Senators and Representatives to which the State may be entitled in the Congress; but no Senator or Representative, or Person holding an Office of Trust or Profit under the United States, shall be appointed an Elector.

[3] The Electors shall meet in their respective States, and vote by Ballot for two Persons, of whom one at least shall not be an Inhabitant of the same State with themselves. And they shall make a List of all the Persons voted for, and of the Number of Votes for each; which List they shall sign and certify, and transmit sealed to the Seat of the Government of the United States, directed to the President of the Senate. The President of the Senate shall, in the Presence of the Senate and House of Representatives, open all the Certificates, and the Votes shall then be counted. The Person having the greatest Number of Votes shall be the President, if such Number be a Majority of the whole Number of Electors appointed; and if there be more than one who have such Majority, and have an equal Number of Votes, then the House of Representatives shall immediately chuse by Ballot one of them for President; and if no Person have a Majority, then from the five highest on the List the said House shall in like Manner chuse the President. But in chusing the President, the Votes shall be taken by States, the Representation from each State having one Vote; A quorum for this Purpose shall consist of a

Member or Members from two thirds of the States, and a Majority of all the States shall be necessary to a Choice. In every Case, after the Choice of the President, the Person having the greater Number of Votes of the Electors shall be the Vice President. But if there should remain two or more who have equal Votes, the Senate shall chuse from them by Ballot the Vice President.

[4] The Congress may determine the Time of chusing the Electors, and the Day on which they shall give their Votes; which Day shall be the same throughout the United States.

[5] No person except a natural born Citizen, or a Citizen of the United States, at the time of the Adoption of this Constitution, shall be eligible to the Office of President; neither shall any Person be eligible to that Office who shall not have attained to the Age of thirty five Years, and been fourteen Years a Resident within the United States.

[6] In case of the removal of the President from Office, or of his Death, Resignation or Inability to discharge the Powers and Duties of the said Office, the Same shall devolve on the Vice President and the Congress may by Law provide for the Case of Removal, Death, Resignation or Inability, both of the President and Vice President, declaring what Officer shall then act as President, and such Officer shall act accordingly, until the Disability be removed, or a President shall be elected.

[7] The President shall, at stated Times, receive for his Services, a Compensation, which shall neither be increased nor diminished during the Period for which he shall have been elected, and he shall not receive within that Period any other Emolument from the United States, or any of them.

[8] Before he enter on the Execution of his Office, he shall take the following Oath or Affirmation: "I do solemnly swear (or affirm) that I will faithfully execute the Office of President of the United States, and will to the best of my Ability, preserve, protect and defend the Constitution of the United States."

Section 2. [1] The President shall be Commander in Chief of the Army and Navy of the United States, and of the militia of the several States, when called into the actual Services of the United States; he may require the Opinion, in writing, of the principal Officer in each of the Executive Departments, upon any Subject relating to the Duties of their respective Offices and he shall have Power to grant Reprieves and Pardons for Offenses against the United States, except in Cases of Impeachment.

[2] He shall have Power, by and with the Advice and Consent of the Senate, to make Treaties, provided two thirds of the Senators present concur; and he shall nominate, and by and with the Advice and Consent of the Senate, shall appoint Ambassadors, other public Ministers and Consuls, Judges of the supreme Court, and all other Officers of the United States, whose Appointments are not herein other-

wise provided for, and which shall be established by Law; but the Congress may by Law vest the Appointment of such inferior Officers, as they think proper, in the President alone, in the Courts of Law, or in the Heads of Departments.

[3] The President shall have Power to fill up all Vacancies that may happen during the Recess of the Senate, by granting Commissions which shall expire at the End of their next Session.

Section 3. He shall from time to time give to the Congress Information of the State of the Union, and recommend to their Consideration such Measures as he shall judge necessary and expedient; he may, on extraordinary Occasions, convene both Houses, or either of them, and in Case of Disagreement between them, with Respect to the Time of Adjournment, he may adjourn them to such Time as he shall think proper; he shall receive Ambassadors and other public Ministers; he shall take Care that the Laws be faithfully executed, and shall Commission all the Officers of the United States.

Section 4. The President, Vice President and all civil Officers of the United States, shall be removed from Office on Impeachment for, and Conviction of, Treason, Bribery, or other high Crimes and Misdemeanors.

Article III

Section 1. The judicial Power of the United States, shall be vested in one supreme Court, and in such inferior Courts as the Congress may from time to time ordain and establish. The Judges, both of the supreme and inferior Courts, shall hold their Offices during good Behaviour, and shall, at stated Times, receive for their Services a Compensation, which shall not be diminished during their Continuance in Office.

Section 2. [1] The judicial Power shall extend to all Cases, in Law and Equity, arising under this Constitution, the Laws of the United States, and Treaties made, or which shall be made, under their Authority;—to all Cases affecting Ambassadors, other public Ministers and Consuls;—to all Cases of admiralty and maritime Jurisdiction;—to Controversies to which the United States shall be a Party;—to Controversies between two or more States;—between a State and Citizens of another State;—between Citizens of different States;— between Citizens of the same State claiming Lands under the Grants of different States, and between a State, or the Citizens thereof, and foreign States, Citizens or Subjects.

[2] In all Cases affecting Ambassadors, other public Ministers and Consuls, and those in which a State shall be a Party, the supreme Court shall have original Jurisdiction. In all the other Cases before mentioned, the supreme Court shall have appellate Jurisdiction, both as to Law and Fact, with such Exceptions, and under such Regulations as the Congress shall make.

[3] The trial of all Crimes, except in Cases of Impeachment, shall be by Jury; and such Trial shall be held in the State where the said Crimes shall have been committed; but when not committed within any State, the Trial shall be at such Place or Places as the Congress may by Law have directed.

Section 3. [1] Treason against the United States, shall consist only in levying War against them, or, in adhering to their Enemies, giving them Aid and Comfort. No Person shall be convicted of Treason unless on the Testimony of two Witnesses to the same overt Act, or on Confession in open Court.

[2] The Congress shall have Power to declare the Punishment of Treason, but no Attainder of Treason shall work Corruption of Blood, or Forfeiture except during the Life of the Person attainted.

Article IV

Section 1. Full Faith and Credit shall be given in each State to the public Acts, Records, and judicial Proceedings of every other State. And the Congress may by general Laws prescribe the Manner in which such Acts, Records and Proceedings shall be proved, and the Effect thereof.

Section 2. [1] The Citizens of each State shall be entitled to all Privileges and Immunities of Citizens in the several States.

[2] A Person charged in any State with Treason, Felony, or other Crime, who shall flee from Justice,

and be found in another State, shall on demand of the executive Authority of the State from which he fled, be delivered up, to be removed to the State having Jurisdiction of the Crime.

[3] No Person held to Service or Labour in one State, under the Laws thereof, escaping into another, shall, in Consequence of any Law or Regulation therein, be discharged from such Service or Labour, but shall be delivered up on Claim of the Party to whom such Service or Labour may be due.

Section 3. [1] New States may be admitted by the Congress into this Union; but no new State shall be formed or erected with the Jurisdiction of any other State; nor any State be formed by the Junction of two or more States, or Parts of States, without the Consent of the Legislatures of the States concerned as well as of the Congress.

[2] The Congress shall have Power to dispose of and make all needful Rules and Regulations respecting the Territory or other Property belonging to the United States; and nothing in this Constitution shall be so construed as to Prejudice any Claims of the United States, or of any particular State.

Section 4. The United States shall guarantee to every State in this Union a Republican Form of Government, and shall protect each of them against Invasion; and on Application of the Legislature, or of the Executive (when the Legislature cannot be convened) against domestic Violence.

Article V

The Congress, whenever two thirds of both Houses shall deem it necessary, shall propose Amendments to this Constitution, or, on the Application of the Legislatures of two thirds of the several States, shall call a Convention for proposing Amendments, which, in either Case, shall be valid to all Intents and Purposes, as part of this Constitution, when ratified by the Legislatures of three fourths of the several States, or by Conventions in three fourths thereof, as the one or the other Mode of Ratification may be proposed by the Congress; Provided that no Amendment which may be made prior to the Year One thousand eight hundred and eight shall in any Manner affect the first and fourth Clauses in the Ninth Section of the first Article; and that no State, without its consent, shall be deprived of its equal Suffrage in the Senate.

Article VI

[1] All Debts contracted and Engagements entered into, before the Adoption of this Constitution, shall be as valid against the United States under this Constitution, as under the Confederation.

[2] This Constitution, and the Laws of the United States which shall be made in Pursuance thereof; and all treaties made, or which shall be made, under the Authority of the United States, shall be the supreme Law of the Land; and the Judges in every

State shall be bound thereby, any Thing in the Constitution or Laws of any State to the Contrary notwithstanding.

[3] The Senators and Representatives before mentioned, and the Members of the several State Legislatures, and all executive and judicial Officers, both of the United States and of the several States, shall be bound by Oath or Affirmation, to support this Constitution; but no religious Test shall ever be required as a Qualification to any Office or public Trust under the United States.

Article VII

The Ratification of the Conventions of nine States shall be sufficient for the Establishment of this Constitution between the States so ratifying the Same.

DONE in Convention by the Unanimous Consent of the States present the Seventeenth Day of September in the Year of Our Lord one thousand seven hundred and Eighty seven and of the Independence of the United States of America the Twelfth. In WITNESS whereof We have hereunto subscribed our Names,

> Go. WASHINGTON—
> *Presidt. and deputy
> from Virginia*

New Hampshire

JOHN LANGDON   NICHOLAS GILMAN

Massachusetts

NATHANIEL GORHAM   RUFUS KING

Connecticut

WM. SAML. JOHNSON

ROGER SHERMAN

New York

ALEXANDER HAMILTON

New Jersey

WIL: LIVINGSTON

WM. PATERSON

DAVID BREARLEY

JONA: DAYTON

Pennsylvania

B. FRANKLIN

THOS. FITZSIMONS

THOMAS MIFFLIN

JARED INGERSOLL

ROBT. MORRIS

JAMES WILSON

GEO. CLYMER

GOUV MORRIS

Delaware

GEO: READ

RICHARD BASSETT

GUNNING BEDFORD jun

JACO: BROOM

JOHN DICKINSON

Maryland

JAMES MCHENRY

DANL. CARROLL

DAN OF ST. THOS. JENIFER

Virginia

JOHN BLAIR

JAMES MADISON, JR.

North Carolina

WM. BLOUNT

HU WILLIAMSON

RICHD. DOBBS SPAIGHT

South Carolina

J. RUTLEDGE

CHARLES PINCKNEY

CHARLES COTESWORTH PINCKNEY

PIERCE BUTLER

Georgia

WILLIAM FEW

ABR BALDWIN

Attest

WILLIAM JACKSON

Secretary

ARTICLES IN ADDITION TO, AND AMENDMENT OF, THE CONSTITUTION OF THE UNITED STATES OF AMERICA, PROPOSED BY CONGRESS, AND RATIFIED BY THE LEG-

ISLATURES OF THE SEVERAL STATES PUR-
SUANT TO THE FIFTH ARTICLE OF THE
ORIGINAL CONSTITUTION.

Amendment I [1791]

Congress shall make no law respecting an establishment of religion, or prohibiting the free exercise
thereof; or abridging the freedom of speech, or of the
press; or the right of the people peaceably to assemble, and to petition the Government for a redress of
grievances.

Amendment II [1791]

A well regulated Militia, being necessary to the
security of a free State, the right of the people to
keep and bear Arms, shall not be infringed.

Amendment III [1791]

No Soldier shall, in time of peace be quartered in any
house, without the consent of the Owner, nor in time
of war, but in a manner to be prescribed by law.

Amendment IV [1791]

The right of the people to be secure in their persons, houses, papers, and effects, against unreasonable searches and seizures, shall not be violated, and
no Warrants shall issue, but upon probable cause,
supported by Oath or affirmation, and particularly
describing the place to be searched, and the persons
or things to be seized.

Amendment V [1791]

No person shall be held to answer for a capital, or otherwise infamous crime, unless on a presentment or indictment of a Grand Jury, except in cases arising in the land or naval forces, or in the Militia, when in actual service in time of War or public danger; nor shall any person be subject for the same offence to be twice put in jeopardy of life or limb; nor shall be compelled in any criminal case to be a witness against himself, nor be deprived of life, liberty, or property, without due process of law; nor shall private property be taken for public use, without just compensation.

Amendment VI [1791]

In all criminal prosecutions, the accused shall enjoy the right to a speedy and public trial, by an impartial jury of the State and district wherein the crime shall have been committed, which district shall have been previously ascertained by law, and to be informed of the nature and cause of the accusation; to be confronted with the witnesses against him; to have compulsory process for obtaining witnesses in his favor, and to have the Assistance of Counsel for his defence.

Amendment VII [1791]

In Suits at common law, where the value in controversy shall exceed twenty dollars, the right of trial by jury shall be preserved, and no fact tried by jury, shall be otherwise re-examined in any Court of the United States, than according to the rules of the common law.

Amendment VIII [1791]

Excessive bail shall not be required, nor excessive fines imposed, nor cruel and unusual punishments inflicted.

Amendment IX [1791]

The enumeration in the Constitution, of certain rights, shall not be construed to deny or disparage others retained by the people.

Amendment X [1791]

The powers not delegated to the United States by the Constitution, nor prohibited by it to the States, are reserved to the States respectively, or to the people.

Amendment XI [1798]

The Judicial power of the United States shall not be construed to extend to any suit in law or equity, commenced or prosecuted against one of the United States by Citizens of another State, or by Citizens or Subjects of any Foreign State.

Amendment XII [1804]

The Electors shall meet in their respective states and vote by ballot for President and Vice President, one of whom, at least, shall not be an inhabitant of the same state with themselves; they shall name in their ballots the person voted for as President, and in distinct ballots the person voted for as Vice President, and they shall make distinct lists of all persons voted for as President, and of all persons voted for as Vice President, and of the number of votes for each, which lists they shall sign and certify, and transmit sealed to the seat of the government of the United States, directed to the President of the Senate;—The President of the Senate shall, in the presence of the Senate and House of Representatives, open all the certificates and the votes shall then be counted;—The person having the greatest number of votes for President, shall be the President, if such number be a majority of the whole number of Electors appointed; and if no person have such majority, then from the persons having the highest numbers not exceeding three on the list of those voted for as President, the House of Representatives shall choose immediately, by ballot, the President. But in choosing the President, the votes shall be taken by states, the representation from each state having one vote; a quorum for this purpose shall consist of a member or members from two-thirds of the states, and a majority of all the states shall be necessary to a choice. And if the House of Representatives shall not choose a President whenever the right of choice shall devolve upon them before the fourth day of March next following, then the Vice President shall act as President, as in the case of the death or other constitutional disability of the President.—The person having the greatest number of votes as Vice President, shall be the Vice President, if such number be a majority of the whole number of Electors appointed, and if no person have a majority, then from the two highest numbers on the list, the Senate shall choose the Vice President; a quorum for the purpose shall consist of two-thirds of the whole number of Senators, and a majority of the whole number shall be necessary to a choice. But no person constitutionally ineligible to the office of President shall be eligible to that of Vice President of the United States.

Amendment XIII [1865]

Section 1. Neither slavery nor involuntary servitude, except as a punishment for crime whereof the party shall have been duly convicted, shall exist within the United States, or any place subject to their jurisdiction.

Section 2. Congress shall have power to enforce this article by appropriate legislation.

Amendment XIV [1868]

Section 1. All persons born or naturalized in the United States, and subject to the jurisdiction thereof, are citizens of the United States and of the State wherein they reside. No State shall make or enforce any law which shall abridge the privileges or immunities of citizens of the United States; nor shall any

State deprive any person of life, liberty, or property, without due process of law; nor deny to any person within its jurisdiction the equal protection of the laws.

Section 2. Representatives shall be apportioned among the several States according to their respective numbers, counting the whole number of persons in each State, excluding Indians not taxed. But when the right to vote at any election for the choice of electors for President and Vice President of the United States, Representatives in Congress, the Executive and Judicial officers of a State, or the members of the Legislature thereof, is denied to any of the male inhabitants of such State, being twenty-one years of age, and citizens of the United States, or in any way abridged, except for participation in rebellion, or other crime, the basis of representation therein shall be reduced in the proportion which the number of such male citizens shall bear to the whole number of male citizens twenty-one years of age in such State.

Section 3. No person shall be a Senator or Representative in Congress, or elector of President and Vice President, or hold any office, civil or military, under the United States, or under any State, who having previously taken an oath, as a member of Congress, or as an officer of the United States, or as a member of any State legislature, or as an executive or judicial officer of any State, to support the Constitution of the United States, shall have engaged in insurrection or rebellion against the same, or given aid or comfort to the enemies thereof. But Congress may by a vote of two-thirds of each House, remove such disability.

Section 4. The validity of the public debt of the United States, authorized by law, including debts incurred for payment of pensions and bounties for services in suppressing insurrection or rebellion, shall not be questioned. But neither the United States nor any State shall assume or pay any debt or obligation incurred in aid of insurrection or rebellion against the United States, or any claim for the loss or emancipation of any slave; but all such debts, obligations and claims shall be held illegal and void.

Section 5. The Congress shall have power to enforce, by appropriate legislation, the provisions of this article.

Amendment XV [1870]

Section 1. The right of citizens of the United States to vote shall not be denied or abridged by the United States or by any State on account of race, color, or previous condition of servitude.

Section 2. The Congress shall have power to enforce this article by appropriate legislation.

Amendment XVI [1913]

The Congress shall have power to lay and collect taxes on incomes, from whatever source derived, without apportionment among the several States, and without regard to any census or enumeration.

Amendment XVII [1913]

[1] The Senate of the United States shall be composed of two Senators from each State, elected by the people thereof, for six years; and each Senator shall have one vote. The electors in each State shall have the qualifications requisite for electors of the most numerous branch of the State legislatures.

[2] When vacancies happen in the representation of any State in the Senate, the executive authority of such State shall issue writs of election to fill such vacancies: *Provided,* that the legislature of any State may empower the executive thereof to make temporary appointments until the people fill the vacancies by election as the legislature may direct.

[3] This amendment shall not be so construed as to affect the election or term of any Senator chosen before it becomes valid as part of the Constitution.

Amendment XVIII [1919]

Section 1. After one year from the ratification of this article the manufacture, sale, or transportation of intoxicating liquors within, the importation thereof into, or the exportation thereof from the United States and all territory subject to the jurisdiction thereof for beverage purposes is hereby prohibited.

Section 2. The Congress and the several States shall have concurrent power to enforce this article by appropriate legislation.

Section 3. This article shall be inoperative unless it shall have been ratified as an amendment to the Constitution by the legislatures of the several States, as provided in the Constitution, within seven years from the date of the submission hereof to the States by the Congress.

Amendment XIX [1920]

[1] The right of citizens of the United States to vote shall not be denied or abridged by the United States or by any State on account of sex.

[2] Congress shall have power to enforce this article by appropriate legislation.

Amendment XX [1933]

Section 1. The terms of the President and Vice President shall end at noon on the 20th day of January, and the terms of Senators and Representatives at noon on the 3d day of January, of the years in which such terms would have ended if this article had not been ratified; and the terms of their successors shall then begin.

Section 2. The Congress shall assemble at least once in every year, and such meeting shall begin at noon on the 3d day of January, unless they shall by law appoint a different day.

Section 3. If, at the time fixed for the beginning of the term of the President, the President elect shall have died, the Vice President elect shall become President. If the President shall not have been chosen before the time fixed for the beginning of his term, or if the President elect shall have failed to qualify, then the Vice President elect shall act as President until a President shall have qualified; and the Congress may by law provide for the case wherein neither a President elect nor a Vice President elect shall have qualified, declaring who shall then act as President, or the manner in which one who is to act shall be selected, and such person shall act accordingly until a President or Vice President shall have qualified.

Section 4. The Congress may by law provide for the case of the death of any of the persons from whom the House of Representatives may choose a President whenever the right of choice shall have devolved upon them, and for the case of the death of any of the persons from whom the Senate may choose a Vice President whenever the right of choice shall have devolved upon them.

Section 5. Sections 1 and 2 shall take effect on the 15th day of October following the ratification of this article.

Section 6. This article shall be inoperative unless it shall have been ratified as an amendment to the Constitution by the legislatures of three-fourths of the several States within seven years from the date of its submission.

Amendment XXI [1933]

Section 1. The eighteenth article of amendment to the Constitution of the United States is hereby repealed.

Section 2. The transportation or importation into any State, Territory, or possession of the United States for delivery or use therein of intoxicating liquors, in violation of the laws thereof, is hereby prohibited.

Section 3. This article shall be inoperative unless it shall have been ratified as an amendment to the Constitution by conventions in the several States, as provided in the Constitution, within seven years from the date of the submission hereof to the States by the Congress.

Amendment XXII [1951]

Section 1. No person shall be elected to the office of the President more than twice, and no person who has held the office of President, or acted as President, for more than two years of a term to which some other person was elected President shall be elected to the office of President more than once. But this Article shall not apply to any person holding the office of President when this Article was proposed by the Congress, and shall not prevent any person who may be holding the office of President, or acting as President, during the term within which this Article becomes operative from holding the office of President or acting as President during the remainder of such term.

Section 2. This article shall be inoperative unless it shall have been ratified as an amendment to the Constitution by the legislatures of three-fourths of the several States within seven years from the date of its submission to the States by the Congress.

Amendment XXIII [1961]

Section 1. The District constituting the seat of Government of the United States shall appoint in such manner as the Congress may direct:

A number of electors of President and Vice President equal to the whole number of Senators and Representatives in Congress to which the District would be entitled if it were a State, but in no event more than the least populous state; they shall be in addition to those appointed by the states, but they shall be considered, for the purposes of the election of President and Vice President, to be electors appointed by a state; and they shall meet in the District and perform such duties as provided by the twelfth article of amendment.

Section 2. The Congress shall have power to enforce this article by appropriate legislation.

Amendment XXIV [1964]

Section 1. The right of citizens of the United States to vote in any primary or other election for President or Vice President, for electors for President or Vice President, or for Senator or Representative in Congress, shall not be denied or abridged by the United States or any State by reason of failure to pay any poll tax or other tax.

Section 2. The Congress shall have power to enforce this article by appropriate legislation.

Amendment XXV [1967]

Section 1. In the case of the removal of the President from office or of his death or resignation, the Vice President shall become President.

Section 2. Whenever there is a vacancy in the office of the Vice President, the President shall nominate a Vice President who shall take office upon confirmation by a majority vote of both Houses of Congress.

Section 3. Whenever the President transmits to the President pro tempore of the Senate and the Speaker of the House of Representatives his written declaration that he is unable to discharge the powers and duties of his office, and until he transmits to them a written declaration to the contrary, such powers and duties shall be discharged by the Vice President as Acting President.

Section 4. Whenever the Vice President and a majority of either the principal officers of the executive departments or of such other body as Congress may by law provide, transmit to the President pro tempore of the Senate and the Speaker of the House of Representatives, their written declaration that the President is unable to discharge the powers and duties of his office, the Vice President shall immediately assume the powers and duties of the office as Acting President.

Thereafter, when the President transmits to the President pro tempore of the Senate and the Speaker of the House of Representatives his written declaration that no inability exists, he shall resume the powers and duties of his office unless the Vice President and a majority of either the principal officers of the executive department or of such other body as Congress may by law provide, transmit within four days to the President pro tempore of the Senate and the Speaker of the House of Representatives their written declaration that the President is unable to discharge the powers and duties of his office. Thereupon Congress shall decide the issue, assembling within forty-eight hours for that purpose if not in session. If the Congress, within twenty-one days after receipt of the latter written declaration, or, if Congress is not in session, within twenty-one days after Congress is required to assemble, determines by two-thirds vote of both Houses that the President is unable to discharge the powers and duties of his office, the Vice President shall continue to discharge the same as Acting President; otherwise, the President shall resume the powers and duties of his office.

Amendment XXVI [1971]

Section 1. The right of citizens of the United States, who are eighteen years of age or older, to vote shall not be denied or abridged by the United States or by any State on account of age.

Section 2. The Congress shall have power to enforce this article by appropriate legislation.

Amendment XXVII [1992]

No Law, varying the compensation for the services of the Senators and Representatives, shall take effect, until an election of Representatives shall have intervened.

CONSTITUTIONAL LAW

IN A NUTSHELL

Third Edition

*

INTRODUCTION:
CONSTITUTIONAL PRINCIPLES

Constitutional law texts are generally divided into two parts. The first part is devoted to a study of the allocation of powers. This entails two basic principles of American constitutionalism-separation of powers and division of powers.

Separation of powers discusses the interaction among the three constituent elements of the national government. Thus, Art. I of the Constitution is devoted to the powers of the legislative arm of the federal government, the Congress. Art. II sets forth the powers of the Executive and Art. III delineates and circumscribes the jurisdiction of the federal courts. But while these powers are institutionally separated, their exercise often overlaps. Thus, there emerges the need for recognition of another vital feature of American constitutional law, the principle of checks and balances. Although Congress can legislate, the President can veto. Similarly, while the President makes treaties, the Senate must give its advice and consent to make them effective. While the federal courts exercise a power of judicial review, it is the Congress which endows those courts with such jurisdiction as it chooses within the given parameters of Art. III.

1

Checks and balances are not limited to the national arena. The principle finds expression in the division of powers between the national and state governments. Federalism embodies an effort to achieve national unity while preserving some degree of local autonomy. It strives at once to provide a structure for a national government and to provide some protection for regional diversity. But a continuing question is the extent to which the values of federalism are to be found in the constitutional allocation of powers or in the actual workings of the political process.

From these principles is derived still another foundation of American constitutionalism, the concept of limited government. Government must be afforded the means to operate efficiently and yet its powers must be sufficiently demarcated in order to preserve individual liberty. It is a basic tenet of Madisonian democracy that concentration of power poses a threat to individual autonomy and freedom. Therefore, to the eighteenth century mind, the mind at least of Jefferson and Madison, the objectives of federalism and separation of powers served the cause of liberty. Both limit and diffuse governmental power. Indeed, in the American system, the totality of power is denied to either the national or the state government or to any component part of our federalism. In the demarcation of national power, the Executive, the Congress, and the federal judiciary are alike denied absolute power.

Preservation of liberty in the American constitutional scheme is, however, not entirely dependent on the allocation of governmental powers. Limited government finds expression in the specification of rights and liberties of the individual. This is the focus of the second part of the constitutional law course. Some of these guarantees were included in the original Constitution. For example, Art. I, Sec. 9 prohibits suspension of the Great Writ, the writ of habeas corpus, except in cases of rebellion and insurrection. Similarly, bills of attainder and *ex post facto* laws are proscribed for both the national and state governments under Art. I, Secs. 9 and 10. But this was insufficient for many of the democrats of the eighteenth century. The First Congress undertook to draft a Bill of Rights, the first ten amendments to the Constitution. These serve as a constant reminder that the newly created federal government must always wield its power in the light of these basic guarantees of individual liberty. This principle has been re-affirmed in most of the subsequent seventeen amendments (with apologies for the Eighteenth or Prohibition Amendment) to the Constitution. Of these latter amendments, it must be said that the post-Civil War Amendments, the 13th, 14th, and 15th Amendments, have been most significant in limiting governmental power in favor of individual liberty. But the amendment process set forth in Art. V is a continuing one as recent proposals for a Balanced Budget Amendment and a school prayer amendment illustrate.

*

PART ONE

THE ALLOCATION OF POWERS

CHAPTER I

JUDICIAL REVIEW AND ITS LIMITS

A. FOUNDATIONS OF JUDICIAL REVIEW

The common law tradition that the lawyers, political theorists, and statesmen who drafted the American Constitution knew was rooted in the concept of Parliamentary supremacy. But there was always an undercurrent in the thinking of those men, trained as they were on John Locke's notion of inalienable rights, that certain actions were denied even to the Legislature. Indeed, in the seventeenth century, Lord Coke in *Dr. Bonham's* case (1610) had written that "the common law will control Acts of Parliament, and sometimes adjudge them to be utterly void." The United States Constitution proclaimed itself to be a product of "We, the people"— a concept of popular rather than Parliamentary supremacy.

The unique contribution of the United States to political theory is the doctrine of judicial review. Under this doctrine, the courts have the power to invalidate governmental action as repugnant to the Constitution. It extends to the acts of the national executive and Congress as well as the activities of state governments.

1.   REVIEW OF FEDERAL ACTIONS

The seminal document in the life of this doctrine of judicial review is the case of *Marbury v. Madison* (1803). In *Marbury,* Marshall emphasized the fact that the Constitution was the expression of the popular will and, therefore, properly controlled the exercise of all governmental power including the Congress. The Constitution is thus supreme over ordinary law and laws in defiance of the Constitution are null and void.

In *Marbury,* Sec. 13 of the Judiciary Act of 1789, which was read, perhaps improperly, to give original jurisdiction in mandamus actions to the Supreme Court of the United States, was held to violate Art. III on the ground that the original jurisdiction of the Supreme Court was set forth with precision in Art. III and did not include mandamus jurisdiction. Therefore, utilizing the canon of construction *expressio unius, exclusio alterius* (the expression of one is the exclusion of all others), Marshall declared that Sec. 13 constituted a transgression of Art. III.

But the real question is who decides that a law is repugnant to the Constitution. For Marshall, the answer was simple. It is emphatically the province and duty of the judicial department to say what the law is. The Constitution is not moral advice; it has the force of law. Indeed, it is fundamental law. But is interpretation of the Constitution equivalent to an interpretation of ordinary law? Congress may correct an erroneous judicial interpretation of a law but only constitutional amendment can revise judicial interpretation of the Constitution. Further, it can be argued that judicial delineation of vague concepts such as equal protection or due process partakes more of a policy or legislative decision than typical judicial interpretation of statute.

There is in fact no explicit textual authority for the doctrine of judicial review in the United States Constitution. While Art. III vests the "Judicial Power," including cases arising under the Constitution, in the federal courts, it nowhere specifies that this judicial power includes the prerogative of invalidating the acts of a co-equal branch of government. Art. VI does establish that "this Constitution and the Laws of the United States which shall be made in Pursuance thereof shall be the supreme Law of the Land," and binds judges of state courts to uphold it "anything in the Constitution or Laws of any State to the contrary notwithstanding." But does this language authorize the courts to determine when laws are in pursuance of the Constitution? It could be argued that the judgment that an action or law conforms to the Constitution already has been made by the popularly elected branches, the Congress and the President. In this view, the courts would be bound by the decision of the legislature that the law is constitutional.

Apart from arguments based on the constitutional text, the question of who should decide whether a law is contrary to the Constitution may be approached historically or functionally. As usual, the historical evidence as to the Framers' intent is indecisive although some form of review appears to have been contemplated. We might simply ask: Who is better able to make the judgment of constitutionality? It has been argued that the courts possess the insulation and expertise to exercise a "sober second thought" and thereby give expression to our most basic values. On the other hand, this very alleged insularity can be said to argue against vesting final authority on the meaning of the Constitution in an unelected body of nine judges holding tenure for life.

While *Marbury v. Madison* might have been read narrowly as holding only that the judiciary could act to protect its own jurisdiction against congressional action, it has not been so limited. Rather, the Court has unanimously declared that it stands for the following proposition: "[*Marbury v. Madison*] declared the basic principle that the federal judiciary is supreme in the exposition of the law of the Constitution, and that principle has ever since been respected by this Court and the Country as a permanent and indispensable feature of our Constitutional system." *Cooper v. Aaron* (1958). Thus, the Supreme Court can review and invalidate acts of the President and other executive officials as well as the Congress. While the Court in *United States v. Nixon* (1974) acknowledged a constitutionally based executive privilege of confidentiality, at the same time it affirmed the judicial prerogative of determining the proper exercise of that privilege: "Notwithstanding the deference that each branch must accord the others, the 'Judicial Power of the United States' can no more be shared with the Executive Branch than the Chief Executive, for example, can share with the Judiciary the veto power."

2. REVIEW OF STATE ACTIONS

Judicial review is not limited solely to review of federal actions and laws. It extends as well to state action. As early as 1810, the Supreme Court in *Fletcher v. Peck* had struck down a state statute as unconstitutional on grounds that the statute offended the Contract Clause of Art. I, Sec. 10. And, in *Martin v. Hunter's Lessee* (1816), the Court established its prerogative of reviewing the judgment on constitutional questions of the highest courts of a state.

The issue in *Martin v. Hunter's Lessee* was the validity of Sec. 25 of the Judiciary Act of 1789 which endowed the Supreme Court with appellate jurisdiction over the state supreme courts. It was contended that Art. III should be read to give the Supreme Court jurisdiction only in cases coming from the lower federal courts. In a decision which has been the linchpin ever since of Supreme Court jurisdiction over the state courts, Mr. Justice Story, speaking for the Court in *Martin,* rejected this contention: "It is the case, and not the court, that gives the jurisdiction."

Under the Supremacy Clause of Art. VI, state judges are bound by the United States Constitution notwithstanding contrary state law. This has been read to confer upon state court judges the power of judicial review even over federal laws. The Art. III subject matter jurisdiction of the Supreme Court includes cases arising under the Constitution. Since the state court has decided the constitutional question originally, the Supreme Court has power to review the issue by way of appellate jurisdiction.

Coupled with this argument based on the constitutional text, Story added a policy justification based on the need for uniformity in federal constitutional interpretation. The Constitution must not mean 50 different things in 50 different jurisdictions. This thesis was later echoed by Holmes when he argued that the Union would not be imperiled if the Court lost its power of judicial review over federal action but would be endangered if it had no such power over state action.

B. FOUNDATIONS OF FEDERAL JURISDICTION

1. THE CONSTITUTIONAL BASIS OF FEDERAL JURISDICTION

Under Art. III, the "federal judicial power" is vested in a Supreme Court and such inferior courts (including the circuit courts of appeals and the federal district courts) as Congress "may" create. Only the existence of the Supreme Court is constitutionally guaranteed. These Art. III courts, as distinguished from courts created by Congress under Art. I, must function within the carefully specified jurisdictional boundaries of Art. III. If a case or controversy does not fall within one of the specified categories of Art. III, Congress cannot constitutionally give the federal courts jurisdiction to entertain the matter and the court must dismiss for lack of jurisdiction. It is very important for the student to realize that Art. III describes the ultimate extent of the jurisdiction of federal courts created under it. Some of the more important examples of Art. III subject matter jurisdiction are cases arising under the Constitution, laws and treaties of the United States (federal question jurisdiction) and cases involving citizens of different states (diversity jurisdiction).

Thus, the jurisdiction of the federal courts, including the twin fountainheads of jurisdiction in the federal courts, federal question jurisdiction and diversity jurisdiction, like the federal judicial power itself, owes its very existence to the Constitution. But the exercise of jurisdiction within these Art. III parameters is at least in broad principle at the pleasure of Congress. While it is the Constitution that provides the fuel, it is Congress that must step on the gas.

2. BASES OF SUPREME COURT JURISDICTION

Art. III vests *original* jurisdiction in the Supreme Court in all cases affecting ambassadors, other public ministers and consuls and those in which a state shall be a party. As *Marbury* so memorably illustrated, Congress may not enlarge upon this constitutional delineation of the Supreme Court's original jurisdiction. Congress has, however, provided that some of this original jurisdiction should be exercised concurrently with the federal district courts. 28 U.S.C.A. § 1251.

Art. III provides, further, that in all other cases to which the federal judicial power extends, the Supreme Court shall have *appellate* jurisdiction "with such Exceptions, and under such Regulations as the Congress shall make." Pursuant to this "Exceptions" provision, Congress must confer, and may withdraw, subjects from the Supreme Court's appellate jurisdiction. The failure of Congress to confer full power within the confines of Art. III is viewed as an implicit exception by Congress to the grant of federal judicial power and, even after the appellate jurisdiction has been conferred, it may be withdrawn. Thus, in *Ex parte McCardle* (1869), the Supreme Court upheld a congressional statute withdrawing Supreme Court appellate jurisdiction to issue writs of habeas corpus even after the case had been orally argued to the Supreme Court. Was the congressional act of repeal in *McCardle* one of those "Exceptions" contemplated by Art. III or was it an impermissible infringement on the separation of powers principle? The Court held that it was an example of an "Exception."

The potential for mischief presented by *McCardle* has been both serious and enduring. *McCardle* has been the basis for recurrent efforts to legitimize erosion of the domain of the federal courts, including that of the Supreme Court, in controversial areas (to select only some of the more contemporary examples) like school busing, school prayer, abortion, internal security, and reapportionment.

McCardle, however, has had many detractors. For one thing, even on its facts, its precedential value is less impressive than appears. *McCardle* did not end all routes to Supreme Court *habeas corpus* jurisdiction but only one (as *Ex parte Yerger* (1868) proved). Similarly, *McCardle* was not a massive blow to an essential function of federal court jurisdiction, such as the power of the Supreme Court to review state court constitutional decisions, which preserves the unity of federal law. Since *McCardle* could be read to involve only a minor exception to Supreme Court jurisdiction, or more narrowly to remove only one remedy, it should not be read to support a radical revision of the contemporary role of the federal judiciary in the American system. Further, even a recognition of a broad congressional power to "except" certain subjects from the federal judicial power does not address possible constitutional limitations on the exercise of that power. For example, would Congress violate the due process guarantee by withdrawing the ability of federal courts to review, on constitutional matters, criminal convictions? Could the equal protection guarantee embodied in Fifth Amendment due process be vitiated by withdrawing from federal courts the power to order the only effective remedies available to vindicate the right (*e.g.,* the power to require busing)?

In short, Mr. Justice Douglas's observations in *Glidden Co. v. Zdanok* (1962), although made in the context of a dissent, has great force: "There is a serious question whether the *McCardle* case could command a majority view today." On the other hand, more literal readers of Art. III may be persuaded by Justice Frankfurter's brutal observation on the fragility of Supreme Court jurisdiction in *National Mutual Insurance Co. v. Tidewater Transfer Co.* (1949): "Congress need not give this Court any appellate power; it may withdraw appellate jurisdiction once conferred and it may do so even while a case is *sub judice.*" Under such a view, it was the intent of the Framers to leave it to Congress to decide whether federal courts, at least those inferior to the Supreme Court, were needed at all and also to decide the occasions when the federal judicial power should be exercised.

3. STATUTORY FORMS OF REVIEW

In 1988 Congress made a major change in the statutes setting forth the basis for Supreme Court jurisdiction. The old distinction between appeal, technically a matter of right, and certiorari, involving the exercise of discretion, is now largely a matter of history. The principal route now for obtaining Supreme Court review of lower court decisions is by means of certiorari. See 28 U.S.C.A. §§ 1254 and 1257. The certiorari jurisdiction is a discretionary one. Therefore, this means that the Supreme Court has almost complete control over whether or not it will take a case. Jurisdiction by appeal, technically a matter of right, still obtains in the limited number of cases where a three judge federal court must be convened. See 28 U.S.C.A. § 1253. But the fundamental point is that the great bulk of cases decided by the Supreme Court come to it by certiorari.

There are a number of grounds for granting certiorari. Perhaps, the clearest case for certiorari arises when federal courts of appeal are in conflict. But the Court has also noted that certiorari is appropriate when lower courts have decided significant novel federal constitutional questions or where a state court has decided a constitutional question in a way which is probably in conflict with prior Supreme Court decisions. The student should note that only four justices have to agree to grant the writ of certiorari. This means that a majority may subsequently decide that the writ was improvidently granted. A denial of certiorari is not a disposition on the merits and does not indicate approval or disapproval of the decision below.

C. CONSTITUTIONAL AND POLICY LIMITATIONS ON JUDICIAL REVIEW

Even if a case appears to fall within the confines of the federal jurisdiction outlined in Art. III, there is no assurance that a federal court will decide the case on the merits. There are a number of doctrines whereby an Art. III court can avoid disposition of the constitutional issue and dismiss the case. These doctrines emanate from two principal sources. First, the doctrine may be grounded in the constitutional text itself. For example, the Eleventh Amendment prohibits, on its face at least, federal courts from entertaining specified cases brought against a state without its consent. Another such textual limitation on judicial review is the requirement of Art. III that the jurisdiction of courts created thereunder be limited to "cases and controversies." The second principal source of limitation is born of the Court's own sense of self-restraint in the exercise of its judicial review powers. In defining its own place within the legal political system, the Court has declared that it will follow "a policy of strict necessity in disposing of constitutional issues." *Rescue Army v. Municipal Court of Los Angeles* (1947).

1. CONSTITUTIONAL LIMITATIONS

a. The Bar of the Eleventh Amendment

In defining the subject matter of the federal courts, Art. III, Sec. 2, indicates a number of instances where a federal court can hear a suit brought against a state. There are indications, however, that it was widely believed that the doctrine of sovereign immunity would prevent any such actions against the state without its consent. But in *Chisholm v. Georgia* (1793), the Supreme Court permitted a citizen of one state to sue another state in a federal court. The notion that the new federal courts could entertain suits against a state which the state as sovereign would not tolerate in its own courts was shocking. As a result, popular reaction to *Chisholm v. Georgia* led to the first new amendment after the Bill of Rights. The Eleventh Amendment rejected *Chisholm* by providing: "The judicial power of the United States shall not be construed to extend to any suit in law or equity commenced or prosecuted against one of the United States by Citizens of another State, or by Citizens or by Subjects of any Foreign State." Judicial interpretation utilizing the doctrine of sovereign immunity extended the bar to suits by a citizen against his own state, *Hans v. Louisiana* (1890), and also suits against the state by citizens of a foreign country.

The Eleventh Amendment, however, has not been the bar to federal judicial review of state action that a literal reading of its text might suggest. First, it is a bar to suit only against the state or its agencies and not local governments and their agencies. *Lake Country Estates, Inc. v. Tahoe Regional Planning Agency* (1979) [Eleventh Amendment held not to bar suit against the Tahoe Regional Planning

Agency since its activities make it more analogous to a county or municipal agency rather than a state agency].

Second, a state may consent to be sued in federal court. This exception does create a logical problem since the Eleventh Amendment purports to preclude "the Judicial power" in a suit against the state. How can a state grant jurisdiction to a federal court when the Constitution says the judicial power shall not extend to that case? The courts have treated the Eleventh Amendment as granting personal immunity founded on the doctrine of sovereign immunity. This personal immunity can be waived. Although this reasoning has satisfied later courts, it is less satisfying to the logical faculty.

Third, and most important, is the principle that when an official acts unconstitutionally the action is not state action at least for the purposes of the Eleventh Amendment. This precept, the doctrine of *Ex parte Young* (1908), is a kind of American analogue to the English common law precept that the King Can Do No Wrong. Under this doctrine, a state can never act unconstitutionally because the Eleventh Amendment provides sovereign immunity from constitutional review. State officials, however, in their individual capacity, can commit constitutional wrongs and in such a case, the Eleventh Amendment provides no refuge from federal jurisdiction. The need to vindicate federal constitutional rights prevails. Thus, the Eleventh Amendment was held not to bar a suit against named state officials for their alleged unconstitutional acts resulting in the death of students at Kent State University. *Scheuer v. Rhodes* (1974). However, the Eleventh Amendment has been interpreted as a bar against a federal court order requiring state officials to conform to state law since, under these circumstances, the state is the real party in interest and there is no need to vindicate federal rights. *Pennhurst State School & Hosp. v. Halderman* (1984).

The *Ex parte Young* exception to the Eleventh Amendment bar has proven of critical importance in the growth of American constitutional law. In the absence of the *Ex parte Young* doctrine, unruly states would have been less easily subjected to the single rule of federal constitutional law. For example, the problem of state legislative malapportionment could not have secured redress in the federal courts against the wishes of recalcitrant states. In short, without *Ex parte Young,* the reapportionment decisions would not have been possible. The mandates of the Fourteenth Amendment would have fallen on the shoals of the Eleventh Amendment. But invocation of the doctrine does raise a logical dilemma. How can the acts of a state official constitute "state action" for purposes of establishing a violation of the Fourteenth Amendment but not constitute state action sufficient to invoke the bar of the Eleventh Amendment? This answer to the question haunts Mr. Justice Peckham's decision in *Ex parte Young* but it is a ghost he failed to exorcise. He simply didn't talk about the problem.

Later federal courts have not worried much about the problem either. Some commentators have suggested that all that is necessary to say by way of explanation is that the Fourteenth Amendment qualifies *pro tanto* the Eleventh Amendment.

Where the relief requested would in fact constitute a retroactive charge against the state treasury, indistinguishable from an award of damages against the state itself, however, the Eleventh Amendment will bar the action. *Edelman v. Jordan* (1974). The *Edelman* exception to the *Ex parte Young* doctrine does not bar prospective remedies, even if they involve expenditures by the state in order to comply with a court order. By way of illustration, in *Hutto v. Finney* (1978), the Court held that the award of attorneys' fees against state prison officials for their bad faith unconstitutional actions would not involve an Eleventh Amendment violation even though the award constituted monies that would be paid by the state. Similarly, judicially imposed state expenditures to implement desegregation orders are treated as ancillary and do not violate the Eleventh Amendment. *Milliken v. Bradley* (1977) (*Milliken II*).

A final exception to Eleventh Amendment immunity arises from congressional power to legislate under the Thirteenth Amendment, Sec. 2, the Fourteenth Amendment, Sec. 5, and the Fifteenth Amendment, Sec. 2. The Civil War Amendments were enacted subsequent to the Eleventh Amendment and imposed specific prohibitions against state action. Pursuant to Congress's textually granted power to enforce these guarantees by appropriate legislation, it may legislate remedies even if they run against the state. *Fitzpatrick v. Bitzer* (1976). Similarly, Congress has power when it legislates under the Commerce Clause to abrogate the states' Eleventh Amendment immunity and to render a state liable for money damages. *Pennsylvania v. Union Gas Co.* (1989). Congressional intent to abrogate state Eleventh Amendment immunity must be "unmistakably clear in the language of the statute." *Atascadero State Hospital v. Scanlon* (1985). It should be noted also that the state itself can intentionally waive its Eleventh Amendment immunity. But such waiver must be done expressly: "Thus, in order for a state statute or constitutional provisions to constitute a waiver of eleventh amendment immunity, it must specify the State's intention to subject itself to suit in federal court." A state's receipt of funds under the federal Rehabilitation Act of 1973 did not without more waive its Eleventh Amendment immunity. *Atascadero State Hospital v. Scanlon* (1985). But the Port Authority of New York and New Jersey waived any Eleventh Amendment immunity when it agreed (1) to the consent to suit provisions in the statutory bi-state compact which created the Port Authority and (2) to a venue provision in the bi-state compact which referred to judicial districts established by the United States. *Port Authority Trans–Hudson Corp. v. Feeney* (1990).

The *Atascadero* case was the occasion for a major but unsuccessful effort by Justice Brennan to limit the scope of the Eleventh Amendment. Justice

Brennan in a lengthy and passionate dissent, joined by Marshall, Blackmun and Stevens, contended that the Eleventh Amendment as a matter of both text and history intended only to bar diversity suits against state governments in federal courts, i.e. suits by a citizen of State B against State A. In 1890, *Hans v. Louisiana* put a gloss on the Eleventh Amendment which also barred suits by a citizen of State A against State A in federal courts. In Brennan's view, the gloss *Hans* imposed on the Eleventh Amendment was wrong and should be reversed. Justice Powell for the Court rebuffed this assault on *Hans* declaring that the Eleventh Amendment exemplified a principle of state sovereign immunity which was rooted in a justified concern for state sovereignty.

Finally, if a suit filed in a state court raises a federal issue, the Eleventh Amendment will not bar Supreme Court review even though the Eleventh Amendment would have barred instituting suit in the federal court in the first place. This result is based on the need for a uniform federal law. *McKesson Corp. v. Division of Alcoholic Beverages* (1990).

b. The "Case or Controversy" Requirement

In defining the subject matter jurisdiction of federal courts, Art. III speaks in terms of cases and controversies. The Court has said that this language requires that litigation be presented to the federal courts in an adversary form and context capable of judicial resolution and that its resolution not violate separation of powers principles limiting the occasions for judicial review. *Flast v. Cohen* (1968). Thus, the Supreme Court will not give advisory opinions on federal constitutional questions—it will decide only "flesh and blood" controversies. Art. III federal courts cannot reach out to resolve even vital constitutional questions, even at the behest of Congress and the President. Congress, therefore, cannot make the United States a defendant in a federal court unless the United States truly has an interest adverse to the plaintiff. *Muskrat v. United States* (1911). Moreover, parties who are interested in securing resolution of a constitutional issue from a federal court cannot by their own agreement confer jurisdiction on the court. If the parties are merely curious about a matter but there is no real adversity between them, the bar of the Constitution—the case and controversy requirement—will require dismissal of the suit.

The "flesh and blood" controversy principle embodied in the ban on advisory opinions indicates one of the great paradoxes of American constitutionalism. The Court has undertaken to fashion broad principles transcending the immediate parties to a controversy but nevertheless insists that such principles be sown from the matrix of an actual dispute between adverse parties. This reflects the Court's commitment to the adversarial system. It also bears witness to reliance on practical empiricism as the wisest means of passing on constitutional issues even when they involve the most fundamental questions. The assumption appears to be that insistence on actual controversy limits and tempers the Court's undoubted power to generate new constitutional doctrine. If the case or controversy requirement is thus analyzed, it becomes apparent that it also serves the ends of the separation of powers principle. The price paid for assuring adversity and restraint in the use of judicial power is that the Court often postpones or indeed sometimes forgoes the exercise of its peculiar competence. Further, the harm done by the operation of an unconstitutional law while we await a case and controversy to move from embryo to reality may never be fully undone by a later decision even if it is forthcoming. Thus, when Chief Justice John Jay refused to give general legal advice on behalf of the Court to Secretary of State Jefferson on treaty questions, more was involved than a mere unwillingness on the part of the Court to do legal research for the Executive.

2. POLICY LIMITATIONS

Closely related to the constitutional restraints flowing from the case and controversy language of Art. III are a variety of policy limitations developed by the federal courts whereby they avoid disposition of constitutional issues on the merits. Thus, in *Ashwander v. Tennessee Valley Authority* (1936), the Supreme Court indicated that it would avoid deciding a constitutional issue raised in friendly non-adversary proceedings. Similarly, a federal court, according to the orthodox canon, will not decide a constitutional issue until it is absolutely necessary. This mode of avoiding decision is often accomplished by relying on alternative non-constitutional grounds for decision, if available, or by construing a statute in such a way as to avoid a constitutional problem. Further, a federal court will presume that legislation is constitutional, imposing on the challenging party the burden of demonstrating its invalidity.

All of these principles reflect the Court's commitment to self-restraint in the exercise of judicial review by the federal judiciary. Many times the Court has been admonished that the only limitation on the Court's power is its own sense of self-restraint. An inventory of factors justifying this policy of self-restraint would include: (1) the delicacy of the judicial function in constitutional cases; (2) the comparative finality of decisions resting on constitutional grounds; (3) the need for appropriate consideration to "other repositories of constitutional power"; (4) the need to preserve the constitutional allocation of powers, including that of the courts; and (5) "the inherent limitations of the judicial process." *Rescue Army v. Municipal Court of Los Angeles* (1947). In respecting such a limitation on the use of judicial power, the Court has asserted that it is providing a firmer foundation for private rights than if it were to involve itself actively in the political process.

Careful consideration of the policy occasions for avoiding unnecessary constitutional decision indicate that they generally overlap with the limitations which flow from the case and controversy requirement in Art. III. This suggests a critical problem underlying most of the discussion which follows. In cases where the Court avoids a decision on the merits, it is often difficult to determine whether the barrier to decision arises from the Constitution or from the Court's self-imposed sense of restraint. Yet the distinction is critical. A policy barrier to decision can be avoided if there are important factors counseling the need for decision. While Congress cannot override a limitation on judicial review which has its origin in the Art. III delineation of "the Judicial Power" (*i.e.,* federal court jurisdiction), the Congress can, by enacting legislation, allow the federal courts to entertain suits where the courts might otherwise refuse to adjudicate on the basis of policy or (as they are now often called) "prudential considerations."

D. SPECIFIC DOCTRINES LIMITING JUDICIAL REVIEW

The case and controversy mandate of Art. III coupled with the closely associated policy considerations have found expression in a number of specific doctrines whereby a federal court dismisses a case without reaching the constitutional merits. These doctrines can be conveniently grouped around three basic questions. First, *WHO* may litigate a constitutional claim (*i.e.,* the question of standing)? Second, *WHEN* may a constitutional question be litigated (the problem of timing, *e.g.,* ripeness, mootness, and abstention)? Third, *WHAT* constitutional questions may be litigated to a federal court (the problem of subject matter, *e.g.*, the political question doctrine)?

1. WHO MAY LITIGATE? —THE PROBLEM OF STANDING

a. Constitutional Requirements for Standing

The problem of who can litigate a constitutional question involves both the requirements of the case and controversy provision and the policy considerations underlying judicial self-restraint. Insofar as the Art. III cases and controversy requirement is concerned, the Supreme Court has required that the parties seeking relief allege "such a personal stake in the outcome of a controversy as to assure that concrete adverseness which sharpens the presentation of issues upon which the Court so largely depends for illumination of difficult constitutional questions." *Baker v. Carr* (1962). In order to demonstrate this "personal stake" the litigant must allege an *injury in fact* which results from the wrong complained of, *i.e.*, that the injury is "fairly traceable" to the government action and is "redressable" by the judicial relief requested. Further, the litigant must demonstrate that he has standing sufficient to justify the particular relief sought. *Los Angeles v. Lyons* (1983) [litigants' past physical injury resulting from police implementation of a departmental choke hold policy does not afford standing for injunctive relief].

(1) *Injury in Fact.* The personal stake requirement does not necessarily mean legal injury. Rather, the requirement is that the litigant demonstrate some factual injury. This may take the form of economic injury, aesthetic or environmental injury, or even intangible injury, such as the ability to live in an integrated community. For example, a physician has personal standing to maintain a civil action challenging state abortion statutes since he may be able to show that he suffers economic injury from the challenged legislation. *Singleton v. Wulff* (1976). A resident of a community in which a nuclear power plant is to be built may be able to show environmental injury in fact sufficient to challenge the constitutionality of a federal statute making construction of the plant possible. *Duke Power Co. v. Carolina Environmental Study Group* (1978). Residents of a neighborhood, and the village in which they reside, have sufficient Art. III standing to challenge realtor's steering practices which impair the ability to develop and maintain a stable racially integrated community. *Gladstone, Realtors v. Village of Bellwood* (1979). Recently, the Court has attempted to insert more rigor in the injury in fact requirement by declaring that injury in fact is demonstrated by the "invasion of a legally protected interest which is (a) concrete and particularized and (b) 'actual or imminent not conjectural' or 'hypothetical.' " *Lujan v. Defenders of Wildlife* (1992).

Lujan involved a regulation issued by the Secretary of the Interior which required other federal agencies to consult with him on federally funded projects in the United States and on the high seas which were likely to jeopardize the existence or habitat of endangered species. There was no such consultation requirement with respect to projects abroad and environmental groups challenged this omission in the regulation.

Two members of the these environmental groups pointed specifically to projects in Egypt and Sri Lanka which might adversely affect endangered species. The Court, per Justice Scalia, rejected their challenge on standing grounds. Standing is not an " 'ingenious academic exercise in the conceivable' ". True, a desire to see or to use an animal specie in some way can constitute cognizable injury in fact. But individual members of groups challenging the failure of the Secretary to extend the consultation requirement to projects abroad must show that they were personally affected in a concrete manner. Otherwise, their claim is too speculative. Statements that the plaintiffs might some day visit the regions of the world affected were simply too vague: " '[S]ome day' intentions—without any description of concrete plans, or indeed even any specification of *when* the some day will be—do not support a finding of the 'actual or imminent' injury that our cases require." *Lujan.*

It should be noted that Congress can by statute, create an interest, the denial of which is said to constitute injury in fact. *Warth v. Seldin* (1975). The "aggrieved person" provisions in the enabling legislation of federal regulatory agencies permitting those aggrieved by federal administrative action to obtain review in the federal courts typify this kind of statute.

A particularly troublesome aspect of *Lujan v. Defenders of Wildlife* (1992) was whether it somehow altered the rule that Congress could by statute provide for standing. The Endangered Species Act, on which the plaintiffs based their claim for standing, contained a provision authorizing "any person" to bring an action to enforce the statute. Statutory creation of standing by Congress was justified on the theory that Congress had by enacting the statute created a legal interest the denial of which constituted injury in fact. Nonetheless, the Court held there was no standing. Generalized grievances about government which cannot be differentiated from that shared by members of the public at large cannot provide a basis for standing. To hold otherwise would permit Congress to transfer the commonly shared interest of the public in the duty of executive officers to comply with the law from the Executive to the Judiciary. The courts would become the monitors of the wisdom of executive action.

Lujan did not contradict, the Court insisted, the principle that the injury in fact which Article III requires for standing may exist "solely by virtue of 'statutes creating legal rights, the invasion which creates standing.'" The broadening by statute of categories of injury that may qualify for standing was distinct from dispensing with the requirement that the plaintiff must herself have suffered injury. In a concurrence, Justice Kennedy, joined by Justice

Souter, sought to make clear that the prior law on the right of Congress to "to define injuries and articulate chains of causation," was not changed by *Lujan*.

Ideological opposition to a government policy is insufficient to satisfy the injury in fact requirement. Such injury must rise above a mere "generalized grievance" against the challenged law. Members of a racial minority or persons of low or moderate income do not have standing to challenge an exclusionary zoning ordinance merely because of their race or income level. They must show some direct or indirect injury to them personally resulting from the law to which they object. Thus, in *Warth v. Seldin* (1975), the litigants were unable to demonstrate that any developer who would build housing suitable to their needs was being excluded by reason of the zoning law. Similarly, the litigants had failed to allege or identify a specific developer with a specific project the furtherance of which had been precluded by the zoning law. On the other hand, in *Village of Arlington Heights v. Metropolitan Housing Development* (1977), a black litigant who desired housing near his employment and who would qualify for the housing that a developer wished to build was held to have standing to challenge the exclusionary official action as racially discriminatory. A non-profit housing developer who was a plaintiff in the same case, who had contracted to purchase land to build racially integrated housing, was also held to have standing since he had suffered economic injury based on financial outlays in connection with the planned housing project. Further, the Court indicated that injury in fact could also be found in the more intangible injury reflected in the "frustration of [the developer's] desire to make suitable low-cost housing available in areas where such housing is scarce."

Finally, a state senator who wanted to exhibit certain foreign films but was required by the federal Foreign Agents Registration Act of 1938 to label the films as "political propaganda" had standing to challenge the Act. The state senator had demonstrated more than a " 'subjective chill' ". He could not exhibit the labeled films without risking injury to his personal, political and professional reputation and without impairing his ability to obtain re-election. A judgment holding that the Act was unconstitutional would provide redress for the threatened injury by freeing the senator from having to choose between exhibiting the films and risking his reputation. *Meese v. Keene* (1987). Note that in these cases standing does not turn on the legal issue being litigated. Instead, standing reflects only the existence of a factual injury.

(2) *The Causal Relation.* In order to have standing, the challenging parties also must demonstrate that the injury in fact is caused by the government action they are challenging. In *Warth v. Seldin* (1975), minority and low income residents of Rochester, New York were held not to have standing to challenge exclusionary zoning by the suburban town of Penfield, New York. These residents were unable to show that a developer who would build

housing there suitable for them was precluded from doing so because of the zoning ordinance. Similarly, developers lacked standing to protest the town's exclusionary zoning since no developer could point to a specific project which was in fact being thwarted by the zoning ordinance. In short, the plaintiffs must "establish that, in fact, the asserted injury was the consequence of the defendant's actions or that prospective relief will remove the harm." *Warth v. Seldin* (1975). They must demonstrate that the alleged injury is fairly traceable to the asserted unlawful government conduct.

Stated in different terms, the plaintiff must demonstrate that there is a "substantial likelihood" that he will personally profit from the requested judicial relief; he must show that the judicial relief requested will redress the alleged injury. This causation requirement has proven to be a significant obstacle where the litigant alleges that the government defendant's action unconstitutionally motivates some third party not before the court to act in a way that produces injury to the litigant. The causation requirement is particularly important since it has been described as a "minimum requirement of Article III." *Warth v. Seldin*.

Candor requires acknowledgement that judicial assessment of the sufficiency of injury in fact or the existence of the requisite causal relationship is susceptible of doctrinal manipulation. Indeed, in dissent in *Warth v. Seldin*, Justice Brennan castigated the Court's approach to injury in fact as explainable "only by an indefensible hostility to the claim on the merits."

Illustrative of the malleability of the causal relationship requirement is *Northeastern Florida Chapter of Associated General Contractors of America v. Jacksonville* (1993). A construction contractors association challenged a city ordinance requiring 10% of the funds spent on city contracts each fiscal year be set aside for Minority Business Enterprises. The contractors association contended that many of its members would have bid on the set aside contracts if permitted to do so. Although the court of appeals had held that the association lacked standing because its members had not demonstrated that but for the set aside program they would have bid successfully for any of the set aside contracts, the Supreme Court, per Justice Thomas, disagreed and held that the association had standing. *Warth* was distinguished because it had not involved a claim "that some discriminatory classification prevented the plaintiff from competing on an equal footing in its quest for a benefit." In *Warth*, the plaintiffs had complained about the exclusionary zoning, not that they could not equally compete with others.

In essence, in *Northeastern Florida Chapter*, the Court relaxed the rigor of the causal relation requirement for standing. When a government classification makes it more difficult for members of one group to obtain a benefit than members of another group, the plaintiff is not obliged to show that the benefit would be available absent the government discrimination.

In *Allen v. Wright* (1984) Justice O'Connor declared to the surprise of many that the causation
requirement implemented separation of powers concerns; the requirement served to prevent judicial
frustration of administrative policies fashioned by
the executive. In *Allen*, the litigants claimed that
the IRS's failure to deny tax-exempt status to racially discriminatory private schools diminished the
ability of their children to receive a racially desegregated education. The Court, per Justice O'Connor,
held 5–3 that the complaint alleged a sufficient
claim of injury, but that the injury was not shown
to be fairly traceable to the IRS's conduct. Although the litigants had named a number of segregated schools enjoying tax exemptions, it was uncertain how many segregated schools benefitted from
tax breaks. Moreover, it was only speculative that
withdrawal of tax benefits would cause a segregated
school to change its admissions policy—parents and
officials would have to respond collectively to produce a significant change in the racial composition
of the schools. The causal connection was "attenuated at best." The litigants also contended that the
tax breaks to racially discriminatory schools imposed a "stigmatizing injury" on the members of
minority groups. This claim was rejected because
the litigants had failed to "allege a stigmatic injury" which they had suffered because they had personally been deprived of equal treatment.

But Justice O'Connor was not finished. Prior
cases had indicated that the Art. III standing involved solely an inquiry into whether the litigant

allen v wright

had sufficient adversity to litigate, and that separation of power concerns over the propriety of judicial intervention were not central to Art. III standing. *Flast v. Cohen* (1968). But Justice O'Connor declared: "[T]he law of Art. III standing is built on a single basic idea—the idea of separation of powers." Suits such as that involved in *Allen* would invite litigation challenging "the particular programs agencies establish to carry out their legal obligations." Such litigation was "rarely if ever appropriate, for federal courts are not the proper forum for general complaints about how government does its business." Justice O'Connor specifically accepted the principle that separation of powers' concerns can be used "to interpret the 'fairly traceable' component of the standing requirement."

Justice Stevens, dissenting, argued first that the injury was "fairly traceable." The very purpose of the tax subsidy is to encourage certain behavior; it follows logically that withdrawal of such subsidies because of particular undesirable conduct would discourage that conduct. Further, basic economics suggested that if segregated education became more expensive, less would be purchased. But more broadly, Justice Stevens challenged the Court's resort to separation of powers principles as part of the standing doctrine. Concerns relating to judicial interference with the way the executive exercises its prerogatives relate to prudential concerns, not jurisdiction: "The strength of the plaintiff's interest in the outcome has nothing to do with whether the relief it seeks would intrude upon the prerogative of other branches of government; the possibility that the relief might be inappropriate does not lessen the plaintiff's stake in obtaining that relief."

On the other hand, the Court has upheld a lower court finding of a causal relation between environmental injury from the operation of nuclear power plants and the federal Price–Anderson Act. The lower court judgment that the injury was "fairly traceable" to the Act's limitation on the potential liability for nuclear accident was not clearly erroneous since the statute made it feasible to construct the plants. While it was possible that the plants would be built even without the federal statute or that the government itself might build its own plants, the Court reasoned that the plaintiff need not eliminate all alternative possibilities. *Duke Power Co. v. Carolina Environmental Study Group* (1978).

The Court's treatment of the causal relationship requirement in *Allen v. Wright* and *Duke Power* suggests the requirement's lack of precision. Causality is a difficult concept whenever it is encountered in the law and it is no less so in the constitutional arena. It is certainly possible to argue that the Court's treatment of the causality issue in *Duke Power* is partially attributable to its greater willingness to decide important constitutional and policy issues involving nuclear power. Perhaps, for this reason *Duke Power* should not be read as involving too great a relaxation of the causal relation requirement. *Allen v. Wright* indicates the potential for using causation requirements as a vehicle for infusing separation of powers concerns over the propriety of using judicial power into the law of standing. While considerations relating to the judicial role are usually handled as prudential considerations under the label of justiciability, *Allen* suggests that they may, in the future, serve as a more formidable jurisdictional impediment to litigating constitutional claims.

b.   Federal Taxpayer Standing

Federal taxpayers generally lack a sufficient personal stake in the spending of federal monies to challenge the constitutionality of federal spending measures. Federal taxes become part of the general revenue and lose any separate identity with a particular taxpayer. If a challenge to a federal spending measure were successful, it is highly unlikely that the judicial remedy striking down or enjoining the program would yield any economic benefit to the taxpayer litigant. As the Court said in *Frothingham v. Mellon* (1923): "The party who invokes the [judicial] power must be able to show that he has sustained or is immediately in danger of sustaining some direct injury as the result of the statute's enforcement, and not merely that he suffers in some indefinite way in common with people generally." It never has been clear, however, whether the *Frothingham* impediment to a federal taxpayer's standing had its origin in the Art. III case and controversy requirement or was a prudential consideration born out of judicial self-restraint.

While the Court never has completely removed this uncertainty, it is now established that a federal taxpayer can challenge spending measures if two conditions are satisfied. First, the taxpayer litigant must be challenging an exercise of the taxing and spending power rather than any incidental appropriation pursuant to a regulatory measure. For example, a taxpayer would not have standing as a taxpayer to challenge a congressional appropriation to fund an agency to enforce federal pollution laws. Second, the taxpayer must allege that the challenged enactment violates a specific constitutional limitation on the taxing and spending power. Thus, in *Flast v. Cohen* (1968), the Court held that a federal taxpayer had standing to challenge federal spending benefiting parochial schools on the ground that such appropriations violated the Establishment Clause of the First Amendment. One of the historic purposes of the prohibition against Establishment was to prevent the use of government monies for religion.

Remaining unclear after *Flast* was the issue of whether the second nexus in the *Flast* test, *i.e.,* the requirement that there be a connection between the legal claim of the plaintiff and the taxing and spending power, originates in Art. III or is merely a prudential consideration which the Court was free to relax. It is now established, however, that the second nexus, focusing on the litigant's legal claim must be satisfied only when federal taxpayer standing is in question. *Duke Power Co. v. Carolina Environmental Study Group* (1978). With respect to standing contentions which are not predicated on federal taxpayer standing alone, the test would still be whether the government enactment has caused the factual injury.

In *Valley Forge Christian College v. Americans United for Separation of Church & State, Inc.* (1982), the Court dramatically demonstrated the narrowness of the *Flast* recognition of federal taxpayer standing. Respondents had challenged an HEW grant of surplus funds to the college as violated the Establishment Clause. The Court held that the respondents lacked standing as federal taxpayers because they were challenging the actions of an administrative agency rather than Congress. Further, the land transfer was made under the Property Clause of Art. IV, and was not an exercise of Congress taxing and spending power.

A state taxpayer who cannot make a showing of "direct injury", such as pecuniary loss, does not have federal standing even though the status of being a state taxpayer may suffice to create standing in the state courts. *Doremus v. Board of Education* (1952). However, where a judgment of a state court causes "direct, specific and concrete" injury to the plaintiff, the Supreme Court may exercise its certiorari jurisdiction. This is so even though the plaintiff might not have been able to meet federal standing requirements when the original action was commenced. *ASARCO Inc. v. Kadish* (1989).

c. Citizen Standing

In the absence of congressional legislation, a citizen lacks standing to challenge federal actions as unconstitutional. The citizen *qua* citizen is said to have only a generalized grievance which cannot be differentiated from that of other citizens. When a complaint is made that a federal agency, for example, is acting contrary to a specific clause of the Constitution, the claim will fail for lack of standing. Thus, a citizen lacks standing to challenge a federal statute which permits the director of the CIA merely to certify expenditures as a violation of Art. I, Sec. 9, cl. 7, requiring a regular accounting of public funds. The assertion that citizens need such information in order to vote intelligently was held to be only a generalized grievance rather than an allegation of particularized injury. *United States v. Richardson* (1974). See *Schlesinger v. Reservists Comm. to Stop the War* (1974) [no citizen standing to challenge practice of members of Congress serving in Armed Forces Reserve as violation of Art. I, Sec. 6, Cl. 2, prohibiting House members from holding any office under the United States].

Nor does the fact that the challenge to federal action is based on the Establishment Clause provide a basis for citizen standing. In *Valley Forge,* the Court of Appeals had held that the Establishment Clause created a personal, but shared constitutional right in citizens distinguishable from other claims of citizen standing. The Supreme Court, per Justice Rehnquist, rejected this effort to have citizen standing vary with the constitutional claim being asserted. A claim that the Constitution has been violated, without more, does not establish the personal injury in fact required by Art. III. The fact that no one would have standing, said Justice Rehnquist, "is not a reason to find standing." To the extent that the impediment to citizen standing is based on Art. III, the ability of Congress to confer standing by statute is limited. But note that Congress may, by statute, create a legal interest in a person. It can be argued that if such a statutory interest is violated, the personal injury in fact required for Art. III standing is present. See *Gladstone, Realtors v. Village of Bellwood* [violation of rights conferred under 1968 Civil Rights Act held sufficient to confer standing].

d. Third Party Standing

Third party standing or, as the courts often call it, *jus tertii,* is as a generality easy to state: A is normally not considered to have standing to raise the legal rights of B. Even if A has sufficient injury in fact to assert his own legal claims, this standing is still insufficient to permit him to assert the legal claims of B. The basis for the rule is grounded in a "best plaintiff" concept. In the normal course of events, B is deemed the most appropriate person to litigate with respect to claims affecting him. The person most directly affected also will be the most likely to insure that the case is adequately presented. The rule has obvious connections with the adversity requirement associated with the case and controversy rule but it also reflects the Court's desire to avoid constitutional questions until decision is necessary (*i.e.,* strict necessity of decision).

In fact, it is now established that the third party standing rule is solely a prudential doctrine. Indeed, this area of the law of standing is now characterized by exceptions that almost negate the rule. If A can offer sufficient reason for allowing him to litigate B's legal claims, he may be permitted to do so. Some of the most frequently cited reasons for allowing standing in third party situations, despite the *jus tertii* rule, are as follows. If it would be difficult if not impossible for B to assert his own legal rights, then A may be allowed to litigate B's claims (assuming A has Art. III standing). If there is a close personal relationship between A and B, the Court is once again likely to relax the third party standing impediment. Thus, a physician has been permitted to raise the privacy rights of his patients in challenging the constitutionality of restrictive abortion laws. The physician-patient relationship is close and personal. Further, it would be difficult for the patient to assert her own rights since she might be chilled from litigating her claim by a desire to avoid publicity. *Singleton v. Wulff* (1976). Since laws discriminating between males and females in their ability to purchase beer impairs the relationship between sellers and potential buyers, the seller will have standing to raise the equal protection challenge to the laws. *Craig v. Boren* (1976).

Organizations can raise the legal rights of their members if the following conditions are met: (1)

the members themselves must have injury in fact for Art. III standing, (2) the interests involved in the litigation must be relevant to the organization's purposes, (3) the claims asserted and the relief requested do not require the participation of the individual members. *Hunt v. Washington State Apple Advertising Com'n* (1977). Organizational standing is one of the liveliest and most important areas where the exception to the *jus tertii* rule can be seen. Environmental litigation, for example, has been characterized by the use of organizational standing.

2.   WHEN CAN CONSTITUTIONAL LITIGATION BE BROUGHT?   THE PROBLEM OF TIMING

a. Rule Against Mootness

When a judicial decision cannot have any practical legal effect because the issues that generated it either have been resolved or disappeared, it is said that the case has become moot. In federal constitutional law, mootness obviously serves what are called prudential considerations in limiting the occasions for judicial review. But there is a constitutional dimension to the mootness doctrine which should be understood. A case or controversy requires a *present* flesh and blood dispute that the courts can resolve. Nevertheless, it should be emphasized that the mootness cases in the Supreme Court are not easily rationalized. Many of the recent mootness decisions suggest that mootness is being used in a tactical way by the Court in order to find refuge from resolving controversial constitutional questions where no one point of view has captured a majority of the justices.

When Marco De Funis challenged the University of Washington Law School's affirmative action admission program, De Funis was in his third year of law school. The University indicated that if he successfully completed the program, he would graduate regardless of the Court's decision. These facts, the Court ruled in *De Funis v. Odegaard* (1974), rendered the case moot. Even if the highly speculative possibility that De Funis were to fail in his exams were realized, he would still not have to face again the initial admissions requirements. The Supreme Court is bound by Art. III requirements even though the state courts of Washington were not; they indeed, had not found mootness to be a barrier to decision.

While the mootness doctrine may be grounded in Art. III, this has not prevented the federal courts from fashioning exceptions to the mootness doctrine which do not entirely cohere with the mootness rationale. For example, if a case is found to be "capable of repetition and yet evading review," a federal court may take review even though the particular fact pattern might otherwise fall under the mootness doctrine. But how does the repetitious quality of the issue diminish the Art. III problem? In short, how is the requirement of present adversity satisfied?

The exemplar of the recurring issue case is the famous abortion decision, *Roe v. Wade* (1973). By the time the case reached the Supreme Court, nine months had long since passed and the case was technically moot. But the Supreme Court said this was a classic example of a case "capable of repetition yet evading review." Even if Mrs. Roe were not to become pregnant again—and she might—all that would be required is that some member of her class be capable of becoming pregnant. Marco De Funis, on the other hand, had not filed a class action. For him, the question of the constitutionality of the law school's admission program would not recur. There was no reason to believe that the issue would again "evade review." If a suit is not filed as a class action, the recurring issue exception applies only if the issue is "capable of repetition" for the litigating party. *First National Bank v. Bellotti* (1978).

Another example of the "capable of repetition yet evading review" exception arose under the federal Education of the Handicapped Act. An emotionally disturbed student sought injunctive relief against school officials who had suspended him for violent and disruptive behavior relating to his handicap. The student involved was 20 but had not yet finished high school. The student was still eligible for educational services under the Act and, given his disability, was still likely to be in need of them. The school officials for their part were still insistent that they had authority to exclude disabled children for violent and disruptive conduct. In the circumstances, the Court held the case was not moot since it was reasonably likely that the action of the school officials which the student complained of was capable of being repeated. On the other hand, a similar challenge by a student no longer eligible because of his age for the benefits of the Act was held to be moot. *Honig v. Doe* (1988).

A second exception to the mootness doctrine which was asserted but also found unavailing in *De Funis* is the principle that the "voluntary cessation of unlawful activities" will not render a case moot at least where there is a reasonable likelihood that the wrong will be resumed. The reason for this exception is that a contrary rule would allow exploitation of the mootness doctrine because a wrongdoer could momentarily halt his mischief to escape judicial review. But again, how does the voluntary cessation exception assure the present adversity mandated by the Art. III case or controversy requirement?

Suppose the defendant changes its conduct after suit is brought? Is the case now moot? In *Northeastern Florida Chapter of Associated General Contractors of America v. Jacksonville* (1993), the city changed its affirmative action program after the Court granted certiorari to consider an equal protection challenge to an earlier affirmative action program. Under the old program, 10% of city contracts were set aside for members of seven different minority groups. Under the new program, participation goals of 5% to 16% were established but the new program applied solely to women and blacks.

Five alternative methods for achieving the participation goals were set forth, only one of which was a set aside program. The city contended that the change in programs rendered the case moot. The Court invoked the voluntary cessation exception to the mootness doctrine and rejected this contention. In this case, there was not just a risk that the city would revert to its allegedly illegal conduct, it had in fact done so. The basis of the contractors' complaint was that the city's affirmative action program disadvantaged their ability to secure city contracts. That was still the case. There is no requirement that "it is only the possibility that the *selfsame* statute will be enacted that prevents a case from being moot."

A third exception arises in those infrequent cases where there are important unsettled collateral consequences that remain unresolved. Thus, a criminal conviction or a finding of insanity can impact on an individual even after he has been released from confinement.

b. Ripeness, Prematurity, and Abstractness

A federal court will not hear a case unless there is present injury or significant threat of imminent injury. Something adverse must be happening to the individual now or in the immediate future. The constitutional underpinnings of the precept that an issue be ripe for judicial resolution is once again the case or controversy requirement of Art. III. The ripeness doctrine was used as a bar to review in *United Public Workers of America v. Mitchell*

(1947), where the Hatch Act banning political activities by government employees was challenged. While one employee who had violated the Act and was being threatened with removal was allowed to challenge (albeit unsuccessfully), other employees who merely wished to engage in political activities but had not yet done so were barred from challenging the act. As to them, the Court said it would be required to speculate as to the nature of the political activity and the probable response of the government to it. For example, for all the Court knew, the government might not choose to act. It is doubtful, however, that a government employee would be required to engage in political activity to the point of inviting job dismissal to raise the constitutional issue—imminent harm is sufficient.

Once again, however, Art. III requirements shade into prudential considerations. Even where the issue may be technically ripe, the Court has found the issues to be excessively premature or abstract. In *Socialist Labor Party v. Gilligan* (1972), the Court dismissed an appeal from an unsuccessful challenge by a minor political party to a state loyalty oath citing the lack of clarity and specificity of harm provided by the pleadings. Even if the technical requirements of standing and ripeness were met, the constitutional issues were not presented in a "clean-cut and concrete form." The Court cited *Rescue Army* on the "insuperable" obstacles to the exercise of the Court's jurisdiction presented by the problems of prematurity and abstractness. The Court could not tell from the pleadings in *Socialist*

Labor Party whether the party had ever refused or now intended to refuse to take the oath and to undergo the consequences that might follow. For example, the Socialist Labor Party had not pleaded that it would not sign the loyalty oath. It was entirely possible that the Party intended to sign the oath and would appear on the ballot.

3. WHAT CAN BE LITIGATED? THE POLITICAL QUESTION DOCTRINE

As early as 1803, in *Marbury v. Madison,* Chief Justice Marshall indicated that there is a class of constitutional cases which federal courts cannot review because "the subjects are political." On the other hand, in 1821 in *Cohens v. Virginia,* Chief Justice Marshall stated: "We have no more right to decline the exercise of jurisdiction which is given, than to usurp that which is not given." Further, it has become clear that jurisdiction is not to be declined merely because the case involves either political values or the political process.

What then is the key to the "non-justiciability" of political questions or, to put it another way, to those situations where the political question doctrine is a barrier to review of a case by the federal courts? In *Baker v. Carr* (1962), precursor to a powerful line of cases resolving the problem of state malapportionment, Justice Brennan provided an authoritative examination of the foundations and the characteristics of the political question doctrine.

Beginning from the premise that "[t]he non-justici-ability of the political question is primarily a func-tion of the separation of powers," Justice Brennan noted that, in part, the doctrine required federal courts to determine whether a question had been committed by the Constitution to another branch of the national government. Further, the doctrine of non-justiciability necessitated an inquiry into whether "the duty asserted can be judicially identi-fied and its reach judicially determined, and wheth-er protection for the right asserted can be judicially molded." While the political question doctrine sug-gests roots in Art. III, it is primarily based on what the Court calls, in the standing context, prudential considerations. See *Rescue Army v. Municipal Court of Los Angeles* (1947), for an elaboration of these prudential concerns.

In a much-quoted passage in *Baker v. Carr*, Jus-tice Brennan set forth criteria, reflecting classic, functional and prudential considerations, for identi-fying a political question case. First, invoking a *classic* concern, Justice Brennan said that a case should be held non-justiciable if there is "a textual-ly demonstrable constitutional commitment of the issue to a coordinate political department." It has been suggested that only such a constitutional com-mitment of an issue to the autonomous discretion of another branch of the national government would justify a federal court in declining the exercise of its Art. III jurisdiction. Other commentators have raised the question whether there is any issue that is totally committed to another branch of government in the sense that the judiciary could not, if it chose, review the matter. In support of this view is Justice Brennan's statement in *Baker v. Carr* describing the Supreme Court as the "ultimate interpreter of the Constitution." Perhaps, the most appropriate resolution of this issue is to recognize that under the classical approach there are subjects which are charged primarily to the discretion of either the executive or the Congress, but that the identification of the subjects so charged and the constitutionality of the exercise of the discretion given remains subject to judicial review.

Other criteria mentioned by Justice Brennan in *Baker* reflect *functional* considerations relating to the capabilities of the judicial department. Thus, Justice Brennan would have federal courts ask whether there is "a lack of judicially discoverable and manageable standards for resolving (the question)" or would have them consider "the impossibility of deciding without an initial policy determination of a kind clearly for non-judicial discretion." Professor Scharpf, in his article *Judicial Review and the Political Question: A Functional Analysis,* 75 Yale L.J. 517 (1966), cites such considerations as the difficulty of acquiring accurate information and the need for uniformity of decision of the respective branches of government as bearing on the justiciability of a particular question.

Stalin asked, "How many divisions has the Pope?" Andrew Jackson, according to an apocryphal story, said: "John Marshall has made his decision. Now let him enforce it." In a similar vein, it was concern that the Supreme Court and the federal courts would fail if they sought to resolve the "mathematical quagmire of reapportionment" that influenced Justice Frankfurter's strong and anguished dissent in *Baker*. As Frankfurter put it, "There is not under our Constitution a judicial remedy for every political mischief, for every undesirable exercise of legislative power." But for the Court, the equal protection challenge to malapportionment involved well developed and familiar Fourteenth Amendment standards. The courts were fully capable of identifying and implementing the constitutional mandate.

Political considerations are reflected in Justice Brennan's references to "the impossibility of a court's undertaking independent resolution without expressing lack of the respect due coordinate branches of government" or "an unusual need for unquestioning adherence to a political decision already made" or "the potentiality of embarrassment for multifarious pronouncements by various departments on one question." The late Professor Alexander Bickel carried this theme even further, arguing that an issue should be deemed non-justiciable because of its strangeness, momentousness, or its "intractability to principled decision-making," anxiety concerning the consequences of judicial involvement, or the "self-doubt of an institution lacking electoral responsibility or enforcement capability." Justice Frankfurter, haunted by the South's "massive resistance" to compliance in *Brown v. Board of Education* (1954) reflected these same concerns in dissent in *Baker* and warned that judicial involvement in political reapportionment threatened the Court's authority even in its established terrain: "The Court's authority possessed of neither the purse nor the sword ultimately rests on sustained public confidence in its moral sanction." Frankfurter implored the Court to exercise complete detachment from political entanglements involving the clash of political forces in order not to jeopardize this public confidence. For him, the forum for such struggles was the electoral and not the judicial process.

Baker v. Carr was a watershed in the evolution of the political question doctrine. The Court in *Baker* made it clear that the federal judiciary would resolve equal protection challenges to malapportionment despite Justice Frankfurter's admonitions that the courts would become enmeshed in a "political thicket".

In another political question case, *Powell v. McCormack* (1969), the Court held that congressional exclusion of an elected representative is justiciable. A specific provision of the constitutional text, Art. I, Sec. 5, making each house "the Judge of the Qualifications of its own members" was not commitment of all questions relating to an elected person's qualifications to take his seat. Instead, it was a limited reference to the qualifications for membership specified in the Constitution, *i.e.*, age, citizenship, and state residence. In *United States v. Nixon* (1974), the Court held the President could be required to respond to judicial process. The fact that the President was a defendant did not render non-justiciable the question of privilege for confidential communications. A plurality of the Court in *Goldwater v. Carter* (1979), reflecting the traditional reluctance to become involved in the foreign affairs sphere, held that the unilateral termination of a treaty by a President was a matter which the overtly political branches of government were quite capable of resolving. Finally, in a pre-*Baker* case concerning the propriety of judicial supervision of the Article V amendment process, the Court invoked the political question doctrine and, by declining to resolve the matter, left problems of ratification to Congress. *Coleman v. Miller* (1939).

The criteria for defining a political question set forth by Justice Brennan in *Baker* have continuing importance. Yet it must be recognized that these criteria are not in themselves always applied in a uniform or predictable way. Some cases, of course, do present issues beyond the competence of the federal judiciary. A federal judge had been impeached by the House of Representatives. Was a Senate rule which allowed a committee of Senators to hear evidence and to report that evidence to the full Senate consistent with the Impeachment Trial Clause, Art. I, Sec. 3, cl. 6, which states that the "Senate shall have the sole Power to try all Impeachments"? The Court held that the question presented was a non-justiciable political question. *Nixon v. United States* (1993). The word "sole" means that the power was "reposed in the Senate and nowhere else." The Senate's power to try

impeachments was subject to the specific requirements of Art. I., Sec. 3, and the other limitations set
forth in the Constitution. In light of the specificity
of these requirements, the Court was disinclined to
add to them and rule "that the Framers used the
word 'try' as an implied limitation on the method
by which the Senate might proceed in trying impeachments." The word "try" in the Impeachment
Trial Clause was too imprecise to provide any judicially manageable standards of review.

In summary, the political question doctrine is
most likely to be invoked in areas of traditional
presidential or congressional competence. The foreign affairs area, the national security context,
questions about the exercise of the war power and
the amendment process are not the traditional fare
of the courts but today comprise the hard core
definition of the political question doctrine.

CHAPTER II

NATIONAL LEGISLATIVE POWERS

A. SCOPE OF CONGRESSIONAL POWER

In *McCulloch v. Maryland* (1819), Chief Justice John Marshall stated: "This government is acknowledged by all to be one of enumerated powers." It follows from this principle that there is in American constitutionalism no doctrine of inherent legislative powers, at least in the domestic arena. Whenever the constitutionality of congressional legislation is at issue, some relationship to a specifically enumerated power in the constitutional text must be shown. Candidly, relationships are sometimes "found" which might not be obvious to the average reasonable person. Indeed, the lack of an inherent powers doctrine and the formal allegiance to an enumerated powers approach is less important in the end result than might appear.

Under our Constitution, all powers not delegated to the national government under the Tenth Amendment are retained by the states and the people. This is a basic premise of the division of powers, "Our Federalism." But it remains to be determined how the scope of the delegated powers should be delineated.

In *McCulloch v. Maryland* (1819), the Court considered whether the constitutional delegation of powers to Congress included a power to incorporate a national bank. Chief Justice Marshall conceded that there was no *express* provision granting such power to Congress and that incorporation was normally a prerogative of the states. There were, however, express powers in Art. I, Sec. 8, to lay and collect taxes, to borrow money, to regulate commerce, to declare and conduct wars, and to raise and support armed forces. Did these powers of sword and purse include a power to incorporate a national bank? Certainly there was nothing in the Constitution expressly prohibiting Congress from enacting such legislation. But John Marshall had emphasized the need for an affirmative grant of power.

Beginning with the great premise, "It is a Constitution we are expounding," Marshall argued for a doctrine of implied powers. A Constitution must be read broadly to provide government with all of the means to effectuate the powers granted in the basic instrument, subject, of course, to the restrictions contained therein. But Marshall did not rely solely on this logical and practical argument (which found support in the Federalist Papers), regarding the nature of the Constitution. Instead, he found specific authorization for implied powers in the Constitution itself. The Necessary and Proper Clause, Art. I, Sec. 8, Cl. 18, provides that Congress shall have power "To make all Laws which shall be necessary and proper for carrying into Execution the foregoing Powers, and all other Powers vested by this Constitution in the Government of the United States, or in any Department or Officer thereof."

Counsel for Maryland, which was seeking to tax the national bank, argued that the Necessary and Proper Clause should be interpreted restrictively by limiting it to those means which are indispensable to the execution of the granted power. But for John Marshall, Necessary and Proper didn't necessarily mean necessary. Our Constitution was "intended to endure for ages to come." The inclusion of the word "proper" with the word "necessary," the placement of the Necessary and Proper Clause among the powers of Congress in Art. I, Sec. 8, rather than in the Art. I, Sec. 9 limitations on congressional powers as well as the language of the Clause itself all led to a single conclusion—the express powers set forth in the Constitution were not to be read narrowly but were to be read broadly in order to accomplish the goal of making this new federal government work.

Marshall himself provided a broad interpretive guide to federal legislative power in *McCulloch* which is still being quoted and used in our courts: "Let the end be legitimate, let it be within the scope of the Constitution, and all means which are appropriate, which are plainly adapted to that end, which are not prohibited, but which consist with the letter and spirit of the Constitution, are constitutional." Applying this principle, the incorporation of a national bank was clearly "a convenient, a useful, and essential instrument" in carrying on the national government's fiscal operations.

The Chief Justice did include one limitation on his broad approach to congressional power. In what has come to be known as the Pretext Principle, Marshall reasoned that if Congress enacted legislation, "for the accomplishment of objects not entrusted to the government," it would become the duty of the courts to declare the law unconstitutional even though Congress purported to be executing its granted powers. While this principle was used in the early part of the twentieth century to overturn congressional legislation allegedly invading the residual powers of the states, unlike the Constitution, this principle has not endured for the ages.

B. THE COMMERCE POWER

1. ESTABLISHING THE FOUNDATIONS

The most important of the express domestic powers of Congress set forth in Art. I, Sec. 8, is the commerce power: "Congress shall have power to regulate commerce among the several states." This clause received its initial interpretation in the great case of *Gibbons v. Ogden* (1824). New York had given an exclusive navigation license to one party. Congress had conferred a license to traverse the same waters to another party. In this case of conflict, which power, state or federal, should prevail?

Chief Justice Marshall had little difficulty in including navigation within the term "commerce" given the Framers' concern with ending trade wars between the states. A greater problem was presented by the phrase "among the several states". *organic theory* Employing what Felix Frankfurter called an organic theory of commerce, Marshall read these words to mean "that commerce which concerns more states than one." Only that commerce which is exclusively internal to a state, which does not affect other states, would be precluded from the reach of the Commerce Clause under this interpretation. And Marshall chose not to extend the congressional power to this internal commerce only because "[s]uch a power would be inconvenient and is certainly unnecessary."

Had Marshall's organic interpretation of the Commerce Clause prevailed, much of subsequent commerce power history might have been different. Limitations placed on the Commerce Clause to frustrate the national economic recovery during the New Deal era, for example, would have been far more difficult. However, the Court gradually developed a territorial approach to the Commerce Clause limiting its reach to interstate commerce, *i.e.*, commerce crossing a state line. Today, through express reliance on the Commerce Clause and the doctrine of implied powers, there has been a return to that broad conception of the commerce power envisioned by Marshall.

Finally, Chief Justice Marshall turned to the meaning of the power "to regulate Commerce."

And once again he employed his broad vision of the constitutional grant of federal powers: "This power, like all others vested in Congress, is complete in itself, may be exercised to its utmost extent, and acknowledges no limitation, other than are prescribed in the Constitution." In short, the power to regulate commerce is "plenary" with respect to the objects of the power. The principal restraint on the exercise of this regulatory power is found in the wisdom and discretion of the Congress where, ironically, after a convoluted constitutional history, it remains today. It is the people exercising their power through the political process that safeguards constitutionally granted legislative powers from abuse.

2. USING THE COMMERCE CLAUSE FOR POLICE POWER ENDS

The Framers of the Constitution considered but rejected a proposal to vest a national police power in the Congress. But the question remained whether Congress, through the exercise of its delegated powers, could regulate to achieve police power objectives. Classically, these police powers concerned health, morals, and well-being. With the rise of the positive state in the twentieth century, such legislation often takes the form of social welfare laws. But John Marshall's Pretext Principle in *McCulloch v. Maryland* appeared to repudiate any effort to use the federal legislative power for social welfare ends. This more limited view of the commerce power is illustrated by *Hammer v. Dagenhart* (1918), in which a federal law restricting the interstate shipping of goods produced by child labor was held unconstitutional as invasive of the reserved powers of the states. For the Court, the congressional regulatory power over interstate commerce, while "ample," was limited by the Tenth Amendment. In this view, the powers reserved to the states served to limit the powers granted to the national government. This was the doctrine of dual federalism.

But even in the heyday of the Pretext Principle, the doctrine was not always followed. For example, in the case of *Champion v. Ames* (The Lottery Case) (1903), fifteen years before *Hammer,* the Court validated federal anti-lottery legislation, clearly a police power measure. The first Justice Harlan, speaking for the Court in *Champion,* said Congress has the power to protect the people of the United States against the pollution of the channels of interstate commerce. In *Hammer,* the *Lottery Case* was distinguished on the ground that the evil being legislated against followed rather than preceded the interstate transaction. For Justice Holmes, dissenting in *Hammer,* this distinction was a casuistry which was hardly persuasive. Justice Holmes concluded that the plenary regulatory power of Congress included the power to prohibit the movement of interstate commerce when it was being used to encourage what Congress in its judgment concluded is a moral evil: "It may carry out its views of public policy whatever indirect effect they may have upon the activities of the states."

The restrictive view of the commerce power adopted in *Hammer* as well as the Pretext Principle itself were conclusively rejected in *United States v. Darby* (1941). In upholding a provision of the Fair Labor Standards Act prohibiting the shipment of goods in interstate commerce which had been produced by employees working for substandard wages or excessive hours as defined by the Act, Chief Justice Stone in *Darby* returned to the Protective Principle fashioned in *Champion:* "Congress, following its own conception of public policy concerning the restrictions which may appropriately be imposed on interstate commerce, is free to exclude from the commerce articles whose use in the states for which they are destined it may conceive to be injurious to the public health, morals, or welfare, even though the state has not sought to regulate their use." It is for Congress to define the conditions for using the channels of interstate commerce.

The function of the Court, reasoned Stone, was not to probe the purpose or motive of Congress in regulating interstate commerce since these are "matters for the legislative judgment upon the exercise of which the Constitution places no restriction and over which the courts are given no control." Nor did the reserved powers of the states limit an otherwise constitutional exercise of the commerce power: "Our conclusion is unaffected by the Tenth Amendment. The Amendment states but a truism that all is retained which has not been surren-

dered." The dual federalism doctrine set forth in
Hammer which so long and so effectively limited
the reach of the federal commerce power was rejected. *Hammer* was overruled; implicitly, the Holmes
dissent in *Hammer* was now the law. Congress
could use the commerce power for social welfare
purposes.

3. THE STREAM OF COMMERCE

Can Congress, using its commerce power, regulate the wages and hours of workers at the Chicago
stockyards? Under the classic view, activity at the
stockyards might be viewed as an entirely local
transaction which would normally fall within the
purview of the state police power. Nevertheless, in
Stafford v. Wallace (1922), the Court upheld such
federal legislation reasoning that "[t]he stockyards
are but a throat through which the current [of
interstate commerce] flows, and the transactions
which occur therein are only incident to this current." The seemingly local activity at the stockyards was in fact part of the stream of interstate
commerce subject to federal control.

But note that the *Stafford* Court addressed itself
only to local activities at the "throat" of interstate
commerce. It did not undertake to approve federal
regulatory power over activities, such as agricultural production and mining, which arguably are antecedent to interstate commerce. Nor did it say that
Congress could regulate activities, such as the sale
and consumption of goods, solely on the ground that

the goods had once traveled in interstate commerce. However, whether or not the "stream of interstate commerce" in fact extends to these activities has not proven critical. Even if such activities are not *in* interstate commerce, Congress can reach them under the Affectation Doctrine. Since the Affectation Doctrine brings a wider range of activity under the scope of federal regulation, it has virtually displaced the "stream of commerce" doctrine.

4.   THE AFFECTATION DOCTRINE

In *McCulloch v. Maryland* (1819), Chief Justice Marshall had made it clear that congressional power is not limited to the express grants of Art. I, Sec. 8, but includes such power as is necessary and proper to the effectuation of the express powers. Using the broad interpretive approach to implied powers adopted by John Marshall, it can be said that the commerce power encompasses federal regulation of local activity when such regulation is reasonably appropriate to the effective regulation of interstate commerce.

In the pre-New Deal era, the Court translated this principle to mean that Congress can regulate local activities which "directly" affect interstate commerce but not those local activities where the effect was only "indirect." This conceptualistic approach had the practical effect of precluding any inquiry into the magnitude of the impact of local transactions on interstate commerce and the need for federal regulation for our national economy.

But beginning with *NLRB v. Jones & Laughlin Steel Corp.* (1937), the Court increasingly began to inquire into the extent of the burden on the free movement of interstate commerce.

The era of the modern affectation doctrine was launched with the case of *Wickard v. Filburn* (1942), upholding federal legislation regulating the most local of all activities—production of wheat for personal consumption on the family farm. Justice Jackson for the Court stated the controlling principle: "[E]ven if [the farmer's] activity be local, and though it may not be regarded as commerce, it may still, whatever its nature, be reached by Congress, if it exerts a substantial economic effect on interstate commerce, and this irrespective of whether such effect is what might at some earlier time have been defined as 'direct' or 'indirect'."

In defining whether the farmer's activities had a substantial adverse effect, the Court introduced the cumulative effects principle. In a context like *Wickard,* the effect must be considered in the light of the farmer's "contribution taken together with that of many others similarly situated." It is the aggregate or cumulative impact of all the individual producers that provided the predicate for congressional regulation.

Applying these principles to the marketing restrictions before them, the Court, in *Wickard,* concluded that Congress could reasonably have found that home consumed wheat would have substantial influence on price and market conditions. First, such wheat would overhang the market and thus introduce an uncontrolled variable on supply and demand. Second, even if never marketed, the wheat would satisfy the needs of the grower thus withdrawing him from the market. A wag of the time, parodying Cardozo's style, said of the hapless farmer in *Wickard:* "Grow it he can, but eat it he cannot."

The modern Affectation Doctrine fashioned in *Wickard* controls Commerce Clause analysis to the present day. Its broad sweep is indicated by the fact that since the New Deal no congressional legislation grounded in the commerce power has been held unconstitutional for want of federal legislative power.

The breadth of the congressional commerce power thus recognized is indicated by two cases upholding the public accommodations provisions of the 1964 Federal Civil Rights Act which was based principally on the federal commerce power. In *Heart of Atlanta Motel v. United States* (1964), the Court held that Congress had power to prohibit racial discrimination in hotels and motels serving interstate travelers. Even though the motel's racial discrimination occurred locally, by discouraging blacks from traveling the discrimination burdened interstate commerce. Justice Clark, for the Court in *Heart of Atlanta* observed: "How obstructions in commerce may be removed—What means are to be employed—is within the sound and exclusive discretion of the Congress. It is subject to only one caveat—that the means chosen by it must be reasonably adapted to the end permitted by the Constitution. We cannot say that its choice here was not so adapted. The Constitution requires no more." The contention that since Congress was legislating against "moral wrongs" the use of the Commerce Clause was improper was similarly rejected in *Heart of Atlanta*. Given the burdensome effect of racial discrimination on commerce, Congress could act. The *Heart of Atlanta* case, therefore, made it clear, if any doubt remained, that a police or social welfare motivation would not in itself render a congressional exercise of the commerce power invalid.

In the companion case, *Katzenbach v. McClung* (1964), the commerce power provided the foundation for the extension of the public accommodations provisions of the Civil Rights Act to Ollie's Barbecue, a small restaurant catering to a local trade. Only forty-six per cent of the food purchased by Ollie's Barbecue came through the channels of interstate commerce. But this was sufficient since Congress could rationally conclude that restaurants practicing racial discrimination sold less interstate goods, that interstate travel was obstructed, and that business in general suffered. While the volume of food purchased by Ollie's from interstate sources might be insignificant, the cumulative effects doctrine dictated that Congress might consider the aggregate impact in determining the burden on the free flow of commerce: "[W]here we find that the legislators, in light of the facts and testimony before them, have a rational basis for finding a chosen regulatory scheme necessary to the protection of commerce, [the Supreme Court's] investigation is at an end." Together with *Heart of Atlanta, Katzenbach v. McClung* demonstrates that the judiciary will extend great deference to a congressional assertion that it is acting under the Commerce Clause. Nevertheless, the Court does not abandon all investigation into the matter. At least a nominal inquiry into the regulated conduct's effect on interstate commerce is conducted.

The Affectation Doctrine also has provided a vehicle for the federalization of criminal law, a traditional bastion of the local police power. For example, in *Perez v. United States* (1971), the Court upheld Title II of the Consumer Credit Protection Act, the criminal sanctions of which were applied to a local loan-sharking situation. Justice Douglas said that Congress could reasonably conclude that local loan-sharking was one of the most lucrative sources of revenue or organized interstate crime.

But had *Perez* any tie-in to interstate criminal organization? In response, Justice Douglas appeared to say that none was needed. He apparently invoked the cumulative effects doctrine: "Where *the class* of activities is regulated, and that *class* is within the reach of federal power, the courts have no power 'to excise, as trivial, individual instances' of the class." But there remained a problem. There was no indication that *Perez* was a member of the class of loan sharks having ties to interstate crime. Justice Stewart observed in a bitter dissent: "[U]nder the statute before us, a man can be convicted without any proof of interstate movement, of the use of the facilities of interstate commerce, or of facts showing that his conduct affected interstate commerce." But in *United States v. Lopez* (1995), for the first time since the New Deal, the commerce power was held inadequate to sustain the law. The Court held 5–4 that the Gun–Free School Zones Act, prohibiting knowing possession of firearms in a school zone, is unconstitutional.

In an opinion that may portend major changes in Commerce Clause jurisprudence, Chief Justice Rehnquist rejected the Government's Affectation Doctrine argument. The Act did not have a jurisdictional nexus requiring that the firearms or the defendant have some connection with interstate commerce. *Lopez* placed a new emphasis on the need for a *substantial* and *commercial* effect. The Act was not limited to "commercial transactions" which in the aggregate, substantially affect interstate commerce.

Congress had made no findings on the effect of school violence on interstate commerce. While findings are not required, their absence makes it more difficult to conclude that such a substantial effect exists. The Government argued that the use of guns in schools affects the national economy because of the substantial cost of violent crime, the impediment violence places on travel and the less productive citizenry produced by a handicapped educational process. Chief Justice Rehnquist responded that accepting such arguments would allow federal regulation of any activity, even in areas such as family law where the states have traditionally been sovereign.

Justice Kennedy, joined by Justice O'Connor, concurred, arguing that the Act is unconstitutional, given its significant interference with state sovereignty, "[a]bsent a stronger connection or identification with commercial concerns that are central to the Commerce Clause."

Justice Breyer, joined by Justices Stevens, Souter and Ginsburg, dissenting, stressed that the specific question was whether Congress could have "a rational basis" for concluding that the regulated act has a "significant" effect on interstate commerce. The absence of findings only deprives the statute of some extra leeway beyond the deference required. Congress could rationally conclude that gun related violence near the schools, through its effect on education, has a significant effect on economic activity. Violence around the schools "is a commercial, as well as a human, problem."

In sum, *Lopez* signifies there are limits to the power of Congress to legislate under the Commerce Clause.

C. THE TAXING POWER

Congress can use taxation as a necessary and proper means for effectuating its delegated powers. Additionally, Art. I, Sec. 8, provides that Congress shall have an independent power to lay and collect taxes. At least in form, this is a fiscal power, not a regulatory power. In the earlier part of this century, the Court struck down nominal taxing powers when it determined that the law in fact imposed a regulatory "penalty." In *Bailey v. Drexel Furniture Co.* (1922), the Court held unconstitutional the federal child labor tax on grounds that "its prohibitory and regulatory effect and purpose [were] palpable." The penalties of the Act were triggered by the guilty knowledge of the employer. Chief Justice Taft observed acidly: "Scienters are associated with penalties not with taxes."

But in modern times the "penalty" doctrine has given way to the doctrine of objective constitutionality. As the Court explained in *United States v. Kahriger* (1953), upholding an occupational tax on gamblers: "Unless there are provisions, extraneous to any tax need, courts are without authority to limit the exercise of the taxing power." As long as the federal law is revenue producing on its face, the Court will not probe to discover hidden regulatory motives and will not be overmuch concerned with whether the effects of the law trespass on the traditional state police power domain.

D. THE SPENDING POWER

While Congress has no express power to legislate for the general welfare, Art. I, Sec. 8, authorizes Congress to use federal monies to provide for the common defense and the general welfare. Federal spending is not simply a means for accomplishing Congress's delegated powers, it is an independent source of federal power. In *United States v. Butler* (1936), Justice Roberts professed to choose Hamilton's construction of the spending power (a power separate and distinct from the other enumerated powers) over Madison's construction (the spending power was only a means for furthering the enumerated power). As the Court said in *Butler,* "the power of Congress to authorize expenditure of public monies for public purposes is not limited by the direct grants of legislative power found in the Constitution."

Once again, spending is a fiscal not a regulatory power. During the New Deal era, this conception of the spending power as fiscal in nature was used to invalidate federal economic recovery legislation. In *United States v. Butler,* the Agricultural Adjustment Act of 1933, which sought to use the taxing and spending power to increase farm prices by controlling farm production, was invalidated as an intrusion on the regulatory powers of the state. Since the power to regulate agricultural production belonged to the states, Congress could not use taxing and spending as a constitutionally permissible means for achieving a non-delegated end. The tax and the federal spending were "but means to an unconstitutional end." Although Hamilton may have prevailed in theory, Madison prevailed in fact.

But this judicially fashioned limitation was not to survive the New Deal. Thus, the Social Security Act of 1935 was upheld against a Tenth Amendment based challenge in *Chas. C. Steward Machine Co. v. Davis* (1937). Today, Congress is free to spend and impose reasonable conditions on receipt of the federal grants. States and localities remain free to reject the federal monies but if they accept them they are taken subject to the conditions imposed by Congress. In *Fullilove v. Klutznick* (1980), upholding a ten per cent set aside of federal construction contracts for minority business concerns, Chief Justice Burger stated that Congress may "further broad policy objectives by conditioning receipt of federal monies upon compliance by the recipient with federal statutory and administrative directives" and may use its spending power "to induce governments and private parties to cooperate voluntarily with federal policy." Today, the spending power is conceived of in a much more expansive fashion than Madison would ever have contemplated. As Chief Justice Burger said in *Fullilove*: "The reach of the Spending Power within its sphere is at least as broad as the regulatory powers of Congress." Theoretically, a condition imposed by Congress which was completely unrelated to any federal interest in the spending program involved would be illegitimate. In a dissent, Justice O'Connor tried to breathe new life into this idea. See *South Dakota v. Dole* (1987). However, this limitation on the spending power is now of little importance since the reach of federal power is so extensive and the judicial review accorded exercises of the spending power so deferential.

A caveat, however, should be noted. Mere hortatory language in federal grants will not be interpreted by the courts as conditions unless the language of the grant setting forth the conditions is sufficiently precise. A federal grant is in the nature of a contract and the parties must be clear in their mutual undertaking. In *Pennhurst State School and Hosp. v. Halderman* (1981), language in federal mental disability legislation calling for treatment in "the setting that is least restrictive of personal liberty" was held not to be a condition for receipt of federal monies to the state institutions involved but only a policy objective.

In the Low–Level Radioactive Waste Policy Amendments Act, Congress provided monetary incentives to states which imposed a surcharge on radioactive wastes generated in other states. *New York v. United States* (1992). Unlike *Pennhurst*, the Court, per Justice O'Connor, said the conditions imposed by Congress on the states were unambiguous. The legislation authorized the Secretary of Energy to collect a portion of the surcharge and place it in an escrow account. The funds in this account were then to be used to provide grants to states which complied with federal deadlines for establishing waste disposal sites within the state. The conditions imposed by the statute were held to be reasonably related to the purpose of the expenditure; they were designed to resolve the difficult question of radioactive waste disposal.

Those challenging the validity of the legislation pointed out that the federal statute (1) required the funds to be collected in a separate escrow account, (2) empowered the Secretary of Energy to hold the funds only as trustee, (3) declared that the funds deposited in the escrow account were not the property of the United States, and (4) noted that the states were largely in control of whether they would pay into the escrow account. Accordingly, it was contended that the legislation did not call for the *spending of federal funds*. The Court rejected this analysis. Congress had power under the spending power to structure federal spending as it had done here. The spending power does not mandate any particular form of accounting: "That the States are able to choose whether they will receive federal funds does not make the resulting expenditures any less federal." Endowing the states with choice is inherent "in any conditional exercise of Congress' spending power." Since the challenged legislation was authorized by the Spending Clause, an affirmative grant of power in the Constitution, the legislation did not violate the Tenth Amendment.

E. INTERGOVERNMENTAL IMMUNITIES

There are two dimensions to the intergovernmental immunities problem. One deals with the power of the state or locality to tax or regulate federal activity. The other deals with the power of the federal government to tax or regulate the states. Both of these situations are greatly affected by the Supremacy Clause of Art. VI which enables the federal government to enjoy a greater immunity from state taxation and regulation and a greater power to tax and regulate state activities.

A state may not directly tax or regulate the federal government or its instrumentalities. *McCulloch v. Maryland* (1819). Moreover, a state may not discriminate against the federal government, or those who deal with the federal government, in the absence of a showing that significant differences between the classes warranted the inconsistent treatment. For example, a Michigan state law exempting from taxation all retirement benefits paid by Michigan to its former employees but which taxed pensions paid to federal retirees in Michigan violated the doctrine of intergovernmental immunities. The differences were insufficient to justify the differing treatment of the two classes of retirees. *Davis v. Michigan Department of Treasury* (1989).

To what extent may the federal government regulate the states and localities themselves? In the past, in the heyday of the doctrine of dual federalism, the Tenth Amendment had been interpreted to be an independent limitation on federal power. But this view of the Tenth Amendment was apparently rejected in *United States v. Darby* (1941). In recent times, however, the principle that the existence of the states imposes some limitation on congressional legislative power was revived by the decision in *National League of Cities v. Usery* (1976).

In holding unconstitutional provisions of the federal Fair Labor Standards Act regulating the wages and hours paid by the state to their employees, the Court in *National League of Cities* resurrected state sovereignty as an affirmative limitation on the congressional commerce power. Congress was not merely displacing police power to regulate wages and hours; Congress was regulating the states as states. Justice Rehnquist, for the Court, declared: "We hold that insofar as the [federal provisions] operate to directly displace the States' freedom to structure integral operations in areas of traditional governmental functions, they are not within the authority granted Congress by Art. I, Section 8, cl. 3." The federal law was seen as displacing the considered policy choices of state officials on how they wish to structure delivery of basic governmental services to their citizens. Determination of the wages of those that the state employs to perform such functions was considered an undoubted "attribute of state sovereignty" since it implicated "functions essential to [the states'] separate and independent existence."

For the four dissenting justices, the Court's decision constituted a startling restructuring of our federal system. Justice Brennan speaking for three of the dissenters noted that "there is no restraint based on state sovereignty requiring or permitting judicial enforcement anywhere expressed in the Constitution; our decisions over the last century and a half have explicitly rejected the existence of any such restraint on the commerce power." For the dissent, it was not judicial enforcement of the Tenth Amendment but the political processes that protect state sovereignty.

Justice Blackmun provided the crucial fifth vote in *National League of Cities*. In a concurring opin-

•

ion, Justice Blackmun expressed his belief that the Court was simply adopting a balancing approach which would allow the federal government to regulate where the federal interest is overriding and the need for state compliance is demonstrable. It was this less than full endorsement of the Court's opinion in *National League of Cities* that led its critics to hope that the decision was not a bellwether of a return to the discarded doctrine of dual federalism.

In subsequent cases, the Court struggled with the nature of the limitation fashioned in *National League*. It declared that a law would be held to violate the doctrine of state sovereignty only if it satisfied each of the following requirements: "First, there must be a showing that the challenged statute regulated 'States as States.' Second, the federal regulation must address matters that are indisputably attributes of state sovereignty. And, third, it must be apparent that the States' compliance with the federal law directly impair their ability to 'structure integral operations in areas of traditional functions.' " Even if these conditions were met, Tenth Amendment concerns could be overridden by a sufficiently compelling national interest. *Hodel v. Virginia Surface Mining and Reclamation Association, Inc.* (1981). In applying these standards to a variety of varying fact contexts, the Court indicated that *National League of Cities* was a unique situation and not an indicator of a new major emphasis on state sovereignty as a limitation on federal legislative power.

In *Garcia v. San Antonio Metropolitan Transit Auth.* (1985), the Supreme Court, 5–4, reversed its position on the limitations on congressional commerce power to enforce wage provisions of the FLSA against the states and overruled *National League of Cities.* Justice Blackmun had switched sides and wrote for the new majority. He had become convinced since *National League* that a determination of state immunity from federal regulation, based on an appraisal by an unelected federal judiciary of what constitutes a traditional or integral governmental function "is not only unworkable but is inconsistent with established principles of federalism."

While accepting in principle that the Constitution's federal structure imposes limitations on the commerce power, he rejected the view that federal courts have a "license to employ free standing conceptions of state sovereignty when measuring congressional power." Rather than focusing on "predetermined notions of sovereign power," as in *National League of Cities,* protection of federalism is to be found in "the built-in restraints that our system provides through state participation in federal governmental action. The political process ensures that laws that unduly burden the states will not be promulgated." The Constitution guarantees a process of decision, not a favorable result for the states. However, the constitutional structure does impose affirmative limits on federal power enforceable by the courts. Justice Blackmun did not explore what such limits on federal incursions into state sovereignty might be other than to assert they "must be tailored to compensate for possible failings in the national political process rather than to dictate a 'sacred province' of state autonomy."

The dissent challenged the assertion that there was no workable standard for the state sovereignty limitation, arguing that the proper approach is a balancing of the respective national and state interests with a sensibility for state autonomy. Political processes, they argued, are inadequate to assure that states would perform their role as an effective counterpoise to overreaching federal power. For example, members of Congress, while locally elected, are still members of the federal government. Most troubling for the dissent was their belief that the Court was implicitly abandoning the teaching of *Marbury* that it is the province of the federal judiciary to say what the law is: "In rejecting the role of the judiciary in protecting the states from federal overreaching, the Court's opinion offers no explanation for ignoring the teaching of the most famous case in our history."

The *Garcia* dissenters expressed hope for a future return to the federalist principles of *National League of Cities*. But at least for the present, the Court has rejected any meaningful judicial role in limiting Congress's power to regulate the states as states; such cases generally are the equivalent of political questions, inappropriate for judicial resolution. Coupled with the broad congressional commerce power over private activity, the national regulatory power is sweeping indeed. Absent any violation of some particular constitutional right or liberty, it is difficult to imagine any judicially enforceable limitation on the exercise of the commerce power. And it is difficult to believe that the Court would treat Congress's fiscal powers any differently.

In *Gregory v. Ashcroft* (1991), a provision of the Missouri Constitution requiring state judges to retire at age 70 was unsuccessfully challenged as violative of the federal Age Discrimination in Employment Act (ADEA). *Gregory* amplified the idea expressed in *Garcia* that there is a certain area of state sovereignty which the federal government may not displace: "[T]he authority of the people of the States to determine the qualifications of their government officials may be inviolate." Under *Garcia*, the political process provides the primary protection for the states against an intrusive exercise of the commerce power by Congress. But the principle of an inviolate core of state sovereignty influenced statutory interpretation in *Gregory*. Invoking the "plain statement" rule, the Court held, per Justice O'Connor, that Congress had not made plain an intention to apply the ADEA to state judges.

In *New York v. United States* (1992), the Court, per Justice O'Connor, held that Congress could not compel the states to regulate. The take title provision of the Low Level Radioactive Waste Policy Amendments of 1985 was invalid. The take title provision gave the states an unwelcome and invalid choice between taking title to radioactive waste or regulating according to the direction of Congress:

"Either type of regulatory action would 'commandeer' state governments into the service of federal regulatory purposes, and would for this reason be inconsistent with the Constitution's division of authority between federal and state governments." Whether one looked at the take title provision as not authorized by the enumerated powers of Congress or as "infringing upon the core of state sovereignty reserved by the Tenth Amendment," the take title provision was inconsistent with the "federal structure of our government established by the Constitution."

Justice O'Connor distinguished *Garcia* by saying that the legislation in that case subjected a "State to the same legislation applicable to private parties" whereas in *New York v. United States* the federal legislation was directed at the state alone. The rationale for the invalidity of the take title provision was the offense it did to political accountability. When the federal government requires the states to regulate, state officials bear the wrath of the citizenry. Yet the federal officials who designed the offending federal legislation remain "insulated from the electoral ramifications of their decision."

Congress, of course, pursuant to its authorized powers, may regulate directly. Congress could validly authorize states with disposal sites to increase costs or deny access to waste generated in states not complying with federal deadlines for the construction of waste disposal sites. Congress could give the states the choice of regulating in accordance with federal standards or having the state law preempted by federal legislation. But political accountability is undermined "when elected state officials cannot regulate in accordance with the views of the local electorate in matters not preempted by federal regulation."

In dissent, Justice White, joined by Justices Blackmun and Stevens, complained that Justice O'Connor had made an end run around *Garcia* on the basis of a distinction without a difference. The political process itself, rather than a doctrine of state autonomy, protected the states. Indeed, the states had been deeply engaged participants in constructing the federal legislation under review in *New York v. United States*. With the departures of two members of the *Garcia* majority—Justices Blackmun and White—it remains to be seen whether the effort in *New York v. United States* to confine the *Garcia* precedent will be expanded.

CHAPTER III

STATE POWER IN AMERICAN FEDERALISM

States have broad police powers to legislate for the health, morals, and well-being of their citizens. But, like the national government, state action is subject to constitutional limitations arising either from specific guarantees or from the constitutional division of powers between the federal and state governments. It is with the working out of the parameters of "Our Federalism" that the present chapter is concerned.

Some constitutional powers are exclusively national in character; they do not admit of concurrent exercise by both the federal and state governments. For example, the war power and the power over foreign affairs are vested in the national government to the point that state regulation in the same area is essentially precluded. See *Toll v. Moreno* (1982) [naturalization power]. Other powers such as the power to raise revenues through taxation and the spending power are concurrent powers.

A. STATE POWER TO REGULATE COMMERCE

1. THE NATURE OF THE POWER

In *Gibbons v. Ogden* (1824), the Court examined the question whether the commerce power is exclusive or concurrent. While John Marshall found "great force" in the argument for exclusivity, it was unnecessary to finally resolve the issue since the state law conflicted with the congressional act. Under the Supremacy Clause of Art. VI, the state law yielded to the federal enactment. In addressing the nature of the commerce power, Marshall considered the basis upon which the states were allowed to enact inspection laws which would appear to constitute regulations of interstate commerce. His conclusion was that such state regulation was an exercise of the police power, not an exercise of the national power over interstate commerce. This distinction would accommodate states' need to regulate the subjects of interstate commerce as part of their effort to protect the health, morals and well-being of their citizens. However, this distinction really avoided the basic issue of the extent to which states could exercise their powers when interstate commerce is affected. Whether a state regulation is called a police power or an exercise of the commerce power, the critical question remains how the state law comports with the national commerce power.

2. THE SUBJECT OF THE REGULATION: THE *COOLEY*-DOCTRINE

Cooley v. Board of Wardens (1851), upheld a Pennsylvania statute requiring vessels entering or leaving Philadelphia to have local pilots. Justice Curtis began from the premise that the law did constitute a regulation of interstate commerce but that the regulation of interstate commerce was a concurrent power. Indeed, the *Cooley* approach may be described as setting forth a doctrine of "selective exclusiveness"—whether the dormant Commerce Clause, *i.e.*, Congress had not legislated, itself precluded state regulation was to be determined on a selective basis by looking to the subject of the regulation.

The Court fashioned what now has come to be known as the *Cooley* Doctrine: "Whatever subjects of this [commerce] power are in their nature national, or admit only of one uniform system, or plan of regulation, may justly be said to be of such a nature as to require exclusive legislation by Congress." Applying this standard to the facts, the *Cooley* Court determined that the regulation of pilotage is best provided for by diverse regulation accommodated to local needs.

But if the *Cooley* Doctrine means that the Court should focus only on the subject matter of the state regulation and not the nature of the regulation, its adequacy as a test of the negative implications of the dormant Commerce Clause is questionable. If the Commerce power is unexercised by Congress—if it is dormant—a critical question still remains: What is the effect of the state law on interstate commerce? This cannot be answered solely by looking to the subject matter of the state law. For one thing, such an approach is likely to end up as a jurisprudence of labels.

3. THE MODERN APPROACH: THE BALANCING OF INTERESTS

The modern approach to commerce power litigation recognizes that the "dormant" Commerce Clause does have "negative implications" limiting state power to regulate. This power is to be determined by the nature of the state regulation, using the following standard:

> Where the statute regulates even-handedly to effectuate a legitimate local public interest, and its effects on interstate commerce, are only incidental, it will be upheld unless the burden imposed on such commerce is clearly excessive in relation to the putative local benefits. If a legitimate local purpose is found, then the question becomes one of degree. And the extent of the burden that will be tolerated will of course depend on the nature of the local interest involved, and on whether it could be promoted as well with a lesser impact on interstate activities. *Pike v. Bruce Church, Inc.* (1970).

This avowed balancing approach replaced the earlier nominalistic test which made the validity of a state law turn upon whether the effect on interstate commerce was deemed to be "indirect" or "direct." Instead, the balancing approach forces a court into a fact-gathering inquiry to determine (1) whether the state law is an even-handed regulation pursuant to a legitimate state objective or is discriminatory against interstate commerce interests; and, (2) if the law is non-discriminatory, whether the state interest in the regulation overrides the adverse effect on interstate commerce. The overriding questions are whether balancing of interests is appropriate for the courts and whether courts are capable of weighing non-legal factors such as economic data and considerations.

a. Discrimination: Purpose, Means, Effects

The modern Dormant Commerce Clause doctrine mandates that the courts initially determine whether a state has a legitimate police power interest in regulating. If the sole objective of the state is to favor local as against out-of-state interests, such discriminatory legislation almost certainly violates the Commerce Clause. The historic purpose of the Commerce Clause was to prevent parochial state legislation which inevitably stimulates reprisals by other states. Further, out-of-state interests which are adversely affected by such discrimination are said to lack recourse to the ordinary legislative means for correcting wrongs—they have no representation in the discriminating state's legislature (the political rationale). It follows that purposeful protectionist regulation is virtually *per se* impermissible.

In *Baldwin v. G.A.F. Seelig, Inc.* (1935), the Court struck down a New York law which prohibited the sale of milk bought out of state at a price lower than the sale price of in-state milk. The Court reasoned that "when the avowed purpose of the obstruction, as well as its necessary tendency, is to suppress or mitigate the consequences of competition between the states, the Commerce Clause is offended." The ultimate principle is "that one state in its dealings with another may not place itself in a position of economic isolation." Even if the state has critical social welfare purposes at stake, it cannot erect trade barriers to the free flow of interstate competition consistent with the Common Market philosophy underlying the Commerce Clause: "The Constitution was framed under the dominion of a political philosophy less parochial in range. It was framed upon the theory that the people of the several states must sink or swim together and that in the long run prosperity and salvation are in union not division."

Even if a state law is designed to serve a legitimate police power objective, that does not mean that it is not discriminatory. As was said in *City of Philadelphia v. New Jersey* (1978), "the evil of protectionism can reside in legislative means as well as legislative ends." In *City of Philadelphia,* the Court held unconstitutional a New Jersey law prohibiting the importation into the state of out-of-state solid or liquid waste. To put the question bluntly, could New Jersey refuse to be a garbage dump for Philadelphia? The Court answered,

"No". New Jersey might refuse to allow the dumping of any more solid or liquid waste within its borders, but it could not set up a barrier solely against out-of-state waste. "[W]hatever New Jersey's ultimate purpose, it may not be accomplished by discriminating against articles of commerce coming from outside the state unless there is some reason apart from their origin to treat them differently." In short, when a state law imposes burdens on the face of its regulation on out-of-state interests which it does not impose on in-state interests, such burdens are likely to be categorized as facially discriminatory means which should be subjected to more searching judicial review.

The non-discrimination principle of *City of Philadelphia* was invoked in *Hughes v. Oklahoma* (1979). An Oklahoma statute prohibiting the out-of-state sale of free swimming minnows, even though in-state sales were permitted, was struck down. Such facially discriminatory legislation, stated Justice Brennan, "invokes the strictest scrutiny of any purported legitimate local purpose and of the absence of non-discriminatory alternatives." Even assuming that the statute served Oklahoma's ecological and environmental concerns, "the means selected were the most discriminatory available." Conservation was achieved by placing the entire burden on out-of-state interests.

The heightened scrutiny test for judging state legislation using facially discriminatory means has been applied in a variety of other contexts. Thus, the test was used to invalidate a state statute requiring utility companies to give a preference to in-state customers for hydroelectric power. The statute employed facially protectionist means, and hence, was invalid. *New England Power Co. v. New Hampshire* (1982).

In some circumstances, however, a state discriminatory means regulation can survive a dormant Commerce Clause challenge. A Maine prohibition on the importation of live-baitfish for fear of parasites not common to Maine fisheries was upheld. A state may use discriminatory means to serve a legitimate state police power interest, i.e., protection of local fisheries, if no less restrictive means are available. *Maine v. Taylor* (1986). But a "plain discrimination against products of out-of-state manufacture" will be struck down. Thus, an Ohio tax credit against its fuel sales tax for each gallon of ethanol sold as a component of gasohol, but only if the ethanol was produced in Ohio or in a state that granted similar tax advantages to Ohio ethanol, was violative of the Dormant Commerce Clause. The reciprocity provisions didn't save the legislation since, if anything, they enhanced the discrimination by seeking more favorable treatment for Ohio ethanol elsewhere. The facial disadvantage imposed on out-of-state sellers was not justified by the speculative health and commerce interests advanced by the state. *New Energy Co. v. Limbach* (1988).

Recently, state and local regulation of solid waste has foundered on the shoals of the dormant Commerce Clause. The Court has been unmoved by appeals to validate such regulation on the ground of local health and safety considerations if the regulation presents barriers to the free flow of interstate commerce. In *Chemical Waste Management, Inc. v. Hunt* (1992), an Alabama statute which imposed an additional fee on out-of-state hazardous waste disposed of inside the state was invalidated. Although local safety and health interests might be legitimate, "only rhetoric, and not explanation" had been offered to explain why Alabama had only targeted interstate hazardous waste to meet these concerns. Furthermore, there were less discriminatory alternatives available. These included a generally applicable additional fee on all hazardous waste disposed of within the state, a per-mile tax on all vehicles transporting hazardous waste on state roads, or an even-handed cap on total tonnage in state landfills.

In *Fort Gratiot Sanitary Landfill, Inc. v. Michigan Dept. of Nat'l Resources* (1992), a Michigan law stating that solid waste generated in another county, state, or country cannot be accepted for disposal unless explicitly authorized in the receiving county's 20 year waste disposal plan was invalidated. The law was impermissibly protectionist. The fact that the law treated waste generated in other Michigan counties no differently from out of state waste did not save the law: "[A] State (or one of its political subdivisions) may not avoid the strictures of the Commerce Clause by curtailing the movement of articles of commerce through subdivisions of the State, rather than through the State itself."

Novel state schemes to banish out-of-state waste from their borders continue to be checkmated. An Oregon statute that imposed a $2.25 per ton surcharge on in-state disposal of waste generated out-of-state but only a $0.85 per ton surcharge on the disposal of waste generated in-state was held to be facially discriminatory. *Oregon Waste Systems, Inc. v. Department of Environmental Quality of the State of Oregon* (1994). Although *Chemical Waste Management* suggested that "a differential surcharge might be valid if based on the costs of disposing of waste from other states," Oregon had failed to provide a legitimate reason for subjecting out-state waste to a discriminatory surcharge three times higher than that imposed on in-state waste. No intrastate tax burden had been identified which would justify the differential in the surcharges.

Nor could the surcharge on out-of-state waste be justified because the state wished to spread the cost of the in-state disposal of Oregon waste to all state citizens. State conferral of a cost advantage on handlers of local waste was invalid economic protectionism. Oregon's argument that its surcharge on out-of-state waste constituted resource—not economic—protectionism was rejected because a state cannot prefer its citizens over out-of-state consumers in providing access to natural resources located within the state.

The invalidity of resource protectionism is illustrated by the invalidation of an Oklahoma law requiring that the state's coal-fired electric generating plants producing power for sale in the state burn a mixture of coal which contain at least 10% Oklahoma coal. The Oklahoma law "on its face and in practical effect discriminates against interstate commerce." *Wyoming v. Oklahoma* (1992). The law's stated preference for coal from domestic sources was "protectionist and discriminatory." The state contention that efforts to sustain the state "coal-mining industry would diminish state reliance on a single source of coal delivered over a single rail line" was rejected. Legitimate goals cannot be secured "by the illegitimate means of isolating the State from the national economy."

If a state law operates to regulate activities outside the state, it is likely to be found discriminatory and subjected to more stringent judicial review. For example, a New York law which required liquor distillers to sell to wholesalers in New York at a price that was no higher than the lowest prices charged wholesalers in other states constituted an impermissible extraterritorial regulation in violation of the Commerce Clause. A state may seek lower prices for its consumers but it can not require that producers or consumers in other states surrender competitive advantages they might otherwise have: "Economic protectionism is not limited to attempts to convey advantages to local merchants; it may include attempts to give local consumers an advantage over consumers in other states." *Brown–Forman Distillers Corp. v. New York State Liquor Authority* (1986).

Even if a statute is facially non-discriminatory and is designed to serve a legitimate social welfare objective, the law still may be discriminatory in its impact on interstate commerce. In *Hunt v. Washington State Apple Advertising Comm'n* (1977), a North Carolina statute requiring that all closed containers of apples sold in the state bear only the U.S. grade was held unconstitutional. While the law on its face appeared to be non-discriminatory in that it applied equally to out-of-state and in-state sellers alike, in fact this was not the case. Application of the North Carolina requirements to the Washington sellers in fact denied the latter the competitive advantage of being able to utilize the state's superior grading system. When a law is found to have a discriminatory impact, "the burden falls on the State to justify it both in terms of the local benefits flowing from the statute and the unavailability of non-discriminatory alternatives adequate to preserve the local interests at stake. *Dean Milk Co. v. Madison.*"

The North Carolina law purported to be a consumer protection measure but it was not. The apple growing state of Washington had developed a more refined system of grading for its apples than the U.S. Department of Agriculture grading systems. The application to the State of Washington's apples of the U.S. grade, therefore, deprived consumers of information which they previously had. There were other, non-discriminatory alternatives available, *e.g.,* banning state grades inferior to the USDA standards.

A town flow control ordinance requiring that all solid waste be processed at a designated transfer station was deemed to have an invalid discriminatory effect even though, like the state law in *Hunt*, it did not facially discriminate on the basis of geographic origin. *C & A Carbone, Inc. v. Clarkstown* (1994). Unlike the statute in *Philadelphia v. New Jersey*, the town contended that its ordinance posed no barrier to the import or export of solid waste but merely required that the waste be channeled through a designated facility. But the article of commerce, the Court declared, was not the solid waste "but rather the processing and disposing of it."

The ordinance had an impermissible discriminatory effect on the processing and disposing of solid waste in interstate commerce. First, the ordinance's requirement that all waste be channeled through a designated facility drove up the costs of waste generated from outside the town. Second, the ordinance barred all but a single favored local facility from processing waste within the town. The ordinance thus prevented out-of-state competitors from competing in the local processing market. The fact that the flow control ordinance was a means of financing the waste disposal transfer facility was irrelevant: "[R]evenue generation is not a local interest that can justify discrimination against interstate commerce." Less discriminatory means such as uniform safety regulations were available to accomplish the town's health and safety objectives.

Another law which did not facially discriminate on the basis of geographical origin but which still had a discriminatory effect was a Massachusetts pricing order imposing an assessment on all fluid milk sold by dealers to Massachusetts retailers. The proceeds were then placed in a fund which was distributed to Massachusetts dairy farmers as a subsidy. The Court, per Justice Stevens, held that the purpose and effect of the pricing order was "to enable higher cost Massachusetts dairy farmers to compete with lower cost dairy farmers in other States." The assessment acted as a tax which served to make out-of-state milk more expensive. Furthermore, although the tax applied to milk produced in Massachusetts, the consequences of the tax as to milk produced in-state were entirely offset because of the subsidy which went only to Massachusetts dairy farmers. Although a "pure subsidy" funded out of general revenue "ordinarily imposes no burden on interstate commerce," the subsidy in this case was funded chiefly from the sale of out-state milk: "By conjoining a tax and a subsidy, Massachusetts has created a program more dangerous to interstate commerce than either part alone." In short, the Massachusetts pricing order was unconstitutional because, like a tariff, it neutralized advantages which belonged to the place of origin, *i.e.*, the lower costs of out-of-state dairy farmers. *West Lynn Creamery v. Healy* (1994).

Of course, it is not always easy to identify a law which has a discriminatory impact on interstate commerce. *Exxon Corp. v. Governor of Maryland* (1978), involved the validity of a state law prohibiting gasoline producers or refiners from operating gasoline retail service stations within Maryland. In upholding the law, the Court rejected the claim that the law was discriminatory, even though Maryland essentially had no local producers or refiners and thus interstate companies would bear the burden of divestiture. The Court reasoned that the Maryland law "creates no barriers whatsoever against interstate independent dealers; it does not prohibit the flow of interstate goods, place added costs upon them, or distinguish between in-state and out-of-state companies in the retail market." The structural character of the market rather than the interstate character of the company determined the law's applicability.

What is the difference between an ad hoc balancing test and a heightened scrutiny test used in these discrimination cases? The state laws which were challenged in the cases set forth above might well have survived an *ad hoc* balancing test. Certainly, the state interests being asserted were of substantial weight. For example, in *Carbone*, Justice Souter in dissent, joined by Chief Justice Rehnquist and Justice Blackmun, applied the *Pike* balancing test and concluded that the town ordinance was valid. The ordinance was free from discriminatory purpose or effect. While it created a local monopoly, local monopolies were subject to challenge under the Sherman Act not the Dormant Commerce Clause. In his view, the town ordinance was valid under *Pike* since the burdens it imposed fell on local residents not on interstate commerce. *Carbone* thus illustrates the difference in result that may obtain in Dormant Commerce Clause cases depending on whether the heightened scrutiny test or the *Pike* balancing test is used. The majority in *Carbone* had applied the heightened scrutiny test and invalidated the ordinance.

The heightened strict scrutiny test dictates the result in a way the balancing test does not. The heavy burden that the state must meet to justify a facially discriminatory statute if the heightened scrutiny test is used (especially the demand that the state show the absence of any less burdensome alternative means) largely dooms the law.

b. Undue Burdens–Ad Hoc Balancing

Even if a law is not discriminatory that does not necessarily mean that it passes Commerce Clause muster. Although a law may be even-handed, it still can run afoul of the Dormant Commerce Clause if it imposes an excessive burden on interstate commerce. How is an "excessive" or undue burden on interstate commerce determined? It is determined by an inquiry into whether the regulatory interests of the state justify or outweigh the law's impediment to the free movement of interstate commerce. Courts employ an *ad hoc* balancing test probing the nature and functions of the regulation, the character of the business involved, and the actual effect of the law on the flow of interstate commerce.

A growing number of Justices, such as Chief Justice Rehnquist and Justice Scalia, believe that judicial balancing of interests in this context is inappropriate. In their view, if the state law is non-discriminatory, then judicial intervention should be foreclosed; a balancing of interests test when discrimination is absent give courts an improper mandate to legislate. In their view, if the problem is a serious one, Congress is available to correct it. Nor is it only the conservatives on the Court who question judicial invalidation of state laws in the absence of discrimination. Justice Brennan, and more recently, Justice Blackmun, took a deferential view of state regulation in this area since they believed regulation of the economy is not the task of judicial review. Justice Souter, as indicated by his deferential attitude toward local regulation in his dissent in *Carbone*, may be moving toward this position.

When using the balancing approach, the courts accord great weight to traditional state police power concerns such as public health and safety, prevention of consumer fraud and the regulation of public highways. But even in these areas of local prerogative, the burden on the free movement of interstate commerce may override the state concern. Protection of the environment and conservation of depletable natural resources are interests not only of the regulating state but also of the nation. Not surprisingly, then, state conservation and environmental protection laws receive marked judicial deference. In *Minnesota v. Clover Leaf Creamery Co.* (1981), the Court upheld a Minnesota law prohibiting the use of plastic milk containers. While the law imposed a more severe burden on the out-of-state plastic industry than on the Minnesota pulpwood industry, the Court did not deem the law either discriminatory or excessively burdensome. All milk retailers, interstate and local, were subject to the ban on plastic containers. The minimal costs of using non-plastic containers in Minnesota was justified by the substantial state interest in conservation of natural resources and reducing the problem of solid waste disposal.

Another state law which survived a challenge as unduly burdensome concerned an Indiana statute. The law provided that when an entity or person acquired controlling stock of an Indiana corporation which had a substantial number of Indiana stockholders, the acquiring party received no voting rights unless the stockholders agreed to give voting rights. The Indiana statute was held not to violate the Commerce Clause. The law was not discriminatory; it applied to all tender offers whether or not the offeror was an Indiana resident. The law applied only to Indiana corporations; therefore, there was no danger that business would be subjected to inconsistent state regulation. The Indiana statute did not impose an undue burden on interstate commerce since the statute was limited to Indiana corporations and was concerned with protecting the stockholders of Indiana corporations, including residents of Indiana, from takeovers. The state legislation was concerned with preventing the corporate form from being used as a shield for unfair business practices. *CTS Corp. v. Dynamics Corp. of America* (1987).

The Supreme Court has long declared that state highway regulation is in a special category justifying a greater presumption of validity than is the case with the general run of state law. Indeed, at times the Court has suggested that the usual balancing-of-interest approach should not be applied to state highway legislation. The standard used should be the deferential rationality approach. This deference is due to the historic and necessarily unique role of local prerogative in this area. While state regulation of the railways is deemed to be more intrusive on the free flow of national commerce [*Southern Pacific Co. v. Arizona* (1945)], state regulation of the highways implicates predominantly local concerns—at least this is the theory.

In fact, state highway laws are judged under the Dormant Commerce Clause. The Court has regularly struck down state regulations where the local interests in highway management have been deemed insufficient to outweigh the burden on interstate commerce. This is especially true when the state legislation grants exceptions or other favorable conditions only to local business or where the particular state law is markedly out of step with the laws of other states governing the same activities.

Kassel v. Consolidated Freightways Corp. (1981), struck down an Iowa law which generally prohibited use of sixty-five foot double-trailer trucks within the state. Even though the state had offered substantial safety evidence to support the law in the trial court, the state's safety interest was characterized as illusory. *Kassel* ruled that the state law significantly impaired the federal interest in efficient and safe interstate transportation. Empirical evidence was closely scrutinized. The Iowa law required the use of a greater number of smaller trucks to be driven through Iowa and forced larger trucks to drive greater distances to bypass Iowa. Various provisions in the law benefitted only Iowa residents and imposed added burdens on neighboring states.

In summary, *Kassel* illustrates that the Court is still wedded to an *ad hoc* balancing approach even when the state interest is very strong, as is the case with state highways. Three justices, it should be noted, dissented in *Kassel*. There continues to be a vocal minority on the Court which insists on the abandonment of the balancing approach at least in highway cases and, perhaps more broadly, for all non-discriminatory state laws. As Justice Rehnquist said in dissent in *Kassel,* the Court's present balancing approach "arrogate(s) to this Court functions of forming public policy, functions which, in the absence of congressional action were left by the Framers of the Constitution to state legislatures."

4.   STATE AS MARKET PARTICIPANT

There is one context, however, when the Dormant Commerce Clause does not apply. When the state is not acting in a regulatory capacity, but is, instead, itself participating in the marketplace as a buyer or a seller, it may regulate free of restrictions flowing from the Dormant Commerce Clause. *Hughes v. Alexandria Scrap Corp.* (1976). The Dormant Commerce Clause does not preclude a state from discriminating in favor of its own citizens in the form of subsidies or through market transactions entered into by the state. However, this market participant exception to the Dormant Commerce Clause may not extend to state discrimination with respect to natural resources which the state has not had time to develop. However, the Court has not yet made an explicit statement to this effect. The lead case in this area did not involve natural resources. Thus, in *Reeves, Inc. v. Stake* (1980), the Court held that the Commerce Clause did not prevent the State of South Dakota from discriminating in favor of its residents with respect to sales from a state-owned cement factory despite the fact that Wyoming businesses had long relied on the output of the factory.

In *Reeves*, the Court, per Justice Blackmun, stated: "The Commerce Clause responds principally to state taxes and regulatory measures impeding free private trade in the national marketplace. There is no indication of a constitutional plan to limit the ability of the states themselves to operate freely in the free market." In addition to this historical basis, support for the market participant principle was found in concern for state sovereignty (*i.e.,* the ability of a state to provide public benefits to its citizens), the ability of an enterprise to choose its customers, the fact that private traders are not subject to Commerce Clause constraints, and the complexity of adjusting competing interests when the state engages in proprietary action. The Court did, however, emphasize that the state's business in this instance involved an extensive undertaking on its part and left open the possibility that restrictions placed on the use of the state's natural resources might be subject to the Dormant Commerce Clause.

A significant problem generated by *Reeves* lies in identifying those occasions when the state is acting as a participant rather than as a regulator. In *White v. Massachusetts Council of Const. Employers* (1983), the Dormant Commerce Clause doctrine was held not to apply to an executive order requiring that all city construction projects be performed by a work force at least half of which were city residents. While the dissent noted that "the economic choices the city restricts in favor of its residents are the choices of private entities engaged in interstate commerce," the Court, per Justice Rehnquist, reasoned that "[i]mpact on out-of-state residents figures in the equation only after it is decided that the city is regulating the market rather than participating in it." Since the city had expended only its *own* funds in entering into construction contracts for *public* projects, it was acting as a market participant. But see *South–Central Timber Dev., Inc. v. Wunnicke* (1984) [plurality expresses view that an Alaskan requirement that timber taken from state lands be processed in Alaska was subject to the Dormant Commerce Clause doctrine. Alaska participated in the timber-selling market but regulated the timber processing market. The state used its leverage in the timber-selling market to exert a regulatory effect in the processing market].

The student should note also that the Court has held that such resident preferences in hiring might violate the Privileges and Immunities Clause of Art. IV, Sec. 2. See *United Bldg. & Const. Trades Council v. Mayor and Council of Camden* (1984).

What is the current status of the market participant doctrine? Some members of the present Court are clearly supporters of the doctrine. In *Oregon Waste Systems*, Chief Justice Rehnquist, joined by Justice Blackmun, dissented and criticized the Court for making no "distinction between publicly and privately owned landfills". They noted that *Philadelphia v. New Jersey* had "specifically left unanswered the question whether a state or local government could regulate disposal of out-of-state solid waste landfills owned by the government."

In dissent in *Carbone*, Justice Souter, joined by Chief Justice Rehnquist and Justice Blackmun, said that the ordinance there did not extend a benefit to local private actors "but instead directly aids the government in satisfying a traditional governmental function." Although the majority in *Carbone* viewed the processing facility as privately operated, Justice Souter contended that functionally it was a municipal facility and that it should be obvious that "favoring state-sponsored facilities differs from discriminating among private economic actors, and is much less likely to be protectionist."

In sum, the Court has not relied on the market participant exception to the Dormant Commerce Clause since the early 1980's. Yet it has not disavowed the doctrine either and it remains available as a doctrinal escape hatch for the states and localities from the rigors of the Dormant Commerce Clause.

5. INTERSTATE PRIVILEGES AND IMMUNITIES

In constitutional law particularly, the same fact pattern may be approached under a number of overlapping constitutional alternatives. Thus, facts that could be resolved through a Commerce Clause analysis may be equally responsive to resolution under the Interstate Privileges and Immunities Clause of Art. IV, Sec. 2. Unfortunately, there is no particular geiger counter which can predict when the courts will use one clause rather than the other or, possibly, use both clauses.

The Privileges and Immunities Clause of Art. IV, Sec. 2, should be distinguished from the Privileges and Immunities Clause set forth in the Fourteenth Amendment, Sec. 1. Art. IV protects out-of-state citizens from unreasonable discrimination in regard to their fundamental national interests—interests which concern the Nation's vitality as single entity. While the Clause does not necessarily guarantee any particular right or privilege, it does require that, when a state confers a benefit on its own citizens, it cannot deny that same benefit to out-of-state citizens unless it demonstrates substantial justification. Substantial justification generally means that a state must establish that non-residents are a particular source of the problem that the state is seeking to remedy and that the law bears a substantial relationship to the eradication of the problem. *Hicklin v. Orbeck* (1978) [Alaska-hire law requiring preferential treatment to be given to state residents in employment held unconstitutional].

It is important to note that Art. IV, Sec. 2, requires that there be fundamental national interests at stake. The crucial question is whether the activity at issue is so "fundamental" to the well-being of the Nation as to be within the privileges and immunities protected by Art. IV, sec. 2. Thus, the Clause has been held to be inapplicable to a Montana statute which discriminated against non-residents in regard to license fees for elk hunting. *Baldwin v. Fish & Game Com'n* (1978). The Court concluded that Art. IV, Sec. 2, was designed only to reach that discrimination which would "hinder the formation, the purpose or the development of a single union of States." Simply, hunting for elk "is not basic to the maintenance or well-being of the Union." *Hicklin v. Orbeck* (1978). Compare *Supreme Court of New Hampshire v. Piper* (1985) [state supreme court rule limiting bar admission to state residents is violation of "National fundamental right" protected under "privileges and immunities" because of the important part which lawyers play in commercial intercourse and the national

economy which the Clause was intended to protect.]
Relying on *Piper*, the Court struck down as violative
of the privileges and immunities clause a Virginia
Supreme Court rule requiring out-of-state lawyers
to become permanent residents of Virginia in order
to become admitted to the Virginia bar without
taking the Virginia bar examination: "[L]awyers
who are admitted in other States are [not] less
likely to respect the bar and further its interests
solely because they are nonresidents." *Supreme
Court of Virginia v. Friedman* (1988).

Similarly, local court rules of the District Court of
the Virgin Islands which required that applicants
for admission to the bar live on the Virgin Islands
for one year and declare an intent to reside and
practice law there following admission were struck
down. On the basis of *Piper*, these requirements
were held violative of the privileges and immunities
clause of Art. IV, Sec. 2. Less restrictive means
were available to meet the demands of legal practice
in the Virgin Islands. For example, even if a nonresident lawyer was not able to make a court appearance, no showing had been made as to why the
government interest could not be met by substituting a local lawyer for the nonresident lawyer. *Bar-
nard v. Thorstenn* (1989).

In *United Building & Const. Trades Council v.
Mayor and Council of Camden* (1984), the Court
held that a city's imposition of a 40% resident
hiring requirement upon all contractors working on
city-funded public works construction projects must
satisfy Art. IV, Sec. 2, analysis. The Court rejected

the argument that municipalities are not bound by Art. IV, Sec. 2, and that conditioning the exercise of the privilege upon municipal rather than state citizenship or residency removed the ordinance from the Clause's reach. The privilege in question is "an out-of-state resident's interest in employment on public-work contracts in another state". Such employment is " 'sufficiently basic to the livelihood of the Nation' "as to fall within the scope of Art. IV, Sec. 2. However, because there was insufficient fact finding at the trial level, the Court did not decide whether Camden's ordinance satisfied the second part of the Privileges and Immunities Clause test. The Court did indicate, however, that if Camden could establish that out-of-state citizens were a particular source of the socioeconomic evils at which the ordinance was aimed and if the ordinance was narrowly tailored to eradicate this evil, Art. IV, Sec. 2, would be satisfied.

B. WHEN CONGRESS SPEAKS

Our prior analysis has been focused on situations when Congress has not legislated in the area in which a state seeks to regulate. In such situations, the restriction on state regulatory power flows from the negative implications of the Dormant Commerce Clause. But what happens when Congress enacts valid legislation in areas where the states also have regulated? Obviously, if Congress says it intends to occupy the field to preclude state action, the Supremacy Clause of Art. VI makes it clear that the valid federal regulatory scheme will prevail. But sometimes Congress legislates in areas where the state also has legislated without declaring its intent. Questions then abound: Did Congress intend its scheme to function concurrently with the state scheme or did Congress intend to occupy the field? Can any inferences be drawn from the congressional silence?

1.   PREEMPTION

If the state law "stands as an obstacle to the accomplishment and execution of the full purposes and objectives of Congress" [*Jones v. Rath Packing Co.* (1977)], under the Art. VI Supremacy Clause, the state law is preempted. Even if the state law is generally compatible with the objectives of the federal legislation, a court may determine that Congress intended to foreclose state action. Unfortunately, there is little by way of general doctrine controlling when preemption will be found. Each case tends to turn on its particular facts.

The Court has provided factors to be considered in determining whether Congress intended to preempt non-conflicting state law. If the area requires uniformity of regulation rather than diversity, preemption is more likely. The pervasiveness of the federal law—whether it appears that Congress sought to regulate all the critical aspects of the subject—will often be of controlling importance. If the subject area is one that historically has been dominated by the state government, the Court is more likely to reject preemption absent some clear indication by the Congress to the contrary. If administration of both the federal and the state law is likely to produce conflict, the courts are more likely to find a congressional intent to exclude the states. Finally, under what is sometimes referred to as the one-master theory, congressional creation of an agency to provide regular superintendence over a regulatory area suggests that continued state action is precluded.

Application of these principles is found in *English v. General Electric Co.* (1990), where a unanimous Court held that an action for intentional infliction of emotional distress based on state law was not preempted by the Federal Energy Reorganization Act which prohibited employers from discharging nuclear plant employees who reported safety violations. Although the federal statute provided a federal remedy for unlawful discharge of whistleblowers, Congress had not explicitly precluded state tort recovery in the federal statute nor did the federal remedy establish a Congressional intent to occupy the field. Concededly, the threat of state tort actions might influence some nuclear safety policy decisions. Yet this consequence was insufficiently direct or substantial to justify a conclusion that the state tort claim fell into the federally preempted field of nuclear safety. Furthermore, there was no "actual conflict" between the state tort claim and the prohibitions of the federal act.

2. LEGITIMIZATION

While Congress may speak to preempt state regulation, Congress alternatively can legislate to legitimize state regulation which might otherwise fail to satisfy the demands of the dormant Commerce Clause. The Court has recognized that the congressional power over interstate commerce is plenary and that Congress in the exercise of this plenary power might choose to leave an area, over which it could otherwise legislate, to state legislation. Even if the Supreme Court has invalidated state legislation on the ground that it conflicts with the negative implications of the Commerce Clause, the Congress may rescue such legislation simply by authorizing it. *Prudential Insurance Co. v. Benjamin* (1946) [state discriminatory taxation of out-of-state insurance companies held valid given federal law authorizing state control]. But before a state violation of the dormant Commerce Clause may be legitimized by Congress, Congress must make unmistakably clear its "unambiguous intent" to do so. *Wyoming v. Oklahoma* (1992).

CHAPTER IV

CONGRESS AND THE EXECUTIVE POWER

Under the Articles of Confederation, executive functions were performed by congressional committees. But the Framers of the Constitution provided in Art. II, Sec. 1: "The Executive Power shall be vested in a President of the United States of America." Was this Vestiture Clause simply a shorthand reference to all of the express executive powers provided in Art. II, or perhaps simply a reference to the choice of a single rather than a plural Executive? Or was it a separate grant of power for the President to perform all functions which are "executive" in character (sometimes called "inherent" executive power). While Presidents have regularly claimed inherent executive power (usually citing the Vestiture Clause), and the claim has received some favorable reaction from the Supreme Court [*United States v. Midwest Oil Co.* (S.Ct.1915); *In re Debs* (1895); *In re Neagle* (1890)] reliance on the Vestiture Clause as an independent source of power has never really been necessary to justify executive action. The broad undefined express powers of Art. II have provided ample room for

116

presidential initiatives. See generally, A.S. Miller, *Presidential Power In A Nutshell* (1977).

A reading of the express powers set forth in Art. II would not begin to provide even a flavor of modern executive power. The need for prompt, informed, and effective action in domestic and foreign affairs has meant that power has tended to flow to the Executive. While many of the vague, open-ended executive powers provided in the Constitution are shared with Congress, presidential initiatives have generally produced only congressional acquiescence and the courts have tended to avoid judicial review of executive actions, especially in the area of foreign affairs and national security. Indeed, it has been suggested that separation of powers questions involving the allocation of powers between Congress and the Executive should generally be treated as political questions inappropriate for judicial resolution. J. Choper, *Judicial Review and the National Political Process* 263 (1980).

What emerges from the Constitution's allocation of powers between the Executive and Congress is a system of separation of powers in which there are separate institutions generally exercising shared or blended powers. The actual relationship of the national institutions is determined more by practical realities and by custom and usage than by formal constitutional language.

Most of the executive powers set forth expressly in the text of the Constitution are stated in quite general terms and involve matters where power is

shared with Congress. Unsurprisingly in such circumstances, executive and congressional power
sometimes collide. In the past, the Executive has
usually tended to prevail in the case of conflict.
Congress, however, has increasingly tried to specify
and structure the division of power between it and
the Executive. This legislation is enacted under
the banner of promoting Executive responsibility
and accountability. But in light of the fact that the
Executive and Legislative Branches have been controlled by different political parties during much of
the post-Lyndon Johnson era, it is also clear that
these legislative efforts have their source in parti-
san or political differences.

When Congress attempts to specify Executive
power, does it trespass on Executive power? Does
Congress thereby usurp the powers it shares with
the other Branches? In the main, it has been left
for the Supreme Court to answer these questions.
The Court's answers to these questions have not
been unequivocal. Indeed, the Court may be said to
have given two sets of answers. One approach may
be called a formalist or textually literal approach.
This approach puts great weight on the text of the
Constitution and on formal observance of a strict
separation of powers. The Court's other approach
is a functional one which highlights the need for
checks and balances and the interdependence of the
Branches. In this view, the Branches of government cannot be approached as air-tight compartments; the constitutional text and the lines between the Branches must on occasion be subordi-

nated to flexibility and function. In the contest between these two approaches—the functional versus the formalist—the functional approach, aided by its formidable spokesman, Chief Justice Rehnquist, has thus far emerged as the dominant one. See *Morrison v. Olson* (1988); *Mistretta v. United States* (1989). But cf. *Bowsher v. Synar* (1986). On the other hand, the formalist approach has found its voice in the powerful but lonely dissents of Justice Scalia in *Morrison* and *Mistretta*.

A. THE DOMESTIC ARENA

1. EXECUTIVE LAWMAKING

Art. I provides that the legislative power is vested in the Congress. The President's formal constitutional power in lawmaking is found primarily in his power to recommend legislation and in the veto power, and even this negative power to refuse to assent to legislation can be overridden by a two-thirds vote of both houses. Art. I, Sec. 7. But again, the Constitution only hints at the lawmaking role of the President. Using the Executive Office to frame legislation and influence legislative deliberations, the President has truly become the Legislator–in–Chief.

The President also "legislates" independent of the formal lawmaking process. Through the issuance of executive orders and proclamations he directs the massive federal bureaucracy. What are the parameters of this executive policy-making? To what extent can the President act independent of (or even contrary to) statutory authorization? Such questions are not readily answered by reference to the Constitution's allocation of powers. Nor have the courts provided much guidance.

Perhaps the most significant judicial effort at providing some answers came in *Youngstown Sheet & Tube Co. v. Sawyer* (The Steel Seizure Case) (1952), in which the Court held unconstitutional President Truman's seizure of the steel mills during the Korean War to prevent a crippling strike. Justice Black, for the Court, noted that Congress had specifically rejected seizure as a method for preventing strikes. But the President wasn't relying on statutory authorization for his action but on the aggregate of his Art. II powers. Focusing on Congress' power to make the laws, Justice Black rejected executive domestic lawmaking: "In the framework of our Constitution, the President's power to see that the laws are faithfully executed refutes the idea that he is to be a lawmaker." The presidential power as Commander–in–Chief (and presumably his foreign affairs powers) could not be extended to mean that the President has "the ultimate power" to seize private property to prevent domestic production stoppages: "This is a job for the Nation's lawmakers, not for its military authorities."

Nevertheless, the *Steel Seizure Case* is as often cited as authority for executive domestic lawmaking as for its rejection of such a presidential prerogative. The reason is that a majority of justices accepted presidential power to take emergency action in the domestic sphere, at least in the absence of a specific congressional negative. Justice Vinson, speaking for three dissenters, cited the Art. II presidential powers to see that the laws are faithfully executed and to act as Commander–in–Chief and a history of executive initiatives lacking statutory authorization, to justify "at least interim action necessary to execute legislative programs essential to the survival of the Nation." Three Justices, while concurring in holding the seizure unconstitutional given the congressional rejection of seizures, nevertheless did not foreclose presidential emergency initiatives. What would constitute an "emergency" was left unanswered.

Justice Jackson's concurring opinion has had an especially enduring value. "Presidential powers," he reasoned, "are not fixed but fluctuate depending upon their disjunction or conjunction with those of Congress." When the President acts with congressional authorization, his constitutional authority is maximized; when he acts contrary to the congressional will, his power is at its lowest ebb. When the President must rely on his own authority, he acts in "a zone of twilight in which he and Congress may have concurrent authority, or in which the distribution is uncertain." In the twilight zone of shared powers, "the imperatives of events and contemporary imponderables rather than abstract thesis of law" determines the meaning of separation of powers.

2. EXECUTIVE IMPOUNDMENT

Art. I vests the powers of the purse in Congress. Nevertheless, presidents have regularly claimed the prerogative of impoundment, *i.e.,* withholding or delaying the expenditure of congressionally appropriated funds. When legislation vests discretion in the Executive to take such action, the constitutional problems are minimal. But in the 1970s, as the President increasingly used impoundments, it was claimed that constitutional power existed to impound funds even though Congress had mandated that they be spent. The argument was made that the President has a constitutional duty to execute all of the laws, including those imposing budgetary and debt limitations, requiring that he reconcile the competing legislative mandates. Further, inherent executive power was said to include the maintenance of fiscal control. Indeed, it was questioned whether Congress itself had constitutional power to mandate spending when the impoundment involved foreign affairs or national security—areas of traditional executive responsibility.

Critics of impoundment argued in response that the power to execute the laws cannot include the power to set aside the policy choices of Congress. "To contend that the obligation imposed on the President to see the laws faithfully executed implies a power to forbid their execution, is a novel construction of the Constitution and entirely inadmissible." *Kendall v. United States ex rel. Stokes,* (1838) [the President could not legally order the

Postmaster General to pay less for services than Congress had mandated]. They argue further that inherent executive power, even if accepted, cannot be stretched to include the prerogative of setting aside the congressional power to make the laws. Finally, opponents claim that the practical effect of impoundment allows the President to exercise an item veto which is not authorized by the Constitution.

While lower court decisions generally have rejected the President's constitutional arguments, the Supreme Court has not reached the constitutional question. See *Train v. New York* (1975). In 1974, Congress enacted the Congressional Budget and Impoundment Control Act which requires either congressional approval or failure to disapprove (depending on the nature of the impoundment) of presidential impoundments. The constitutionality of the Act, however, is subject to question. Does it excessively intrude on executive power, especially in the areas of foreign affairs and national security or is it only a reasonable allocation of roles in exercising shared powers? Does it embody a legislative veto proscribed by *Immigration & Naturalization Service v. Chadha* (1983)?

3. DELEGATION AND LEGISLATIVE VETO

A venerable precept of American constitutionalism with deep roots in the separation of powers principle is the idea that that which has been delegated cannot be redelegated. Obviously, this non-delegation doctrine has not been applied too literally or our modern administrative state would not be possible. Given the complexity of the modern state, the nondelegation doctrine has been interpreted with understandable latitude. Thus, when Congress created the United States Sentencing Commission, placed it in the Judicial Branch and delegated power to the Commission to promulgate Sentencing Guidelines which would be binding on the federal courts, it was held that the nondelegation doctrine was not violated. The nondelegation doctrine is not violated so long as Congress sets forth an intelligible principle to which those exercising the delegated authority are directed to conform. Since the law establishing the United States Sentencing Commission set forth policies and principles to govern the substantive formulation of the Sentencing Guidelines, delegation of rulemaking authority to the Commission to promulgate Sentencing Guidelines did not violate the nondelegation doctrine. *Mistretta v. United States* (1989).

Although it has been relatively easy for Congress to delegate legislative authority, it has been more difficult for it to retain control over that which has been delegated. The Legislative Veto has been a major weapon in the congressional arsenal for preserving executive accountability. Congress enacts legislation containing a broad delegation of power to the Executive but then provides for congressional review and veto of executive actions taken pursuant to the grant. In *Immigration & Naturalization*

Service v. Chadha (1983), the Court, per Chief Justice Burger, held 7–2, that a one-House veto of executive orders involving deportation of aliens is unconstitutional.

Chadha was an unfortunate case for making the constitutional decision since it didn't involve agency rule-making or executive policy choices, but rather a deportation decision in a particular case. Chadha, an East Indian, admitted that he was deportable for overstaying his student visa. In 1974, he sought and obtained an Attorney–General suspension of the deportation order as permitted under the Immigration and Nationality Act because of the hardship such deportation would involve. However, the same Act authorized either the Senate or the House by resolution to "veto" the executive decision. The House of Representatives passed a resolution vetoing the suspension. In 1976, Chadha was ordered to be deported and he appealed to the courts.

The Supreme Court held the Legislative Veto provision unconstitutional. While the Court might have overturned the congressional action in *Chadha* on narrow grounds that the particular Legislative Veto in question violated the separation of powers, the Court instead chose to attack the Legislative Veto device itself. The Legislative Veto was held to violate the Presentment (Art. I., Sec. 7, cl. 3) and Bicameralism (Art. I, Secs. 1 and 7) Clauses which are "integral parts of the constitutional design for the separation of powers."

Chief Justice Burger began from the premise that presentment of legislation to the President for his signature before becoming law and the presidential veto were considered by the Framers as imperative to permit the President to defend himself against Congress. Further, presentment was designed to protect against "oppressive, improvident, or ill-considered" laws and to engraft a "national perspective" on the legislative process. The President's veto power was similarly checked by providing that two-thirds of both Houses could override the President's veto. Like the Presentment Clause, bicameral consideration was intended to assure "that legislation should not be enacted unless it has been carefully and fully considered by the Nation's elected officials." The legislative power "would be exercised only after opportunity for full study and debate in separate settings." Dividing authority between two houses also protected against "legislative despotism," reflected the Framer's fears "that special interests could be favored at the expense of public needs" and responded to the concerns of both the large and small states over congressional representation.

Legislative power, then, must "be exercised in accord with a single, finely wrought and exhaustively considered procedure." But was the House's Veto action an exercise of the "legislative power"? Examining the action of the House in this case indicated that "it was essentially legislative in purpose and effect." The House's actions altered the legal rights, duties and relations of persons. Further, absent the veto, the Attorney General's action rejecting deportation could have been overridden, if at all, only by legislation requiring deportation.

Since the House's actions were "legislative," presentment and bicameral consideration were required and the Legislative Veto was unconstitutional. Concluding that the Legislative Veto provision was severable from the rest of the legislation delegating the power to suspend deportation orders to the executive, the Court held that the Attorney General's suspension order was effective.

Justice White, dissenting, stressed the value of the Legislative Veto in overcoming Congress's dilemma, *i.e.*, either to undertake the hopeless task of writing detailed statutes specifying future action in endless specific circumstances or "to abdicate its lawmaking function to the executive branch and independent agencies." The Veto, he reasoned, "is a necessary check on the unavoidably expanding power of the agencies, both executive and independent, as they engage in exercising authority delegated by Congress." The concerns that underlie Art. I, Sec. 7, simply were not in issue. Neither Art. I nor separation of powers is violated by a mechanism designed to preserve Congress's lawmaking role and make separation of powers effective.

The Court's reliance on Art. I in *Chadha* places into jeopardy all of the nearly 200 laws containing Legislative Veto provisions. Both the War Powers Resolution and the Impoundment Control Act of 1974, for example, use this device to control Executive action. In reviewing the validity of such provisions, it will be necessary to determine: (1) is the Veto provision an exercise of the legislative power requiring bicameral consideration and presentment; and (2) if the Veto is considered lawmaking by extra-constitutional means, and hence, is invalid, is the Veto provision severable? If the latter question is answered no, then the whole delegation of power to the Executive or independent agency fails. Thus far, the Executive Branch has chosen to treat Legislative Veto provisions as still effective rather than entering into a confrontation with Congress.

4. APPOINTMENT AND REMOVAL

The checks and balances which characterize the tripartite nature of American government are illustrated in the constitutional provisions for appointment and removal of government officers. The strength of these provisions is in the limits they place on absolute power in any one Branch by dividing authority between Branches; the difficulty with them is in their silence on crucial questions.

Congress may not vest the Appointment Power in persons other than those indicated in Art. II, Sec. 2, cl. 2 which provides: "[The President] shall nominate, and by and with the advice and consent of the Senate, shall appoint Ambassadors, other public Ministers and Consuls, Judges of the Supreme Court, and all other Officers of the United States, whose appointments are not herein otherwise provided for, and which shall be established by law, but the Congress may by law vest the Appointment of such inferior Officers, as they think proper, in the President alone, in the Courts of Law, or in the Heads of Departments." Congress cannot vest the appointment power in persons other than those indicated in the foregoing provision. Thus, a federal statute providing that the voting members of the Federal Election Commission should be appointed by the President pro tem of the Senate and the Speaker of the House was struck down because these Congressional leaders did not come within the terms "Courts of Law" or "Heads of Departments" as mandated by Art. II, Sec. 2, cl. 2. Congress cannot vest the Appointment Power in itself since this would constitute an impermissible usurpation of power. *Buckley v. Valeo* (1976).

Military officers of the United States are appointed under the Appointments Clause. Do military officers need yet another appointment pursuant to the Appointments Clause in order to serve as military judges? The Court, per Chief Justice Rehnquist, held "No." All military officers play a role in the military justice system. Military judges are assigned unrelated non-judicial duties and exercise judicial authority only when serving on a court-martial. Essentially, the task of serving as a military judge is just one of many tasks to which a military officer may be detailed. *Weiss v. United States* (1994).

A critical question in the Appointment Power context is this—what is the basis for distinguishing a principal officer from an inferior officer? This question is best answered by a functional inquiry into whether the officer is subordinate or independent, the scope and breadth of the officer's jurisdiction and the extent of the duties performed.

The importance of this distinction is illustrated by a constitutional challenge to a federal statute, the Ethics in Government Act which vested the appointment of an Independent Counsel in a Special Division of the United States Court of Appeals for the District of Columbia; the Independent Counsel was charged with investigating certain Executive Branch officials. If the Independent Counsel was an inferior officer, this interbranch appointment was permissible unless it impaired the ability of the Executive Branch to perform its functions or was otherwise incongruous. The statute was upheld. The Independent Counsel was declared to be an "inferior officer", subject to removal for good cause by the Attorney General, and possessed of a limited jurisdiction. Chief Justice Rehnquist emphasized for the Court that the Independent Counsel performed only limited duties of investigation and prosecution and did not make general policy. Moreover, the office of Independent Counsel under the statute was limited in term to the completion of the specified task. *Morrison v. Olson* (1988).

When does the President have the power to remove Executive Branch officials? In the past, the answer to this question turned on whether an official was categorized as a "purely executive official"—in which case the President's power of removal was seen as "incident to the power of appointment." *Myers v. United States* (1926). However, if the official was categorized as one who exercised "quasi-legislative" or "quasi-judicial" power, then the separation of powers principle precluded placing an "illimitable power of removal" in the President. *Humphrey's Executor v. United States* (1935).

While not rejecting these categories, the Court has criticized reliance on the literal and excessive use of these "rigid categories" because they obscure the "real question"—are the restrictions on removal imposed by Congress "of such a nature that they impede the President's ability to perform his constitutional duty?" Applying this approach in *Morrison v. Olson* (1988), the Court held that the provision in the Ethics in Government Act that the Attorney General can remove an Independent Counsel only for good cause did not impermissibly burden the President's duty to faithfully execute the laws. Conceding that law enforcement functions belong to the Executive Branch, Chief Justice Rehnquist concluded, nevertheless, that the President's need to control the exercise of discretion of an inferior officer such as the Independent Counsel was not so central to the operation of the Executive Branch "as to require as a matter of constitutional law that the counsel be terminable at will by the President." Congressional limitation of the Attorney General's power to remove the Independent Counsel was "essential" if she was to have the necessary independence to perform her task. Misconduct on the part of the Independent Counsel was still nonetheless a ground for removal. In the circumstances, Congress has not usurped the President's removal power over executive officials.

When Congress can remove officials by means other than impeachment, can Congress also vest executive functions in such officials? This issue was presented by some provisions of the Gramm–Rudman Act, enacted to control the burgeoning federal deficit, which vested in the Comptroller General authority to specify spending reductions binding on the President. The Act gave final authority to the Comptroller General to decide which budget cuts should be made. The Court held that the Act vested executive authority in the Comptroller General since he was placed in the position of interpreting and implementing the legislation. Such action constituted execution of the laws—an executive function. At an earlier time, however, Congress had enacted legislation providing that the Comptroller General could be removed for certain specifically stated, if generally phrased, reasons such as inefficiency and neglect of duty. This rendered the Comptroller General an agent of Congress since he could be removed by Congress for defying its will. Congress had, therefore, impermissibly inserted its own agent over the execution of the Gramm–Rudman Act. Congress had thereby invalidly usurped an executive function in violation of the principle of separation of powers. *Bowsher v. Synar* (1986).

5. SEPARATION OF POWERS GENERALLY

Separation of powers problems will sometimes be analyzed in terms of the general separation of powers principle itself. When this approach is undertaken, the Court examines the extent of the intrusion on the constitutional functions of the other Branch, gauges the extent to which the challenged action aggrandizes in one Branch power that should properly be shared, and balances the competing interests at stake.

In *Morrison v. Olson* (1988), the Court analyzed the Ethics in Government Act from this perspective. From an overall point of view, the Act's appointment of an Independent Counsel to investigate and prosecute high executive officials did not unduly thwart the functioning of the Executive Branch. Nor did Congress wrongfully arrogate to itself any Executive Branch functions. The Attorney General retained sole and unreviewable power to request the appointment of the Independent Counsel and could remove her for good cause. He still retained several means for supervising and controlling the Independent Counsel's prosecutorial powers. Although it was true that the Independent Counsel was freer from executive direction than most federal prosecutors, the Ethics in Government Act still afforded the Executive Branch "sufficient control" to enable the President to perform his constitutionally assigned duties. In the last analysis, that was the dispositive point.

B. THE FOREIGN ARENA

While the Court generally has reacted negatively to assertion of inherent domestic governmental powers, the claim of extra-constitutional national powers in external relations has received a far more sympathetic judicial response. In *United States v. Curtiss–Wright Export Corp.* (1936), the Court upheld a congressional resolution delegating broad power to the President to prohibit arms sales to certain countries. Justice Sutherland, for the Court, indicated that the normal constraints on broad delegation of legislative powers do not apply in the foreign arena since "the investment of the federal government with the powers of external sovereignty did not depend upon the affirmative grants of the Constitution." He reasoned that upon our separation from Great Britain, the powers of external sovereignty passed directly from the Crown to the *Union* of States, since foreign affairs powers are "necessary concomitants of nationality." The Constitution, however, allocates only the powers previously lodged in the *separate* states. While this declaration of inherent foreign affairs powers, operating independently of the Constitution, represents a questionable interpretation of history, it has never been rejected by the Court and has, on occasion, been embraced. See, *e.g., Perez v. Brownell* (1958).

1.   ALLOCATING THE FOREIGN RELATIONS POWER

In *Curtiss–Wright,* Justice Sutherland argued for executive primacy in the exercise of foreign relations powers, both constitutional and extra-constitutional. While this presidential power must be exercised consistent with the Constitution, Justice Sutherland asserted, the President acts "as the sole organ of the Federal Government in the field of international relations." What is the basis for this assertion of executive prerogative in the foreign arena? Certainly, the constitutional grants of power do not indicate an intent to vest the President with such a dominant position. Rather, the formal constitutional grants of foreign relations power are allocated between the President and Congress. In addition to the general presidential powers, Art. II vests in the President the powers to recognize and withdraw recognition from foreign governments, to make treaties, and to serve as Commander–in–Chief. Further, it is generally accepted that the President has implied power to represent the Nation in day-to-day negotiations with foreign countries. From these powers and from custom and usage flows the broad presidential role in the making and execution of foreign policy. But the Congress also has express foreign affairs powers, such as the power to regulate foreign commerce, to raise and maintain armies, and to declare war as well as its general law-making powers, including the critical powers to tax and spend. The Constitution then appears to envision a sharing of power in the foreign arena.

Curtiss–Wright's claim for executive primacy appears to rest primarily on the respective capabilities of the branches and the teachings of history. The President's abilities to acquire information, maintain secrecy and respond quickly to events was specifically cited by Justice Sutherland as necessitating executive discretion in foreign affairs independent of congressional authorization. Certainly, the historical expansion of presidential foreign affairs powers vis-a-vis Congress cannot be denied.

Nevertheless, it is questionable that these considerations would provide an adequate justification for presidential action in the foreign arena *contrary* to congressional legislation. Perhaps the best explanation of the allocation of foreign affairs powers remains that provided by Justice Jackson in the *Steel Seizure Case.* When the President acts pursuant to authorization from Congress, as he did in *Curtiss–Wright,* his authority is maximized; when he acts contrary to the will of Congress, his power is at its lowest ebb. And when the President acts without any congressional authorization or denial of authority, he acts in a twilight zone where the distribution of powers remains uncertain. Coupled with the fact that courts are more reluctant to intrude into foreign affairs decision-making (*i.e.*, the political question doctrine), the predicate for a free congressional-executive interplay in the foreign affairs arena is apparent.

2. TREATIES AND EXECUTIVE AGREEMENTS

Art. II, Sec. 2, authorizes the President, with the advice and consent of two-thirds of the Senators present, and subject to any Senate reservations, to make treaties (*i.e.,* the President negotiates and "ratifies" a treaty). There is no constitutional provision dealing with the question of how treaties are to be terminated and the issue whether the President can unilaterally abrogate an existing treaty has been a subject of controversy. See *Goldwater v. Carter* (1979) [p. 51 *supra*]. If a treaty is executory, congressional legislation will be necessary to make the treaty effective domestically. Coupled with the necessary and proper clause, a treaty can provide the constitutional basis for congressional legislation that might otherwise be of doubtful validity. *Missouri v. Holland* (1920).

While the Constitution in Art. II speaks only of treaties, the President, often with congressional participation, today makes more use of international agreements and compacts than formal treaties. In fact, executive agreements can be used to speedily and privately commit the United States to action in the foreign arena without the need for any congressional involvement, *i.e.,* a "pure" executive agreement. Increasing executive reliance on international accords rather than treaties has generated congressional efforts to control and limit their use. While most such efforts have failed, Congress has enacted legislation requiring that Congress at least be notified of the existence of the agreement.

Both treaties and executive agreements enjoy Art. VI supremacy over contrary state law. *United States v. Belmont* (1937); *United States v. Pink* (1942). While the language of Art. VI might appear to make treaties equal with the Constitution, it is now generally accepted that international agreements of all kinds are subject to constitutional limitations. *Reid v. Covert* (1957). The Tenth Amendment reserved powers clause, however, is not such a limit on the federal power. *Missouri v. Holland* (1920). If acts of Congress conflict with treaty provisions, the later in time will be given effect domestically. *Whitney v. Robertson* (1888). Whether an executive agreement made solely on the basis of presidential power, without any congressional involvement, has legal effect when it conflicts with congressional legislation has not been decided by the Supreme Court, although it seems doubtful that the agreement would prevail.

An excellent example of the importance of executive agreements, and of the continuing vitality of Justice Jackson's approach to shared powers in the *Steel Seizure Case,* is provided by *Dames & Moore v. Regan* (1981). Pursuant to an agreement between the governments of the United States and Iran for the release of embassy personnel held hostage in Iran, President Reagan ratified executive orders nullifying certain attachments and ordering the transfer to Iran of Iranian assets held frozen in United States banks. An executive agreement also obligated the United States to terminate all legal proceedings in United States courts against Iran.

The Court, per Justice Rehnquist, found specific congressional authorization for the presidential action nullifying attachments and ordering the transfer of assets. The order therefore enjoyed "the strongest of presumptions and the widest latitude of judicial interpretation." The challenger failed to satisfy its heavy burden to prove that "the federal government as a whole lacked the power exercised by the President."

While the Court found no similar specific congressional authorization for presidential suspension of pending court claims, a history of congressional acquiescence in independent presidential action in emergencies indicated an intent to accord the President broad discretion, at least in the absence of any contrary expression of congressional intent. Congressional acquiescence in the use of executive agreements to settle foreign claims, the character of existing federal legislation in the area of claims settlement, and the judicial acceptance of the legality of executive agreements, led the Court to uphold this particular presidential action as a necessary incident to resolving a major foreign policy dispute.

3. ALLOCATING THE WAR POWER

Art. II declares that the President is Commander-in-Chief of the armed force. But Congress has the power to declare war and to maintain the armed forces. To what extent can the President acting pursuant to his role as Commander-in-Chief and his other executive powers commit the armed might of the Nation in foreign ventures without congressional authorization? While the question is of critical importance, neither the Constitution nor the Court has provided very much by way of an answer. Indeed, the Court regularly avoided review of challenges to the validity of the Viet Nam War that might have provided guidelines for the exercise of the shared war power.

The debate over presidential-congressional roles in using the war powers frequently focuses on the War Powers Resolution which restricts presidential commitment of the armed forces absent congressional authorization. 50 U.S.C.A. §§ 1541–48. The Resolution contains consultation and reporting requirements for presidential involvement in hostilities and provides for termination of the use of the armed forces 60 days after reporting absent congressional action. For some, the Act is an unconstitutional intrusion into the Executive's war powers; for others, the Resolution is a proper use of Congress's implied powers to define the proper use of the shared war power.

To what extent do the Militia Clauses, Art. I, Sec. 8, cl. 15, 16, limit the war powers of Congress? The Congress, in the so-called "Montgomery Amendment" provided, contrary to a federal statutory requirement that had been in place since 1952, that Congress could authorize the President to order a state's National Guard units on active duty for training missions outside the United States without either the consent of the state's Governor or the declaration of a national emergency. The

Governor of Minnesota challenged the constitutionality of the Amendment under the Militia Clauses. However, the Court upheld the Amendment. The Militia Clauses do not limit the war power of Congress; they provide Congress with "additional grants of power" and recognize "the supremacy of federal power in the area of military affairs." *Perpich v. Department of Defense* (1990).

Aside from presidential interaction with Congress concerning the war power, what is the nature of the President's war power itself? Advocates of a broad reading of the presidential war power tend to stress custom and usage. It does seem clear that the President has power to repel an invasion. *The Prize Cases* (1863). There is also ample historical evidence, which is fortified by custom and usage, that the President can act unilaterally to preserve our neutrality and to protect American citizens abroad and possesses an ill-defined power to act in an "emergency." Finally, presidential initiatives are frequently defended by invoking collective security agreements or congressional actions such as the Gulf of Tonkin Resolution.

Those seeking to limit presidential war powers emphasize that the original intent of the Framers was to make the President "top general and top admiral," *The Federalist* No. 69 (A. Hamilton). "[G]enerals and admirals even when they are 'first' do not determine the practical purpose for which troops are to be used; they command them in the execution of policy made by others." L. Henkin, *Foreign Affairs and the Constitution* 50–51 (1972).

C. PROMOTING EXECUTIVE RESPONSIBILITY

1. EXECUTIVE PRIVILEGE

While there is no provision in the Constitution establishing an executive privilege to withhold information from a judicial forum, a unanimous Supreme Court in *United States v. Nixon* (1974), found "constitutional underpinnings" for a conditional privilege relating to confidential communications between the President and his advisers on domestic matters. President Nixon, an unindicted co-conspirator, had asserted a claim of privilege in refusing to turn over tapes and other memoranda to a special grand jury investigating the Watergate break-in. The Court accepted the existence of a constitutionally based privilege flowing "from the supremacy of each branch within its own assigned area of constitutional duties" and from "the nature of the enumerated powers." However, the Court rejected the President's claim (at least in cases not involving military, diplomatic or sensitive national security matters) that invoking the privilege was vested absolutely in the Executive free of judicial review.

Chief Justice Burger, speaking for the Court, instead invoked *Marbury v. Madison* (1803) for the proposition that "it is emphatically the province and duty of the judicial department to say what the law is"—a duty which the courts could not share with the Executive Branch. To accept a claim of absolute privilege, stated the Chief Justice, "would upset the constitutional balance of 'a workable government' and gravely impair the role of the courts under Art. III." While the claim of executive privilege was presumptively valid, the courts must determine, through *in camera* inspection, whether the claimed privilege should yield to some overriding interest in disclosure.

Applying these principles, the Court concluded: "[W]hen the ground for asserting privilege as to subpoenaed materials sought for use in a criminal trial is based only on the generalized interest in confidentiality, it cannot prevail over the fundamental demands of due process of law in the fair administration of criminal justice. The generalized assertion of privilege must yield to the demonstrated, specific need for evidence in a pending criminal trial." The order of the district court requiring that the subpoenaed materials be turned over to it was affirmed. However, the Court stressed that in determining what materials should be released or published, the district court was not to treat the President as "an ordinary individual" but was "to afford presidential confidentiality the greatest protection consistent with the fair administration of justice."

Executive privilege arose again in *Nixon v. Administrator of Gen. Servs.* (1977), upholding the constitutionality of a federal statute governing public access to confidential papers, tape recordings, and other materials produced during the Nixon administration. Justice Brennan, writing for the Court, rejected President Nixon's challenge to the law, characterizing it as reflecting an "archaic view of the separation of powers as requiring three air tight departments of the government." The proper inquiry, said Justice Brennan, required a determination whether the challenged Act would prevent the Executive Branch from accomplishing its constitutionally assigned functions. In this instance, President Ford had signed the Act into law and President Carter had urged its validity, indicating that the Executive Branch was a partner in the Act's disposition of the presidential material. Further, the Executive Branch, through the GSA, remained in full control of the materials. Nor was the Act a violation of the executive privilege recognized in *United States v. Nixon* (1974) since it involved "a very limited intrusion by personnel in the Executive Branch sensitive to executive concerns." As in *United States v. Nixon* (1974) the claim for confidentiality yielded to an overriding interest—the important congressional interest in preserving access to confidential materials for lawful government and historical use.

2. EXECUTIVE IMMUNITY

United States v. Nixon (1974) and *Marbury v. Madison* (1803) establish that, at least in some instances, executive officers, including the President, are amenable to judicial process. But the extent of this judicial oversight is less clear. For example, could the courts have issued a coercive order if President Nixon had chosen to disobey the judicial order to turn over the Watergate tapes? Was President Nixon amenable to criminal processes while still in office or after he left office for acts done while President? The disposition of such issues under the separation of powers doctrine remains unanswered.

The Court has had occasion to address the question whether the President and his aides could be held civilly liable for their actions. *Nixon v. Fitzgerald* (1982), involved a suit by Fitzgerald, an Air Force management analyst, against former President Nixon and various executive officials, claiming that he had been illegally fired in retaliation for his testimony before a congressional committee. The Court, per Justice Powell, held 5–4 that the former President enjoyed absolute immunity from damages liability for acts within the "outer perimeter" of his official responsibility while in office. Presidential immunity was defined as "a functionally mandated incident of the President's unique office, rooted in the constitutional tradition of the separation of powers and supported by our history."

Justice Powell found support for the principle in the absolute immunity accorded judges and prosecutors. Given the adversarial character of the presidential duties and the resulting probability of civil law suits, a qualified immunity would not provide an adequate guarantee to assure the effective performance of the President's duties. The interests of the civil litigant were outweighed by the separation of powers dangers of judicial intrusion "on the authority and functions of the Executive Branch."

Alternative checks, such as impeachment, press and congressional scrutiny, Presidential concerns with maintaining influence and with reelection, reasoned Justice Powell, provided adequate assurance that the President would not be "above the law." The dismissal of an employee as part of a reorganization was found to be well within the outer perimeter of the President's official responsibility.

In a companion case, *Harlow v. Fitzgerald* (1982), the Court held that White House aides enjoy only a qualified immunity. "Government officials performing discretionary functions are shielded from liability for civil damages insofar as their conduct does not violate clearly established statutory or constitutional rights of which a reasonable person would have known." See *Mitchell v. Forsyth* (1985) [Attorney General entitled only to qualified immunity].

PART TWO

INDIVIDUAL RIGHTS AND LIBERTIES

Limited government in the United States is achieved not only through the constitutional allocation of powers but also through the recognition of rights and liberties. The original Constitution contained few such specific guarantees. Art. I, Secs. 9 & 10, prohibit Congress and the states respectively from enacting bills of attainder, *i.e.,* legislative punishment without the benefit of judicial trial. The same sections proscribe federal and state enactment of retroactive legislation, *i.e., ex post facto* laws. The *Ex Post Facto* Clause, interestingly enough, has been interpreted to apply only to criminal legislation (even though the text is not so limited) and only if the effect of the law is to significantly burden the offender. *Weaver v. Graham* (1981) [state statute retroactively reducing a prisoner's gain time for good conduct held unconstitutional]. Art. I, Sec. 10 also provides that states shall not pass laws impairing the obligations of contract. This limitation operates on the federal government through the Due Process Clause of the Fifth Amendment.

147

None of these guarantees, however, have been interpreted so broadly as to extend meaningful protection to the fundamental interests of individuals. Indeed, many of the Framers felt that no specification of basic rights was needed since the national government could exercise only the limited powers delegated in the Constitution. For example, since Congress had no power to regulate the press, there was no need to guarantee freedom of the press. For the Framers, the limited powers of the federal government was the assurance of freedom. But the Antifederalists were fearful. As the price of ratification, they demanded the addition of what we now call the Bill of Rights.

In *Barron v. Mayor and City Council of Baltimore* (1833), the argument was made that the Bill of Rights was a limitation on the state governments as well as the federal government. John Marshall disagreed and ruled that, both as a matter of text and history, the states were not limited by the Bill of Rights. But a significant limitation on the state power was introduced into American constitutional law with the enactment of the Fourteenth Amendment which was to become the vehicle through which much of the contents of the Bill of Rights were made binding on the states.

The Fourteenth Amendment guarantee that no state shall deny the privileges or immunities of citizens of the United States might have served as a vehicle for applying the guarantees of the Bill of Rights to the states. At least it might have done so were it not for the Court's decision in the *Slaugh-*

terhouse Cases (1872). Justice Miller, for the Court, began with the premise that the first sentence of the Fourteenth Amendment creates two types of citizenship, federal and state. He then read the second sentence of the Amendment as extending federal constitutional protection only to the privileges and immunities of national citizenship. But what are the privileges and immunities attaching to federal and state citizenship? Justice Miller's answer was that the fundamental rights of the individual were derived from state law. The federal guarantee was limited to those rights peculiar to the citizen's relationship to the federal government, *e.g.,* to petition Congress, to use the navigable waters of the United States, the right to interstate travel, etc. An alternative interpretation, *e.g.,* that the privileges and immunities clause was meant to extend all the fundamental rights traditionally associated with state citizenship to the national citizen as a guarantee of federal law would, in Miller's view, upset the historic relation of the federal government to the states. Congress and the Court would become the perpetual censors of state legislation.

But arguably the precise intent of the Fourteenth Amendment, as Justice Field stated in dissent, was to upset the historic relationship of the states to the federal government, particularly in relation to protection of the rights and liberties of the citizen. After all, the Fourteenth Amendment in all its sections was designed to bring legal freedom and equality to the recently emancipated slaves. The

Privileges and Immunities Clause, in this view, was a means by which this objective was to be accomplished. Justice Miller's interpretation, however, gave the Clause no significance. Essentially all the rights that he was willing to find within it already had been recognized as federally guaranteed.

On the other hand, Justice Field, dissenting in the *Slaughterhouse Cases,* perceived the Fourteenth Amendment Privileges and Immunities Clause as guaranteeing those rights which belong to citizens of all free governments. "The fundamental rights, privileges and immunities which belong to him as a free man and as a free citizen, now belong to him as a citizen of the United States, and are not dependent upon his citizenship in any state."

The practical effect of the *Slaughterhouse Cases* was to read out the Privileges and Immunities Clause as a meaningful constitutional guarantee. While the Clause is occasionally invoked in support of peculiarly federal rights, *e.g.* the right to vote in federal elections, it is of little practical significance today.

CHAPTER V

DUE PROCESS OF LAW

A. THE PROCESS OF INCORPORATION

The Fourteenth Amendment Privileges and Immunities Clause failed as a vehicle for expanded federal constitutional limitations on the states. Instead, the Fourteenth Amendment Due Process Clause became the tool whereby various fundamental guarantees of the Bill of Rights were "incorporated" and made applicable to the states. But while there has been agreement on the Court that various parts of the Bill of Rights are embodied in the due process guarantee, there has been little unanimity on what rights are included or the character of the incorporation process.

In *Adamson v. California* (1947), two major due process methodologies were joined in combat. One theory—that defended by Justice Frankfurter in his concurring opinion in *Adamson*—argued that the Due Process Clause has an "independent potency" of its own, not defined by the Bill of Rights. The commands of due process were to be determined on a case-by-case basis by asking whether the particular procedures used by government "offend those canons of decency and fairness which express the

notions of justice of English-speaking peoples."
This theory, in Frankfurter's view, did not simply
implement the idiosyncratic standards of the particular judge but rather involved a quest to identify
"accepted notions of justice."

For Justice Black, the *ad hoc* approach of Frankfurter would only lead to the revival of discredited
notions of natural law. The Fourteenth Amendment, taken as a whole, he argued, required the
application of the entire Bill of Rights to the states,
nothing more and nothing less. This "total incorporation" approach provided the guarantee of judicial objectivity. If it were argued that, unlike the
Frankfurter *ad hoc* theory, the Black theory had no
dynamic quality, Justice Black would respond: Precisely. For him, total incorporation assured certainty, objectivity, and conformance to the historical
intent of the Framers of the Fourteenth Amendment.

As often happens in the history of ideas, neither
the Frankfurter nor the Black theory in its pure
form prevailed. While the *ad hoc* approach enjoyed
a temporary ascendancy during the late fifties, its
demise quietly began in *Mapp v. Ohio* (1961). Later, the new theory fashioned in *Mapp* was more
boldly proclaimed under the name "selective incorporation," meaning that some of the Bill of Rights
were binding on the states in accord with the teachings of Justice Black but the mode of their selection
was more in keeping with the flexible due process
theories of Justice Frankfurter.

In implementing this selective incorporation approach, the Court, at times, has asked whether the particular guarantee of the Bill of Rights is "implicit in the concept of ordered liberty." More recently, the Court has asked, instead, whether the guarantee in question is "fundamental to the American scheme of justice," even though a "fair and enlightened system of justice" would be possible without the guarantee. *Duncan v. Louisiana* (1968) [Sixth Amendment right to jury trial incorporated as a part of due process liberty under the Fourteenth Amendment]. Through this process of selective inclusion, the states have been subjected to most of the principal guarantees of the Bill of Rights. The only provisions thus far not incorporated are the Second, Third, and Seventh Amendments, the right to grand jury indictment in the Fifth Amendment, and the Eighth Amendment's guarantee of freedom from excessive bail.

Duncan v. Louisiana (1968) set forth another basic principle of the incorporation approach. The Court held that an "incorporated" Bill of Rights guarantee applies against the states to the same extent and in the same manner that it binds the federal government. This approach, however, presents a problem. The Sixth Amendment guarantee of trial by jury, for example, had been thought to imply the use of a twelve-person jury and a unanimous verdict. But were the states to be fettered by these requirements? In a somewhat confusing line of cases, the Court has answered, "No". In *Williams v. Florida* (1970), the Court held that a twelve-person jury is not required under either the Sixth or the Fourteenth Amendment. In subsequent cases, it was held that a jury of five persons would violate due process [*Ballew v. Georgia* (1978)] as would a state conviction by a non-unanimous six-person jury [*Burch v. Louisiana* (1979)]. In *Apodaca v. Oregon* (1972), the Court held that the requirement of unanimity was not a demand of Fourteenth Amendment due process. But a split among the justices left it uncertain whether the federal government itself was still bound by a Sixth Amendment requirement of unanimity in a federal criminal prosecution. Many commentators examining these cases conclude that the Court has simply watered down the guarantees of the Bill of Rights to accommodate the values of federalism. So, perhaps, in the Court's post-*Duncan* due process cases, Frankfurter's flexible due process theory had a final inning.

B. SUBSTANTIVE DUE PROCESS

1. TRADITIONAL SUBSTANTIVE DUE PROCESS

The due process liberty clause incorporates not only the procedural guarantees of the Bill of Rights but the substantive limitations of the Bill of Rights as well. Thus, a state law burdening freedom of speech can be attacked as an infringement of the First and Fourteenth Amendment guarantee of freedom of expression. But is the substantive limitation of due process liberty limited to the express, or even the implied, guarantees of the Bill of Rights?

a. The Early Rise and Demise of Economic Due Process

Historically, business interests have sought a basis in the Constitution to protect property against the state economic regulation and intervention. A favored constitutional locus for this protection has been the Due Process Clause of the Fourteenth Amendment. Illustrative is the famous case of *Lochner v. New York* (1905), invalidating 5–4 a New York law prohibiting employers from employing workers in bakeries more than ten hours per day and sixty hours per week.

Justice Peckham, for the Court, found the law to be a significant interference with the liberty of contract protected by the Due Process Clause since "[t]he right to purchase or to sell labor is part of the liberty protected by this amendment." How did one know that the right to contract for one's labor was part of the content of the word "liberty" in the Due Process Clause? The Court had said so and this made it so. [See, *e.g., Allgeyer v. Louisiana* (1897)]. But even if the New York law was an interference with the guarantee of liberty, so construed, that did not necessarily mean that the law was unconstitutional since the state still might have latitude to legislate under its police powers. As Justice Peckham said: "Both property and liberty are held on such reasonable conditions as may be imposed by the governing power of the state." The due process issue, then, was whether the New York law was "an unreasonable, unnecessary, and arbitrary interference with the right of the individual to his personal liberty."

Applying this standard, the Court initially considered whether the law furthered the police power interest of the state. While the law under review in *Lochner* purported to be for the health of the workers, Justice Peckham questioned whether this was its real object and purpose. For him, the real legislative objective was the regulation of private labor contracts which was not within the realm of the state's police power. The ordering of private economic relationships was simply not a matter of the general welfare which the state was empowered to protect. This unjudicial probing for the true legislative purpose has been cited by many commentators as constituting one of the principal defects of the *Lochner* approach.

But Justice Peckham declared further that even if the law were considered as a health measure, the law was unconstitutional. The Court found no reasonable foundation for holding that the law was necessary or appropriate for safeguarding the health of the public or the employees. An act "must have a more direct relation as a means to an end." But why was there no direct relationship here? Was the problem in *Lochner* only one of a deficiency of evidence? Perhaps counsel had simply failed to provide sufficient facts to establish that the maximum hours law furthered the permissible health interests of the state. After all, in other cases from the same period, the Court upheld maximum hour laws applied to the mining industry [*Holden v. Hardy* (1898)] and to maximum hours for women in the workplace [*Muller v. Oregon* (1908)]. In these cases, the health dangers arguably were either more apparent or were supported by a "Brandeis brief" detailing the factual basis for the reasonableness of the law in promoting the public health.

We would suggest, however, that the problem presented in *Lochner* transcended proof of reasonableness. *Lochner* closely scrutinized the *appropriateness* of the legislative means for promoting health interests of the workers. Justice Peckham examined alternatives that the legislature might have selected but chose not to. Simply, there was no deference to the legislative judgment during the reign of *Lochner*-style substantive due process but rather an intrusion of the judicial economic value choices in preference to those selected by the legislature.

It was this close judicial scrutiny of the legislative judgment that drew the impassioned dissents written by Justice Holmes and the first Justice Harlan. For Justice Harlan, there was adequate evidence whereby the legislature could reasonably conclude that long hours working in a bakery might endanger the health of the workmen. Only if economic enactments were "plainly, palpably, beyond all question" inconsistent with due process liberty should the Court, in Harlan's view, invalidate a legislative enactment.

Justice Holmes characterized the majority's decision as being based "upon an economic theory which a large part of the country does not entertain" and chastised the majority for importing into the Fourteenth Amendment "Mr. Herbert Spencer's Social Statics." For Holmes, the majority will, as expressed by the legislature, prevails "unless it can be said that a rational and fair man necessarily would admit that the statute proposed would infringe fundamental principles as they have been understood by the traditions of our people and our law." There was no question in the present case that a reasonable man could conclude that the New York maximum hour law for bakers served a legitimate and permissible health interest of the state.

The judicial approach to economic due process in *Lochner* provided the dominant motif for the early part of the twentieth century. *Adair v. United States* (1908); *Coppage v. Kansas* (1915); *Adkins v. Children's Hospital* (1923). But it was the judicial deference to the legislative judgment in economic cases preached by Justices Holmes and Harlan in their dissents which ultimately prevailed.

Constitutional doctrines usually do not die all at once but slowly show signs of mortality. So it was with *Lochner*-style substantive due process. A significant instance of the decline of Lochnerism is found in *Nebbia v. New York* (1934), upholding a New York minimum price law for milk. Gone was the active probing of the legislative objective. Price regulation, even though it involved the private economic relationship of a buyer and a seller, was held to be still within the state's police power concern. Further, "a state is free to adopt whatever economic policy may reasonably be deemed to promote public welfare." If the means selected "have a reasonable relation to a proper legislative purpose, and are neither arbitrary nor discriminatory, the requirements of due process are satisfied, and judicial determination to that effect renders a court *functus officio.*"

While this may sound like the reasonableness test employed in *Lochner,* the minimal judicial scrutiny of the legislative work product left little doubt that the Court was exercising a degree of deference to the legislature in marked contrast to the judicial activism of *Lochner.* Courts were not to judge the wisdom of the policy or the adequacy or practicability of the law for achieving that policy since they were "both incompetent and unauthorized" to do so. Only if the means were "demonstrably irrelevant" to the permissible state policy would the law violate due process. In this instance, the Court found that there was extensive legislative fact finding on the dangers of price instability in the milk industry that demonstrated the reasonableness of the milk price control law.

Nebbia began a process that was to result not merely in the demise of Lochnerism (judicial activism in socioeconomic cases under the guise of interpreting the Due Process Clause of the Fourteenth Amendment) but with a complete judicial role reversal. Where once there had been judicial activism, there was now candid judicial abdication.

b. Economic Regulation: Substantive Due Process Today

The judicial deference begun in *Nebbia* was soon transformed into a total withdrawal from review in economic regulation cases. The modern approach proceeds from principles such as those set forth in *Ferguson v. Skrupa* (1963), holding constitutional against a substantive due process attack a state law limiting the business of debt adjusting to lawyers exclusively. Justice Black, for the Court, stated: "We have returned to the original constitutional proposition that courts do not substitute their social and economic beliefs for the judgment of legislative bodies, who are elected to pass laws. Whether the legislature takes for its textbook, Adam Smith, Herbert Spencer, Lord Keynes, or some other, is no concern of ours. [R]elief if any be needed lies not with us but with the body constituted to pass laws."

This principle finds expression today in the rational basis approach which at least nominally is the test used for reviewing socioeconomic legislation. A law is presumed constitutional and the burden is on the challenging party to prove that the law is not rationally related to a permissible governmental interest. Further, "the existence of facts supporting the legislative judgment is to be presumed." *United States v. Carolene Products Co.* (1938). In practice, the review afforded is essentially no review at all. Illustrative is *North Dakota State Board of Pharmacy v. Snyder's Drug Stores, Inc.* (1973), where the Court upheld a state law requiring that applicants for pharmacy permits be limited either to those who were pharmacists or were corporations the majority of whose stock was owned by pharmacists. *Louis K. Liggett Co. v. Baldridge* (1928), had struck down very similar legislation. *Liggett* was overruled in *Snyder's Drug Stores*. The North Dakota legislature could rationally conclude that there was some relation between the legislative means and the end that pharmacies not be owned by those who knew nothing about them. This was so even though the means and the end were hardly a perfect fit.

It is important for the student to note that this deferential standard of due process review, or more precisely, judicial abdication, is used primarily for socioeconomic laws. It is not applicable when legislation burdens the exercise of fundamental rights. In the absence of a meaningful burden on a fundamental personal right, the student should use the deferential rational basis standard of review in analyzing the constitutionality of laws challenged on due process grounds. And, this means that the law is invariably upheld.

In discrete areas involving non-fundamental rights, however, a form of review slightly more exacting than the rational basis test may be used. Such a development appears to be in the making in the punitive damages area. A challenge to punitive damages awards based on both procedural and substantive due process involved a jury award of $10 million in punitive damages when the actual damages in the case awarded were only $19,000. Although the punitive damages award was sustained, the plurality opinion declined to adopt a rational basis approach that would sustain any punitive damages award no matter how large as long as it served some legitimate state interest in deterring or punishing wrongful conduct. The due process clause of the Fourteenth Amendment imposes a substantive standard of reasonableness which acts as a limitation on punitive damages awards. *TXO Production v. Alliance Resources Corp.* (1993). Nor can punitive damages be left to the unreviewable discretion of a jury. A state law which prohibited judicial review of a punitive damages award was deemed to violate the due process clause. *Honda Motor Co. v. Oberg* (1994).

c. The Takings Alternative

Deprivations of property caused by governmental action obviously invoke consideration of the applicability of the due process clause. Such situations could also invoke analysis of the "takings" alternative. Both the federal and state governments have the power of eminent domain, *i.e.* authority to take private property for public use. The Fifth Amendment specifically deals with takings by the federal government and provides that private property shall not be taken for public use without just compensation. The states are bound to provide compensation for takings of private property pursuant to the Just Compensation Clause of the Fifth Amendment as made applicable to the States through the Due Process Clause of the Fourteenth

Amendment. *First English Evangelical Lutheran Church v. Los Angeles County* (1987).

The law on what constitutes a "taking" is fairly complex. A reasonable exercise of government power which may result in the reduction of property values does not in itself create a compensable "taking." "[W]hile property may be regulated to a certain extent, if regulation goes too far it will be recognized as a taking." *Pennsylvania Coal Co. v. Mahon* (1922). Factors which are relevant in determining whether a law is a "reasonable" regulation or a compensable taking include (1) the economic impact of the regulation on the party protesting it, (2) the extent to which the regulation interferes with distinct investment expectations, and (3) the nature of the governmental action, e.g. a physical occupation of the property. For example, a municipal zoning ordinance, enacted after the plaintiff has purchased the land in question, which limited the use of the land did not constitute a "taking." *Agins v. Tiburon* (1980). Residential uses for the land in question were still possible. The fact that the economically optimal use was foreclosed still did not extinguish beneficial use of the land. The significant point was that the fundamental attributes of ownership remained intact.

Even a "temporary" loss of use of private property will constitute a taking requiring compensation for the period during which use of the property was denied. *First English Evangelical Lutheran Church v. Los Angeles County* (1987). But one crucial determination is whether the regulation can be classified as a taking at all. Some of the more recent Supreme Court case law evidences a greater concern for property rights than in the past. It is possible that economic substantive due process may have taken new root in the Takings Clause.

A landowner who bought property on a South Carolina barrier island intending to develop it was prevented from doing so by state regulation banning construction in order to preserve the state's beaches. Despite the public interest served by the ban, there is a categorical rule in takings cases that total regulatory takings—depriving a property owner of all beneficial use of the property—must be compensated. An exception to this doctrine would exist if the state could show that regulation at issue is inherent in the landowner's title under state property or nuisance law. *Lucas v. South Carolina Coastal Council* (1992).

Lucas dealt with a total taking but the Takings Clause also may limit the conditions government may impose on land use. When a California couple applied for a permit to tear down the house on their ocean-front property and build a new one, the state Coastal Commission said that a permit would be issued only on condition that the couple grant a public easement across the beach to allow people to move back and forth to other public beaches. The state might have denied the permit if it had determined that the proposed development would impair legitimate state concerns. But conditioning the permit would be valid only if the condition served the same governmental purpose as the ban.

"[L]ack of nexus between the condition and the original purpose of the building restriction converts that purpose to something other than what it was." The Court invalidated the public easement condition imposed by the state as an uncompensated taking. *Nollan v. California Coastal Commission* (1987).

Although *Nollan* may have set the stage, a doctrine of unconstitutional conditions under the Takings Clause was clearly established in *Dolan v. City of Tigard* (1994). A hardware store owner in a small Oregon city sought a building permit to expand her store and pave a parking lot on her property. The city said it would grant the permit if the landowner would dedicate part of her property for flood control and traffic improvements. This involved dedication of land for a public greenway along a creek and a pedestrian bicycle pathway. Could the landowner be forced to choose between the building permit and her constitutional right to just compensation? The Court, per Chief Justice Rehnquist, struck down the condition 5–4: "[T]he government may not require a person to give up a constitutional right—here the right to receive just compensation when property is taken for a public use—in exchange for a discretionary benefit conferred by the government where the property sought has little or no relationship to the benefit."

Dolan established a two-part framework for analyzing whether a condition is a reasonable regulation or a taking requiring just compensation. The first part—based on *Nollan*—asks whether there is an essential nexus between a legitimate state interest and the condition at issue. The second inquiry requires "rough proportionality." The government must make an "individualized determination that the required dedication" is roughly proportionate to the impact of the proposed development. There was an essential nexus between legitimate government interests and the conditions imposed. Dedication of land for a greenway would minimize flooding. Dedication of a pathway would reduce congestion. But the rough proportionality inquiry was *not* satisfied. Why was a *public* easement necessary? Why not a *private* greenway? Similarly, the city had not sufficiently documented that additional traffic congestion flowing from the proposed development necessitated the pedestrian bicycle pathway. No precise mathematical formula was required but the city had to make some effort to quantify its traffic findings.

In summary, *Dolan's* two-part test for conditions sets forth a more demanding standard of review than rational basis. Indeed, Justice Stevens complained in dissent that the "regulatory takings" doctrine resurrected *Lochner*. Has economic substantive due process taken new root in the Takings Clause? Clearly, recent Supreme Court case law evidences a greater concern for property rights than in the past.

2.   SUBSTANTIVE DUE PROCESS REVISITED: FUNDAMENTAL PERSONAL RIGHTS

a.   In General

When federal or state legislation burdens the exercise of fundamental personal rights, the courts forsake the rational basis test in favor of more searching standards of review. When, for example, First Amendment rights are burdened by a law, the courts will not uphold the legislation even if it is rationally related to a permissible governmental objective. Rather, the courts will demand that government establish that the law is narrowly tailored to a compelling or substantial governmental interest.

This is a standard of review most unlike the toothless rationality standard of review used presently in economic due process. In the fundamental rights area, the standard of review is truly searching. Nevertheless, even here, the standard employed is not always uniform. In many fundamental rights cases, the courts demand that the state establish that the law is necessary to a compelling state interest, *i.e.*, strict scrutiny. But, in other instances, the standard of review appears more tempered. Generally, it may be said that the degree of justification required of government tends to increase as the severity of the burden on the protected right increases. For example, a law totally prohibiting the exercise of the right is likely to be tested by a far more exacting standard than a law that only regulates the manner in which the right is exercised. See Chap. VII, *infra,* on freedom of expression.

But what are the "fundamental personal rights" that will trigger this exacting judicial scrutiny? The concept clearly includes express constitutional rights. For example, when First Amendment rights are burdened by state action, the courts will not apply simple rationality review, but will employ a more demanding standard of judicial review. It is also clear today that "fundamental personal rights" includes some non-enumerated rights. But it is very unclear how these rights are to be determined.

The modern debate is generally framed in terms of interpretivism v. noninterpretivism. Interpretivists argue that all constitutional rights must be found through interpretation of the Constitution itself. For example, freedom of association and belief can be implied from the express guarantees of the First Amendment. *N.A.A.C.P. v. Alabama* (1958). Interpretivists debate among themselves concerning the extent to which it is appropriate to go beyond the text of the Constitution to consider history and the constitutional structure and relationships established by the Framers (*e.g.,* the need to assure open political processes). They also debate over the closeness of the relationship demanded before new rights are implied from express rights. But, interpretivists all do agree that the only legitimate source for values and principles of decision is the Constitution itself. See J.H. Ely, *Democracy and Distrust* (1980).

Noninterpretivism, on the other hand, accepts that constitutional principles and norms can be found outside of the constitutional document. Noninterpretivists cite favorably early Court decisions such as *Meyer v. Nebraska* (1923) [state law barring the teaching of foreign languages to young children held to violate due process liberty of teachers and students] and *Pierce v. Society of the Sisters* (1925) [state law requiring all students to attend public schools held an unconstitutional interference with the liberty of parents to control their children's education]. See also *Skinner v. Oklahoma* (1942) [holding a law requiring sterilization of certain criminals violative of equal protection, but emphasizing the importance of marriage and procreation]. But noninterpretivists differ on what extra-constitutional sources are legitimate in discovering and fashioning these extra-constitutional rights. The two approaches which have received most judicial acceptance are, first, reliance on values drawn from tradition and custom, and, second, a dynamic approach identifying those values which are implicit in the concept of ordered liberty. Some commentators have urged the use of principles of morality, logic, and reason. See *e.g.*, M. Perry, *The Constitution, the Courts and Human Rights* (1982). Others simply argue that some interests are of such importance to the individual or society that they demand constitutional protection. These varying strands of noninterpretivism have played a vital part in the debate over the right of privacy discussed below.

The basis for the departure from the rationality standard of review when fundamental personal rights are burdened is difficult to ascertain. If a law burdens an express constitutional right, perhaps more active review is understandable even though the right applies to state action only through its incorporation as part of Fourteenth Amendment liberty. But if the right is only judicially implied from the express rights, or is cut whole cloth through judicial use of extra-constitutional sources, what considerations justify judicial activism? In short, if *Lochner* was wrong, what makes close judicial scrutiny proper when the Court determines that the conduct being regulated involves an unenumerated fundamental personal right? After all, the *Lochner* Court invoked a right of contract implied from the liberty and property guarantees of the Fourteenth Amendment. For many critics of the fundamental rights approach, the invocation of a stricter standard of review at least where used to protect non-express interests such as privacy, travel, marriage or family life, is nothing more than substantive due process in new clothes. And, these critics continue, this use of the judicial power is nothing but natural law jurisprudence in a new form.

Some commentators have sought to justify active judicial scrutiny where fundamental personal rights are concerned by arguing that personal rights such as speech, association and belief, travel or privacy are more deserving of special judicial solicitude than purely economic property rights. They suggest a hierarchy or, at least, a tiering of constitutional rights. But see, *Lynch v. Household Finance Corp.* (1972), criticizing such a double standard. Sometimes this argument is bolstered by the claim that ordinary political processes may be inadequate to protect such personal rights. See *United States v. Carolene Products Co.* (1938) [Justice Stone's footnote 4]. A closely related justification is to focus on the judicial capabilities vis-a-vis the legislature. Legislatures have a higher degree of competence than courts in socioeconomic matters. But, the insularity and sensitivity of courts to minority beliefs and practices, it is argued, require that courts exercise special solicitude when personal rights are burdened.

A number of fundamental personal rights will be considered in the chapters on Equal Protection and First Amendment Rights. In the present chapter, the focus is on a range of interests involving marriage, family, sex, procreation, treatment, and care and protection. Sometimes these interests are treated together under the single rubric of a Right of Privacy. In any case, it is in the context of these intimate interests that the problems generated by the "fundamental personal rights" approach to due process review become most apparent.

b. Contraception, Abortion and Sodomy

There is no right of privacy specifically guaranteed by the Constitution. Indeed, the Constitution does not mention marriage, family, or procreation. Nevertheless, in *Griswold v. Connecticut* (1965), the

Court held, 7–2, that a criminal law prohibiting the use or the aiding or abetting of the use of contraceptives violated a constitutional right of privacy.

Justice Douglas for the Court was at pains to distinguish *Lochner* where the Court had sat as superlegislature.   Unlike *Lochner* which had involved only economic conditions, the Connecticut law "operates directly on an intimate relation between husband and wife and their physician's role in one aspect of that relation."   The substantive due process of the *Lochner* era was to be distinguished, according to Justice Douglas, because, unlike the freedom of contract values cherished by Justice Peckham in *Lochner,* the privacy value had a textual constitutional source.

What was the textual source for a constitutional right of privacy?   Justice Douglas found the right of privacy in the penumbras and emanations of the First, Third, Fourth, Fifth, and Ninth Amendments. In fact, Justice Douglas relied on two key concepts derived from the express rights.   First, he emphasized a right of association flowing from the First Amendment which he concluded encompassed a protected status for the marital relationship.   Second, enforcement of the criminal proscriptions against the use of contraceptives could involve police intrusion into the marital bedroom, which would implicate the privacy guarantees of the Third, Fourth, and Fifth Amendments.   Since the state law employed means having a severe destructive impact on the privacy of the marital relationship, the Connecticut law was unconstitutionally overbroad.

Justice Douglas provided little explanation as to why the First Amendment's implied rights of political association extends to the marital relationship other than the fundamental importance to society of protecting the marital relationship. Further, since the defendants in the *Griswold* case were a physician and an official of the Planned Parenthood organization, there was no question in this case of the invasion of the marital bedroom. Why, then, did Justice Douglas feel the need to bring the right of privacy within the confines of the guarantees of the Bill of Rights? The answer is that Justice Douglas accepted Justice Black's premise that Fourteenth Amendment liberty incorporated all of the guarantees of the Bill of Rights but nothing else. In short, Justice Douglas tried to do homage to what today would be called an interpretivist approach. On the other hand, Justice Black, in dissent, remained faithful to the vaunted literalism of his *Adamson* dissent. The Bill of Rights was binding on the states by virtue of the enactment of the Fourteenth Amendment. But it was a more literal Bill of Rights that was binding on them. Justice Black said he liked his privacy as well as the next one, but this predilection did not mean that he could read privacy into the Bill of Rights when it was not there.

Concurring opinions in *Griswold* by Justices Goldberg and Harlan adopted a non-interpretivist approach in fashioning a right of privacy. The liberty guarantee, said Justice Goldberg, "is not restricted to rights specifically mentioned in the first eight amendments" but includes fundamental personal rights that have their source directly in the "liberty" clause of the Fourteenth Amendment. Justice Goldberg cited the Ninth Amendment as a specific recognition that not all rights protected by the Constitution are specifically enumerated in the Constitution. How are fundamental rights to be identified? Justice Goldberg said the Court must look to the "traditions and (collective) conscience of our people" to determine fundamental principles, as well as experience regarding the requirements of a free society. For Justice Goldberg, "the entire fabric of the Constitution and the purposes that clearly underlie its specific guarantees demonstrate that the rights to marital privacy and to marry and raise a family are of a similar order and magnitude as the fundamental rights specifically protected."

Similarly, Justice Harlan contended that the Connecticut law violated basic values "implicit in the concept of ordered liberty." Fourteenth Amendment liberty, independent of any reliance on the Bill of Rights, embodied the traditional values of our society. Marital privacy was one of those values. In an earlier contraceptives decision, *Poe v. Ullman* (1961), Justice Harlan had stressed that tradition is a "living thing" and urged that certain liberty interests "require particularly careful scrutiny of the state needs asserted to justify their abridgment."

For the majority of the *Griswold* Court, a law that so intruded on protected marital privacy could not be justified on the basis of its rationality. As Justice White stated in a concurring opinion, when a law regulates "sensitive areas of liberty," the courts apply a strict scrutiny standard of review to the fundamental right protected by the liberty clause of the Fourteenth Amendment. The law must serve a subordinating state interest which is compelling and no less drastic means must be available to the state, if the law under review is to be upheld. In the *Griswold* situation, the state interest in discouraging extra-marital relations could not justify the intolerable burden placed on the marital relationship especially in light of the adultery and fornication laws available to protect the state interests.

Griswold v. Connecticut is firmly grounded in the traditional values associated with the marital relationship. Privacy, as fashioned in *Griswold,* is essentially an associational right born of the relation recognized by the state between marital partners. As such, it does not provide a basis for extending a right of privacy to non-marital relationships or personal sexual privacy generally. A key step toward the judicial recognition of an expanded right of sexual privacy came in *Eisenstadt v. Baird* (1972), holding unconstitutional a Massachusetts statute prohibiting the distribution of contraceptives to unmarried persons. While the case was decided on equal protection grounds, Justice Brennan, for the Court, provided a basis for breaking the privacy right loose from its marital moorings: "[T]he marital couple is not an independent entity with a mind and heart of its own, but an association of two individuals each with a separate intellectual and emotional make-up. If the right of privacy means anything, it is the right of the individual, married or single, to be free from unwarranted governmental intrusion into matters so fundamentally affecting a person as the decision whether to bear or beget a child."

It was this expanded concept of personal privacy that was to find expression in *Roe v. Wade* (1973), invalidating, 7–2, a Texas law prohibiting abortion except to save the life of the mother. Adopting a noninterpretivist position, Justice Blackmun for the Court concluded: "This right of privacy, whether it is founded in the Fourteenth Amendment's concept of personal liberty and restrictions upon state action, as we feel it is, or, as the District Court determined, in the Ninth Amendment's reservation of rights to the people is broad enough to encompass a woman's decision whether or not to terminate her pregnancy." What was the basis for this conclusion? Justice Blackmun cited all the detrimental consequences to a single woman such as Jane Roe which might result from being denied the ability to terminate an unwanted pregnancy. This suggested to many commentators that Justice Blackmun was asserting that the importance of an interest to a person was sufficient in itself to give the value a constitutional dimension—at least when enjoyment of the interest involved was being prohibited or burdened by state action.

The right of personal privacy, Justice Blackmun noted, is not absolute but must be considered in light of the state's interest in regulation. Given the fundamental character of the right involved, and the severity of a criminal penalty on the right, state limitations could be justified only by a "compelling state interest," and the state enactment "must be narrowly drawn to express only the legitimate state interests at stake." While the Court might have held simply that the Texas abortion law proscribing all abortions except those necessary to save the life of the mother was unconstitutionally overbroad, Justice Blackmun instead fashioned a trimester test. This approach attracted scathing criticism. The trimester approach was seen as a statute in the guise of a judicial opinion and therefore, in effect, a judicial usurpation of the role and power of the legislature.

In applying the strict scrutiny standard, Justice Blackmun initially dismissed the claim that the rights of the fetus to life should be included in the balance. The term "person" in the Fourteenth Amendment Due Process Clause, he reasoned, was not intended by its Framers to include the unborn. Turning instead to the state interests supporting abortion laws, Justice Blackmun concluded that the state has a compelling interest in maternal health, permitting reasonable regulation of abortions, only after the first trimester. Prior to that time, abortion produces less mortality than normal childbirth.

During this initial trimester, "the attending physician in consultation with his patient is free to determine without regulation by the state, that, in his medical judgment, the patient's pregnancy should be terminated." Critics of *Roe,* however, ask why the state may not regulate abortion procedures during the first trimester in order to promote the health of the mother. Why are only the mortality tables relevant?

Justice Blackmun then went on to hold that the government has a compelling interest in the potentiality of life from the point of viability, *i.e.,* when the fetus can live apart from its mother: "If the State is interested in protecting fetal life after viability, it may go so far as to proscribe abortion during that period except when it is necessary to preserve the life or health of the mother." Again, it may be asked, why does the state interest in potential life become "compelling" only at viability? Certainly, a legislature could reasonably conclude that potential life begins at conception. In any case, under the *Roe* trimester standards, the Texas statute clearly swept too broadly.

For Justice Rehnquist, this decisional emperor clearly had no clothes. While accepting the premise that the Fourteenth Amendment guarantee of liberty includes more than the rights set forth in the Bill of Rights, that liberty is protected only against deprivation without due process. Social and economic legislation is to be judged solely by whether the law "has a rational relation to a valid state objective." For example, if the state law were to prohibit abortions even where a mother's life is at stake, Justice Rehnquist would agree that such a law violated the Due Process Clause of the Fourteenth Amendment. Thus, while Justice Rehnquist rejects the rationale of the majority as a return to *Lochner,* he does not reject all substantive judicial review under the Due Process Clause. It is the strict scrutiny of the compelling interest standard and the trimester approach in effect making the Court a judge of the wisdom of the legislative policies of the legislature, to which his criticism is directed.

In the years following *Roe,* its opponents continued to insist that abortion was a non-constitutional issue. The Court was repeatedly asked to reconsider its decision and return the fashioning of abortion law to the state legislatures. The Court regularly rejected the invitation, reaffirming its holding in *Roe.* See, *e.g., City of Akron v. Akron Center for Reproductive Health, Inc.* (1983). The Court was required to apply *Roe* and its trimester scheme to a variety of state regulations which limited access to abortions. Some were upheld, but most were rejected under the stringent standards of *Roe.*

In 1989, the Court upheld a Missouri state abortion law which presented a major challenge to *Roe v. Wade.* In *Webster v. Reproductive Health Services* (1989), a three-Justice plurality, consisting of Justices Kennedy, Rehnquist and White, would have overruled the trimester framework. Justice Scalia, although also an advocate of scrapping the trimester framework, would have overruled *Roe* entirely. Much to the chagrin of Justice Scalia, Justice O'Connor, one of the new conservative appointees to the Court, saved the fragile shell that *Roe* had now become. While Justice O'Connor acknowledged that the *Roe* trimester was "problematic," she limited her concurrence by saying that Missouri's law did not violate the Court's precedents including *Roe*. Relying on policies of adherence to stare decisis and judicial restraint, Justice O'Connor declined to "reexamine Roe." In her opinion, the Missouri abortion law did not require such reexamination.

In 1992, the Court in *Planned Parenthood of Southeastern Pennsylvania v Casey* considered yet another challenge to *Roe*. Retirements on the Court gave new hope to its opponents that *Roe*, clearly weakened by *Webster*, would at long last collapse altogether. Two stalwart adherents of *Roe*—Justices Marshall and Brennan—had left the Court. They were replaced respectively by Justices Thomas and Souter. Only Justice O'Connor's vote had saved *Roe* in *Webster*. Would the two new Justices provide the majority for overruling it altogether?

In the end result, a joint opinion for the Court, authored by Justices O'Connor, Kennedy and Souter, declared their adherence to the core—but not the whole—of *Roe*. The joint opinion reduced the protection afforded the woman's abortion decision. Why didn't the joint opinion reverse it altogether? The Court's answer to this was based in part on a fidelity to *stare decisis* and in part on a desire to protect the institutional image of the Court by not retreating under fire. Changing societal circumstances may require new constitutional responses and warrant departures from a rigid adherence to *stare decisis*. That was not the case here for several reasons. A whole generation had relied on *Roe* and structured its conduct accordingly. Moreover, the factual background underpinnings of *Roe* remained constant as had society's understanding of it.

Abortion was a unique act involving the "most intimate and personal choices a person may make in a lifetime." This dimension of personal liberty was what *Roe* sought to protect. The joint opinion in *Casey* based the constitutional protection for abortion in the liberty protected by the Fourteenth Amendment. The student will note that, despite the formal allegiance to *Roe*, the abortion decision in *Casey* does not use the terminology of "fundamental rights" in general or "right to privacy" in particular.

The joint opinion combined with support provided by the separate opinions of Justices Blackmun and Stevens forged a fragile majority of five to save *Roe's* "essential holding" which was described as having three parts: First, a woman has a right to choose to have an abortion prior to viability of the fetus and that choice can be exercised without undue interference by the state. Second, the state has a right to restrict abortions after fetal viability so long as the state regulation provides an exception to those pregnancies which endanger a woman's life or health. Third, from the very beginning of the pregnancy, the state has an interest in protecting the health of the woman *and* the life of the fetus that may become a person.

The joint opinion in *Casey* rejected the trimester scheme. Opinions by Justices Rehnquist and Scalia also rejected it, establishing a majority for repudiating the trimester scheme. This prompted Justice Scalia, who concurred in part and dissented in part, to characterize the Court's version of *stare decisis* as "keep-what-you-want-and-throw-away the rest." Nor was the trimester scheme the only part of *Roe* scuttled by the joint opinion. The strict scrutiny standard was also abandoned. In its place, the plurality said it would use an undue burden test. What is an undue burden? The joint opinion described it: "An undue burden exists, and therefore a provision of law is invalid, if its purpose or effect is to place a substantial obstacle in the path of a woman seeking an abortion before the fetus attains viability."

How does the undue burden test work in practice? The Pennsylvania Abortion Control Act which was under review in *Casey* contained five provisions which were challenged as violative of *Roe*. Four of the five provisions were held not to constitute an undue burden:

— A provision that a woman seeking an abortion must give her informed consent with an exception for medical emergencies prior to the abortion procedure was not an undue burden. Prior decisions had validated such a regulation so long as it was not designed to coerce the woman's choice. Indeed, informed consent was standard medical procedure.

— A provision that a woman be provided with certain information prescribed by the state 24 hours before the abortion proceeding was performed was not an undue burden. The state was permitted to insist that reflection precede the abortion decision. Insofar as *City of Akron v. Akron Center for Reproductive Health* (1983) had invalidated a 24 hour waiting period, it was repudiated. The Court did concede that some applications of this provision might yield a different result, *i.e.*, a poor woman who would not be able to have an abortion because she could not afford the expense of a waiting period. But this did not render the provision facially unconstitutional.

— A provision requiring the consent of at least one parent or, failing that, permission by a court in the case of a minor seeking an abortion was held not to be an undue burden. Such provisions had been upheld in the past. See, *infra*, *Hodgson v. Minnesota* (1990); *Ohio v. Akron Center for Reproductive Health* (1990).

— A provision that physicians give certain specified information about the nature of the abortion procedure, its health risks and the gestational age of the fetus was not an undue burden. The information in question was truthful and not misleading. The key to the conclusion that mandating such information does not constitute an undue burden is that the woman is still permitted to make the ultimate choice—to have an abortion. Even if the state seeks to promote childbirth, all the state is doing is to make sure that she is aware of a competing choice. To the extent that *City of Akron* and *Thornburgh v. American College of Obstetricians and Gynecologists* (1986) held otherwise, they were repudiated.

— The only regulation struck down as an undue burden in *Casey* dealt with spousal notification. Requiring a woman to secure a statement that she has notified her husband of her decision to have an abortion is an undue burden. Such a requirement places a substantial obstacle in the path of a woman since fear of spousal abuse might inhibit the abortion decision altogether.

The Court's holding on what was and what was not an undue burden put in sharp relief the difference between the undue burden standard of *Casey* and the strict scrutiny standard of *Roe*. State mandates requiring a 24 hour waiting period and that specified information be provided the woman by the physician had been struck down in *Thornburgh* and *City of Akron*. In those cases, the strict scrutiny standard had been employed. Clearly—at least as used in *Casey*—the undue burden standard was far more generous to state regulation of abortion than *Roe's* strict scrutiny standard.

Four Justices—Rehnquist, Thomas, Scalia and White—would have reversed *Roe* in its entirety. Justice Blackmun would have adhered to *Roe* in its entirety. Although an adherent of *Roe*, Justice Stevens said he would invalidate the very regulations upheld by the joint opinion and he would do so using the undue burden standard. This is because in applying the undue burden test, Stevens would weigh the woman's constitutional interest in deciding whether to go to full term more heavily than the state's non-constitutional interest in life. This approach may prove to have significance in the future.

For nearly twenty years the question about *Roe* was—would it survive? The new question is how hardy will the undue burden test of *Casey* prove to be. After all, it was only subscribed to by a plurality of the Court. Two of the Justices who participated in *Casey*—Blackmun and White—are no longer on the Court. Their successors are Breyer and Ginsburg. Whether they will join with O'Connor, Kennedy and Souter in employing the undue burden test or whether they will employ some alternative approach to abortion regulation is as yet unclear.

Justice Scalia castigated the "inherently standardless" quality of the undue burden inquiry. This standard has been criticized because its predictive quality—unlike the situation with the strict scrutiny test or the rational basis test—is not high. But paradoxically, the imprecision of the undue burden test may enable it to endure as the measure of regulation in the abortion area. As a test, it is sufficiently malleable to meet the purposes of both the proponents and the opponents of abortion regulation.

A significant body of abortion case law has addressed the constitutional issues raised by the privacy rights of minors. While the Court has consistently recognized that "[m]inors as well as adults are protected by the Constitution and possess constitutional rights," it has also established that "the power of the state to control the conduct of children reaches beyond the scope of its authority over adults." *Carey v. Population Services International* (1977). Thus, the Court has employed a less demanding standard than strict scrutiny in reviewing state legislation limiting the access of minors to contraceptives and abortions. Nevertheless, in *Carey,* the Court struck down a total prohibition against non-prescription sales of contraceptives to minors since the law served no significant state interest not present in the case of an adult. Similarly, a blanket requirement in state law that a parent has an "absolute veto" over the abortion decision of a minor child is unconstitutional. *Planned Parenthood of Central Missouri v. Danforth* (1976). On the other hand, some parental or judicial consent substitutes for immature minors are constitutional.

A Minnesota parental notification statute which required that a physician notify both parents of a female minor seeking an abortion but which did not provide for a judicial bypass was unconstitutional. Requiring notification of both parents serves no legitimate state interest and could have harmful

effects on the pregnant minor—particularly in the
case of divorced or separated parents or of an abusive or dysfunctional family. However, the Minnesota statute also provided that a judicial bypass
procedure would go into effect if the dual parent
notification requirement was struck down. This
bypass provision was constitutional and saved the
statute. The judicial bypass procedure enables the
minor to show a court that she possesses sufficient
maturity to make an informed choice or it may
allow her to show that parental notification was not
in her best interests. Consequently, the bypass
procedure corrects the infirmities which would have
otherwise rendered the statute unconstitutional.
Hodgson v. Minnesota (1990).

A significant limitation on the privacy rights
forged in *Roe* is indicated in the abortion funding
cases. It is one thing to hold that the constitutional
right of privacy inhibits the state's power to limit
the abortion decision of a woman. However, it is
another and different step to say that the right is
not only protected but the state is obligated to make
the right effective if the woman is indigent. Thus,
in *Maher v. Roe* (1977), the Court held, per Powell,
J., that the state is under no constitutional obligation to provide public funding for abortions of
state welfare recipients. And this is true even
though the state provides funding for normal childbirth: "The Connecticut regulation places no obstacles—absolute or otherwise—in the pregnant woman's path to an abortion. An indigent woman who
desires an abortion suffers no disadvantage as a

consequence of Connecticut's decision to fund childbirth. While the state may have made childbirth a
more attractive alternative than abortion, it has
imposed no restriction on the woman's decision to
terminate her pregnancy that was not already present." But Justice Brennan declared in dissent:
"What is critical is that the State has inhibited [the
indigent woman's] fundamental right to make that
choice free from state interference." In the view of
the dissenters, the financial pressure exerted on the
woman to bear the child constitutes a restraint
making the exercise of the right more difficult and
thus infringes the fundamental right established by
Roe.

The principle of *Maher v. Roe* was pushed even
further in *Harris v. McRae* (1980). The Hyde
Amendment prohibits the use of federal funds even
for medically necessary abortions. Justice Stewart
invoked the principle of *Maher* and concluded for
the Court that the Hyde Amendment "places no
governmental obstacle in the path of a woman who
chooses to terminate her pregnancy, but rather, by
means of unequal subsidization of abortion and
other medical services, encourages alternative activity deemed in the public interest." In short, the
Roe right does not include "a constitutional entitlement to the financial resources to avail herself of
the full range of protected choices." In dissent,
Justice Brennan protested that both "by design and
in effect" government was coercing indigent pregnant women to bear children that they did not
want. Justice Stevens, dissenting, objected that the

government was not employing neutral criteria in distributing its medical benefits: "If a woman has a constitutional right the exercise of that right cannot provide the basis for the denial of a [medical] benefit to which she would otherwise be entitled." Having decided to provide medically necessary benefits to indigent women, the government could not constitutionally exclude benefits for the exercise of what was, after all, a protected right. The majority in *Harris v. McRae* did not agree.

Webster v. Reproductive Health Services (1989) made clear just how little in the way of obligation is imposed on the state to make the abortion decision effective—a Missouri state law prohibiting public employees and public facilities from being used for facilitating abortions not necessary to save the life of the mother was upheld. States are not obliged to commit any resources to facilitate abortions.

The Court has thus far rejected efforts to extend the privacy right protecting contraceptive and abortion choices to sexual privacy or matters of personal autonomy generally. *Bowers v. Hardwick* (1986) upheld, 5–4, a Georgia statute criminalizing sodomy against a constitutional attack by a homosexual engaged in homosexual activity in the privacy of his home. There was no fundamental due process right conferred on homosexuals to engage in sodomy. At the time the *Bowers* case came before the Court, 24 states and the District of Columbia had statutes punishing sodomy. It was insupportable, therefore, to contend that homosexual conduct was " 'deeply rooted in this Nation's history and tradi-

tion' or 'implicit in the concept of ordered liberty'."
There should be "great resistance to expanding the
substantive reach" of due process. Having disposed
of the fundamental rights issue, the Georgia sodomy
law was upheld as a rationally based moral choice
by its citizens. In *Roe v. Wade,* the Court expressed
doubt that the right of privacy could be extended to
include the unlimited right to do with one's body as
one pleases. The Court's treatment of private homosexual relations in *Bowers* confirms these
doubts.

In *Bowers,* Justice Blackmun wrote a strong dissent, joined by three other Justices. The issue was
not a fundamental right to engage in homosexual
sodomy but a far more inclusive right to be let
alone. The Georgia statute punished sodomy
whether homosexual or heterosexual. The Court's
obsessive focus had been on homosexual sodomy.
But the case really involves the privacy right of the
defendant and the intrusion which targeted enforcement of the statute against homosexuals presented
to the right of intimate association. The state had
violated the fundamental due process right to be let
alone—a right which embraced the right to privacy,
the right to intimate association and the right to
make critical personal choices. In addition, the
Court should have considered whether the state
statute contravened the Ninth Amendment or the
Equal Protection Clause or the Eighth Amendment.
Justice Powell, concurring, had suggested that the
prohibition against cruel and unusual punishment
might have been violated if there had been a crimi-

nal prosecution given the severe sentence which the state statute imposed. In short, *Bowers* itself exhibited portents of fragility.

The controversy about whether homosexuals may claim constitutional protection against governmental action which discriminates against them was certainly not silenced by the bare majority in *Bowers* which held against such protection. The lower courts have not been awed by the majority opinion in *Bowers*. Indeed, in the years since *Bowers*, lower court cases have extended constitutional protection to homosexuals using the Equal Protection Clause. In addition, the presence of new Justices on the Court and the departure of others suggests that the Supreme Court may decide to take a new look at this issue.

c. Marital and Familial Rights

A right to marry has been judicially accepted as a guarantee of due process. Thus, in *Loving v. Virginia* (1967), a state statute prohibiting interracial marriage was struck down on both equal protection and due process grounds. Chief Justice Warren declared: "The freedom to marry has long been recognized as one of the vital personal rights essential to the orderly pursuit of happiness by free men. Marriage is one of the 'basic civil rights of man,' fundamental to our very existence and survival." So vital a right could not be abridged by statutes designed to accomplish invidious racial discrimination. Similar issues are often disposed of by the Court under the rubric of equal protection rather than due process. See *Zablocki v. Redhail* (1978), where Justice Stewart, concurring, referred to the Court's use of equal protection doctrine as "no more than substantive due process by another name." The calculus for determining which clause will be used is not readily apparent.

The Court has stated: "This Court has long recognized that freedom of personal choice in matters of marriage and family life is one of the liberties protected by the Due Process Clause of the Fourteenth Amendment." *Cleveland Board of Education v. LaFleur* (1974). When a law significantly burdens the exercise of critical choices in marriage and family life, the rationality standard of review is inappropriate and a stricter standard of review should be used.

Thus, in *Moore v. East Cleveland* (1977), the Court stated: "[W]hen the government intrudes on choices concerning family living relationships, this Court must examine carefully the importance of the governmental interest advanced and the extent to which they are served by the challenged regulation." This standard, which sounds more like the intermediate standard of review than the strict scrutiny standard, was invoked by the Court to strike down an ordinance limiting housing occupancy to members of a single family. Family was defined in such a way as to exclude the grandchild of a grandmother living in the house. In *Moore,* Justice Powell in a plurality opinion, did not invoke the right of privacy but instead adopted a substantive due process approach to protect "family rights."

The *Moore* facts, reasoned Powell, J., unlike *Lochner*, involved the basic values of our society. "Our decisions establish that the Constitution protects the sanctity of the family precisely because the institution of the family is deeply rooted in this Nation's history and tradition. It is through the family that we inculcate and pass down many of our most cherished values, moral and cultural." Nor was this constitutional protection limited to the nuclear family. The tradition of the extended family "has roots equally venerable and equally deserving of constitutional recognition."

In *Moore*, the city tried to defend its occupancy limitation ordinance as a reasonable means of preventing overcrowding with its ensuing burden on the community. While these were legitimate goals, the ordinance only marginally served them. Powell noted, for example, that the ordinance would permit a husband, wife and unmarried children to live together even "if the family contains a half-dozen licensed drivers each with his or her own car."

The four dissenters in *Moore* challenged both the judicial activism of the substantive due process methodology employed by Powell as well as the conclusions derived therefrom. In dissent, Justice White argued that the "judge-made constitutional law, employed by the plurality would intrude excessively into the ability of Congress and the state legislatures to respond to a changing social order."

He warned: "What the deeply rooted traditions of the country are is arguable; which of them deserves the protection of the Due Process Clause is even more debatable." Justice Stewart, dissenting, questioned whether the interest of a person in sharing living quarters with a relative was of constitutional dimension. "To equate this interest with the fundamental decisions to marry and to bear and raise children is to extend the limited substantive contours of the Due Process Clause beyond recognition."

In *Michael H. & Victoria D. v. Gerald D.* (1989), a California statute which established a presumption that a child born to a married woman living with her husband is a child of the marriage if the husband is not impotent or sterile was upheld against a substantive due process claim. The statute was upheld despite the fact that blood tests performed on the putative natural father indicated a 98.07% probability of paternity, that the natural father had established a parental relationship with the child, and that the natural father had brought a filiation action to establish paternity and a right to visitation. In a plurality opinion, Justice Scalia for the Court, rejected the substantive due process claims of the natural father. Justice Scalia said that what was decisive was that the states did not in fact confer substantive parental rights on the "natural father of a child conceived within and born into an extant marital union that wishes to embrace the child." Michael H. had failed to prove a liberty interest. Persons in the situation of *Michael H.*

and his married lover had never been "treated as a protected family unit under the historic practices of our society."

Justice Scalia would have gone further in *Michael H.* and fashioned a new and restrictive test for substantive due process. He argued in a footnote, in which he was joined only by Chief Justice Rehnquist, that the inquiry to determine whether a right was fundamental for substantive due process purposes should "refer to the most specific level at which a relevant tradition protecting, or denying protection to, the asserted right can be identified." In his view, there was such a specific tradition and it "unqualifiedly" denied protection to a parent in the situation of Michael H.

In *Reno v. Flores* (1993), Justice Scalia's analysis for the Court looked very much like his "most specific level" approach even though its use was not acknowledged. At issue in *Flores* was an Immigration and Naturalization Service (INS) regulation stating that alien juveniles in custody and facing deportation could be released to parents, guardians and adult relatives not in INS detention. In certain unusual and compelling circumstances, the juvenile could be released to another adult. Otherwise the INS could place the child in a government custodial facility which met federal standards. The alien juveniles launched a facial challenge to the regulation on the ground that it violated their right to "freedom from physical restraint." The Court upheld the regulation.

Justice Scalia asserted that the right of alien juveniles in *Flores* was not a fundamental right to freedom from physical restraint but a far narrower and hitherto unrecognized right. "[T]he right at issue is the alleged right of a child who has no available parent, close relative, or legal guardian, and for whom the government is responsible, to be placed in the custody of a willing-and-able private custodian rather than of a government-operated or government-selected child-care institution." The novelty of the claim was itself evidence that substantive due process did not require it. This alleged right was certainly not " 'so rooted in the traditions and conscience of our people as to be ranked as fundamental.' " This would be so even if the right at issue were characterized as the alien juvenile's fundamental right to an individualized hearing to ascertain whether private placement would be in the juvenile's *best interest*. No such fundamental right exists as long as the government was providing adequate care for the alien juvenile. Substantive due process does not require the government to substitute private placement for institutional custody where possible.

In *Michael H.*, Justice Scalia's narrow "most specific level" approach to substantive due process had only attracted the support of Chief Justice Rehnquist. *Reno v. Flores* suggests at first blush that it may have more of a future than was originally thought. But it should be noted that Justice O'Connor, joined by Justice Souter, concurring in *Flores*, recognized that there *was* a core liberty interest in freedom from institutional confinement. Nevertheless, they felt that the INS regulation survived the heightened scrutiny that substantive due process imposed. Moreover, in dissent, Justices Blackmun and Stevens asserted that the only novelty in *Flores* was Scalia's analysis. They objected to the Court's "narrow reading of the right at issue." The right at issue was nothing less than the right not to be detained at all. In short, the effort begun by Justice Scalia in *Michael H.*, and continued in *Flores*, to make substantive due process a less fertile source for the recognition of new constitutional rights and interests can still be expected to meet substantial resistance on the Court.

d.   Right to Care and Protection

As the abortion funding cases indicate, the Court has generally insisted that there is no affirmative constitutional duty on the part of government to effectuate rights. Yet a right to care and protection by the government has occasionally been recognized. In the limited context where the State has custody of an individual, the due process clause has been found to impose a duty on government to assume a measure of responsibility for that person's care and well-being. *Youngberg v. Romeo* (1982) held that a profoundly retarded individual who had been involuntarily committed to a state institution for the mentally retarded had some substantive due process rights. When the state institutionalizes such a wholly dependent person, the state then has a duty to provide certain services and care. The person in the state's custody has a liberty interest which would have to be balanced against the relevant state interests. In the context of *Youngberg,* the liberty interest would require the state to provide "minimally adequate or reasonable training to ensure safety and freedom from undue restraint." The judgment of medical professionals in such circumstances would be presumptively valid. That judgment could be validly superseded only when there was a showing of a "substantial departure from accepted professional judgment."

The Rehnquist Court has been unwilling to extend the *Youngberg v. Romeo* analysis very far. Thus, the state has been held not to deprive a child of his "liberty" when it failed to protect him from the physical abuse of his father. Complaints about physical abuse of the child had been made known to the county department of social services. Yet when the child was so badly beaten by his father that he suffered permanent brain damage, the state was held not to be sufficiently implicated to violate the due process guarantee. Chief Justice Rehnquist said that, unlike *Youngberg*, the harms suffered by the child did not occur while he was in the state's custody but while he was in the custody of his natural father. Even though the county department of social services had investigated the case, and might have removed the child, there was no affirmative right to government aid. The father was not a state actor: "While the State may have been aware of the dangers that Joshua faced in the free world, it played no part in their creation, nor did it do anything to render him more vulnerable to them." In dissent, Justice Brennan protested the Court's failure to understand "that inaction can be every bit as abusive of power as action, that oppression can result when a State undertakes a vital duty and then ignores it." *DeShaney v. Winnebago County Dept. of Social Services* (1989).

A city sanitary worker died of asphyxia while working in a manhole. The city had not trained its employees about the dangers of working in sewers nor had it provided safety equipment or even warnings. The city employee did not have a right under the Due Process Clause to be free from unreasonable risk of harm and to protection from the city's deliberate indifference. The appropriate level of resources to be allocated to the training of sewer maintenance employees is a matter for local government and not for the federal judiciary. "[T]he Due Process Clause does not impose an independent federal obligation upon municipalities to provide certain minimal levels of safety and security in the workplace." *Collins v. City of Harker Heights* (1992).

e.   The Right to Refuse Treatment

An individual has a significant due process liberty interest in refusing unwanted medical treatment. However, the state's regulatory interest may sometimes outweigh the burden on the protected liberty interest. For example, a state does not violate substantive due process if it authorizes the involuntary treatment with drugs of a prisoner who suffers

from a mental disorder, is gravely disabled, and
presents a likelihood of serious harm to others or
their property. There was a valid rational relationship between the prison regulation and the government interest asserted to support it. The absence
of a ready alternative to involuntary medication
furnished additional evidence of the state policy's
reasonableness: "[T]he Due Process Clause permits
the State to treat a prison inmate who has serious
mental illness with antipsychotic drugs against his
will, if the inmate is dangerous to himself or others
and the treatment is in the inmate's medical interests." *Washington v. Harper* (1990).

Does a person have a "right to die" or at least to
refuse life preserving treatment? This difficult issue was presented when the parents of a young
woman, a victim of an automobile accident, unsuccessfully sought an order from a Missouri court
directing the withdrawal of their daughter's artifi-
cial feeding and hydration equipment because it was
clear that "she had virtually no chance of recovering her cognitive faculties." The Supreme Court
held, per Chief Justice Rehnquist, that a state may
constitutionally require clear and convincing evidence that the patient herself desires that life-
sustaining treatment be withdrawn. A patient has
a significant liberty interest in refusing unwanted
medical treatment. But the state has an interest in
the preservation of human life and in protecting the
personal element in the choice of life or death.
These state interests were sufficient to justify the
imposition of heightened evidentiary standards.

Such standards protect against abuse, promote more accurate fact finding and reflect the importance of the decision to withdraw medical life supports. *Cruzan v. Director, Missouri Dept. of Health* (1990).

Cruzan teaches that the state is not constitutionally required to confer decisional power in such matters on anyone but the patient. The state is not constitutionally obliged to accept the substituted judgement of even close family members. But, the Court was not called upon to resolve the question whether a state would be required to defer to the decision of a surrogate if evidence clearly established that the patient wanted the surrogate to make the decision to withdraw life supports for her.

f. Other Fundamental Rights

The constitutional protection afforded personal decisions involving abortion, contraception, marriage and family life indicates the general principle that laws significantly burdening fundamental personal rights are subjected to stricter judicial scrutiny. This principle will be reflected again in subsequent sections of this Nutshell dealing with First Amendment freedoms made applicable to the states through the Due Process Clause of the Fourteenth Amendment. This fundamental rights principle is also used to protect both rights that may be fairly implied from the constitutional text as well as rights that are judicially created, *e.g.,* the right of interstate travel. *Shapiro v. Thompson* (1969). Finally, the fundamental rights principle has provided the foundation for stricter review of governmental action under the Equal Protection Clause.

C. PROCEDURAL DUE PROCESS

Substantive due process is addressed to what government can do. Procedural due process inquires into the way government acts and the enforcement mechanisms it uses. When government deprives a person of an already acquired life, liberty or property interest, the Due Process Clauses of the Fifth and Fourteenth Amendments require procedural fairness. In testing the adequacy of government procedures, two questions are asked: First, is there a life, liberty or property interest at stake? Second, what procedures must be afforded to assure fair treatment?

1. LIFE, LIBERTY AND PROPERTY INTERESTS

At one time, the due process mandate of procedural fairness did not apply when governmental benefits or privileges rather than constitutional rights were denied. *McAuliffe v. Mayor of New Bedford* (1892) [dismissal of a policeman for political activities held to be solely a matter of government discretion]. But with an increasing appreciation of the adverse impact of government action on the individual, this right-privilege dichotomy eroded. Today, whether an interest is a right or a privilege, when it is intentionally denied, procedural due process must be afforded. *Goldberg v. Kelly* (1970) ["The Constitutional arguments cannot be answered by an argument that public assistance benefits are 'a privilege and not a right' "]. Further, government cannot condition receipt of public benefits on surrender of constitutional rights (*i.e.*, the Unconstitutional Conditions Doctrine).

But this does not mean that due process applies whenever government action intentionally denies an interest of value. In fact, the terms "life, liberty or property" have received an increasingly narrow interpretation in recent years. Indeed, many commentators would argue that the Court has restored the right-privilege dichotomy by giving highly restrictive meaning to the terms "liberty" and "property."

a. Property Interests

"Property" includes a wide range of significant, legally-recognized proprietary interests. The key concept in defining property today is "entitlement." When the government recognizes that an individual is legally entitled to a benefit, it thereby creates an expectancy that the benefit will not be arbitrarily terminated. A property interest is created. But note that entitlement applies only to "presently enjoyed" rights or interests; due process does not protect the person applying for benefits. *Board of Regents v. Roth* (1972).

The vital role played by entitlement can be appreciated by comparing *Roth* with *Perry v. Sindermann* (1972). In *Roth*, the Court held that a state untenured teacher, hired under a fixed one-year term, could be dismissed without reasons or a hearing. In concluding that the teacher had no property interest, Justice Stewart, for the Court, stressed that it is "the nature of the interest at stake," not the weight, that is critical. Property interests, he explained, "are created and their dimensions are defined by existing rules or understandings that stem from an independent source such as state law—rules or understandings that secure certain benefits and that support claims of entitlements to those benefits." In this case, there was no contractual provision for renewal of Roth's employment; no state statute or University policy "secured his interest in re-employment" or "created any legitimate claim" to re-employment. Simply, the state had not created any entitlement qualifying as a property interest.

In a companion case, *Perry v. Sindermann* (1972), the Court discovered such an entitlement in a school official Faculty Guide which could reasonably be interpreted to create a de facto tenure system. Property interests, said Justice Stewart, can arise from "mutually explicit understandings" that support a claim of entitlement. Thus, a teacher who had been employed for 12 years under a series of one year contracts could attempt to prove that the college, while lacking a formal tenure system, had in practice created an "unwritten common law" which was the equivalent of tenure.

In other cases, "property interests" have been found when government has aided in the collection of debts [*Sniadach v. Family Finance Corp. of Bay View* (1969) (wage garnishment)]; or in pre-judgment seizures [*North Georgia Fin., Inc. v. Di–Chem, Inc.* (1975) (the use and enjoyment of goods)]; or has terminated statutorily created welfare benefits [*Goldberg v. Kelly* (1970)]; or has imposed a ten-day suspension from a state guaranteed education [*Goss v. Lopez* (1975)]; or has terminated public employment [*Perry v. Sindermann* (1972)]; or has suspended a driver's license [*Bell v. Burson* (1971)]; or has terminated a state-created cause of action [*Logan v. Zimmerman Brush Co.* (1982)].

A troublesome area in defining "property" arises when the state creates an interest but prescribes various procedures for terminating it or otherwise conditions the interest. While a state is free to stipulate restrictions on a claim, it is the judicial function to determine whether the conditioned claim constitutes a "property" interest. For example, when the state conditions public employment to an extent that it is terminable at will, rather than "for cause," it has been held that the employment does not constitute a property interest. *Bishop v. Wood* (1976). But in *Cleveland Board of Education v. Loudermill* (1985), a statute entitling classified civil servants to retain their positions absent "misfeasance, malfeasance, or nonfeasance in office" was held to create a property interest in continued employment even though the state provided procedures for termination. Justice White, for the Court, stressed that the question of the substantive right of liberty or property is distinct from the procedural question: " 'Property' cannot be defined by the procedures provided for its deprivation any more than can life or liberty." The question of what procedures are due is a constitutional issue, not to be determined by the state statute.

b. Liberty Interests

The concept of "liberty" is far more amorphous than that of property, embodying principles of freedom that lie at the roots of our legal system. The Court has said that liberty "denotes not merely freedom from bodily restraint but also the right of the individual to contract, to engage in any of the common occupations of life, to acquire useful knowledge, to marry, establish a home and bring up children, to worship God according to the dictates of his own conscience and generally to enjoy those privileges long recognized as essential to the orderly pursuit of happiness by free men." *Meyer v. Nebraska* (1923). Using this statement as a guide, liberty interests generally fall under one of the following headings: (1) freedom from bodily restraint or "physical liberty"; (2) substantive constitutional rights; (3) other fundamental freedoms.

Liberty interests are burdened when physical freedom is curtailed by commitment, imprisonment, or when bodily integrity is impaired [*Ingraham v. Wright* (1977), corporal punishment of students by teachers]. Thus, the Constitution mandates extensive procedural protection for the accused in the criminal justice system and juvenile justice system. When the state seeks to revoke parole [*Morrissey v.*

Brewer (1972)], or probation [*Gagnon v. Scarpelli* (1973)], due process must be afforded. Involuntary civil commitment to a mental institution demands due process. *Addington v. Texas* (1979) ["clear and convincing" evidence of dangerousness required for commitment]; *Parham v. J.R.* (1979) [parental commitment of child involves protectable liberty interest, requiring neutral fact finder's determination that admission requirements are satisfied]. Transfer of an incarcerated prisoner to a mental hospital involving stigma and subjection to mandatory treatment procedures requires written notice and a hearing with extensive procedural protections. *Vitek v. Jones* (1980).

However, the Court has indicated that not every "grievous loss" inflicted on a prisoner implicates a liberty interest. Once criminal due process is satisfied and a person is imprisoned, liberty has already been significantly curtailed and subsequent adverse action does not necessarily constitute a significant deprivation of liberty. Thus, transfer of a prisoner to a different institution [*Meachum v. Fano* (1976); *Olim v. Wakinekona* (1983)]; or rescission of discretionary parole prior to release [*Jago v. Van Curen* (1981)]; or, administrative segregation of prisoners [*Hewitt v. Helms* (1983)], have been held not to involve liberty requiring due process procedures.

Similarly, in *Kentucky Department of Corrections v. Thompson* (1989), the Court held that Kentucky prison regulations governing visitation did not create a liberty interest when visiting privileges for certain visitors were suspended. No entitlement had been created by the prison regulations. The regulations did not create by mandatory language the "substantive predicate" that would lead prisoners to reasonably expect that a visit would be allowed. Denial of access to particular visitors was well within the terms of confinement associated with imprisonment.

On the other hand, state law can create a specific entitlement to designated procedures for prisoners before adverse actions are taken by prison authorities. *Greenholtz v. Inmates of Nebraska Penal & Correctional Complex* (1979) [statute requiring parole for eligible inmate absent finding of designated grounds for denial of parole creates an entitlement].

Liberty also includes all of the incorporated rights (*e.g.,* freedom of expression and religion), as well as those substantive rights which have been implied from, or have been read into the Constitution (*e.g.,* association and belief, privacy). If a public employee is discharged because of her exercise of speech rights, liberty is burdened and procedural fairness is required. *Perry v. Sindermann* (1972) [But see, *Mt. Healthy City School Dist. Bd. of Educ. v. Doyle* (1977), indicating due process is not required if the employee would have been discharged for permissible reasons]. When parental rights in the care, custody and management of their children are terminated, due process is required. *Santosky v. Kramer* (1982) ["clear and convincing" evidence of unfitness required before terminating parental rights]. In short, when constitutional rights are severely burdened by government action, due process must be provided.

Finally, due process "liberty" encompasses a variety of fundamental interests relating to personal autonomy and choice. It is in this context that liberty is most ill-defined and tends to produce most conceptual confusion with "property" interests. Discharge from a particular job may not involve a property entitlement but government action which denies access to the common occupations of the community may well implicate due process liberty. See *Board of Regents v. Roth* (1972). Termination of one's ability to practice a profession can involve not only property but liberty interests as well.

The confusion in this murky area of liberty and property is best illustrated by the Court's treatment of reputational interests. Early cases had indicated that when government action "stigmatizes" a person, impairing her good name, reputation, honor, or integrity, the liberty clause requires that due process be afforded. See, *e.g., Wisconsin v. Constantineau* (1971) [public posting of names of persons causing problems because of excessive drinking]. But in *Paul v. Davis* (1976), the Court indicated that injury to reputation, without more, does not require due process.

Paul v. Davis involved reputational injury resulting from police distribution of a flyer identifying Davis as an "active shoplifter." In fact, while Davis had been arrested, he was subsequently acquitted. Rather than suing for defamation in state court, Davis sued in federal court claiming a violation of his due process rights since he had not been afforded any hearing on the charges prior to circulation of the flyer. The Court, 5–4, rejected the claim "that reputation alone, apart from some more tangible interests such as employment, is either 'liberty' or 'property' by itself sufficient to invoke the procedural protection of the Due Process Clause." Justice Rehnquist, for the Court, instead indicated that interests attain the constitutional status of liberty or property "by virtue of the fact that they have been initially recognized and protected by state law." The public posting in *Constantineau,* explained Justice Rehnquist, had altered the plaintiff's legal right to purchase liquor. In the present case, the action of the police did not produce "a deprivation of any 'liberty' or 'property' recognized by state or federal law nor has it worked any change of respondent's status as theretofore recognized under the state's laws."

Taken literally, *Paul v. Davis* would limit "liberty" to constitutional rights and physical liberty. Beyond these interests only state created entitlements (*i.e.,* "property") would invoke the due process guarantee. Perhaps, *Paul* may simply reflect the Court's federalism concern with preserving state created causes of action—Rehnquist warned against making "the Fourteenth Amendment a font of tort law to be superimposed upon whatever systems may already be administered by the states."

2. THE PROCESS THAT IS DUE

Having determined that a liberty or property interest is significantly burdened, the Court must next assess what procedures are required in order to provide fundamental fairness. The answer to this inquiry depends heavily on the particular fact context involved, *e.g.*, welfare, prisons, schools. The important item for the constitutional law student is to understand the methodology employed by the courts in providing the answer. Remember that the inquiry into what process is due is a federal constitutional question to be answered by the courts in interpreting the meaning of "due process." The fact that the state has defined procedures for terminating an interest is not determinative of the demands of the federal Constitution. *Vitek v. Jones* (1980); *Logan v. Zimmerman Brush Co.* (1982); *Cleveland Board of Education v. Loudermill* (1985). Compare *Arnett v. Kennedy* (1974) (plurality opinion).

An example of the way in which the due process clause can override state definitions is the conclusive presumption doctrine. A statute creates such a presumption when it conclusively presumes that certain facts exist which permit categorizing individuals into a class and subjecting them to burdens not visited on others. The conclusive presumption doctrine holds that since the presumption may not be valid for each member of the class, denial of an opportunity to challenge the presumption violates due process. When critical due process interests of the individual are at stake, an opportunity for an individualized hearing to challenge the presumption must be provided. For example, school board rules requiring every pregnant school teacher to take a maternity leave without pay for a specified number of months before the expected birth of her child violated due process. Individualized determinations are necessary for due process to be satisfied. *Cleveland Board of Education v. La Fleur* (1974). A plurality of the Court contends that the conclusive presumption doctrine does not have its source in the requirements of procedural due process. The doctrine instead, it is argued, is based on the lack of fit between the classification established by the law and the policy underlying the classification, i.e. equal protection or a challenge to the policy itself, e.g. substantive due process. *Michael H. & Victoria D. v. Gerald D.* (1989).

While the Court has not provided systematic guidance on the values and objectives underlying the due process inquiry, primary emphasis has been given to assuring accuracy and avoiding arbitrariness in government decision-making. *Codd v. Velger* (1977) [employee claiming due process right to a hearing because of stigma resulting from discharge must allege that the charges are false]. Commentators have argued that this approach excessively narrows the judicial inquiry; the due process inquiry should also focus on process values such as individual dignity, participation, and equality of treatment. Once it is determined that due process interests have been adversely affected, the individual has at least the right, absent an emergency, to reasonable notice and some form of hearing on his claim.

The scope of the procedural protection afforded beyond this minimum is determined by balancing the interests favoring summary determination against the interests of the individual in additional procedural protection. *Goss v. Lopez* (1975). Courts making this balancing determination employ a three-part test fashioned in *Mathews v. Eldridge* (1976), focusing on the following factors:

First, the private interest that will be affected by the official action; second, the risk of an erroneous deprivation of such interest through the procedures used, and the probable value, if any, of additional or substitute procedural safeguards; and finally, the government's interest, including the function involved and the fiscal and administrative burden that the additional or substitute procedural requirements would entail.

Applying these standards in *Mathews v. Eldridge,* in the context of termination of disability benefits, the Court found significant differences from *Goldberg v. Kelly* (1970), where the Court had required extensive procedural protection and a hearing prior to termination of welfare benefits under the Aid to Families with Dependent Children (AFDC) program. First, whereas AFDC benefits are based upon need, disability benefits are grounded upon findings unrelated to the worker's financial needs; there is likely to be less hardship on the disability claimant. Second, termination of AFDC benefits turns upon decisions by social workers that involve a high risk of error. Continued eligibility for disability, on the other hand, involves medical decisions having a higher degree of accuracy. Finally, a full administrative hearing in disability cases would involve high costs taken from scarce resources which might well decrease benefits.

The cost benefit calculus involved in using this balancing formulation is also illustrated by the Court's treatment of student discipline. In *Goss v. Lopez* (1975), involving a ten-day suspension from school for students engaged in misconduct, the Court balanced the need of the schools for discipline and order through immediate, effective action in combating misconduct against the stigma and loss of schooling suffered by students subjected to even a short 10–day suspension. At least minimal presuspension procedural protection, *i.e.,* an explanation of the charges and an informal opportunity to reply, was required.

The Court displayed an even greater reluctance to excessively intrude on school administration and to constitutionalize school procedures in *Board of Curators v. Horowitz* (1978). Charlotte Horowitz had failed to graduate from medical school because of poor performance in clinical courses and concern for her personal hygiene. Although the Court acknowledged the severity of Ms. Horowitz's plight, it denied her claim to personally appear before the school's administrative board to defend her interests. The Court was unanimous in determining that due process had been satisfied by affording her a hearing and an appeal at which she could make her case in writing. But the Court was not unanimous on whether the procedures which had been provided were constitutionally required. Justice Rehnquist, for the Court, emphasized the differences between academic evaluation and the fact-finding and adversariness characteristic of adjudication, concluding "that the school went beyond [constitutionally required] due process." Justice Marshall, concurring, rejected this "dicta suggesting that respondent was entitled to even less procedural protection than she received." Instead, he compared the present case with *Goss,* stressing the greater severity of the personal harm, the risk of error in academic evaluation and the absence, compared to *Goss,* of any government interest in discipline and order.

When a medicated and disoriented patient was admitted to a state mental hospital as a "voluntary" admission where, as alleged, the state employees should have known otherwise, the failure of the state employees to follow a state statutory procedure for the involuntary admission of mentally ill patients was sufficient to state a claim under the Due Process Clause. In such circumstances, post-deprivation remedies were inadequate and due process mandated a proper predeprivation hearing. *Zinermon v. Burch* (1990).

But a state policy which established a nonjudicial procedure, staffed by medical professionals, for deciding the involuntary treatment with antipsychotic

drugs of mentally ill felons did not violate procedural due process. Although the prisoner enjoyed a
significant liberty interest in avoiding the unwanted
administration of antipsychotic drugs, the state procedure, given the inmate's threat to the security of
the prison environment, satisfied due process. The
procedure afforded the inmate notice, the right to
cross-examine witnesses, and the opportunity to
attend the hearing. Since medical personnel would
be making the treatment decision, a clear and convincing standard was not required and would not be
helpful. *Washington v. Harper* (1990).

A new development in the law of institutional due
process is that a state may not punish by involuntary commitment to a mental institution a person
who has not been convicted and who is not now
mentally ill. A state statute which permitted an
individual acquitted on grounds of insanity to be
committed to a mental institution until he was able
to demonstrate that he was not dangerous to himself or others even though he was not mentally ill
was invalid. The state has no punitive interest to
justify involuntary commitment in these circumstances. But a state may confine a mentally ill
person if it shows by clear and convincing evidence
that the individual is presently mentally ill and
dangerous. *Foucha v. Louisiana* (1992).

A state statute permitted guardians and members
of the immediate family of a mentally retarded
person who is the subject of an involuntary commitment to participate in the proceeding as if they
were full parties. Applying *Mathews v. Eldridge*,

the Court held that such participation by third parties did not violate due process. Their participation did not increase "the risk of an erroneous deprivation" of the mentally retarded person's liberty interest. Close relatives and guardians might be able to offer valuable insights concerning the mentally retarded person which would increase the accuracy of the commitment decision. The presence of additional parties in the commitment proceeding might, it is true, increase the likelihood of commitment if those parties favor commitment. But the due process clause does not require that a state adopt an alternative procedure just because the alternative might produce a result more favorable to the party challenging the existing procedure. *Heller v. Doe* (1993).

While the *Mathews v. Eldridge* balancing test suggests an objective measure of the demands of due process, the above cases indicate the subjective value choices that are actually involved. Further, many commentators find in the Court's calculus a utilitarian bias that denigrates the intrinsic worth of constitutional rights. Use of the calculus arguably ignores the effects of governmental action on particular individuals and focuses on claimants generally. Finally, in assessing the Court's efforts to objectively measure the costs and benefits of administrative actions, a serious question is raised over the capacity of courts to weigh the competing interests at stake.

CHAPTER VI

EQUAL PROTECTION

The Fourteenth Amendment guarantees that "[n]o State shall make or enforce any law which shall deny to any person within its jurisdiction the equal protection of the laws." While there is no corresponding provision applicable to the federal government, the Fifth Amendment Due Process Clause applies the same limitation to the federal government. *Bolling v. Sharpe* (1954). While it has been argued that the Equal Protection Clause was intended only to require equal enforcement of the laws, it is established today that the Clause is a guarantee of equal laws, *i.e.,* that the law itself may be challenged as violating equal protection.

But what is the nature of this equal protection right? The Clause cannot be a proscription against legal classification since different treatment of persons and things that are not similarly situated is essential to lawmaking. Men and women, adults and children, aliens and citizens need not always be treated alike under the law. But it is also clear that these classes cannot be treated differently on an arbitrary basis. The Court's answer has been that a legal classification must be reasonable in relation to the objectives of the law. "A reasonable classification is one which includes all persons who are similarly situated with respect to the purpose of the law." Tussman & TenBroek, The Equal Protection of the Laws, 37 *Calif.L.Rev.* 341 (1944).

In developing this general demand for reasonableness in government classifications, the Court has employed three different standards of review. During the Warren Court era, the Court developed a two-tiered system of equal protection review. In most socioeconomic cases, the Court employs a traditional rationality standard. If the classification is rationally related to a permissible government objective, equal protection is satisfied. But when a law intentionally employs a "suspect classification" or when a classification significantly burdens the exercise of a "fundamental right," strict scrutiny is applied. The burden is on the government to establish that the classification is necessary to a compelling governmental interest; there must be no less onerous alternative available. During the Burger Court years, a third approach emerged. Used mostly in gender and illegitimacy cases (quasi-suspect classifications), the "intermediate" standard of review requires that a classification be substantially related to an important government interest.

In fact, the Rehnquist Court may be moving towards an abandonment of a rigid three-tiered approach to equal protection review. In the main, the law of equal protection has consisted largely in working out the standards for judicial scrutiny of legal classifications. For a time, it appeared that a more indeterminate "reasonableness" standard might emerge in which the degree of judicial scrutiny would vary depending on the identity of the classes (or nature of the classifying trait, *e.g.*, race, sex, age), the severity of the burden imposed by the classification, and the nature of the government interests supporting the classification (*e.g.*, national security and foreign affairs will produce increased judicial deference. *Rostker v. Goldberg* (1981) [male only draft registration upheld]). From time to time various Justices—Marshall, Stevens, Rehnquist—have suggested that there is really only one standard of review and that the degree of judicial scrutiny should vary with the nature of the discrimination and the significance of the burden on fundamental interests. Whether these later variations or departures from the three-tiered theme will capture a majority of the Court is uncertain. At the present, the three-tiered approach remains dominant.

A. TRADITIONAL EQUAL PROTECTION

The traditional approach to equal protection review has been marked by extreme judicial self-restraint and a marked concern for limiting the judicial role vis a vis the legislature. While the Court occasionally frames the traditional equal protection standard in terms of whether a classification is based upon some difference having a "fair and substantial relation" to the legislative objective [*F.S. Royster Guano Co. v. Commonwealth of Virginia* (1920)], the standard most frequently used imposes on the challenging party the burden of proving that the classification is not "rationally related to furthering a legitimate government interest." *Massachusetts Board of Retirement v. Murgia* (1976) [state law requiring retirement of police officers at age 50 held constitutional under rational basis test]. The judicial deference embodied in this test has almost invariably resulted in socioeconomic laws being upheld against equal protection challenges.

Government must have a *legitimate interest* in imposing a classification; the objective of the law cannot itself violate the Constitution. But what if the real objective of the law is impermissible or if the classification is not rationally related to the law's true purpose. The courts have shown extreme deference requiring only that the law serve some conceivable legislative purpose. As long as the classification rationally serves a legitimate objective that the legislature *might* have had, it will be upheld. *United States Railroad Retirement Bd. v. Fritz* (1980) [since there was a "plausible reason" for the congressional enactment, it was "constitutionally irrelevant whether this reasoning in fact underlay the legislative decision"]. This deference reflects concern over the propriety of judicial probing of the legislative purpose, the problem of identifying and proving the actual purpose of a collegial lawmaking body and concern that the legislature would simply re-enact the law while masking its impermissible objectives.

The classification must be *rationally related* to the law's objective. In challenging a law, the litigant might argue that the classification is under- or over-inclusive or a combination of the two. Under-inclusion arises when a law does not burden or benefit all those who are similarly situated. Over-inclusive classifications extend the benefit or burden of the law not only to those who are similarly situated with respect to the objective of the law but to others as well (*e.g.*, dragnet searches, internment of Japanese–Americans during World War II because of the danger of sabotage).

However, neither of these conditions is likely to make a classification unreasonable if the rationality standard is applied; only if the law is totally arbitrary will it fail. Perfectly drawn classifications in lawmaking are essentially impossible. The Court has stated: "A classification having some reasonable basis does not offend [equal protection] merely because it is not made with mathematical nicety or because in practice it results in some inequality." *Lindsley v. Natural Carbonic Gas Co.* (1911). Further, the *Lindsley* Court noted that "if any state of facts reasonably can be conceived that would sustain the classification, the existence of that state of facts at the time the law was enacted must be assumed." More recently, the Court has captured this principle by holding that a challenging party cannot prevail where an issue remains debatable. *Minnesota v. Clover Leaf Creamery Co.* (1981). The state need not choose the best means to accomplish its purpose but only select a rational means.

The judicial deference in rationality review is suggested by the Court's decision in *Railway Ex-*

press Agency v. New York (1949). A city ordinance banning advertising on trucks but exempting those advertising their own wares on their trucks was held not to violate equal protection. The law was designed to promote the permissible objective of public safety, stated Justice Douglas for the Court, and the local authorities "may well have concluded" that those advertising their own products would not present the same traffic problem in light of the nature and extent of their advertising. The Court deferred to the legislative capacity to assess "practical considerations based on experience." Nor was the fact that the city had not banned even more vivid displays relevant. "It is no requirement of equal protection that all evils of the same genus be eradicated or none at all." Government must be able to experiment and may deal with a problem one step at a time.

Justice Jackson, concurring, rejected the Court's rationale since there was not even a pretense that traffic hazards posed by the two classes of truck advertising differed. Instead, he urged that the legislature may also have had the objective of curbing the nuisance posed by truck advertising and that legitimate objective would make the classification rational. "[T]here is a real difference between doing in self-interest and doing for hire, so that it is one thing to tolerate action from those who act on their own and it is another thing to permit the same action to be promoted for a price."

This same deference exhibited in *REA* was employed by the Burger Court in rejecting a challenge to a state ban on nonreturnable milk containers while permitting use of other nonreturnable containers, *e.g.,* paperboard cartons. The legislature might have concluded that even a limited ban would foster greater use of environmentally desirable alternative containers. *Minnesota v. Clover Leaf Creamery Co.* (1981). A grandfather clause exempting two vendors from a general ban on pushcart dealers in the New Orleans French Quarter was sustained against an equal protection challenge. The city could rationally conclude that the exempted vendors had become part of the distinctive charm of the Quarter. *New Orleans v. Dukes* (1976).

A federal statute denying food stamps to strikers was sustained on traditional equal protection analysis. The federal statute denied eligibility for food stamps to households while a member was on strike; the statute also precluded an increase in the allotment of food stamps even though the striker's income had decreased. Conceding that the statute was harder against strikers than "voluntary quitters," the Court nonetheless upheld the statute since it bore a rational relationship to the legitimate government objective of avoiding favoritism in labor disputes. *Lyng v. International Union, UAW* (1988).

While invocation of the traditional rationality test in modern economic regulation cases has regularly resulted in rejection of the equal protection challenge, the Court is capable of putting some teeth into rationality review. This was presaged in a concurring opinion by Justice Blackmun in *Logan v.*

Zimmerman Brush Co. (1982): "The State's rationale must be something more than the exercise of a strained imagination; while the connection between means and ends need not be precise, it, at the least, must have some objective basis." In *Metropolitan Life Insurance Co. v. Ward* (1985), the state interest in promoting domestic business was deemed not to be a legitimate purpose under the Equal Protection Clause when achieved through the imposition of a discriminatory domestic preference tax statute. And, in *City of Cleburne v. Cleburne Living Center* (1985), the Court held that requiring a special use permit for a proposed group home for the mentally retarded was not rationally related to any permissible government purpose and therefore violated equal protection.

Also illustrative of this less deferential approach is a state tax case where a West Virginia county assessed real property on the basis of its recent purchase price. The county made only minor modifications to assessments of properties not recently sold. This valuation scheme was held to violate equal protection since it resulted in a gross disparity in the assessed value of comparable properties over a long period of time. Equal protection tolerates some margin for mistake in the valuation of property for tax purposes and does not require constant reevaluation of all assessed properties on the basis of the latest market developments. But seasonal attainment of a rough equality among similarly situated taxpayers is required by equal protection. *Allegheny Pittsburgh Coal Co. v. County Commission* (1989). The Court, thus, has demonstrated that it will sometimes use in socio-economic cases a non-deferential "reasonableness" test which involves a real evaluation of the state interests supporting a classification and a true balancing of the competing interests.

The traditional deferential rationality test, however, is still the norm in economic regulation. A California property tax, Proposition 13, employed an acquisition value taxation scheme resulting in long-time owners paying lower taxes based on historic property values while newer owners paid higher taxes based on more recent values. The California tax law did not violate equal protection. The distinction between new owners and long-time owners met the rationality test. First, discouraging rapid turnover in ownership helped neighborhood stability. Second, new owners had no reliance interest in a pre-existing system of taxation as did the long-time owners. *Nordlinger v. Hahn* (1992). Similarly, a federal statute subjecting satellite master antenna television (SMATV) facilities that serviced separately owned and managed buildings to regulation but exempting from regulation SMATV facilities servicing buildings owned and managed by a single owner was upheld. The statutory distinction was rational because Congress might have concluded that commonly owned facilities were small in size and that costs of regulation would exceed the benefits to be derived therefrom. In addition, the legislature is not required "to articulate its reasons for enacting a statute" and it is irrelevant whether the rationale justifying legislation "actually motivated the legislature." *FCC v. Beach Communications, Inc.* (1993).

A Kentucky law requiring a more demanding procedure for the involuntary commitment of the mentally ill than the mentally retarded was upheld, 5–4, against an equal protection challenge. The Kentucky law made two distinctions between the two classes. First, the burden of proof for the involuntary commitment of the mentally retarded was clear and convincing evidence but the burden of proof required for the mentally ill was beyond a reasonable doubt. Second, guardians and immediate relatives of mentally retarded persons were permitted to participate in the involuntary commitment proceedings of a mentally retarded person but not in such proceedings for a mentally ill person. Citing *Cleburne*, rational basis review was applied to the classification. Less demanding procedures for the mentally retarded than the mentally ill were rational because mental retardation was a static condition and was easier to diagnose. In addition, treatment of the mentally retarded tends to be less invasive than the treatment accorded to the mentally ill. Classifications which do not involve fundamental rights or "proceed along suspect lines" are accorded a "strong presumption of validity." *Heller v. Doe* (1993).

B. THE NEW EQUAL PROTECTION

1. CLASSIFYING TRAITS

While the traditional ratiohality test is generally used for equal protection review, the courts will employ a stricter scrutiny when government employs a suspect or quasi-suspect classification. For example, when the government intentionally acts on the basis of race or national origin (and sometimes alienage), strict scrutiny will be used. And when intentional gender or illegitimacy classifications are employed, the law will be tested using intermediate review. The judicial deference normally accorded governmental action is no longer appropriate when the government intentionally confers benefits or imposes burdens on the basis of such classifying traits.

But why isn't deference appropriate? What justification is there for judicial activism when such classifications are involved? Perhaps the suspect treatment of racial classifications could be explained simply as a matter of history: "[T]he clear and central purpose of the [Equal Protection Clause] was to eliminate all official state sources of invidious racial discrimination in the States." *Loving v. Virginia* (1967) [miscegenation laws held violative of equal protection and due process]. But this explanation would probably justify only judicial activism in race cases. A broader rationale can be found in the concept of "stigma" or "caste." When a particular group is regularly treated as inferior, ["implying inferiority in civil society," *Strauder v.*

West Virginia (1880)], special judicial solicitude is appropriate. This concern is enhanced when the discrimination visited on the class is pervasive in the society. It is argued that government must treat persons on the basis of merit and not on the basis of immutable traits or stereotypes. See *Regents of the Univ. of California v. Bakke* (1978).

Another approach to the rationale making certain classifications suspect is grounded on Justice Stone's famous footnote four in *United States v. Carolene Products Co.* (1938): "[P]rejudice against discrete and insular minorities may be a special condition, which tends seriously to curtail the operation of those political processes ordinarily to be relied upon to protect minorities, and may call for a more searching judicial scrutiny." These specially disadvantaged groups, these insular minorities, have a special claim to judicial protection since the ordinary political processes for redressing injury are closed to them because of prejudice.

The discrimination that entails heightened judicial scrutiny may be contained in legislation. In *Loving v. Virginia* (1967), the Court held that a statute prohibiting marriages between the races violates equal protection. Chief Justice Warren, for the Court, noted that "the fact of equal application does not immunize a statute from the very heavy burden of justification which the Fourteenth Amendment has traditionally required of state statutes drawn according to race." The Court found "no legitimate overriding purpose independent of invidious racial discrimination that might justify the racial classification." See *Strauder v. West Virginia* (1880) [murder conviction of a Black by a jury from which Blacks were excluded by state law violates equal protection].

Alternatively, discrimination may be found in the administration of a racially-neutral law. *Yick Wo v. Hopkins* (1886) dealt with a law requiring a permit to operate a laundry unless the laundry was located in a brick or stone building. Yick Wo, a Chinese alien, was convicted for operating a laundry without a permit. His conviction was reversed. Whatever the merits of the statute itself, the law had been administered in a discriminatory manner. Statistics demonstrated that permits were denied to Chinese applicants while being granted to others. "Though the law itself be fair on the face yet, if it is applied and administered by public authorities with an evil eye and unequal hand, the denial of equal justice is still within the prohibition of the Constitution." The Court found no reason for the discrimination other than hostility to the race and nationality of the Chinese applicants. The administration of the law, therefore, violated equal protection.

Whether it is a law or its enforcement that is the subject of the litigation, the challenger must establish that the classification is intentional [de jure] before a stricter standard of judicial review will be used. While the discriminatory effect or impact of a law or administrative action may be evidence of discriminatory intent, "[a] purpose to discriminate must be present. Standing alone, [disproportionate impact] does not trigger the rule that racial classifications are to be subjected to the strictest scrutiny and are justifiable only by the weightiest of considerations." *Washington v. Davis* (1976) [fact that police qualifying test produces racially discriminatory results held insufficient to establish equal protection violation]. Discrimination need not be the sole or even the primary basis for the law, but it must be one of the objectives. *Village of Arlington Heights v. Metropolitan Housing Dev. Corp.* (1977). While discriminatory effects may suffice for some congressional civil rights statutes [*Griggs v. Duke Power Co.* (1971)], the key for constitutional litigation is whether the discrimination is intentional. *Hunter v. Underwood* (1985) [state constitutional provision disenfranchising persons convicted of a crime of moral turpitude held violative of equal protection because, while racially neutral on its face, the original enactment was motivated by a desire to discriminate against Blacks].

The fact that the government adopts a policy knowing discrimination will result does not satisfy this requirement of intent. In *Personnel Adm. of Massachusetts v. Feeney* (1979), a state law granting a preference for veterans in state employment was challenged as discriminating against women since veterans are overwhelmingly males. In rejecting the equal protection challenge, the Court stated: " 'Discriminatory purpose' implies more than intent as volition or intent as awareness of consequences. It implies that the decision-maker selected or reaffirmed a particular course of action at least in part 'because of,' not merely 'in spite of,' its adverse effects upon an identifiable group." While the state legislature could foresee that use of the preference policy would disadvantage women, its objective was to benefit veterans, male or female—it acted "in spite of" the negative effect on women.

Discrimination may be overt or covert. A statute or a formal administrative rule or regulation may be discriminatory on its face. In *Palmore v. Sidoti* (1984), the Court, per Chief Justice Burger, held that a state court's overt consideration of community racial bias in determining child custody (the white mother was cohabiting with a black male) violated equal protection. Chief Justice Burger noted that the state court "was entirely candid and made no effort to place its holding on any ground other than race." While the objective of granting custody based on the best interests of the child represented a substantial interest, "[t]he effects of racial prejudice, however real, cannot justify racial classification."

Similarly, in a case involving a black accused, it was held that a prosecutor could not, consistent with equal protection, use peremptory challenges to exclude black jurors solely on their race. A showing of purposeful discrimination in selection of a jury makes out a prima facie case for the defendant. The state then has the burden of coming forward with a neutral explanation for its use of peremptory challenges against black jurors. *Batson v. Kentucky* (1986). [But cf. *Holland v. Illinois* (1990), where the equal protection issue was not raised by the defendant. Instead the defendant unsuccessfully contended that the use of peremptory challenges to exclude all black jurors from the petit jury of a white defendant violated his Sixth Amendment right to trial by an impartial jury: "The Sixth Amendment requirement of a cross-section on the venire is a means of asserting, not a representative jury (which the constitution does not demand), but an impartial one (which it does)"]. *Batson* has been extended to race-based peremptory challenges by the defense on the theory that enforcement of such challenges by the judicial process constitutes state action. *Georgia v. McCollum* (1992). Similarly, the rule of *Batson* prohibiting race-based peremptory challenges also applies to civil litigation. *Edmonson v. Leesville Concrete Co.* (1991).

If the discriminatory intent is not overt, the challenger seeking to secure stricter review must prove that the facially neutral government action is, in fact, covert discrimination. Statistical impact may provide useful evidence of discriminatory intent, but absent a stark pattern of impact, unexplainable on other grounds, "impact alone is not determinative and the Court must look to other evidence." *Village of Arlington Heights.* Similarly, foreseeability or knowledge of discriminatory impact can provide evidence of covert prejudice. *Personnel Adm. of Massachusetts v. Feeney* (1979). Proof of discriminatory purpose can sometimes be found in the historical context in which government actions are taken, in departures from the usual substantive or procedural policies employed, or from contemporaneous statements by government decision-makers. *Village of Arlington Heights.*

In voting discrimination cases challenging use of at-large electoral systems, the courts have looked to the "totality of the circumstances" to determine if there is discriminatory intent. In *Rogers v. Lodge* (1982), the Court upheld a lower court finding of discriminatory intent by county officials based on evidence of the failure of any Black candidate to be elected, the impact of past discrimination on Black political participation, the failure of elected officials to consider the needs of the Black community, past racial discrimination in contexts other than voting, the socioeconomic conditions of the county's Blacks and electoral requirements minimizing the voting strength of racial minorities in the county.

If the challenger proves discrimination was *a* factor motivating the government's action, the burden shifts to the government. The state may seek "to rebut the presumption of unconstitutional action" by showing that discriminatory purpose was not the basis for the discriminatory impact. *Washington v. Davis* (1976). It may also be possible for the state to avoid strict scrutiny by proving that it *would* (not could) have reached the same result even if discrimination had not been involved. *Village of Arlington Heights.* Essentially, the state argues that its racially-motivated action did not cause the harm. Alternatively, the state must overcome the strict standard of equal protection review.

a. Race and Ethnic Origins

Race is the paradigm suspect classification. As Chief Justice Burger explained in *Palmore v. Sidoti* (1984): "A core purpose of the Fourteenth Amendment was to do away with all governmentally-imposed discrimination based on race. Classifying persons according to their race is more likely to reflect racial prejudice than legitimate public concerns; the race, not the person, dictates the category." Simply, race should generally be a neutral factor in allocating public benefits and burdens. When race is used, the law is suspect and "subject to the most exacting scrutiny." *Palmore*. The government has the burden of proving that the classification is necessary to a compelling interest. Application of this standard of review generally results in a holding that the law violates equal protection. But see *Korematsu v. United States* (1944) [exclusion of Japanese–Americans from areas of West Coast during World War II upheld on grounds of extreme military danger from sabotage]. The same strict scrutiny treatment has been given to discrimination based on national origin. *Hernandez v. Texas* (1954) [discrimination against Mexican Americans in selection for jury service, reflecting "community prejudice," held unconstitutional].

(1) *Segregation in Education.* Through most of the 20th century, even officially-sanctioned racial segregation in matters of "social, as distinguished from political equality," was held not to violate the Equal Protection Clause. *Plessy v. Ferguson* (1896) [law requiring "equal but separate" railway accom-

modations for whites and blacks upheld]. But in
Brown v. Board of Educ. (1954), the Court held that
"[s]eparate educational facilities are inherently unequal and that laws requiring or permitting racial
segregation of schools violate equal protection."
While the Court in *Brown I* emphasized the harm to
children from educational segregation, the rejection
of state sanctioned racial segregation was summarily extended to other public facilities.

Would racial segregation in the schools that was
not attributable to government action violate equal
protection? Today *Brown I* is treated by the courts
as a condemnation *only* of intentional or de jure
state segregation. *Keyes v. School Dist. No. 1*
(1973). Racial segregation in the schools which is
not proven to be the product of intentional government action (*i.e.*, de facto segregation) does not
violate equal protection even if it is proven that
children suffer from the educational racial segregation. The state has no constitutional duty to remedy racial segregation in schools which it has not
caused. Thus, even a formerly de jure segregated
school system which has desegregated is not constitutionally required to remedy segregation produced
by changing social conditions. *Pasadena City Bd. of
Educ. v. Spangler.* (1976).

Determining when a school has "desegregated"
has produced an uncertain standard. The Court
has held that a public school district which has been
under a judicial order to desegregate may still implement a new busing plan which would result in
one race schools. But the school district must have

complied in good faith with the initial judicial order and the vestigial remnants of past de jure discrimination must have been eradicated as far as practicable. Regulatory control of a federal court over a public school system should not continue beyond the time necessary to remedy consequences of "past intentional discrimination." *Board of Education of Oklahoma City v. Dowell* (1991). Moreover, the federal district court may relinquish supervision and control over a school district in incremental stages. The court's objective must be to remedy the violation and to restore to the local authorities a school system which is operating in compliance with the constitution. "A transition phase in which control is relinquished in a gradual way is an appropriate means to this end." *Freeman v. Pitts* (1992).

If a school district is found to have engaged in de jure racial segregation, what remedy is appropriate? The remedy in the *Brown* litigation might have been simply to order the immediate admission of members of the plaintiff class to the schools on a nonracial basis. But in *Brown v. Board of Educ.* (1955) (*Brown II*), the Court, perhaps anticipating strong public reaction, ordered only desegregation "with all deliberate speed." However, federal courts were instructed to retain jurisdiction, apply equitable principles (no specific standards were provided) and to assure that school boards engaged in good faith compliance to desegregate "as soon as practicable." *Brown II* is generally credited (or blamed) for having launched modern public law litigation where courts engage in large scale institutional reform to remedy a generalized injury to a large class.

The aftermath of *Brown II* was a slow process of resistance and desegregation. Eventually, the Court held that "[c]ontinued operation of segregated schools under a standard of allowing 'all deliberate speed' for desegregation is no longer constitutionally permissible. Under explicit holdings of this Court, the obligation of every school district is to terminate dual systems at once and to operate now and hereafter only unitary schools." *Alexander v. Holmes County Bd. of Educ.* (1969).

Today, if the courts find that a school system has engaged in de jure, intentional racial segregation, the school system has an affirmative duty to desegregate—"to take whatever steps might be necessary to convert to a unitary system in which racial discrimination would be eliminated root and branch." *Green v. County School Bd. of New Kent County* (1968). Any actions by a school board under this affirmative duty which have even the *effect* of impeding desegregation violate equal protection. *Wright v. Council of Emporia* (1972). Again, note that school systems that are only de facto segregated have no affirmative duty to desegregate and can act even if their actions have disparate racial impact. This same principle governs segregation between city and suburbs (*i.e.,* interdistrict litigation). A challenger must show "that racially discriminatory acts of the state or local school districts, or of a single school district have been a substantial cause of interdistrict segregation." *Milliken v. Bradley*

(1974). De jure, intentional segregation establishes the constitutional wrong creating the affirmative duty to desegregate.

Even though a state has established race neutral policies to govern its system of state supported colleges, the state has not necessarily met its affirmative obligation to dismantle a de jure system of segregated higher education. Thus, admission requirements for Mississippi's public universities required higher standardized test scores for its historically white institutions than for its historically black institutions. Similarly, the historically white institutions offered more comprehensive programs and graduate degrees. These policies and practices, attributable to a heritage of de jure segregated higher education, have segregative effects, including the continuing racial identifiability of colleges within the state system and thus constitute impermissible state action. *United States v. Fordice* (1992).

When segregation is a product of a law requiring a dual school system as in *Brown II,* de jure segregation is clearly present. But as the courts began to confront northern style segregation involving covert racial discrimination, finding intentional or purposeful discrimination has been more problematical. Generally, the courts engage in a fact-based inquiry into purpose, focusing on policies and actions of the school board. In addition, certain judicially-crafted presumptions have proven valuable. If it is established that a substantial part of a school system is de jure segregated, there is a presumption that other segregation in the district is de jure. To rebut this presumption, the school board must prove that the de jure segregation was an isolated event, not affecting other parts of the system. *Keyes v. School Dist. No. 1* (1973). The existence of past de jure segregation in a district creates a presumption that present segregation is attributable to the past conduct. Further, "actions having a foreseeable and anticipated disparate impact are relevant evidence to prove the ultimate fact, forbidden purpose." *Columbus Bd. Educ. v. Penick* (1979); *Dayton Bd. of Educ. v. Brinkman* (1979) (*Dayton II*).

When de jure segregation is established, the federal courts have broad equity powers to remedy the constitutional wrong. In *Swann v. Charlotte–Mecklenburg Bd. of Educ.* (1971), the Court provided guidance to lower courts for "balancing of the individual and collective interests." While lower courts may not require racial balance in the schools, the Chief Justice concluded that numerical ratios based on the racial composition of the students in the system (which were used by the lower court) provide "a useful starting point" in fashioning an effective remedy. A reasonable amount of busing where needed to remedy past discrimination was also approved. But the Chief Justice warned against use of busing where the time and distance involved threatens the health or education of the children.

Judicial approval of busing has provided a rash of federal and state efforts to curb use of this remedy. Congressional measures which simply curb use of federal funds for busing or limit the executive in seeking busing orders may be constitutional. But there is greater doubt whether Congress can prevent a federal court from ordering busing where it is the only effective way of remedying de jure segregation. In such cases, denial of the remedy can be viewed as effectively denying the constitutional right or might intrude on the judicial function in violation of the separation of powers.

State laws prohibiting the use of busing, at least when de jure segregation is present, are unconstitutional. *North Carolina State Bd. of Educ. v. Swann* (1971). State legislative efforts to curb *voluntary* busing programs aimed at de facto segregation have failed to generate any general principle. When the legislation alters the usual process for making school policy decisions by denying a school board the power to order busing, the law is based on the racial characteristic of the policy and violates equal protection. *Washington v. Seattle School Dist. No. 1* (1982). But a state constitutional amendment which would prevent state courts from ordering busing to remedy de facto segregation was upheld. The law was racially neutral on its face and was not enacted for a discriminatory purpose. School boards could still order busing. Equal protection does not prevent repeal of a particular judicial remedy which goes beyond the federal constitutional mandate. *Crawford v. Board of Educ. of Los Angeles* (1982).

The scope and the limits on a federal district court's power to remedy de jure racial segregation

were delineated by Justice White for the Court in
Missouri v. Jenkins (1990). A federal district
court's order increasing local taxes to satisfy a
school desegregation decree violates the principles
of federal/state comity. Although the federal district court may not itself raise taxes, it may order
local governments to do so if it is necessary to
implement its school desegregation decree even
though the increase will exceed the limit on taxes
imposed by state statute. The latter holding was
objected to by four dissenters who complained, per
Justice Kennedy, against the Court's "casual embrace of taxation imposed by the unelected, life-
tenured federal" judiciary because of its disregard
of "fundamental precepts for the democratic control
of public institutions."

Missouri v. Jenkins (1990) held that the federal
court may enjoin the operation of state laws where
they obstruct conformance with federal constitutional guarantees. Further, the ability of the federal courts to enforce the Fourteenth Amendment
was in no way diminished by the reservation in the
Tenth Amendment of nondelegated powers to the
states. The Fourteenth Amendment is by its very
language addressed to the states. The federal
courts are, therefore, permitted to "disestablish local government institutions that interfere with the
[Fourteenth Amendment's] commands."

Spallone v. United States (1990) outlined some
further do's and don'ts for federal courts in the
context of judicially imposed desegregation orders.
A federal district court order which imposed mone-

tary sanctions upon individual Yonkers city council members for failure to vote to implement a housing desegregation order was invalidated as an abuse of discretion. Judicial imposition of such sanctions on legislators constituted a perversion of the normal functioning of the legislative process because it caused legislators "to vote, not with a view to the interest of their constituents or of the city, but with a view solely to their own personal interest." On the other hand, imposition of a daily fine on the city for the duration of the contempt had a reasonable likelihood of success and was valid. In the event the sanction against the city failed to bring compliance with the judicial order, imposition of contempt citations against individual legislators until they voted to implement the judicial order would presumably be valid.

(2) *Affirmative Action.* Courts regularly use race as a basis for remedying past de jure segregation. *Swann v. Charlotte–Mecklenburg Bd. of Educ.* (1971). But a government agency may also voluntarily adopt race-conscious policies in awarding benefits in order to benefit racial minorities. Further, government frequently requires private parties who have not been found to have personally engaged in racial discrimination to take action that would benefit racial minorities. Is strict scrutiny appropriate for these intentional racial classifications? In short, what is the status of affirmative action programs under the equal protection guarantee?

In *Regents of the Univ. of California v. Bakke* (1978), the Court considered the validity of a special minority admissions program at University of California–Davis medical school. Under the plan, a separate committee considered applicants from four designated minority groups for 16 out of 100 available places. Alan Bakke, a white, was denied admission even though he had higher numerical scores than some special program applicants who were admitted. The Court held 5–4 that the Davis plan violated Title VI of the 1964 Civil Rights Act. More significantly, five Justices accepted the principle that a public university can use a race-conscious admissions program; that the use of racial considerations will not *per se* violate equal protection. But there was not agreement among these five justices on when a race conscious admissions program would pass constitutional muster.

Justice Powell, providing the critical swing vote, argued for the use of strict scrutiny in reviewing discrimination even if whites as a class are disadvantaged. Arguing for a principle of individualized justice, Powell stressed that equal protection is a personal right of an individual to be judged on the basis of individual worth and merit and not on the basis of class membership. Applying strict scrutiny, Powell concluded that, while remedying societal discrimination may be a compelling interest for some governmental institutions, a state medical school was not in a position to fashion an appropriate remedial program. Decisions based on race must be made by government policy makers in a position to narrowly tailor the race-conscious program to further the compelling interest with the least burden to the disadvantaged race (*i.e.*, structural due process). Promoting diversity in the student body, on the other hand, is a compelling interest for a university. However, the Davis quota system, in which consideration for 16 places was based solely on race, was not a "necessary" means for promoting diversity. Race could simply be considered a plus factor in admissions decisions. The Davis program, Powell concluded, violated both Equal Protection and Title VI and he joined with four other Justices who decided only that the Civil Rights Act was violated.

Four other Justices (led by Justice Brennan) argued for intermediate equal protection review. Whites as a class do not have any of the traditional factors of suspectness. They are not the special beneficiaries of the Fourteenth Amendment nor have they historically experienced pervasive discrimination. They are not politically insular. And, most important, the racial classification imposes no stigma on them; whites are not viewed as a caste, as morally inferior. While strict scrutiny was therefore inappropriate, rationality review was also inadequate. Benign classification often masks race prejudice. Preferential treatment tends to foster race consciousness in government and racial stereotypes that run counter to the ideal of success based on individual merit and achievement. Brennan concluded that benign racial classification "must serve important governmental objective and must be substantially related to achievement of those objectives." Since "minority underrepresentation is substantial and chronic, and the handicap of past discrimination is impeding access of minorities to medical school," the Davis program was substantially related to government's interest in remedying the discriminatory effects of societal discrimination.

In *Fullilove v. Klutznick* (1980), seven Justices again accepted the principle that race conscious programs to remedy discrimination may be constitutional. The Court 6–3 upheld, against a Fifth Amendment challenge, a congressional statute requiring that 10% of federal public work project funds be used by a grantee to purchase services or supplies from businesses controlled by designated minorities. Chief Justice Burger, in a plurality opinion joined by Justices White and Powell, applied a "most searching examination," concluding that the program would satisfy either the strict scrutiny or intermediate review tests. Stressing the broad remedial powers of Congress, the Chief Justice noted that the program was limited in extent and duration and was narrowly-tailored to the end of remedying discriminatory treatment of minorities on public works projects.

Justice Powell, concurring, reaffirmed his support for a strict scrutiny standard which he found satisfied. Justices Marshall, Brennan and Blackmun, using their *Bakke* intermediate test, concurred. Justice Stevens dissented based on his conclusion that the Act was not narrowly tailored to achieve any remedial objective. Only Justices Stewart and Rehnquist, dissenting, adopted the view that "the government may never act to the detriment of a person solely because of that person's race. The color of a person's skin and the country of his origin are immutable facts that bear no relation to ability, disadvantage, moral culpability or any other characteristics of constitutionally permissible interest to government. In short, racial discrimination is by definition invidious discrimination." Even a race-conscious judicial decree is permitted only to remedy "the actual effects of illegal race discrimination."

In *City of Richmond v. J. A. Croson Co.* (1989), a city ordinance requiring prime contractors awarded city construction contracts to subcontract at least 30% of the dollar amount of each contract to "Minority Business Enterprises" was held, per Justice O'Connor, to violate equal protection. A key development in *Croson* was its holding that the "standard of review under the Equal Protection Clause is not dependent on the race of those burdened or benefitted by a particular classification." Strict scrutiny should therefore be applied to all racial classifications: "Absent searching judicial inquiry into the justification for such race-based measures, there is simply no way of determining what classifications are 'benign' or 'remedial' and what classifications are in fact motivated by illegitimate notions of racial inferiority or simple racial politics." Justices Marshall, joined by Justices Blackmun and Brennan, dissented. They still adhered to use of an intermediate standard of review for remedial racial classifications.

Could a municipal minority set aside program ever meet a strict scrutiny standard? Justice

O'Connor responded to this question in *Croson* by saying that elimination of government's passive support for private racial discrimination would be a compelling interest. However, Richmond's ordinance was not based on a record that showed specific statistical findings that the city was actually remedying specific past acts of illegal racial discrimination by the city. In addition, the city's plan was not narrowly drawn. Racial quotas should not be used where other means such as case-by-case consideration was possible. Rather than race-conscious remedies racially neutral alternatives should be used. The city is required to consider the effects of its remedial program on third parties. It is also bound to limit the program's scope and duration.

Croson's larger meaning for the future of affirmative action has stimulated considerable controversy. The minority set aside upheld on the federal level in *Fullilove* was distinguished on two grounds. First, Congress has unique legislative enforcement powers under Sec. 5 of the Fourteenth Amendment. Second, Congress included a waiver procedure in its set aside program showing that Congress clearly recognized that the scope of the discrimination problem would vary from market to market. A question *Croson* was silent on, however, was whether its view that strict scrutiny applied to all racial classifications undermined the race conscious remedy upheld in the context of public university education in *Bakke*. However, *Bakke* is arguably distinguishable on the ground that, even under the *Croson* framework, the value of diversity in education represented by the use of race as a factor in admissions is a compelling governmental interest.

The status of state mandated race-conscious programs in non-educational contexts was rendered even more problematic by a ruling throwing doubt on the validity of North Carolina redistricting legislation which had created a district so irregular in shape that it resembled a " 'bug splattered on a windshield.' " White constituents alleged that the district was formed without regard to " 'compactness, contiguousness, geographical boundaries or political subdivisions.' " The Court concluded that where state redistricting legislation is inexplicable on any other grounds than race, *i.e.*, the creation of a black Congressional district, such legislation should be accorded the same strict scrutiny that would be extended to other state legislation which classified citizens on the basis of their race, the fact that the district was created as a remedial response to the federal Voting Rights Act notwithstanding. On remand, if the charge of racial gerrymandering remained uncontradicted, the district court was ordered to consider whether the North Carolina plan was narrowly tailored to further a compelling governmental interest. *Shaw v. Reno* (1993).

Croson had held that the strict scrutiny standard should be used for state mandated local racial classifications. *Fullilove* had stressed that race-conscious programs mandated by Congress warrant more deferential treatment. This deference to Congress was underscored when two FCC minority preference policies aimed at encouraging diversity of viewpoint in broadcast programming were held, 5–4, not to violate equal protection. One FCC policy at issue gave an "enhancement" to a license applicant which could show minority participation and management in its ownership. This "enhancement" was then weighed with other factors when the FCC had to make a comparative choice among competing applicants for the same license. The other minority preference policy at issue was the "distress sale" policy which allowed a licensee facing revocation or non-renewal to transfer the license to a qualified minority-controlled firm without having to undergo an FCC hearing as would normally be required. Both of these FCC policies had been specifically required and approved by Congress. The policies served First Amendment values and implemented the important government interest in promoting diversity of information and views in broadcast programming. Both the FCC and Congress had found that there was a substantial nexus between the minority preference programs and increasing minority ownership and participation in broadcasting. Moreover, the programs did not involve quotas and nonminorities were still able to compete for licenses. *Metro Broadcasting, Inc. v. FCC* (1990).

In short, the teaching of *Metro Broadcasting, Inc. v. FCC* (1990), per Justice Brennan, is that in light of the deference that should be accorded Congressionally mandated benign race-conscious programs, such programs, if substantially related to the achievement of an important governmental interest do not violate equal protection so long as they do not impose "undue burdens on nonminorities." The two challenged FCC minority preference programs did not have to satisfy the strict scrutiny standard of review. Instead, in such circumstances, an intermediate standard of review should be applied. Of the five Justices who comprised the majority in *Metro Broadcasting*, three—Brennan, Marshall and White—are no longer on the Court. Whether their successors will adhere to their view that a standard of review more relaxed than strict scrutiny should apply where congressionally mandated benign race-conscious programs are involved remains to be seen.

b. Alienage: The "Sometimes Suspect" Classification

The status of alienage classifications is confused. Generally, it can be said that when a state awards public benefits to citizens, but denies them to aliens, such classification is "inherently suspect and subject to close judicial scrutiny." Aliens are "a prime example, of a single 'discrete and insular' minority for whom such heightened judicial solicitude is appropriate." *Graham v. Richardson* (1971) [15 year durational residency requirement for alien eligibility for welfare benefits violates equal protection]. Critics of the use of strict scrutiny argue that alienage is not an immutable characteristic and that citizenship requirements are frequently used in the Constitution.

Application of the strict scrutiny standard has resulted in the invalidation of statutes barring aliens from competitive civil service positions [*Sugarman v. Dougall* (1973)] and from eligibility for membership in the state bar [*In re Griffiths* (1973)]. In *Nyquist v. Mauclet* (1977), a statute barring resident aliens from state financial assistance for education unless they indicated an intent to apply for citizenship was invalidated. See also *Plyler v. Doe* (1982) [discrimination against illegal aliens in providing free education held to violate equal protection].

Nevertheless, the Court has fashioned an important "political function" exception to this strict scrutiny principle. When aliens are excluded from voting or from positions "that are intimately related to the process of democratic self-government" [*Bernal v. Fainter* (1984), state law barring aliens from eligibility to become notaries public held unconstitutional], only rationality is required. When the government job relates to "political" rather than "economic" functions and involves broad discretion in the formulation and implementation of the state's self-definition, the state can choose to exclude those who are not part of the political community. Thus, a state may require that police be citizens since police officers "are clothed with authority to exercise an almost infinite variety of discretionary powers" involving the public. *Foley v. Connelie* (1978). The critical role played by teachers in shaping pupils for their roles as citizens and in preserving basic values was stressed by the Court in upholding the exclusion of aliens from public school teaching. *Ambach v. Norwick* (1979). Probation officers, like police and school teachers, were held to exercise official discretion over individuals, thus qualifying for the "political function" exception in *Cabell v. Chavez–Salido* (1982).

But the fact that a state designates a public official as occupying a critical political function will not be decisive. *Bernal v. Fainter* (1984) held 8–1 that the position of notary public does not qualify for the political function exception. Justice Marshall for the Court applied a two part test. First, Justice Marshall examined the specificity of the classification to determine if it was substantially over or under-inclusive which "tends to undercut the governmental claim that the classification serves legitimate political ends." While the exclusion applied to only one particular post and thus was not over-inclusive, there was greater concern over whether the law was under-inclusive since citizenship was not required for many state jobs involving similar functions. But the Court found a second inquiry dispositive—a notary public does not "perform functions that go to the heart of representative government." Justice Marshall characterized the functions of a notary as clerical and ministerial. Such officials are not, he said, "invested with policy-making responsibility or broad discretion in the execution of public policy" involving authority over individuals. The state failed to show that the law "furthers a compelling state interest by the least restrictive means practically available."

Strict scrutiny is thus a "sometimes" test when state alienage classifications are challenged. Also, strict scrutiny does not apply to federal laws based on alienage. The federal power over immigration and naturalization produces greater judicial deference. When federal classifications are challenged as violative of the Fifth Amendment, the courts ask only whether the classification is reasonable. *Mathews v. Diaz* (1976) [alien eligibility for federal medical assistance benefits conditioned on 5–year residency and application for permanent residence upheld]. This federal prerogative in matters involving immigration and naturalization has also been used as a basis for finding federal preemption of state laws burdening aliens. *Toll v. Moreno* (1982) [state university policy denying tuition benefits to certain aliens conflicts with federal immigration policy].

c. Gender Classification: Intermediate Review

It is doubtful that the framers of the Fourteenth Amendment ever contemplated that the Equal Protection guarantee would become a vehicle for challenging legal disabilities imposed on women. Prior to the 1970's, gender classifications were generally upheld against equal protection challenge using the highly-deferential rationality standard of review. The discriminatory laws being challenged generally reflected a paternalistic attitude regarding the need to protect "the weaker sex" and assumptions about a woman's proper place in society. *Goesaert v.*

Cleary (1948) [state law excluding women from being licensed as bartenders, but exempting wives and daughters of male bar owners, upheld]. But in 1971 a major shift occurred. In *Reed v. Reed* (1971), the Court unanimously struck down a state law giving men a preference over women as administrators of estates. The state claimed that the law rationally served the public interests in avoiding disputes and in limiting the workload of the probate courts. Chief Justice Burger, however, castigated the preference as "the very kind of arbitrary legislative choice forbidden by the Equal Protection Clause." While the opinion used the language of rationality, the review was more searching and demanding. But if not rationality, what standard should govern gender classification?

Justice Brennan, for a plurality in *Frontiero v. Richardson* (1973) [federal law allowing male servicemen to claim their spouse as dependent but requiring servicewomen to prove the spouse's dependency held unconstitutional], argued for strict judicial scrutiny. He cited the historic discrimination against women, the numerous "gross, stereotypical distinctions between the sexes" in the laws, the "pervasive, although at times more subtle, discrimination" against women today, and the immutability of the sex characteristic which "frequently bears no relation to ability to perform or contribute to society," as rendering sex classifications "inherently suspect." But critics of strict scrutiny for gender classifications have challenged Justice Brennan's efforts to analogize discrimination against

women with the suspectness accorded race and ethnicity classifications. Justice Powell in *Bakke* as-
serts that "the perception of racial classifications as
inherently odious stems from a lengthy and tragic
history that gender-based classifications do not
share." While gender-based laws do often reflect
stereotypical thinking about women, critics argue
that there is no stigma imposed nor does the classification reflect any assumption that women as a
class are morally inferior. And, critics add, women
are not a "discrete and insular minority"—they
have been guaranteed the vote since 1920 and constitute a numerical majority.

The challenge to a stricter review standard for
gender classifications is more compelling when the
discrimination is visited upon males as a class.
Certainly men have not been politically insular,
have not suffered from pervasive historical discrimination and bear no stigma or sense of inferiority
from separate treatment. On the other hand, any
allocation of government benefits or burdens based
on gender, rather than merit, challenges the ideal of
individualized justice. Use of the immutable characteristic of sex, whether the discrimination is directed against women or men, often perpetuates
gender stereotypes.

Today, gender classifications are subject to an
intermediate standard of review: "Classifications
by gender must serve important governmental objectives and must be substantially related to
achievement of those objectives." *Craig v. Boren*
(1976). *Craig* held unconstitutional a law prohibit-

ing the sale of 3.2% beer to males under the age of 21 and to females under 18. While the state had an important interest in traffic safety, statistics offered by the state on the incidence of drunk driving among males and females did not establish that the gender discrimination was closely related to that objective. Justice Rehnquist in dissent challenged the Court's use of a new standard of equal protection review. Both the phrases "important objective," and "substantial relation," he argued, "are so diaphanous and elastic as to invite subjective judicial preferences or prejudices."

A useful example of intermediate review is *Mississippi University for Women v. Hogan* (1982), where the Court struck down (5–4) a women-only admissions policy at a state nursing school. While the plaintiff Hogan could audit courses at the women's school, in order to obtain credits he would have to travel a considerable distance to a state-supported coeducational nursing school: "A similarly situated female would not have been required to choose between foregoing credit and bearing that inconvenience." While the state claimed that the admissions policy served compensatory objectives (*i.e.*, affirmative action), Justice O'Connor for the Court concluded that the state had failed to establish that this was its actual objective given the lack of any disadvantage suffered by women in entering nursing. Instead, the policy tended to perpetuate stereotypic notions and that, she asserted, is illegitimate. Even if the policy were intended as compensatory, Justice O'Connor added, the state had not proven that the policy was "substantially and directly related to its proposed compensatory objective." Allowing males to audit classes undermined any claim that women would be adversely affected by the presence of males. Since the state did not provide a males-only nursing school, the Court did not address the validity of such a "separate but equal" policy.

For the dissent, the fact that the state policy added to the educational choices available to women with only a minimal personal inconvenience to the plaintiff meant that only rationality review was appropriate. There simply was no stereotyping involved and no sex class discrimination involved. Even using heightened review, the dissent argued that the state policy was substantially related to promoting diversity in educational choices.

In *J.E.B. v. Alabama* (1994), the Court extended *Batson v. Kentucky* and its ban on race-based peremptory challenges to gender-based peremptories: "[G]ender, like race, is an unconstitutional proxy for juror competence and impartiality." Gender-based peremptories by state actors perpetuated "invidious, archaic and overbroad" stereotypes about the relative abilities of men and women. Aren't *all* peremptory challenges based on social stereotypes? Peremptory challenges not based on group characteristics such as race or gender do not reinforce historical patterns of state and socially imposed race and gender discrimination. Justice O'Connor concurred but urged that *J.E.B.* should be confined to the use by *government* of gender-based peremptory strikes. In light of *Shelley v. Kraemer* (1948), it is doubtful that *J.E.B.* can be so cabined.

The student should not assume that the stricter review used in gender cases mirrors strict scrutiny and will necessarily result in a determination of invalidity. At times, the Court not only hedged on the appropriate degree of scrutiny in middle tier equal protection but has engaged in an analysis markedly similar to rationality review. In *Michael M. v. Superior Court of Sonoma County* (1981), the Court held 5–4 that California's statutory rape law, making only men liable for the criminal conduct, does not violate equal protection. Justice Rehnquist's plurality opinion, while reciting the *Craig* intermediate review test, described this standard as simply giving "sharper focus" to the traditional rationality standard. Noting that men as a class are not "in need of the special solicitude of the courts," Justice Rehnquist stressed that a gender classification which "realistically reflects the fact that the sexes are not similarly situated in certain circumstances," will be upheld.

While *Craig* and *Hogan* appeared to probe for the actual or true legislative purpose in enacting the law, *Michael M.* tends to stress the reality of mixed legislative objectives and avoids judicial probing of the claimed state objective. The Court, however, did not suggest that any conceivable purpose would support the gender classification. The state's proffered objective, *i.e.*, preventing illegitimate teenage pregnancies, was to be accepted since it was "at least one of the 'purposes' of the statute." That the law may also have been enacted for "an alleged illicit legislative motive" of protecting the virtue and chastity of young women could not be used to strike down the otherwise constitutional law.

Turning to the relation of the gender classification to the state's "strong" social welfare objective, Justice Rehnquist stressed that men and women are not similarly situated with respect to the law since only women could become pregnant. It followed that the state could direct deterrence to males who do not suffer from the consequences of their illicit conduct. This was not a law that "rests on the baggage of sexual stereotypes" but a law that "reasonably reflects the fact that the consequences of sexual intercourse and pregnancy fall more heavily on the female than on the male."

To the claim that a gender neutral statute, punishing both male and female offenders, would be at least equally effective as a deterrent, Justice Rehnquist replied: "The relevant inquiry, however, is not whether the statute is drawn as precisely as it might have been, but whether the California Legislature is within constitutional limitations. Further, a gender neutral statute might not be as effective since the exemption of females enhances the statute's enforceability by encouraging disclosure."

The above cases suggest that in applying middle tiered review, the Court will generally not invalidate laws for want of an important legislative objective. Instead, whether the classification substantially serves the important objective is the focal point of dispute. The more a law is perceived as resting on archaic stereotypes rather than on identifiable differences between the sexes, the more it is likely to be held violative of equal protection.

(1) *Affirmative Action.* Gender classification, like race classification, can be employed for the benign objective of compensating women for past discrimination. However, the problem of identifying if an allegedly benign law is actually a product of romantic paternalism and reflects sexual stereotypes has proven difficult. As *Mississippi Univ. for Women v. Hogan* indicates, the Court will not simply accept a state claim of affirmative action but will probe to determine if the law is truly compensatory. See *Califano v. Goldfarb* (1977) [presumption that widows but not widowers are dependent used in determining Social Security death benefits is based on an "archaic and overbroad generalization." Discrimination against female workers who receive less insurance protection for their spouses than male workers, violates equal protection].

Even if a law is treated as a benign classification favoring women, the Court will employ an intermediate standard of review in determining if the discrimination against males is justified—the classification must be shown to be substantially related to the compensatory objective. Remedying past discrimination against women is invariably held to be an important interest. But once again, the problem is whether the gender classification is sufficiently related to the compensatory end. In *Orr v. Orr* (1979), the Court struck down a state law authorizing alimony awards to wives but not husbands. While the objective of helping needy spouses and compensating women for past discrimination during marriage were deemed sufficiently important, the Court determined that sex, in this instance, was not "a reliable proxy for need." Since individualized determinations of financial need were already part of the divorce proceedings, there was no reason to presume that women generally were needy. "Where as here, the State's compensatory and ameliorative purposes are as well served by a gender neutral classification as one that gender-classifies and therefore carries with it the baggage of sexual stereotypes, the State cannot be permitted to classify on the basis of sex." See *Wengler v. Druggists Mut. Ins. Co.* (1980) [law presuming wives dependency for determining workers' compensation health benefits held unconstitutional. While providing for needy spouses is an important objective, the administrative convenience achieved by presuming dependence is an inadequate justification].

While the above cases establish that the state's invocation of a benign objective will not invariably survive equal protection scrutiny, a truly benign classification has a fairly good chance of surviving stricter scrutiny. Compensation for past discrimination is accepted as an important government interest. And if the law is tailored to remedying specific past discrimination against women, it will be upheld. See, *e.g., Kahn v. Shevin* (1974) [state property tax exemption for female widows, but not male widowers, upheld]; *Schlesinger v. Ballard*

(1975) [law providing for later mandatory discharge for female military officers, because of lesser opportunities for women officers to be promoted, upheld]; *Califano v. Webster* [social security formula permitting women to exclude more low wage earning years than men, based on past discrimination against women, upheld]. But, once again, if the law is simply stereotyping, or if it is merely administratively convenient to use gender, the law will probably fail the stricter scrutiny standard.

(2) *Mothers and Fathers.* Laws built on stereotypes concerning the roles of mothers and fathers in relation to their children are likely to be held violative of equal protection under intermediate review. For example, a law permitting the mother, but not the father, of an illegitimate child, to veto the child's adoption, regardless of the child's development or the relation of the father to the child, violates equal protection. *Caban v. Mohammed* (1979). However, when a law is perceived by the Court, not as a gender classification, but as discrimination within a particular class, a rationality test has been used. Thus in *Parham v. Hughes* (1979), the Court held that a law barring a father who has not legitimated a child from suing for wrongful death as a means of promoting legitimization does not violate equal protection. Only the father, not the mother, could legitimate the child. Men and women therefore were not similarly situated and need not be treated alike. The law discriminates only against those fathers who have failed to legitimate their child.

d. Illegitimacy Classification: Intermediate Review

Illegitimacy classifications, while not subject to strict scrutiny, have been reviewed under a middle tier standard since the 1960's. *Levy v. Louisiana* (1968) [law barring unacknowledged illegitimates from recovering for wrongful death of mother held to violate equal protection]; *Weber v. Aetna Casualty & Surety Co.* (1972) [law barring illegitimates from collecting death benefits violates equal protection]. However, the Court has been highly ambivalent over the precise standard to be applied [see *Labine v. Vincent* (1971), upholding an intestate succession law subordinating illegitimate children to other relatives, using a deferential form of judicial review] and even more uncertain as to how heightened review is to be applied in particular fact contexts. While the rationale for a heightened judicial scrutiny has sometimes been found in the "fundamental personal rights" attached to the familial relationship, the Court has more often emphasized the questionable character of illegitimacy as a classifying trait: "the legal status of illegitimacy is, like race and national origin, a characteristic determined by causes not within the control of the illegitimate individual and bears no relation to the individual's ability to participate in and contribute to society."

The ambiguity in application of heightened review in illegitimacy cases is indicated by comparing *Trimble v. Gordon* (1977) and *Lalli v. Lalli* (1978). In *Trimble,* the Court 5–4 struck down an Illinois law barring illegitimate children from inheriting intestate from their fathers unless they were acknowledged and the parents married; the law was not substantially related to a permissible state interest. While the state interest in protecting legitimate family relationships was proper, this end could not be pursued by means of sanctions against illegitimate children. The state had "substantial" interests in dealing with the difficulty of proving paternity and the danger of spurious claims but the law was not "carefully tuned to alternative considerations." The law broadly disqualified illegitimate children even where paternity could be established.

But in *Lalli,* the state interest in a just and orderly disposition of property on death and the problems of proving paternity were sufficient to uphold a state law providing that illegitimate children could inherit intestate from the father only if a court had determined paternity during the father's lifetime. The law was upheld even though it admittedly barred inheritance by some illegitimates where paternity could clearly be established. In a plurality opinion, Justice Powell stated that unlike the law in *Trimble,* the means were not "so tenuous that [the law] lacks the rationality contemplated by the Fourteenth Amendment; it did not disqualify an unnecessarily large number of [illegitimate] children."

In spite of *Lalli,* the Court has continued to apply intermediate review. In *Mills v. Habluetzel* (1982), a Texas law requiring that a paternity suit to establish child support had to be brought before the illegitimate child is one year old was unanimously held "not substantially related to a legitimate state interest." And, in *Pickett v. Brown* (1983), a unanimous Court held a two year statute was not "substantially related" to the state interest in avoiding stale or fraudulent claims. In *Clark v. Jeter* (1988), Pennsylvania's state statute requiring suits to establish paternity to be brought within six years of an illegitimate child's birth was invalidated on equal protection grounds. Even a six year period of limitation did not necessarily provide a reasonable opportunity to assert a claim on behalf of an illegitimate child. *Jeter* applied the intermediate standard of review. The six year period was not substantially related to the state's interest in preventing litigation of stale or fraudulent claims. Other Pennsylvania statutes permitted paternity to be litigated much longer than six years after the illegitimate child's birth.

While it is difficult to draw any principles from the Court's application of heightened equal protection review in illegitimacy cases, it does appear that laws based on stereotypes or prejudice against illegitimates or that impose insurmountable or extremely burdensome obstacles to illegitimates securing equal treatment with legitimate children will be held unconstitutional. While the state may be able to cite important interests which support the laws, the Court will determine that the means used are not "substantially related" to the achievement of the state objective.

e. Other Bases of Classification

It is unlikely that the present Court will add new classifying traits to the lists of suspect and quasi-suspect classifications. Age classifications [*Massachusetts Board of Retirement v. Murgia* (1976)] and wealth classifications [*James v. Valtierra* (1971) public housing referendum, *Harris v. McRae* (1980), abortion funding for indigents], for example, are not suspect and are subject only to rationality review.

In rejecting mental retardation as a suspect classification in *City of Cleburne v. Cleburne Living Center* (1985), Justice White, for the Court, stated: "[W]here individuals in the group affected by a law have distinguishing characteristics relevant to interests the state has authority to implement, the Courts have been very reluctant, as they should be in our federal system and with our respect for separation of powers, to closely scrutinize legislative choices as to whether, how and to what extent those interests should be pursued. In such cases, the Equal Protection Clause requires only a rational means to serve a legitimate end." Since mental retardation is a characteristic that government can legitimately employ in many decisions, *e.g.,* benign laws to aid the retarded, the Court would not treat legislative action embodying differential treatment as suspect. Using a non-deferential rational basis standard, the Court held that the application of the zoning law to exclude a group home for the mentally retarded was not rationally related to a legitimate government purpose.

2. FUNDAMENTAL RIGHTS

Suspect classifications analysis focuses on the basis on which classifications are drawn. But stricter equal protection review can also be triggered by what is lost as a result of a classification. If a classification significantly burdens the exercise of a fundamental right, strict judicial scrutiny will be applied, *i.e.*, the classification must be necessary to a compelling government interest. Again the student should note the Court's increasing discontent with a rigid tiered approach to equal protection law. There are indications that the Justices are moving towards a sliding scale approach similar to substantive due process review.

The clearest example of fundamental rights equal protection law arises when a law discriminates in the right to engage in protected constitutional activity. For example, when a classification significantly burdens the exercise of express First Amendment rights, traditional rationality review is inappropriate. If a law bars all picketing of schools [*Police Dept. of Chicago v. Mosley* (1972)] or residences [*Carey v. Brown* (1980)], except for labor picketing, such content-based discrimination is more closely scrutinized. "When government regulation discriminates among speech related activities in a public forum the Equal Protection Clause mandates that the legislation be finely tailored to serve substantial state interests, and the justifications offered for any distinctions, its draws must be carefully scrutinized." *Ibid.* See *Larson v. Valente* (1982) [charitable solicitation law operating to discriminate against non-traditional religion such as Moonies held violative of the Establishment Clause].

Similarly, if a law discriminates in the exercise of implied rights a stricter mode of judicial review will be applied. As indicated below, laws significantly burdening the right of interstate travel [*Shapiro v. Thompson* (1969)] or the right to marry [*Zablocki v. Redhail* (1978)], have been subjected to a more probing judicial scrutiny.

The most challenging aspect of fundamental rights equal protection involves stricter review of classifications burdening the exercise of rights derived from the Equal Protection Clause itself. When government classification significantly burdens equality of access to the exercise of the franchise or equality of access to criminal or civil justice, strict scrutiny will be used even though there is no independent right. The Equal Protection Clause itself protects against discrimination in regard to these fundamental interests. While the Court has not repudiated the Warren Court legacy in this area of fundamental rights and interests, the Court has shown little inclination to use the Equal Protection Clause as a font for equalizing social inequalities. See *Dandridge v. Williams* (1970) [welfare]; *San Antonio Ind. School Dist. v. Rodriguez* (1973) [education].

a. Interstate Travel

There is no express right to travel in the Constitution. Nevertheless, in holding that a one-year durational residency requirement for welfare assistance violates equal protection, the Court stated: "Since the classification here touches on the fundamental right of interstate movement, its constitutionality must be judged by the stricter standard of whether it promotes a *compelling* state interest." *Shapiro v. Thompson* (1969). The source of this fundamental right to travel interstate has never been clearly established by the Court although it is generally treated as an implication of our federalist system embodied in the very structure of the Constitution. In any case, when a state requires that newcomers live in the state for a fixed period of time as a condition of eligibility for benefits otherwise available on an equal basis to residents, the Court has generally invoked fundamental rights equal protection and closely scrutinized the laws. *Memorial Hospital v. Maricopa County* (1974) [one year durational residency requirement for indigents receiving public medical care held violative of equal protection]; *Dunn v. Blumstein* (1972) [one year durational residency requirement for voting held violative of equal protection]; *Shapiro*.

But not every burden on interstate migration is subjected to strict scrutiny review. *Bona fide* residency requirements are generally upheld using rationality review. *McCarthy v. Philadelphia Civil Service Com'n* (1976) [law requiring city employees to be city residents upheld]; *Martinez v. Bynum* (1983) [residence requirement for free public education upheld]. Such laws do not discriminate on the basis of travel but upon whether or not the claimant has acquired residence. Upon achieving such residence, the person participates fully in the program.

In *Sosna v. Iowa* (1975), the Court applied rationality review in upholding a one-year durational residency requirement for divorce. In distinguishing previous durational residency requirements held invalid, Justice Rehnquist explained that the recent traveler was not "irretrievably foreclosed from obtaining some part of what she sought; her access to the courts was merely delayed." The distinction appears to turn on the significance of the burden on the right of interstate migration. When the state law deters or imposes a significant "penalty" on the exercise of the right, strict scrutiny is used. *Shapiro* involved loss of basic necessities of life. Justice Marshall in *Maricopa County* stated: "Whatever the ultimate parameters of the Shapiro penalty analysis, it is at least clear that medical care is as much a 'basic necessity of life' to an indigent as welfare assistance. And, government privileges or benefits necessary to basic sustenance have often been viewed as being of greater constitutional significance than less essential forms of governmental entitlements." Apparently, delay in securing a divorce is not a sufficient "penalty" on travel as to merit strict scrutiny. See *Starns v. Malkerson* (1971) [one year durational residency requirement for lower tuition rates at state universities upheld]; *Jones v. Helms* (1981) [distinctions in the sanction for a parent who abandons a child which depends on whether the defendant left or remained in the state upheld since defendant's own conduct qualified his right to travel].

In some travel cases, the Court has verbally employed the rationality test but struck down the state law. For example, the Court in *Zobel v. Williams* (1982), held that a statutory scheme, whereby Alaska distributed income derived from its natural resources to adult citizens based on the length of each citizen's residence violated equal protection. Unlike the durational residency cases, no Alaska resident was totally denied benefits for failure to satisfy a threshold waiting period. Instead, "fixed permanent distinctions between an ever increasing number of perpetual classes of *bona fide* residents, based on how long they have been in the State" determined the amount of benefits. In this case, the state interests in creating an incentive for establishing residence in Alaska and encouraging prudent management of the funds and resources were not rationally served by distinctions drawn between those already resident in the state. The asserted state interest in recognizing past contributions of citizens was "not a legitimate state purpose" since it would "open the door to state apportionment of other rights, benefits and services according to length of residence." Since the discriminatory treatment could not pass even the rationality test, the Court found it unnecessary to determine if "enhanced scrutiny" would be appropriate. Thus the Court did not determine whether discrimination in access to funds not earmarked for any particular purpose such as welfare or medical services would constitute a "penalty" on the fundamental right triggering strict scrutiny.   See *Attorney Gen. v. Soto–Lopez* (1986) [state employment preference limited to veterans residing in the state at the time of entering military service held unconstitutional. Plurality used strict scrutiny, citing right to travel and equal protection.   Concurring justices used a rationality test].

b. Marriage and Family Life

Zablocki v. Redhail (1978), involved a Wisconsin criminal statute requiring court approval for marriage of any parent having child support obligations. Approval would not be given if support obligations were not being met or if the individual could not prove that the out of custody children would not become public charges.   In invalidating the law, Justice Marshall, for the Court, stated: "[Since] the right to marry is of fundamental importance, and since the classification at issue here significantly interferes with the exercise of that right, we believe that 'critical examination' of the state interests advanced in support of the classification is required."   As a result of the Wisconsin classification, persons (especially the poor) could be coerced into foregoing their right to marry or be absolutely prevented from getting married.   This impact was a significant burden on the right.   While the state interests in counseling parents regarding support obligations and assuring the welfare of out of custody children were "sufficiently important state interests," the means were not "closely tailored to effectuate only those interests."

But as *Zablocki* suggests, if the challenged classification does not significantly interfere with the decision to marry, only rationality review is appropriate. *Califano v. Jobst* (1977) [exception to rule terminating disability benefits upon marriage, providing continued benefits for persons who marry another disabled entitled to benefits, upheld using rationality review]. Consider also the abortion funding cases, involving funds for maternity care but not for abortion. In *Harris v. McRae* (1980), the Court held that since there was no violation of the constitutionally protected substantive right, (*i.e.*, no significant burden) the rational basis test was applicable. The Hyde Amendment was rationally related to the legitimate government objective of protecting potential life.

c. Voting

The Fifteenth Amendment, § 1, prohibits abridgment of the franchise by the federal or state government on the basis of race, color or previous condition of servitude. *Gomillion v. Lightfoot* (1960) [racially discriminatory gerrymander held violative of Fifteenth Amendment]. But the Court has never held that there is a general constitutionally protected right to vote. States possess broad power to define residence, age and citizenship qualifications and may choose to fill offices by appointment rather than election. However, if the state does grant the franchise, then the Equal Protection Clause requires equality of access to the franchise.

Is the equal protection mandate satisfied if the government acts rationally? The Court has held that the right to vote is a fundamental interest in democratic society because it is "preservative of other civil and political rights," *Reynolds v. Sims* (1964). When government classification significantly burdens its exercise a more searching review is usually required. This principle applies whether the electoral scheme denies or merely dilutes the franchise.

(1) *Voting Qualifications.* In *Harper v. Virginia State Bd. of Elections* (1966), the Court held state poll taxes violative of equal protection. While Justice Douglas, for the Court, relied in part on wealth discrimination as suspect, it was his treatment of voting discrimination that has endured. While noting the close relation of voting to express First Amendment rights, Justice Douglas did not deem it necessary to fashion a right to vote: "For it is enough to say that once the franchise is granted to the electorate, lines may not be drawn which are inconsistent with the Equal Protection Clause." The states could not fix voter qualifications that "invidiously discriminate." Nor was rationality review appropriate. Since voting was fundamental, "classifications which might restrain [it] must be closely scrutinized and carefully confined." Since wealth or fee paying had no relation to one's ability to participate intelligently in the electoral process, the poll tax requirement violated equal protection.

Limiting the franchise for school district elections to parents of school children and property owners and lessees was held violative of equal protection in *Kramer v. Union Free School Dist. No. 15* (1969). Chief Justice Warren, stressing the importance of non-discriminatory participation in the electoral process to representative government, employed strict scrutiny review. The ordinary presumption of constitutionality, he argued, was based on the assumption that the state law-making institutions are structured fairly. When this assumption is challenged in the lawsuit, "exacting judicial scrutiny" is required. Applying this standard, the disenfranchisement failed. Assuming that the state might limit the vote to those primarily interested in the electoral outcome, the classification was not tailored to achieve that goal. The classification included many with only a limited interest in the election while excluding many citizens having a distinct interest in school district decisions. See *Cipriano v. Houma* (1969) [limitation of franchise to property taxpayers for approving issuance of revenue bonds held unconstitutional]; *Phoenix v. Kolodziejski* (1970) [restriction of voting for general obligation bonds to property taxpayers held unconstitutional]. The basic principle is that when state classifications restrict the franchise on grounds other than residence, age, and citizenship, the law cannot stand unless the state can demonstrate that the limitation serves a compelling state interest. *Hill v. Stone* (1975) [requiring majority of property tax-payers to approve sale of bonds for city library held unconstitutional].

But there is an exception to this basic principle for "special interest" elections. In *Salyer Land Co. v. Tulare Lake Basin Water Storage Dist.* (1973), the Court applied the rational basis test in upholding an electoral scheme which limited the franchise to landowners and allocated votes by the assessed value of the land. Strict scrutiny was deemed inappropriate for reviewing the water district's election system because of "its special limited purpose and of the disproportionate effect of its activities on landowners as a group." Essentially the water district was not an entity exercising general governmental powers and a limitation of the franchise to those with a "special interest" in its activities was reasonably related to achieving the statutory objectives. See *Ball v. James* (1981) [limitation of franchise to landowners and weighted voting scheme for electing directors of a large water reclamation district upheld under the rationality test]. But *Ball* should be compared with *Quinn v. Millsap* (1989) where a Missouri constitutional provision requiring ownership of real property as a condition for membership on a board of freeholders was held to violate equal protection on the basis of a rationality standard of review. That the board did not exercise general governmental powers was deemed irrelevant. The right to be considered for public service is guaranteed by equal protection even if the board only recommends proposals and does not enact laws directly. Appreciation for community issues and

concern for the community does not rationally depend on property ownership. State objectives could
have been achieved by more narrowly tailored
means. *Ball* was distinguished in *Millsap* on the
ground that the water reclamation district at issue
in the former had a peculiarly narrow function and
a special relationship to the class of landowners.

Durational residency requirements provides another context in which fundamental rights equal
protection has been used to overturn restrictions on
the franchise. While *bona fide* residency requirements for voting do not violate equal protection,
durational residency requirements which significantly burden both the fundamental interest in
voting and the right to travel are frequently held
invalid using strict scrutiny. *Dunn v. Blumstein*
(1972) [one year state residency requirement held
to violate equal protection]. But some limited term
durational residency requirements shown to be necessary to serve the state interest in preventing
election fraud have survived searching review.
Marston v. Lewis (1973) [50 day durational residence requirement upheld].

(2) *Diluting the Franchise.* Equal protection also
safeguards against electoral schemes which significantly burden the *effectiveness* of the votes of particular classes of voters. For example, state apportionment schemes which undervalue the votes of
particular voters deny "the opportunity for equal
participation by all voters." *Reynolds v. Sims*
(1964). In *Reynolds,* the Court held that the Equal
Protection Clause requires that the seats in both

houses of a bicameral state legislature must be apportioned on a population basis. This "one-person, one-vote" principle was applied to congressional districting in *Wesberry v. Sanders* (1964) pursuant to Art. I, Sec. 2, which requires that members of Congress be chosen "by the people of the several states." While the principle applies to all local government units [*Hadley v. Junior College Dist.* (1970)], the unit may be so specialized in purpose and limited in powers as not to qualify as governmental. See *Salyer Land Co.*

But the *Reynolds* Court also indicated that "mathematical exactness or precision is hardly a workable constitutional requirement. Somewhat more flexibility may be constitutionally permissible with respect to state legislative apportionment than in congressional districting." In fact, the courts have required that states "come as nearly as practicable to population equality" in congressional districting. In rejecting a .7% maximum percentage deviation between districts in *Karcher v. Daggett* (1983), the Court noted that the state must show "with some specificity that a particular objective required the specific deviation in its plan." In state districting, however, the Court has permitted minor deviations without any state justification [*White v. Regester* (1973), upholding average deviation of 2% and maximum deviation of 9.9%] and substantial deviation when justified by the state's interest in preserving its traditional political boundaries. *Mahan v. Howell* (1973) [16.4% deviation upheld]; *Brown v. Thomson* (1983) [16% average deviation and maximum deviation of 89% upheld where grant of a single seat to a county entitled to it numerically was not a significant cause of the population deviations].

Multimember districting, while it may impede particular groups from achieving political power proportionate to their numbers, does not, without more, violate equal protection. *City of Mobile v. Bolden* (1980). But when an examination of the "totality of the circumstances" establishes that the electoral scheme was borne of an intent to racially discriminate (*i.e.,* a suspect classification), the Fourteenth Amendment is violated. *Rogers v. Lodge* (1982). Similarly, giving a minority disproportionate political power by requiring an extraordinary majority [*Gordon v. Lance* (1971), 60% referenda approval for incurring bond indebtedness upheld] or concurrent majorities [*Town of Lockport v. Citizens for Community Action* (1977), separate majority of urban and rural voters required for new county charters upheld], does not necessarily violate equal protection.

Another method by which the value of the franchise can be diluted is through limitations on access of candidates and parties to the ballot. Restrictions prevent voters from expressing their preferences through their vote. In fact, such restrictions on access place "burdens on two different, although overlapping, kinds of rights—the right of individuals to associate for the advancement of political beliefs and the right of qualified voters, regardless of their political persuasion, to cast their votes effectively." *Williams v. Rhodes* (1968) [variety of state requirements limiting the access of new political parties to ballot held violative of equal protection because it gave Democrats and Republicans "a complete monopoly"]. On the other hand, restrictions on access are said to serve important state interests "in protecting the integrity of their political process from frivolous or fraudulent candidacies, in ensuring that their election processes are efficient, in avoiding voter confusion caused by an overcrowded ballot, and in avoiding the expense and burden of run-off elections." *Clements v. Fashing* (1982) [state laws limiting an office holder from running for a different office held not violative of equal protection using a rational basis test].

In most cases, the Court has applied strict scrutiny to such access restrictions, requiring the state to demonstrate that the differential treatment is "necessary to further compelling state interests." But a plurality of the Court in *Clements v. Fashing* stated: "Not all ballot access restrictions require 'heightened' equal protection scrutiny." The plurality argued that it is necessary to examine each law to determine the extent of the burden it imposes—"The inquiry is whether the challenged restriction unfairly or unnecessarily burdens 'the availability of political opportunity.' *Lubin v. Panish*."

The imposition of filing fees on indigent candidates as a necessary condition of access (*i.e.,* no alternative means of access is provided) is likely to be held unconstitutional. *Bullock v. Carter* (1972); *Lubin v. Panish* (1974). But the fate of laws requiring that candidates or parties demonstrate a certain level of community support in order to secure access is far less certain. If the law "affords minority political parties a real and substantially equal opportunity for ballot qualification," it can be upheld even under a strict scrutiny standard. *American Party of Texas v. White* (1974) [ballot access requirement that parties which had not demonstrated significant voter support in previous elections provide petitions signed by 1% of voters and limiting pool of signatories to those who had not participated in another party's primary or nominating process upheld]; *Storer v. Brown* (1974) [one year disaffiliation provision upheld as furthering state's compelling interest in the stability of its political system]. On the other hand, if the provisions are virtually exclusionary of independents and minority parties, the requirements will be held invalid. *Anderson v. Celebrezze* (1983) [early filing deadlines for petitions of independent candidates seeking ballot access but not for candidates of major parties held to violate freedom of political association but relying heavily on equal protection cases]; *Williams v. Rhodes*. The Court's approach in the *Anderson* case suggests that the First Amendment analysis might receive increased attention from courts as an alternative to fundamental rights equal protection.

d. Access to Justice

A highly confused area of equal protection law involves the treatment of economic obstacles such as fee requirements limit... civil justice. The primary s... proper role of equal protection... process analysis. In *Griffin v. I*... Court held that the state must pr... scripts to indigent criminal defenda... transcript was required to obtain "ad... a effective" appellate review. Justice Black, ...and rality opinion, invoked both due process and... protection principles. On the latter issue, he... knowledged that the state was under no constitutional duty to provide appellate review. But while there was no constitutional right to appeal, "that is not to say that a state that does grant appellate review can do so in a way that discriminates against some convicted defendants on account of their poverty. There can be no equal justice where the kind of trial a man gets depends on the amount of money he has."

Justice Harlan, dissenting, challenged the plurality's reliance on equal protection analyses, asserting "that the basis for that holding is simply an unarticulated conclusion that it violates 'fundamental fairness for a State which provides for appellate review [not] to see to it that such appeals are in fact available to those it would imprison for serious crimes.' That of course is the traditional language of due process." His critique of the plurality's use of equal protection has vital importance for fundamental rights equal protection analysis generally. The plurality, he argued, even while acknowledging the absence of any constitutional right to an appeal,

the Equal Protection Clause it-
was dra〉 ve duty to lift the handicaps flow-
self "a ence in economic circumstances."
ing fr ion, he argued, demands equal treat-
Equa〉es not require a state to "give to some
men〉quires others to pay for."

wh〉qual protection approach to the problem of
〉 to criminal justice was even more clearly
a〉pted by the Court in *Douglas v. California*
963). In upholding the right of indigent criminal
defendants to appointed counsel on their first state
appeal as of right, the Court, per Justice Douglas,
branded the state's refusal to provide counsel as
"discrimination against the indigent." Justice
Douglas acknowledged that "absolute equality" in
access to justice was not constitutionally required,
but contended that counsel was of critical importance in the *"one and only appeal* an indigent has
as of right." The state had drawn "an unconstitutional line between rich and poor." *Compare Ross
v. Moffitt* (1974) [no right to appointed counsel for
indigent on discretionary appeal].

And once again Justice Harlan challenged the
Court's reliance on equal protection analysis. He
accepted that the Clause prohibited discrimination,
"between 'rich' and 'poor' *as such.*" But he argued
that this was very different from saying that equal
protection "prevents the State from adopting a law
of general applicability that may affect the poor
more harshly than it does the rich, or, from making
some effort to redress economic imbalances while
not eliminating them entirely." While the states

may have a moral obligation to alleviate the effects of poverty, "[t]o construe the Equal Protection Clause as imposing an affirmative duty to cure economic disparities," he argued, "would be to read into the Constitution a philosophy of leveling that would be foreign to many of our basic concepts of the proper relations between government and society." Indeed, he questioned whether the state could ever satisfy an affirmative duty to equalize access to the justice system.

Griffin–Douglas focused on an ill-defined vital interest in equal access to criminal justice coupled with an obvious concern for discrimination against indigents. Yet there was no independent constitutional right at stake in the cases and wealth was not identified as a suspect classifying trait. It is the combination of the important interest and the indigency classification that demanded closer judicial scrutiny under the Equal Protection Clause and which provided the unique theme of *Griffin–Douglas*. *Williams v. Illinois* (1970) [provisions for "working off" a fine, resulting in confinement beyond the statutory maximum held to violate indigent's equal protection rights]; *Tate v. Short* (1971) [imprisonment alternative to fine held violative of equal protection]. *Compare Ross v. Moffitt; Fuller v. Oregon* (1974) [state recoupment of funds expended to provide counsel to an indigent if a convicted indigent is able to repay upheld].

The exact relationship of equal protection and due process in cases involving access to criminal justice remains problematical. Recently, the Court reiterated that both clauses are implicated. Due process applies because of its demand for a fair opportunity to obtain an adjudication on the merits; equal protection applies because of the differential treatment of two classes of defendants. *Evitts v. Lucey* (1985) [due process right to *effective* assistance of counsel on first appeal as of right was violated]. In *Ake v. Oklahoma* (1985), the Court used the Due Process Clause as the basis for requiring states to provide free psychiatric assistance to indigent defendants in some criminal cases. The Court employed the *Mathews v. Eldridge* procedural due process test, balancing the defendant's interest in psychiatric assistance, the government interest that would be affected by affording the safeguard and the risk of erroneous deprivation if psychiatric assistance was not provided. The Court concluded: "[W]here a defendant demonstrates to the trial judge that his sanity at the time of the offense is to be a significant factor at trial, the state must, at a minimum, assure the defendant access to a competent psychiatrist who will conduct an appropriate examination and assist in evaluation, preparation, and presentation of the defense." The Court also held that the critical importance of a psychiatrist to the defendant in the sentencing phase of a capital case when the state presents psychiatric evidence of his future dangerousness, required access to free psychiatric assistance.

The problem of indigent access to justice has also arisen in the civil context. In *Boddie v. Connecticut* (1971), the Court struck down a state imposition of fees on welfare recipients seeking a divorce. Justice Harlan, for the Court, employing the Due Process Clause, emphasized two key factors: (1) the importance of the marriage relationship in our society's hierarchy of values; and, (2) the state monopolization of the means for ending that relationship. But what if these conditions were not present in other fee cases? In *United States v. Kras* (1973), the Court upheld a $50 fee for bankruptcy proceedings. The interest of the debtor in discharge of the debt burden was not deemed as "fundamental" as the marriage interest in *Boddie* and there were alternative means of debt settlement available to the debtor. Due process was not violated. See *Ortwein v. Schwab* (1973) [filing fee for appeal from adverse welfare board decisions upheld]. The importance of the two part *Boddie* inquiry was most recently indicated in *Little v. Streater* (1981), where the Court held that Connecticut's failure to pay for blood grouping tests for indigent defendants in paternity actions violated due process: "Because appellant has no choice of an alternative forum and his interest, as well as those of the child, are constitutionally significant, this case is comparable to *Boddie* rather than to *Kras* and *Ortwein*."

e. The Limits of Fundamental Rights

The fundamental rights strand of equal protection law fashioned by the Warren Court appeared to offer an alternative to substantive due process and its taint of "Lochnerism." Indeed, it was sometimes called "Substantive Equal Protection." Further, the developing case law suggested that the states might be under an affirmative constitutional duty to equalize access to important government benefits and services such as welfare, education, housing and medical care. Perhaps the Equal Protection Clause could be a vehicle for attacking economic inequalities in the society.

But the Burger Court sharply curtailed these expansive interpretations of equal protection. In *San Antonio Ind. School Dist. v. Rodriguez* (1973), the Court considered whether Texas violated equal protection by funding education through property taxes, producing marked interdistrict disparities in per pupil expenditures, because of the disparate property values in the districts. The Court, per Justice Powell, employed rational basis analysis and held 5–4 that equal protection was satisfied.

In rejecting strict scrutiny, Justice Powell first determined that the law did not operate to the disadvantage of a suspect class. There was no showing that the poor as an identifiable class live in property poor districts. Nor had it been shown that they suffered "an absolute deprivation of the desired benefit"; Justice Powell noted that equal protection "does not require absolute equality or precisely equal advantages." Finally, discrimination based on school district wealth was not suspect. District wealth possessed "none of the traditional indicia of suspectness." Justice Powell concluded that the Texas funding scheme "does not operate to peculiar disadvantage of any suspect class." See *Maher v. Roe* (1977) and *Harris v. McRae* (1980), the abortion funding cases, rejecting wealth as suspect.

The Court similarly rejected strict scrutiny based on fundamental rights analysis. While acknowledging that education may be the most important function of state government, Justice Powell asserted that "the importance of a service performed by the state does not determine whether it must be regarded as fundamental for purposes of examination under the Equal Protection Clause." The critical conclusion was that there is no "right to education explicitly or implicitly guaranteed by the Constitution." Efforts to link education to First Amendment rights and voting failed since the Constitution does not guarantee "the most *effective* speech or the most *informed* electoral choice."

Justice Powell did note that even if it were assumed that there is a constitutional right to "some identifiable quantum of education," there was no evidence that this basic minimum was not provided. Indeed, whereas prior cases had involved deprivations or interferences with free exercise of a right, Texas was affirmatively seeking to extend education. Since Texas has made a rational choice on allocating its scarce tax resources in a way to protect local autonomy over education, it was not the function of the courts to override its choices. See *Dandridge v. Williams* (1970) [state maximum grant law setting a ceiling on AFDC welfare benefits upheld using rational basis test].

Nevertheless, it was Justice Powell who provided the crucial fifth vote in *Plyler v. Doe* (1982), holding that Texas' failure to provide undocumented school age children the free public education that it provides to citizens and legally admitted aliens violates equal protection. Justice Brennan, a dissenter in *San Antonio,* now wrote for the Court. While he acknowledged that "public education is not a 'right' granted to individuals by the constitution," he observed that "education has a fundamental role in maintaining the fabric of our society." Justice Brennan similarly accepted that illegal aliens are not a suspect class. But the children of illegal entrants are special members of an "underclass," part of a "permanent caste" denied the benefits provided to citizens and lawful residents. In language reminiscent of that used in illegitimacy cases, Justice Brennan noted that the Texas law "imposes a lifetime of hardship on a discrete class of children not accountable for their disabling status." In light of the costs of lost education that the discrimination visited on "innocent" undocumented children, the law could "hardly be considered rational unless it furthers some substantial goal of the state." Applying this intermediate standard of review, the Court found the Texas law unconstitutional.

Justice Powell, concurring in *Plyler,* distinguished *Rodriguez* on grounds that, in *Rodriguez,* "no group of children was singled out by the state and then penalized because of their parent's status." Further, in *Rodriguez* there was not "any group of children totally deprived of all education as in this case."

Plyler is a noteworthy departure from rationality review absent any suspect classification or fundamental right. *Plyler* could be seen as providing an alternative to the strict tiered equal protection review used by the Warren Court—the degree of scrutiny varies with the nature of the classifying trait and the importance of the interest burdened as well as the severity of the burden (*e.g.*, is the law a "penalty" on a fundamental interest). But *Plyler* more likely should be seen, as the dissent contended, as simply a result-oriented case, providing minimal doctrinal development in equal protection law. See *Martinez v. Bynum* (1983) [state *bona fide* residency requirement denying free tuition benefits to children living in the district for the primary purpose of attending free public schools upheld using rationality review].

In *Kadrmas v. Dickinson Pub. School* (1988), the Court, 5–4, per Justice O'Connor, upheld, as against an equal protection challenge, a North Dakota statute authorizing school districts which chose not to "reorganize" into larger districts to charge a fee for school bus service. Unlike the situation in *Plyler*, the school child in *Kadrmas* was not being disadvantaged by the state because of the illegal conduct of her parents. The child was denied access to the school bus "only because her parents would not pay the same user fee charged to all other families". Furthermore, the statute was rationally related to the state's legitimate interest in fulfilling the expectation of residents of reorganized districts that a consequence of reorganization would be free busing arrangements.

Kadrmas refused to apply either the strict scrutiny standard or the less exacting "heightened scrutiny" standard which had been applied in *Plyler*. Indeed, *Plyler* was pointedly described as not having been extended beyond its "unique circumstances."

In summary, the future of fundamental rights equal protection analysis appears to be a limited one. Strict scrutiny analysis is unlikely to be extended to reach new interests not already protected. The Rehnquist Court appears, if anything, even less disposed than the Burger Court to expand further the domain of the fundamental rights branch of the new equal protection.

CHAPTER VII

FREEDOM OF EXPRESSION

A. THE BASIC DOCTRINE

1. THE RATIONALE OF SPEECH PROTECTION

The First Amendment provides that "Congress shall make no law abridging the freedom of speech." The text of the First Amendment clearly has Congress, *i.e.,* the federal government, as its addressee. It probably was not intended to reach the states. But in 1925 the Supreme Court declared that the Due Process Clause of the Fourteenth Amendment protected freedom of expression against state infringement. *Gitlow v. New York* (1925).

What is the nature of the guarantee of freedom of expression? It cannot reasonably be claimed that the Constitution extends its protection to all verbal and non-verbal communication. As Holmes said: "The most stringent protection of free speech would not protect a man in falsely shouting fire in a theatre and causing a panic." *Schenck v. United States* (1919). But why not? There are no qualifications to the guarantee of freedom of speech in the text of the First Amendment. The key is that the Constitution prohibits laws "abridging the freedom of speech" and not all laws restricting communication.

What does "the freedom of speech" embrace? The historical intent of the Framers is disputed and does not provide much guidance. But some guidance can be obtained after the fact, as it were, by considering the functions the First Amendment serves. For some, freedom of expression is a vital ingredient of the pursuit of truth, especially political truth. Thus, Justice Holmes believed that "the best test of truth is the power of the thought to get itself accepted in the competition of the market." *Abrams v. United States* (1919). This marketplace of ideas rationale for free expression had its origins in English constitutional history. Thus, in the seventeenth century, John Milton, in a famous essay, *The Areopagitica,* protested government licensing and censorship of the press: "[W]ho ever knew truth put to the worse, in a free and open encounter?" Modern refinement of this doctrine contends that the state must allow dialogue to continue no matter how noxious that dialogue. Only when the social order is drastically threatened is government permitted to punish a speaker. As Justice Brandeis put it in *Whitney v. California* (1927): "Only an emergency justifies repression."

But is the marketplace of ideas model of the First Amendment realistic? Critics question the notion of absolute truth as the objective of political dialogue. The marketplace theory rests on a presumption of rationality—a citizenry of intelligent decisionmakers seeking and empowered to govern a free society. But is this how twentieth century society really functions? Free societies threatened by totalitarian adversaries may not dare to wait. Critics of the marketplace argue that in an age of concentration of control of the mass media there are too few stalls in the market for the marketplace theory still to be viable.

Alexander Meiklejohn posited an influential rationale for free expression. He said that the Framers were interested in political freedom and in making democracy work. The citizen-critic of government must be given the information to enable him to do his political duty. Otherwise he cannot control his governors. As Meiklejohn put it, "public speech", speech involving the political arena, is absolutely protected. Speech involving private life—business communications, for example—is not absolutely protected but is to be accorded only the general protection provided by the Due Process Clause. Critics ask: Is the Meiklejohn theory meant to be descriptive of reality or is it only a utopian ideal?

An alternative to these social utilitarian models is the view that freedom of speech is valuable in itself in promoting individual self-realization and self-determination. The rational individual requires information and an opportunity to express his own ideas if she is to grow. This theory may be called the individual liberty or self-realization model.

From these theories flows the principle that laws limiting freedom of expression are not to be reviewed under the deferential rationality test. Rather, such laws are to be subjected to the regimen of stricter judicial scrutiny. From this modern principle of searching scrutiny of governmental action infringing free expression we derive the basic doctrines and tests of First Amendment law.

2. A DOCTRINAL OVERVIEW

a. Content Control v. Indirect Burdens

The Supreme Court has stated that "above all else the First Amendment means that government has no power to restrict expression because of its message, its ideas, its subject matter, or its content." *Police Department of Chicago v. Mosley* (1972). Nevertheless, the Court has frequently upheld laws imposing content-based restrictions on speech. Two approaches are used to reconcile such holdings. First, some speech has been thought of as categorically excluded from First Amendment protection or at least is given a lesser degree of protection under the First Amendment. In *Chaplinsky v. New Hampshire* (1942), the Court stated: "There are certain well-defined and narrowly limited classes of speech, the prevention and punishment of which have never been thought to raise constitutional problems." Thus, as a general rule, one does not ask whether particular obscene publications are protected by the First Amendment. Obscenity has been considered the kind of expression with which "the freedom of speech" is not concerned. Laws restricting its availability were therefore not restricted by the First Amendment.

The categorical approach to free expression problems received a significant qualification in *R.A.V. v. City of St. Paul* (1992) where an ordinance sanctioning fighting words in the context of race, religion or gender was struck down.   Justice Scalia for the Court held that no category of expression was "entirely invisible" to the First Amendment.   Obscenity may be regulated, it is true, but only with regard to its "distinctly proscribable content."   Thus, a city council ordinance prohibiting "only those legally obscene words that contain criticism of the city government" would violate the First Amendment. Three justices, concurring, deplored this revisionism in the traditional understanding of the First Amendment status of unprotected categories of expression.   They insisted that since such categories involved speech that was worthless in First Amendment terms, government could regulate as it chose. But the *R.A.V.* majority held that content discrimination within a particular category of even otherwise unprotected expression merited First Amendment protection and was subject to strict scrutiny review.

A second approach is to employ a weighted form of "balancing" test to determine whether the government content control constitutes an impermissible "abridgement" of "the freedom of speech." The balancing or justification approach may be cast as a formula such as the clear and present danger doctrine.   Or it may come in the form, as is often the case today, of a court extending strict scrutiny to content-based legislation, *i.e.*, government must demonstrate that the law under review is narrowly tailored to meet some overriding or compelling governmental interest. Finally, the judicial inquiry may amount to little more than *ad hoc* balancing of the speech and governmental interest in conflict even when the law is content-based.

Alternatively, government regulation may be content-neutral and impose only an indirect burden on freedom of speech. In such cases, a less demanding form of judicial review is used. Justice Harlan writing for the Court in *Konigsberg v. State Bar of California* (1961) [refusal to answer lawful inquiries concerning bar applicants' qualifications is a permissible basis for denying admission], stated: "[G]eneral regulatory statutes, not intended to control the content of speech but incidentally limiting its unfettered exercise, have not been regarded as the type of law the First or Fourteenth Amendment forbade Congress or the states to pass, when they have been found justified by subordinating valid governmental interests, a prerequisite to constitutionality which has necessarily involved a weighing of the governmental interest involved."

The courts engage in a balancing of the competing interests to determine if a content neutral regulation is reasonable. For example, a broad municipal ordinance governing sound trucks, vesting extensive discretion in police officials, was held unconstitutional. *Saia v. New York* (1948). A more narrowly-drawn sound truck ordinance, prohibiting "loud and raucous noises" on the streets, was constitutional. *Kovacs v. Cooper* (1949). Similarly, a

New York City ordinance which regulated the volume of amplified music at a bandshell in Central Park by requiring use of sound-amplification equipment and a sound technician provided by the city was constitutional. Here again the regulation was deemed narrowly tailored because the substantial governmental interest in controlling the sound volume was served in a direct and effective way by requiring use of the city's sound technician but allowing the sponsor autonomy concerning the sound mix. *Ward v. Rock Against Racism* (1989).

A total ban on residential canvassing, handbilling, and solicitation [*Martin v. Struthers* (1943)] or a law vesting excessive discretion in officials over the content of such solicitation [*Hynes v. Mayor and Council of Oradell* (1976)], is unreasonable—it approximates content control. On the other hand, a limited reasonable regulation designed to protect the privacy of homeowners will be upheld. *Breard v. Alexandria* (1951) [ban on residential magazine sales without homeowners consent upheld]; *Rowan v. United States Post Office Dept.* (1970) [statute permitting homeowners to stop offensive home mailings is constitutional]. Narrowly drawn, reasonable content-neutral regulations of the time, place and manner of public protest, designed to promote valid local interests such as traffic flow and public safety, will be upheld. *Grayned v. City of Rockford* (1972).

The student should be aware that the degree of judicial scrutiny in this balancing of interests can vary markedly from case to case. Perhaps the most frequently used standard for measuring the reasonableness of such indirect regulation is that fashioned in *O'Brien v. United States* (1968): "A government regulation is sufficiently justified if it furthers an important or substantial government interest; if the governmental interest is unrelated to the suppression of free expression; and if the incidental restriction of alleged First Amendment freedoms is no greater than is essential to the furtherance of that interest."

Finally, a helpful guide to the rationale for subjecting content-neutral regulations to intermediate rather than strict scrutiny is provided by *Turner Broadcasting System, Inc. v. FCC* (1994). Unlike content-based regulations, content-neutral regulations present less risk that they will exclude particular ideas or points of view from public discourse. In *Turner*, "must carry" obligations imposed by federal legislation requiring cable systems to carry a designated number of local broadcast signals were reviewed under the *O'Brien* intermediate level of scrutiny "applicable to content-neutral restrictions that imposed an incidental burden on speech." Clearly, distinguishing content-neutral from content-based regulations is difficult. Indeed, the Court pointed out that content-neutral regulations that appeared to be neutral on their face could be deemed content-based if their "manifest purpose is to regulate speech because of the message it conveys." But the must carry regulations were not imposed to regulate on the basis of the subject-matter or viewpoint of a message but because Congress believed that the future of free broadcasting was placed in economic jeopardy because of the "physical characteristics of cable transmission."

The fact that a regulation is content-neutral and is subject to a less exacting standard of scrutiny than a content-based one does not necessarily mean that it will be upheld against a First Amendment challenge. Thus, when a city ordinance prohibited homeowners from displaying all signs except residence identification signs, "for sale" signs and signs warning of safety hazards, the Court struck it down. Since the city justified the ordinance on aesthetic and related grounds, the Court was prepared to assume that the ordinance was content-neutral. Nonetheless, the city had virtually shut down a "venerable means of communication that is both unique and important." Entirely too much protected expression was prohibited by the ordinance. Political, religious and personal messages were completely precluded from being communicated by means of residential signs. Since such signs were an unusually inexpensive and effective means of communication, it was doubtful that an adequate substitute existed. *City of Ladue v. Gilleo* (1994).

Finally, unlike the more deferential treatment given to content-neutral regulations, content-based regulations are scrutinized much more strictly. New York's "Son of Sam" law creating a mechanism applying the income from works of criminals who describe their crimes first to the criminal's victims and then to creditors was struck down. There was no doubt that the "Son of Sam" law was content-based. The state imposed a burden on income derived from expressive activity placed on no other income. Further, the burden was placed only on activity with a particular content, *i.e.*, works in which an author described his crimes. A content-based law is presumptively invalid under the First Amendment. Such a law could be upheld only if it met the strict scrutiny standard. Did the law serve a compelling state interest? Was it narrowly drawn to achieve those interests? Although the state interests in victim compensation and preventing criminals from profiting from their crimes were compelling, the law was not narrowly drawn. Indeed, it was impermissibly overinclusive. For example, the law applied even to works of authors describing crimes for which they had never been convicted. *Simon & Schuster, Inc. v. Members of the New York State Criminal Victims Board* (1991).

b. Vagueness and Overbreadth

In most First Amendment litigation, the constitutional challenge is directed at the validity of the law "as applied" to the particular litigant. Under this "as applied" approach, a judicial determination of unconstitutionality does not render the law itself invalid but only renders void the particular application of the law. The law must be unconstitutional as applied to the plaintiff. Pursuant to the third party standing rule, a litigant will not be permitted to challenge possible but unrelated unconstitutional applications to others of an otherwise valid law.

There is, however, another vitally important approach. In addition (or as an alternative) to challenging the validity of the application of the law to himself, the litigant may challenge the validity of the law itself by arguing that the law is facially unconstitutional in that it is vague and/or overbroad. A court decision in the plaintiff's favor in such circumstances results in the invalidation of the law. Further, the litigant is allowed to raise the rights of third parties not before the Court who could not be reached under a properly drawn law. This is so even though the litigant himself is not affected by the overbreadth and could be validly regulated by a statute that was neither overbroad nor vague. Because of concern about the chilling effect of vague and overbroad laws on protected constitutional expression, an exception is made to the third party standing rule.

The doctrines of vagueness and overbreadth are closely related but distinct. Vagueness is concerned with the clarity of the law. A law must be drawn with sufficient clarity so that it informs people of the conduct they must take to avoid the sanction of the particular law. Under procedural due process, a statute is not constitutionally fair if it fails to give such information. However, an unclear statute may have First Amendment as well as a procedural due process impact. A law regulating expression has to be especially clear because, if it is not specific, protected expression may be chilled or suppressed.

The doctrine of overbreadth is concerned with the precision of a law. A law may be facially clear but may sweep too broadly if it indiscriminately reaches both protected and unprotected expression. For example, a law that prohibits three or more persons from congregating on a street corner and engaging in activity that is "annoying" to passers-by is both vague and overbroad. *Coates v. Cincinnati* (1971). Protected expression can be chilled or suppressed by such a law. Administrators are permitted to roam free and curtail protected expression. Herein lies the vice of overbreadth. Even though the litigant might be engaged in unprotected expression, the statute could be applied to protected speech.

Closely related to the overbreadth doctrine is the less burdensome alternatives test, often used in First Amendment litigation. Even if the government has a compelling objective, if that objective could be achieved by a law less burdensome on protected expression, the First Amendment demands that these less drastic means be used.

The overbreadth doctrine is under attack within the Court. It has been described as "strong medicine" to be "employed by the Court sparingly and only as a last resort." *Broadrick v. Oklahoma* (1973). The judicial critics challenge the propriety of a court's invalidation of a law based on possible, imagined applications of the statute that may in fact never arise. They point out that it is not an appropriate judicial function to anticipate constitutional issues which are not directly presented by parties actually affected.

Broadrick v. Oklahoma (1973), fashioned a significant exception to the overbreadth doctrine. "[W]here conduct and not merely speech is involved, we believe that the overbreadth of a statute must not only be real but substantial as well, judged in relation to the statute's plainly legitimate sweep." While this principle, as formulated, applied only to speech-related conduct and not pure speech, the potential scope of this demand for "substantial overbreadth" was left essentially uncharted. It has always been clear that not any possible unconstitutional application of a statute would render it facially invalid. *Broadrick,* however, suggests a sharp limitation on those occasions when the overbreadth doctrine will be invoked. In fact, there has been an increasing tendency to invoke the requirement of "substantial overbreadth" even when reviewing a law burdening pure speech. And the word "substantial" in the phrase "substantial overbreadth" has a chameleon-like quality that proves mischievous.

c. The Doctrine of Prior Restraint

Historically, freedom from prior restraint was what English lawyers meant when they spoke of freedom of the press. Indeed, the earliest understanding of the First Amendment was that it provided freedom from prior restraint. This freedom protected the printed word prior to publication and forbade prior administrative restraint. In other words, the doctrine of prior restraint forbade censorship in advance of publication. This should be distinguished from subsequent punishment through breach of the peace, disorderly conduct, or tort damages, all of which might be imposed *after* expression has taken place.

Freedom from prior restraint has been deemed in the past more important than freedom from subsequent punishment. Why is this? The bias against prior restraint is grounded in large part on the fact that the expression never enters the marketplace of ideas. In the case of subsequent punishment, on the other hand, at least the public has been given an opportunity to hear and judge the communication in controversy. The speaker in a system of subsequent punishment remains responsible for the consequences of his speech. Since concern for the marketplace is a primary motivating force underlying the bias against prior restraint, it is not surprising that the modern doctrine of prior restraint reaches a variety of forms of government restraint which operate prior to expression. Thus, even an injunction issued by a court which bears a special responsibility for protecting freedom of expression falls within its parameters. *Near v. Minnesota ex rel. Olson* (1931). Similarly, in more recent times, forms of expression other than printed materials have been accorded freedom from prior restraint. *Walker v. Birmingham* (1967) [street demonstration].

In its modern form, the doctrine provides that prior restraints are highly suspect both substantively and procedurally and are subject to a rebuttable presumption of unconstitutionality. In seeking to justify use of such a restraint the government bears a heavy burden of proof. Generally, the Court has professed to employ the clear and present danger doctrine in reviewing such prior restraint systems. *Nebraska Press Association v. Stuart* (1976). Such cases also involve controls on speech content which independently require use of strict judicial scrutiny.

In *Nebraska Press*, the gag order designed to prevent prejudicial pretrial publicity was aimed at journalists. Where a gag order targeted lawyers, the Court did not use the clear and present danger doctrine. Instead, since lawyers were officers of the court, the gag order was evaluated under the less demanding "substantial likelihood of material prejudice" standard. *Gentile v. State Bar of Nevada* (1991).

In a brief *per curiam* decision, the Court, 6–3, in *New York Times Co. v. United States (The Pentagon Papers Case)* (1971) invalidated a lower court restraint on the publication of a classified study dealing with the Vietnam war policy of the United States. The Court's *per curiam* decision did little more than cite the failure of the government to meet the heavy burden of justification for the use of a prior restraint. This was followed by nine separate opinions detailing each Justice's views on the issue presented.

A difficulty with evaluating the role of the prior restraint doctrine in the case is that a number of the justices were deeply troubled by the issuance of a restraint against the press in the absence of a federal statute authorizing such a restraint. Some of the justices felt that the presence of a statute, coupled with a fact pattern involving an alleged threat to national security, might satisfy the heavy burden of justification necessary to authorize a prior restraint. In the absence of such a statute, the simple declaration by the Executive that publication would involve a "grave and irreparable threat to the public interest" was insufficient to override the heavy presumption against prior restraint.

Since the First Amendment grants "greater protection from prior restraints than from subsequent punishment," it has been deemed essential to define the characteristics of prior restraint with precision. *Alexander v. United States* (1993). For example, when the government seized $9,000,000 worth of books and videos belonging to the owner of businesses dealing with sexually oriented materials pursuant to the forfeiture provisions of RICO (the federal Racketeer Influenced and Corrupt Organizations Act), the owner contended that since his RICO conviction was based on prior convictions under federal obscenity laws the RICO forfeiture constituted prior restraint. A prohibition of "future presumptively protected expression in retaliation for prior unprotected speech" was, in this view, a prior restraint. Indeed, most of the seized materials had not been adjudicated to be obscene. Nonetheless, the forfeiture was held not to be a prior restraint but a valid criminal sanction which had been preceded by a full criminal trial. To characterize the forfeiture as a prior restraint would blur "the time-honored distinction between barring speech in the future and penalizing past speech." The punishment was for past acts not future speech. The owner was still free to engage in expressive activities in the future. *Alexander v. United States* (1993).

The *Alexander* case was a refusal to extend prior restraint doctrine. In *Madsen v. Women's Health Center* (1994), the Court, per Chief Justice Rehnquist, eroded traditional prior restraint doctrine by refusing to characterize a state court injunction as an impermissible prior restraint. The injunction prohibited antiabortion protesters from demonstrating within a 36 foot buffer zone around a health clinic that performed abortions as an impermissible prior restraint. Although some injunctions are prior restraints, "not all injunctions which may incidentally affect expression" are prior restraints. The injunction was not content-based, as in the *Pentagon Papers* case. The protesters were not prevented from expressing their views but were just prohibited from doing so in the buffer zone around the clinic. In dissent, Justice Scalia, joined by Justices Kennedy and Thomas bitterly criticized the view that injunctions are not prior restraints if they merely restrain speech in a designated area or if their issuance is not based on content. *Madsen v. Women's Health Center, Inc.* (1994).

3. THE CLEAR AND PRESENT DANGER DOCTRINE

Perhaps the most significant formulation of First Amendment doctrine has been the clear and present danger doctrine. As used by Justice Holmes in *Schenck v. United States* (1919), the doctrine dealt with what evidence is admissible to establish violation of the Espionage Act. Holmes' answer was that a publication could be used to convict when "the words used are used in such circumstances and are of such a nature as to create a clear and present danger that they will bring about the substantive evils that Congress has a right to prevent. It is a question of proximity and degree." It is doubtful that Holmes was really reformulating First Amendment doctrine in *Schenck*. Indeed, he seemed to adopt the prevailing "bad tendency" test, then in its ascendancy, since he states: "If the act (speaking, or circulating a paper), its tendency and the intent with which it is done are the same, we perceive no ground for saying that success alone warrants making the act a crime."

But by the time of *Whitney v. California* (1927), Justice Brandeis, in a concurrence which became more influential than the opinion of the Court, provided a statement of the danger test which yielded a greater measure of protection to free expression than the *Schenck* formulation. Brandeis said that for government to suppress speech, "[t]here must be reasonable ground to believe the danger apprehended is imminent. There must be the probability of serious danger to the State." For Brandeis, speech could not be denied protection "where the advocacy falls short of incitement and there is nothing to indicate that the advocacy would be acted on." Further, the danger test was now used by Holmes and Brandeis not merely as an evidentiary standard but as a test for judging the validity of a law even where the legislature had determined the speech in question to be dangerous.

In *Gitlow v. New York* (1925), the Court, per Justice Sanford, upheld a New York statute punishing criminal anarchy. Justice Sanford began from the premise that when the legislature determines that speech is so inimical to the general welfare "every presumption is to be indulged in favor of the validity of the statute." It is only where the statute is an "arbitrary and unreasonable" use of state police power that it violates freedom of expression. Since the legislature could reasonably conclude that utterances inciting to the overthrow of government by unlawful means are to be suppressed, "[the legislature] may, in the exercise of its judgment, suppress the threatened danger in its incipiency." Justices Holmes and Brandeis objected to this reasoning and dissented. For them, the clear and present danger test was fully applicable to judicial review of the legislative judgment. As Justice Brandeis explained in *Whitney,* the legislative declaration regarding the need for legislating "creates merely a rebuttable presumption that these conditions have been satisfied."

The *Whitney* formulation of the danger test by Brandeis received both formal espousal and a near trashing in the famous case of *Dennis v. United States* (1951), where a plurality opinion by Chief Justice Vinson upheld the validity of the federal anti-subversive law, the Smith Act, against First Amendment attack. Chief Justice Vinson declared that the formulation of the danger test which the Court accepted was the test announced by Brandeis in *Whitney*. But, it is doubtful that Brandeis would have claimed the test for his own in light of the application it received. Vinson placed heavy emphasis on the need for government to respond to the Communist threat; the danger test could not mean that government "must wait until the *putsch* is about to be executed, the plans have been laid, and the signal awaited." Rather, government could move against the conspiracy or attempt at overthrow, even though the attempt was obviously doomed at the outset. Probability of success could not be the criterion and imminence could not be the measure of government power. The Court adopted a new formulation of the danger test fashioned by Chief Judge Learned Hand in the federal court of appeals below: "In each case [courts] must ask whether the gravity of the 'evil', discounted by its improbability, justifies such invasion of free speech as is necessary to avoid the danger."

Even this watered-down version of the danger test was unacceptable for Justice Frankfurter who concurred in the judgment. No formula could capture the delicate balance of interests. Rather, the demands of national security are better served "by candid and informed weighing of the competing interests within the confines of the judicial process than by announcing dogmas too inflexible for the non-Euclidean problems to be solved." While this statement would appear to envision judicial balancing of the competing speech and national security interests, in fact Justice Frankfurter argued that the balancing was the function of the Congress. The judicial function was limited to assuring that there was a reasonable basis for the legislative judgment. Shades of Justice Sanford in *Gitlow!!*

The emasculation of the danger test in *Dennis* was somewhat mitigated by *Yates v. United States* (1957), which also involved the Smith Act. Interestingly, *Yates* was not technically speaking a First Amendment case. The legal issue presented was a statutory question—the meaning of the prohibition against advocacy of violent overthrow of the government in the Smith Act. What kind of "advocacy" did the Smith Act prohibit? Justice Harlan for the Court in *Yates* repaired some of the damage to free expression done by *Dennis* by interpreting the statute to proscribe "advocacy of action" rather than "advocacy of abstract doctrine or ideas." Now this was an approach reminiscent not of Justice Sanford but of the Brandeis formulation of the danger test in *Whitney*. This liberalizing decision may have been due to the waning support for the rabid anti-Communism of McCarthyism. In any event, it was not a thorough resurrection of the Holmes–Brandeis test since Justice Harlan never purported to use the danger test in *Yates*. Similarly, there is no mention of imminence or probability of success.

The true Brandeis–Holmes faith achieved a fuller but still somewhat altered restoration in the case of *Brandenburg v. Ohio* (1969).

In *Brandenburg,* the Court, *per curiam,* invalidated a state statute punishing criminal syndicalism, *i.e.,* the advocacy of violence in industrial disputes in the workplace. For the Court, *Dennis–Yates* had established the principle that freedom of expression does not permit a state "to forbid or proscribe advocacy of the use of force or of law violation except where such advocacy is directed to inciting or producing imminent lawless action and is likely to incite or produce such actions." The *Brandenburg* Court never mentioned the danger test and cited only cryptically to *Dennis* and *Yates.*

Some commentators interpret *Brandenburg* as adopting an "incitement" test which focuses on the nature of the speech in question. Freedom of speech is absolutely protected, they argue, but speech which incites to the violent overthrow of government is not First Amendment speech. Such expression is categorically excluded from protection. Other commentators read *Brandenburg* as a merger of the Holmes–Brandeis danger test, which focuses on the context in which the speech occurs, with an incitement test. In order to punish speech, the speaker must both use the language of action and the context must be sufficient to establish imminence and the probability of the occurrence of the serious substantive evil which the government is seeking to prevent.

The debate over the meaning of *Brandenburg* is indicative of the continuing controversy over the value of the danger test itself. For some critics the test provides inadequate protection for First Amendment interests offering little more protection to the speaker than ad hoc balancing provides. Other critics see the danger test as affording inadequate protection to vital governmental interests. Hidden within the language of the danger test, they argue, is found functionally a strict scrutiny standard. In this view, demanding judicial superintendence of the legislative judgment in areas such as national security is inappropriate because it curtails the democratic will. In any case, it may well be that where in the past the danger test was invoked, the courts today will use the strict scrutiny test.

4. SYMBOLIC CONDUCT

Conduct is frequently used as a means of communicating messages, *e.g.,* picketing, handbilling, advertising. This "speech plus conduct" is subject to reasonable regulation. But conduct can also constitute the message itself. Conduct can embody an idea: "Symbolism is a primitive but effective way of communicating ideas. The use of an emblem or flag to symbolize some system, idea, institution, or personality, is a short cut from mind to mind." *West Virginia State Bd. of Educ. v. Barnette* (1943) [compulsory flag salute law held unconstitutional]. But not all conduct is meant to be communicative and not all expressive conduct is protected by the

First Amendment. The anarchist who shoots a public official to express opposition to government cannot wrap himself in the protective cloak of the Constitution. What standards determine when symbolic conduct will enjoy First Amendment protection?

The initial task is to define when conduct will be treated as speech for First Amendment purposes. In fact, when the Court does not wish to apply First Amendment protection to conduct, it will sometimes simply assume arguendo that even if the conduct is "speech," the law is a reasonable regulation of the "speech." *United States v. O'Brien* (1968) [draft card burning during Vietnam War protests assumed to be symbolic speech]; *Clark v. Community for Creative Non–Violence* (1984) [overnight sleeping in public park as part of protest assumed to be expressive conduct]. Even in cases where First Amendment protection is extended to conduct, the Court often fails to discuss why the conduct constitutes speech. *Tinker v. Des Moines Independent Community School Dist.* (1969), merely stated that the wearing of black armbands by public high school students to protest the Vietnam War is "closely akin to 'pure speech.'" Unfortunately this approach often ignores the importance of the conduct in question as a means of expressing the speaker's message. *Spence v. Washington* (1974), overturning a flag misuse statute applied to a protestor who had affixed a peace symbol on the flag and flown it from his window, did confront the task of defining symbolic speech. The Court examined the factual context and environment in which the conduct took place, and determined that (1) there was an intent to communicate a particularized message of opposition to war and violence, and (2) the message would be received and understood by others.

Assuming that the conduct at issue qualifies as First Amendment speech under *Spence,* what degree of constitutional protection should such symbolic speech receive? Does expressive conduct enjoy the same constitutional protection as oral speech? In *Tinker,* the Court said that the conduct (black armbands) enjoyed "comprehensive protection under the First Amendment." The ban, which appears to have been treated as a content-based regulation, was unconstitutional absent a showing that the exercise of the right would "materially and substantially interfere with the requirements of appropriate discipline in the operation of the school." This latter showing is the real test set forth in *Tinker.* While this test appears to require something less than the clear and present danger test requires, that was probably due to the school house context in which the expression occurred.

United States v. O'Brien (1968), most clearly defines the governing standards. In *O'Brien,* Chief Justice Warren, for the Court, began from the premise that when speech and nonspeech are combined in conduct, an incidental restriction of expression resulting from regulating the nonspeech element could be justified only if the following conditions are satisfied: (1) the regulation must further an important or substantial governmental interest, (2) the government interest must be unrelated to the suppression of free expression; and, (3) the incidental restriction on alleged freedom must be no greater than is essential to the furtherance of that interest. The *O'Brien* test is of major importance since it is one of the most frequently-used standards for reviewing content-neutral laws which incidentally burden speech.

In applying this balancing standard, the *O'Brien* Court refused to probe the congressional motive in proscribing draft-card burning which might have proven that the law was based on the content of the speech, requiring a more stringent standard of review. Instead, the law was said to serve the content-neutral, important objective of promoting the effective operation of the Selective Services System. Even assuming that this was the objective of law, the challengers argued that it was already adequately served by other laws—the incremental advantages gained by one more law was not worth the added burden on First Amendment rights. *O'Brien* adopted a less demanding approach to means-end analysis. Since no alternative law would as effectively serve the governmental interest, the law was valid. This watered-down approach to balancing has been severely criticized but it has emerged as the dominant judicial approach for reviewing content-neutral regulation.

The *O'Brien* approach to interest balancing is also reflected in *Clark v. Community for Creative Non–Violence* (1984). While the National Park Service permitted the erection of tent cities in Lafayette Park and on the Mall in Washington, D.C., as part of a demonstration on the problems of the homeless, the Service invoked regulations against camping in the parks in rejecting requests to allow the demonstrators to sleep in the tents. The Court, per Justice White, rejected the claim that this refusal violated the First Amendment. Justice White in *Clark* invoked *O'Brien*'s rules for symbolic conduct as well as the standards for judging the reasonableness of regulation of the manner of expression in the public forum concluding that the two standards were essentially the same.

The dissenters in *Clark* leveled an objection frequently made against the Court's application of the *O'Brien* standards: "[T]he Court has dramatically lowered the scrutiny of government regulations once it has determined that such regulations are content-neutral." The challenge of the critics is not to the *O'Brien* standards themselves but to the Court's use of them, especially its assessment of the relation of the law to the admittedly important government interest. Critics assert that the Court does not give sufficient weight to First Amendment values in the balance and that the Court does not ask whether the added incremental effectiveness afforded by using the law in question is really worth the costs in freedom of expression. More generally, the critics question whether the Court is not diluting the standards of First Amendment review because the expression takes the form of conduct rather than pure oral speech.

But the student should not assume that symbolic expression is never accorded full protection. When the government regulates the content of symbolic expression, it constitutes a direct and significant burden on expression. In such circumstances the *O'Brien* rules do not apply because those rules apply only to incidental burdens. For example, when a demonstrator as a means of political protest burned an American flag at the Republican National Convention in Texas, his conviction under a Texas statute which prohibited desecration of a venerated object was set aside as inconsistent with the First Amendment. The expressive and overtly political nature of the flag burner's conduct at the convention was obvious. The state may not presume that provocative or offensive words will produce disorder. The flag burning did not constitute "fighting words." An interest in preventing breach of the peace was not served when no disturbance occurred or was threatened. The state's asserted interest in preserving the flag as a symbol of "nationhood and national unity" proved too much because such concerns come to the fore only when the "person's treatment of the flag communicates a message." The precept that government cannot "prohibit expression simply because it disagrees with its message" is not conditional on the mode chosen for expression of the idea. Government cannot limit the symbols which the people use to communicate their messages. The contention that the flag cannot be used for communicating has no limiting principle. Can the Presidential seal or the

Constitution itself be similarly placed off limits? The Court, applying the strict scrutiny standard of review, held, 5–4, that the state interests asserted did not justify criminally punishing a person for communicating political protest by means of burning a flag. *Texas v. Johnson* (1989).

After the decision in *Texas v. Johnson*, the Congress passed the Flag Protection Act of 1989 which made criminal the conduct of anyone who "knowingly mutilates, defaces, physically defiles, burns, maintains on the floor or ground, or tramples upon" the United States flag. The United States prosecuted certain individuals for violating the Act by setting fire to the American flag. Was the new Flag Protection Act sufficiently different from the Texas law? The Texas law had "targeted expressive conduct on the basis of the content of its message." Nevertheless, it was clear that the interest of Congress in the Act was related to the suppression of free expression. The language of the statute revealed Congress's interest "in the communicative impact of flag destruction." Almost every term used in the statute was concerned with disrespectful treatment of the flag. The Flag Protection Act was cast in broader terms than the Texas law; yet it still suffered from the same fatal infirmity. It suppressed expression because of concern for its "likely communicative impact." Once again the Court held, 5–4, that the prosecutions for flag burning could not stand consistent with the First Amendment. *United States v. Eichman* (1990).

The controversy over flag burning resulted in a renewed emphasis on a fundamental principle: "If there is a bedrock principle underlying the First Amendment, it is that the Government may not prohibit the expression of an idea simply because society finds the idea offensive or disagreeable." *Texas v. Johnson* (1989). When regulation of symbolic activity is content based, the most exacting level of scrutiny will be applied. *United States v. Eichman* (1990).

The First Amendment status of expressive activity may be in more flux, however, than the flag desecration cases indicate. A state law which prohibited non-obscene nude dancing was upheld 5–4 even though such dancing was conceded to be expressive activity protected by the First Amendment. This concession seemed to deprive the activity of protection at the same time it conceded it. Chief Justice Rehnquist in a plurality opinion described the prohibited non-obscene nude dancing as "expressive conduct within the outer perimeters of the First Amendment, though only marginally so." Perhaps because of its "outer perimeter" First Amendment status, the plurality concluded that the state law could be evaluated under the *O'Brien* test. The substantial state interest prong of *O'Brien* was satisfied since the law furthered the state interest in "order and morality." The critical prong of *O'Brien* requiring that the law be unrelated to the suppression of free expression was said to be satisfied since the law was deemed to be directed at public nudity not at any erotic message communicated by the dancing. The plurality indicates a willingness to accord a lower degree of protection to some forms of hitherto protected expressive activity such as indecent dancing. Justice Souter concurred on the ground that under the doctrine of *Renton v. Playtime Theatres, Inc.* (1986) the state law could be justified as directed at preventing the adverse secondary effects flowing from adult entertainment establishments. Justice Scalia concurred on the ground that the law banning non-obscene nude dancing did not present First Amendment issues at all since it was a general law not directed at expression. *Barnes v. Glen Theatre, Inc.* (1991).

5. FREEDOM OF ASSOCIATION AND BELIEF

a. The Source of the Right

Freedom of association is not specifically mentioned in the Constitution. As early as the seventeenth century, John Locke wrote of the importance of private associations in checking concentrations of power and protecting liberty. In modern society, association is a vital means for competing in the marketplace of ideas and controlling government. Interest groups and political parties compete for public attention and support and, in that process, they further the values of democratic government. As the Supreme Court stated in *N.A.A.C.P. v. Alabama* (1958): "[I]t is beyond debate that freedom to engage in association for the advancement of beliefs and ideas is an inseparable aspect of the 'liberty' assured by the Due Process Clause of the Fourteenth Amendment, which embraces freedom of speech."

But when a city ordinance restricts admission to certain dance halls to persons between the ages of 14 and 18, the exclusion of adults from these dance halls does not violate any First Amendment right of association. There is no generalized right of "social association." It is expressive association to further First Amendment objectives which the First Amendment protects. Protecting the opportunity for minors and adults to dance together does not fall in that category. *City of Dallas v. Stanglin* (1989).

Similarly, freedom of belief is not an express constitutional guarantee. But, like association, it has developed into a right implied from the First Amendment guarantee and due process liberty. "If there is any fixed star in our constitutional horizon, it is that no official, high or petty, can proscribe what shall be orthodox in politics, nationalism, religion, or other matters of opinion." *West Virginia State Bd. of Educ. v. Barnette* (1943).

b. Membership and Associational Action

Suppose government were to make it a crime to be a member of the Ku Klux Klan? Such a law, if approached *in vacuo*, would violate freedom of association and belief. Associations often have multiple objectives, some might be legal and some might not be. To punish mere membership alone is essentially to create guilt by association. Thus, freedom of association precludes the consideration in a capital sentencing hearing of defendant's membership in a white racist organization which had neither committed nor endorsed unlawful or violent acts. The First Amendment prevents the use of defendant's abstract beliefs in a sentencing proceeding when those beliefs have no relevance to it. *Dawson v. Delaware* (1992).

In *Scales v. United States* (1961), the Court held that individual membership in an association could be criminally punished only if the government were required to show, (1) knowledge or scienter of the illegal objectives of the association; (2) specific intent to further those illegal objectives; and (3) "active" membership. It is probable that the reference to illegal objectives would be synchronized by a contemporary court to meet the requirements of the modern revised clear and present danger doctrine. *Brandenburg v. Ohio* (1969). The group must be shown to have a specific intent to incite, not merely to advocate illegal conduct. *Noto v. United States* (1961). The severity of these requirements have effectively terminated government prosecution of group membership. The student should note, however, that as stringent as these requirements are, they do not require that punishment be based on actual harmful conduct.

If constitutional protection of association is to be meaningful, it must extend to activities in furtherance of the group's objectives. Legislation burdening lawful activities must be judicially scrutinized. In *Aptheker v. Secretary of State* (1964), the Court struck down a federal law prohibiting members of so-called subversive action organizations from even applying for a passport. The law violated the freedom of travel found to be embodied in the freedom of association, an instance, it might be said, of a right twice derived. In *N.A.A.C.P. v. Claiborne Hardware Co.* (1982), the Court held that neither the NAACP nor its members could be held liable for damages arising from a civil rights boycott, absent a showing of illegal conduct causing the resultant harm. "The right to associate does not lose all constitutional protection merely because some members of the group may have participated in conduct or advocated doctrine that itself is not protected." Damages could not be imposed based on the results of non-violent protected activity. Unless the government established that the NAACP had authorized the illegal conduct causing the injury, imposing liability would "impermissibly burden the rights of political association."

A protected political boycott like the one in *Claiborne* should be distinguished from an unprotected economic boycott. A boycott by an association of court-appointed lawyers representing indigents for the purpose of obtaining an increase in their compensation was a restraint of trade under the antitrust laws. The lawyer boycott's expressive element was insufficient to merit shelter under the First Amendment. Participants in this illegal boycott sought an economic advantage for themselves and were unlike the civil rights protestors in *Claiborne* who had sought no "special advantage for themselves." *FTC v. Superior Court Trial Lawyers Association* (1990).

The student should not assume that the principles set forth above require government to treat all groups equally. For example, the fact that government chooses to extend certain tax breaks to some groups but refuses to support the lobbying activities of others via tax advantages does not violate the First Amendment. "Congress has simply chosen not to pay for [the organization's] lobbying. We again reject the 'notion that First Amendment rights are somehow not fully realized unless they are subsidized by the State.'" *Regan v. Taxation With Representation of Washington* (1983).

The idea expressed in *Regan* that the "legislature's decision not to subsidize the exercise of a fundamental right does not infringe the right" was relied on again in *Lyng v. International Union, UAW* (1988). A federal statute provided (1) that no household would be eligible to participate in the food stamp program while any of its members was on strike and (2) that no household would be permitted to receive an increase in its food stamp allotment because the income of a striking member of the household had decreased because of the strike. The statute was upheld against contentions that the statute infringed a striker's right to associate with her family as well as the freedom of association rights of strikers and their unions. The statute did not order individuals not to dine together nor did it directly and substantially interfere with family life. Similarly, the statute did not order union members "not to associate together for the purpose of conducting a strike." Concededly, strikers would be better off if food stamps were available during a strike but freedom of association did not "require the Government to furnish funds to maximize the exercise" of the "striker's right of association."

Federal regulations governing federally funded family planning grantees explicitly barred them from providing abortion counseling or making referrals to abortion clinics. The regulations also barred the grantees from the encouragement, promotion or advocacy of abortion. Also, the grantees were required to organize themselves so that they were " 'physically and financially separate' " from abortion related activities. The regulations did not constitute impermissible viewpoint discrimination. Government had simply chosen "to fund one activity to the exclusion of the other." Just because a government decision to fund a program to accomplish certain lawful goals thereby discourages competing goals does not invalidate such government choices or subsidies. Abortion is a right but government is not obliged to fund it. Nor does the conferral of grants with such conditions violate the unconstitutional conditions doctrine. The condition runs to the program. The recipient is still free to exercise the constitutional right in question. *Rust v. Sullivan* (1991).

c. Group Registration and Disclosure

A vital aspect of freedom of association and belief is the right to maintain privacy regarding those beliefs and group ties. Anonymity is a vital means of avoiding the chilling effect of threats and harassment. Nevertheless, the Court has not forged a consistent doctrine indicating when the First Amendment will protect against compelled disclosure of group membership or other information concerning group activities. Cases from an earlier era dealing with subversive organizations tended to adopt an *ad hoc* balancing analysis giving extreme deference to legislative justifications based on national security. *Barenblatt v. United States* (1959) [contempt conviction for refusing to answer congressional committee's questions concerning witness' associational relationships upheld]; *Communist Party of the United States v. Subversive Activities Control Bd.* (1961) [compelled registration and disclosure of Communist Party membership list upheld].

However, other cases, typically dealing with groups perceived as "legitimate," have been reviewed under a strict scrutiny standard. *Gibson v. Florida Legislative Investigation Comm.* (1963) held that before a state legislature could compel the NAACP to disclose membership list information, it had to "convincingly show a substantial relation between the information sought and a subject of overriding and compelling state interest." In explaining the basis for heightened review, the Court noted that the state was not seeking to secure information about Communist activity. Rather, it was the NAACP, which was in no way alleged to be a subversive organization, that was the focal point of the state's inquiry. "The strong associational interest in maintaining the privacy of membership lists of groups engaged in the constitutionally protected free trade in ideas and beliefs may not be substantially infringed except upon a substantial state showing of justification." *Gibson; Brown v. Socialist Workers* (1982).

How are these two lines of cases to be reconciled? One interpretation would be that the *ad hoc* balancing test and its susceptibility to allowing disturbing exceptions to freedom of association has been overtaken by the strict scrutiny standard of the later cases. Another view is that each line of cases is still creditable; *Barenblatt* and its government-favored balancing approach has neither been reversed nor discredited by the Court. The more stringent standard of review is reserved by the Court to protect activities deemed "legitimate" under the First Amendment. This suggests the view that the right of association implied from and protected by the First Amendment is to join together to pursue objectives consistent with the goals of the First Amendment. It is not a general right of association.

d. Public Benefits and Government Employment

Governmental benefits and public employment have traditionally been treated as privileges rather than rights. If government employment and public benefits are privileges, it is argued, it follows that government is free to impose such conditions on the receipt of such benefits as it deems appropriate. Today, this right-privilege dichotomy has been largely discarded and replaced by principles such as the unconstitutional conditions doctrine. Government cannot condition the receipt of public benefits or enjoyment of public employment upon the surrender of constitutional rights.

In the context of freedom of association and belief, unconstitutional conditions reasoning means that the government cannot freely condition an individual's access to benefits from the public sector on the basis of what would constitute interference with her political and associational freedom. Of course, this does not mean that government must open sensitive job positions to obvious national security risks. But it does require that governmental rules and regulations concerning access to public employment, for example, be narrowly drawn with precision and clarity. Illustrative is *United States v. Robel* (1967), which invalidated provisions of federal law prohibiting members of communist-action organizations from engaging in "any employment in any defense facility." The Court, per Chief Justice Warren, struck down this statutory prohibition as a vague and overbroad intrusion on First Amendment rights: "[T]he statute sweeps indiscriminately across all types of associations with communist-action groups, without regard to the quality and degree of membership." The government must, said the Chief Justice, use "means which have a 'less drastic' impact on the continued vitality of First Amendment freedoms."

Unfortunately, the use of the overbreadth doctrine in *Robel* to invalidate the sweeping federal law did little to illuminate how a properly drawn loyalty-security program might be framed. Paradoxically, if the Court had chosen to put a savings construction on the statute, the *Robel* decision might have provided greater clarification on the line between permissible and impermissible conditions. As a consequence of the Court's approach, the *Robel* decision is now usually dismissed as a form of interest balancing even though the Court specifically refused to adopt a balancing test.

How should a loyalty security program be drafted to withstand First Amendment attack? It appears that a statute must satisfy the requirements outlined in *Scales v. United States* (1961). Although *Scales* arose in a criminal setting, even in the civil context of a *Robel*-type situation, the requirements of *Scales* apply, *i.e.*, there must be individual *scienter* of the organization's illegal objectives and specific intent to further those objectives, and active membership. If the statute meets these demanding criteria, it is likely to survive First Amendment scrutiny. Conversely, if the statute is not narrowly drawn in these terms, or if it is not drawn with clarity, it is likely to be held unconstitutionally vague and overbroad. The student should remember that even if a law survives such a facial inquiry, it still must be applied to particular individuals in a constitutional manner, *e.g.*, whether the law is limited to sensitive government employment.

The principles used in the public employment cases have also found expression in cases involving loyalty oaths and bar admission requirements. Positive oaths whereby the individual promises support of the Constitution are generally upheld since a properly drawn positive oath, reasonably related to the individual's capacity or fitness for office, involves only a minimal intrusion on protected association and belief. On the other hand, a broader oath directed at past associations and beliefs involves a more questionable intrusion on First Amendment values. For example, the oath in *Baggett v. Bullitt* (1964), requiring teachers to swear that they would "by precept and example promote respect for the flag and the institutions of the [United States]" and that they were not members of a "subversive organization," was held to be facially invalid since it "was vague, uncertain and broad." In *Keyishian v. Board of Regents of Univ. of N.Y.* (1967), the Court held that a statute proscribing knowing membership in a seditious organization without any requirement of seditious intent was unconstitutionally vague and overbroad. Less drastic means were available to the government. "Because First Amendment freedoms need breathing space to survive, government may regulate in the area only with narrow specificity." It should be noted that even a loyalty oath which appears to be vague and overbroad can be given a savings construction. For example, in *Cole v. Richardson* (1972), the Court determined that a statute requiring a loyalty oath which could have been read as fatally overbroad should be accorded a narrower savings reading to merely require a positive oath.

A series of bar admission cases further illustrates the conflict between government's desire to control access to its benefits and associational freedom. Generally, the bar can inquire into an applicant's fitness for membership and it can deny admission to an applicant who refuses to cooperate with a lawful inquiry into matters relevant to fitness; the bar cannot be held responsible for the performance of its members if it cannot fully inform itself of their character and fitness prior to their admission. *Konigsberg v. State Bar of California* (1961). But a broad-ranging inquiry into associations and beliefs directly intrudes on protected freedoms. *Baird v. State Bar* (1970) struck down denial of admission to the bar of an applicant who had refused to answer questions about his associational ties. The essential limiting factor was clarified in the companion case, *Law Students Civil Rights Research Council Inc. v. Wadmond* (1971), establishing that the bar association could inquire into an applicant's membership in groups advocating the violent overthrow of government so long as this was preliminary to further inquiries into the nature of that membership. The inquiry into past associations must be limited by scienter and specific intent.

In addition to the First Amendment problems raised by government efforts to force disclosure of group memberships and political beliefs, public inquiries may also raise issues of self-incrimination. May government force its employees to disclose incriminating information under threat of discharge? *Garrity v. New Jersey* (1967), held that confessions given under such coercion cannot be used as a basis for subsequent criminal prosecution. Further, the employee cannot be forced to surrender his privilege against self-incrimination as a condition of continued employment. *Gardner v. Broderick* (1968). But if the employee is granted full immunity from criminal prosecution, and the questions asked are relevant to the job, she cannot refuse to answer. Refusal to cooperate with a lawful inquiry here as in the bar cases can become an independent basis for either denial of a public benefit or discharge from public employment.

e. The Right Not to Associate–Compelled Speech

The corollary of freedom to speak, to believe, and to associate is the freedom not to speak, not to believe, and not to associate. In part, recognition of these corollary rights reflects concern with freedom of conscience. When government intrudes into the private realm, its activities must necessarily be more restricted than when it regulates public conduct or expression. *Stanley v. Georgia* (1969) [private possession of obscene matter cannot constitutionally be made a crime]. The corollary rights also reflect appreciation of the need to allow an individual to determine for herself what identity or personality she will present to the world. Government cannot force an individual to identify with a belief or idea with which she disagrees. "A system which secures the right to proselytize religious, political, and ideological causes must also guarantee the concomitant right to decline to foster such beliefs." *Wooley v. Maynard* (1977). But these corollary rights are not absolute. As the Court said in *Roberts v. United States Jaycees* (1984): "Infringements may be justified by regulations adopted to serve compelling state interests, unrelated to the suppression of ideas, that cannot be achieved through means significantly less restrictive of associational freedoms."

In *Abood v. Detroit Board of Education* (1977), the Court held that compulsory service fees charged under a closed shop agreement (permitted by state law) which were used for the ideological or political objectives of the union (which were not necessarily shared by those paying fees) were unconstitutional. "[A]t the heart of the First Amendment is the notion that the individual should be free to believe as he will, and that in a free society one's beliefs should be shaped by his mind and his conscience rather than coerced by the State."

Similarly, an "integrated state bar" (which conditions the right to practice on membership in and payment of dues to the state bar) cannot use the dues of its members to finance political and ideological activities with which its members disagree. The Court rejected an attempt to distinguish *Abood* by reliance on the "government speech" doctrine which provides that government necessarily must take positions if it is to govern effectively. Use by the state bar of mandatory dues for political and ideological purposes could not be so justified. Unlike a government agency, the funds of the state bar came from dues not legislative appropriations and its functions were essentially advisory. The "integrated bar" was held to be governed by *Abood*. The state bar could fund activities which were germane to its goals but it could not fund activities of an ideological nature. *Keller v. State Bar of California* (1990).

And in *Wooley v. Maynard* (1977), the Court held unconstitutional the application of criminal sanctions to Jehovah's Witnesses who covered over the motto on their New Hampshire automobile license plate, "Live Free or Die." Their claim that they should not be compelled to proclaim agreement on their private property (*i.e.,* the license plate) with a state-composed message that offended their deepest religious and ideological convictions was upheld. The Court concluded that the state's interests in fostering appreciation of state history and state pride were insufficiently compelling to override the First Amendment rights at stake.

The principle that not every burden on the interests of a group to choose its members freely, or of an individual who declines to provide any support for an idea, will be protected, is reflected in *PruneYard Shopping Center v. Robins* (1980). *PruneYard* presented the question whether the California court's interpretation of the free expression provisions of its own Constitution could be used to force shopping center owners to permit pamphleteering within the shopping mall. The shopping center owner claimed a First Amendment right of non-association against being compelled to provide a forum on his property for the speech of others. The Supreme Court upheld the decision of the California court's ruling that the owner's First Amendment rights had not been infringed.

How is *PruneYard* to be distinguished from *Abood, Keller* and *Wooley?* First, *Wooley* involved ideas coming from the state itself. Second, the shopping center, by the choice of the Shopping Center owners, was open to the public. Third, there was little likelihood that the views expressed by the pamphleteers would be identified with those of the owners. Fourth, to the extent that such a danger was present, the owners could simply disavow the views being expressed. In short, the more a government regulation compelling some activity imposes a personal and direct burden on the rights of association and belief, the more it is likely to infringe the First Amendment right. See *Pacific Gas & Elec. Co. v. Public Util. Com'n* (1986) [state utility commission order requiring a private utility company to provide space in its billing envelopes four times a year to a private interest group critical of the utility held unconstitutional. The utility may be forced either to appear to agree with the group's message or to respond].

In some cases, the governmental interest in the regulation may be so overriding as to justify an admitted intrusion on the corollary rights. In the

Abood case, for example, the Court upheld compulsory fees used for collective bargaining purposes even though some workers might be opposed to collective bargaining or strikes. *Abood* concluded that the legislative assessment of the important contribution of the union shop to industrial peace constitutionally justified the interference with associational rights.

Roberts v. United States Jaycees (1984), upheld an interpretation of the Minnesota Human Rights Act barring gender discrimination by public business entities to apply to the males-only membership rules of the United States Jaycees. The Jaycees attacked the Act as a vague and overbroad intrusion on First Amendment rights. Justice Brennan for the Court in *Roberts,* distinguished two senses of freedom of association. First, the Jaycees' exclusion of women did not involve the constitutional protection afforded "intimate human relationships." Unlike marriage, family, or childbirth, "the local chapters of the Jaycees are neither small nor selective. Moreover, much of the activity central to the formation and maintenance of the association involved the participation of strangers to that relationship." Second, while the Act did burden the right to associate for expressive purposes protected by the First Amendment by interfering with the internal organization and affairs of the group, "Minnesota's compelling interest in eradicating discrimination against its female citizens justifies the impact that application of the statute to the Jaycees may have on the male members' associational freedoms." Brennan stressed the state's strong commitment to eliminating discrimination in public accommodations, the serious social and personal harms caused by gender discrimination, the need to remove barriers to economic advancement and political and social integration, and the use by the state of the least restrictive means of achieving its ends.

Similarly, a New York City law prohibiting discrimination in clubs with over four hundred members which provided benefits to businesses and non-members was not unconstitutionally overbroad. The law on its face did not significantly diminish "the ability of individuals to form associations that will advocate public or private viewpoints." If there was any overbreadth in the New York law, cure would have to await case-by-case analysis of situations where such overbreadth was in fact present. *New York State Club Association v. City of New York* (1988).

In summary, claims based on the right not to associate may be defeated by a finding that there is no significant intrusion on the right or by the determination that a burden is justified by a compelling governmental interest. *PruneYard* indicates that not every form of compelled expression significantly intrudes on First Amendment rights. *Roberts* suggests that where a state policy of requiring freedom from gender discrimination collides with associational freedom, the state policy can override the liberty claim. Although the Court did not say so in *Roberts*, the case is certainly capable of being seen as an example of equal protection policy triumphing over liberty considerations. See also *Runyon v. McCrary* (1976) [discrimination in private schools on the basis of race held to violate civil rights laws even as against claims of privacy, educational freedom, and associational freedom].

B. THE DOCTRINE APPLIED

1. EXPRESSION IN THE LOCAL FORUM

In the "fifties" and "sixties," a civil rights social revolution occurred in the United States. Through sit-ins, demonstrations, parades, and picketing, civil rights demonstrators protested the continuing survival of Jim Crow legislation in the southern and border states. When the states and municipalities involved responded through legislation, the demonstrators usually found successful refuge in the First Amendment. *Edwards v. South Carolina* (S.Ct. 1963); *Cox v. Louisiana* (1965); *Brown v. Louisiana* (1966). In 1977, the American Nazis announced plans to march through Skokie, Illinois, a predominantly Jewish suburb of Chicago. Skokie's population included many survivors of Nazi concentration camps. When the village of Skokie responded by seeking injunctions and announcing new ordinances to prevent such marches, the Nazis contended that these measures offended the First Amendment. These contentions prevailed. *Collin v. Smith* (1978).

Whatever one's reaction to these events, they dramatically illustrate the dilemma of reconciling the rights of speech and assembly in the public forum with a community's right to maintain peace and order. Indeed, the context of the Skokie cases is particularly troubling. Who may properly claim freedom of speech? For what modes of expression? In order to answer these questions, it is necessary first to draw a distinction based on the nature of the regulation. It must be determined whether the local community is seeking to regulate the content of the speech, *i.e.,* the message being communicated, or is merely seeking to regulate the conditions under which the expression will occur in a content-neutral way, *e.g.,* regulating the time, place, and manner under which expression, regardless of its content, can occur.

a. Controlling Speech Content: Inciting, Provocative and Offensive Language

Whenever government undertakes to regulate speech and assembly because of the content of what is being communicated, it bears a heavy burden of justification. Frequently, the courts invoke the modern clear and present danger test in reviewing convictions under a breach of the peace or disorderly conduct law. For example, *Hess v. Indiana* (1973), reversed a disorderly conduct conviction of a demonstrator in an antiwar protest who had used words such as "we'll take the fucking street later." *Hess* declared that such language was nothing more than advocacy of illegal action at some future time. Since there was no incitement to imminent disorder, or indeed any evidence of an intent to produce such imminent disorder, the fact that the words might have a tendency to lead to violence was inadequate to meet the requirements of the modern clear and present danger test. *Brandenburg v. Ohio* (1969). See also *Cohen v. California* (1971), where the Court held that the defendant could not be convicted of disturbing the peace absent a showing of intent to incite to illegal conduct.

An alternative approach can be found in *Chaplinsky v. New Hampshire* (1942), where a Jehovah's Witness called the town constable "a goddamned racketeer and a damned fascist." A breach of the peace conviction was upheld because the state supreme court had given a curative gloss to the breach of the peace law limiting it to words with a "direct tendency to cause acts of violence by the persons to whom individually the remark is addressed." The U.S. Supreme Court explained in *Chaplinsky* that there are some categories of expression which are not protected freedom of speech, including fighting words, "those words which by their very utterance inflict injury or tend to incite an immediate breach of the peace." Such expression is "of such slight social value as a step to truth that any benefit that may be derived is clearly outweighed by the social interest in order and morality." In short, fighting words, like obscenity, do not fall within the protected scope of the freedom of speech.

The student should note the important features of the fighting words doctrine as it operates. First, as defined by *Chaplinsky*, the doctrine had two parts. It encompassed offensive or abusive language which by its very utterance inflicts injury. It also included language which by its very nature, judged by the probable reaction of a person of common intelligence, is likely to produce a violent reaction. Second, the doctrine, as framed, was limited to face-to-face verbal encounters which at the moment they are uttered invite physical reprisal or otherwise are likely to produce disorder. Third, the doctrine does not look to the actual danger of the particular situation but focuses on the abstract character of the words—are they of a kind likely to provoke retaliation by the average addressee?

The fighting words doctrine, however, has been severely limited since its announcement in *Chaplinsky*. The doctrine suggested that a speaker could be restricted because of the reactions of the audience. It thus seemed to endorse the concept of a heckler's veto. *Terminiello v. Chicago* (1949), rejected the principle that the hostile reaction of a crowd would provide justification, consistent with the First Amendment, for silencing a speaker. Justice Douglas said in fact that it was the purpose of the First Amendment to invite dispute. "[The First Amendment] may indeed best serve its high purpose when it induces a condition of unrest, creates dissatisfaction with conditions as they are, or even stirs people to anger." Speech can neither be censored nor punished "unless shown likely to produce a clear and present danger of a serious substantive evil that rises far above public inconvenience, annoyance, or unrest."

But *Feiner v. New York* (1951), appeared to endorse a broader version of *Chaplinsky*. Irving Feiner spoke at the American Legion picnic in Syracuse, New York. Among other things, he called the Mayor "a champagne-sipping bum." The crowd moved toward the speaker. Who should be arrested, the speaker or the crowd? The police arrested the speaker. The Supreme Court, 5–4, upheld the conviction by drawing a distinction between Feiner's situation and a hostile audience scenario. While a speaker could not be silenced merely because of the reactions of a hostile audience, in this case the speaker was deemed to have been inciting a riot. *Feiner* had created a "clear and present danger of disorder." But is this only after-the-fact rationalization? Logistically, it is always easier to arrest the speaker than the crowd. Similarly, it is not difficult to portray a noisy and insulting speaker as inciting. The dissenters found no danger of imminent disorder on the *Feiner* facts; the majority did. *Feiner* shows that the clear and present danger test can be manipulated to silence offensive speakers.

Nevertheless, *Feiner* has increasingly been read narrowly. When a speaker intentionally provokes a hostile reaction and imminent disorder is probable, his speech is not protected, and the police may move against him. See *Cohen v. California* (1971). But if a speaker is engaged in protected expression, if he is not intentionally inciting the crowd to violence, he is to be protected. Police must then move against the hostile crowd. *Gregory v. Chicago* (1969). What happens if the police cannot control the crowd and violence is imminent remains unclear. In such an emergency, whether or not the speaker should be stopped, he usually will be.

There was a second part to the *Chaplinsky* "fighting words" doctrine. The Court had indicated that insulting or abusive language (*i.e.*, words which by their very utterance inflict an injury) also fell outside the First Amendment. But *Cohen v. California* severely undermined this concept. Cohen had been convicted of disturbing the peace by "offensive conduct" for wearing a jacket bearing the words "Fuck the Draft" in a Los Angeles courthouse. In reversing the conviction, Justice Harlan rejected the proposition that the Court could excise, as offensive conduct, particularly scurrilous expression from the public discourse. There was a great danger in government selecting certain expression and placing it off-limits: "[O]ne man's vulgarity is another's lyric." Further, Justice Harlan stressed that speech often serves an emotive, non-cognitive value. In prohibiting a certain manner of expression, there was great danger that the ideas themselves would be suppressed. See *Erznoznik v. Jacksonville* (1975): "[T]he Constitution does not permit our government to decide which types of otherwise protected speech are sufficiently offensive to require protection for the unwilling listener or viewer."

The fighting words doctrine, although it has been altered, has never been overturned. The prohibition against punishing offensive language, while a source of dispute on the present Court, remains unaltered. The line between fighting words and offensive language is ill-defined. Yet it is an important distinction. Fighting words—absent content discrimination among subsets of fighting words [*R.A.V. v. City of St. Paul* (1992) *infra*]—can be prohibited consistent with the First Amendment. Offensive speech cannot be. The reason that the nature of fighting words has not been clarified is, in part, that the Court has increasingly used the devices of vagueness and overbreadth to invalidate disorderly conduct and breach of the peace statutes on their face.

In *Gooding v. Wilson* (1972), a Georgia breach of the peace statute was held unconstitutionally overbroad in that the Georgia courts had not limited the statute to fighting words as defined in *Chaplinsky*. The Court concluded that the statute as interpreted made it "a 'breach of the peace' merely to speak words offensive to some who hear them, and so [swept] too broadly." The defendant in *Gooding* had shouted epithets such as "white son-of-a-bitch, I'll kill you" during an anti-Vietnam war demonstration at an induction center. Whether this would constitute fighting words was not relevant to the disposition of the case since the statute was itself not limited to fighting words.

The *Gooding* technique of using vagueness and overbreadth to invalidate a statute, thereby avoiding the need to define fighting words with particularity, has been employed frequently in subsequent cases. See, *e.g.*, *Lewis v. New Orleans* (1972) (*Lewis I*), *Lewis v. New Orleans* (1974) (*Lewis II*), *Rosenfeld v. New Jersey* (1972). Indeed, Justice Blackmun joined by Chief Justice Burger and Justice Rehnquist, dissenting in *Lewis II,* stated: "Overbreadth and vagueness in the field of speech have become result-oriented rubber stamps attuned to the easy and imagined self-assurance that 'one man's vulgarity is another's lyric.' " To pass muster under the prevailing judicial doctrine, then, a statute must be limited to fighting words used in personal face-to-face encounters, or incitement to imminent and probable illegal conduct. The laws must not cross the line to reach speech which is merely offensive or annoying. The student should remember that if a statute is narrowly drawn, it would then become necessary to determine whether the defendant's words in the particular case are constitutionally protected words (*i.e.,* is the law constitutional "as applied").

In addition to the many limitations which have been placed on the "fighting words" doctrine since its inception, a major limitation was added in *R.A.V. v. City of St. Paul* (1992). Justice Scalia declared for the Court 5–4 that there were "no categories of speech entirely invisible to the Constitution." A St.Paul ordinance which punished fighting words that insult or provoke violence "on the basis of race, color, creed, religion, or gender" was unconstitutional on its face. The ordinance had been applied to white youths who had burnt a cross in the yard of a black family. The city was unsuccessful in defending the ordinance on the ground that it punished fighting words. Categories of speech may be regulated consistent with the First Amendment "because of their constitutionally proscribable content." For example, libel can be made actionable because of the damage it inflicts on reputation but libel actions cannot be limited only to those actions where government officials have been criticized. All "fighting words" can be punished but a subset of fighting words which is punished because of the viewpoint they express cannot be. Such regulation of fighting words is impermissible content discrimination.

The St. Paul ordinance in *R.A.V.* could not be justified as a "secondary effect" [See *Renton v. Playtime Theaters, Inc.* (1986)] because of the city's interest in protecting vulnerable minority groups which had suffered discrimination. The consequences of the proscribed speech flowed from the listener's reaction to the speech—an impermissible ground for the regulation of speech. Although the ordinance served a compelling interest in promoting racial, religious and ethnic harmony, the ordinance was still invalid since there were content-neutral alternatives available, *i.e.*, the proscription of all fighting words.

Justice Scalia's opinion for the Court in *R.A.V.* drew fire from the concurring justices on two grounds. First, the holding undermined the entire categorical approach to free expression problems. Justice White, concurring, said the holding contradicted "repeated statements [in earlier cases] that certain categories of expression are 'not within the area of constitutionally protected speech.'" Justice White said the Court's new underbreadth doctrine served no useful function because it protects expressive activity that is "evil and worthless in First Amendment terms" simply because government had not regulated more rather than less speech. Second, *R.A.V.* undermined the purpose of strict scrutiny analysis in First Amendment cases since a narrowly drawn law which met the strict scrutiny standard was nevertheless invalid since it had not regulated *enough* speech. Such an approach to strict scrutiny analysis robbed it of all utility as a First Amendment tool. In sum, *R.A.V.* takes a radically new approach to the fighting words doctrine and to the categorical approach to First Amendment problems in general. *R.A.V.* suggests that hitherto unprotected categories of expression will merit First Amendment protection if regulation of them reflects impermissible content-based discrimination.

Similarly, *R.A.V.* affects the future of new candidates for unprotected First Amendment category status such as hate speech. Some legal scholars have argued that racial epithets, and hate speech in general, serves to perpetuate the subordinate status of minority groups. Hate speech does not invite discussion but instead produces a demeaning silence on the part of its victims. Some universities have developed hate speech codes and legislatures have considered enacting legislation punishing hate speech. At an earlier time, when hate speech was known as group defamation, an Illinois criminal libel statute punishing group defamation was upheld 5–4. *Beauharnais v. Illinois* (1952). Justice Frankfurter suggested for the Court that racial libel constituted unprotected expression because it robbed members of minority groups of human dignity and deprived them of economic and educational opportunities. However, *Beauharnais* proved to be a First Amendment dead end. The Illinois statute was repealed and *Beauharnais* has not met with favor in subsequent Supreme Court decisions.

Since *R.A.V.* held that a content-based proscription of a subset of "fighting words" such as hate speech is impermissible, the future of hate speech regulation just dealing with "fighting words" is not bright. Even if racist speech as a broad category were proscribed, such regulation would likely fall afoul of the doctrine of *Cohen v. California* that offensive speech may not be proscribed simply on the ground of its offensiveness.

For the proponents of hate speech regulation, a development which provides some encouragement, however, is *Wisconsin v. Mitchell* (1993) which upheld a Wisconsin law enhancing criminal penalties when the victim of the crime has been selected because of race. Motive is an appropriate factor in sentencing and when the motivation for crime is the racial identity of the victim, such motivation can be considered. *R.A.V.* was distinguished on the ground that the law struck down there was aimed at expression while enhanced penalties for racial crimes were by definition directed at non-speech conduct.

b. Access to Public Property

While government regulation of protected First Amendment speech in the public forum because of its content is subject to strict scrutiny, content-neutral regulation which only indirectly burdens free speech is not seen as imposing as severe a burden on First Amendment values. *Greer v. Spock* (1976). Thus, time, place and manner regulation of the context in which speech occurs (*i.e.*, an indirect burden on free speech, *supra*) is subjected to a less searching balancing inquiry. *Perry Education Ass'n v. Perry Local Educators' Ass'n* (1983). The degree of judicial scrutiny of the government regulation frequently turns on the nature of the place being regulated. Public property may be characterized as a traditional public forum, a limited or designated public forum, or a nonpublic forum.

Streets, sidewalks, and parks are "quintessential public forums" which "have immemorially been held in trust for the use of the public, and, time out of mind, have been used for purposes of assembly, communicating thoughts between citizens, and discussing public questions." *Hague v. CIO.* See *Edwards v. South Carolina* (1963) [state capitol grounds are a traditional place for public protest]. While these traditional public fora are open for speech, the right of access must be exercised "in subordination to the general comfort and convenience, and in consonance with peace and good order." *Hague.* In short, competing uses of the forum must be harmonized.

Because traditional public fora are "natural and proper places for the dissemination of information and opinion" [*Schneider v. State of New Jersey* (1939), ordinance forbidding all handbilling is not justified by concern over street littering], any restriction based on the *content* of the message must be narrowly tailored to serve a compelling state interest. *Carey v. Brown* (1980) [prohibition on residential picketing except for labor picketing held unconstitutional]. But even an indirect government regulation of the context of expression is subject to stringent standards. Government may "enforce reasonable time, place and manner regulations as long as the restrictions are content-neutral, are narrowly tailored to serve a significant government interest, and leave open alternative channels of communication." *United States v. Grace* (1983) [law barring all picketing and leafletting on the sidewalks surrounding the Supreme Court held unconstitutional].

In the context of the traditional public forum, the distinction between a content-based regulation and a content-neutral time, place or manner regulation is a crucial one. Exemplifying this distinction is *Boos v. Barry* (1988), which invalidated under the First Amendment a District of Columbia regulation prohibiting the display of signs within 500 feet of a foreign embassy if the signs tended to bring the embassy's government into disrepute. Although not viewpoint-based, the sign prohibition was a content-based regulation of core political expression. Even assuming the regulation's justification that shielding embassy personnel from critical speech protected their dignity was compelling, the regulation was not narrowly tailored since less restrictive alternatives were available to protect the dignity interest.

But a regulation permitting dispersal of demonstrators within 500 feet of an embassy was valid. The lower court had narrowly interpreted this congregation clause to permit dispersal of demonstrators only when the police reasonably believed that a threat to the security of the embassy was present. So interpreted, this content-neutral regulation was not facially overbroad; it was instead a reasonable place and manner regulation.

The Court has held that a right of minimum and equal access to the public forum for expression extends beyond the traditional public forum to government property designated as a "limited public forum." But what is the scope of this limited public forum? Not all public property is open to speech and protest by the public generally: "The State, no less than a private owner of property, has power to preserve the property under its control for the use to which it is lawfully dedicated. [People who want to propagandize do not] have a constitutional right to do so whenever and however and wherever they please." *Adderley v. Florida* (1966).

In an effort to more clearly define the scope of the "public forum," the Court at times has applied a generalized inquiry into the compatibility of the expressive activity with the normal use to which the property is put. *Brown v. Louisiana* (1966) [quiet sit-in protest in a public library held to be constitutionally protected]; *Grayned v. City of Rockford* (1972) [school property may be part of public forum subject to reasonable time, place and manner regulation].

A more narrow, but increasingly dominant approach, is to look to the government's intent: "[A] public forum may be created by government designation of a place or channel of communication for use by the public at large for assembly and speech, for use by certain speakers, or for the discussion of certain speakers, or for the discussion of certain subjects." *Cornelius v. NAACP Legal Def. and Educ. Fund* (1985) [challenge to law excluding legal defense and political advocacy groups from participation in a charity drive among federal employees generally upheld but case remanded to determine if the law was applied in a viewpoint neutral fashion]. Under this designated forum approach, the compatibility of the expressive activity with the nature of the property is only one factor to be considered along with the relevant policies and practices of the government to ascertain whether the government intended to designate the place as a limited public forum. *See, e.g., Widmar v. Vincent* (1981) [university policy of opening meeting facilities to student groups created a limited public forum from which religious groups could not be constitutionally excluded].

An example of limited public forum analysis is provided by *Heffron v. International Society for*

Krishna Consciousness (1981). A state fair rule
limiting the sale or distribution of goods and materials to fixed locations was challenged by the Hare
Krishnas, who sought more personal encounters.
The rule was held to be a reasonable time, place
and manner regulation. A state fair held on public
property, reasoned the Court, involves a limited
public forum designed to efficiently present the
products and views of a great number of exhibitors
to a large number of people in a limited area. The
fixed location rule was applied even-handedly to all
distributors; it was therefore content-neutral. It
was narrowly-tailored to serve the significant government interest in maintaining orderly movement
of the crowds. No alternative regulation would deal
adequately with the problem. The Court rejected a
selective access approach exempting the Krishnas
from the fixed place rule-other religious and nonre-
ligious groups seeking support for their activities
were equally entitled to access as the Krishnas.
Finally, the rule did not prevent communication; it
did not deny access to the forum nor prevent the
Krishnas from pursuing their personal encounters
outside the fairgrounds.

Recently, the Court has increasingly avoided this
somewhat demanding form of judicial scrutiny by
characterizing the public property subject to the
regulations as not being part of the public forum.
In *Cornelius v. NAACP Legal Def. & Educ. Fund*
(1985), Justice O'Connor stated: "Control over access to a nonpublic forum can be based on subject
matter and speaker identity so long as the distinc-

tions drawn are reasonable in light of the purpose served by the forum and are viewpoint neutral." Thus, the city may limit access to the advertising space on city buses. *Lehman v. Shaker Heights* (1974). Military bases are not ordinarily a part of the public forum even when they are open to the public. *Greer v. Spock* (1976); *United States v. Albertini* (1985) [protestor who had been banned on security grounds from access to a base because of past protest activity could be excluded even during military open house]. Jail house grounds are not part of the public forum. *Adderley v. Florida* (1966). There is no right of public access to home mail boxes for unstamped mail. *United States Postal Service v. Council of Greenburgh Civic Ass'ns* (1981).

Nonpublic forum analysis is exemplified by *Perry Education Ass'n v. Perry Local Educators' Ass'n* (1983). A local school district had entered into an agreement with the exclusive bargaining agent for the teachers to deny access to the teachers' mailboxes to a rival union. The Court, 5–4, upheld the school district's action. Justice White, for the Court, began by rejecting the rival union's efforts to invoke the public forum doctrine. The district did not have a policy of unrestricted public access to the mailboxes. Selective access afforded certain civic groups engaged in activities of interest to students did not render the property open to the general public—at most the district had created a limited forum open to groups of a similar character.

Applying principles used for a nonpublic forum, Justice White concluded that the restriction on access turned "on the status of the respective union rather than their views," *i.e.*, it was viewpoint neutral; there was no ideological bias. The restriction was reasonable in serving the district's interest in preserving the property for its designated use—only the exclusive bargaining agent had responsibility to all of the teachers. The rival union retained "substantial alternative channels" for communication with the teachers.

For the four dissenters, the case involved an "equal access claim" which should not turn on whether the mailboxes were designated a public forum. Justice Brennan argued that the teachers would hear only the message of the dominant union while being denied the critical perspectives of the rival union—no other group but the rival union was explicitly denied access to this effective channel of communication. Applying a strict scrutiny standard, the dissenters concluded that, while the exclusive bargaining agent's status was relevant to assuring the dominant union access to teachers, it did not justify a policy of exclusive access.

The problem of determining whether a facility, even though public property, constitutes a public forum is itself an intensely difficult one. For example, a postal service regulation barred solicitation of contributions on postal premises. Did the application of the regulation to prohibit solicitation of contributions by a political advocacy group on the post office sidewalk violate the First Amendment?

Justice White held for a plurality that it did not. The postal sidewalk was not a traditional public forum; it lacked the characteristics of a general public sidewalk. It was not a public thoroughfare but led only from the parking lot to the post office. Even though some individuals and groups had been permitted to speak, leaflet, and picket on postal premises in the past, there was also a regulation extant prohibiting disruption. The sum of these factors did not dedicate postal property to expressive activity. Relying on *Perry*, the plurality declared that selective access did not transform public property into a public forum. *United States v. Kokinda* (1990).

Just as the postal sidewalk in *Kokinda* was not a public forum, so an airport terminal operated by a public authority was not a public forum either. Why were these facilities categorized as nonpublic forums? The distinction between public and nonpublic fora was governed by whether government was acting as a lawmaker or as a proprietor. The heightened review which applied when the government managed a public facility as a regulator or licensor would not be invoked when the government functioned as a proprietor managing the internal operations of a public facility. *International Society for Krishna Consciousness, Inc. v. Lee* (1992).

Airport terminals were not traditional public fora. Airport terminals unlike the village green had not been historically open to expressive activity. Airport terminals existed to facilitate air travel not expression. In such circumstances the no-solicitation rule was a reasonable content-neutral regulation. For an airport terminal to be categorized as a limited or designated public forum, government must have an intention to open the facility to public discourse. Justice Kennedy in a concurrence rejected the idea that the public forum category should be confined to those facilities which had historically been so categorized. The purpose of the public forum doctrine was to protect expression from government interference. Closing off recognition of new public facilities as public forums ran counter to this objective. The First Amendment had responded to changing technologies in other contexts and it should do so here as well. Justice Kennedy contended instead that the use of the public facility should dictate whether it was a public forum. If physical characteristics and easy public access made a public facility appropriate and suitable for expressive activity, then it should be characterized as a public forum.

Kokinda held the challenged regulation's application to sidewalk solicitation valid using the reasonableness standard applied in the case of nonpublic fora. The regulation did not involve content or viewpoint discrimination. Solicitation was inherently disruptive of the business of the postal service and impeded normal traffic flows. Furthermore, a categorical ban on solicitation was reasonable since it would be too difficult to enforce more limited regulations for all the nation's post offices. Justice Kennedy concurred but reached that result after using the heightened review standard applied to content-neutral time, place and manner regulation, *i.e.,* is the regulation narrowly tailored to serve significant government interests? Does it leave open alternative channels of communication?

Similarly, in *International Society for Krishna Consciousness v. Lee* (1992), a government operated airport terminal regulation which prohibited the solicitation and receipt of funds within the terminal did not violate the First Amendment. But a public authority-operated airport terminal regulation banning the distribution of written or printed materials violated the First Amendment. *Lee v. International Society for Krishna Consciousness* (1992). Using the foregoing public forum analysis, four Justices ruled that so extensive a prohibition was not narrowly drawn nor did it leave open ample alternative means of communication. Justice O'Connor using *nonpublic* forum analysis reached the same conclusion. The total ban on the distribution of leaflets or pamphlets was invalid because it was unreasonable. Unlike the disruption associated with solicitation such as pedestrian traffic delay and congestion, the peaceful distribution of leaflets or pamphlets was clearly not incompatible "with a large, multi-purpose forum" such as an airport terminal.

The student should note that while the above discussion focuses on regulations of the *place* for expression, government may also impose narrowly drawn, reasonable regulation of the *time* and *manner* of protest. In focusing on the manner of expression, the Court has suggested that "speech plus" conduct does not enjoy the same constitutional protection as "pure speech." Thus, Justice Goldberg in *Cox v. Louisiana* (1965) [obstructing public passage law held facially vague and overbroad] rejected any suggestion that the Constitution affords "the same kind of freedom to those who would communicate ideas by conduct such as patrolling, marching, and picketing [as] to those who communicate ideas by pure speech." While balancing is employed in such "speech plus" cases, the Court tends to weigh the scales in favor of regulation.

In balancing the competing interests in these public forum cases, the Court will frequently use the standard fashioned in *O'Brien:* "A government regulation is sufficiently justified if it furthers an important or substantial government interest; if the governmental interest is unrelated to the suppression of free expression; and if the incidental restriction of alleged First Amendment freedoms is no greater than is essential to the furtherance of that interest." The Court has characterized this test as involving essentially the same inquiry as is used in public forum analysis. See *Clark v. Community for Creative Non-Violence* (1984).

In *Members of City Council of Los Angeles v. Taxpayers for Vincent* (1984), the Court used *O'Brien* in upholding an ordinance prohibiting the posting of signs on public property including lamp posts. Justice Stevens, for the Court, characterized the law as a regulation of the *manner* of communication. The law was said to serve aesthetic interests, *i.e.,* barring a visual assault on citizens, which were "basically unrelated to the suppression of ideas." The ordinance was not substantially broader than necessary since it was aimed at the exact source of the evil. Visual clutter is a product of the medium itself; the substantive evil is not merely a byproduct of the conduct, *e.g.*, litter from handbilling. Borrowing from the public forum cases, the Court noted that adequate alternative channels of effective communication, at the public places where the signs would have been posted, were available, *e.g.*, handbilling. But Justice Stevens found no support for the challenger's invocation of the public forum doctrine. Rather, he suggested that lamp posts would not qualify as a traditional or limited public forum.

While the Court's balancing approach in the public forum cases or under *O'Brien* purports to be searching, the application of the test appears much less demanding. The "significance" of the government's interest often is little more than a requirement of a real, not imagined interest; the Court does not generally weigh the government's interest in a particular law against any increased intrusion on First Amendment values from its use; while a narrow tailoring of means to ends is verbally endorsed, the availability of alternative means of expression tends to diminish the demand for a close fit. With the development of the nonpublic fora concept, the protection available for open and equal access is even more restricted. Content neutrality is abandoned in favor of viewpoint or ideological neutrality; reasonableness of means often is little more than a minimal rationality standard; selectivity of access to the forum is accepted. A geographic fixation with the location of the speech replaces balanced assessment of the competing interests.

In summary, when government regulates expressive activity in the public forum, time, place and manner controls must be precise and must be able to be justified without reference to the content of the speech. A control, however, does not become content-neutral just because it incidentally burdens some speakers more than others. *Renton v. Playtime Theatres, Inc.* (1986). In addition, the Court has declared that although time, place and manner controls must be narrowly tailored to accomplish the substantial government interests they professedly serve, "narrowly tailored" does not mean the same thing as a "least restrictive alternative" test. The inquiry as to whether the control is narrowly tailored is less demanding than a less restrictive alternative test would be. All that is required is a showing that the government interest to be served would be accomplished less effectively in the absence of the control or regulation. *Ward v. Rock Against Racism* (1989).

c. Access to Private Property

State action is a key concept in imposing constitutional obligation. But is it possible that the First Amendment creates rights of access even in the context of private property? Can private property ever become part of the public forum? The possibility that the First Amendment can create a right of public access against an owner's consent was suggested by *Marsh v. Alabama* (1946). In reviewing a trespass conviction of a Jehovah's Witness for handbilling on the streets of a business district of a company town, the Court stated: "The more an owner, for his advantage, opens up his property for use by the public in general, the more do his rights become circumscribed by the statutory and constitutional rights of those who use it."

Marsh's suggestion that privately owned property could be dedicated to the public use generated a tortured series of cases involving access for speech purposes to privately owned shopping centers. In *Amalgamated Food Employees Union Local 590 v. Logan Valley Plaza, Inc.* (1968), an injunction barring informational picketing at the center was overturned. The shopping center was deemed a "functional equivalent" of the business district in *Marsh;* property rights of the store owners were closer to public property than to the private property rights of homeowners.

A caveat to the access rights recognized in *Logan Valley* came in *Lloyd Corp. v. Tanner* (1972). Only if there is a relationship between the object of the protest and the site of the protest, *i.e.,* the shopping center, do First Amendment rights attach—there was "no open-ended invitation to the public for any and all purposes." Then, in *Hudgens v. N.L.R.B.* (1976), *Logan Valley* was overruled. Conditioning access to the shopping center on the subject of the protest, reasoned the Court, constituted an invalid content-based restriction on expression.

Marsh apparently survives but in a highly limited form. Only when privately owned property has taken on essentially all of the attributes of a public property does it become subject to constitutional obligations. Absent some legally imposed duty, private property remains private, subject to the dominion of the owner to exclude those he chooses. But note that a right of access to private property can be created by state law. *PruneYard Shopping Center v. Robins* (1980) [state guarantee of public access for speech purposes to privately owned shopping center does not violate owner's right not to associate].

The fact that private property is not part of the public forum does not mean that government is free to bar access by the public to the homeowner. When a speaker seeks to communicate with homeowners through handbilling, solicitation, etc., First Amendment rights must be balanced with the state interest in protecting the interests of the homeowner, especially the interest in privacy and freedom from annoyance. A total government ban on door-to-door handbilling has been held invalid. *Martin v. Struthers* (1943). But in *Breard v. Alexandria* (1951), a more limited ban on commercial solicitation without the homeowner's consent was upheld. Soliciting the homeowner, then, is subject to reasonable regulation designed to protect citizens against crime and undue annoyance. But any such regulation must be drawn with "narrow specificity." *Hynes v. Mayor and Council of Oradell* (1976).

When a regulation, is found to impose a "direct and substantial limitation on protected activity," it can be justified only if the government demonstrates that it serves "a sufficiently strong, subordinating interest that [government] is entitled to protect." In *Village of Schaumburg v. Citizens for a Better Environment* (1980), the Court invalidated an ordinance of the Village prohibiting charitable solicitations unless the charity used at least 75% of its receipts for charitable purposes. The law only peripherally promoted the state's admittedly substantial interest in protecting the public from fraud, crime, and annoyance. Less intrusive means than banning solicitation were available.

But a content-neutral ordinance banning targeted picketing, i.e., picketing "before or about" any residence, is constitutional. As construed, the ordinance only reached picketing focused on, or taking place in front of, a particular residence. The regulation of such focused picketing served the significant government interest in the protection of residential privacy: "The devastating effect of targeted picketing on the quiet enjoyment of the home is beyond doubt." As construed, the ordinance left open ample alternative means of communicating a message. The prohibition on targeted picketing was narrowly tailored since it eliminated no more than the precise evil it sought to correct—targeted picketing of "captive" residents presumptively unwilling to receive the message. *Frisby v. Schultz* (1988).

d. Licensing, Permits and Injunctions

A narrowly drawn, content-neutral, reasonable time, place and manner control is constitutional even if it comes in the form of a prior restraint. *Cox v. New Hampshire* (1941) [city requirement for a fee and license for parades or processions held constitutional]. But, as is the case for prior restraints generally, when government employs licensing or permit systems, it bears a heavy burden of justification. *Organization for a Better Austin v. Keefe* (1971) [state court injunction against distribution of leaflets charging blockbusting overturned]. One aspect of the suspectness of such controls is the requirement that adequate standards be provided in the law to guide the administrator. Broad delegations of authority, even when cast as content-neutral, indirect controls, invite censorship of unpopular views.

A licensing system that provides no standards is overbroad and invalid on its face. *Kunz v. New York* (1951). If standards are provided, they must be clear and precise regardless of the way in which the law is applied. In *Shuttlesworth v. Birmingham* (1969), the city ordinance provided for issuance of a parade permit unless the administrator determined that "the public welfare, peace, safety, health, decency, good order, morals or convenience require that it be refused." The defendant, who had marched without a permit, successfully argued that the law was invalid on its face. As the Court concluded, it vested "virtually unbridled and absolute power" in the administrator. While the state courts had narrowly construed the law, the Supreme Court determined that it was impossible for protestors to anticipate this limited interpretation at the time of protest.

Similarly, a facial challenge to a Lakewood, Ohio ordinance which gave the Mayor unfettered discretion to deny a permit for the placement of coin-operated newspaper dispensing devices on city sidewalks was upheld. Under the ordinance, the Mayor could deny such a permit whenever he deemed it in the public interest. No reasons were required to be stated. Unlimited authority to condition a permit on any terms the licensor deemed "necessary and reasonable" violated the First Amendment. Neutral licensing criteria are required: "Therefore, a facial challenge lies whenever a licensing law gives a government official or agency substantial power to discriminate based on the content or viewpoint of speech by suppressing disfavored speech or disliked speakers." *City of Lakewood v. Plain Dealer Publishing Co.* (1988).

A facial challenge to a Forsyth County, Georgia ordinance requiring applicants for a permit to conduct a parade or assembly on public property to pay a permit fee of up to $1000 to the county administrator was unconstitutional. As in *City of Lakewood*, an overly broad licensing discretion had been impermissibly lodged in a government official. Ostensibly, the amount of the license fee was based on the costs of providing security for the parade. But this meant that the fee could in fact depend on the administrator's estimate of the degree of hostility the expressive activity, *i.e.*, the parade, was likely to generate in the community. That there was a $1000 cap on the permit fee did not make it content-neutral. Censorship was still possible since the amount of the fee could clearly be related to the content of the speech. Four justices joined in a dissent in which Chief Justice Rehnquist accused the majority of reaching out to invalidate the ordinance. In his view, the case should have been remanded to the lower courts for consideration of whether the ordinance was invalid for lack of adequate standards to guide discretion or for incorporation of a "heckler's veto." *Forsyth County, Georgia v. Nationalist Movement* (1992).

Injunctions are also prior restraints subject to close judicial scrutiny; precision of regulation is required of the judicial order as well as the municipal ordinance. *Near v. Minnesota ex rel. Olson* (1931). Nevertheless, courts have tended to be more tolerant of this form of control. At least the decision that the expression is subject to regulation is made by a judicial decision-maker. One aspect of this tolerance lies in the obligation to obey the facially invalid injunction. In *Shuttlesworth*, Justice Stewart, for the Court, said that a person faced with a facially invalid licensing law "may ignore it, and engage with impunity in the exercise of the right of free expression for which the law purports to require a license." But in *Walker v. Birmingham* (1967), involving an injunction issued during the same demonstration, Justice Stewart rejected the right of the protestors "to ignore all the procedures of the law and carry their battle to the streets." The theory appears to be that the rule of law requires at least an initial respect for the judicial injunction. If there is a judicial process available allowing prompt review of the injunction and the protestor fails to use it, he is barred from collateral attack in the contempt proceeding. But note that if the state fails to provide strict procedural safeguards, including "immediate appellate review," the injunction does not bind. See *National Socialist Party of America v. Village of Skokie* (1977). A similar principle governs the right to disobey a facially valid law which is being applied unconstitutionally. The protestor must seek judicial review of the administrative action before taking to the streets. *Poulos v. New Hampshire* (1953).

2. COMMERCIAL SPEECH

In 1942, the Supreme Court read "purely commercial advertising" out of the First Amendment. *Valentine v. Chrestensen* (1942) [municipal anti-litter ordinance could be constitutionally applied to handbilling containing both political and commercial messages]. However, the Court provided no rationale for this categorical exclusion of commercial speech from First Amendment protection nor did it define the meaning of commercial speech. What would be the status of a paid advertisement in a newspaper containing a political message but soliciting funds? See *New York Times v. Sullivan*

(1964). Should an offer to buy or sell, *i.e.*, purely commercial speech, be excluded from "the freedom of speech" protected by the Constitution?

Some commentators have argued against extending First Amendment protection to commercial speech. They point to the minimal value of commercial advertising to the citizen-critic in the process of self-government and the limited role such communication has in self-development. The potential effect of extending full First Amendment protection to commercial speech given the plethora of government regulation of economic transactions also has been of concern. Nevertheless, in *Virginia State Bd. of Pharmacy v. Virginia Citizens Consumer Council, Inc.* (1976) [state statute prohibiting pharmacists from advertising the price of prescription drugs held unconstitutional], speech which does "no more than propose a commercial transaction" was brought within First Amendment protection. Justice Blackmun, for the Court, focused on the interests of the advertiser, consumers (especially poor and aged consumers), and the society, in drug price advertising. It is in the "public interest," he contended, to assure that private economic decisions regarding the allocation of resources in our free enterprise economy "in the aggregate, be intelligent and well informed. To this end, the free flow of commercial information is indispensable." The importance of this free information flow in fashioning intelligent opinion regarding how the economic system should be regulated was cited to indicate the value of commercial speech in self-governing. See generally *Linmark Assocs., Inc. v. Willingboro* (1977) [town's prohibition on posting of "For Sale" and "Sold" signs on real estate as a means of curbing white flight held unconstitutional].

To bring commercial speech within the freedom of speech guarantee, however, does not mean that such speech enjoys the same degree of First Amendment protection as "core" First Amendment expression, *e.g.,* political speech. *Virginia Pharmacy* characterized commercial speech as having greater hardiness and objectivity and as being easier to verify than other kinds of protected speech. Thus more extensive government regulation is acceptable than for more sensitive forms of expression. One consequence flowing from this conclusion is that false, misleading, and deceptive commercial speech enjoys no First Amendment protection. *Friedman v. Rogers* (1979) [state statute prohibiting practicing optometry under a trade name upheld]. Compare *New York Times v. Sullivan* (1964) [false defamatory speech protected under First Amendment, absent a showing of actual malice]. Similarly, commercial speech that proposes an illegal transaction is not protected speech. *Pittsburgh Press Co. v. Human Relations Com'n* (1973) [ban on sex-designated help wanted ads upheld].

But the unwillingness of the Court to equate commercial speech and political speech is not limited to erroneous expression. In commercial speech cases, the Court foregoes the ordinary strict scrutiny standard of review applied to content regulation in favor of a less stringent balancing analysis. *Central Hudson Gas & Electric Co. v. Public Service Com'n* (1980) [total state ban on promotional advertizing by utilities held unconstitutional], established that commercial speech may be restricted only to further a substantial government interest and only if the means used directly advance that interest. Even if these requirements are met, the regulation must not be more extensive than is necessary. However, a regulation, if narrowly tailored, can meet the "necessary" prong of the *Central Hudson* test even though the regulation is not the least restrictive means of furthering the substantial government interests. *Board of Trustees of State University of New York v. Fox* (1989).

Fox did not signify that the means selected to achieve a governmental goal were entirely without significance in commercial speech cases. Thus the Court struck down a municipal ban, which in the interest of safety and esthetics, banned commercial newsracks but not newspaper newsracks. The ban affected only 62 commercial newsracks but left 1500 to 2000 newsracks still on the streets. Clearly, the safety and aesthetic benefits to be derived from a ban with such minimal impact were marginal. The city had failed to calculate the costs and benefits flowing from the burden on speech which it had imposed. *Fox* required a "reasonable fit" between the government goal and the means selected to achieve it. *Cincinnati v. Discovery Network, Inc.* (1993).

Some First Amendment rules have less—or no— force in the context of commercial speech. Given the lesser danger of chill of hardy commercial speech, the overbreadth doctrine [*Bates v. State Bar of Arizona* (1977)], and the prior restraint doctrine [*Central Hudson Gas v. Public Service Commission* (1980)], do not apply to commercial speech. A challenge to a regulation of commercial speech on its face will not be invalidated on overbreadth grounds.

Lawyer advertising has proven an especially fruitful area for litigation probing the parameters of the constitutional protection afforded commercial speech. Shortly after *Virginia Pharmacy, Bates v. State Bar of Arizona* (1977) held that a blanket ban on lawyer price advertising in newspapers for routine legal services violates freedom of speech. But the Court acknowledged concern over deception of the consumer and stressed the narrow confines of its ruling. *Bates* was dealing with a total prohibition on price advertising and not a narrowly tailored regulation. Nor was it addressing the "peculiar problems" posed by advertisements relating to the quality of the legal services offered or broadcast advertising.

The concern with the danger of deception of consumers manifested in *Bates* found expression in the judicial imprimatur given state prophylactic regulation of in-person solicitation for pecuniary gain (*i.e.,* ambulance chasing). *Ohralik v. Ohio State Bar Ass'n* (1978). Compare *In re Primus* (1978) [ACLU lawyer may "further political and ideological goals of the association," *i.e.,* core political values, by informing potential clients of the possibility of litigation free from state sanction based on the *potential* danger of deception]. While prophylactic measures were approved in the context of face to face solicitation, state efforts to curtail potential deception have generally not fared well. *Zauderer v. Office of Disciplinary Counsel of Supreme Court of Ohio* (1985), struck down a state court reprimand of an attorney for newspaper ads soliciting business from those injured by using Dalkon Shields. There was no showing that the ads were false or misleading. Nor could the state sanction the use of illustrations of the shields in the ad since the representation was not inaccurate; the fear of potential public deception and the state interest in the dignity of the profession were deemed insufficient to justify a total ban on illustrations. A law designed to further the state's interest in preventing consumer confusion by curbing potentially misleading advertising must be "no broader than is reasonably necessary to prevent the deception." See *In re R.M.J.* (1982). For example, *Peel v. Attorney Registration and Disciplinary Commission of Illinois* (1990) held that a categorical state prohibition on advertising a lawyer's certification as a trial specialist failed to meet the heavy burden required where "dissemination of actual factual information to the public" was involved even though there was some potential for misleading consumers.

May an attorney who was also a CPA and a certified financial planner (CFP) use those designations after her name in advertising? A Florida state agency which had reprimanded an attorney for so doing was held to violate the First Amendment. The prong of the *Central Hudson* test which required that the regulation at issue must directly advance a substantial state interest was not served by the reprimand. The advertising was not misleading nor had there been any showing that any member of the public had been misled. There was a constitutional presumption which favored "disclosure over concealment." *Ibanez v. Florida Department of Business and Professional Regulation, Board of Accountancy* (1994).

In *Zauderer*, the Court did uphold state discipline of the attorney for failure to disclose in his ads that a client might be liable for litigation costs if the lawsuit failed: "Because the extension of First Amendment protection to commercial speech is justified principally by the value to consumers of the information such speech provides, [the lawyer's] constitutionally protected interest in *not* providing any particular factual information in his advertising is minimal." Rejecting the *Central Hudson* test for evaluating this minimal burden on speech from disclosure laws, the Court asked only if the requirements were reasonably related to the state interest in preventing deception of consumers.

Generally, lawyer advertising in the form of mailed solicitation receives more First Amendment protection than does in-person solicitation. A state ban on in-person solicitation by Certified Public Accountants was held to violate one of the prongs of

the *Central Hudson* test. *Edenfield v. Fane* (1993).
The Court distinguished *Ohralik* where a ban on in-
person solicitation by lawyers was upheld. The
state in *Edenfield* had not shown that its ban
directly advanced a substantial state interest. Unlike lawyers, CPA's are not schooled in the art of
persuasion. Therefore, CPA in-person solicitation
was not inherently susceptible to overreaching nor
were innocent people likely to be misled.

In *Shapero v. Kentucky Bar Association* (1988), a
state regulation prohibiting lawyers from sending
truthful nondeceptive letters to potential clients
facing particular types of legal problems was invalidated. The risk of overreaching and undue influence from mailed solicitation was deemed less than
would be the case with in-person solicitation. A
targeted letter invaded the recipient's privacy no
more than at-large mailing of the same letter.

The *Central Hudson* test will permit the regulation of truthful advertising about lawful but potentially harmful activity. Thus regulation of advertising of legalized casino gambling which prohibited
such advertising directed at Puerto Rico residents
but permitted the same advertising directed to residents on the mainland was upheld. Deference to
the legislature should be accorded to the legislature
as to the appropriateness of the means used to
accomplish the state's interest under *Central Hudson*. After all, Puerto Rico could have banned
gambling altogether. If government has the authority to completely ban the activity, it necessarily
has "the lesser power to ban advertising" of that

activity. *Posadas de Puerto Rico Associates v. Tourism Company of Puerto Rico* (1986).

Given that commercial speech is subject to a less demanding standard of review than other protected speech, it might be expected that the Court would have fashioned a fairly clear definition of what constitutes "commercial speech." But such is not the case. In *Bolger v. Youngs Drug Prods. Corp.* (1983), the Court considered the constitutionality of a federal law prohibiting the mailing of unsolicited advertisements for contraceptives as applied to certain promotional and informational material. Most of the mailings were held to fall "within the core notion of commercial speech—'speech which does no more than propose a commercial transaction.'" But much of the material did more than offer to deal, thus presenting "a closer question." Clearly the fact that the expression was embodied in an advertisement did not necessarily make it commercial speech. See *New York Times v. Sullivan* (1964). Neither the references to products nor the economic motivation for the mailings rendered the speech commercial. However, "[t]he combination of *all* these characteristics" provided a basis for invoking the *Central Hudson* test. The fact that the advertising sought to link the product to current public debate was deemed inadequate to elevate the expression to the fully protected category. Applying *Central Hudson,* neither the government interest in barring offensive material from unwilling recipients nor its interest in aiding parents of minor children justified the law's sweeping prohibition of the mailings at issue.

In retrospect, the resolution in the extent of First Amendment protection to be accorded to commercial speech signified by *Virginia Pharmacy* has proven to be less dramatic than originally anticipated. The refusal to apply many of the traditional protective doctrines of First Amendment law and the decision to categorically exclude false and misleading commercial speech from any constitutional protection certainly limits the constitutionalization of commercial speech. Further, the strict scrutiny regimen has not been followed in reviewing this mode of content control. Although there are occasional deviations, the *Central Hudson* test remains the dominant approach for the resolution of commercial speech problems.

3. DEFAMATION AND PRIVACY

a. Rise of the Public Law of Defamation

New York Times v. Sullivan (1964), declared that where an elected public official sues a "citizen critic" of government for defamation, the First Amendment should alter the normal operation of a state's private law of libel. Analogizing the rendition of heavy damages in a civil libel action in such circumstances to the old and discredited crime of seditious libel, the Court, per Justice Brennan, concluded in a famous passage that the "central meaning" of the First Amendment guaranteed the right of the "citizen critic" to criticize his government. The First

Amendment was said to reflect this nation's "profound commitment to the principle that debate on public issues should be uninhibited, robust, and wide-open, and that it may well include vehement, caustic, unpleasantly sharp attacks on government and public officials." Just as the government official enjoys immunity to freely perform his governmental duties, so also the "citizen critic" must enjoy a qualified immunity from civil damages in order to permit him to perform his duty in a democratic government.

A difficult task was presented to the Court in *Sullivan*. How to reconcile the reputational interest of the public official plaintiff with the interest in freedom of expression of the citizen critic, in this case the *New York Times?* Since the Court was not prepared, even in these circumstances, to obliterate the reputational interest, it created a qualified immunity for the citizen critic defamation defendant. This qualified privilege, as described by Justice Brennan, required proof of actual malice by the defamation plaintiff if he is to be successful: "The constitutional guarantees require a federal rule that prohibits a public official from recovering damages for a defamatory falsehood relating to his official conduct unless he proves that the statement was made with 'actual malice'—that is, with knowledge that it was false or with reckless disregard of whether it was false or not." Justice Brennan, by using the actual malice test, essentially reads out from First Amendment protection defamatory expression that meets the actual malice standard. In this sense, the "actual malice" test performs a similar function to the definition of obscenity in First Amendment law; the definition of obscenity separates what is protected speech from what is not.

The Supreme Court has held that a lower court finding of actual malice must be independently reviewed by appellate courts since the actual malice finding is a question of constitutional fact. *Bose Corp. v. Consumers Union* (1984). Although an appellate court must examine the statement at issue and the surrounding circumstances to decide whether it constitutes protected speech, a jury's credibility determinations are reviewed under the "clearly erroneous standard" and not a de novo review standard. *Harte–Hanks Communications, Inc. v. Connaughton* (1989). Furthermore, *Herbert v. Lando* (1979), declined to recognize an editorial privilege precluding pre-trial discovery into actual malice. Actual malice involves judgments about state of mind and the journalistic process which makes it necessary for a plaintiff to have access to such information in order to prove actual malice.

The doctrine set forth in *Sullivan* rapidly expanded. It was applied to non-elected public officials. *Rosenblatt v. Baer* (1966). It was then expanded to private sector public figures even though the analogy to seditious libel appeared to be stretched to the breaking point. *Curtis Publishing Co. v. Butts* (1967). These developments were not applauded by everyone on the Court. Justice Douglas asked cryptically in *Rosenblatt* whether the night watchman was a government official for purposes of *Sullivan*. What he suggested was that the content of the defamation was more important than the status of the plaintiff. This view found expression in a plurality opinion of the Court in *Rosenbloom v. Metromedia, Inc.* (1971). Three of the Justices—Brennan, Blackmun, and Burger—were willing to see the actual malice privilege extended to matters of public interest generally. In their view, the public interest in the communication in controversy should be the touchstone for the applicability of the actual malice privilege rather than the status of the plaintiff.

b. The Modern Public Law of Defamation

The *Rosenbloom* plurality's desire to make the content of the defamation the critical factor in the new public law of libel was rejected in *Gertz v. Robert Welch, Inc.* (1974). The Court held, 5–4, per Justice Powell: "[S]o long as they do not impose liability without fault, the States may define for themselves the appropriate standard of liability for a publisher or broadcaster of defamatory falsehood injurious to a private individual."

Justice Powell reasoned that the reputational interest of the private plaintiff enmeshed in the defamation controversy permitted a greater degree of state action. The private plaintiff lacked the means of self help available to the public plaintiff. Further, there was "compelling normative consideration" for a different rule—the private figure had not voluntarily entered the vortex of public controversy or debate. On the other hand, concern for the dangers of self-censorship by the citizen-critic faced with a potential defamation action led to the extension of constitutional protection even to the private figure defamation plaintiff. States cannot impose strict liability. Further, at least in matters where there is a public interest, presumed and punitive damages would be precluded absent a showing of actual malice. Compensatory damages would still be available as long as the standard of liability was not a strict one. Although presumed damages were thus curtailed, compensatory damages were defined in such a way as to include some of the former domain of presumed damages. For example, the Court made it clear that damages for embarrassment, humiliation, and pain and suffering would be included under the rubric of compensatory damages.

Gertz, a milestone case, further extended the reach of the First Amendment into the private law of libel. Particularly significant was its rule that the First Amendment would not tolerate strict liability and that the minimum for liability would be negligent misstatement. The states, however, were free to create a rule more generous to the defamation defendant than negligent misstatement.

Gertz had not indicated whether its limitations on state defamation law were applicable in all private plaintiff defamation actions. Did the rules, for example, apply to non-media defendants? A case which seemed to pose this issue precisely was *Dun & Bradstreet, Inc. v. Greenmoss Builders, Inc.*

(1985). A credit reporting agency had inaccurately reported that a construction company had filed for bankruptcy. Arguably, the credit reporting agency was not a media defendant. Were presumed and punitive damages therefore available in the absence of proof of actual malice? In a plurality opinion, the Court said such damages were available and the ordinary rules of Vermont libel law should apply. However, the plurality opinion said that the critical distinction was not whether the defendant was a media defendant. The critical issue was whether the public communication involved a matter of public interest. The *Gertz* rules apply only to matters of public concern that are "at the heart of the First Amendment's protection." Justice Powell reasons that "speech on matters of purely private concern is of less First Amendment concern." In the view of the *Dun & Bradstreet* plurality, the credit rating of a construction company which had been communicated only to a very small group of people was not a matter of public interest.

In a concurring opinion, Justice White made an extended attack on the entire evolution of the public law of libel from *Sullivan* to *Gertz*. After *Dun & Bradstreet*, some of the state rules of libel law which might have been thought to have been altered by *Gertz* apparently are restored. For example, it is not clear that the rule of no strict liability in private plaintiff defamation cases which do not involve a matter of public concern still endures. Even more important after *Dun & Bradstreet*, however, is the question whether the *Sullivan–Gertz* rules, even as modified by *Dun & Bradstreet,* will endure. *Philadelphia Newspapers, Inc. v. Hepps* (1986), ruled 5–4 that plaintiffs suing newspapers for libel in matters of public concern must prove that the statements complained of are false. However, the Court did observe that when the defamatory matter is of exclusively private concern and the plaintiff is a private figure, constitutional requirements do not necessarily demand such special protection for the media.

Hepps was used to reject a First Amendment privilege for matters of opinion in defamation cases. Liability for a statement of opinion which includes or implies false, defamatory statements of fact is not barred by the First Amendment. *Milkovich v. Lorain Journal Co.* (1990). First Amendment interests were sufficiently protected by the *Hepps* rule that the plaintiff prove falsity and by the requirement that the plaintiff must prove fault. *Milkovich* emphasized that a defamation action cannot prevail unless the statement at issue can reasonably be interpreted as stating actual facts about an individual. This may allow defense counsel to find shelter in a modified opinion privilege by contending that the opinion expressed should not have been interpreted to have asserted actual facts.

The *Milkovich* case constitutes a major reaffirmation of the *New York Times–Gertz* rules. Another such reaffirmation is illustrated by the Court's refusal to allow the tort of infliction of emotional distress to do an end run around the Times doctrine. Hustler Magazine, a "skin" magazine, published a parody of right-wing evangelist Rev. Jerry Falwell portraying him having a sexual encounter with his mother in an outhouse. A judgment awarding damages to Falwell for emotional distress was unanimously reversed by the Supreme Court. Public plaintiffs—public officials and public figures—could not recover for intentional infliction of emotional distress in the absence of a showing that the publication complained of contained a false statement of fact which was published with actual malice. One of the elements of emotional distress is "outrageousness." But such a showing in a First Amendment context was too subjective because it would enable juries to impose liability based on the content of the publication or the identity of the parties. Moreover, the publication had been labeled "parody"; it could not reasonably have been interpreted as stating facts concerning Falwell. *Hustler Magazine v. Falwell* (1988). In summary, despite its many critics and its myriad technicalities, the *Times* doctrine still reigns.

c. Identifying the Public Figure Plaintiff

Since the focal point of the *Gertz–Sullivan* rules is still the status of the defamation plaintiff, it becomes critically important to understand the criteria for identifying who is a public figure. In *Gertz,* Justice Powell stated: "In some instances an individual may achieve such pervasive fame or notoriety that he becomes a public figure for all purposes and in all contexts. More commonly, an individual voluntarily injects himself or is drawn into a particular public controversy and thereby becomes a public figure for a limited range of issues. In either case, such persons assume special prominence in the resolution of public questions." Drawing on this dichotomy, subsequent cases have distinguished the all-purpose pervasive public figure from the limited-purpose public figure.

The pervasive public figure concept has been severely limited by the courts. Before an individual will be totally exposed to media attention, the courts require that his name almost be a household word, *e.g.*, Johnny Carson. Such a personality, it is thought, has access to the media to rebut defamatory attacks and has voluntarily thrust himself into the public spotlight.

The limited purpose public figure has proven more difficult to identify. *Time, Inc. v. Firestone* (1976), rejected efforts to apply the public figure label to Dorothy Firestone, Palm Beach socialite, who was involved in a racy divorce scandal. Justice Rehnquist, for the Court, applied a bifurcated test. First, in order for a person to be a public figure, the defamation must involve public controversy. Second, the plaintiff's involvement in that controversy must be voluntary. Applying these standards, Justice Rehnquist refused to equate matters of public controversy with matters of public interest. While the public might be keenly interested in Mrs. Firestone's marital travails, her divorce did not involve questions of overriding public concern. She had not voluntarily sought out public attention to make her divorce a matter of public debate. Her appearances in society pages did not in themselves make her a public figure. It would, of course, have been a different case if Mrs. Firestone had used the divorce litigation in which she was involved as the launch-pad for airing her own views on divorce and mar-riage.

Hutchinson v. Proxmire (1979) refused to extend the public figure label to a scientist, a federal grant recipient, who sued Senator Proxmire for criticism concerning the value of his research. The scientist had neither sought public attention nor was he sufficiently well known to have access to the media. Similarly, in *Wolston v. Reader's Digest Association, Inc.* (1979), the plaintiff, who had pled guilty to a contempt citation for refusing to respond to a sub-poena, sued Reader's Digest for falsely describing him, many years later, as a Soviet agent who had been found guilty of contempt. Wolston's activities may have made him newsworthy in that he attract-ed media attention. But this did not mean that he voluntarily thrust himself into a particular public controversy sufficient to make him a public figure. While Justice Powell in *Gertz* had suggested that a person might involuntarily become a public figure, these later cases failed to develop such a motion.

d. The Public Law of Privacy

There is a public law of defamation. Has the law of privacy also been constitutionalized? Does the First Amendment limit the state's ability to award civil damages for other tortious conduct involving expression such as invasion of privacy? *Time, Inc.*

v. Hill (1967), considered this question in the context of the state award of civil damages for inaccurate portrayal of the plaintiff to the public in a way highly offensive to the reasonable person, *i.e.*, false light privacy.   Life Magazine had done a picture story of the ordeals of the Hill family who had been held hostage by escaped convicts.   While the story was newsworthy, parts had been fictionalized.   Under New New law, Hill had a cause of action for privacy regardless of whether the publication was defamatory.

The Supreme Court, per Justice Brennan, set aside the damage award: "[T]he constitutional protection for speech and press preclude the application of the New York statute to redress false reports of matters of public interest in the absence of proof that the defendant published the report with knowledge of its falsity or in reckless disregard of the truth."   A new public law of privacy was created. Its foundations reflected the principles of *New York Times v. Sullivan* (1964).   Fear of damage awards, reasoned Justice Brennan, would yield self-censorship; negligence-based liability provided inadequate protection for the press.   First Amendment guarantees "are not for the benefit of the press so much as for the benefit of all of us.   A broadly defined freedom of the press assures the maintenance of our political system and an open society."   On the other side of the scales, the plaintiff's privacy interest was given short shrift since exposure of one's self is part of modern life—"The risk of this exposure is an essential incident of life in a society which places a primary value on freedom of speech and the press."

Brennan's majority opinion in *Time, Inc.* reflects the public interest issue orientation that characterized the *Rosenbloom* plurality's approach to the private plaintiff defamation action. The dissenters in *Time, Inc.*, on the other hand, stressed the lack of self-help of the private plaintiff, a normative concern that the plaintiff had not sought out the public spotlight, and the need to assume greater accuracy in reporting, *i.e.*, the themes used in *Gertz* to reject the public interest issue approach. Does *Gertz*, then, implicitly overturn *Time, Inc.?* Is it the status orientation of *Gertz* rather than *Time, Inc.'s* emphasis on the public interest that defines the constitutional limits of false light privacy? The Court, thus far, has not provided any answer. Perhaps the fact that the potential invasion of the false light privacy interest is often less apparent to the publisher than a defamatory content might serve to distinguish *Gertz*, *i.e.*, the need to protect the press from self-censorship is enhanced.

Time, Inc. deals with false light privacy which is closely related to defamation. But what of the "true" privacy action involving accurate publicity given to intimate facts concerning the private life of the plaintiff in a way offensive to a reasonable man? *Restatement (Second) of Torts*, Sec. 652 D. In *Cox Broadcasting Corp. v. Cohn* (1975), involving public disclosure of a rape victim's name in violation of state law, the Supreme Court reversed an award of damages. But the Court limited its holding to accurate disclosures of matters of public record; the victim's name had appeared in the indictment. Similarly, *Florida Star v. B.J.F.* (1989) invalidated under the First Amendment a damages award against a newspaper for negligently publishing the name of a rape victim obtained from a public police report. The report had been released in violation of police department procedures and of a state statute banning the publication of the names of rape victims. An award of civil damages was not a narrowly tailored means of protecting privacy. Other means less restrictive of protected speech were available to government. The Court strongly relied on a principle that had been set forth earlier in *Smith v. Daily Mail Publishing Co.* (1979): "If a newspaper lawfully obtains truthful information about a matter of public significance then state officials may not constitutionally punish publication of the information absent a need to further a state interest of the highest order." Reflecting a similar emphasis on public access to information, a state cannot consistent with the First Amendment permanently prohibit a grand jury witness from disclosing his testimony after the expiration of the grand jury term. *Butterworth v. Smith* (1990).

Thus there has been no Supreme Court answer to the fundamental question: can liability be imposed for truthful disclosure of private facts? Lower courts grappling with the problem have generally rejected any absolute constitutional privilege for truthful publication. Instead, they have tended to focus on the public interest in disclosure and the "outrageousness" of the disclosure. It is likely that such a balancing of the First Amendment with the interests underlying the privacy tort will generate some form of qualified privilege for disclosure of matters of legitimate public concern.

4. OBSCENITY AND INDECENCY

Roth v. United States (1957) determined that, as a matter of history and function, obscenity was "utterly without redeeming social importance." Obscenity was "not within the area of constitutionally protected speech or press." Since obscenity is categorically excluded from First Amendment protection, it enjoys only the protection afforded by the due process mandate of rationality in law-making. Obscenity control, apart from protecting juveniles and unconsenting adult passersby from exposure, serves the legitimate state interests in maintaining "the quality of life and the total community environment, the tone of commerce in the great city centers, and possibly, the public safety itself." *Paris Adult Theatre I v. Slaton* (1973).

Since *Roth,* the central constitutional task in obscenity cases has been identifying what expression qualifies as "obscenity." It is a question of definition. Today, each element of a three-part test must be satisfied. It must be determined: "(a) whether the average person, applying contemporary community standards, would find that the work, taken as a whole, appeals to the prurient interest, (b) whether the work depicts or describes, in a patently offensive way, sexual conduct specifically defined by the applicable state law, and (c) whether the work, taken as a whole, lacks serious literary, artistic, political, or scientific value." *Miller v. California* (1973). While the *Miller* formulation is designed to limit the Supreme Court's censorial role and promote local determination of obscenity, First Amendment values are to be protected "by the ultimate power of appellate courts to conduct an independent review of constitutional claims when necessary." See *Jenkins v. Georgia* (1974) [obscenity conviction for showing film "Carnal Knowledge" reversed since nude scenes did not constitute "hard core" sexual conduct].

The first part of the inquiry, the prurient interest test, was derived from *Roth*. Prurience is constitutionally defined as material appealing to a shameful or morbid interest in sex. It does not include a normal interest in sex. But see *Brockett v. Spokane Arcades, Inc.* (1985) [overbroad definition of prurient to include lust does not support holding that the entire statute is facially invalid]. *Roth* rejected the earlier *Regina v. Hicklin* (1868) standard that focused on the possible impact of the material, or even isolated parts of a work, on those persons most susceptible to its negative influences. In *Roth*, Justice Brennan, for the Court, determined that the *Hicklin* approach provided inadequate protection to material protected by the First Amendment. The Court instead required consideration of the effect of the work, taken as a whole, on the "average person, applying contemporary community standards."

However, if the material is targeted to appeal to the peculiar susceptibilities of a particular group, courts will apply a variable obscenity standard measuring the impact on such a group. *Ginsberg v. New York* (1968) [minors]; *Pinkus v. United States* (1978) [sexually deviant groups]. See *Erznoznik v. Jacksonville* (1975) [state cannot proscribe exposure to all nudity, even for minors].

Obscenity is limited to "patently offensive" representations of sexual conduct (not violence) which is specifically defined by applicable law. Patently offensive refers to depiction of sexual conduct that "goes substantially beyond customary limits of candor and affronts contemporary community standards of decency." *Miller.* See *Manual Enterprises, Inc. v. Day* (1962). *Miller* undertook to provide examples: "(a) patently offensive representations or descriptions of ultimate sexual acts, normal or perverted, actual or simulated, (b) patently offensive representations or descriptions of masturbation, excretory functions, and lewd exhibitions of the genitals." While this listing is not exhaustive [*Jenkins v. Georgia* (1974)], obscenity controls must be written or judicially interpreted to be limited to such material or the law suffers from overbreadth. See *Ward v. Illinois* (1977) [state statute read to embody *Miller* standards and applied to materials describing sado-masochistic acts held constitutional]. Patent offensiveness, coupled with the pruriency test, is generally considered as restricting obscenity to hard-core pornography.

Both pruriency and patent offensiveness are determined by "contemporary community standards." But what is the relevant community? In *Miller*, the Court rejected the contention that only a national community standard, free of local biases, would provide adequate First Amendment protection and allowed lower courts to use local standards in defining what is obscene. Subsequent cases have made it clear that the state may choose to omit reference to any particular geographic community, state or local, although it may do so. If a geographic reference is omitted, each juror is free to ascertain the contemporary community standard. *Jenkins v. Georgia* (1974); *Hamling v. United States* (1974) [federal prosecutions]. The relevant community includes all adults, including sensitive persons, but excludes children. *Pinkus v. United States* (1978). Since the jury is applying community standards in determining pruriency and patent offensiveness, expert evidence is not required. *Paris Adult Theatre I v. Slaton* (1973).

One of the notable effects of *Miller* was its rejection of an earlier test requiring that material be "utterly without redeeming social value" in order to be labeled obscene. *Memoirs (A Book Named "John Cleland's Memoirs of A Woman of Pleasure") v. Attorney General of Comm. of Massachusetts* (1966). Chief Justice Burger, for the *Miller* Court, castigated this as "a burden virtually impossible to discharge under our criminal standards of proof" since it requires proof of a negative. In its place, *Miller* asks whether the work in question lacks "*serious* literary artistic, political or scientific value." Unlike the other two tests which involve fact determinations for the jury, the redeeming serious value element appears to involve an increased judicial role and not to be governed by the open-ended community standards. See *Smith v. United States* (1977).

There is one exception to the *Miller* tripartite test. Even if material does not satisfy the standards, the material may be rendered obscene by the way in which it is published. A distributor can be convicted of selling obscene material if he exploits the sexually provocative aspects of the material, *i.e.,* pandering. *Ginzburg v. United States* (1966) [mailings from Intercourse and Blueball, PA. and Middlesex, N.J. evidenced the "leer of the sensualist" which permeated the advertising].

Miller represents the first time since *Roth* that a majority of the Court agreed on a test of obscenity. Justice Brennan, the author of the opinion in *Roth,* recanted in dissent in *Miller* accepting the bankruptcy of the search for a sufficiently specific and clear definition of obscenity. He concluded that the concept was inherently vague, producing a lack of fair notice, a chill on protected speech and a constant institutional stress. For him the answer was to limit obscenity control to the context of protecting juveniles and unconsenting adults. *Paris Adult Theatre I v. Slaton* (1973) (Brennan, J., dissenting). A majority of the Court, however, continues to adhere to the path defined in *Roth–Miller.*

Although the Court has gone so far as to hold that there is no constitutional bar to the inclusion of substantive obscenity offenses under a state criminal RICO law, *Sappenfield v. Indiana* (1989), the state power to regulate obscenity recognized in *Roth–Miller* does not provide a *carte-blanche* to government. Obscenity control must be pursued consistent with other constitutional values. For example, the State may not invade the privacy of the home or a person's private thoughts by punishing a person for the mere possession of obscene materials in his home—"If the First Amendment means anything, it means that a State has no business telling a man, sitting alone in his own house, what books he may read or what films he may watch." *Stanley v. Georgia* (1969). *Stanley*, however, did not extend to a state law prohibiting the possession or viewing of child pornography; the state interest in the physical and psychological well-being of minors served to distinguish *Stanley*. The state had a compelling interest in protecting child pornography victims and in destroying the "market for the exploitative use of children." *Osborne v. Ohio* (1990). Furthermore, the right of privacy protected in *Stanley* appears to be limited to the home. The First Amendment provides no protection to consenting adults seeking to view obscene films in an adult movie theater. *Paris Adult Theatre I v. Slaton* (1973).

A corollary of the demand for specific limits on states in defining obscenity is that government cannot generally proscribe "indecent" publications consistent with the First Amendment. Whether cast as a criminal prosecution or a civil regulation, the *Miller* three-part test governs. *Paris Adult Theatre I v. Slaton* (1973). For example, a law condemning drive-ins showing films containing nudity as a public nuisance when visible from the public streets was held to be an excessive intrusion on First Amendment values. *Erznoznik v. Jacksonville* (1975). A zoning ordinance which excludes all live entertainment including non-obscene nude dancing while permitting other commercial activity, has been held to be an overbroad intrusion on First Amendment rights. *Schad v. Mount Ephraim* (1981). Compare *New York State Liquor Auth. v. Bellanca* (1981) [state may ban nude dancing in establishments serving liquor pursuant to its police powers to prevent disturbances and the 21st Amendment].

But when the state undertakes to regulate the location of adult-only establishments pursuant to its zoning powers, the Court has treated such laws as time, place and manner controls rather than as content regulations requiring stricter scrutiny. Such laws imposing only an indirect burden on speech must serve a substantial government interest and must leave open reasonable alternative avenues of communication. *Young v. American Mini Theatres, Inc.* (1976), upheld 5–4 Detroit's "Anti–Skid Row" ordinance requiring dispersal of places of adult entertainment. The Court, per Justice Stevens, stressed that the law was a reasonable means of furthering the city's important interest in regulating land use for commercial purposes in order to preserve the quality of urban life. Unlike *Schad, supra,* there was evidence of harm from the regulated conduct. See *Renton v. Playtime Theatres, Inc.* (1986) [regulating the location of adult theaters by concentrating or dispersing them was aimed at the "secondary effects" of adult theaters; a city may rely on any evidence reasonably believed to be relevant and need not develop independent evidence of harm]. The Detroit law in *American Mini Theatres* was perceived as involving only a minimal indirect burden on First Amendment values since there was no claim that adult establishments were denied access to the market or that the law was ideologically biased.

In a controversial portion of the opinion which did not win majority support, Justice Stevens contended that non-obscene erotic expression enjoys a lesser degree of First Amendment protection than political speech: "[F]ew of us would march our sons and daughters off to war to preserve the citizen's right to see 'Specified Sexual Activities' exhibited in theaters of our choice." It followed, he reasoned, that the indecent content of the speech could be considered by Detroit in regulating the location of the establishments. Justice Powell concurred on grounds that the innovative land use ordinance involved only an "incidental and minimal" burden on the First Amendment but he did not address Justice Stevens' endorsement of levels of protected speech. Four justices in dissent expressly rejected Justice Stevens' bid for a two-tier approach to the value of speech: "The fact that the 'offensive' speech here may not address 'important' topics— 'ideas of social and political significance,' in the Courts terminology—does not mean that it is less worthy of constitutional protection."

The two-tiered approach to indecent expression again won only plurality support in *FCC v. Pacifica Foundation* (1978). The Court endorsed FCC sanctions against a radio broadcaster for airing a program involving indecent, but not obscene, language. A majority of Justices were content with emphasizing the "uniquely pervasive presence" of broadcasting in our lives rendering us captive to unexpected programming and the unique accessibility of broadcasting to children. But Justice Stevens, for a three-judge plurality, again argued that the indecent content of the speech permitted greater government consideration of the expression's social value in the particular context. Two justices, concurring, and two justices, dissenting, rejected the assertion that the case should turn on the social value assigned by the Court to the speech. Two other justices did not reach the question.

Justice Stevens observed in *Pacifica* that "of all forms of communication, it is broadcasting that has received the most limited First Amendment protection." This lesser protection should not be applied indiscriminately, however, to all electronic media. For example, a total Congressional ban on dial-a-porn, *i.e.*, sexually-oriented indecent, but not obscene telephone messages, was held unconstitutional. The total ban was subjected to the more exacting form of review used for content control and was invalidated because it was not narrowly tailored to achieve a compelling government interest and because it failed to use the least restrictive means. *Pacifica* was distinguished. Dial-a-porn requires more of an affirmative act by the recipient than just turning on the television set. There was no captive audience. Unwilling listeners could avoid exposure to it. Furthermore, there were technological means available to protect children short of a total ban. *Sable Communications of California, Inc. v. FCC* (1989).

There is one context in which the Court has accepted indecency as sufficient for government suppression. In *New York v. Ferber* (1982), the Court upheld a New York statute prohibiting knowing promotion of photographic or other visual reproductions of live performances of children engaged in non-obscene sexual conduct. The *Miller* standards were not applied; instead, the Court treated child pornography as "category of material outside the protection of the First Amendment." While the Court specifically indicated that the *Miller* pruriency and patent offensiveness tests did not apply to child pornography, the status of the "serious social value" test in the new category remains unclear. While the Court acknowledged the possibility that some educational, medical or artistic work might fall within the New York statute, it concluded that the problem could be handled on a case by case basis and that there was no "substantial overbreadth." Justice White, for the Court, in justifying categorical exclusion of child pornography, stressed the compelling state interest in protecting minors, the close relation of the distribution of the films and photographs to the sexual abuse of children and the motivation for the production of such materials resulting from sales and advertising revenues.

Another example of the Supreme Court's solicitude toward child pornography legislation involved an Ohio statute criminalizing the possession and viewing of child pornography. The statute might have succumbed to an overbreadth challenge since it punished "simple nudity, without more". However, the Ohio Supreme Court had given the statute a narrowing construction so that it only reached nudity "where such nudity constitutes a lewd exhibition or involves a graphic focus on the genitals". As narrowed, the statute was not impermissibly overbroad. *Osborne v. Ohio* (1990).

While the discussion in this section focuses on the substantive law of obscenity, the student should note that procedural problems are especially prevalent in obscenity regulation. For example, while the prior restraint doctrine is applicable to obscenity regulation [*Bantam Books, Inc. v. Sullivan* (1963); *Vance v. Universal Amusement Co.* (1980), heavy burden on government to justify issuance of injunction on future filming based on past showing of obscene films], the courts have upheld film censorship. *Times Film Corp. v. Chicago* (1961). However, when administrative or judicial censorship is used, the Court requires that defined proce-

dural norms be satisfied. These norms, set forth in
Freedman v. Maryland (1965), require that three
procedural requirements must be met: (1) the government authority or censor has the burden of
demonstrating that the material is unprotected; (2)
there must be a prompt judicial proceeding if a valid
final restraint on publication is to be imposed; and
(3) the government authority or censor must either
issue a license for publication or exhibition or go to
court to justify the refusal to do so. The *Freedman*
standards reflect a clear preference for a judicial
determination of the question of obscenity in order
to protect First Amendment values.

If the regulatory or licensing scheme does not
involve the exercise of administrative discretion
with respect to the content of the publication or
movie at issue, there is some disagreement about
whether all the *Freedman* requirements must be
met. A Dallas ordinance regulating zoning, licensing and inspections of "sexually oriented businesses" such as adult bookstores, video centers and
theatres was invalidated as constituting a prior
restraint which failed to meet the *Freedman* requirements. The Dallas ordinance was held invalid
since it failed to place limits on the time within
which the decision maker may issue the license and
failed to provide for prompt judicial review as required by *Freedman*. Three members of the Court
believed, however, that since no censorship was
involved in the Dallas licensing scheme, the *Freedman* requirement that the city must go to court to
justify the restraint need not be met. Three jus-

tices would have applied all three *Freedman* standards. Three others believed that none of the *Freedman* standards were applicable where content censorship was not present. *FW/PBS, Inc. v. City of Dallas* (1990).

5. FREEDOM OF THE PRESS

The First Amendment protects against abridgment of the freedom of speech "or of the press." Does this clause provide special protection to the media as an institution? The Court has not accepted the idea that the Press Clause has a meaning independent of the Speech Clause. See *First Nat. Bank of Boston v. Bellotti* (1978) (Burger, C.J., concurring, criticizing the theory that the Press Clause has a separate meaning). Claims for special press privileges and immunities not available to ordinary citizens have been rejected. *Branzburg v. Hayes* (1972). But this does not mean that the press enjoys no special constitutional protection as the eyes and ears, the surrogate, of the public on matters of public interest. We have already seen the constitutional protection afforded the press against prior restraints (*i.e., Pentagon Papers; Nebraska Press*) and post hoc burdens on publication (*e.g., New York Times v. Sullivan*, involving defamation law). Further, laws which treat the press differently are subjected to stricter judicial scrutiny. See *Minneapolis Star & Tribune Co. v. Minnesota Com'r of Rev.* (1983) [special state use tax imposed solely on the use of paper and ink in publishing invalid absent "a counterbalancing interest of compelling importance that it cannot achieve without differential taxation" even though press enjoyed favored tax treatment].

a. Newsgathering

Is the constitutional protection afforded the media limited only to publication or does the Constitution also provide protection to the process of gathering the news? In *Branzburg v. Hayes* (1972), this question arose in the context of a claim for a "journalist's privilege" to resist disclosure of information to a grand jury. The Court, per Justice White, accepted the premise that "newsgathering is not without its First Amendment protection" for "without some protection for seeking out the news, freedom of the press could be eviscerated." But this did not mean the press enjoyed some special immunity or "a constitutional right of access to information not available to the public generally." The First Amendment, said Justice White, did not require invalidating every "incidental burdening of the press."

The Court 5–4 rejected any absolute or qualified journalist privilege to refuse disclosure of the names of informants or other information beyond that enjoyed by any citizen. Justice White noted that reporters remain free to seek out the news by legal means; any inhibition from forced disclosure was deemed "widely divergent and to a great extent speculative." Against this "consequential, but uncertain burden" on information-gathering, the public interest in "fair and effective law enforcement"—the interest of the public to every person's evidence—was held to be sufficiently overriding. As long as the grand jury inquiry is conducted in good faith, the questions asked are relevant and there is no harassment, the journalist must cooperate. Further, *Branzburg* expressed concern that if such a privilege were recognized, the courts would face the administrative difficulty of defining what constitutes "the press." See also *Zurcher v. Stanford Daily* (1978) [issuance of ex parte search warrant authorizing search of student news offices for photographs of riot held constitutional].

A crucial, and subsequently highly influential, swing vote in *Branzburg* was cast by Justice Powell. In a separate concurrence, Justice Powell indicated that a claim of privilege might be available on a case-by-case basis as a result of balancing the competing interests in disclosure and confidentiality. Indeed, Powell asserted that the Court's opinion meant that "the courts will be available to newsmen under circumstances where legitimate First Amendment interests require protection." Many commentators suggest that as a result of Powell's position, a majority of the *Branzburg* Court actually endorsed a qualified privilege.

Justice Stewart, for three dissenters in *Branzburg,* urged recognition of a qualified journalist privilege requiring government seeking to force disclosure to prove: (1) that there is probable cause to believe that the journalist possesses clearly relevant evidence relating to law violation; (2) the absence of any means of acquiring the evidence less destructive of First Amendment rights; and (3) that there is "a compelling and overriding interest in the information." This approach has enjoyed marked success in lower courts especially in the civil context where law enforcement interests are not as pronounced.

Another context in which the constitutional protection afforded newsgathering arises is that of access to government institutions, documents and other information in possession of the government. Unlike most First Amendment issues, which involve the limits on government coercive powers, the issues in this area have a decided affirmative orientation. Is government under an affirmative constitutional duty to provide media access to information in its possession? Is there a constitutional right to know what government is doing?

Once again the Court has been unreceptive to special rights of access for the press. As long as there is no discrimination against the press, "newsmen have no constitutional right of access to prisons or their inmates beyond that afforded to the general public." *Pell v. Procunier* (1974) [state prison regulations prohibiting press interviews with specific inmates upheld as reasonable regulation, at least where alternative methods of communication are available]. See *Saxbe v. Washington Post Co.* (1974) [similar holding for federal prisons]. But note that neither *Pell* nor *Saxbe* determined whether the public has a First Amendment right of access which the media would share as "the necessary representative of the public's interest in the context and the instrumentality which affects the public's right." (Powell, J., dissenting). In both *Pell* and *Saxbe,* the public did enjoy visitation rights and mail privileges with prisoners. [See *Procunier v. Martinez* (1974), prison mail censorship must be no greater than is necessary to further the substantial government interests in security, order and inmate rehabilitation].

Houchins v. KQED, Inc. (1978), revealed the sharp divisions in the Court on the access question. Chief Justice Burger, joined by Justices White and Rehnquist, found the *Pell* requirements of equal access to prisons satisfied and went on to suggest that the public could be denied any prison access. The Chief Justice stressed the absence of any constitutional guidelines for confining judges in fashioning and applying such a right of public access. Justices Stevens, Brennan, and Powell, dissenting, argued for a public right of access: "The preservation of a full and free flow of information to the general public has long been recognized as a core objective of the First Amendment to the Constitution." Justice Stewart, concurring, appeared to reject a constitutional duty on government to provide public access to information but argued that, if public access is provided, " 'effective access' may require different rules for the media than for the general public," *e.g.,* cameras and recording equipment and more frequent interview schedules may be required. As this suggests, the subject of access to the prisons for public and press alike remains uncertain. Perhaps the best that can be said is that if the public is given access, the press may not be denied access and may be entitled to preferences in the name of "equal and effective access."

The claim of a constitutional right of access to government institutions has slowly found substantial acceptance in the context of judicial proceedings. *Gannett Co., Inc. v. De Pasquale* (1979), held that the Sixth Amendment guarantee of the accused to a public trial gives neither the press nor the public an enforceable right of access to a pretrial suppression hearing. But after this initial setback, *Richmond Newspapers, Inc. v. Virginia,* a landmark decision, recognized 7–1 that the First Amendment limits the power to close a criminal trial. *Richmond Newspapers, Inc.* held that "[a]bsent an overriding interest, articulated in findings, the trial of a criminal case must be open to the public." Since no findings had been made to justify closure, the trial court erred in closing the trial.

But the Court in *Richmond Newspapers* became fragmented in defining the nature of the emerging access right. Chief Justice Burger, for the Court, joined by Justices Stewart and White, emphasized the historic foundation of a "presumption of openness" in criminal trials as the basis for an implied right to attend criminal trials. Focusing on the guaranteed rights of speech, press and assembly, he concluded: "The explicit, guaranteed rights to speak and to publish concerning what takes place at a trial would lose much meaning if access to observe the trial could, as it was here, be foreclosed summarily."

Justice Brennan, joined by Justice Marshall, concurring, was willing to recognize a First Amendment "public right of access" based on the "structural role [that the First Amendment plays] in securing and fostering our republican system of self-government." Emphasizing the citizen-critic's role in democratic government, Brennan urged that both communication and "the indispensable conditions of meaningful communication" must be safeguarded. "[V]aluable public debate—as well as other civic behavior—must be informed." But recognizing the need to define limits, Justice Brennan urged attention to historic and current assessment of the importance of access to the particular process involved. He concluded: "[Our] ingrained tradition of public trials and the importance of public access to the broader purposes of the trial process, tip the balance strongly towards the rule that trials be open." The present law which left the question of closing to the unfettered discretion of the trial judge was inadequate to satisfy the presumption of openness.

In subsequent cases, the Court has reaffirmed this qualified right of access to at least some criminal justice proceedings and employed a heightened scrutiny standard in reviewing trial court closures. In *Globe Newspaper Co. v. Superior Court* (1982), a state statute requiring that trials of designated sex offenses be closed during the testimony of minor witnesses was held unconstitutional. While accepting that the state interest in protecting the physical and psychological well-being of minors is compelling, Justice Brennan, for the Court, concluded that the law was not "a narrowly tailored means" of achieving the objective case-by-case determination of the need for closure.

Chief Justice Burger, for the Court in *Press–Enterprise Co. v. Superior Court* (1984) [*Press-Enterprise I*], held *Richmond Newspapers* applicable to voir dire examination of prospective jurors as a vital part of the criminal trial: "The presumption of openness may be overcome only by an overriding interest based on findings that closure is essential to preserve higher values and is narrowly tailored to serve that interest. The interest is to be articulated along with findings specific enough that a reviewing court can determine whether the closure order was properly entered." The trial court's failure to consider alternatives to closure was considered critical in the case.

The presumption of openness also attaches to at least some pretrial criminal proceedings. After considering the history of openness of preliminary hearings and the values of public access to such proceedings, the Court recognized a qualified First Amendment right of access. *Press-Enterprise Co. v. Superior Court* (1986) [*Press-Enterprise II*]. Only specific findings that there is a substantial probability of prejudice to the defendant's fair trial rights and the absence of reasonable alternatives would justify closure under the standards of *Press-Enterprise I*.

Similarly, a blanket Puerto Rico rule that the preliminary hearing should be private unless the defendant chooses otherwise violates the First Amendment. Despite the contention that the unique history and traditions of Puerto Rico show a special sensitivity for the honor and reputation of the citizenry, the "established and widespread tradition of open preliminary hearings among the states" controls. As in *Globe Newspaper Co.*, the concern that publicity will prejudice the rights of the defendant if the preliminary hearing is open must be dealt with on a case-by-case basis. *El Vocero de Puerto Rico v. Puerto Rico* (1993).

In summary, newsgathering may enjoy some constitutional protection but not too much. Unlike the broad First Amendment protection provided when government controls expression or publication, the courts have been hesitant in granting protection to the newsgathering process. In fact, it may be preferable to speak of information-gathering since the Press Clause adds little, if anything, to the Speech Clause and journalists are largely fungible with other citizens. To the limited extent that the First Amendment creates a qualified privilege to resist forced disclosure of information to the government, it is a right of citizens generally. If there is an affirmative right of access to government institutions and information in government hands, which seems doubtful outside of the courtroom context, it is a right of the public.

b. Public Access to the Media

The most common scenario for government restraint on publication arises when government seeks to prevent or punish the media for publication. But what if the government seeks to compel the media to publish messages that would not otherwise be adequately presented in the marketplace? The First Amendment protects not only the rights of the speaker but also "the right of the public to receive suitable access to social, political, aesthetic, moral, and other ideas and experiences." *Red Lion Broadcasting Co. v. FCC* (1969) [FCC fairness doctrine, requiring discussion of public issues and fair coverage to competing positions, held constitutional]. In *Red Lion,* the Court added: "It is the right of the viewers and listeners, not the rights of the broadcasters, which is paramount." Can a legislature force the media to publish material in the national interest in order to further this First Amendment right of the public?

In the case of the print media, the Court has rejected a First Amendment right of public access. In *Miami Herald Publishing Co. v. Tornillo* (1974), the Court unanimously held unconstitutional a state statute granting political candidates a right of reply to published criticism. Chief Justice Burger, after documenting the case of media concentration distorting the marketplace of ideas, nevertheless rejected use of government coercion to force the press to print what they would otherwise not print. While "a responsible press is an undoubtedly desirable goal, press responsibility is not mandated by the Constitution and like many other virtues it cannot be legislated." The Chief Justice reasoned that coerced publishing penalizes the press for past publication by adding to the costs of printing and by occupying valuable newspaper space. The fear of such sanctions, he warned, might lead editors to avoid controversial publications. Editorial control and judgment over the size and content must remain with the press, not with the government. See *Pacific Gas & Elec. Co. v. Public Utilities Com'n* (1986) [compelled access for private group to private utility's billing envelopes violates principles of *Tornillo*]. Whether a right of reply statute, as an affirmative remedy for defamation, would be valid under *Tornillo* has not been decided. See *Rosenbloom v. Metromedia, Inc.* (1971).

A First Amendment based right of public access to the broadcast media was rejected in *CBS v. Democratic Nat. Comm.* (1973), where the Court, per Chief Justice Burger, upheld an FCC ruling that a broadcaster who meets his statutory responsibilities for fair coverage is not required to accept editorial advertisements. The FCC was justified in concluding that such a right of access would not serve the public interest since it would be weighted in favor of the financially affluent with the means to purchase editorial time. While broadcasting is subject to government regulation, the Chief Justice stated that editing is what editors are for. Finally, Chief Justice Burger expressed concern that FCC monitoring of a constitutional right of access would intrude the government "into a continuing case-by-case determination of who should be heard and when." The Court concluded that the dangers of greater government surveillance of journalistic discretion outweighed any public access benefits to be gained.

While *CBS v. Democratic National Committee* declared that the First Amendment of its own force did not mandate a right of access to the electronic media, the Court pointed out that it left open situations where the statute or the FCC by regulation might mandate some form of public access. Although *Tornillo* stressed journalistic freedom over newspaper content, broadcasting is subject to greater government regulation in the public interest. In upholding the fairness doctrine against First Amendment challenge in *Red Lion,* the Court noted the scarcity of radio frequencies as justifying government regulation aimed at preventing monopolization of the media marketplace by private broadcast licensees. In other cases, the Court has stressed the pervasiveness of broadcasting in our lives and its accessibility to children as justifying greater government control over content. See *FCC v. Pacifica Foundation* (S.Ct.1978).

CBS v. FCC (1981) recognized the legitimacy of specific as compared with general rights of access; the Court upheld the Federal Election Campaign Act establishing a statutory right of reasonable access for federal political candidates. *CBS v. FCC* stressed that the statute only "creates a *limited* right to 'reasonable' access that pertains only to legally qualified federal candidates and may be invoked by them only for the purpose of advancing their candidacies once a campaign has commenced." This was not a "general right of access to the media" significantly impairing journalistic discretion regarding what to air, but a limited law designed "to assure that an important resource—the airwaves—will be used in the public interest."

What is the appropriate First Amendment standard for new electronic technologies such as cable television? In *Turner Broadcasting System, Inc. v. FCC* (1994), the Court considered a First Amendment challenge to provisions of federal cable legislation which imposed so-called must-carry obligations on cable operators. These requirements obliged cable systems to transmit the signals of a certain number of local over-the-air broadcast stations. The cable operators contended that their First Amendment rights were violated since these provisions required them to transmit that which they would prefer not to transit. The Court declared that cable operators are engaged in speech and that the *Red Lion* approach to broadcast regulation which allowed substantial government regulation was not appropriate for cable. The multi-channel capacity of cable contrasted sharply with the spectrum limitation problems which characterized over-the-air-broadcasting.

Nevertheless, the *Turner* Court held that the must-carry legislation constituted content-neutral regulation which should be evaluated under the *O'Brien* test. Substantial governmental interests were served by the must-carry provisions such as ensuring that "broadcast television remains available as a source of video programming for those without cable." *Tornillo* did not govern since the must-carry provisions were content-neutral in application. Unlike the right of reply statute in *Tornillo*, must-carry obligations were not activated by any particular message transmitted by cable operators. Nor did the must-carry provisions impose any content-based penalty. But the must-carry rules may suppress more speech than was necessary. Therefore, the Court remanded the case to the district court in order to develop a more complete factual record on issues such as whether, without must-carry, local over-the-air free broadcasting would be placed in economic jeopardy.

In summary, while the Court has recognized that the First Amendment includes the right of the public to hear, this has not been converted into a constitutional right of access to the media. For print and broadcast media alike, the Court has emphasized the importance of journalistic discretion over content. While broadcasting is subject to a greater degree of government regulation than the print media, the Court has increasingly emphasized the limited nature of the federal government's regulatory authority. The Court even seemed to introduce a heightened standard of review with respect to government content controls on broadcasting. In *FCC v. League of Women Voters* (1984) [federal statute forbidding broadcasters receiving grants for public broadcasting from engaging in editorializing held unconstitutional], the Court stated that only when a restriction is narrowly tailored to further substantial governmental interests will such content regulation be upheld. Nevertheless, as *CBS* indicates, a limited statutory right of reasonable access to the broadcast media can survive First Amendment scrutiny. Similarly, the Court's willingness in *Turner* to view statutorily imposed must-carry obligations on cable systems as content-neutral illustrates that some measure of regulation of new electronic media such as cable is permissible.

6. SPEECH IN THE ELECTORAL PROCESS

Political speech is at the core of First Amendment concerns. It is not surprising, therefore, that the Court applies strict scrutiny when a state undertakes to regulate the content of speech during an election campaign. *Brown v. Hartlage* (1982) [application of a state law against vote buying to void the election of a candidate who had promised to take a lower salary than fixed by law if elected held unconstitutional]. Similarly state regulation of national political parties has been closely scrutinized on the basis of the right of political association. *Democratic Party of United States v. Wisconsin ex rel. LaFollette* (1981) [Wisconsin open primary law cannot be used to force DNC to seat delegates selected contrary to party rules]. A Colorado statute which prohibited the use of paid circulators to obtain the number of qualified voter signatures required to place an initiative on the general election ballot violates the right to engage in political speech protected by the First Amendment. Restrictions on circulating petitions concerning political change infringes on " 'core political speech' " and will be subjected to "exacting scrutiny". *Meyer v. Grant* (1988).

Application of the strict scrutiny standard to electoral process regulation does not invariably result in invalidation. A Tennessee law which prohibited the solicitation of votes and the display of campaign materials within 100 feet of the entrance to a polling place on election day was a content-based time-place-manner regulation. Noting that all 50 states had provided "for a restricted zone around the voting compartments," the Court subjected the regulation to strict scrutiny and still upheld it. The state interests advanced in support of the statute—prevention of voter intimidation and election fraud—were held to be compelling. *Burson v. Freeman* (1992).

When the Republican Party in Connecticut adopted a rule that permitted independent voters to vote in Republican primaries despite a state statute requiring voters in party primaries to be registered members of that party, the Court struck down the statute because it deprived the state Republican Party of the right to enter into political association with individuals of its own choice. A state statute which placed limits on the registered voters whom a political party could ask to participate in a basic party function such as selecting candidates impermissibly burdens freedom of association. *Tashjian v. Republican Party of Connecticut* (1986).

Similar over-regulation of the political process was set aside by the Court when it struck down provisions of the California Electoral Code which prohibited the official governing bodies of political parties from making primary endorsements and which mandated the organization and composition of those governing bodies. Such provisions were directed at speech at the core of the electoral process, did not serve a compelling governmental interest, and could not be justified by state interests such as the stability of government and protecting voters from undue influence and confusion. A state should not censor "the political speech a political party shares with its members." The regulation of party governance was also invalid since the state had no more business to tell a political party what its internal structure should be than it had to tell a party what it could say to its members. *Eu v. San Francisco County Democratic Central Committee* (1989).

On the other hand, a more generalized balancing test was used in reviewing regulations governing access to the ballot of independent and minority parties in *Anderson v. Celebrezze* (1983). *Anderson* held 5–4 that Ohio's March filing deadline for November elections placed an unconstitutional burden on the supporters of independent presidential candidate John Anderson. Major political parties which had demonstrated vote support were assured a place on the ballot and were able to select their candidate after the March filing deadline.

Justice Stevens, for the Court, focused on "the character and magnitude of the asserted injury" to the First Amendment rights of the voters (not the candidate). An early filing date was seen as severely limiting the ability of disaffected voters to coalesce around an independent candidate and as impeding the ability of voters to respond to major events. Since the major parties were not subject to the March deadline, the Ohio law had a differential impact on an identifiable class of voters, *i.e.,* those who chose not to align with the major parties; it discriminated against independent voters.

While political stability would be a legitimate state objective, less burdensome means were available. Greater precision of regulation than the discriminatory Ohio law was possible. *Anderson* concluded that the burden on independent voting "unquestionably outweighs the State's minimal interest in imposing the March deadline." Compare *Storer v. Brown* (1974) [one year disaffiliation provision held to further State's compelling interest in political stability].

Freedom of association includes the right of likeminded voters to join in pursuit of shared political goals and to form new political parties. State regulation restricting access to the ballot of new parties must be narrowly drawn to advance state interests of compelling importance. An Illinois state law which conditioned ballot access for a new party on securing 25,000 signatures in *each* political subdivision and which prohibited the use of the name of a party established in one political subdivision from being used in another—even with the party's permission—failed to meet this standard. Although the state has strong interests in the prevention of misrepresentation and confusion among voters, these restrictions violated the right of political association since they swept more broadly than was necessary to protect the electoral process. A more narrowly tailored law could have served the state interests as well. *Norman v. Reed* (1992). Laws that place severe burdens on the right to vote warrant strict scrutiny. But reasonable and non-discriminatory regulation of the right to vote is presumptively valid. For example, where state law provides for easy access to the ballot, a prohibition against write-in voting to prevent "unrestrained factionalism at the general election" is valid. *Burdick v. Takushi* (1992).

Perhaps the most controversial area of First Amendment electoral law involves the status of restrictions on campaign spending by individuals and groups. In *Buckley v. Valeo* (1976), a divided Court held, *per curiam,* that a federal law limiting individual *contributions* to candidates for office served the state's compelling interest in limiting the actuality and appearance of corruption. However, a law limiting *expenditures* by candidates, individuals, and groups was unconstitutional.

The Court's *per curiam* opinion first rejected efforts to characterize the spending law as a regulation of conduct, only incidentally burdening speech. Money is a form of speech and the law regulated speech itself. Even if the funding limits were treated as a regulation of conduct, strict scrutiny was appropriate since, although ideologically neutral, the law was directed at the harmful content of the communication, *i.e.,* it was content-based regulation. The government's interest, reasoned the Court, "arises in some measure because communication allegedly integral to the conduct is itself thought to be harmful." Unlike simple time, place and manner regulation, the dollar limitations involved "direct quantity restrictions on political communication and association."

Having concluded that speech is significantly burdened on the basis of content by spending restrictions, it might have been expected that the strict scrutiny test would be applied. Instead, in an analysis suggestive of a balancing test, a distinction was drawn between the severity of the burden imposed by contribution and expenditure limits. While close scrutiny was applicable to both contributions and expenditures, the expenditure ceilings were said to impose "significantly more severe restrictions on protected freedoms." A limit on the amount a person or group can spend "necessarily reduces the quantity of expression," impacting on the quality and diversity of political speech. Limitations on contributions, on the other hand, impose only a "marginal restriction on the contributor's ability to communicate." The Court reasoned that "[t]he quantity of communication by the contributor does not increase perceptively with the size of his contribution"; it is the symbolic act of contribution itself that is communicative. While a contribution may be used to increase the quality of a recipient's speech, this was "speech by someone other than the contributor," *i.e.*, speech by proxy.

The Court then considered the governmental interest in maintaining contribution and expenditure limitations, focusing on the interest in preventing corruption. Large contributions are often given to secure political favors and Congress should be allowed to limit the opportunity for abuse, *i.e.*, seek to prevent "political quid pro quos," or dollars for political favors. On the other hand, limitations on expenditures on behalf of a candidate were seen as less clearly serving the anti-corruption interests. The lack of control by the candidate over independent spending limited the possibility that such spending would be given as a quid pro quo for political influence. For Justice White, dissenting, limiting independent expenditures was justifiable to prevent evasion of the contribution limits—the candidate would still be aware of the expenditures for his benefit.

The government's argument that the expenditure limits could be justified as serving the interest in equalizing the ability of individuals and groups to exercise electoral influence was rejected. "[T]he concept that government may restrict the speech of some elements of our society in order to enhance the relative voice of others is wholly foreign to the First Amendment, which was designed to secure the widest possible dissemination of information. The First Amendment's protection against governmental abridgment of free expression cannot properly be made to depend on a person's financial ability to engage in public discussion." Simply, the desire for greater equality could not be achieved by sacrificing the liberty interests in free speech. Justice White, dissenting, argued that First Amendment interests in free dialogue are actually promoted by spending limitations, by controlling the "overpowering advantage" of the wealthy and by "encouraging the less wealthy." In short, it is big money that distorts the electoral marketplace.

Cases following *Buckley,* have struggled with the imprecision created by its dichotomy between limitations on campaign expenditures and contributions. In *California Medical Ass'n v. FEC* (1981), a federal law limiting the amount an incorporated association can contribute to a multi-candidate political committee was upheld. Such spending was viewed, not as independent political speech, but rather as "speech by proxy." Thus, the spending was deemed analogous to group contributions to a candidate which can be regulated.

FEC v. National Conservative Political Action Comm. (1985) held 6–3 that a provision of the Federal Election Campaign Fund Act prohibiting political action committees (PAC) from expending more than $1000 to further the candidacy of a candidate who chooses to receive public financing violated the First Amendment. As in *Buckley,* "the expenditures at issue in this case produce speech at the core of the First Amendment" necessitating a "rigorous" standard of review. Justice Rehnquist, for the Court, likened the restriction to allowing a speaker in a public hall to express his views while denying him use of an amplifier. Both limitations reduce the quantity and quality of expression. Nor was this simply a restriction on "speech by proxy." Although contributors do not control the particular use of their funds, "the contributors obviously like the message they are hearing from these organizations and want to add their voice to that message; otherwise they would not part with their money." Concluding that PAC expenditures are entitled to full First Amendment protection, the Court could find no governmental interest sufficiently strong to justify restricting PAC expenditures. Here, as in *Buckley,* independent expenditures, not coordinated with candidate's political campaign, were seen as presenting a lesser danger of political quid pro quos. The Court rejected an effort to support the statutory limitation on expenditures on the basis of the special treatment historically accorded to corporations. In this instance, the terms of the Campaign Fund Act "apply equally to an informal neighborhood group that solicits contributions and spends money on a presidential election as to the wealthy and professionally managed PACs involved in the this case."

In *FEC v. Massachusetts Citizens for Life (MCFL)* (1986), the application of a provision of the Federal Election Campaign Act prohibiting direct expenditure of corporate funds to a nonprofit, voluntary political association concerned with elections to public office was struck down as inconsistent with the First Amendment. Protected political speech could not be so infringed in the absence of a compelling governmental interest—an interest clearly absent in the case of application of the provision to a small voluntary political association which refused to accept contributions from either business corporations or labor unions. Moreover, the association had no shareholders and was not engaged in business. In such circumstances, the regulation was a limitation on speech which failed to use narrowly tailored means to achieve its end.

However, the application of a Michigan statute prohibiting corporations from making campaign contributions from their general treasury funds to a nonprofit corporation was held not to violate the First Amendment. The nonprofit corporation involved, the Michigan Chamber of Commerce, lacked three of the distinctive features of the organization protected in *MCFL*: (1) The Chamber of Commerce, unlike MCFL corporation, was not formed just for the purpose of political expression; (2) The members of the Chamber of Commerce had an economic reason for remaining with it even though they might disagree with its politics; and (3) the Chamber, unlike *MCFL*, was subject to influence from business corporations which might use it as a conduit for direct spending which would pose a threat to the political marketplace. Use of the corporate form did not, of course, remove corporate speech from the scope of First Amendment protection. But the Michigan statute's burden on corporate political speech was justified by the state's compelling interest in preventing political corruption or the appearance of undue influence. Unlike the situation in *MCFL*, the statute was precisely targeted, *i.e.*, narrowly tailored, to achieve its goal. The Michigan statute did not prohibit all corporate spending and corporations were permitted to make independent expenditures for political purposes from segregated funds but not from their general treasuries. *Austin v. Michigan Chamber of Commerce* (1990).

The *Austin* case marks an important development in the First Amendment law governing the electoral process. In short, states may regulate corporate spending in the political process if the regulation is drawn with sufficient specificity to serve the compelling state interest in reducing the threat that "huge corporate treasuries," accumulated with the help of the state conferred corporate structure, will distort the political process and "influence unfairly the outcome of elections."

The anti-corruption interest of the government relied on in *Buckley* to uphold spending limits on contributions is not applicable to spending limits on contributions in referenda. In *Citizens Against Rent Control v. City of Berkeley* (1981), a local ordinance placing a $250 limitation on contributions to committees formed to support or oppose ballot measures submitted to a popular vote was held unconstitutional. It violated both the right of association (*i.e.*, it limited individuals wishing to band together in advancing their views while placing no limit on individuals acting alone) and individual and collective rights of free expression (*i.e.*, it limited the quantity of expression). Since the ordinance did not advance a significant state interest sufficient to satisfy the Court's "exacting scrutiny," the law failed.

Given the long history of political patronage in America, a surprising development in recent years is the extent to which the whole field of political patronage has come to be governed by the strictures of the First Amendment. In *Branti v. Finkel* (1980), it was held that lawyers employed by a county public defender's office could not be dismissed on purely political grounds. The First Amendment protection accorded to political belief and association prevented such purely political dismissals. They constituted the imposition of an unconstitutional condition on receipt of a government benefit.

Branti dealt with dismissals but its principle has been extended. Promotion, transfer, recall, and hiring decisions involving public employment have been held to be decisions for which party affiliation is not a permissible requirement. The infirmity of patronage practices in all these matters is that they condition government service on membership in or support of a particular political party. Such conduct is constitutionally invalid for two reasons. First, it impermissibly coerces belief. Second, it invalidly imposes significant penalties on the exercise of protected First Amendment rights. The challenged party affiliation requirements were not narrowly tailored to serve the government interests asserted since less intrusive means were available.

For example, the government interest in securing employees who will faithfully implement its policies "can be adequately met by choosing or dismissing certain high level employees on the basis of their political views." Justice Brennan opined for the Court: "To the victor belong only those spoils that may be constitutionally obtained." Justice Scalia complained in dissent that the new First Amendment based antipatronage principle "will be enforced by a corps of judges (the Members of this Court included) who overwhelmingly owe their office to its violation." *Rutan v. Republican Party of Illinois* (1990).

CHAPTER VIII

FREEDOM OF RELIGION

The First Amendment guarantee of freedom of religion "was adopted to curtail the power of Congress to interfere with the individual's freedom to believe, to worship, and to express himself in accordance with the dictates of his own conscience." *Wallace v. Jaffree* (1985) [silent prayer law held unconstitutional]. The two components of the freedom of religion guarantee, *i.e.,* the Free Exercise Clause and the Anti–Establishment Clause, have both been applied to the states through incorporation into the Fourteenth Amendment due process guarantee of liberty. [*Cantwell v. Connecticut* (1940), free exercise; *Everson v. Board of Educ.* (1947), Anti–Establishment].

But while both components are part of our constitutional freedom of religion, the clauses often appear to conflict. Exemption from generally applicable laws when such laws burden a particular religion may serve the interests of religious freedom, but such exemptions can be perceived as government support for religion violative of the Establishment Clause. The proscription against religious establishment may bar government support for religion and religious institutions, but denial of public benefits and services (especially given the important role played by government in our lives), may impose hardships on religion presenting free exercise problems. A continuing problem is how to reconcile these potentially-conflicting constitutional demands. While some have argued for the primacy of free exercise when the two clauses conflict, the Court has not thus far clearly accepted this approach. Rather, the basic command has been that government maintain a position of "neutrality." The Rehnquist Court is much less insistent on the strictness with which government must maintain this neutrality and is much more willing to entertain government accommodation of religion. This is particularly true of the newer appointees to the Court such as Justices Kennedy and Scalia.

A. THE ESTABLISHMENT CLAUSE

The First Amendment prohibits the making of laws "respecting the establishment of religion." This has not been read simply as a prohibition against a government sponsored church [*but see Wallace v. Jaffree* (Rehnquist, J., dissenting)] or as simply a demand of equal treatment of religions (*i.e.*, an anti-discrimination guarantee) but as a broader prohibition against laws "which aid one religion, aid all religions, or prefer one religion over another." *Everson.*

What constitutes impermissible aid? At times, the Court has stated that the Clause erects a "wall of separation" between church and state. *Reynolds v. United States* (1878). At other times, the Court has referred to the wall metaphor as "not a wholly accurate description of the practical aspects of the relationship that in fact exists between church and state" [*Lynch v. Donnelly* (1984)] and has asserted that the Constitution "affirmatively mandates accommodation, not merely tolerance, of all religions and forbids hostility towards any." *Id.*

In most cases, the Court requires that each part of a three-part test be satisfied in order to withstand an Establishment Clause challenge: (1) the law must have a secular legislative purpose; (2) the principal or primary effect of the law must neither advance nor inhibit religion; and, (3) the law must not foster "an excessive government entanglement with religion." *Lemon v. Kurtzman* (1971).

The *Lemon* test has been severely criticized. Further, the Court has departed from the test in upholding prayers opening legislative sessions, emphasizing instead the historical acceptance of the challenged practice making it a "part of the fabric of our society" *Marsh v. Chambers* (1983); *Walz v. Tax Com'n of New York* (1970) [emphasizing historic practices in upholding state tax exemptions for property and income of religious institutions]. *Larson v. Valente* (1982), also avoided *Lemon* in invalidating a state law imposing disclosure requirements only on religious organizations soliciting more than 50% of funds from non-members on the ground that it discriminated against non-traditional religions in violation of the Establishment Clause. *Larson* used the strict scrutiny test for laws discriminating against some religions in favor of others.

Whether the tripartite *Lemon* test will survive is not clear. There are new trends that have become apparent. Increasingly, the Court is asking whether the law at issue constitutes an endorsement of religion or a particular religious belief. Justice O'Connor has indicated that she believes that this is a more useful test than *Lemon*. *Lynch v. Donnelly* (1984). Justice Kennedy, on the other hand, believes that endorsement is too imprecise a concept and that the appropriate inquiry is whether the state is proselytizing so that the government action is coercive. *Board of Education of Westside Community Schools v. Mergens* (1990) (Kennedy, J., concurring.) As of now, the *Lemon* test has not yet been repudiated. But *Lee v. Weisman* (1992), *infra*, which did not apply *Lemon* at all, suggests that the issue remains open.

1. PUBLIC AID TO RELIGION

A recurring problem in Establishment Clause jurisprudence is the extent to which government can provide financial and other assistance to religious institutions. The aid may be directly to the institution itself. Alternatively, religious institutions may benefit only indirectly through assistance to citizens using the services of the religious institution, *e.g.,* tax breaks for parents of students attending private religious schools. Disposition of such cases has produced case-by-case decisions that resist efforts to formulate generally applicable principles. But it does appear that the Court is more tolerant of aid programs providing benefits to citizens generally than those involving aid directly to the religious institutions.

Everson v. Board of Educ. (1947), upheld a local program for reimbursing parents for funds spent in transporting their children to school by public buses. The law was "a general program to help parents get their children, regardless of their religion, safely and expeditiously to and from accredited schools." The public welfare benefit was available to all students and any aid to religion was only incidental. In short, the law had a secular purpose and a secular primary effect. Similarly, state approved, secular textbooks may be loaned to private school students, including parochial school students. *Board of Educ. v. Allen* (1968). A law which imposes a general obligation on the state to provide a sign language interpreter for a deaf student can be applied to a student at a Catholic high school. The Establishment Clause is not violated just because a sectarian institution receives an "attenuated financial benefit" from a government program which neutrally distributes benefits. *Zobrest v. Catalina Foothills School District* (1993) [providing a sign language interpreter for a deaf student in a Catholic high school does not violate the Establishment Clause]. On the other hand, loan of instructional materials, (*e.g.,* maps, magazines, tape recorders) and providing public transportation for field trips to parochial school students, have been struck down. *Wolman v. Walter* (1977). *Wolman* concluded: "In view of the impossibility of separating the secular education function from the sectarian," the state aid presented too great a danger of advancing the religious teaching mission of the parochial schools. See *Meek v. Pittenger* (1975) [state loan of non-textbook instructional material and equipment to private schools held unconstitutional].

Mueller v. Allen (1983) upheld 5–4 a Minnesota program permitting parents to deduct from their state tax certain expenses incurred in educating their children. Justice Rehnquist, for the Court, noted that the educational deduction was only one of many deductions designed to equalize tax burdens and encourage desirable expenditures. Most important, unlike an earlier tax break program for parents of private school children which the Court had invalidated [*Committee for Public Educ. v. Nyquist* (1973)], the Minnesota tax break was available to *all* parents, including those whose children attend public schools. Justice Rehnquist commented: "[A] program that neutrally provides state assistance to a broad spectrum of citizens is not readily subject to challenge under the Establishment Clause." The argument that the bulk of deductions would be claimed by parents who pay high tuition at sectarian schools was dismissed—"Such an approach would scarcely provide the certainty that this field stands in need of, nor can we perceive principled standards by which such statistical evidence might be evaluated." Further, Justice Rehnquist saw no significant danger of "comprehensive discriminating, and continuing state surveillance" in the religious schools which might excessively entangle the state in religion.

Justice Rehnquist placed special emphasis on the benefits provided to society by parents supporting private schools. Tax benefits to such parents serves the secular purposes of educating children and of assuring the continuing financial health of private schools. The private school system relieves the burden on public schools, serves as a benchmark for public schools and provides an educational alternative promoting diversity. Any unequal effects of the program could be viewed as "a rough return for the benefits" provided to the state and taxpayers generally.

For Justice Marshall, dissenting, the Minnesota law, like any tax benefit system subsidizing tuition payments to sectarian schools, had "a direct and immediate effect of advancing religion."

Programs of direct assistance to private elementary and secondary schools have produced a checkered, but essentially a negative, response from the Court. Parochial schools particularly have been characterized as being permeated with religious objectives and activities. Aid to religious schools involves young, immature students who are susceptible to religious indoctrination. Political divisiveness over aid to religious schools is common. In short, the probability that state aid will have a primary effect of advancing religion is enhanced. Increased state surveillance of the religious schools to prevent sectarian use of the funds becomes necessary and this threatens church-state entangle-ment.

Nevertheless, aid to religious elementary and sec-ondary schools does not necessarily violate the *Lem-on* test. The nature of the aid will be considered (*e.g.*, whether it affords an opportunity for ideologi-cal persuasion); whether the aid is administered by and requires personal involvement of private school personnel or whether it is state-run; and, whether the aid is provided in the private school building or on publicly-owned property. While such consider-ations provide no bright-line standard, they reflect concerns over the danger that the religious mission of sectarian schools will intrude into the operation of the state aid program.

Just such considerations were cited in *Lemon v. Kurtzman* (1971), in striking down state salary sup-plements to teachers of secular subjects at private schools. Noting that "parochial schools involve substantial religious activity and purpose" and cit-ing the difficulty of assuring that the teachers would not engage in religious teaching, it was found unnecessary to consider the "primary effect" of aid. The need for state monitoring to assure that the aid was not used for advancing religion violated *Lem-on's* third prong: "The cumulative impact of the entire relationship involves excessive entanglement between government and religion."

State programs to provide auxiliary services to private schools or to reimburse private schools for testing, record-keeping and reporting have produced a myriad of program-by-program results yielding few general principles. *Levitt v. Committee for Public Educ.* (1973), rejected state reimbursement of parochial schools on a lump sum per project basis for costs of administering tests where some of the tests were prepared by the private school teachers— there was little control to assure that funds would not be used to advance religion. But in *Committee for Public Educ. v. Regan* (1980), state payments to private schools for administering standardized tests and for other state mandated record-keeping and reporting was upheld. In this instance, the state retained control over the tests which "serves to prevent the use of the test as part of religious teaching." The state mandated services were "ministerial" and "lacking in ideological content or use." Entanglement concerns were dismissed since the services "are discrete and clearly identifiable," not requiring excessive government monitoring.

Wolman v. Walter (1977) approved furnishing of speech, hearing, and psychological diagnostic services by public employees, even though the aid was located in the private school. Diagnostic services are non-ideological, have no educational content and are not closely associated with the educational mission of the school. Further, the diagnostician has a limited relationship with the student, limiting further the "risk of the fostering of ideological views." It followed that there would be no need for excessive state surveillance, involving impermissible entanglement. On the other hand, therapeutic services, guidance counseling and remedial education, involving a greater danger of ideological persuasion, can be offered only at religiously-neutral locations off the private school premises. The danger of advancing religion arises "from the nature of the institution, not from the nature of the pupils." If the program is conducted outside of the religious school, "[i]t can hardly be said that the supervision of public employees performing public functions on public property creates an excessive entanglement between church and state." *Wolman*. See *Meek v. Pittenger* (1975), invalidating programs involving provision of such services *at the private school*.

School Dist. of Grand Rapids v. Ball (1985), invalidated a shared time and a community education program which provided classes financed by the public school system, taught by teachers hired by the public school system, held in classrooms leased from private schools. Stressing the "pervasively sectarian" of almost all of the private schools involved, Justice Brennan, for the Court, identified three factors as establishing that the programs had the primary effect of advancing religion.

"First, the teachers participating in the programs, may become involved in intentionally or inadvertently inculcating particular religious tenets or beliefs." Even though many of the teachers in the shared time program had never worked in religious schools and the courses were supplemental and secular in content, the religious atmosphere of the schools could influence the instructors to conform to the environment. The private school students would be receiving the instruction in the usual religious environment "thus reinforcing the indoctrinating effect."

"Second, the program may provide a crucial symbolic link between government and religion, thereby enlisting—at least in the eyes of impressionable youngsters—the powers of government to the support of the religious denomination operating the school." A core purpose of the Establishment Clause, stated Justice Brennan, is to avoid any message of government approval of religion. Young religious school students, moving from religious to secular classes in the same religious-school building, would be unlikely to be able to discern the "crucial difference" between the religious-school classes and the public-school classes. This would have the effect of promoting "the symbolic union of government and religion in one sectarian enterprise."

"Third, the programs may have the effect of directly promoting religion by impermissibly providing a subsidy to the primary religious mission of the institutions affected." A public subsidy was involved since the public schools assumed responsibility for providing a substantial portion of the teaching of the private school students. Not only instructional material as in *Meek* and *Wolman* was involved, but "also the provision of instructional services by teachers in a parochial school building." The primary effect was the "direct and substantial advancement of the sectarian enterprise."

Aguilar v. Felton (1985), a companion case, invalidated a program involving the use of federal funds to pay the salaries of public school teachers who provided remedial instruction and clinical and guidance services to educationally deprived low income children in parochial schools. Efforts to distinguish *Ball* by emphasizing the use of public monitoring to prevent religious influences failed. While this might avoid the religious effects prong of *Lemon,* the Court found that the ideological nature of the aid and the religious character of the institution receiving the aid threatened excessive government entanglement in religion. "[T]he scope and duration of [the] program would require a permanent and pervasive State presence in the sectarian schools receiving aid."

Government aid programs directed at higher education have generally been upheld by the Court. For example, *Tilton v. Richardson* (1971), upheld federal construction grants for buildings to be used for secular purposes at private colleges. Chief Justice Burger, for the Court, noted that "college students are less impressionable and less susceptible to religious indoctrination." There is less likelihood "that religion will permeate the area of secular education." Since construction aid involves a one-time grant, there is minimal need for government surveillance and less danger of church-state entanglement. Even annual noncategorical grants to private colleges have been upheld if there are assurances that the funds will not be used for sectarian purposes. *Roemer v. Board of Public Works of Maryland* (1976) [upholding annual noncategorical grants]. Such a continuing assistance program, however, does require government surveillance to assure that the conditions imposed limiting the aid to secular activities are enforced and this enhances the dangers of entanglement.

2. RELIGION IN THE SCHOOLS

Is any breach in the wall of separation resulting from the recognition of religion and religious values by public education a violation of the Establishment Clause? Does denial of the ability to pray in the classroom, to teach creationism as an alternative to evolution, to include religious values in the curriculum and educational programs, constitute hostility to religion violative of the Free Exercise Clause and establish a religion of secularism? Such are the contours of the modern debate over the extent to which religion can be accommodated in the classroom. Once again, the uncertain application of the *Lemon* test provides the structure for analysis. And, once again, there are few bright line answers.

One of the more settled areas involves the release of students from public schools for religious instruction. If the released time for religious education occurs in the public school building, so that the state could be perceived as endorsing the religious message thereby advancing religion, the Establishment Clause is violated. *McCullom v. Board of Educ.* (1948). But if the instruction occurs outside the public school, the program is a permissible accommodation of religion. Such a program "respects the religious nature of our people and accom-

modates the public service to their spiritual needs."
The Establishment Clause does not embody "a philosophy of hostility to religion." *Zorach v. Clauson*
(1952).

A far less well-settled and more divisive issue
involves the question of school prayer. *Engel v.
Vitale* (1962), struck down a prayer composed by
the Board of Regents on the basis of the principle
that "it is no part of the business of government to
compose official prayers for any group of the American people to recite as a part of a religious program
carried on by government." *Abington School Dist.
v. Schempp* (1963), extended *Engel* beyond officially
composed prayers to prohibit Bible reading and
recitation of the Lord's Prayer. Even if it were
assumed that the activity was for the secular purposes of promoting mortality, combatting material-
ism and teaching literature, "the laws require religious exercises and such exercises are being conducted in direct violation of [the Establishment
Clause]." While a study of the Bible or of religion
as part of the educational program is permissible,
state-run "religious exercises" violate the First
Amendment mandate "that the Government maintain strict neutrality, neither aiding nor opposing
religion." The fact that children could be excused
from participating was not determinative—"a violation of the Free Exercise Clause is predicated on
coercion while the Establishment Clause violation
need not be so attended." Nor would exclusion of
religious exercises establish a religion of secularism
violative of the majority's rights—the Free Exercise

Clause "has never meant that a majority could use the machinery of the State to practice its beliefs."

With the rejection of school prayer, there has been increasing interest in moments of silent prayer or quiet meditation. *Wallace v. Jaffree* (1985), involved the validity of an Alabama law requiring a 1-minute period of silence "for meditation or voluntary prayer." Applying the first prong of the *Lemon* test, Justice Stevens, for the Court, asked "whether government's actual purpose is to endorse or disapprove of religion." The Court concluded 6-3 that the sole purpose for enacting the law was to express "the State's endorsement of prayer activities for one minute at the beginning of each school day." The State's inclusion of the prayer alternative indicated an intent "to characterize prayer as a favored practice." It followed that the State had violated the principle that government must follow a course of "complete neutrality towards religion."

The Court, as well as the concurring opinions in *Jaffree,* indicated that a religiously-neutral moment of silence law, not enacted solely for sectarian purposes, might well be constitutional. Justice O'Connor, concurring, noted that, unlike the prayer cases, "a moment of silence is not inherently religious" and does not require the dissenter to compromise his or her beliefs. Such a law could serve the secular purpose of devotional activities—"It is difficult to discern a serious threat to religious liberty from a room of silent, thoughtful children." Justice Powell, concurring, expressed the view "that the 'effect' of a straightforward moment-of-silence statute is unlikely to 'advanc[e] or inhibi[t] religion' " nor would it "foster 'an excessive government entanglement with religion.' "

While released time and prayer in the schools have proven to be recurring Establishment Clause issues for the Court, there have been other problem cases. The Court employed the first *Lemon* prong in holding that a state statute barring the teaching of evolution violated freedom of religion. *Epperson v. Arkansas* (1968). Excluding a particular theory or segment of a body of knowledge from the school curriculum because it conflicts with dominant religious doctrine is inconsistent with the mandate of neutrality. The posting of the Ten Commandments, even though privately funded, was determined to be for a "plainly religious" purpose and hence violative of the Establishment Clause in *Stone v. Graham* (1980). Efforts to characterize the Ten Commandments in secular terms as a part of our legal heritage failed. On the other hand, the Court struck down an effort by a state university to avoid Establishment Clause problems by denying student groups access to university facilities "for purposes of religious worship and teaching." *Widmar v. Vincent* (1981). A policy of equal access serves the secular purpose of promoting the free exchange of ideas in the public forum. It would not have a primary effect of advancing religion since there is no symbolic state approval of the religious message and the access is available to all groups, secular and sectarian. Enforcement of a policy of excluding "religious" groups would involve an even greater threat of church-state entanglement. The thin line separating moral and religious values and the ambiguity of what constitutes a religion suggests that the subject of religion in the school curriculum will be a recurring issue.

Could *Widmar* be extended to the public high schools? Congress thought so and enacted the Equal Access Act of 1984 which prohibited discrimination against religious student speech. The Act provided that if a public high school allowed "noncurriculum related groups" to meet on school premises a "limited open forum" was created. A school would then be prohibited from denying the request of student religious groups to meet on school premises during noninstructional time. Denial of such access to school premises to a student Christian club by a public high school violated the Equal Access Act; the Act was triggered because other noncurriculum related groups were recognized by the school. Moreover, the Act's principle of equal access for religious groups to school facilities under such circumstances did not violate the Establishment Clause. *Board of Education of the Westside Community Schools v. Mergens* (1990).

The plurality opinion for the Court in *Mergens* applied the *Lemon* test. The Congressional purpose behind the Equal Access Act was "undeniably secular" since it prohibited discrimination against political or philosophical speech as well as political speech on the basis of content. The Act was neutral toward religion; it does not constitute an endorsement of religion. The Act did not have the primary effect of advancing religion. High school students were mature enough to understand that a school does not endorse speech merely because speech is allowed on a nondiscriminatory basis. The wide variety of clubs assured that no official endorsement or favoritism was present. Involvement by school officials was minimal. The limited monitoring role of school officials did not constitute an impermissible entanglement with religion. In short, high school students were not so much less mature than university students to make the precepts of *Widmar* inapplicable.

A public school board may not consistent with the Establishment Clause deny use of public school premises to a church group which wishes to show a film series on child rearing. Such action violates the Freedom of Speech Clause since it is viewpoint discrimination to permit school property to be used for the airing of all views about child rearing except those views on that topic which have a religious orientation. Furthermore, the exhibition of the child rearing film by the church group would not offend the Establishment Clause. The film was not shown during school hours, was not sponsored by the school and was open to the general public. As in *Widmar*, there was no "realistic danger" that the community would think the school endorsed religion or any religious denomination. Any benefit to the religious group flowing from the showing of the film was entirely incidental. Finally, the Court observed that the permitting the exhibition of the film on school property in these circumstances did not constitute a violation of the Establishment Clause using the tripartite *Lemon* test. *Lamb's Chapel v. Center Moriches School District* (1993).

Finally, despite the *pro forma* profession of adherence to *Lemon* in *Lamb's Chapel*, it should be noted that the use of the *Lemon* test as the measure of the validity of public school "efforts to accommodate religion" has become intensely controversial. Thus inclusion of a prayer offered by a clergyman selected by a public high school for a graduation baccalaureate ceremony was held, 5–4, to violate the Establishment Clause. Justice Kennedy for the Court declined to reconsider the *Lemon* test as requested by the Bush Administration. But he didn't use it either. Instead, he used a coercion test. Peer and public pressures to attend the baccalaureate ceremony exerts coercive if subtle pressure on students particularly in view of the school's involvement in the ceremony. The high school sponsored the religious exercise and chose the clergyman. The fact that students were not required to attend did not diminish the force of that pressure. *Lee v. Weisman* (1992).

Four concurring justices in *Lee* contended that an endorsement test should be used for Establishment Clause issues—does the challenged government related practice endorse religion? An endorsement test was preferable to a coercion test since the problem of coercion is already dealt with by the Free Exercise Clause. Four justices in a dissent by Justice Scalia contended that *Lemon* should be abandoned altogether and that Justice Kennedy's definition of coercion was too broad since no penalties attached to non-attendance at the ceremony. The baccalaureate ceremony was merely an aspect of a civic religion long understood to be nonsectarian in character.

3. ESTABLISHMENT OUTSIDE THE SCHOOLS

While the educational forum has provided a fruitful source of church-state issues, Establishment Clause jurisprudence casts a broader shadow. When the state vests "substantial governmental powers" in religious institutions, excessive church-state entanglement is present. *Larkin v. Grendel's Den, Inc.* (1982) [law barring issuance of liquor license to facilities within 500 feet of a church or school if the church or school objects held unconstitutional]. The *Larkin* Court stressed that the law provided no assurance that the system would be used in a religiously neutral way and that it provided a "significant symbolic benefit to religion" by sharing state power with religious institutions.

A New York state law creating a state school district coterminous with a village populated by Satmar Hasidim, an Orthodox Jewish sect, violated the Establishment Clause since it allocated political power on the basis of a religious criterion. The separate public school district was set up just to run a special education program for handicapped children. The other village children went to parochial schools in the village. Although *Larkin* was a rare illustration of an impermissible attempt to unite civic and religious authority, the law creating the Kiryas Joel school district still resembled it. Here the delegation was of civic power to the qualified voters of the village rather than to a church parish council. But this was a distinction that made no constitutional difference. The state law defined a political subdivision in religious terms thus creating an invalid *Larkin*-type fusion of government and religious functions. It was not clear what the next religious group seeking a separate school district from the legislature would receive. Such special favored treatment on the basis of religion violated the Establishment Clause. *Board of Education of Kiryas Joel School District v. Grumet* (1994).

Sunday Closing Laws have long been upheld against Establishment Clause challenge. *McGowan v. Maryland* (1961). *McGowan* reasoned that the laws have a secular purpose and effect in promoting a common day of rest. See *Estate of Thornton v. Caldor, Inc.* (1985) [state law affording employee with an absolute unqualified right not to work on the Sabbath of their choice "has a primary effect that impermissibly advances a particular religious practice" violative of Establishment Clause]. The law in *Thornton* did not relieve the Sabbatarian from any government imposed obligation. Instead, "[t]he employer and others must adjust their affairs to the command of the State whenever the statute is invoked by an employee."

However, when Congress in Title VII prohibited discrimination in employment but provided an exemption for religion, it was held that such an exemption does not violate the Establishment Clause because it is a "mere accommodation for religion." The *Lemon* analysis permits government to alleviate "significant governmental interference with their religious missions." *Corporation Presiding Bishop of the Church of Jesus Christ of Latter–Day Saints v. Amos* (1987).

Lynch v. Donnelly (1984), upheld, 5–4, a municipality's erection of a creche or Nativity scene as part of an annual Christmas display. For the majority, per Chief Justice Burger, the display served the secular purpose of celebrating the holiday and of depicting the origins of the holiday. Noting the frequent government recognition of religious holidays and events, the Court focused on the increasing secularization of Christmas. Further, the religious effects were no more egregious here than in many of the public aid programs approved by the Court. The Chief Justice concluded that any benefit to religion was "indirect, remote and incidental." The absence of any ongoing day-to-day interaction between church and state made any entanglement concerns *de minimis*. Fear of political divisiveness alone could not serve to invalidate otherwise permissible municipal conduct.

Justice Brennan, dissenting, applied the *Lemon* criteria, as did the majority, but reached a very different conclusion: "[T]he City's action should be recognized for what it is: a coercive, though perhaps small, step towards establishing the sectarian preferences of the majority at the expense of the minority, accomplished by placing public facilities and funds in support of religious symbolism and theological tidings that the creche conveys." State endorsement of the "distinctively religious elements" of the secular holiday provided the primary religious effect violative of the Establishment Clause.

Placement of a Christmas creche on the Grand Staircase, the most public and most beautiful part of the Allegheny County Courthouse violates the Establishment Clause. However, the placement at the entrance to the City–County Building of an eighteen foot Chanukah menorah next to the City's Christmas tree and a sign celebrating liberty did not violate the Establishment Clause. *Allegheny County v. ACLU* (1989).

Justice Blackmun explained for the Court the seemingly anomalous result in *Allegheny County*. The creche stood by itself with no other secular symbols of the holiday season. The County thereby "sends an unmistakable message that it supports and promotes the Christian praise to God that is the creche religious message." The teaching of *Lynch* is that "government may celebrate Christmas in some manner and form, but not in a way that endorses Christian doctrine." The menorah display, on the other hand, was permissible under the Establishment Clause because its display along with the tree and the sign simply constitutes a recognition "that both Christmas and Chanukah are part of the same winter-holiday season." This season has achieved a secular status in American society.   The menorah was not an endorsement of religion but rather a secular celebration of "cultural diversity."

Another non-academic context in which the meaning of the Establishment Clause has arisen involves the tax liability of religious organizations. Does the grant of an exemption violate the Establishment Clause? *Walz v. Tax Com'n of New York* (1970) held that a property tax exemption for places of religious worship did not violate the Establishment Clause given the historical acceptance of such exemptions.   But *Texas Monthly v. Bullock* (1989) held that where a state grants exemptions from sales and use taxes only to religious periodicals, such exemptions violate the Establishment Clause. These exemptions constitute an impermissible endorsement of religious beliefs.   Such an exclusive subsidy to religion lacks both the requisite secular purpose or the primary secular effect.

On the other hand, *Hernandez v. Commissioner of Internal Revenue* (1989) held that a refusal by the IRS to recognize as charitable contributions payments made by members of the Church of Scientology to that Church did not violate the Establishment Clause. The charitable contributions provisions of the Internal Revenue Code made no explicit distinction between religious and non-religious organizations. Since the provision applied to all religious entities, there was no impermissible denominational preference.

Similarly, a state sales and use tax applied to a religious organization selling religious materials in the state did not violate the Establishment Clause. Using the *Lemon* test, it was held that the tax was generally applicable and was neutral and nondiscriminatory with respect to matters of religious belief. Moreover, there was no excessive governmental entanglement either. Since the state sales and use tax was imposed without an exemption for religious organizations, the state was not required to look into the religious content of the materials sold but only with the question of whether there had been a sale or use. *Jimmy Swaggart Ministries v. Board of Equalization* (1990).

B. FREE EXERCISE OF RELIGION

Coercion of religious beliefs or conduct is the essence of a claim under the Free Exercise Clause. "The freedom to hold religious beliefs and opinions is absolute." *Braunfeld v. Brown* (1961). See *Torcaso v. Watkins* (1961) [test oath requiring profession of a belief in God for public employment held violative of free exercise]. See U.S. Const., art. VI, proscribing use of religious tests for federal employment. When an individual is required to engage in conduct which violates his religious beliefs or opinions, he may seek refuge in the First Amendment. *West Virginia State Bd. of Educ. v. Barnette* (1943), involved a Jehovah's Witness' challenge to a law requiring him to salute the flag—a practice which he believed violated the Scriptures. In striking down the law, the Court declared that government may not prescribe what shall be orthodox in politics, nationalism, religion or other matters of opinion.

While the Court initially indicated that government could regulate religious conduct without any Free Exercise Clause constraints [*Reynolds v. United States* (1878), federal law criminalizing bigamy held constitutional], this view was quickly abandoned. Freedom to believe would be a hollow right without freedom to act pursuant to that belief. Even religiously-neutral laws which significantly burden religious practices must satisfy the demands of the Free Exercise Clause. *Cantwell v. Connecticut* (1940) [conviction for religious soliciting without a license reversed]. On the other hand, does the First Amendment require government to grant exemptions from religiously-neutral laws because conformity to the law burdens religious practices? *Cantwell* stated that while the freedom to believe is absolute, freedom to act pursuant to one's religion cannot be. "Conduct remains subject to regulation for the protection of society." Further, the grant of a religious exemption raises Establishment Clause problems—such an exemption would be granted for the purpose of aiding a particular religion.

In attempting to define standards for determining what accommodation to religion is required by the Free Exercise Clause, the Court has sometimes distinguished between direct and indirect burdens on religion. Direct burdens, *e.g.*, laws which make a religious practice unlawful, impose an especially severe burden on freedom of religion. In *Braunfeld v. Brown* (1961), in upholding Sunday Closing laws against free exercise attack, the Court distinguished laws imposing direct burdens from laws which only indirectly burden religious practices. Since the closing law imposed only an economic burden on Orthodox Jewish merchants who closed on Saturdays for religious reasons, the burden was indirect. Such a burden is constitutional, "unless the State may accomplish its [secular] purpose by means which do not impose such a burden." Granting an exemption to Sabbatarians, the Court concluded, could have undermined the States religiously-neutral purpose of promoting a uniform day of rest.

But the judicial deference manifested in *Braunfeld* to laws imposing only indirect burdens on religious practices was lost in *Sherbert v. Verner* (1963). The Court, per Justice Brennan, who had dissented in *Braunfeld,* struck down the denial of state unemployment benefits to a Seventh Day Adventist for refusing to work on Saturday, the Sabbath day of her faith. While the burden on her religion was admittedly indirect, the coercive effect of the law imposed a significant burden, a penalty, on her religious liberty: "The ruling forces her to choose between following the precepts of her religion and forfeiting benefits on the one hand, and abandoning one of the precepts of her religion in order to accept work, on the other." Government imposition of such a choice could be justified only by showing a "compelling state interest" and "that no alternative form of regulation" would suffice. The State failed to meet this burden. For Justice Brennan, this accommodation was not violative of establishment principles but only an effort to maintain neutrality between Sunday and Saturday Sabbatarians.

Justice Harlan, dissenting, argued that in spite of Justice Brennan's use of the overriding state interest in *Braunfeld* to distinguish that case, *Sherbert* "necessarily overruled *Braunfeld*." The state was being "constitutionally compelled" to fashion an exception to its general rules of eligibility even though the burden on religion was only indirect and remote.

Sherbert was deemed controlling in *Thomas v. Review Board of the Indiana Employment Sec. Div.* (1981). The Court, per Chief Justice Burger, overturned Indiana's denial of unemployment benefits to a Jehovah's Witness who left his job producing armaments because of a sincere belief that such work violated his religion. The fact that other Jehovah's Witnesses continued to work did not defeat the free exercise claim: "The guarantee of free exercise is not limited to beliefs which are shared by all members of a religious sect." Thomas was coerced in his religious beliefs and that constituted a substantial burden, albeit indirect, in the free exercise of his religion. "Where the state conditions receipt of an important benefit upon conduct proscribed by a religious faith, or where it denies such a benefit because of conduct mandated by a religious belief, thereby putting substantial pressure on an adherent to modify his behavior and to violate his beliefs; a burden upon religion exists."

The state failed to show that it had used "the least restrictive means of achieving some compelling state interest."

A denial of state unemployment compensation benefits to a Seventh–Day Adventist who was fired by her private employer for refusing to work on Friday evenings and Saturdays violated the Free Exercise Clause. No compelling state interest was served by placing pressure on the claimant to modify her behavior and to violate her religious beliefs. It did not matter that the claimant converted to the Seventh Day Adventist faith after she commenced her employment. *Hobbie v. Unemployment Appeals Compensation Commission of Florida* (1987). However, where the government chose to use numbers in administering its social security system, a free exercise challenge based on religious opposition to the use of a social security number failed to demonstrate a significant burden on free exercise. Religious belief does not entitle a claimant to dictate the internal processes of government. *Bowen v. Roy* (1986) But where a Christian who did not belong to any specific Christian denomination was denied unemployment compensation benefits because he refused to take a job which would entail working on Sunday, eligibility for those benefits could not be conditioned on requiring him to violate his beliefs. Absent a compelling state interest an individual in such circumstances could not be forced to choose between his faith and state unemployment benefits. *Frazee v. Illinois Department of Employment Security* (1989).

However, benefits can be denied if denial is the incidental effect of a generally applicable and otherwise valid criminal law. Strict scrutiny would not be used in such circumstances. Where the general criminal law has the consequence of prohibiting a religious practice, imposing the lesser burden of denying of unemployment compensation benefits to persons violating the criminal law is constitutional. *Employment Division v. Smith* (1988) (*Smith I*).

While indirect burdens on religion are sufficient to invoke strict scrutiny review, laws which compel an individual "to perform acts undeniably at odds with fundamental tenets of their religious beliefs" (*i.e.*, direct burdens) are especially coercive of religious liberty. *Wisconsin v. Yoder* (1972). In *Yoder,* the Court invalidated application of Wisconsin's law requiring compulsory school attendance until age 16 to Amish children. The Amish refused to send their children to public schools beyond the eighth grade, based on their "deep religious convictions" about the way to live. "Only those interests of the highest order and those not otherwise served can overbalance legitimate claims to the free exercise of religion." *Braunfeld* had concluded that an exception would undermine the state's interest in a uniform day of rest. But in the case of the Amish in *Yoder,* the state's interests in promoting self-reliant and self-sufficient participants in society were not undermined by an exemption for the Amish. Most Amish children stayed in the community and were well-suited for life in their society. The state interest in including the Amish under the law was not sufficiently overriding to justify the significant burden on religious liberty.

Finding of a significant burden on religious liberty does not invariably result in invalidation of the law. *United States v. Lee* (1982), upheld the federal government's refusal to exempt an Amish employer from participating in the social security system. While accepting that the law significantly burdened a sincerely held religious belief, the government met its burden of demonstrating that denial of the exemption was "essential to accomplish an overriding governmental interest." Mandatory and continuous participation in the social security system is vital to the integrity of the system and "it would be difficult to accommodate the comprehensive social security system with myriad exceptions flowing from a wide variety of religious beliefs." Further, it would be hard to cabin such an exception to social security: "[t]he tax system could not function if denominations were allowed to challenge the tax system because tax payments were spent in a manner that violates their religious beliefs." See *Tony & Susan Alamo Found. v. Secretary of Labor* (1985) [application of Fair Labor Standards Act to commercial activities of nonprofit religious organization and employees receiving no cash salaries held not to involve a significant burden on free exercise or to violate Establishment Clause]. The Free Exercise Clause requires an exemption from a government program only if the mandates of the program actually burdened the complainant's free exercise rights. The Fair Labor Standards Act did not require the workers in *Alamo* to accept wages nor did it prevent them from returning those wages to their religious organization. Similarly, a state sales and use tax on religious materials did not violate the Free Exercise Clause. The religious beliefs of the individuals involved did not forbid them from paying the tax. The state is not required to provide an exemption for a religious organization to a generally applicable tax when there is no significant burden imposed by the state on their free exercise rights. *Jimmy Swaggart Ministries v. Board of Equalization* (1990).

The foregoing cases have used a two step approach that dates back to Sabbatarian cases like *Sherbert v. Verner* in the 1960's. This approach makes two inquiries. First, it measures the severity of the burden the law places on the individual's free exercise. If that burden is a significant one, then the government must show that the law is narrowly tailored to achieve a compelling state interest. The less burdensome alternatives or less restrictive means test, often used in the free expression context, will be applied. The question then posed is this—Could the state's interest be accomplished by less burdensome means? In practice, the use of this test has sometimes meant that this strict scrutiny standard of review exempted individuals making a free exercise claim from compliance even with laws that are religiously neutral. This result has obtained because once this two step test is applied the effect of the law at issue has been deemed to significantly burden an individual's free exercise of religion.

However, the doctrinal approach in this area may be undergoing major change. In *Lyng v. Northwest Indian Cemetery Protective Association* (1988) and *Employment Division v. Smith* (1990) (*Smith II*), the Court held that the strict scrutiny approach just described did not apply to a generally applicable and otherwise valid law. This conclusion was reached despite the fact that application to the law in question in both cases incidentally imposed a substantial burden on free exercise. It was feared that these cases were the harbingers of a radical doctrinal change which would no longer use a strict scrutiny standard of review for religiously neutral laws having only an incidentally burdensome effect on free exercise.

When the federal government allowed timber harvesting and road construction in a national forest which had been used for religious purposes by Indian tribes, a free exercise challenge of the government action was rejected. The effect of the governmental action was incidental in nature. Even though the consequences of the governmental action might destroy the religious practice, such "indirect coercion or penalties" on free exercise did not invoke the use of a strict scrutiny standard. The government after all owned the land and had not directly prohibited any specific Indian religious practice. *Lyng v. Northwest Indian Cemetery Protective Association* (1988).

A state may validly deny unemployment compensation to Indian workers who were fired from their jobs because of work-related misconduct resulting from the use of the drug peyote while participating in the rites of the Native American Church. Such denial does not infringe on free exercise. Under Oregon law use of the drug peyote was a criminal violation and the Oregon unemployment compensation law forbade the payment of benefits for work-related misconduct. These laws were religiously neutral and, therefore, presumptively valid. A free exercise claim does not free an individual from compliance with a generally applicable religiously neutral criminal law which is otherwise valid. Strict scrutiny is not triggered when a free exercise challenge is directed to a generally applicable criminal prohibition. This result is not altered even if the religious practice the free exercise claim is designed to protect is central to the religious faith of which the complainant is a member. It is inappropriate for courts to investigate whether a particular religious practice is or is not central to a religious faith. Furthermore, use of strict scrutiny in this context would invite requests for the creation of "constitutionally required religious exemptions from civic obligation of almost every conceivable kind." Moreover, exemptions from legislation based on a desire to accommodate religion is a more appropriate task for the legislature than for the judiciary. *Employment Division v. Smith* (1990) (*Smith II*).

Certainly, if the doctrinal approach of *Lyng* and *Smith II* were clearly adopted by the Court to the exclusion of the two step approach, a decisive question would be whether the governmental action at issue in a free exercise case is an incidental or a direct burden on free exercise. The problems attached to such an inquiry are reminiscent of the now long discarded direct indirect inquiry in the interstate commerce area. Such analysis in that context proved to be doctrinally unworkable and essentially conclusionary in nature. Similarly unsatisfactory results can be expected in this area. Incidental burdens on free exercise would be insufficient to trigger the strict scrutiny standard. Thus, the conclusion that the burden was incidental would be dispositive of the free exercise claim.

In the Religious Freedom Restoration Act of 1993, Congress sought to undo the holding in *Smith II* by restoring the use of the compelling governmental interest test, as set forth in *Sherbert* and *Yoder*, in cases presenting a substantial burden to the free exercise of religion. The Religious Freedom Restoration Act provides that government is precluded from imposing substantial burdens on free exercise even if they result from laws of general applicability unless such laws further a compelling governmental interest and are the least restrictive means of accomplishing that interest. The statute itself presents a substantial constitutional law issue since it is not clear that Congress can impose a substantive rule of decision on the judiciary consistent with the doctrine of separation of powers.

Not all substantial burdens on free exercise will escape invalidation even if the laws of general applicability approach of *Smith II* endures. It would still be open to show that a law was not a law of general applicability. Thus municipal ordinances which prohibited animal sacrifice but exempted non-religious animal slaughtering were held to violate the Free Exercise Clause. The ban against animal sacrifice could not be placed under the rubric of a law of general applicability because of the municipality's interest in promoting and preventing animal cruelty and protecting public health. Although these were secular objectives, they were "pursued only with respect to conduct motivated by religious beliefs." The challenged ordinances were not neutral and were aimed at the Santeria religion which practices animal sacrifice. Justice Kennedy noted: "[T]he texts of the ordinances were gerrymandered with care to proscribe religious killings of animals but to exclude almost all secular killings." The ordinances were invalid since they directly burdened religion. Applying strict scrutiny, it was clear—given the exemptions afforded to non-Santerian animal practices—that the municipal ordinances at issue were not narrowly tailored to serve a compelling governmental interest. *Church of the Lukumi Babalu Aye, Inc. v. Hialeah* (1993).

A fundamental problem runs throughout the field of freedom of religion: what *is* a religion? The Court has not directly answered this question. It has, however, indicated that non-theistic beliefs can qualify for constitutional protection. *Torcaso;*

United States v. Seeger (1965) [conscientious objector status available to person having a sincere, meaningful belief which "occupies a place in the life of its possessor parallel to that filled by the orthodox belief in God"]. See *Welsh v. United States* (1970) [Court plurality extends C.O. status to those having strong moral or even public policy objections]. On the other hand, the Court rejected conscientious objector status for those objecting to a particular war. *Gillette v. United States* (1971). *Wisconsin v. Yoder* stressed that a person is not allowed to convert his own personal standards on matters of conduct into a religious belief requiring constitutional protection. The Amish claim, by contrast, was said to reflect "deep religious conviction, shared by an organized group, and intimately related to daily living." Yet a free exercise claim will be upheld even where the claimant is not a member of organized religion or any particular sect. All that is required is a sincerely held "religious belief." *Frazee v. Illinois Department of Employment Security* (1989). While commentators frequently suggest that religion should be given a broader definition in Free Exercise cases, the question of what constitutes a religion remains open.

In the past the two-step approach worked as follows. First, it was necessary to determine if the law significantly burdened the free exercise of religion. Then the Court had to consider the extent to which the belief was sincerely held [*Thomas*] and the importance of the practice or belief (*i.e.*, centrality) in the religion [*Yoder*]. But it declined to consider the truth or falsity of the belief or doctrine [*United States v. Ballard* (1944)] or choose between doctrinal viewpoints within a religion [*Thomas*]. See *Jones v. Wolf* (1979) [state court may decide property disputes between contending church groups if it does not require an inquiry into religious doctrine]. However, in *Employment Division v. Smith* (1990) the Court observed that it is "no more appropriate for judges to determine the 'centrality' of religious belief before applying a 'compelling interest' test in the free exercise field than it would be for them to determine the 'importance' of an idea before applying the 'compelling interest' test in the free speech field." These observations raise the question whether the inquiry into centrality in the free exercise field will soon be eliminated altogether.

Second, in the past, if religious liberty was significantly burdened then the government could justify its denial of an exemption only if it could demonstrate that comprehensive coverage was essential to achieve an overriding or compelling government interest. But see *Goldman v. Weinberger* (1986) [application of Air Force dress codes "reasonably and evenhandedly" to prevent Orthodox Jew from wearing a yarmulke as required by his religion held constitutional, citing "far more deferential" standard of review in military cases]. Apparently the Establishment Clause and the demand for government neutrality is not violated when the Free Exercise Clause does mandate the religious accommodation. *Lyng* and *Smith II*, however, did not require the state to meet a compelling state interest standard where the free exercise challenge was directed to a valid, generally applicable, religiously neutral law which only imposed an incidental burden on the free exercise of religion. Whether the *Lyng-Smith II* approach will be extended to the free exercise field generally remains to be seen.

CHAPTER IX

STATE ACTION

A. INTRODUCTION

With the exception of the Thirteenth Amendment, the guarantees of the Constitution run only against the national and state governments. Absent congressional legislation extending these rights to private conduct, "state action" is required. In part, this demand for governmental involvement to make the constitutional protections work is a matter of constitutional language, *e.g.*, the First and Fourteenth Amendments specifically refer to government wrongs. But the state action doctrine also reflects the nature of the Constitution as organic law. It defines the relation of persons and citizens to their government rather than to each other. Further, the requirement of state action is perceived by many as a vital protection for personal liberty, limiting governmental interference with freedom of action and association, including the ability to freely use one's own property. Finally, the state action doctrine is argued by some to further the values of federalism by forcing recourse to state rather than federal law.

Problems arise, however, in defining when seemingly private action is truly private. Privately owned corporations today often exercise power over persons comparable to that of government agencies and much of that private power is attributable to benefits provided by government. Government may be "significantly intertwined" with nominally private individuals, groups, clubs, and associations; their conduct may be authorized or so encouraged by official action as to make the label "private action" inappropriate. Some functions these groups perform may be so public in character that the activity remains essentially governmental even when performed by a private actor. In such cases, the question arises whether the private conduct should be treated as "state action."

B. FRAMING THE STATE ACTION DOCTRINE

In the *Civil Rights Cases* (1883), the Court, per Justice Bradley, held the Civil Rights Act of 1875, proscribing racial discrimination in places of public accommodation, unconstitutional. Since the case was decided well before the commerce power reached its present expansive proportions, and since the Act was not limited to interstate commerce, the Court examined whether the enforcement clauses of the Thirteenth and Fourteenth Amendments gave Congress power to enact the law.

Justice Bradley began from the premise that Sec. 1 of the Fourteenth Amendment prohibited only state action: "Individual invasion of individual rights is not the subject matter of the Amendment."

What then was the scope of congressional power under Sec. 5 of the Amendment? Simply, to enforce the limited prohibition against state action: "To adopt appropriate legislation for correcting the effects of such prohibited state laws and statutes, and thus to render them effectually null, void and innocuous." The power was strictly corrective or remedial, *i.e.*, to provide remedies for what the courts determined to be substantive rights but not to define the substantive rights themselves. Congressional power was limited to correcting government misconduct.

Concern for personal liberty and for federalism motivated the Court. To extend the guarantees of the Amendment further would be to allow Congress "to establish a code of municipal law regulative of all private rights between man and man in society. It would be to make Congress take the place of the state legislatures and to supersede them." Private wrongs, "not sanctioned in some way by the state, or done under state authority" should be vindicated by state law. Since the 1875 law operated directly on private actions and itself defined what was the substantive wrong, it was beyond Congress's legislative power.

For the first Justice Harlan, dissenting, the 1875 law was a valid enforcement of the Citizenship Clause set forth in the first sentence of the Fourteenth Amendment, which was "of a distinctly affirmative character." The citizenship thus conferred on Blacks by this affirmative grant, he argued, could be protected by congressional legislation "of a

primary direct character." Section 5 of the Fourteenth Amendment gave Congress the power to
enforce both the prohibitive and the affirmative
provisions of the Amendment. What did the grant
of citizenship include? It included, at least, "exemption from race discrimination in respect of any
civil right belonging to citizens of the white race in
the same state." The Amendment was designed to
protect these privileges and immunities not only
from unfriendly state legislation, but also from the
hostile action of corporations and individuals. Alternatively, Justice Harlan argued that the owners
of places of public accommodation are "agents of
the state, because amenable, in respect of public
duties and functions, to public regulation." Since
the rights recognized in the 1875 Act were legal, not
social rights, the Act was a valid exercise of Congress's Fourteenth Amendment power.

The Court in the *Civil Rights Cases* also rejected
the claims that the Act was constitutional under the
Thirteenth Amendment. Justice Bradley did accept
that Sec. 1 of that Amendment abolished slavery,
"established universal freedom," and was self-exe-
cuting against private misconduct. Congress pursuant to Sec. 2 of the Amendment could enact
"primary and direct" legislation "abolishing all
badges and incidents of slavery in the United
States." But these expansive premises were then
undercut by the conclusion that an act of racial
discrimination at a place of public accommodation
"has nothing to do with slavery or involuntary
servitude, and that if it is violative of any right of

the party, his redress is to be sought under the laws of the State." The Court rejected the premise that Sec. 1 of the Thirteenth Amendment was violated.

Again, Justice Harlan's dissent directly took issue with the Court. The Thirteenth Amendment, he asserted, was designed to protect the former slave "against the deprivation, on account of their race, of any civil rights enjoyed by other freemen in the same state." Congress correctly determined that racial discrimination by corporations and individuals in the exercise of their public or quasi-public functions, constitute a "badge of servitude"—the Act was a constitutional exercise of Congress' power under Sec. 2 to enforce the Thirteenth Amendment guarantee.

Had Justice Harlan's approach to the meaning of the Civil War Amendments been accepted, much of the confused history of the state action doctrine might have been avoided. Similarly, if the Court had been willing to accept the argument that state failure to protect the Thirteenth or Fourteenth Amendments was itself a wrong (*i.e.,* the amendments impose an affirmative duty on the states), correctable by congressional legislation, constitutional protection against a broader range of conduct might have become available. But the Court in the *Civil Rights Cases* forged a far more limited doctrine for bringing the constitutional guarantee into play. While much of the impediment to federal protection fashioned in the case has been eroded (especially that pertaining to congressional enforcement), its essential principle that, apart from the

Thirteenth Amendment, governmental action is necessary to implicate constitutional rights, remains a formidable obstacle to a party seeking to claim constitutional protection against nominally private action.

C. FINDING STATE ACTION

The continuing vitality of the state action doctrine forged in the *Civil Rights Cases* has produced a mass of confusing litigation designed to avoid its strictures. It is clear that the acts of officials, federal or state, even if the acts violate the law, constitute "state action." Further, the term covers the action of all governmental subdivisions and agencies. Or, if government officials participate in the management or administration of an enterprise, the government is responsible for its activities. Indeed, even though Congress stated in its governing legislation that Amtrak was not a government agency, the judiciary is not bound by that determination. When government creates a corporation like Amtrak and reserves for itself the permanent authority to appoint a majority of its directors, such an entity is a public actor. Therefore, when Amtrak refused to let an artist display his billboard in New York City's Penn station, that decision is subject to judicial review to ascertain whether it violated the First Amendment. *Lebron v. National Railroad Passenger Corp.* (1995).

But state involvement is usually far more indirect and unclear than in these official misconduct cases.

When can private action qualify as state action? This is the critical question in state action cases. During the Warren Court years, the Court seemed so willing to find state action in nominally private conduct that commentators began to speak of the twilight of the state action doctrine. It seemed as if the doctrine was being merged into the issue of whether the right was violated rather than serving as a threshold issue of whether the constitutional right was even implicated. But with the coming of the Burger Court, the state action doctrine has been restored—and with a vengeance. Generally today, the state action cases resolve into three questions: (1) whether an activity is a "public function;" (2) whether the government is so significantly involved with the private actor as to make the government responsible for the private conduct; (3) whether the government may be said to have approved or authorized (or perhaps, significantly encouraged) the challenged conduct sufficiently to be responsible for it.

1. PUBLIC FUNCTIONS

The Court has never accepted the argument that the Fourteenth Amendment imposes affirmative duties on the state so that government failure to use its regulatory power to protect the guaranteed rights constitutes state action. However, the Court has accepted the proposition that a function may be so governmental in character that the state may not disclaim responsibility for its performance—the state's failure to act where it has a duty to prevent the wrong becomes a form of action.

When electoral processes such as primaries are performed by private political parties, the group's actions constitute state action under the Fourteenth and Fifteenth Amendments. *Smith v. Allwright* (1944); *Terry v. Adams* (1953) [primaries conducted in a racially discriminatory manner]. Whether the actions of political parties always constitute state action has not been decided but does seem unlikely. When privately-owned property has taken on the essential characteristics of a municipality, *e.g.,* company towns, state action is present. *Marsh v. Alabama* (1946) [use of trespass laws to prevent distribution of religious literature]. While it seemed that shopping centers might also come under this "public function" principle [*Amalgamated Food Employers Union Local 590 v. Logan Valley Plaza, Inc.* (1968), informational picketing related to activities at the shopping center constitutionally protected], later cases first circumscribed [*Lloyd Corp. v. Tanner* (1972), handbilling unrelated to shopping center activities held not protected] and then rejected the view that a privately owned shopping center is "the functional equivalent of a municipality." *Hudgens v. N.L.R.B.* (1976) [*Logan Valley* overruled; distinction based on whether the speech was related to shopping center activities would be an impermissible discrimination based on speech content]. In short, only when privately owned property is the "functional equivalent" of a municipality is there state action.

The difficulty of the public function approach is demonstrated not only by the shopping center cases but also by *Evans v. Newton* (1966). *Evans* held that racial discrimination at a park managed by private trustees violated the Fourteenth Amendment. Justice Douglas, for the Court, described the case as requiring the reconciliation of "the right of the individual to pick his own associates" and "to fashion his private life" with the constitutional ban "against state-sponsored racial inequality." While Justice Douglas might have rested the Court's decision that the government was responsible solely on the finding that the municipality remained "entwined in the management or control of the park," *i.e.,* public administration, he also relied the public function approach, reasoning that "the service rendered even by a private park of this character is municipal in nature." Analogizing the services provided by a park to those of a fire or police department, Justice Douglas concluded that "the predominant character of the park is municipal."

Justice Harlan, dissenting, argued that the Court's public function theory was "a catch-phrase approach as vague and amorphous as it is far-reaching." Reasoning by analogy, the Court's approach could be extended to encompass education, orphanages, libraries, garbage collection, detective agencies, and a host of other parallel activities. Expressing concern for federalist values, Harlan concluded that the ill-defined theory "carries the seeds of transferring to federal authority vast areas of concerns whose regulation has wisely been left by the Constitution to the States."

While the Court continues to accept the public function theory of state action, its doctrinal scope has been severely restricted. Presently, the public function theory is limited solely to functions which are "traditionally exclusively reserved to the State." Applying this restrictive standard, the Court refused to find state action in the running of a privately-owned public utility. *Jackson v. Metropolitan Edison Co.* (1974) [the state is not obligated to furnish utility services; supplying utility service "is not traditionally the exclusive prerogative of the State"]. Nor does state approval of the sale of stored goods pursuant to a warehouseman's lien as a means of resolving a dispute delegate "an exclusive prerogative of the sovereign," given the variety of remedies available to the debtor. *Flagg Bros., Inc. v. Brooks* (1978). And the operation of a private school for maladjusted high school students is not state action for purposes of an action by a teacher challenging the constitutionality of the school's decision to discharge him. The education of the maladjusted is not the exclusive province of the state. *Rendell–Baker v. Kohn* (1982). Nor is the state responsible for decisions regarding the transfer or discharge of patients at a privately-operated nursing home. Even if the state had been obligated under its laws to provide nursing care (which it was not), "it would not follow that decisions made in the day-to-day administration of a nursing home are the kind of decisions traditionally and exclusively made by the sovereign for and on behalf of the public." *Blum v. Yaretsky* (1982).

2. SIGNIFICANT INVOLVEMENT/JOINT PARTICIPATION

Another approach to finding state action is to look to the nature of the relationship between government and the nominally private actor. In *Burton v. Wilmington Parking Auth.* (1961), the Warren Court was asked to determine this question: Is a city constitutionally responsible for racial discrimination practiced by a privately-owned restaurant which rented space in its municipal parking garage? Justice Clark, for the Court, answered this question in the affirmative. He cited the public ownership of the facility, the financing of its operations through municipal obligations, its public upkeep and maintenance and, referring to a factor that was to assume critical future importance, he noted the "mutual benefits" derived from the operation. The public might patronize the restaurant because they had a place to park; they might park at the garage in order to dine at the restaurant: "The state has so far insinuated itself into a position of interdependence with [the restaurant] that it must be recognized as a joint participant in the challenged activity." The aggregate of all of the contacts between the state and the restaurant provided the basis for finding state action: "Addition of all these activities, obligations and responsibilities of the Authority, the benefits mutually conferred indicates that degree of state participation and involvement in discriminatory action which it was the design of the Fourteenth Amendment to condemn."

While *Burton* suggested an expansive approach to the state action doctrine, subsequent cases have not fulfilled the promise. Instead of aggregating all of the State's contacts with the private actor, the Court has tended to treat each contact seriatim. Further, the Court has demanded that the State be a partner or joint venturer in the challenged activity. Finally, the Court has increasingly focused on the state's relationship to the particular conduct being challenged (*i.e.,* a "nexus" between the state and the challenged act is required).

The fact that the state licenses and pervasively regulates the private actor is insufficient for a finding of state action. *Moose Lodge No. 107 v. Irvis* (1972) [racial discrimination in services by a private club held not to involve the "symbiotic relationship" found in *Burton*]. The fact that government financial support is critical to the existence of a private entity does not make the state responsible for its actions. Thus, in *Blum v. Yaretsky* (1982), the Court stated: "That programs undertaken by the state result in substantial funding of the activities of a private entity is no more persuasive than the fact of regulation of such an entity in demonstrating that the state is responsible for decisions made by the entity in the course of its business." In *Blum,* the Court held that state subsidization of the operating costs of a nursing home and the financing of the medical expenses of 90% of its patients did not make the state responsible for the institution's decisions regarding the transfer or discharge of patients. And, in *Rendell–Baker v. Kohn* (1982), the fact that over 90% of the operating expenses of a private high school for maladjusted students was paid by government did not make the state responsible for the decision of the school to discharge teachers. Bear in mind, however, that there are some earlier decisions, involving state assistance to racially segregated private schools, that were based on a lower threshold of state responsibility. See *Norwood v. Harrison* (1973) [state financial support available to racially segregated schools for the purchase of textbooks constitutes state action]; *Gilmore v. Montgomery* (1974) [city under desegregation order held to violate equal protection by permitting exclusive use, even on a temporary basis, of recreational facilities by segregated private schools]. These decisions may be explainable as reflecting a more stringent Court attitude towards racial discrimination or as simply as a product of an earlier, more lenient attitude towards the state action mandate.

3. ENCOURAGEMENT, AUTHORIZATION AND APPROVAL

A state is also responsible for private action when it has "exercised coercive power" over the challenged action or "has provided such significant encouragement, either overt or covert, that the choice must in law be deemed that of the state." *Blum v. Yaretsky* (1982). Again, the student should be aware of the tightening of the state action mandate under the Burger Court. Increasingly, "encouragement" of private action is giving way to a requirement that the state "command" the particular decision or action being challenged.

The Court's decision in *Shelley v. Kraemer* (1948), suggested to some commentators that any state enforcement of private racial discrimination would constitute state action. *Shelley* involved the question whether state court enforcement of a racially discriminatory restrictive covenant in a deed constituted state action. The Court, per Chief Justice Vinson, held that while the private restrictive covenant itself would not violate the Fourteenth Amendment, court enforcement of the agreement did violate the Constitution. But it is important to note that the effect of the state court action in *Shelley* was to force willing white sellers to racially discriminate against willing Black buyers. Thus, the state was making available "the full coercive power of government to deny to [Black buyers], on the grounds of race or color, the enjoyment of property rights in premises which [Black buyers] are willing and financially able to acquire and which the [white sellers] are willing to sell." By invoking its common law policy to aid the covenantors in preventing the sale, the state had used its coercive powers to enforce racial discrimination.

State action is present, then, when government forces unwilling parties to racially discriminate. On the other hand, neutral state enforcement of its laws in a way that does not force or coerce persons to discriminate does not constitute state action. The fact that enforcement of the laws may aid a person seeking to racially discriminate is unlikely, without more, to constitute state action. Thus in *Evans v. Abney* (1970), a state's application of its trust laws to allow a testamentary grant of land to revert to the estate when the terms of the bequest (*i.e.,* that the land be used as a park "for whites only") could not be implemented, was not unconstitutional state action.

But when government actively "significantly encourages" private racial discrimination, the Court has, at least in the past, found the requisite state action. In the sit-in cases of the 1960s, actions by city officials instigating private restaurant owners to refuse service to Blacks made the state responsible for the discrimination. *Lombard v. Louisiana* (1963). And, in *Reitman v. Mulkey* (1967), the high point of this "encouragement approach" to state action, the Court held 5–4 that a referendum amendment (Proposition 14) of the California Constitution prohibiting governmental interference with a person's right to racially discriminate in the sale or rental of housing constituted state action.

Justice White, for the Court in *Reitman,* rejected the dissent's position that Proposition 14 was simply an assertion of official neutrality regarding private discrimination; that the law was "simply permissive in purpose and effect, and inoffensive on its face." Instead, the Court deferred to the finding of the California Supreme Court that the "design and effect" of Proposition 14 was to overturn the state's fair housing laws and to authorize private racial discrimination—it would "significantly encourage and involve the State in private discrimination." This was no policy of state neutrality or simply a repeal of existing fair housing laws or merely a state failure to prevent private racial discrimination. The effect of Proposition 14 was to embody a "right to discriminate" on racial grounds in the State's basic Charter. Private racial discrimination could now operate "free from censure or interference of any kind from official sources." Private discrimination had been given constitutional status.

The dissent in *Reitman* warned that, in relying on "encouragement," the Court was "forging a slippery and unfortunate criterion." Whatever the merits of this evaluation, the "encouragement" thesis has not really been employed in later cases. While lip service is still paid to "significant encouragement" as a basis for finding state action, the Court is increasingly demanding a showing of "authorization and approval" of the challenged private action.

By the early 1970's, however, it became clear that the generous interpretation of the state action concept which had characterized Warren Court era cases like *Reitman* was coming to a close. A series of cases in the early seventies made it clear that it was going to be much more difficult to reach private conduct through judicial expansion of state action. This approach begun in the era of the Burger Court, and ascendant now under the Rehnquist Court, requires a significant increase in the degree of government involvement in private conduct to justify the conclusion that state action is present. Litigants are now required to show that a close nexus exists between the private action at issue and government. From the state action perspective, the domain of the private sector is now significantly increased.

For example, in *Jackson v. Metropolitan Edison Co.* (1974), the Court considered a procedural due process challenge to termination of services for non-payment by a privately-owned utility company. Even though the state had reviewed the utility's tariff schedule providing for the challenged termination, the Court found no state action. While there was state "failure to overturn the practice," the state "has not put its own weight on the side of the proposed practice by ordering it." State toleration of a practice does not place the state's imprimatur on it. In *Flagg Bros. Inc. v. Brooks* (1978), the Court rejected "mere acquiescence" or "inaction" by the state in a warehouseman's sale of goods without notice or hearing to the debtor as sufficient to constitute state action. Even though the state's UCC law specifically *permitted* such a sale, the state had "merely announced the circumstances under which its courts will not interfere with a private sale." In *Rendell–Baker v. Kohn* (1982), the Court found no evidence that the private school's challenged discharge of employees was "compelled or influenced by any state regulation." And in *Blum v. Yaretsky* (1982), there was insufficient evidence that state regulations "dictate the decision to discharge or transfer [the nursing home patients] in a particular case." While there was pervasive state regulation, including adjustment of state financial benefits based on the nursing home's decisions, this did not "constitute approval or enforcement of that decision."

In each of these above cases, there was inadequate showing of official involvement in the particular challenged action—the state had not sanctioned it. However, when a deprivation of a federal right is caused by the exercise of some right or privilege created by the state or by a rule of conduct imposed by the state, *and* where the party charged with the deprivation may fairly be said to be a state actor, state action will be found. Or, at least, this is what the Court held 5–4 in *Lugar v. Edmondson Oil Co.* (1982). Acting pursuant to state law, Edmondson had obtained, *ex parte,* a prejudgment attachment of some of debtor Lugar's property. The writ of attachment was issued by a court clerk and executed by the sheriff. The Court held both requirements for state action were present. Lugar was claiming that the statute, which defined a "rule of conduct" for prejudgment attachment, was depriving him of due process. The second element, *i.e.,* involvement of a state actor, resulted from the "joint participation," by the state officials with the private party. For the dissent, this official action was simply neutral state action since invocation of state law, without more, does not make the state a partner to the crime.

Lugar appears to be a narrow crack in the formidable wall to constitutional litigation created by the modern state action doctrine. State responsibility for the particular private action being challenged has become a critical focus. And the factual predicates for finding state responsibility are increasingly limited. But race-based peremptory challenges by private litigants constitutes state action. Such challenges meet the two-part *Lugar* test. First, such challenges were authorized by state law. Second, a government official, a judge, conducts the *voir dire* and administers the use of such challenges. Therefore, the requisite joint participation between state and private actors is satisfied. *Edmonson v. Leesville Concrete Co.* (1991).

Even a close working relationship between the public action and the private party will sometimes on close examination be found insufficient to show the requisite joint action. When the National Collegiate Athletic Association (NCAA) threatened the University of Nevada–Las Vegas(UNLV), a state university, with sanctions unless it took disciplinary action against its basketball coach, Jerry Tarkanian, the NCAA conduct was held not to constitute state action. *National Collegiate Athletic Association v. Tarkanian* (1988).

The *Tarkanian* case was the "mirror image" of *Burton v. Wilmington Parking Authority, supra.* *Burton* had involved state encouragement of private action. *Tarkanian* involved private encouragement of state action. It turned out to be a significant difference. The NCAA did not act as an agent of the state university but in response to its obligation to its other members to enforce its rules. UNLV was under no compulsion to stay in the NCAA. No power had been delegated by the state to the NCAA to discipline a state university employee, the basketball coach. The NCAA sanctions were not created or required by Nevada law. The Court noted that UNLV had resisted the effort by the NCAA to have it impose sanctions. A crucial point was that the state university and the NCAA were not willing joint actors but adversaries.

CHAPTER X

CONGRESSIONAL LEGISLATION IN AID OF CIVIL RIGHTS AND LIBERTIES

A. SOURCES OF CONGRESSIONAL POWER

Congress can draw on a variety of constitutional provisions when it seeks to legislate in aid of civil rights and liberties. For example, Congress has used its commerce power to provide remedies against racial discrimination in places of public accommodation. *Heart of Atlanta Motel, Inc. v. United States* (1964); *Katzenbach v. McClung* (1964). In Title VI of the 1964 Civil Rights Act, Congress employed its spending power to prohibit racial discrimination by grantees of federal funds and it has used that same power to require the use of minority businesses in public works projects funded with federal monies. *Fullilove v. Klutznick* (1980). Congress may also legislate to protect "federal rights" arising from the relationship of citizens to the national government as it did in providing remedies against private interference with the right of interstate movement [*Griffin v. Breckenridge* (1971)] and in its prohibition of the use of residency requirements in presidential and vice presidential elections which similarly interfered with the right to interstate movement. *Oregon v. Mitchell* (1970). In legislating under these various constitutional sources of power, Congress may legislate against even private misconduct.

Various constitutional amendments also recognize congressional legislative power to implement their guarantees. The Thirteenth, Fourteenth, Fifteenth, Nineteenth [women's right to vote], Twenty-third [vote for the District of Columbia in presidential elections], Twenty-fourth [abolishing the poll tax], and Twenty-sixth [eighteen year old vote] Amendments all have provisions authorizing Congress to enforce their guarantees by appropriate legislation. In construing the congressional power under these constitutional grants, the Court has adopted the same broad perspective of congressional power that characterizes its treatment of the commerce and spending powers. So long as Congress could reasonably conclude that the legislation is in furtherance of the constitutional guarantee, Congress has power to legislate. *McCulloch v. Maryland* (1819).

B. ENFORCING THE THIRTEENTH AMENDMENT

The Thirteenth Amendment, Sec. 2, provides that Congress shall have power to enforce the Amendment's prohibition against slavery or involuntary servitude by "appropriate legislation." While the Court has taken a highly restrictive view of its own power to remedy private and state misconduct as violative of the Thirteenth Amendment, Sec. 1, it has read the Thirteenth Amendment, Sec. 2, to give Congress broad power to enact legislation necessary and proper for eradicating all "badges and incidents of slavery in the United States." Since the Thirteenth Amendment, Sec. 1, proscribes even private action violative of the right guaranteed, Congress can enact legislation reaching private imposition of badges of slavery.

Jones v. Mayer (1968), upheld an 1866 federal law which was read to prohibit even private discrimination in the sale or rental of real and personal property. In addressing the issue of Congress' constitutional power, Justice Stewart, for the Court, held that the enabling clause of the Thirteenth Amendment "clothed 'Congress with power to pass all laws necessary and proper for abolishing all badges and incidents of slavery in the United States.' " Since Congress could rationally conclude that the burden and disabilities of slavery include restraints upon the essence of civil freedom, *i.e.,* the right to purchase and lease property, the law was constitutional. "When racial discrimination herds men into ghettos and makes their ability to buy property turn on the color of their skin, then it is a relic of slavery." The dissent limited itself to challenging the Court's interpretation of the 1866 civil rights law to reach private discrimination, not the Court's exegesis on the constitutional grant of power.

Again, in *Runyon v. McCrary* (1976), the Court upheld congressional power under Sec. 2 of the Thirteenth Amendment to prohibit discrimination against blacks in their ability to "contract" on the same basis as white citizens. The legislation was interpreted to prohibit discrimination against blacks by private, commercially operated, non-sectarian schools. While the dissent challenged the Court's interpretation of the federal law to reach private racially motivated refusals to contract rather than state legal rules disabling persons from making or enforcing contracts, it did not challenge the Court's interpretation of the Thirteenth Amendment to sanction Congress' proscription of racial discrimination.

Runyon also rejected arguments that the federal law violated freedom of association. Parents retained the freedom to send their children to schools that teach racial segregation but the Constitution did not protect the school's practice of excluding racial minorities. *Runyon* left open the question whether Congress could prohibit racial discrimination based on religious grounds. The Court similarly rejected the contention that the law infringed privacy rights. While the right of privacy might extend to a genuinely private social club, it did not insulate private schools advertising and offering their services to members of the general public from appropriate federal legislation.

However, in *Memphis v. Greene* (1981), the Court rejected a challenge based on the Thirteenth Amendment and federal legislation to a decision by

Memphis to close a road which traversed a white residential community from outside traffic coming from black neighborhoods. First, the Thirteenth Amendment was not violated because the disparate impact of the closing on black citizens "could not be fairly characterized as a badge or incident of slavery." There was no showing of racially discriminatory motivation and the adverse impact on blacks was not deemed sufficient to offend the Thirteenth Amendment since such a holding "would trivialize the great purpose of that great charter of freedom. Proper respect for the dignity of the residents of any neighborhood requires that they accept the same burdens as well as the same benefits of citizenship regardless of their racial or ethnic origin." Turning to the congressional enactment, the Court simply found that the actions of Memphis did not involve any discrimination impairing the kind of property interests that the legislation was designed to proscribe. There was no showing that Memphis officials had granted benefits to white citizens that would have been refused to black citizens or that the official action significantly depreciated the value of property owned by black citizens.

C. ENFORCING THE FOURTEENTH AMENDMENT

1. CONGRESS' REMEDIAL POWERS

Sec. 5 of the Fourteenth Amendment provides that Congress can enact appropriate legislation to enforce the guarantees of that Amendment. Pursuant to this enabling clause, Congress can provide remedies for violations of Fourteenth Amendment rights as they have been defined by the courts.

In Sec. 4(e) of the Voting Rights Act of 1965, Congress provided that no state could deny the franchise because of an inability to read or write English to a person who had successfully completed the sixth grade in a Puerto Rican school. In upholding the constitutionality of this provision on the basis of the Fourteenth Amendment, Sec. 5, *Katzenbach v. Morgan* (1966), invoked the broad standards of *McCulloch v. Maryland*: "Correctly viewed, Sec. 5 is a positive grant of legislative power authorizing Congress to exercise its discretion in determining whether and what legislation is needed to secure the guarantees of the Fourteenth Amendment."

Sec. 4(e) could be regarded as a reasonable means to secure non-discriminatory treatment by government in basic public services. It was for Congress to weigh the enhanced political power for the Puerto Rican community against the intrusion on the constitutionally based state power to set voter qualifications. "It is not for [the Court] to review the congressional resolution of these factors. It is enough that the [the Court is] able to perceive a basis upon which Congress might resolve the conflict as it did."

2. CONGRESS' SUBSTANTIVE POWERS

But Justice Brennan, writing for the Court in *Katzenbach,* did not stop merely with an affirmation of Congress' power to provide remedies for judicially recognized Fourteenth Amendment rights. Instead, the opinion could be read to indicate that Congress could itself make the substantive determination that state literacy requirements violate the equal protection guarantee, even though the Court previously had held that such voting qualifications did not violate the Amendment. "A construction of Sec. 5 that would require a judicial determination that the enforcement of the state law precluded by Congress violated the Amendment, as a condition of sustaining the Congressional enactment, would depreciate both Congressional resourcefulness and Congressional responsibility for implementing the Amendment. It would confine the legislative powers in this context to the insignificant role of abrogating only those state laws that the judicial branch was prepared to adjudge unconstitutional, or of merely informing the judgment of the judiciary by particularizing the 'majestic generalities' of Sec. 1 of the Amendment." Sec. 4(e) could be upheld as legislation aimed at eliminating invidious discrimination in state voter qualifications. Congress had applied its "specially informed legislative competence": "[I]t was Congress' prerogative to weigh [the] competing considerations. [I]t is enough that [the Court] perceive a basis upon which Congress might predicate a judgment that the application of New York's literacy requirement to deny the right to vote constituted an invidious discrimination in violation of the Equal Protection Clause."

For Justice Harlan, joined by Justice Stewart, dissenting, the Court's premise that the Sec. 5 power extended beyond remedies to defining substantive rights was an unacceptable abdication of the judicial role. "When recognized state violations of federal constitutional standards have occurred, Congress is of course empowered by Sec. 5 to take appropriate remedial measures to redress and prevent the wrongs. But it is a judicial question whether the condition with which Congress has sought to deal is in infringement of the Constitution, something that is the necessary prerequisite to bringing the Sec. 5 power into play at all." John Marshall had said in *Marbury v. Madison* that it was "the province and duty of the judicial department to say what the law is." Therefore, Justice Harlan argued, it was for the judicial branch to determine if New York's application of its literacy test violated equal protection. While Congress might inform the judicial judgment, it could not substitute its interpretation of the Constitution for that of the Court. Justice Harlan concluded: "To allow a simple majority of Congress to have final say on matters of constitutional interpretation is fundamentally out of keeping with the constitutional structure."

Another construction of the *Katzenbach* cases gives less far reaching legislative power to Congress under the Fourteenth Amendment. In this view, *Katzenbach* means only that when Congress exercises its remedial power under Sec. 5 of the Fourteenth Amendment, it may on the basis of an examination of the facts conclude that a state lacks sufficient justification for the action which Congress has chosen to correct by legislation. For example, New York state in *Katzenbach* lacked sufficient justification for the voting discrimination practiced by the literacy test; therefore, Congress has legislative power under Sec. 5 to take corrective action through the Voting Rights Act.

Justice Harlan also argued in his *Katzenbach* dissent that the Court's reading of Sec. 5 would allow Congress "to exercise its Sec. 5 'discretion' [to enact] statutes so as in effect to dilute equal protection and due process decisions of [the] Court." But Justice Brennan, in a footnote, rejected any congressional power to dilute the constitutional guarantees. "We emphasize that Congress' power under Sec. 5 is limited to adopting measures to enforce the guarantees of the Amendment; Sec. 5 grants Congress no power to restrict, abrogate, or dilute these guarantees." This is the "ratchet theory"— Congress' Sec. 5 powers operate in only one direction, *i.e.,* it is a power "to enforce" or extend rights, not to dilute Fourteenth Amendment rights. Congressional legislation authorizing state use of racially segregated schools, suggested Justice Brennan, would not be a reasonable means for enforcing the equal protection guarantee. In *Mississippi University for Women v. Hogan* (1982), the Court, per Justice O'Connor, endorsed this view in rejecting the argument that Congress, in enacting the Education Amendments of 1972, had expressly authorized the University to continue its single sex policy: "Although we give deference to congressional decisions and classifications, neither Congress nor the state can validate a law that denies the rights guaranteed by the Fourteenth Amendment."

The ratchet theory has been justified by some commentators on the basis that, while Congress has superior ability at fact finding, it has no special capacity for making normative constitutional judgments regarding the limitations on governmental power. It has also been suggested that, while the Court should defer to congressional judgments involving federalism, *i.e.*, what level of government should regulate the conduct, judicial deference in cases involving substantive personal rights would be inappropriate. Other commentators question the soundness of the ratchet theory. If Congress has discretion and fact-finding abilities to determine the balancing of competing considerations, they argue that there is no necessary reason why Congress can't balance in favor of less extensive interpretation of constitutional rights. There also has been the problem of determining what constitutes a dilution. A proposed Human Life Statute defining "persons" in the Fourteenth Amendment purported to extend the benefits of the Fourteenth Amendment to the unborn fetus. But for critics of the proposal, it was a thinly disguised effort to dilute the privacy rights established in *Roe v. Wade*.

The expansive view of Congress's Sec. 5 powers adopted in *Katzenbach* has never been clearly rejected. However, it has been established that the congressional power under the enabling clauses is not unlimited. In *Oregon v. Mitchell* (1970), a badly-fragmented Court held unconstitutional, 5–4, a provision of the 1970 Voting Rights Act lowering the voting age in state elections to age 18. But no opinion commanded majority support. At most, the case stands for the limited principle that Congress cannot use its Sec. 5 powers to violate other constitutional provisions, *i.e.,* Art. 1, Sec. 2, gives the states the power to define the qualifications of voters for state officers and thus limits Congress' power to override state age requirements for state elections.

3.   REACHING PRIVATE CONDUCT

In the *Civil Rights Cases* (1883), the Court held that Congress' enforcement power under the Civil War Amendments was limited to providing remedies against conduct proscribed by the amendments. Congress was authorized only "to provide modes of redress against the operation of state laws, and the actions of state officers, executive or judicial." Private rights were secured by the Amendment only to the extent that Congress could provide legislative remedies to correct state wrongs against private persons. To allow Congress to legislate directly against private action would allow that body "to establish a code of new municipal law regulative of all private rights between man and man in society. It would be to make Congress take the place of the state legislatures and to supersede them."

But this seemingly absolute prohibition against congressional use of Sec. 5 of the Fourteenth

Amendment to reach private conduct was at least brought into question in *United States v. Guest* (1966). Justice Stewart's opinion for the Court rested on the premise that the indictments alleging violation of federal civil rights laws contained an allegation of state involvement or alleged an interference with the right of interstate travel, a fundamental constitutional right which is not limited to state action. However, six justices concurring in *Guest,* indicated that Congress had power under Sec. 5 to legislate against private interference with the Fourteenth Amendment right to use state-owned facilities free from racial discrimination. Justice Brennan, joined by Chief Justice Warren and Justice Douglas, for example, asserted that Sec. 5 "authorizes Congress to make laws that it concludes are reasonably necessary to protect a right created by and arising under [the Fourteenth] Amendment; Congress is thus fully empowered to determine that punishment of private conspiracies interfering with the exercise of such a right is necessary to its full protection." He specifically disapproved of the premise that Congress' power was limited to enacting corrective legislation against state action. "Viewed in its proper perspective, Sec. 5 of the Fourteenth Amendment appears as a positive grant of legislative power, authorizing Congress to exercise its discretion in fashioning remedies to achieve civil and political equality for all citizens."

The scope of congressional power to protect civil rights through the Commerce Clause, the Spending

Power, and the Thirteenth Amendment, has made it unnecessary to determine the full scope of congressional power to reach private action under Fourteenth Amendment, Sec. 5. See *Griffin v. Breckenridge* (1971), upholding application of a federal civil rights statute authorizing damages against private individuals interfering with various constitutional rights on the basis of the Thirteenth Amendment and the right of interstate movement. The Court specifically noted that the allegations of the complaint did not require consideration of the scope of congressional power under Sec. 5 of the Fourteenth Amendment.

D.　ENFORCING THE FIFTEENTH AMENDMENT

Like the other Civil War amendments, Sec. 2 of the Fifteenth Amendment gives Congress the power to enforce the guarantees of the article by appropriate legislation. In interpreting this grant of power, the Court again has applied the mandate of *McCulloch v. Maryland*. So long as Congress could reasonably conclude that the legislation will effectuate the constitutional prohibitions against racial discrimination in voting, the legislation is constitutional. Thus in *South Carolina v. Katzenbach* (1966), the Court upheld the 1965 Voting Rights Act prohibiting voter registration requirements which Congress had determined to be racially discriminatory. The Court stated: "As against the reserved powers of the States, Congress may use any rational means to effectuate the Constitutional prohibition of racial discrimination in voting." Congress could reasonably conclude that the unique remedial devices fashioned in the Voting Rights Act were justified because of the failure of case-by-case litigation to combat wide-spread and persistent voting discrimination. Again, in *Oregon v. Mitchell* (1970), the Court upheld provisions of the 1970 Voting Rights Act prohibiting the use of literacy tests noting that Congress had before it a long history of the discriminatory use of literacy tests to disenfranchise voters on account of their race.

In *City of Rome v. United States* (1980), the Court upheld provisions of the 1965 Voting Rights Act as applied by the Attorney General in disapproving electoral changes made by the City of Rome, Georgia, on grounds that the changes would have had a discriminatory effect. The City of Rome argued that, since the Fifteenth Amendment, Sec. 1, prohibited only purposeful racial discrimination in voting, Congress was similarly limited in fashioning remedial provisions under the Fifteenth Amendment, Sec. 2. But the Court stated: "It is clear that under Sec. 2 of the Fifteenth Amendment Congress may prohibit practices that in and of themselves do not violate Sec. 1 of the Amendment, so long as the prohibitions attacking racial discrimination in voting are 'appropriate,' as that term is defined in *McCulloch v. Maryland.*" Congress could have rationally concluded that, "because electoral changes by jurisdictions with a demonstrable history of intentional racial discrimination in voting create the risk of purposeful discrimination, it was proper to prohibit changes that have a discriminatory impact."

An opportunity for reaffirmation of *City of Rome* was provided when a North Carolina apportionment scheme for its state legislature using multi-member districts was challenged. Black voters contended that the scheme gave them less opportunity than white voters to elect representatives of their choice. They challenged the multi-member district scheme under the 1982 amendments to the Voting Rights Act. The Act established "the 'results' test" as "the relevant legal standard." Sec. 2, as amended, of the Act directed that this standard should be applied through a "totality of the circumstances" approach. This approach inquires into whether the voting scheme in question impairs the opportunity of members of racial minorities to participate in the political process. The Court interpreted the Act, as amended, to reach discriminatory effects, accepting that the Act, so interpreted, was a constitutional exercise of Congressional power under Sec. 2 of the Fifteenth Amendment regardless of whether Sec. 1 of the Fifteenth Amendment requires a showing of discriminatory purpose or not. *Thornburg v. Gingles* (1986).

*

INDEX

References are to Pages

507

†